# The Photographic History
## of The Civil War

TWO VOLUMES IN ONE.
The Opening Battles

IMPORTANT
BATTLEGROUNDS
OF THE
CIVIL WAR

Actual Battlefields
are indicated by stars ★

STATUTE MILES

PREPARING FOR WAR—A CONFEDERATE PHOTOGRAPH OF '61

Florida Opens the Grim Game of War.    On a sandy point at the entrance to Pensacola Bay over two hundred years ago, the Spaniards who so long held possession of what is now the Gulf coast of the United States had built a fort.    On its site the United States Government had erected a strong fortification called Fort Barrancas.    Between this point and a low-lying sandy island directly opposite, any vessels going up to Pensacola must pass.    On the western end of this island was the strongly built Fort Pickens.    Early in 1861 both forts were practically ungarrisoned.    This remarkable picture, taken by the New Orleans photographer Edwards, in February, 1861, belongs to a series hitherto unpublished.    Out of the deep shadows of the sally port we look into the glaring sunlight upon one of the earliest warlike moves.    Here we see one of the heavy pieces of ordnance that were intended to defend the harbor from foreign foes, being shifted preparatory to being mounted on the rampart at Fort Barrancas, which, since January 12th, had been in possession of State troops.    Fort Pickens, held by a mere handful of men under Lieutenant Slemmer, still flew the Stars and Stripes.    But the move of State troops under orders from Governor Perry of Florida, in seizing Fort Barrancas and raising the State flag even before the shot that aroused the nation at Fort Sumter, may well be said to have helped force the crisis that was impending.

# The Photographic History of The Civil War

*Complete and Unabridged*

TWO VOLUMES IN ONE.

## Volume 1
*The Opening Battles
Two Years of Grim War

## Contributors

WILLIAM H. TAFT
President of the United States

HENRY WYSHAM LANIER
Art Editor and Publisher

EBEN SWIFT
Lieutenant-Colonel, U. S. A.

FRENCH E. CHADWICK
Rear-Admiral, U. S. N.

GEORGE HAVEN PUTNAM
Major, U. S. V.

MARCUS J. WRIGHT
Brigadier-General, C. S. A.

HENRY W. ELSON
Professor of History, Ohio University

JAMES BARNES
Author of "David G. Farragut"

## THE BLUE & GREY PRESS

# PHOTOGRAPHIC HISTORY OF THE CIVIL WAR

Vol.1
The Opening Battles
Two Years of Grim War

Two Volumes in One.

Printed in the United States of America.

ISBN: 1-55521-174-7

# CONTENTS

# Contents

## Part IV

## Part V

## Part VI

# FOREWORDS

---

## GREETING FROM PRESIDENT TAFT

---

## DEDICATION

---

## ACKNOWLEDGMENT

---

## EDITORIAL INTRODUCTORY

---

THE WHITE HOUSE
WASHINGTON

We have reached a point in this country when we can look
back, not without love, not without intense pride, but without
partisan passion, to the events of the Civil War. We have
reached a point, I am glad to say, when the North can admire
to the full the heroes of the South, and the South admire to
the full the heroes of the North. There is a monument in
Quebec that always commended itself to me - a monument to commemorate the battle of the Plains of Abraham. On one face
of that beautiful structure is the name of Montcalm, and on
the opposite side the name of Wolfe. That always seemed to
me to be the acme of what we ought to reach in this country;
and I am glad to say that in my own alma mater, Yale, we have
established an association for the purpose of erecting within
her academic precincts a memorial not to the Northern Yale men
who died, nor to the Southern Yale men who died; but to the
Yale men who died in the Civil War.

# Dedicated

FIFTY YEARS AFTER

FORT SUMTER

TO THE MEN IN BLUE AND GRAY

WHOSE VALOR AND DEVOTION

HAVE BECOME THE

PRICELESS HERITAGE

OF A UNITED

NATION

# ACKNOWLEDGMENT

TO Mr. Francis Trevelyan Miller the publishers of these books must confess an obligation quite apart from the usual editorial services. Seldom indeed has it been possible to construct the text of such an extended history in accordance with a single broad idea. Yet it is true that the contributions throughout the entire ten volumes of the PHOTOGRAPHIC HISTORY are a direct outgrowth of the plan created years ago by Mr. Miller, and urged since by him with constant faith in its national importance—to emphasize in comprehensive form those deeds and words from the mighty struggle that strike universal, noble human chords. This was a conception so straightforward and so inspiring that the opportunity to give it the present embodiment has become a lasting privilege.

Readers as well as publishers are also indebted to the collectors, historical societies, and others who have furnished hundreds of long-treasured photographs, unwilling that the HISTORY should appear without presenting many important scenes of which no actual illustrations had ever before been available to the public. Hence the Civil War-time photographs in the present work are not only several times as numerous as those in any previous publication, but also include many hundreds of scenes that will come as a revelation even to historians and special scholars—photographs taken within the lines of the Confederate armies and of the hosts in the Mississippi Valley, whose fighting was no less momentous than the Eastern battles, but in the nature of things could not be as quickly or as fully heralded. With these additions to the "Brady-Gardner" collection—the loss and rediscovery of which Mr. Henry Wysham Lanier's introductory narrates—it is now possible for the first time to present comprehensively the men and scenes and types of the American epic, in photographs.

Deep acknowledgment is due the owners of indispensable pictures who have so generously contributed them for this purpose. Especial mention must be given to: Mrs. W. K. Bachman; Mr. William Beer; Mr. James Blair, C. S. A.; Mr. George A. Brackett; Mr. Edward Bromley; Mr. John C. Browne; Captain Joseph T. Burke, C. S. A.; Captain F. M. Colston, C. S. A.; Colonel E. J. Copp, U. S. V.; Colonel S. A. Cunningham, C. S. A.; The Daughters of the Confederacy; Mr. Charles Frankel; Mr. Edgar R. Harlan; Colonel Chas. R. E. Koch, U. S. V.; Miss Isabel Maury; Mr. F. H. Meserve; The Military Order of the Loyal Legion; Colonel John P. Nicholson, U. S. V.; General Harrison Gray Otis, U. S. V.; Captain F. A. Roziene, U. S. A.; General G. P. Thruston, U. S. V.; The University of South Carolina; The Washington Artillery, and the various State historical departments, state and government bureaus, military and patriotic organizations which courteously suspended their rules, in order that the photographic treasures in their archives should become available for the present record.

# EDITORIAL INTRODUCTORY

ON this semi-centennial of the American Civil War—the war of the modern Roses in the Western World—these volumes are dedicated to the American people in tribute to the courage and the valor with which they met one of the greatest crises that a nation has ever known—a crisis that changed the course of civilization. We look back at Napoleon through the glamor of time, without fully realizing that here on our own continent are battle-grounds more noble in their purport than all the wars of the ancient regimes. The decades have shrouded the first American Revolution in romance, but the time has now come when this second American revolution, at the turning point of its first half century, is to become an American epic in which nearly three and a half million men gathered on the battle-line to offer their lives for principles that were dear to them.

It is as an American "Battle Abbey" that these pages are opened on this anniversary, so that the eyes of the generations may look upon the actual scenes—not upon the tarnished muskets, the silenced cannon, nor the battle-stained flag, but upon the warriors themselves standing on the firing-line in the heroic struggle when the hosts of the North and the legions of the South met on the battle-grounds of a nation's ideals, with the destiny of a continent hanging in the balance. And what a tribute it is to American character to be able to gather about these pages in peace and brotherhood, without malice and without dissension, within a generation from the greatest fratricidal tragedy in the annals of mankind. The vision is no longer blinded by heart wounds, but as Americans we can see only the heroic self-sacrifice of these men who battled for the decision of one of the world's greatest problems.

In this first volume, standing literally before the open door to the "Battle Abbey," in which the vision of war is to be revealed in all its reality, I take this privilege to refer briefly to a few of the intimate desires that have led to this revelation of THE PHOTOGRAPHIC HISTORY OF THE CIVIL WAR. As one stands in the library of the War Department at Washington, or before the archives of the American libraries, he feels that the last word of evidence must have been recorded. Nearly seven thousand treatises, containing varying viewpoints relating to this epoch in our national development, have been written —so Dr. Herbert Putnam, Librarian at the Congressional Library at Washington, tells me; while in my home city of Hartford, which is a typical American community, I find nearly two thousand works similar to those that are within the reach of all the American people in every part of the country.

With this great inheritance before us, military writers have informed me that they cannot understand why the American people have been so little interested in this remarkable war. Great generals have told how they led their magnificent armies in battle; military tacticians have mapped and recorded the movements of regiments and corps with technical accuracy, and historians have faithfully discussed the causes and the effects of this strange crisis in civilization—all of which is a permanent tribute to American scholarship. I have come to the conclusion that the lack of popular interest is because this is not a military nation. The great heart of American citizenship knows little of military maneuver, which is a science that requires either life-study or tradition to cultivate an interest in it.

The Americans are a peace-loving people, but when once aroused they are a mighty moral and physical fighting force. It is not their love for the art of war that has caused them to take up arms. It is the impulse of justice that permeates the Western World. The American people feel the pulse of life itself; they love the greater emotions that cause men to meet danger face to face. Their hearts beat to the martial strain of the national anthem "The Star Spangled Banner" and they feel the melody in that old Marseillaise of the Confederacy, "Dixie," for in them they catch mental visions of the sweeping lines under floating banners at the battle-front; they hear the roar of the guns and the clatter of cavalry; but more than that—they feel again the spirit that leads men to throw themselves into the cannon's flame.

THE PHOTOGRAPHIC HISTORY OF THE CIVIL WAR comes on this anniversary to witness a people's valor; to testify in photograph to the true story of how a devoted people whose fathers had stood shoulder to shoulder for the ideal of liberty in the American Revolution, who had issued to the world the declaration that all men are created politically free and equal, who had formulated the Constitution that dethroned mediæval monarchy and founded a new republic to bring new hope to the races of the earth—parted at the dividing line of a great economic problem and stood arrayed against each other in the greatest fratricidal tragedy that the world has ever witnessed, only to be reunited and to stand, fifty years later, hand in hand for the betterment of mankind, pledging themselves to universal peace and brotherhood.

This is the American epic that is told in these time-stained photographs—an epic which in romance and chivalry is more inspiring than that of the olden knighthood; brother against brother, father against son, men speaking the same language, living under the same flag, offering their lives for that which they believed to be right. No Grecian phalanx or Roman legion ever knew truer manhood than in those days on the American continent when the Anglo-Saxon met Anglo-Saxon in the decision of a constitutional principle that beset their beloved nation. It was more than Napoleonic, for its warriors battled for principle rather than conquest, for right rather than power.

This is the spirit of these volumes, and it seems to me that it must be the spirit of every true American. It is the sacred heritage of Anglo-Saxon freedom won at Runnymede. I recall General Gordon, an American who turned the defeat of war into the victory of citizenship in peace, once saying: "What else could be expected of a people in whose veins commingled the blood of the proud cavaliers of England, the blood of those devout and resolute men who protested against the grinding exactions of the Stuarts; the blood of the stalwart Dissenters and of the heroic Highlanders of Scotland, and of the sturdy Presbyterians of Ireland; the blood of those defenders of freedom who came from the mountain battlements of Switzerland, whose signal lights summoned her people to gather to their breasts the armfuls of spears to make way for liberty." It was a great battle-line of Puritan, of Huguenot, of Protestant, of Catholic, of Teuton, and Celt—every nation and every religion throwing its sacrifice on the altar of civilization.

The causes of the American Civil War will always be subject to academic controversy, each side arguing conscientiously from its own viewpoint. It is unnecessary to linger in these pages over the centuries of economic growth that came to a crisis in the American nation. In the light of modern historical understanding it was the inevitable result of a sociological system that had come down through the ages before there was a republic on the Western continent, and which finally came to a focus through the conflicting interests that developed in the upbuilding of American civilization. When Jefferson and Madison construed our constitution in one way, and Washington and Hamilton in another, surely it is not strange that their descendants should have differed. There is glory enough for all—for North, for South, for East, for West, on these battle-grounds of a people's traditions—a grander empire than Cæsar's legions won for Rome.

To feel the impulse of both the North and the South is the desire of these volumes. When, some years ago, I left the portals of Trinity College, in the old abolition town of Hartford, Conn., to enter the halls of Washington and Lee University in historic Lexington in the hills of Virginia, I felt for the first time as a Northerner, indigenous to the soil, what it means to be a Southerner. I, who had bowed my head from childhood to the greatness of Grant, looked upon my friends bowing their heads before the mausoleum of Lee. I stood with them as they laid the April flowers on the graves of their dead, and I felt the heart-beat of the Confederacy. When I returned to my New England home it was to lay the laurel and the May flowers on the graves of my dead, and I felt the heart-beat of the Republic—more than that, I felt the impulse of humanity and the greatness of all men.

When I now turn these pages I realize what a magnificent thing it is to have lived; how wonderful is man and his power to blaze the path for progress! I am proud that my heritage runs back through nearly three hundred years to the men who planted the seed of liberty in the New World into which is flowing the blood of the great races of the earth; a nation whose sinews are built from the strong men of the ages, and in whose hearts beat the impulses that have inspired the centuries—a composite of the courage, the perseverance, and the fortitude of the world's oldest races, commingled into one great throbbing body. It is a young race, but its exploits have equalled those of the heroic age in the Grecian legends and surpass Leonidas and his three hundred at Thermopylæ.

In full recognition of the masterly works of military authorities that now exist as invaluable historical evidence, these volumes present the American Civil War from an entirely original viewpoint. The collection of photographs is in itself a sufficient contribution to military and historical record, and the text is designed to present the mental pictures of the inspiring pageantry in the war between the Red and the White Roses in America, its human impulses, and the ideals that it represents in the heart of humanity.

# Editorial Introductory

The military movements of the armies have been exhaustively studied properly to stage the great scenes that are herein enacted, but the routine that may burden the memory or detract from the broader, martial picture that lies before the reader has been purposely avoided. It is the desire to leave impressions rather than statistics; mental visions and human inspiration rather than military knowledge, especially as the latter is now so abundant in American literature. In every detail the contradictory evidence of the many authorities has been weighed carefully to present the narrative fairly and impartially. It is so conflicting regarding numbers in battle and killed and wounded that the Government records have been followed, as closely as possible.

The hand of the historian may falter, or his judgment may fail, but the final record of the American Civil War is told in these time-dimmed negatives. The reader may conscientiously disagree with the text, but we must all be of one and the same mind when we look upon the photographic evidence. It is in these photographs that all Americans can meet on the common ground of their beloved traditions. Here we are all united at the shrine where our fathers fought—Northerners or Southerners—and here the generations may look upon the undying record of the valor of those who fought to maintain the Union and those who fought for independence from it—each according to his own interpretation of the Constitution that bound them into a great republic of states.

These photographs are appeals to peace; they are the most convincing evidence of the tragedy of war. They bring it before the generations so impressively that one begins to understand the meaning of the great movement for universal brotherhood that is now passing through the civilized world. Mr. William Short, the secretary of the New York Peace Society, in speaking of them, truly says that they are the greatest arguments for peace that the world has ever seen. Their mission is more than to record history; it is to make history—to mould the thought of the generations as everlasting witnesses of the price of war.

As the founder of this memorial library, and its editor-in-chief, it is my pleasure to give historical record to Mr. Edward Bailey Eaton, Mr. Herbert Myrick, and Mr. J. Frank Drake, of the Patriot Publishing Company, of Springfield, Mass., owners of the largest private collection of original Brady-Gardner Civil War negatives in existence, by whom this work was inaugurated, and to Mr. Egbert Gilliss Handy, president of The Search-Light Library of New York, through whom it was organized for its present development by the Review of Reviews Company. These institutions have all co-operated to realize the national and impartial conception of this work. The result, we hope, is a more friendly, fair, and intimate picture of America's greatest sorrow and greatest glory than has perhaps been possible under the conditions that preceded this semi-centennial anniversary.

To President William Howard Taft, who has extended his autographed message to the North and the South, the editors take pleasure in recording their deep appreciation; also to Generals Sickles and Buckner, the oldest surviving generals in the Federal and Confederate armies, respectively, on this anniversary; to General Frederick Dent Grant and

# The Photographic History of the Civil War

General G. W. Custis Lee, the sons of the great warriors who led the armies through the American Crisis; to the Honorable Robert Todd Lincoln, former Secretary of War; to James W. Cheney, Librarian in the War Department at Washington; to Dr. Edward S. Holden, Librarian at the United States Military Academy at West Point, for their consideration and advice, and to the officers of the Grand Army of the Republic, the Military Order of the Loyal Legion, the United Confederate Veterans, the Daughters of the Confederacy, and the other memorial organizations that have shown an appreciation of the intent of this work. We are especially indebted to Mr. John McElroy, editor of the *National Tribune;* General Bennett H. Young, the historian of the United Confederate Veterans; General Grenville M. Dodge; Colonel S. A. Cunningham, founder and editor of the *Confederate Veteran;* General Irvine Walker, General William E. Mickle, and to the many others who, in their understanding and appreciation have rendered valuable assistance in the realization of its special mission to the American people on this semi-centennial.

This preface should not close without a final word as to the difficulty of the problems that confronted the military, historical, and other authorities whose contributions have made the text of THE PHOTOGRAPHIC HISTORY OF THE CIVIL WAR, whose names are signed to their historical contributions throughout these volumes, and the spirit in which, working with the editorial staff of the Review of Reviews, they have met these problems. The impossibility of deciding finally the difference of opinion in the movements of the Civil War has been generously recognized. With all personal and partisan arguments have been set aside in the universal and hearty effort of all concerned to fulfil the obligations of this work. I ask further privilege to extend my gratitude to my personal assistants, Mr. Walter R. Bickford, Mr. Arthur Forrest Burns, and Mr. Wallace H. Miller.

And now, as we stand to-day, fellowmen in the great republic that is carrying the torch in the foreranks of the world's civilization, let us clasp hands across the long-gone years as reunited Americans. I can close these introductory words with no nobler tribute than those of the mighty warriors who led the great armies to battle. It was General Robert E. Lee who, after the war, gave this advice to a Virginia mother, "Abandon all these animosities and make your sons Americans," and General Ulysses S. Grant, whose appeal to his countrymen must always be an admonition against war: "Let us have peace."

FRANCIS TREVELYAN MILLER,
*Editor-in-Chief.*

HARTFORD, CONNECTICUT,
  Fiftieth Anniversary
    Lincoln's Inauguration.

## THE CARTOON OF BRADY BY NAST

MANY CELEBRITIES OF THE CIVIL WAR PERIOD WERE CARICA-
TURED BY THOMAS NAST, DEAN OF AMERICAN CARTOONISTS. BRADY,
MAKER OF FASHIONABLE PORTRAITS, THEN PIONEER PHOTOGRAPHER
OF SOLDIERS AND ARMY LIFE, WAS FAIR GAME FOR NAST'S TELL-
ING YET KINDLY PENCIL AS THIS REPRODUCTION ILLUSTRATES.

FIRST PREFACE

# PHOTOGRAPHING
# THE
# CIVIL WAR

THE WAR PHOTOGRAPHER BRADY (WEARING STRAW
HAT) WITH GENERAL BURNSIDE (READING NEWSPA-
PER)—TAKEN WHILE BURNSIDE WAS IN COMMAND
OF THE ARMY OF THE POTOMAC, EARLY IN 1863,
AFTER HIS ILL-FATED ATTACK ON FREDERICKSBURG

THE FLANKING GUN

This remarkably spirited photograph of Battery D, Second U. S. Artillery, was, according to the photographer's account, taken just as the battery was loading to engage with the Confederates. The order, "cannoneers to your posts," had just been given, and the men, running up, called to the photographer to hurry his wagon out of the way unless he wished to gain a place for his name in the list of casualties   In June, 1863, the Sixth Corps had made its third successful crossing of the Rappahannock, as the advance of Hooker's movement against Lee. Battery D at once took position with other artillery out in the fields near the

"COOPER'S BATTERY"  (SEE PAGE 32)

This is another photograph taken under fire and shows us Battery B, First Pennsylvania Light Artillery, in action before Petersburg, 1864. Brady, the veteran photographer, obtained permission to take a picture of "Cooper's Battery," in position for battle. The first attempt provoked the fire of the Confederates, who supposed that the running forward of the artillerists was with hostile intent. The Confederate guns frightened Brady's horse which ran off with his wagon and his assistant, upsetting and destroying his chemicals.   In the picture to the left, Captain James H. Cooper himself is seen leaning on a sword at the

"LOAD!"

ruins of the Mansfield house. In the rear of the battery the veteran Vermont brigade was acting as support. To their rear was the bank of the river skirted by trees. The grove of white poplars to the right surrounded the Mansfield house. With characteristic coolness, some of the troops had already pitched their dog tents. Better protection was soon afforded by the strong line of earthworks which was thrown up and occupied by the Sixth Corps. Battery D was present at the first battle of Bull Run, where the Confederates there engaged got a taste of its metal on the Federal left

READY TO OPEN FIRE

extreme right. Lieutenant Miller is the second figure from the left. Lieutenant Alcorn is next, to the left from Captain Cooper. Lieutenant James A. Gardner, just behind the prominent figure with the haversack in the right section of the picture, identified these members almost forty-seven years after the picture was taken. This Pennsylvania battery suffered greater loss than any other volunteer Union battery; its record of casualties includes twenty-one killed and died of wounds, and fifty-two wounded—convincing testimony of the fact that throughout the war its men stood bravely to their guns.

# THE FIRST PHOTOGRAPH OF IRONCLADS IN ACTION

# A DARING CAMERA-TRIUMPH OF 1863

On the highest point of the battered dust heap that was the still untaken fortress of Sumter, the Confederate photographer, Cook, planted his camera on September 8, 1863, and took the first photograph of ironclads in action—the monitors *Weehawken, Montauk* and *Passaic,* as they were actually firing on the Confederate batteries at Fort Moultrie. The three low-freeboarded vessels, lying almost bows-on, at the distance of nearly two miles, look like great iron buoys in the channel, but the smoke from their heavy guns is drifting over the water, and the flames can almost be seen leaping from the turret ports. Although Fort Moultrie was the aim of their gunners, Cook, with his head under the dark cloth, saw on the ground glass a shell passing within a few feet of him. Another shell knocked one of his plate-holders off the parapet into the rain-water cistern. He gave a soldier five dollars to fish it out for him. He got his picture—and was ordered off the parapet, since he was drawing upon the fort the fire of all the Union batteries on Morris Island. It seems incredible that such a daring photographic feat, and one of such historic interest, could have remained unpublished for nearly half a century—until one recalls the absence of any satisfactory method for reproducing photographs direct during the generation succeeding the war. Before photo-engraving became perfected, thirty years or more had passed, and most of the few negatives taken by Confederates had vanished through fire, loss, and breakage. Fortunately, this has been preserved—one of the most vivid of any war.

A CONFEDERATE SECRET SERVICE PHOTOGRAPH OF THE FIRST INDIANA HEAVY ARTILLERY

This remarkable photograph is here published for the first time. It is but one of the many made by A. D. Lytle in Baton Rouge during its occupancy by the Federals. With a courage and skill as remarkable as that of Brady himself this Confederate photographer risked his life to obtain negatives of Federal batteries, cavalry regiments and camps, lookout towers, and the vessels of Farragut and Porter, in fact of everything that might be of the slightest use in informing the Confederate Secret Service of the strength of the Federal occupation of Baton Rouge. In Lytle's little shop on Main Street these negatives remained in oblivion for near half a century. War photographs were long regarded with extreme disfavor in the South and the North knew nothing of Lytle's collection, which has at last been unearthed by the editors of the "Photographic History." The value of Lytle's work to the Confederate Secret Service is apparent from this view, clear in every detail, of the Federal artillery drilling on the Parade Grounds of the Arsenal. The strength of the force, the number of the guns, the condition of the men, are all revealed at a glance. Many other "Lytle" photographs—gunboats, camps, infantry and cavalry—appear in the present work.

PERILOUS PHOTOGRAPHY AT THE FRONT

Here in imagination we may stand with Brady on the bank of the Rappahannock while he calmly focussed his cameras upon the town across the stream. The mighty Union army had arrived before Fredericksburg, and Brady, ever anxious to be in the thick of things, was early at his work. The only indication of war in the picture is the demolished railroad bridge, but behind the windows of the old mill at its farther end and in most of the houses of the town were Confederate sharpshooters, while along the river bank wooden barricades sheltered soldiers prepared to dispute the crossing of the river. No sooner had Brady placed his queer looking cameras in position than he and his assistants became the target for hundreds of rifles, but he calmly proceeded with his work and in accordance with his usual luck secured his pictures and returned uninjured. Almost a month of delay ensued before Burnside's futile crossing of the river furnished the photographers with a wealth of stirring scenes, many of which again had to be caught under fire.

## CONFEDERATES BEFORE A UNION CAMERA

The single known instance in which the Union photographers succeeded in getting a near view of the Confederate troops. After Burnside's fatal attempt to carry the heights back of Fredericksburg he had retreated across the Rappahannock leaving more than 12,000 dead and wounded on the field. A burial truce was then agreed upon with Lee and afforded Brady and his men the sad opportunity to record many a gruesome spectacle. Near the end of the railroad bridge in Fredericksburg was secured a view of the living men of Lee's army which had inflicted such terrible punishment upon the Union forces but a short time before. They were evidently quite willing, during the suspension of hostilities, to group themselves before Brady's camera set up on the partially repaired end of the bridge. Here we get a nearer view of the old mill in the preceding picture. A cannon has been placed in one of its upper windows for defense. Although these houses had escaped injury from the Federal bombardment, other Brady photographs record the ruins of the little town.

## A WASHINGTON BELLE IN CAMP

From Bull Run to Gettysburg the Federal capital was repeatedly threatened by the advances of the Confederates, and strong camps for the defense of Washington were maintained throughout the war. It was the smart thing for the ladies of the capital to invade these outlying camps, and they were always welcomed by the officers weary of continuous guard-duty. Here the camera has caught the willing subject in handsome Kate Chase Sprague, who became a belle of official society in Washington during the war. She was the daughter of Salmon P. Chase, Lincoln's Secretary of the Treasury. At this time she was the wife of Governor William Sprague, of Rhode Island, and was being entertained in camp by General J. J. Abercrombie, an officer of the regular army, well known in the capital.

## A HORSE AND RIDER THAT WILL LIVE

Here is an extraordinary photograph of a spirited charger taken half a century ago. This noble beast is the mount of Lieut.-Col. C. B. Norton, and was photographed at General Fitz John Porter's headquarters. The rider is Colonel Norton himself. Such clear definition of every feature of man and horse might well be the envy of modern photography, which does not achieve such depth without fast lenses, focal-plane shutters, and instantaneous dry plates, which can be developed at leisure. Here the old-time wet-plate process has preserved every detail. To secure results like this it was necessary to sensitize the plate just before exposing it, uncap the lens by hand, and develop the negative within five minutes after the exposure.

# PHOTOGRAPHING THE CIVIL WAR

## By Henry Wysham Lanier

EXTRAORDINARY as the fact seems, the American Civil War is the only great war of which we have an adequate history in photographs: that is to say, this is the only conflict of the first magnitude[1] in the world's history that can be really "illustrated," with a pictorial record which is indisputably authentic, vividly illuminating, and the final evidence in any question of detail.

Here is a much more important historical fact than the casual reader realizes. The earliest records we have of the human race are purely pictorial. History, even of the most shadowy and legendary sort, goes back hardly more than ten thousand years. But in recent years there have been recovered in certain caves of France scratched and carved bone weapons and rough wall-paintings which tell us some dramatic events in the lives of men who lived probably a hundred thousand years before the earliest of those seven strata of ancient Troy, which indefatigable archeologists have exposed to the wondering gaze of the modern world. The picture came long before the written record; nearly all our knowledge of ancient Babylonia and Assyria is gleaned from the details left by some picture-maker. And it is still infinitely more effective an appeal. How impossible it is for the average person to get any clear idea of the great struggles which altered the destinies of nations and which occupy so large a portion of world history! How can a man to-day really understand the siege of Troy, the battles of Thermopylæ or Salamis, Hannibal's crossing of the Alps, the famous fight at Tours when Charles "the Hammer" checked the Saracens, the Norman

[1] There have been, of course, only two wars of this description since 1865: the Franco-Prussian War was, for some reason, not followed by camera men; and the marvellously expert photographers who flocked to the struggles between Russia and Japan were not given any chance by the Japanese authorities to make anything like an adequate record.

The indomitable war photographer in the very costume which made him a familiar figure at the first battle of Bull Run, from which he returned precipitately to New York after his initial attempt to put into practice his scheme for picturing the war. Brady was a Cork Irishman by birth and possessed of all the active temperament which such an origin implies. At Bull Run he was in the thick of things. Later in the day, Brady himself was compelled to flee, and at nightfall of that fatal Sunday, alone and unarmed, he lost his way in the woods near the stream from which the battle takes its name. Here he was found by some of the famous company of New York Fire Department Zouaves, who gave him a sword for his defense. Buckling it on beneath his linen duster, Brady made his way to Washington and thence to New York. In the picture we see him still proudly wearing the weapon which he was prepared to use for the protection of himself and his precious negatives.

Photo taken July 22d 1861

BRADY The Photographer returned from Bull Run

BRADY, AFTER BULL RUN

Below is the gallery of A. D. Lytle—a Confederate photographer—as it stood on Main Street, Baton Rouge, in 1864, when in the employ of the Confederate Secret Service Lytle trained his camera upon the Federal army which occupied Baton Rouge. It was indeed dangerous work, as discovery of his purpose would have visited upon the photographer the fate of a spy. Lytle would steal secretly up the Observation Tower, which had been built on the ruins of the capitol, and often exposed to rifle shots from the Federals, would with flag or lantern signal to the Confederates at Scott's Bluff, whence the news was relayed to New Orleans, and provision made for smuggling the precious prints through the lines. Like Brady, Lytle obtained his photographic supplies from Anthony & Company of New York; but unlike Cook of Charleston, he did not have to depend upon contraband traffic to secure them, but got them passed on the "orders to trade" issued quite freely in the West by the Federal Government.

THE GALLERY OF A CONFEDERATE SECRET-SERVICE PHOTOGRAPHER, BATON ROUGE, LOUISIANA, 1864

conquest of England, the Hundred Years' or Thirty Years' Wars, even our own seven-year struggle for liberty, without any first-hand picture-aids to start the imagination? Take the comparatively modern Napoleonic wars where, moreover, there is an exceptional wealth of paintings, drawings, prints, and lithographs by contemporary men: in most cases the effect is simply one of keen disappointment at the painfully evident fact that most of these worthy artists never saw a battle or a camp.

So the statement that there have been gathered together *thousands of photographs* of scenes on land and water during those momentous years of 1861 to 1865 means that for our generation and all succeeding ones, the Civil War is on a basis different from all others, is practically an open book to old and young. For when man achieved the photograph he took almost as important a step forward as when he discovered how to make fire: he made scenes and events and personalities immortal. The greatest literary genius might write a volume without giving you so intimate a comprehension of the struggle before Petersburg as do these exact records, made by adventurous camera-men under incredible difficulties, and holding calmly before your eyes the very Reality itself.

To apply this pictorial principle, let us look at one remarkable photograph, Cooper's Battery in front of the Avery house, during the siege of Petersburg, of which we have, by a lucky chance, an account from one of the men in the scene. The lifelikeness of the picture is beyond praise: one cannot help living through this tense moment with these men of long ago, and one's eyes instinctively follow their fixed gaze toward the lines of the foe. This picture was shown to Lieutenant James A. Gardner (of Battery B, First Pennsylvania Light Artillery), who immediately named half a dozen of the figures, adding details of the most intimate interest. He stated:

I am, even at this late day, able to pick out and recognize a very large number of the members of our battery, as shown in this photograph. Our battery (familiarly known as Cooper's Battery) belonged to the Fifth Corps, then commanded by Gen. G. K. Warren.

Our corps arrived in front of Petersburg on June 17, 1864, was put into position on the evening of that day, and engaged the Confederate batteries on their line near the Avery house. The enemy at that time

THE PHOTOGRAPHER WITH THE ARMY

Here are two excellent views in which we see the conditions under which the army photographer worked in the field. The larger picture is of Barnard, the Government photographer under Captain O. M. Poe, Chief Engineer of the Military Division of the Mississippi. Barnard was engaged to take photographs of the new Federal fortifications being constructed under Captain Poe's direction at Atlanta, September–October, 1864. Captain Poe found the old Confederate line of defense of too great extent to be held by such a force as Sherman intended to leave as garrison of the town. Consequently, he selected a new line of much shorter development which passed through the northern part of the town, making necessary the destruction of many buildings in that quarter. Barnard is here at work sensitizing his plates in a light-proof tent, making his exposures, and developing immediately within the tent. His chemicals and general supplies were carried in the wagon showing to the right. Thus, as the pioneer corps worked on the fortifications, the entire series of photographs showing their progress was made to be forwarded later to Washington by Captain Poe, with his official report. In the background we see the battle-field where began the engagement of July 22, 1864, known as the battle of Atlanta, in which General McPherson lost his life. Thus Brady and all the war photographers worked right up to the trenches, lugging their cumbersome tents and apparatus, often running out of supplies or carrying hundreds of glass plates over rough roads or exposed to possible shells. To the many chances of failure was added that of being at any time picked off by some sharpshooter. In the smaller picture appears a duplicate of Brady's "What-Is-It," being the dark-room buggy of Photographer Wearn. In the background are the ruins of the State Armory at Columbia, South Carolina. This was burned as Sherman's troops passed through the city on their famous march through the Carolinas, February, 1865. The photographer, bringing up the rear, has preserved the result of Sherman's work, which is typical of that done by him all along the line of march to render useless to the Confederate armies in the field, the military resources of the South.

RUINS OF STATE ARMORY, COLUMBIA, 1865

was commanded by General Beauregard. That night the enemy fell back to their third line, which then occupied the ridge which you see to the right and front, along where you will notice the chimney (the houses had been burnt down). On the night of the 18th we threw up the lunettes in front of our guns. This position was occupied by us until possibly about the 23d or 24th of June, when we were taken further to the left. The position shown in the picture is about six hundred and fifty yards in front, and to the right of the Avery house, and at or near this point was built a permanent fort or battery, which was used continuously during the entire siege of Petersburg.

While occupying this position, Mr. Brady took the photographs, copies of which you have sent me. The photographs were taken in the forenoon of June 21, 1864. I know *myself*, merely from the position that I occupied at that time, as gunner. After that, I served as sergeant, first sergeant, and first lieutenant, holding the latter position at the close of the war. All the officers shown in this picture are dead.

The movement in which we were engaged was the advance of the Army of the Potomac upon Petersburg, being the beginning of operations in front of that city. On June 18th the division of the Confederates which was opposite us was that of Gen. Bushrod R. Johnson; but as the Army of Northern Virginia, under General Lee, began arriving on the evening of June 18th, it would be impossible for me to say who occupied the enemy's lines after that. The enemy's position, which was along on the ridge to the front, in the picture, where you see the chimney, afterward became the main line of the Union army. Our lines were advanced to that point, and at or about where you see the chimney standing, Fort Morton of the Union line was constructed, and a little farther to the right was Fort Steadman, on the same ridge; and about where the battery now stands, as shown in the picture, was a small fort or works erected, known as Battery Seventeen.

When engaged in action, our men exhibited the same coolness that is shown in the picture—that is, while loading our guns. If the enemy is engaging us, as soon as each gun is loaded the cannoneers drop to the ground and protect themselves as best they can, except the gunners and the officers, who are expected to be always on the lookout. The gunners are the corporals who sight and direct the firing of the guns.

In the photograph you will notice a person (in civilian's clothes). This is Mr. Brady or his assistant, but I think it is Mr. Brady himself.

It is now almost forty-seven years since the photographs were taken, yet I am able to designate at least fifteen persons of our battery, and point them out. I should have said that Mr. Brady took picture No. 1 from a point a little to the left, and front, of our battery; and the second one was taken a little to the rear, and left, of the battery. Petersburg lay immediately over the ridge in the front, right over past

## THE FIELD DARK–ROOM

Here we get an excellent idea of how the business of army photography, invented by Brady and first exemplified by him at Bull Run, had become organized toward the close of the war. In the lower picture we see the outfit with which Samuel A. Cooley followed the fortunes of the campaigners, and recorded for all time the stirring events around Savannah at the completion of the March to the Sea. Cooley was attached to the Tenth Corps, United States Army, and secured photographs at Jacksonville, St. Augustine, Beaufort, and Charleston during the bombardment. Here he is in the act of making an exposure. The huge camera and plate-holder seem to eyes of the present day far too cumbersome to make possible the wonderful definition and beautiful effects of light and shade which characterize the war-time negatives that have come down to us through the vicissitudes of half a century. Here are Cooley's two means of transportation. The wagon fitted to carry the

[A—3]

THE CIVIL WAR PHOTOGRAPHERS' IMPEDIMENTA

supply of chemicals, glass plates, and the precious finished negatives includes a compartment for more leisurely developing. The little dark-room buggy to the left was used upon occasions when it was necessary for the army photographer to proceed in light marching order. In the smaller picture we see again the light-proof developing tent in action before the ramparts of Fort McAllister. The view is of the exterior of the fort fronting the Savannah River. A few days before the Confederate guns had frowned darkly from the parapet at Sherman's "bummers," who could see the smoke of the Federal gunboats waiting to welcome them just beyond. With Sherman looking proudly on, the footsore and hungry soldiers rushed forward to the attack, and the Stars and Stripes were soon floating over this vast barrier between them and the sea. The next morning, Christmas Day, 1864, the gunboats and transports steamed up the river and the joyful news was flashed northward.

the man whom you see sitting there so leisurely on the earthworks thrown up.

A notice in *Humphrey's Journal* in 1861 describes vividly the records of the flight after Bull Run secured by the indefatigable Brady. Unfortunately the unique one in which the reviewer identified "Bull Run" Russell in reverse action is lost to the world. But we have the portrait of Brady himself three days later in his famous linen duster, as he returned to Washington. His story comes from one who had it from his own lips:

He [Brady] had watched the ebb and flow of the battle on that Sunday morning in July, 1861, and seen now the success of the green Federal troops under General McDowell in the field, and now the stubborn defense of the green troops under that General Jackson who thereby earned the sobriquet of "Stonewall." At last Johnston, who with Beauregard and Jackson, was a Confederate commander, strengthened by reenforcements, descended upon the rear of the Union troops and drove them into a retreat which rapidly turned to a rout.

The plucky photographer was forced along with the rest; and as night fell he lost his way in the thick woods which were not far from the little stream that gave the battle its name. He was clad in the linen duster which was a familiar sight to those who saw him taking his pictures during that campaign, and was by no means prepared for a night in the open. He was unarmed as well, and had nothing with which to defend himself from any of the victorious Confederates who might happen his way, until one of the famous company of "Fire" zouaves, of the Union forces, gave him succor in the shape of a broadsword. This he strapped about his waist, and it was still there when he finally made his way to Washington three days later. He was a sight to behold after his wanderings, but he had come through unscathed as it was his fate to do so frequently afterwards.

Instances might be multiplied indefinitely, but here is one more evidence of the quality of this pictorial record. The same narrator had from Brady a tale of a picture made a year and a half later, at the battle of Fredericksburg. He says:

Burnside, then in command of the Army of the Potomac, was preparing to cross the Rappahannock, and Longstreet and Jackson, commanding the Confederate forces, were fortifying the hills back of the right bank of that river. Brady, desiring as usual to be in the thick of things, undertook to make some pictures from the left bank. He placed cameras in position and got his men to work, but suddenly found him-

THE CAMERA
WITH
THE ARMY

IN RETREAT
AND
ADVANCE

The plucky Brady-Gardner operatives stuck to the Union army in the East,
whether good fortune or ill betided it.  Above, two of them are busy with
their primitive apparatus near Bull Run, while Pope's army was in retreat,
just before the second battle on that fateful ground.  Below is a photographer's portable dark-room, two years later, at Cobb's Hill on the Appomattox.
Near here Grant's army had joined Butler's, and before them Lee's veterans
were making their last stand within the entrenchments at Petersburg.

(ABOVE)

PHOTOGRAPHERS

AT BULL RUN

BEFORE THE

SECOND

FIGHT

(BELOW)

PHOTOGRAPHERS

AT BUTLER'S

SIGNALING

TOWER

1864

self taking a part very different from that of a non-combatant. In the bright sunshine his bulky cameras gleamed like guns, and the Confederate marksmen thought that a battery was being placed in position. They promptly opened fire, and Brady found himself the target for a good many bullets. It was only his phenomenal good luck that allowed him to escape without injury either to himself and men or to his apparatus.

It is clearly worth while to study for a few moments this man Brady, who was so ready to risk his life for the idea by which he was obsessed. While the war soon developed far beyond what he or any other one man could possibly have compassed, so that he is probably directly responsible for only a fraction of the whole vast collection of pictures in these volumes, he may fairly be said to have fathered the movement; and his daring and success undoubtedly stimulated and inspired the small army of men all over the war-region, whose unrelated work has been laboriously gathered together.

Matthew B. Brady was born at Cork, Ireland (not in New Hampshire, as is generally stated) about 1823. Arriving in New York as a boy, he got a job in the great establishment of A. T. Stewart, first of the merchant princes of that day. The youngster's good qualities were so conspicuous that his large-minded employer made it possible for him to take a trip abroad at the age of fifteen, under the charge of S. F. B. Morse, who was then laboring at his epoch-making development of the telegraph.

Naturally enough, this scientist took his young companion to the laboratory of the already famous Daguerre, whose arduous experiments in making pictures by sunlight were just approaching fruition; and the wonderful discovery which young Brady's receptive eyes then beheld was destined to determine his whole life-work.

For that very year (1839) Daguerre made his " daguerreotype " known to the world; and Brady's keen interest was intensified when, in 1840, on his own side of the ocean, Professor Draper produced the first photographic portrait the world had yet seen, a likeness of his sister, which required the amazingly short exposure of *only ninety seconds!*

Brady's natural business-sense and his mercantile training showed him the chance for a career which this new invention opened, and it was but a short time before he had a gallery

## WASHING THE NEGATIVES

Photographers' Headquarters at Cold Harbor, Virginia.—In the lull before the fierce engagement which Grant was about to meet here in his persistent pushing forward upon Richmond, the cameraists were engaged in fixing, washing, and storing their negatives.

## BEFORE SECOND BULL RUN

Brady's headquarters with his "What Is It?" preparing for the strenuous work involved in the oncoming battle.

## AT WORK IN SUMTER, APRIL, 1865

At last the besiegers were in Charleston, and the Union photographers for the first time were securing views of the position.

## BRADY'S "WHAT IS IT?" AT CULPEPER, VIRGINIA

on Broadway and was well launched upon the new trade of furnishing daguerreotype portraits to all comers. He was successful from the start; in 1851 his work took a prize at the London World's Fair; about the same time he opened an office in Washington; in the fifties he brought over Alexander Gardner, an expert in the new revolutionary wet-plate process, which gave a negative furnishing many prints instead of one unduplicatable original; and in the twenty years between his start and the Civil War he became the fashionable photographer of his day—as is evidenced not only by the superb collection of notable people whose portraits he gathered together, but by Bret Harte's classic verse (from " Her Letter ") :

Well, yes—if you saw us out driving
 Each day in the Park, four-in-hand—
If you saw poor dear mamma contriving
 To look supernaturally grand,—
If you saw papa's picture, as taken
 By Brady, and tinted at that,—
You'd never suspect he sold bacon
 And flour at Poverty Flat.

Upon this sunny period of prosperity the Civil War broke in 1861. Brady had made portraits of scores of the men who leaped into still greater prominence as leaders in the terrible struggle, and his vigorous enthusiasm saw in this fierce drama an opportunity to win ever brighter laurels. His energy and his acquaintance with men in authority overcame every obstacle, and he succeeded in interesting President Lincoln, Secretary Stanton, General Grant, and Allan Pinkerton to such an extent that he obtained the protection of the Secret Service, and permits to make photographs at the front. Everything had to be done at his own expense, but with entire confidence he equipped his men, and set out himself as well, giving instructions to guard against breakage by making two negatives of everything, and infusing into all his own ambition to astonish the world by this unheard-of feat.

The need for such permits appears in a " home letter " from E. T. Whitney, a war photographer whose negatives, unfortunately, have been destroyed. This letter, dated March 13, 1862, states that the day before " all photographing has

ESTABLISHING COMMUNICATION

Here the camera has caught the U. S. Military Telegraph Construction Corps in action, April, 1864. The 150-odd men composing it were active throughout the war in planting poles and stringing wires in order to keep the Central Telegraph Office in direct communication with the armies at all times. Lincoln spent many an evening in the War Department Building at the capital reading the despatches from the front handed to him by the operators. The photograph but faintly indicates the flexible insulated wire, which by this time had come into use, and in the picture is being strung along by the two men on the poles and the three in advance of them in the left foreground.

been stopped by general orders from headquarters." Owing to ignorance of this order on the part of the guard at the bridge, Whitney was allowed to reach the Army of the Potomac, where he made application to General McClellan for a special pass.

We shall get some more glimpses presently of these adventurous souls in action. But, as already hinted, extraordinary as were the results of Brady's impetuous vigor, he was but one of many in the great work of picturing the war. Three-fourths of the scenes with the Army of the Potomac were made by Gardner. Thomas G. Roche was an indefatigable worker in the armies' train. Captain A. J. Russell, detached as official camera-man for the War Department, obtained many invaluable pictures illustrating the military railroading and construction work of the Army of the Potomac, which were hurried straightway to Secretary Stanton at Washington. Sam A. Cooley was attached to the Tenth Army Corps, and recorded the happenings around Savannah, Fort McAllister, Jacksonville, St. Augustine, Beaufort, and Charleston during the bombardment; George M. Barnard, under the supervision of General O. M. Poe (then Captain in the Engineer Corps), did yeoman's service around Atlanta.

S. R. Siebert was very busy indeed at Charleston in 1865. Cook of Charleston, Edwards of New Orleans, and other unknown men on the Confederate side, working under even greater difficulties (Cook, for instance, had to secure his chemicals from Anthony in New York—who also supplied Brady —and smuggle them through), did their part in the vast labor; and many another unknown, including the makers of the little *cartes de visite,* contributed to the panorama which to-day unfolds itself before the reader.

One most interesting camera-man of unique kind was A. D. Lytle, of Baton Rouge, Louisiana, who made a series of views (covering three years and several campaigns—and consequently scattered through the present work) for the specific use of the Confederate Secret Service. That is to say, he was a "camera spy," and a good one, too. He secured his chemicals from the same great firm of Anthony & Co., in New York, but instead of running the blockade with them, they were supplied on "orders to trade." In many cases, for instance, the necessary iodides and bromides masqueraded as

## A TRIUMPH OF THE WET-PLATE

It seems almost impossible that this photograph could have been taken before the advent of modern photographic apparatus, yet Mr. Gardner's negative, made almost fifty years ago, might well furnish a striking exhibit in a modern photographic salon.   The view is of Quarles' Mill, on the North Anna River, Virginia. In grassy fields above the mill the tents of the headquarters of Grant and Meade were pitched for a day or two during the march which culminated in the siege of Petersburg.   Among the prisoners brought in while the army was here in camp was a woman clad in Confederate gray, apparently performing the duties of a scout.   She was captured astride of a bony steed and asserted that she belonged to a battery of artillery. This wild creature, with her tangled black locks hanging down her neck, became the center of interest to the idlers of the camp.   At these she would occasionally throw stones with considerable accuracy, particularly at the negroes, who gave her a wide berth.   As the faithful camera indicates, the river current at this point is strong and rapid.   While General Thomas L. Crittenden's division of the Federal Ninth Corps was crossing the North Anna (June 24, 1864) by fording the mill-dam, many sturdy foot-soldiers as well as horsemen were swept over the falls.   However, the division got across in good fighting shape and formed a line of battle around the ford on the southern bank just in time to head off a bold Confederate dash for the same coign of vantage.   Crittenden's advance guard was hotly engaged in the woods beyond the mill and being roughly handled when the rear of the column reached the southern bank.

quinine.[1] Mr. Lytle's son relates that his father used to signal with flag and lantern from the observation tower on the top of the ruins of the Baton Rouge capitol to Scott's Bluff, whence the messages were relayed to the Confederates near New Orleans; but he found this provided such a tempting target for the Federal sharpshooters that he discontinued the practice.

There are contemporary comments on the first crop of war photographs—which confirm several points already made. *Humphrey's Journal* in October, 1861, contained the following:

### PHOTOGRAPHS OF WAR SERIES

Among the portraits in Brady's selection, spoken of in our last number, are those of many leading generals and colonels—McClellan, McDowell, Heintzelman, Burnside, Wood, Corcoran, Slocum, and others. Of the larger groups, the most effective are those of the army passing through Fairfax village, the battery of the 1st Rhode Island regiment at Camp Sprague, the 71st Regiment [New York] formed in hollow square at the Navy Yard, the Engineer Corps of the New York Twelfth at Camp Anderson, Zouaves on the lookout from the belfry of Fairfax Court House, etc., etc.

Mr. Brady intends to take other photographic scenes of the localities of our army and of battle-scenes, and his collection will undoubtedly prove to be the most interesting ever yet exhibited. But why should he monopolize this department? We have plenty of other artists as good as he is. What a field would there be for Anthony's instantaneous views and for stereoscopic pictures. Let other artists exhibit a little of Mr. Brady's enterprise and furnish the public with more views. There are numerous photographers close by the stirring scenes which are being daily enacted, and now is the time for them to distinguish themselves.

We have seen how far Brady came from " monopolizing " the field. And surely the sum total of achievement is triumphant enough to share among all who had any hand in it.

And now let us try to get some idea of the problem which confronted these enthusiasts, and see how they tackled it.

[1] This statement is historically confirmed. Professor Walter L. Fleming, of the University of Louisiana, states he has seen many such orders-to-trade, signed by President Lincoln, but not countersigned by Secretary Stanton.

## A SNAPSHOT IN THE WAR REGION

Another remarkable example of the results achieved by the old collodion process photographers quite indistinguishable from the instantaneous photographs of the present day. Although taken under the necessity of removing and replacing the lens cap, this negative has successfully caught the waterfall and the Federal cavalryman's horse which has been ridden to the stream for a drink. The picture was taken at Hazel Run, Virginia, above the pontoon bridge constructed for the crossing of the Federal troops. During the advances and retreats, while the Federal armies were maneuvering for position, the photographers were frequently at a loss for material. At such times, true to the professional instinct, they kept in practice by making such views as this. Less important from the strictly military viewpoint, these splendid specimens of landscape photography give us a clear conception of the character of the country over which the Federal and Confederate armies passed and repassed during the stirring period of the war.

Imagine what it must have meant even to get to the scene of action—with cumbersome tent and apparatus, and a couple of hundred glass plates whose breakage meant failure; over unspeakable back-country roads or no roads at all; with the continual chance of being picked off by some scouting sharp-shooter or captured through some shift of the armies.

The first sight of the queer-looking wagon caused amazement, speculation, derision. "What is it?" became so inevitable a greeting that to this day if one asks a group of soldiers about war-photographs, they will exclaim simultaneously, "Oh, yes, the 'what-is-it' wagon!" It became a familiar sight, yet the novelty of its awkward mystery never quite wore off.

Having arrived, and having faced the real perils generally attendant upon reaching the scenes of keenest interest, our camera adventurer was but through the overture of his troubles. The most advanced photography of that day was the wet-plate method, by which the plates had to be coated in the dark (which meant in this case carrying everywhere a smothery, light-proof tent), *exposed within five minutes*, and developed within five minutes more! For the benefit of amateur members of the craft here are some notes from the veteran photographer, Mr. George G. Rockwood:

First, all the plain glass plates in various sizes, usually 8 x 10, had to be carefully cleaned and carried in dust-proof boxes. When ready for action, the plate was carefully coated with "collodion," which carried in solution the "excitants"—bromide and iodide of potassium, or ammonia, or cadmium. Collodion is made by the solution of gun-cotton in about equal parts of sulphuric ether and 95° proof alcohol. The salts above mentioned are then added, making the collodion a *vehicle* for obtaining the sensitive surface on the glass plate. The coating of plates was a delicate operation even in the ordinary well-organized studio. After coating the plate with collodion and letting the ether and alcohol evaporate to just the right degree of "stickiness," it was lowered carefully into a deep "bath holder" which contained a solution of nitrate of silver about 60° for quick field-work. This operation created the sensitive condition of the plate, and had to be done in total darkness except a subdued yellow light. When properly coated (from three to five minutes) the plate was put into a "slide" or "holder" and exposed to the action of the light in the camera. When exposed, it was returned to the dark-room and developed.

[46]

AMENITIES OF THE CAMP IN 1864

This photograph, taken at Brandy Station, Virginia, is an excellent example of the skill of the war photographers. When we remember that orthochromatic plates were undreamed of in the days of the Civil War, the color values of this picture are marvelous. The collodion wet-plate has caught the sheen and texture of the silk dresses worn by the officers' wives, whom we see on a visit to a permanent camp. The entrance to the tent is a fine example of the rustic work with which the Engineer Corps of the various armies amused themselves during periods which would otherwise be spent in tedious inactivity. The officers' quarters received first attention. Thus an atmosphere of indescribable charm was thrown about the permanent camps to which the wives of the officers came in their brief visits to the front, and from which they reluctantly returned without seeing anything of the gruesome side of war. A review or a parade was usually held for their entertainment. In the weary waiting before Petersburg during the siege, the successful consummation of which practically closed the war, the New York engineers, while not engaged in strengthening the Federal fortifications, amused themselves by constructing a number of rustic buildings of great beauty. One of these was the signal tower toward the left of the Federal line of investment. Near it a substantial and artistic hospital building was erected, and, to take the place of a demolished church, a new and better rustic structure sprang into being.

Mr. Rockwood also knew all about Brady's wagon, having had a similar contrivance made for himself before the war, for taking pictures in the country. He "used an ordinary delivery wagon of the period, much like the butcher's cart of to-day and had a strong step attached at the rear and below the level of the wagon floor. A door was put on at the back, carefully hung so as to be light-proof. The door, you understand, came down over the step which was boxed in at the sides, making it a sort of well within the body of the wagon rather than a true step.

"The work of coating or sensitizing the plates and that of developing them was done from this well, in which there was just room enough to work. As the operator stood there the collodion was within reach of his right hand, in a special receptacle. On his left also was the holder of one of the baths. The chief developing bath was in front, with the tanks of various liquids stored in front of it again, and the space between it and the floor filled with plates.

"With such a wagon on a larger scale, large enough for men to sleep in front of the dark-room part, the phenomenal pictures of Brady were made possible. Brady risked his life many a time in order not to separate from this cumbrous piece of impedimenta.

"On exceptional occasions in very cold weather the life of a wet plate might be extended to nearly an hour on either side of the exposure, the coating or the development side, but ordinarily the work had to be done within a very few minutes, and every minute of delay resulted in loss of brilliancy and depth in the negative."

Some vivid glimpses of the war-photographers' troubles come also from Mr. J. Pitcher Spencer, who knew the work intimately:

We worked long with one of the foremost of Brady's men, and here let me doff my hat to the name of M. B. Brady—few to-day are worthy to carry his camera case, even as far as ability from the photographic standpoint goes. I was, in common with the "Cape Codders," following the ocean from 1859 to 1864; I was only home a few months —1862–63—and even then from our boys who came home invalided we heard of that grand picture-maker Brady, as they called him.

When I made some views (with the only apparatus then known, the "wet plate"), there came a large realization of some of the immense

[48]

DIGGING UNDER FIRE AT DUTCH GAP—1864

Here for a moment the Engineering corps of General Benjamin F. Butler's army paused while the camera of the army photographer was focussed upon it. In August, 1864, Butler, with his army then bottled up in Bermuda Hundred, began to dig a canal at Dutch Gap to save a circuit of six miles in the bend of the James River and thus avoid the batteries, torpedoes, and obstructions which the Confederates had placed to prevent the passage of the Federal fleet up the river toward Richmond. The difficulties of this engineering feat are here seen plainly in the photograph. It took Butler's men all the rest of the year (1864) to cut through this canal, exposed as they were to the fire of the Confederate batteries above. One of the last acts of General Butler was an unsuccessful effort to blow up the dam at the mouth of this canal, and by thus admitting water to it, render it navigable.

difficulties surmounted by those who made war-pictures. When you realize that the most sensitive of all the list of chemicals are requisite to make collodion, which must coat every plate, and that the very slightest breath might carry enough "poison" across the plate being coated to make it produce a blank spot instead of some much desired effect, you may perhaps have a faint idea of the care requisite to produce a picture. Moreover, it took unceasing care to keep every bit of the apparatus, as well as each and every chemical, free from any possible contamination which might affect the picture. Often a breath of wind, no matter how gentle, spoiled the whole affair.

Often, just as some fine result looked certain, a hot streak of air would not only spoil the plate, but put the instrument out of commission, by curling some part of it out of shape. In face of these, and hundreds of minor discouragements, the men imbued with vim and forcefulness by the " Only Brady " kept right along and to-day the world can enjoy these wonderful views as a result.

Still further details come from an old soldier and photographic expert, Mr. F. M. Rood:

The plate "flowed" with collodion was dipped *at once* in a bath of nitrate of silver, in water also iodized, remained there *in darkness* three to five minutes; still in darkness, it was taken out, drained, put in the dark-holder, exposed, and developed in the dark-tent *at once.* The time between flowing the collodion and developing should not exceed eight or ten minutes. The developer was sulphate of iron solution and acetic acid, after which came a slight washing and fixing (to remove the surplus silver) with solution of cyanide of potassium; and then a final washing, drying, and varnishing. The surface (wet or dry), unlike a dry plate, could not be touched. I was all through the war from 1861–65, in the Ninety-third New York regiment, whose pictures you have given. I recognized quite a number of the old comrades. You have also in your collection a negative of each company of that regiment.

Fortunately the picture men occasionally immortalized each other as well as the combatants, so that we have a number of intimate glimpses of their life and methods. In one the wagon, chemicals and camera are in the very trenches at Atlanta, and they tell more than pages of description. But, naturally, they cannot show the arduous labor, the narrow escapes, the omnipresent obstacles which could be overcome only by the keenest ardor and determination. The epic of the war-photographer is still to be written. It would compare favorably with the story of many battles. And it does not

## CAMP LIFE OF THE INVADING ARMY

This picture preserves for us the resplendent aspect of the camp of McClellan's Army of the Potomac in the spring of 1862. On his march from Yorktown toward Richmond, McClellan advanced his supply base from Cumberland Landing to White House on the Pamunkey. The barren fields on the bank of the river were converted as if by magic into an immense city of tents stretching away as far as the eye could see, while mirrored in the river lay the immense fleet of transports convoyed up by gunboats from Fortress Monroe. Here we see but a small section of this inspiring view. In the foreground, around the mud-spattered forge, the blankets and knapsacks of the farriers have been thrown carelessly on the ground. Farther on the patient army mules are tethered around the wagons. In the background, before the camp of the Fifth New York Volunteers (Duryée's Zouaves), a regiment of infantry is drawn up in columns of companies for inspection drill. From the 15th to the 19th of May the Army of the Potomac was concentrated between Cumberland Landing and White House. While in camp an important change was made in the organization of the army. The divisions of Porter and Sykes were united into the Fifth Corps under Porter, and those of Franklin and Smith into the Sixth Corps under Franklin. On May 19th the movement to Richmond was begun by the advance of Porter and Franklin to Tunstall's Station.

[A—4]

require much imagination, after viewing the results obtained in the face of such conditions, to get a fair measure of these indomitable workers.

The story of the way in which these pictures have been rescued from obscurity is almost as romantic a tale as that of their making. The net result of Brady's efforts was a collection of over seven thousand pictures (two negatives of each in most cases); and the expenditure involved, estimated at $100,000, ruined him. One set, after undergoing the most extraordinary vicissitudes, finally passed into the Government's possession, where it is now held with a prohibition against its use for commercial purposes. (The $25,000 tardily voted to Mr. Brady by Congress did not retrieve his financial fortunes, and he died in the nineties, in a New York hospital, poor and forgotten, save by a few old-time friends.

Brady's own negatives passed in the seventies into the possession of Anthony, in default of payment of his bills for photographic supplies. They were kicked about from pillar to post for ten years, until John C. Taylor found them in an attic and bought them; from this they became the backbone of the Ordway-Rand collection; and in 1895 Brady himself had no idea what had become of them. Many were broken, lost, or destroyed by fire. After passing to various other owners, they were discovered and appreciated by Edward Bailey Eaton, of Hartford, Connecticut, who created the immediate train of events that led to their importance as the nucleus of a collection of many thousand pictures gathered from all over the country to furnish the material for this work.

From all sorts of sources, from the Atlantic to the Pacific, from Maine to the Gulf, these hidden treasures have been drawn. Historical societies, Government and State bureaus, librarians, private collectors, military and patriotic organizations, old soldiers and their families have recollected, upon earnest insistence, that they did have such things or once knew of them. Singly and in groups they have come from walls, out of archives, safes, old garrets, often seeing the light of day for the first time in a generation, to join together once more in a pictorial army which daily grew more irresistible as the new arrivals augmented, supplemented, and explained. The superb result is here spread forth and illuminated for posterity.

## THE PASSING WAGON TRAIN

This historic bridge crossed Antietam Creek on the turnpike leading from Boonsboro to Sharpsburg. It is one of the memorable spots in the history of the war. The photograph was taken soon after the battle of Antietam; the overturned stone wall and shattered fences, together with the appearance of the adjacent ground, are mute witnesses of the conflict that raged about it on September 16–17, 1862, when the control of this bridge was important to both McClellan and Lee. The former held it during the battle; and the fire of his artillery from the ridges near the bridge enabled the disordered Union lines to recover in time to check the ferocious assaults of the Confederates.

Apart from all the above considerations, these invaluable pictures are well worth attention from the standpoint of pictorial art. We talk a great deal nowadays about the astonishing advances of modern art-photography; and it is quite true that patient investigators have immeasurably increased the range and flexibility of camera methods and results. We now manipulate negatives and print to produce any sort of effect; we print in tint or color, omitting or adding what we wish; numberless men of artistic capacity are daily showing how to transmit personal feeling through the intricacies of the mechanical process. But it is just as true as when the cave-man scratched on a bone his recollections of mammoth and reindeer, that the artist will produce work that moves the beholder, no matter how crude may be his implements. Clearly there were artists among these Civil War photographers.

Probably this was caused by natural selection. It took ardor and zest for this particular thing above all others to keep a man at it in face of the hardships and disheartening handicaps. In any case, the work speaks for itself. Over and over one is thrilled by a sympathetic realization that the vanished man who pointed the camera at some particular scene, must have felt precisely the same pleasure in a telling composition of landscape, in a lifelike grouping, in a dramatic glimpse of a battery in action, in a genre study of a wounded soldier watched over by a comrade—that we feel to-day and that some seeing eye will respond to generations in the future. This is the true immortality of art. And when the emotions thus aroused center about a struggle which determined the destiny of a great nation, the picture that arouses them takes its proper place as an important factor in that heritage of the past which gives us to-day increased stature over all past ages, just because we add all their experience to our own.

# SECOND PREFACE

---

# THE PHOTOGRAPHIC
# RECORD
# AS HISTORY

---

WITH THE DEFENDERS OF WASHINGTON IN 1862 ;
THE SALLY-PORT AT FORT RICHARDSON

## "HISTORY BROUGHT AGAIN INTO THE PRESENT TENSE"

The value of "The Photographic Record as History" is emphasized in the contribution from Mr. George Haven Putnam on page 60. This photograph of a dramatic scene was taken on a July day after the photographer's own heart—clear and sunny. The fort is at the end of Peach Tree Street, Atlanta, to the north of the city. Sherman had just taken possession, and the man at the left is a cavalryman of his forces. The mire-caked wheels of the guns show that they have been dragged through miles and miles of muddy

## CONFEDERATE EARTHWORKS BEFORE ATLANTA, 1864

roads. The delays Sherman had met with in his advance on Atlanta resulting in constant and indecisive fighting without entrapping Johnston, had brought about a reaction at the North. A large party wished to end the war. Election Day was approaching. Lincoln was a presidential candidate for the second time. He had many enemies. But the news of Sherman's capture of Atlanta helped to restore confidence, and to insure the continuation of the administration pledged to a vigorous prosecution of the war.

A STRIKING WAR PHOTOGRAPH OF '63

The introduction on page 30, "Photographing the Civil War," remarks on the genius required to record such vivid action by camera in the days of '61. The use of the instrument had not then become pastime; it was a pioneer science, requiring absolute knowledge, training, and experience. Only experts like the men that Brady trained could do such work as this. There were no lightning shutters, no automatic or universal focus. In positions of danger and at times when speed and accuracy were required, there was the delicacy of the old-fashioned wet plate to consider, with all its drawbacks. No wonder people were surprised that pictures such as this exist; they had grown used to the old woodcut and the often mutilated attempts of pen and pencil to portray such scenes of action. There are many who never knew that photography was

## ARTILLERY "REGULARS" BEFORE CHANCELLORSVILLE

possible in the Civil War. Yet look at this Union battery, taken by the shore of the Rappahannock, just before the battle of Chancellorsville. Action, movement, portraiture are shown. We can hear the officer standing in front giving his orders; his figure leaning slightly forward is tense with spoken words of command. The cannoneers, resting or ramming home the charges, are magnificent types of the men who made the Army of the Potomac—the army doomed to suffer, a few days after this picture was taken, its crushing repulse by the famous flanking charge of "Stonewall" Jackson; yet the army which kept faith and ultimately became invincible in the greatest civil war of history. Within sixty days after the Chancellorsville defeat the troops engaged won a signal triumph over the self-same opponents at Gettysburg.

# THE PHOTOGRAPHIC RECORD AS HISTORY

By GEORGE HAVEN PUTNAM

*Adjutant and Brevet Major 176th New York Volunteer Infantry*

'TIS fifty years since. The words recall the opening sentence of Scott's famous romance, "Waverley," and Scott's reference, like my own, had to do with the strenuous years of civil war.

To one examining the unique series of photographs which were secured, during the campaigns of our great war, by the pluck and persistence of Brady and Gardner, and the negatives of which have, almost miraculously, been preserved through the vicissitudes of half a century, comes, however, the feeling that these battles and marchings were the events not of fifty years back, but of yesterday, if not, indeed, things of to-day. These vivid pictures bring past history into the present tense; the observer sees our citizen soldiers as they camped, as they marched, and as they fought, and comes to know how they lived and how they died. There are revealed to the eye through these lifelike photographs, as if through a vitascope, the successive scenes of the great life-and-death drama of the nation's struggle for existence, a struggle which was fought out through four eventful years, and in which were sacrificed of the best of manhood of the country, North and South, eight hundred thousand lives.

In September, 1862, I landed in New York from the Bremen steamer *Hansa,* which was then making its first transatlantic trip. I had left my German university for the purpose of enlisting in the Union army, and, with the belief that the

"CITIZEN SOLDIERS"—THE 93D NEW YORK.

This informal photograph of the Ninety-Third New York Infantry was taken in 1862 just before Antietam. In it we see the quality of the men who dropped the pursuits of civil life and flocked to form the armies of the North. Thus, in camp and on the battlefield the camera did its work and now takes us back over the four terrible years, showing us to the minutest detail how our men marched and lived and fought. The youth of the troops is strikingly evident in this picture as they stand assembled here with their arms hastily stacked for the ever-pleasurable experience of having their pictures taken.

war could hardly be prolonged for many further months, I had secured leave of absence from my university only for the college year. I have to-day a vivid recollection of the impression made upon the young student by the war atmosphere in which he found his home city. In coming up from the steamship pier, I found myself on Broadway near the office of the *Herald,* at that time at the corner of Ann Street. The bulletin board was surrounded by a crowd of anxious citizens, whose excitement was so tense that it expressed itself not in utterance but in silence. With some difficulty, I made my way near enough to the building to get a glimpse of the announcement on the board. The heading was, "A battle is now going on in Maryland; it is hoped that General McClellan will drive Lee's army back into the Potomac."

I recall to-day the curious impressiveness of the present tense, of the report of a battle that was actually "going on." To one who reads such an announcement, all things seem to be possible, and as I stood surrounded by men whose pulses were throbbing with the keenest of emotions, I felt with them as if we could almost hear the sound of the cannon on the Potomac. The contrast was the stronger to one coming from the quiet lecture-rooms of a distant university to the streets of a great city excited with twelve months of war, and with the ever-present doubt as to what the hours of each day might bring forth. The fight that was then "going on" is known in history as the battle of Antietam. History tells us that Lee's army was not pushed into the Potomac. There were two causes that prevented this result—George B. McClellan and Robert E. Lee. McClellan was a skilled engineer and he knew how to organize troops, but he never pushed an enemy's army before him with the energy of a man who meant to win and who had faith that he could win. It was his habit to feel that he had made a brilliant success when, having come into touch with the foe, he had succeeded in withdrawing his own army without undue loss; and it is fair to say that when the enemy

## THE PRESIDENT INVESTIGATES

Lincoln at McClellan's Headquarters, October 1, 1862.—The serious, impassive features of the President give no hint of the thoughts that were coursing through his mind as his calm eyes gazed upon the General and his staff. He knew that "Little Mac," as the soldiers fondly termed him, was the idol of the army and had the staunch support of his officers. Lincoln also knew that he and McClellan differed radically as to the conduct of the war. Politics had crept into the Army of the Potomac, the politics which during the campaign of 1864 opposed McClellan to Lincoln as a candidate for the presidency. As he stood there before the General's tent the Commander-in-chief could have summarily removed McClellan, but in accordance with his patient policy of leaving the future event to justify his course, Lincoln merely inspected the camp, talked with McClellan and his officers, and pondered all he saw and heard in an effort to find some military reason for the strange failure of the splendid army to end the war by a decisive campaign.

was Robert E. Lee, such a successful withdrawal might almost be considered as a triumph.

A fresh and vivid impression of the scene of the bloody struggle at Antietam Creek is given in one of the photographs in this great war series. The plucky photographer has succeeded in securing, from the very edge of the battle-field, a view of the movements of the troops that are on the charge; and when, on the further edge of the fields, we actually see the smoke of the long lines of rifles by which that charge is to be repulsed, we feel as if the battle were again " going on " before our eyes, and we find ourselves again infused with mingled dread and expectation as to the result.

In looking at the photographs, the Union veteran recalls the fierce charge of Burnside's men for the possession of the bridge and the sturdy resistance made by the regiments of Longstreet. He will grieve with the Army of the Potomac and with the country at the untimely death of the old hero, General Mansfield; he will recall the graphic description given by the poet Holmes of the weary week's search through the battle-field and the environs for the " body " of his son, the young captain, who lived to become one of the scholarly members of the national Supreme Court; and he may share the disappointment not only of the army, but of the citizens back of the army, that, notwithstanding his advantages of position, McClellan should have permitted the Confederate army to withdraw without molestation, carrying with it its trains, its artillery, and even its captured prisoners.

Another photograph in the series, which is an example of special enterprise on the part of Mr. Brady, presents Lincoln and McClellan in consultation some time after this bloody and indecisive battle. The pose and the features of the two men are admirably characteristic. Two weeks have elapsed since Lee's withdrawal across the river, but the Army of the Potomac, while rested and fully resupplied, has been held by its young commander in an inexplicable inaction. Lincoln's per-

## THE BATTLE FOG AT ANTIETAM

The sulphur smoke of the guns, covering the field like a sea mist, tells us to-day as clearly as it told the photographer on September 17, 1862, that a battle is in progress off to the right. It was indeed the bloodiest single day's action of the war, and there probably exists no finer picture of an actual engagement than this remarkable photograph. Down in the meadow are seen the caissons of the artillery; the guns are engaged less than a quarter of a mile away. At the moment of exposure the firing must have been terrific.

The battle-field of Antietam was the first that remained in complete possession of the Union troops since the disasters that began to overtake them after Fair Oaks in June. On Antietam were staked the Confederate hopes for the conquest of Maryland. The battle proved, however, to be the turning-point in establishing the sovereignty of the Union. Lincoln had awaited a Union victory to justify a proclamation of emancipation. This he issued September 22, 1862, almost before the sound of the mighty battle had died away.

sistent demand for an advance and his reiterated inquiries as to the grounds for the delay have met with no response. The President finally comes to the camp for a personal word with the commander in the field. How the photographer secured the opportunity of being present at such an interview one does not know, but that he was there is unmistakable.

These vivid photographs which constitute the great historic series bring again into the present tense, for the memories of the veterans, all of the dramatic scenes of the years of war; and even to those who are not veterans, those who have grown up in years of peace and to whom the campaigns of half a century back are but historic pages or dim stories, even to them must come, in looking at these pictures of campaigns, these vivid episodes of life and death, a clearer realization than could be secured in any other way of what the four years' struggle meant for their fathers and their grandfathers.

The fine views of Fort Stevens and Fort Lincoln recall the several periods in which, to the continuing anxieties of the people's leader, was added immediate apprehension as to the safety of the national capital. On the 19th of April, 1861, the Massachusetts Sixth, on its way to the protection of Washington, had been attacked in Baltimore, and connections between Washington and the North were cut off. A few hundred troops represented all the forces that the nation had for the moment been able to place in position for the protection of the capital.

I have stood, as thousands of visitors have stood, in Lincoln's old study, the windows of which overlook the Potomac; and I have had recalled to mind the vision of his tall figure and sad face as he stood looking across the river where the picket lines of the Virginia troops could be traced by the smoke, and dreading from morning to morning the approach of these troops over the Long Bridge. There must have come to Lincoln during these anxious days the dread that he was to be the last President of the United States, and that the torch, representing the life of the nation, that had been transmitted

[ 66 ]

## THE COMMANDER-IN-CHIEF

Here the gaunt figure of the Great Emancipator confronted General McClellan in his headquarters two weeks after Antietam had checked Lee's invasion of Maryland and had enabled the President to issue the Emancipation Proclamation. Brady's camera has preserved this remarkable occasion, the last time that these two men met each other. "We spent some time on the battlefield and conversed fully on the state of affairs. He told me that he was satisfied with all that I had done, that he would stand by me. He parted from me with the utmost cordiality," said General McClellan. The plan to follow up the success of Antietam in the effort to bring the war to a speedy conclusion must have been the thought uppermost in the mind of the Commander-in-Chief of the Army as he talked with his most popular General in the tent. A few days later came the order from Washington to "cross the Potomac and give battle to the enemy or drive him South." McClellan was relieved in the midst of a movement to carry out the order.

[A—5]

to him by the faltering hands of his predecessor was to expire while he was still responsible for the continuity of the flame.

And it was not only in 1861 that the capital was imperiled. The anxiety of the President (never for himself, but only for his country and his responsibilities) was to be renewed in June, 1863, when Lee was in Maryland, and in July, 1864, at the time of Early's raid. It was during Early's hurried attack that Lincoln, visiting Fort Stevens, came into direct sight of the fighting by which Early's men were finally repulsed. For the President, the war must indeed at this time have been something in the present tense, something which meant dread possibilities always impending.

The month of July, 1863, marked the turning point of the great contest. If the Federal lines had been broken at Gettysburg, Lee would have been able, in placing his army across the highways to Baltimore and to Philadelphia, to isolate Washington from the North. The Army of the Potomac would, of course, have been reconstituted, and Lee would finally have been driven across the Potomac as he was actually compelled to retire after the decision of the battle. But such a check to the efforts of the North, after two years of war for the maintenance of the nation, would in all probability have secured success for the efforts of the Confederate sympathizers in Europe and have brought about recognition and intervention on the part of France and of England. Such an intervention would have meant the triumph of the Confederacy and the breaking up of the great Republic. The value for the cause of the success of Meade in repelling, with heavy loss, the final assaults of Lee was further emphasized by a great triumph in the West. On the very day on which Lee's discomfited army was making its way back to the Potomac, the troops of General Grant were placing the Stars and Stripes over the well-defended works of Vicksburg.

A beautiful little picture recalls the sharp fight that was made, on July 2, 1863, for the possession of Little Round

FORT RICHARDSON—DRILL AT THE BIG GUNS, 1862 Copyright by Review of Reviews Co.

OFFICERS OF THE FIFTY-FIFTH NEW YORK VOLUNTEERS

DEFENSES OF WASHINGTON—CAMP OF THE FIRST CONNECTICUT HEAVY ARTILLERY

Here we see some of the guardians of the city of Washington, which was threatened in the beginning of the war and subsequently on occasions when Lincoln, looking from the White House, could see in the distance the smoke from Confederate camp fires. Lincoln would not consent to the withdrawal of many of the garrisons about Washington to reinforce McClellan on the Peninsula. There was little to relieve the tedium of guard duty, and the men spent their time principally at drill and in keeping their arms and accouterments spick and span. The troops in the tents and barracks were always able to present a fine appearance on review. In sharp contrast was that of their battle-scarred comrades who passed before Lincoln when he visited the front. Foreign military attachés often visited the forts about Washington. In the center picture we see two of them inspecting a gun.

Top. It was the foresight of General Warren that recognized the essential importance of this position for the maintenance of the Union line. After the repulse of Sickles's Third Corps in the Peach Orchard, Longstreet's men were actually on their way to take possession of the rocky hill from which the left and rear of the Union line could have been enfiladed. No Union force was for the moment available for the defense, but Warren, with two or three aides, raised some flags over the rocks, and the leader of Longstreet's advance, getting an impression that the position was occupied, delayed a brief spell for reenforcements.

This momentary respite gave Warren time to bring to the defense of the hill troops from the nearest command that was available, a division of the Fifth Corps. A few minutes later, came the first attack, followed by a series of fierce onsets that continued through the long summer afternoon. With some advantages of position, and with the realization that the control of the hill was absolutely essential for the maintenance of the line, the Federals held their own; but when darkness fell, the rocks of Devil's Den and the slopes of the hill were thickly strewn with dead, the bodies of the Blue and the Gray lying closely intermingled. A beautiful statue of Warren now stands on Little Round Top at the point where, almost single-handed, he placed his flag when there were no guns behind it. The general is looking out gravely over the slope and toward the opposite crest, where have been placed, in grim contrast to the smiling fields of the quiet farm behind, the Confederate field-guns that mark the position of Longstreet's lines.

The editors have fortunately been able to include with the great Brady series of army photographs a private collection, probably unique, of more than four hundred views of the gunboats on the rivers of the West. Each of these vessels represents a history of its own. One wishes for the imagination of a Homer which could present with due effectiveness a new "catalogue of the ships."

## LITTLE ROUND TOP—THE KEY TO GETTYSBURG.

A "slaughter pen" at Gettysburg. On this rocky slope of Little Round Top, Longstreet's men fought with the Federals in the second day's conflict, July 2, 1863. From boulder to boulder they wormed their way, to find behind each a soldier waiting for the hand-to-hand struggle which meant the death of one or the other. After the battle each rock and tree overshadowed a victim. The whole tangled and terrible field presented a far more appalling appearance than does the picture, which was taken after the wounded were removed. Little Round Top had been left unprotected by the advance of General Sickles' Third Corps. This break in the Federal line was discovered by General Warren just in time. Hastily procuring a flag, with but two or three other officers to help him he planted it on the hill, which led the Confederates to believe the position strongly occupied and delayed Longstreet's advance long enough for troops to be rushed forward to meet it. The picture tells all too plainly at what sacrifice the height was finally held.

Admiral Farragut, while accepting the armored vessels as possessing certain advantages and as apparently a necessity of "modern warfare," had the impatience of the old-fashioned sailor against any such attempt at protection. He preferred for himself the old type of wooden frigate of which his flag-ship, the famous *Hartford,* was the representative. "Why," said he, "if a shell strikes the side of the *Hartford* it goes clean through. Unless somebody happens to be directly in the path, there is no damage, excepting a couple of easily plugged holes. But when a shell makes its way into one of those 'damned tea-kettles,' it can't get out again. It sputters round inside doing all kinds of mischief." It must be borne in mind, apart from the natural exaggeration of such an utterance, that Farragut was speaking half a century ago, in the time of slow-velocity missiles. His phrase "damned tea-kettles" came, however, to be the general descriptive term for the ironclads, applied not only by the men in the ranks but by the naval men themselves.

There were assured advantages given by the armor in time of action against most of the fire that was possible with the weapons of the day, but for the midsummer climate of Louisiana, the "tea-kettles" were most abominable abiding places. During the day, the iron of the decks would get so hot that the hand could barely rest upon it. At night, sleep was impossible. The decks were kept wetted down, and the men lay on them, getting, toward the morning hours when the hulls had cooled down, such sleep as could be secured.

The progress of the armored transports making their way up the Red River under fire from the shore was an interesting feature of that campaign. The steepness of the banks on the Red River gave peculiar advantages for such fire, as it was frequently the case that the guns of the boats could not be elevated so as to reach the foe's position. It was difficult to protect the man at the wheel from such plunging fire, but bales of cotton were often placed around the upper

## THE FATEFUL FIELD

No picture has ever been painted to equal this panorama of the very center of the ground over which surged the struggling troops 'mid shot and shell during the thickest of the fighting at Gettysburg. The camera was planted on Little Round Top, and through its eye we look northward over the valley toward and beyond the little town of Gettysburg. Across the plain in the middle distance, over the Federal breastworks near the crest, and up to the very muzzles of the guns on Cemetery Ridge which were belching forth grape and canister, swept the men in gray under General Pickett in the last brave but unsuccessful assault that left Meade in possession of the field on Independence Day, 1863. The daring gallantry, utter coolness, and grim determination with which that charge was made have rarely been paralleled in history. The spirit of complete devotion to the conviction which prompted Pickett and his men is one of the most precious heritages of a united nation.

works which were sufficient to keep off at least musketry fire. This improvised armor proved, however, not only insufficient but a peril when the enterprising Confederate gunners succeeded in discharging from their field-pieces red-hot shot. It happened more than once (I recall witnessing one such incident) that the cotton was brought into flames by such shot and it became necessary to run the vessel ashore.

A photograph in the series which presents a picturesque view of the famous Red River dam recalls some active spring days in Louisiana. The photograph gives an excellently accurate view of a portion of the dam, through the building of which Admiral Porter's river fleet of eleven "turtles" was brought safely over the rapids at Alexandria, and the army of General Banks, repulsed and disappointed but by no means demoralized, was able to make its way back to the Mississippi with a very much lessened opposition. Through a sudden fall of the river, the "turtles" had been held above the rapids at Alexandria. Without the aid of Porter's guns to protect the flank of the army retreating along the river road, it would have been necessary to overcome by frontal attacks a series of breastworks by which this road was blocked.

The energetic Confederate leader, General Taylor, had managed to cut off all connections with the Mississippi, and, while we were feeding in the town of Alexandria the women and children whose men folks were fighting us from outside, we had rations sufficient for only about three weeks. The problem was, within the time at our disposal and with the material available (in a country in which there was no stone), to increase the depth of water on the rapids by about twenty-two inches. The plan submitted by the clever engineer officer, Lieut.-Colonel Bailey, of the Fourth Wisconsin, was eagerly accepted by General Banks. Under Bailey's directions, five wing-dams were constructed, of which the shortest pair, with the widest aperture for the water, was up-stream, while the longest pair, with the narrowest passage for the water, was

### WHERE REYNOLDS FELL AT GETTYSBURG.

At this spot Major-General John F. Reynolds met his death.   During the first day's fighting this peaceful cornfield was trampled by the advancing Confederates.   The cupola of the seminary on the ridge held at nightfall by Lee's forces is visible in the distance.   The town of Gettysburg lies one mile beyond.   General Reynolds' troops, advancing early in the day, had encountered the Confederates and had been compelled to fall back.   Later, the Federal line by hard fighting had gained considerable advantage on the right.   Impatient to retrieve the earlier retrograde movement at this point, General Reynolds again advanced his command, shoving back the enemy before it, and his line of skirmishers was thrown out to the cornfield in the picture.   Riding out to it to reconnoiter, General Reynolds fell, pierced by a Confederate bullet, near the tree at the edge of the road.

placed at the point on the rapids where the increased depth was required. The water was thrown, as it were, into a funnel, and not only was the depth secured, but the rush downward helped to carry the vessels in safety across the rocks of the rapids. As I look at the photograph, I recall the fatiguing labor of "house-breaking," when the troops were put to work, in details on alternate days, in pulling down the sugar-mills and in breaking up the iron-work and the bricks.

On the further side of the river, a territory claimed by the sharpshooters of our opponents, men selected from the Western regiments, protected more or less by our skirmish line, are applying their axes to the shaping of the logs for the crates from which the dams were constructed. The wood-chopping is being done under a scattered but active fire, but while hastened somewhat in speed, it loses none of its precision.

I recall the tall form of the big six-footer, Colonel Bailey, leading the way into the water where the men had to work in the swift current at the adjustment of the crates, and calling out, "Come along, boys; it's only up to your waists."

As in duty bound, I marched after the colonel into the river, calling upon my command to follow; but the water which had not gone very much above the waist of the tall colonel, caught the small adjutant somewhere above the nostrils, with the result that he was taken down over the rapids. He came up, with no particular damage, in the pool beyond, but in reporting for the second time, wet but still ready for service, he took the liberty of saying to the Wisconsin six-footer, "Colonel, that was hardly fair for us little fellows."

After the hot work of tearing down the sugar-mills, the service in the cool water, although itself arduous enough, was refreshing. The dams were completed within the necessary time, and the vessels were brought safely through the rapids into the deep water below.

The saving of the fleet was one of the most dramatic incidents of the war, and the method of operation, as well as the

The army engineers laughed at this wide-browed, unassuming man when he suggested building a dam so as to release Admiral Porter's fleet imprisoned by low water above the Falls at Alexandria at the close of the futile Red River expedition in 1864. Bailey had been a lumberman in Wisconsin and had there gained the practical experience which taught him that the plan was feasible. He was Acting Chief Engineer of the Nineteenth Army Corps at this time, and obtained permission to go ahead and build his dam. In the undertaking he had the approval and earnest support of Admiral Porter, who refused to consider for a moment the abandonment of any of his vessels even though the Red River expedition had been ordered to return and General Banks was chafing at delay and sending messages to Porter that his troops must be got in motion at once.

COLONEL JOSEPH BAILEY IN 1864

THE MAN WHO SAVED THE FLEET

Bailey pushed on with his work and in eleven days he succeeded in so raising the water in the channel that all the Federal vessels were able to pass down below the Falls. "Words are inadequate," said Admiral Porter, in his report, "to express the admiration I feel for the ability of Lieut. Colonel Bailey. This is without doubt the best engineering feat ever performed. . . . The highest honors the Government can bestow on Colonel Bailey can never repay him for the service he has rendered the country." For this achievement Bailey was promoted to colonel, brevetted brigadier general, voted the thanks of Congress, and presented with a sword and a purse of $3,000 by the officers of Porter's fleet. He settled in Missouri after the war and was a formidable enemy of the "Bushwhackers" till he was shot by them on March 21, 1867. He was born at Salem, Ohio, April 28, 1827.

READY FOR HER BAPTISM

This powerful gunboat, the *Lafayette*, though accompanying Admiral Porter on the Red River expedition, was not one of those entrapped at Alexandria. Her heavy draft precluded her being taken above the Falls. Here we see her lying above Vicksburg in the spring of 1863. She and her sister ship, the *Choctaw*, were side-wheel steamers altered into casemate ironclads with rams. The *Lafayette* had the stronger armament, carrying two 11-inch Dahlgrens forward, four 9-inch guns in the broadside, and two 24-pound howitzers, with two 100-pound Parrott guns astern. She and the *Choctaw* were the most important acquisitions to Porter's fleet toward the end of 1862. The *Lafayette* was built and armed for heavy fighting. She got her first taste of it on the night of April 16, 1863, when Porter took part of his fleet past the Vicksburg batteries to support Grant's crossing of the river in an advance on Vicksburg from below. The *Lafayette*, with a barge and a transport lashed to her, held her course with difficulty through the tornado of shot and shell which poured from the Confederate batteries on the river front in Vicksburg as soon as the movement was discovered. The *Lafayette* stood up to this fiery christening and successfully ran the gantlet, as did all the other vessels save one transport. She was commanded during the Red River expedition by Lieutenant-Commander J. P. Foster.

## THE BATTLE WITH THE RIVER

Colonel Bailey's wonderful dam—which, according to Admiral Porter, no private company would have completed within a year. Bailey's men did it in eleven days and saved a fleet of Union vessels worth $2,000,000. Never was there an instance where such difficulties were overcome so quickly and with so little preparation. The current of the Red River, rushing by at the rate of nine miles an hour, threatened to sweep away the work of the soldiers as fast as it was performed. The work was commenced by building out from the left bank of the river with large trees cross-tied with heavy timber and filled in with brush, brick, and stone. We see the men engaged upon this work at the right of the picture. Coal barges filled with brick and stone were sunk beyond this, while from the right bank cribs filled with stone were built out to meet the barges. In eight days Bailey's men, working like beavers under the broiling sun, up to their necks in water, had backed up the current sufficiently to release three vessels. The very next

## THE MEN WHO CAPTURED THE CURRENT

morning two of the barges were swept away.   Admiral Porter, jumping on his horse, rode to the upper falls and ordered the *Lexington* to come down and attempt the passage of the dam.   The water was rapidly falling, and as the *Lexington*, having squeezed through the passage of the falls, approached the opening in the dam through which a torrent was pouring, a breathless silence seized the watchers on the shore.   In another instant she had plunged to safety, and a deafening cheer rose from thirty thousand throats.   Porter was afraid that Colonel Bailey would be too disheartened by the accident to the dam to renew work upon it.   The other three vessels were at once ordered to follow the *Lexington's* example, and came safely through.   But Bailey was undaunted and "his noble-hearted soldiers, seeing their labor swept away in a moment, cheerfully went to work to repair damages, being confident now that all the gunboats would be finally brought over."   Their hopes were realized when the last vessel passed to safety on May 12, 1864.

whole effect of the river scene, are admirably indicated in the cleverly taken photographs.

A view of Fort McAllister recalls a closing incident of Sherman's dramatic march from Atlanta to the sea. The veterans had for weeks been tramping, with an occasional interval of fighting, but with very little opportunity for what the boys called a square meal. By the time the advance had reached the line of the coast, the commissary wagons were practically empty. The soldiers had for days been dependent upon the scattered supplies that could be picked up by the foraging parties, and the foragers, working in a country that had been already exhausted by the demands of the retreating Confederates, gave hardly enough return, in the form of corn on the cob or an occasional razor-backed hog, to offset the " wear and tear of the shoe-leather."

The men in the division of General Hazen, which was the first command to reach the Savannah River, could see down the river the smoke of the Yankee gunboats and of the transports which were bringing from New York, under appointment made months back by General Sherman, the much-needed supplies. But between the boys and the food lay the grim earthworks of Fort McAllister. Before there could be any eating, it was necessary to do a little more fighting. The question came from the commander to General Hazen, " Can your boys take those works? " and the answer was in substance, " Ain't we jest obleeged to take them? "

The assault was made under the immediate inspection of General Sherman, who realized the importance of getting at once into connection with the fleet, and the general was properly appreciative of the energy with which the task was executed.

"See my Bummers," said Old Sherman with most illigant emotion.
"Ain't their heads as horizontal as the bosom of the ocean?"

The raising of Old Glory over the fort was the signal for the steaming up-stream of the supply ships, and that evening

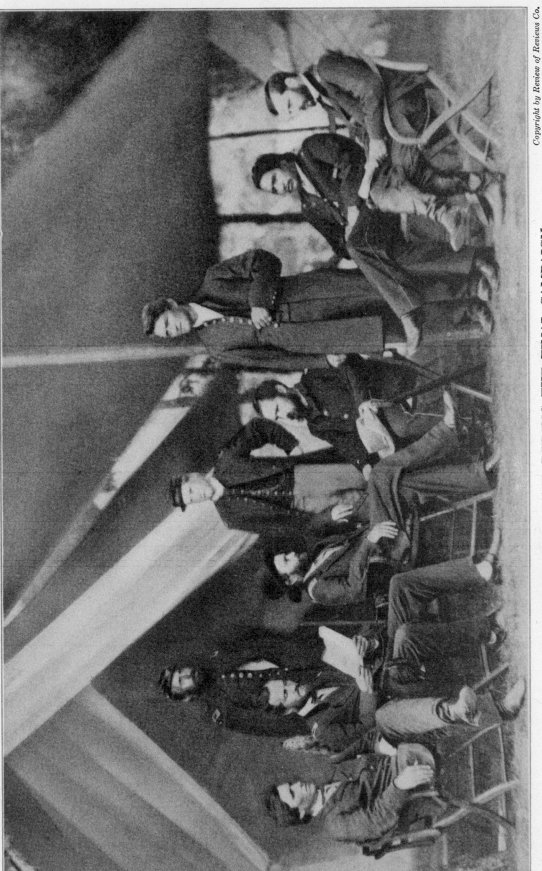

## GRANT AND HIS STAFF—DURING THE FINAL CAMPAIGN

Just as the veterans in Blue and Gray were lining up for the final struggle—before Petersburg, June, 1864—this photograph was taken of the future victor, at his City Point headquarters, surrounded by his faithful staff. They are (from left to right, sitting) Colonel John A. Rawlins, Adjutant-General; Colonel C. B. Comstock, A. D. C.; Lieutenant-General U. S. Grant; Major M. M. Morgan, Chief Commissary; Colonel Ely S. Parker, Military Secretary; Colonel O. E. Babcock, A. D. C.; (standing) Captain Henry Janes, Quartermaster for Headquarters; Captain William S. Dunn, A. D. C.; Major Peter Hudson, A. D. C.

witnessed for the advance division a glorious banquet, with real beef and soft bread.

The following day, which happened to be the 25th of December, General Sherman was able to report to President Lincoln that he had secured for him, or for the nation, a Christmas present in the shape of the city of Savannah.

The preponderance of capable military leaders was an important factor in giving to the Southern armies the measure of success secured by these armies during the first two years; but even during this earlier period, military capacity developed also on the side of the North, and by the middle of the war the balance of leadership ability may be considered as fairly equal. It may frankly be admitted, however, that no commander of the North had placed upon him so stupendous a burden as that which was carried by Lee, as the commander of the Army of Northern Virginia, through the weary and bloody campaigns of three years. For the last year of that period, Lee was fighting with no forces in reserve and with constantly diminishing resources. With great engineering skill, with ingenuity in utilizing every possible natural advantage for defense, with initiative and enterprise in turning defense at most unexpected moments into attack, with a sublime patience and persistence and with the devotion and magnificent fighting capacity of the men behind him, Lee accomplished with his Army of Northern Virginia a larger task in proportion to the resources at his command than has, I believe, ever been accomplished in modern warfare. The higher we place the ability of the Southern commander and the fighting capacity of the men behind him, the larger, of course, becomes the task of the leaders and armies of the North through whose service the final campaigns were won and the cause of nationality was maintained.

In going to England in the years immediately succeeding the war, I used to meet with some sharp criticism from army men and from others interested in army operations, as to the time that had been taken by the men of the North to overcome

LEE—WITH HIS SON, G. W. C. LEE, AND COLONEL TAYLOR

No military leader in any country, not even excepting General Washington himself, ever became so universally beloved as Robert E. Lee throughout the South before the close of the war. Rising from the nominal position of Superintendent of Fortifications at Richmond, he became the military adviser of Jefferson Davis and finally the General-in-Chief of the Confederate forces. From the time that Lee began to drive back McClellan's forces from Richmond in the Seven Days' Battles the hopes of the Confederates were centered in their great general. So hastily arranged was that first and final meeting with Grant to discuss the terms of surrender that no photograph was obtained of it, but here are preserved for us the commanding figure, keen eyes, and marvelously moulded features of General Lee as he appeared immediately after that dramatic event. He has just arrived in Richmond from Appomattox, and is seated in the basement of his Franklin Street residence between his son, Major-General G. W. C. Lee, and his aide, Colonel Walter Taylor.

[A—6]

their opponents and to establish their control over the territory in rebellion. Such phrases would be used as: "You had twenty-two millions against nine millions. You must have been able to put two muskets into the field against every one of your opponents. It was absurd that you should have allowed yourselves to be successfully withstood for four years and that you should finally have crushed your plucky and skilful opponents only through the brute force of numbers." I recall the difference of judgment given after the British campaigns of South Africa as to the difficulties of an invading army.

The large armies that were opposed to the plucky and persistent Boers and the people at home came to have a better understanding of the nature and extent of the task of securing control over a wild and well-defended territory, the invaders of which were fighting many miles from their base and with lines of communication that were easily cut. By the constant cutting and harassing of the lines of communication, and a clever disposition of lightly equipped and active marching troops who were often able to crush in detail outlying or separated troops of the invaders, a force of some forty thousand Boers found it possible to keep two hundred thousand well-equipped British troops at bay for nearly two years. The Englishman now understands that when an army originally comprising a hundred thousand men has to come into action at a point some hundred of miles distant from its base, it is not a hundred thousand muskets that are available, but seventy thousand or sixty thousand. The other thousands have been used up on the march or have been left to guard the lines of communication. Without constantly renewed supplies an army is merely a helpless mass of men.

It is probable, in fact, that the history of modern warfare gives no example of so complex, extensive, and difficult a military undertaking as that which was finally brought to a successful close by the armies of the North, armies which were contending against some of the best fighting material and the ablest military leadership that the world has known.

# THE SOUTH AND
# THE FEDERAL NAVY

# THE SOUTH AND
# THE WAR RECORDS

*With Many Photographs
of '61–'65 Taken Inside
the Confederate Lines*

THE SOUTHERN FLAG FLOATING OVER SUMTER ON APRIL 16, 1861—SOUTH
CAROLINA TROOPS DRILLING ON THE PARADE, TWO DAYS AFTER FORCING
OUT ANDERSON AND HIS FEDERAL GARRISON—THE FLAG IS MOUNTED ON
THE PARAPET TO THE RIGHT OF THE FORMER FLAGSTAFF, WHICH HAS BEEN
SHATTERED IN THE COURSE OF THE BOMBARDMENT FROM CHARLESTON

BEGINNING OF THE BLOCKADE, 1861—THE STARS AND BARS OVER BARRANCAS

INSIDE FORT BARRANCAS

In these hitherto unpublished Confederate photographs appear the first guns trained upon the Federal fleet at the beginning of the blockade. The fort lay about a mile west of the United States Navy Yard at Pensacola and commanded the inner channel to Pensacola Bay. When Florida seceded, January 10, 1861, about 550 Florida and Alabama State troops appeared before the barracks of Company G, 1st U. S. Artillery, 60 men. These retired into Fort Barrancas, after an attack upon that fort about midnight had been repelled. This was the first fighting of the war. Meanwhile Lieut. A. J. Slemmer, commander at Fort Pickens across the inlet, was removing the Barrancas garrison and their families. He succeeded in getting all safely across in a vessel to Fort Pickens, and the guns of Fort Barrancas bearing upon the channel were spiked. The Florida and Alabama troops occupied the fort on the 12th and began mounting twenty-five 32-pounders, which threatened Fort Pickens until the Confederates abandoned the works, May 9, 1862.

## THE SPIRIT OF RESISTANCE

Here a Confederate camera has caught the spirit of the Southern soldiers at the outbreak of the war. These are Captain G. W. Dowson's Perote Guards manning the Perote Sand Batteries at Mobile, January, 1861. On the 11th of January, 1861, the ordinance of secession was passed by the Alabama convention at Montgomery. Its announcement was received with great excitement throughout the State. In Mobile the Cadets and the Independent Rifles marched to the public square and fired salvos of artillery. Alabama was early active in organizing volunteer militia and gave liberally of her sons to the Confederate cause throughout the war. On January 9th, at the request of the Governor of Florida, two days before Alabama seceded, two regiments of Alabama troops were sent to co-operate in the seizure of the navy yard and forts at Pensacola Bay

# THE FEDERAL NAVY AND THE SOUTH

By FRENCH E. CHADWICK,

*Rear-Admiral, United States Navy*

Who shall estimate the value to the United States of the services of its navy which thus isolated the Confederacy, cut it off from communication with the outside world, and at the same time compelled it to guard every point against a raid like that which had destroyed the Capitol of the United States in 1814?  Had the Confederacy instead of the United States been able to exercise dominion over the sea ; had it been able to keep open its means of communication with the countries of the Old World, to send its cotton abroad and to bring back the supplies of which it stood so much in need ; had it been able to blockade Portland, Boston, Newport, New York, the mouth of the Delaware, and the entrance of Chesapeake Bay ; had it possessed the sea power to prevent the United States from despatching by water into Virginia its armies and their supplies, it is not too much to say that such a reversal of conditions would have reversed the outcome of the Civil War.—*Hilary A. Herbert, Colonel 8th Alabama Volunteers, C.S.A., ex-Secretary of the Navy, in an address, "The Sea and Sea Power as a Factor in the History of the United States," delivered at the Naval War College, August 10, 1896.*

NOW that half a century has passed since the Civil War, we have come to a point where we can deal calmly with the philosophy of the great contest without too great disturbance of the feeling which came near to wrecking our nationality.  The actualities of the struggle will be dealt with in the photographic history.  Meanwhile it is not amiss in these pages to look into the causes of the South's failure to set up a nation and thus justify Gladstone's surety of Southern success in his Newcastle speech in 1862.

It has been, as a rule, taken for granted that the South was worsted in a fair fight in the field.  This is so in a moderate

A BLOCKADE RUNNER, THE SWIFTEST CRAFT OF HER DAY

With the regularity of express trains, swift vessels like this one left Nassau and Bermuda and traveled direct for their destination, timed to arrive in the night. So great were the profits of blockade running that in some cases one successful voyage out and back would more than repay the owners for the loss of the vessel. Under these circumstances it can be easily seen that men were tempted to take risks that ordinarily they would avoid.

A CHARLESTON VOLUNTEER COMPANY AT DRILL UNDER THE WALLS OF CASTLE PINCKNEY

In pipe-clayed cross belts and white gloves, with all their accoutrements bright and shining, here we see a volunteer company of young Confederates standing at "Present Arms" and posing before the camera. The four officers standing in front of the line are Captain C. E. Chichester, Lieutenant E. John White, Lieutenant B. M. Walpole and Lieutenant R. C. Gilchrist. Gilchrist is curving his Damascus scimitar—a blade so finely tempered that its point would bend back to form a complete loop.

degree only; for the fight was not wholly a fair one. Difference of forces in the field may be set aside, as the fight being on the ground of the weaker, any disproportion in numbers was largely annulled. But the army of the North was lavishly equipped; there was no want of arms, food, raiment, ammunition, or medical care. Everything an army could have the Federal forces had to overflowing. On the other hand the Southern army was starved of all necessaries, not to speak of the luxuries which the abounding North poured forth for its men in the field. The South was in want of many of these necessaries even in the beginning of the war; toward the end it was in want of all. It was because of this want that it had to yield. General Joseph E. Johnston, writing General Beauregard in 1868, said truly: "We, without the means of purchasing supplies of any kind, or procuring or repairing arms, could continue this war only as robbers or guerillas." The Southern army finally melted away and gave up the fight because it had arrived at the limit of human endurance through the suffering which came of the absolute want brought by the blockade.

Some few historians have recognized and made clear this fact, notably General Charles Francis Adams, himself a valiant soldier of the war. Another is Mr. John Christopher Schwab, professor of political economy in Yale University. The former, analyzing six reasons for the South's failure, given by a British sympathizer in Blackwood's Magazine for July, 1866, says: "We are . . . through elimination brought down to one factor, the blockade, as the controlling condition of Union success. In other words that success was made possible by the undisputed naval and maritime superiority of the North. Cut off from the outer world and all exterior sources of supply, reduced to a state of inanition by the blockade, the Confederacy was pounded to death."[1] The "pounding"

[1] Charles Francis Adams, *Proceedings, Massachusetts Historical Society,* 1905, vol. xix, 224.

THE FIRST TASTE OF CAMP LIFE

This rare Confederate photograph preserves for us the amusements of the Alabama soldiers in camp near Mobile on a spring day in 1861.   To the left we see a youth bending eagerly over the shoulder of the man who holds the much-prized newspaper in his hands. To the right a group of youngsters are reading letters from home, while in the background still others are playing the banjo and the violin to relieve the tedium of this inactive waiting for the glorious battles anticipated in imagination when they enlisted.   These men are clad in the rough costume of home life, and can boast none of the bright new uniforms with shining brass buttons that made the Federal camps resplendent.   Here and there a cap indicates an officer.   Yet even these humble accessories were much better than the same troops could show later on, when the ruddy glow on their faces had given place to the sallowness of disease.

ON PARADE

Here a Confederate photographer has caught the Orleans Cadets, Company A, parading before their encampment at Big Bayou, near Pensacola, Florida, April 21, 1861.   This was the first volunteer company mustered into service from the State of Louisiana.   The Cadets had enlisted on April 11, 1861.   Although their uniforms are not such as to make a brilliant display, it was with pride and confidence for the future that their commander, Captain (afterwards Lieut. Colonel) Charles D. Dreux, watched their maneuvers on this spring day, little dreaming that in less than three months he would fall in battle, the first but one among army officers to offer up his life for the Southern cause.   The hopes now beating high in the hearts of both officers and men were all to be realized in deeds of bravery but only at further cost of human life here seen at its flood tide.

was mainly done by the army; the conditions which permitted it to be effectively done were mainly established by the navy.

"The blockade," says Mr. Schwab in his "Financial and Industrial History of the South during the Civil War," "constituted the most powerful tool at the command of the Federal Government in its efforts to subdue the South. The relentless and almost uniformly successful operations of the navy have been minimized in importance by the at times more brilliant achievements of the army; but we lean to ascribing to the navy the larger share in undermining the power of resistance on the part of the South. It was the blockade rather than the ravages of the army that sapped the industrial strength of the Confederacy."

The South was thus beaten by want; and not merely by force of arms. A nation of well on to 6,000,000 could never have been conquered on its own ground by even the great forces the North brought against it but for this failure of resources which made it impossible to bring its full fighting strength into the field.

We know that there was a total of 2,841,906 enlistments and reenlistments in the army and navy of the North, representing some 1,600,000 three-year enlistments; we shall, however, never know the actual forces of the South on account of the unfortunate destruction of the Southern records of enlistments and levies. That some 1,100,000 men were available is, of course, patent from the fact that the white population of the seceding states was 5,600,000, and to these were added 125,000 men, who, as sympathizers, joined the Southern army. The South fought as men have rarely fought. Its spirit was the equal of that of any race or time, and if the 325,000 Boers in South Africa could put 80,000 men into the field, the 5,600,-000 of the South would have furnished an equal proportion had there been arms, clothing, food, and the rest of the many accessories which, besides men, go to make an army. The situation which prevented an accomplishment of such results as

CONFEDERATES ENLISTING AT THE NATCHEZ COURTHOUSE, EARLY IN 1861

This rare Confederate photograph preserves a lively scene that was typical of the war preparations in the South in the spring of 1861. The fresh recruits are but scantily supplied with arms and accouterments, for only the Federal arsenals in the South could supply munitions of war. The military population of Mississippi at the opening of the war has been estimated at seventy thousand, and that of Louisiana at eighty thousand. It is believed that nearly a hundred thousand from each State enlisted in the Southern armies. The two scenes on this page were duplicated in hundreds of towns throughout the Southland as the war opened.

RECRUITING AT BATON ROUGE—1862

those in South Africa, and it was impossible in the circumstances that they could be, was the result of the blockade of the Southern coast, a force the South was powerless to resist.

What has been said shows how clear was the rôle of the navy. The strategic situation was of the simplest; to deprive the South of its intercourse with Europe and in addition to cut the Confederacy in twain through the control of the Mississippi. The latter, gained largely by the battles of Farragut, Porter, Foote, and Davis, was but a part of the great scheme of blockade, as it cut off the supply of food from Texas and the shipments of material which entered that State by way of Matamoras. The question of the military control of Texas could be left aside so long as its communications were cut, for in any case the State would finally have to yield with the rest of the Confederacy. The many thousand troops which would have been an invaluable reenforcement to the Southern armies in the East were to remain west of the Mississippi and were to have no influence in the future events.

The determination to attempt by force to reinstate the Federal authority over a vast territory, eight hundred miles from north to south and seventeen hundred from east to west, defended by such forces as mentioned, was truly a gigantic proposition, to be measured somewhat by the effort put forth by Great Britain to subdue the comparatively very small forces of the South African republic. It was as far from Washington to Atlanta (which may be considered as the heart of the Confederacy) as from London to Vienna. The frontier of the Confederacy, along which operations were to begin, was fifteen hundred miles in length. Within the Confederacy were railways which connected Chattanooga with Lynchburg, in Virginia, on the east and with Memphis, on the Mississippi, on the west; two north and south lines ran, the one to New Orleans, the other to Mobile; Atlanta connected with Chattanooga; Mobile and Savannah were in touch with Richmond through the coast line which passed through Wilmington and Charleston. No

WAITING FOR THE SMELL OF POWDER—CONFEDERATES BEFORE SHILOH

Some very youthful Louisiana soldiers waiting for their first taste of battle, a few weeks before Shiloh. These are members of the Washington Artillery of New Orleans. We see them at Camp Louisiana proudly wearing their new boots and their uniforms as yet unfaded by the sun. Louisiana gave liberally of her sons, who distinguished themselves in the fighting throughout the West. The Fifth Company of the Washington Artillery took part in the closely contested Battle of Shiloh. The Confederates defeated Sherman's troops in the early morning, and by night were in possession of all the Federal camps save one. The Washington Artillery served their guns handsomely and helped materially in forcing the Federals back to the bank of the river. The timely arrival of Buell's army the next day at Pittsburg Landing enabled Grant to recover from the reverses suffered on that bloody "first day"—Sunday, April 6, 1862.

part of the South, east of the Mississippi, was very distant from railway transportation, which for a long period the South carried on excepting in that portion which ran from Lynchburg to Chattanooga through the eastern part of Tennessee, where the population was in the main sympathetic with the Union.

Thus the South had the great advantage, which it held for several years, of holding and operating on interior lines. Its communications were held intact, whereas those of the Federals, as in the case of Grant's advance by way of the Wilderness, were often in danger. It was not until Sherman made his great march to the sea across Georgia, a march which Colonel Henderson, the noted English writer on strategy, says " would have been impossible had not a Federal fleet been ready to receive him when he reached the Atlantic," that the South felt its communications hopelessly involved.

To say that at the outset there was any broad and well-considered strategic plan at Washington for army action, would be an error. There was no such thing as a general staff, no central organization to do the planning of campaigns, such as now exists. The commanders of Eastern and Western armies often went their own gait without any effective coordination. It was not until Grant practically came to supreme military command that complete coordination was possible.

Four Unionist objectives, however, were clear. The greatly disaffected border states which had not joined the Confederacy must be secured and the loyal parts of Virginia and Tennessee defended; the southern ports blockaded; the great river which divided the Confederacy into an east and west brought under Federal control, and the army which defended Richmond overcome. At the end of two years all but the last of these objectives had been secured, but it was nearly two years more before the gallant Army of Northern Virginia succumbed through the general misery wrought in the Confederacy by the sealing of its ports and the consequent inability of

OFFICERS OF MISSISSIPPI'S "FIGHTING NINTH."

In this long-lost Confederate photograph we see vividly the simple accoutrements which characterized many of the Southern regiments during the war. These men of Company B of the Ninth Mississippi enlisted as the Home Guards of Marshall County, and were mustered into the State service at Holly Springs, February 16, 1861. Their checked trousers and workday shirts are typical of the simple equipment each man furnished for himself. The boots worn by Colonel Barry, at the right, were good enough for the average Confederate soldier to go through fire to obtain later on in the war. Lacking in the regalia of warfare, the Ninth Mississippi made a glorious record for itself in Chalmers' Brigade at Shiloh, where it lost its gallant Colonel, William A. Rankin. "Never," said General Bragg, "were troops and commander more worthy of each other and their State."

# The Federal Navy and the South

the Southerners to hold their own against the ever increasing, well-fed and well-supplied forces of the North. To quote again the able Englishman just mentioned, " Judicious indeed was the policy which, at the very outset of the war, brought the tremendous pressure of the sea power to bear against the South, and had her statesmen possessed the knowledge of what that pressure meant, they must have realized that Abraham Lincoln was no ordinary foe. In forcing the Confederates to become the aggressors, and to fire on the national ensign, he had created a united North; in establishing a blockade of their coasts he brought into play a force which, like the mills of God, ' grinds slowly, but grinds exceedingly small.' " It was the command of the sea which finally told and made certain the success of the army and the reuniting of the States.

[To the discussion presented above by Admiral Chadwick may be added the following expression of opinion by one of the foremost military students of modern Europe: "The cooperation of the United States navy with their army in producing a decisive effect upon the whole character of the military operations is akin to what happens with us in nearly every war in which we engage. An English general has almost always to make his calculations strictly in accordance with what the navy can do for him. The operations by which the Federal navy, in conjunction with the army, split the Confederacy in two and severed the East from the West, must always, therefore, have for him a profound interest and importance. The great strategical results obtained by this concentration of military and naval power, which were as remarkable as the circumstances under which the successes were gained, deserve our closest study."—*Field-Marshal, the Right Honorable Viscount Wolseley.*—Editors.]

## SUMTER BECOMES A FEDERAL TARGET

The eastern barracks inside Fort Sumter during the Bombardment of Sept. 8, 1863.—The guns of the Federal blockading fleet had now been pounding the fort for many weeks. This but recently re-discovered picture is the work of G. S. Cook, the Charleston photographer. The view is to the right of the exploding shell in the picture on page 100. The flag and guns shown in the earlier picture have been swept away. The upper casemate to the left has been demolished. The lower ones remained intact, however, and continued to be used and even armed to the end of the Confederate's defense. The guns here bore on the channel nearly opposite Fort Moultrie. The bake oven of the barracks—on the chimney of which are a couple of Confederate soldiers—was frequently used for heating solid shot. In one of the lower rooms of the barracks, seen to the right, the ruins later fell upon a detachment of sleeping soldiers.

[A—7]

Copyright by Review of Reviews Co.

## THE EXPLODING SHELL

A wonderful war photograph preserved by the Daughters of the Confederacy of Charleston, S. C. The picture is fully described in Major John Johnson's authoritative work, "The Defense of Charleston Harbor," where a drawing based on the photograph was published. It is believed that the photograph itself has never been reproduced before its appearance here. All during August, Sumter was subjected to a constant bombardment from the Federal batteries. On September 7th, Admiral Dahlgren sent to demand the surrender of Sumter. Major Stephen Elliott replied: "Inform Admiral Dahlgren that he may have Fort Sumter when he can take and hold it." That night the Admiral sent a boat party. It was disastrously repulsed. The very same night, under cover of the darkness, George S. Cook, a Charleston photographer, was being rowed across to Fort Sumter and the next morning set up his camera. After securing what is probably the most daring photograph ever taken during the Civil War (see page 24), Cook proceeded to attempt some views of the interior of the fort and luckily caught the one reproduced above. It is quite as successful a picture as could have been made by the instantaneous photographic apparatus of the present day. We see centrally in the parade the explosion of a shell, which has just been dropped over the gorge wall by the stranded monitor *Weehawken*. She, though dangerously exposed, took a vigorous part in the engagement.

NOTE.—The extraordinary conditions under which this photograph was taken made it desirable for the artist to retouch slightly. The photograph is printed here as Cook left it, notwithstanding the rule that none of the illustrations in the PHOTOGRAPHIC HISTORY may be retouched in any way. The thousands of scenes reproduced are from photographs taken direct from nature. The retouching in this one exception has in no way marred the historical accuracy, as will be seen by comparison with the illustrations on the opposite page and page 99, which are nearer views of the left and right of this picture. They also were taken by George S. Cook. The series forms a faithful and unique presentation of Sumter in war-time.

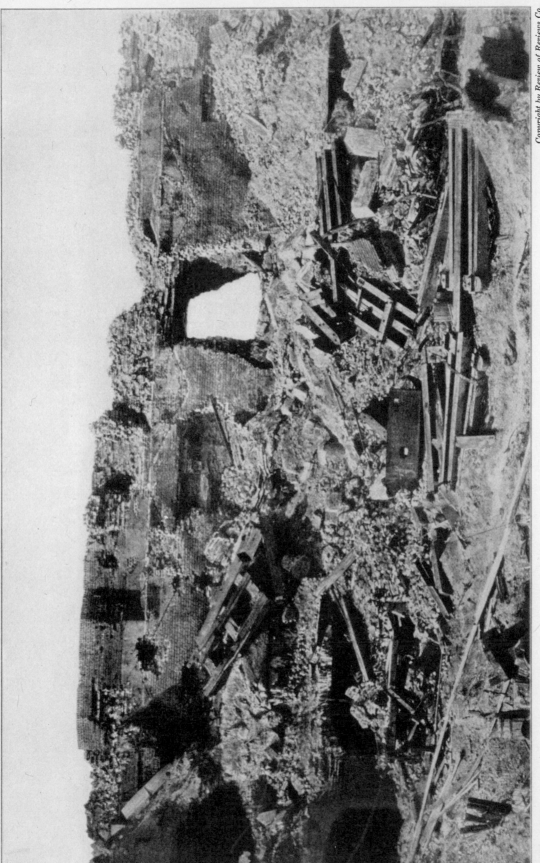

## THE FIRST BREACH

Within the Walls of Sumter—September 8, 1863.—The parapet shows the terrific havoc wrought by the almost continuous bombardment by the Federal fleet and land batteries during August. It culminated on September 8th when photographer Cook secured this view, made under more favorable conditions than the one above and consequently much clearer. The breach is seen to the left in the opposite picture. It was probably first made by a shot from the battery on Morris Island, the fire from which passed centrally through the fort. According to an eye witness, "it indicated the focus of all the breaching guns as they were, from all positions on Morris Island, trained upon the mass of the fort." This breach was steadily widened during the day—September 8th. Expecting another boat attack that night, Major Elliott stationed Captain Miles and his company to defend this formidable breach. The attack came an hour after midnight and was handsomely repelled. Sumter, though almost demolished, could not yet be had for the asking.

# RECORDS OF THE WAR BETWEEN THE STATES

By MARCUS J. WRIGHT, Brigadier-General, C.S.A.

*Agent of the United States War Department for the Collection of Military Records*

THE war which was carried on in the United States in 1861–5, called " The War of the Rebellion," " The Civil War," " The War of Secession," and " The War Between the States," was one of the greatest conflicts of ancient or modern times. Official reports show that 2,865,028 men were mustered into the service of the United States. The report of Provost-Marshal General Fry shows that of these 61,362 were killed in battle, 34,773 died of wounds, 183,287 died of disease, 306 were accidentally killed, and 267 were executed by sentence. The Adjutant-General made a report February 7, 1869, showing the total number of deaths to be 303,504.

The Confederate forces are estimated from 600,000 to 1,000,000 men, and ever since the conclusion of the war there has been no little controversy as to the total number of troops involved. The losses in the Confederate army have never been officially reported, but the United States War Department, which has been assiduously engaged in the collection of all records of both armies, has many Confederate muster-rolls on which the casualties are recorded. The tabulation of these rolls shows that 52,954 Confederate soldiers were killed in action, 21,570 died of wounds, and 59,297 died of disease. This does not include the missing muster-rolls, so that to these figures a substantial percentage must be added. Differences in methods of reporting the strength of commands, the absence of adequate field-records and the destruction of those actually

SOUTH CAROLINA MEN IN BLUE, SPRING 1861     *Copyright by Review of Reviews Co.*

These officers of the Flying Artillery we see here entering the Confederate service at Sullivan's Island, Charleston Harbor, still wearing the blue uniforms of their volunteer organization. It was one of the state militia companies so extensively organized throughout the South previous to the war. South Carolina was particularly active in this line. After the secession of the State the Charleston papers were full of notices for various military companies to assemble for drill or for the distribution of arms and accoutrements. Number 2 of this group is Allen J. Green, then Captain of the Columbia Flying Artillery (later a Major in the Confederate service). No. 4 is W. K. Bachman, then a 4th Lieutenant, later Captain in the German Volunteers, a state infantry organization that finally entered the artillery service and achieved renown as Bachman's Battery. No. 3 is Wilmot D. de Saussure; No. 7 is John Waites, then Lieutenant and later Captain of another company. After 1863, when the Confederate resources were waning, the Confederate soldiers were not ashamed to wear the blue clothing brought in by the blockade runners.

TWO YEARS AFTERWARD   *Copyright by Patriot Pub. Co.*

Confederate Uniforms at Gettysburg, July 1–3, 1863.—According to a Northern authority, Lee's veterans in 1863 were "the finest infantry on earth!" In this picture we see three of them taken prisoners at Gettysburg and caught by the camera of a Union photographer. These battle-stained Confederates had no glittering uniforms to wear; they marched and fought in any garb they were fortunate enough to secure and were glad to carry with them the blankets which would enable them to snatch some rest at night. Their shoes—perhaps taken in sheer necessity from the dead on the field—worn and dusty as we see them, were unquestionably the envy of many of their less fortunate comrades. Lee could only make his daring invasion of the North in 1863 by severing his connection with any base of supplies; and, unlike Sherman in his march to the sea, he had no friendly force waiting to receive him should he prove able to overcome the powerful army that opposed him. "Never," says Eggleston, "anywhere did soldiers give a better account of themselves. The memory of their heroism is the common heritage of all the people of the great Republic."

made are responsible for considerable lack of information as to the strength and losses of the Confederate army. Therefore, the matter is involved in considerable controversy and never will be settled satisfactorily; for there is no probability that further data on this subject will be forthcoming.

The immensity and extent of our great Civil War are shown by the fact that there were fought 2,261 battles and engagements, which took place in the following named States: In New York, 1; Pennsylvania, 9; Maryland, 30; District of Columbia, 1; West Virginia, 80; Virginia, 519; North Carolina, 85; South Carolina, 60; Georgia, 108; Florida, 32; Alabama, 78; Mississippi, 186; Louisiana, 118; Texas, 14; Arkansas, 167; Tennessee, 298; Kentucky, 138; Ohio, 3; Indiana, 4; Illinois, 1; Missouri, 244; Minnesota, 6; California, 6; Kansas, 7; Oregon, 4; Nevada, 2; Washington Territory, 1; Utah, 1; New Mexico, 19; Nebraska, 2; Colorado, 4; Indian Territory, 17; Dakota, 11; Arizona, 4; and Idaho, 1.

It soon became evident that the official record of the War of 1861–5 must be compiled for the purposes of Government administration, as well as in the interest of history, and this work was projected near the close of the first administration of President Lincoln. It has continued during the tenure of succeeding Presidents, under the direction of the Secretaries of War, from Edwin M. Stanton, under whom it began, to Secretary Elihu Root, under whose direction it was completed. Colonel Robert N. Scott, U.S.A., who was placed in charge of the work in 1874, prepared a methodical arrangement of the matter which was continued throughout. Officers of the United States army were detailed, and former officers of the Confederate army were also employed in the work. The chief civilian expert who continued with the work from its inception was Mr. Joseph W. Kirkley. The total number of volumes is 70; the total number of books, 128, many of the volumes containing several separate parts. The total cost of publication was $2,-858,514.67.

## THE LAST TO LAY DOWN ARMS

Recovered from oblivion only after a long and patient search, this is believed to be the last Confederate war photograph taken. On May 26, 1865, General E. Kirby Smith surrendered the troops in the Trans-Mississippi Department. Paroled by that capitulation these officers gathered in Shreveport, Louisiana, early in June to commemorate by means of the camera their long connection with the war. The oldest of them was but 40. The clothes in which they fought were worn to tatters, but each has donned the dress coat of an unused uniform carefully saved in some chest in the belief that it was to identify him with a victorious cause and not as here with a lost one. The names of those standing, from left to right, are: David French Boyd, Major of Engineers; D. C. Proctor, First Louisiana Engineers; unidentified; and William Freret. The names of those seated are: Richard M. Venable; H. T. Douglas, Colonel of Engineers; and Octave Hopkins, First Louisiana Engineers.

In view of the distrust with which the South for a while naturally regarded the efforts made by the Government to procure the records of the Confederacy, the work of the department to obtain this material at first met with slight success.

In 1878, the writer, a Confederate officer, was appointed as agent of the War Department for the collection of Confederate archives. Through his efforts the attitude of the Southern people became more cordial, and increased records were the result. By provision of Congress, certain sets of the volumes were distributed, and others held for sale at cost.

The history of this official record is mentioned in these pages as it indicates a wide-spread national desire on the part of the people of the United States to have a full and impartial record of the great conflict, which must form, necessarily, the basis of all history concerned with this era. It is the record of the struggle as distinguished from personal recollections and reminiscences, and its fulness and impartial character have never been questioned. The large number of these volumes makes them unavailable for general reading, but in the preparation of " The Photographic History of the Civil War " the editors have not only consulted these official reports, but give the equally permanent testimony of the photographic negative. Therefore, as a successor to and complement of this Government publication, nothing could be more useful or interesting than " The Photographic History of the Civil War." The text does not aim at a statistical record, but is an impartial narrative supplementing the pictures. Nothing gives so clear a conception of a person or an event as a picture. The more intelligent people of the country, North and South, desire the truth put on record, and all bitter feeling eliminated. This work, it is believed, will add greatly to that end.

## YOUNG ARTILLERISTS OF THE CONFEDERACY, 1863

This remarkable Confederate photograph instantly recalls Lincoln's oft-quoted saying that "war robbed both the cradle and the grave." Charleston was, throughout the war, active in providing for her own defense, and the women of the city constantly busied themselves in making flags and uniforms for the troops. This home company was much better equipped than the troops in the field at this stage of the war. The youth of some of the men here is noticeable. The standard-bearer is a mere boy— hardly sixteen. As early as April 16, 1862. the Confederate Congress conscripted all men over 18 and under 45 to serve during the war. The Charleston artillery, because Charleston was one of the principal ports for blockade runners, was well equipped with guns and ammunition. At many critical moments, as at Gettysburg, Confederate batteries in the field ran entirely out of ammunition, hence artillerymen stationed near the source of supply were most fortunate.

THE LAST EXCHANGE. CAMP FISK, FOUR MILE BRIDGE (VICKSBURG), APRIL, 1865

At the close of the war, Camp Fisk was established near Vicksburg for the general exchange of prisoners captured during the operations of the armies in the West. Here we see one of the daily meetings of the officers on both sides for this purpose. The Federal transport *Sultana* was busily engaged during the spring of 1865 in carrying the released Federal soldiers from Vicksburg to the North on their way to their homes. In the smaller picture we see her at Helena wharf loaded with the last shipment of paroled Union soldiers to the number of 2,134. The same day, April 27, 1865, she arrived at Memphis. While steaming along some 90 miles above that

THE ILL-FATED *SULTANA*, HELENA, ARKANSAS, APRIL 27, 1865

point, her boilers suddenly exploded and she sunk almost immediately. During the war the levees on both sides of the river had been so demolished that all the bottom lands were inundated, and at this point were covered with water to a width of 50 miles. But few of the ill-fated Union soldiers managed to save their lives. About 1,900 of them perished. A survivor relates that while clinging to a log with three other men, one committed suicide rather than endure the agony caused by the icy water. At Memphis the Federal authorities gathered all the floating bodies they could. Many were found as far below the scene of the disaster as Helena.

# THE STRATEGY
# OF THE
# WAR LEADERS

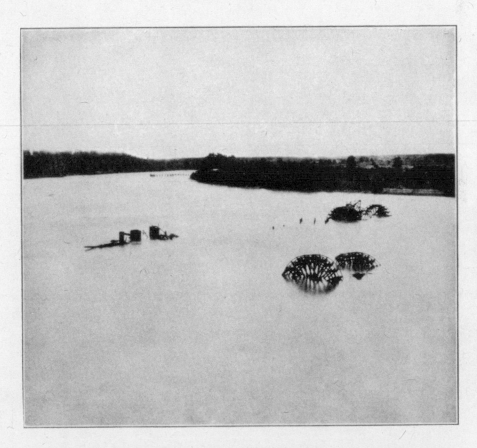

A CENTRAL STRATEGICAL POINT—THE APPROACH TO RICHMOND *VIA*
JAMES RIVER, AS IT LOOKED IN WAR-TIME, BLOCKED BY THE CONFEDERATE
RAM "VIRGINIA," AND GUNBOATS "PATRICK HENRY" AND "JAMESTOWN,"
SUNK IN THE CHANNEL TO HOLD THE FEDERAL FLEET FROM RICHMOND
(SEE TWO PAGES FOLLOWING FOR ANOTHER VIEW OF THIS SCENE)

OBSTRUCTIONS RENDERED USELESS

The superior navy of the Federals at the beginning and throughout the war enabled them to gain the advantage of penetrating the rivers leading into the interior of the Confederacy and thus support the military forces in many telling movements. To this fact the surrender of Forts Henry and Donelson and the ultimate control of the Mississippi by the Union forces gives eloquent testimony. In the East the regions between Washington and Richmond were traversed by streams, small and large, which made aggressive warfare difficult. For this reason McClellan chose the James River Peninsula for his first advance upon the Confederate Capital. Far more dreaded than the advance of the army was the approach of the powerful *Monitor* and the *Galena* up the James River, and the

JAMES RIVER, VIRGINIA, NEAR DREWRY'S BLUFF.—1862

first thought of the Confederates was to hold this danger in abeyance. Hence the obstructions (shown on the opposite page) sunk in the bend of the James River near Drewry's Bluff, where a powerful battery known as Fort Darling was hastily but effectively constructed. These blocked the attempts of the Federals to invest the Confederate capital until Grant's superior strategy in 1864 rendered them useless by throwing his army across the James in one of his famous flanking movements and advancing toward Richmond in a new direction. The campaign developing into a siege of Petersburg on the Appomattox, the Federal vessels confined their activities to the lower James.

# THE STRATEGY OF THE CIVIL WAR

## By Eben Swift
### *Lieutenant-Colonel 8th Cavalry, United States Army*

But strategy, unfortunately, is a very unpopular science, even among soldiers, requiring both in practice and in demonstration constant and careful study of the map, the closest computation of time and space, a grasp of many factors, and the strictest attention to the various steps in the problems it presents. At the same time, it is a science which repays the student, although he may have no direct concern with military affairs; for not only will a comprehension of its immutable principles add a new interest to the records of stirring times and great achievements, but will make him a more useful citizen.—*"Stonewall Jackson and the Civil War," by Lieutenant-Colonel G. F. R. Henderson, C.B.*

THE student has great advantage over the actor in war, particularly when he makes his study after a lapse of fifty years. His point of view is illuminated then by the stories as told by both contestants, by the disputes and explanations of many participants. He also pursues his investigations without any of the distracting influences of war itself. It may not, therefore, be entirely fair to take each man's act before the bar of history and to require him to justify himself to the critics of a later day. In a larger sense, though, it is right, because past experience gives the best lessons and guides for the future. Until we have another war, we shall continue to study the great conflict of 1861–5, and to read the secrets of our future in its tale of failure or success.

" Strategy " is a comparatively recent addition to our language. It is derived from the Greek στρατηγία, meaning generalship, and has several valuable derivatives, as " strategic " and " strategist," which make it a more useful word than

[112]

## WAR STUDENTS OF TWO CONTINENTS

What an excellent example of open-air group portraiture—the work of Gardner's camera! But photography can add nothing to the fame of these men, gathered together in an idle hour to chat about the strategy of the war. Seated in the center is Count Zeppelin, of the Prussian Army, later the winner of honors with his airship and then on a visit to America to observe the Civil War. To his left is Lieutenant Rosencranz, a Swedish officer, on leave of absence, observing the war at close range as General McClellan's personal aide-de-camp. He successively served Burnside, Hooker and Meade in the same capacity. His brave and genial disposition made him a universal favorite. The other men are Americans, conspicuous actors as well as students in the struggle. On the ground, to the left, sits Major Ludlow, who commanded the colored brigade which, and under his direction, in the face of a continual bombardment, dug Dutch Gap Canal on the James. The man in the straw hat is Lieut. Colonel Dickinson, Assistant Adjutant General to Hooker, a position in which he served until the Battle of Gettysburg, where he was wounded. Standing is Captain Ulric Dahlgren, serving at the time on Meade's staff. Even the loss of a leg could not quell his indomitable spirit, and he subsequently sacrificed his life in an effort to release the Federal prisoners at Libby and Belle Isle.

generalship. It means the art of the general and indicates the time, place, and way to fight battles.

The War of the States was viewed at first with indifference by foreign military men. For many years past, however, it has claimed their close attention, because they have come to realize that new conditions were tested then, and that new influences, which changed the art of the general even from the respected models of Napoleon fifty years before, were at work. Ironclads, entrenchments, railroads, the breech-loader, a new kind of cavalry were the fresh factors in the problem.

Although hostilities at first began over an area half as large as Europe, the region of decisive operations was, on account of lack of communication, narrowed to the country between the Atlantic and the Mississippi, about seven hundred miles in an air-line. The line was unequally divided by the towering barrier of the Alleghany Mountains, about two hundred miles wide, over which communication was difficult. The eastern section of the country beyond the range was about one hundred miles wide and the western section was about four hundred miles wide. In Maryland, northwestern Virginia, Kentucky, and Missouri sentiment was divided between the Union and the Confederacy. The Mississippi River separated three of the seceding States from the remaining eight.

The immense amount of supplies needed for a great army caused military operations on a large scale to be confined to rail and water lines. Of the former, both the North and South had several routes running east and west for lateral communication, and the South had several running north and south in each section, which could be used for lines of military operations. In respect to water routes, the North soon demonstrated its complete control of the sea and was thus able to choose its points of attack, while interior water routes were available by the Mississippi, Tennessee, Cumberland, and James rivers. The advantage of the water route over that by rail was at once utilized by the Northern generals.

A KING'S SON IN CAMP

In 1861 there arrived the first great opportunity to study warfare in the field since the campaigns of Napoleon, and these young men of royal blood expected at no distant day to be the leaders of a war of their own to recover the lost Bourbon throne of France. The three distinguished guests of the Army of the Potomac seated at the farther end of the camp dinner-table are, from right to left, the Prince de Joinville, son of King Louis Phillipe, and his two nephews, the Count de Paris and the Duc de Chartres, sons of the Duc d'Orleans. They came to Washington in September, 1861, eager to take some part in the great conflict for the sake of the experience it would give them. President Lincoln welcomed them, bestowed upon each the honorary rank of Captain, and assigned them to the staff of General McClellan. Officially merely guests at headquarters, they acted as aides-de-camp to McClellan, bearing despatches and the like, frequently under fire. They distinguished themselves at the battle of Gaines' Mill. The Prince de Joinville made a painting of that engagement which became widely published.

In the lower picture the Count de Paris and the Duc de Chartres are trying their skill at dominoes after dinner. Captain Leclerc, on the left, and Captain Mohain, on the right, are of their party. A Union officer has taken the place of the Prince de Joinville. It was to perfect their skill in a greater and grimmer game that these young men came to America. At Yorktown they could see the rehabilitated fortifications of Cornwallis, which men of their own blood had helped to seize, now amplified by the latest methods of defensive warfare. Exposed to the fire of the Napoleon field pieces imported by the Confederacy, they could compare their effectiveness with that of the huge rifled Dahlgrens, the invention of an American admiral. General McClellan testified that ever in the thick of things they performed their duties to his entire satisfaction. At the close of the Peninsula Campaign the royal party returned to France, but watched the war with great interest to its close.

LEARNING THE GAME

It was not so vulnerable to attack as the railroad. All navigable rivers within the area of operations were used for this purpose, and McClellan, Burnside, and Grant used the Chesapeake Bay and its tributaries to carry their base of supplies close to Richmond. The operations of the Confederates, on the other hand, were greatly restricted by being confined to railroad lines.

Several natural features which were certain to influence events to a great extent are to be noticed. In Virginia, numerous rivers, running parallel to the direct line of advance, form good lines for defense and also obstacles to an advance. Several mountain valleys leading north at the eastern ranges of the Alleghanies gave opportunities for leading large forces safely into Pennsylvania from Virginia, or vice versa. Within the mountain district, a railroad from Lynchburg, Virginia, to Chattanooga, in Tennessee, about four hundred miles long, gave an opportunity for transferring troops from one section to the other, while the corresponding distance at the North was three times as great. In the western section, the Tennessee and Cumberland rivers are separated at one place by a narrow neck about two miles wide, thus somewhat simplifying the problem of controlling these two important streams. The strategic chess-board, then, gave great opportunities to skilful generalship. The Virginia rivers gave strength to long defensive lines, screened marches from east to west, and forced the Northern generals to seek the flank rather than the front attack. The Shenandoah valley afforded a safe approach to Washington from the rear. This was availed of by Lee, Jackson, and Early to keep many thousand men of the army of the North in idleness. In the West, the long line defended by scattered troops was weak at every point and was quite easily broken by Grant, particularly when the South was slow in grasping the situation there. The advantage of the Richmond-Chattanooga railroad was not used by the Confederates until too late for success.

There is no mistaking the nationality of these Military Attachés with their tartans and Dundreary whiskers. They were accompanying the Army of the Potomac on its Peninsula Campaign. In the center of the group of Englishmen stands the Prince de Joinville. From the observations of these men both France and England were to learn many military lessons from a new conflict on the soil over which the soldiers of both nations had fought in a former generation. The armies of both North and South were being moved and maintained in the field in a manner and upon a scale undreamed of by Napoleon, to say nothing of Howe and Cornwallis. The Count de Paris wrote a very comprehensive and impartial history of the war, and in 1890 revisited America and gathered together some 200 or more surviving officers of the Army of the Potomac at a dinner in the old Hotel Plaza, New York City. Not half the veterans that were his guests more than two decades ago are still alive, and the Duc himself joined the majority in 1894.

WATCHING THE WAR

YORKTOWN EIGHTY YEARS AFTER

Here are some English and other foreign military officers with General Barry and some of his staff before Yorktown in May, 1862. European military opinion was at first indifferent to the importance of the conflict as a school of war. The more progressive, nevertheless, realized that much was to be learned from it. The railroad and the telegraph were two untried elements in strategy. The ironclad gunboat and ram introduced serious complications in naval warfare. At first the influence of Napoleon I was manifest in the field, but as the struggle proceeded both armies developed distinctly new ideas of their own. The sight of Sherman maintaining railroad and telegraphic communications with a base 138 miles away was a new one to the world, while his cutting loose from any base whatever in his March to the Sea was only less remarkable than Lee's invasion of Pennsylvania under similar conditions, to which was added a superior opposing force. In these and many other examples the war set the pace for later development.

The strategy, on account of political and other influences, was not always chosen according to the best military principles. Such influences always exist, and it is the duty of the soldier to conform and to make his plan to suit as best he can.

Under the head of policy would come Lee's several invasions of the North, undertaken with insufficient forces and too far from his base of supplies. Numerous causes have been given for these campaigns, the most plausible of which were of a political and not of a strategic nature. It was thought that a victory won on Northern soil might lead to intervention on the part of foreign nations, or that it would increase the disaffected element in the North to such an extent that the South could dictate a peace.

The policy of making military operations conform to the desire to help Northern sympathizers in eastern Tennessee had a powerful influence on the entire war. In the spring of 1862, it would have taken Buell into eastern Tennessee, instead of to the assistance of Grant and would have changed the course of events in the Mississippi valley. Three months later, it was one of the potent influences that led to the breaking up of Halleck's army at Corinth. It finally caused Buell's relief from command because of his disapproval. It caused Burnside's army to be absent from the battle of Chickamauga.

In 1864, the campaigns of Price in Missouri and Hood in Tennessee are said to have been intended to affect the presidential election at the North by giving encouragement to the party which was claiming that the war was a Federal failure. If that was not the case might not Hood have done better by marching in the track of Longstreet through Knoxville, Tennessee, and Lynchburg, Virginia, to join Lee, while Sherman was marching to the sea, entirely out of reach?

An unreasonable importance, from a military point of view, was given to the capital of each government. The capital of the United States had been captured in two wars without producing more than local effect, but every plan in

[118]

## SCENE OF A PECULIAR MILITARY SITUATION

A remarkable panoramic view of a scene on James River taken in 1865, fifteen miles from Richmond. Farrar's Island is a point of land enclosed by an almost complete loop of the winding James. It is fifteen miles on a direct line from the former Confederate Capital, and by water, owing to the bends of the stream, some seven or eight miles more. When General Butler's Federal army had retreated from its futile attack on Drewry's Bluff, in May, 1864, to its strong entrenchments at Bermuda Hundred, southward, the military authorities, were in great fear that the Confederate flotilla and the ironclad ram *Virginia No. 2* that was just being completed at Richmond would come down the stream, divide the army and separate it from its base. Much against the advice of many of the naval officers who commanded vessels of the Federal flotilla, obstructions were built across the channel almost from shore to shore at Trent's Reach, a broad stretch of water south of Farrar's Island. Further to strengthen the position, four strong Federal batteries were constructed on the river bank, batteries Wilcox, Parsons, Spofford and Sawyer. Only a mile and a half away to the west was the powerful Confederate Battery "Dantzler," known as "Howlett's" to the Federal forces; from thence could be seen Forts Spofford and Sawyer. A peculiar situation was developed here. The Union obstructions and batteries were intended to prevent the Confederate fleet from coming down, and the Confederate engineers had placed mines and torpedoes in Trent's Reach to hinder the Federal fleet from coming up. The various strong forts along the river were for the same purpose, and at Chaffin's Bluff, less than three miles above Dutch Gap, the neck of Farrar's Island, the Confederate flotilla had penned itself in with obstructions quite as formidable as those below. Grant's later operations farther up the James and before Petersburg rendered much of the Federal work unnecessary.

Virginia was contingent upon the safety of Washington, thus causing the diversion of many thousand soldiers for that single duty. On the Southern side the correct military decision would have been to abandon Richmond as soon as Petersburg was invested, but the Government delayed, for political reasons, until it was too late, and the defending army surrendered as a consequence.

In the distribution of troops the Federal authorities were hampered by the rival claims of the border States, which thought they required protection. Hence, Ohio sent an army into West Virginia; Pennsylvania, into the Shenandoah valley; the national Government concentrated troops for the protection of its capital; the Western States gathered along the Ohio River and in Missouri. This great dispersion existed on both sides and continued more or less till the end of the war. The advantage it gave was in the protection of the friendly portion of the population and in the good recruiting ground thus secured. The great difficulty of holding troops in service, whose home country had been overrun, was appreciated by both sides and exercised a strong influence on the plans of the generals. These conditions dictated much of the strategy which is subject to criticism, and should not be forgotten.

The policy of furloughing great numbers of soldiers during the war, as an inducement to reenlist, was probably unavoidable, but it helped to cause inactivity during many months and in the case of Sherman's Atlanta campaign it caused the absence of two of his divisions. Absenteeism is one of the inevitable consequences of a long war, with troops untrained in time of peace by modern methods. Lincoln complained of it and the generals seemed powerless to limit or prevent it. Probably the latter are entitled to most of the blame. It was not uncommon for a general to call for reenforcements at a time when large numbers of his troops were absent.

The armies were indeed long in getting over the

## THE KEY TO WASHINGTON

From Chattanooga, Tennessee, to Harper's Ferry, Virginia, lay the Alleghany Mountains, an almost impassable barrier to the movement of armies. Here we see them sloping toward the gap at Harper's Ferry on the Potomac. The approach to this was made easy from the South by the Shenandoah Valley, the facile and favorite avenue of advance by the Confederates when threatening invasion of the enemy's territory. The scene is of the dismantled bridge across Armstrong Run. Driving General Banks' forces up the Valley and forcing him across the Potomac, Jackson saved Richmond from McClellan in 1862. Up the Valley came Lee the following year, striking terror to the North by the invasion that was only checked at Gettysburg. This eastern gap, provided by nature in the Alleghanies, became a veritable gateway of terror to the Federals, for through it lay open the path for sudden approach upon Washington on the part of the Confederates.

characteristics of raw troops, but the generals in their early movements do not appear much better than the troops. Every man who had been graduated from West Point was regarded as a "trained soldier," which was a mistake, because West Point was a preparatory school, and such men as had studied the art of high command had done so by themselves. The trade of the general was new to all, and had to be learned in the hard school of experience.

In four of the early campaigns in which the Federal troops were practically unopposed, they marched on an average of less than seven miles per day, while, in case of opposition by a greatly inferior force, the average was down to a mile a day, as in the Peninsula campaign and the advance on Corinth.

The plans for the early battles were complicated in the extreme, perhaps due to the study of Napoleon and his perfect army opposed by poor generals. Bull Run, Wilson's Creek, Seven Pines, Glendale, Malvern Hill, Shiloh, Gaines' Mill were of this kind, and failed. Even at Gettysburg, July 2, 1863, Lee's failure to execute his echelon attacks showed that his army was not yet ready to perform such a delicate refinement of war.

As an example of improvement, however, take Jackson's march of fourteen miles on a country road and the battle fought on May 2, 1863, all between daylight and dark of one day. In battles, also, we notice the fine play of early campaigns replaced by a savage directness and simplicity at a later period, in the Wilderness by Lee and at Spottsylvania by Grant. Thus it was that both leaders had ceased to count on the inefficiency of the enemy. At the beginning of the movement on Richmond both Lee and Grant seemed reckless in the risks they took. It was not so earlier.

The earliest form of strategy was the practice of ruse, stratagem, and surprise, but they have long been considered as clumsy expedients which are no longer effective against

RICHMOND IN RUINS, OCCUPIED BY THE FEDERALS

POLITICAL OBJECTIVES, WASHINGTON

In these two pictures appear the two capitals that were mistakenly made the goals of the military operations on both sides. The Confederates threatened Washington at the outset of the war, and realizing the effectiveness of such a move in giving moral rather than military support to their cause, similar movements were repeated throughout the war. For a like reason "On to Richmond" was the cry at the North until Grant took command and made the army of Lee and its ultimate reduction to an ineffective state his controlling purpose. With the investment of Petersburg by the Federals, Lee's proper military move would have been the abandonment of Richmond and the opposing of Grant along other lines.

the best troops and commanders. Among instances which are often classed in this category are Shiloh, Chancellorsville, and the Wilderness.

Some forms of strategy have not changed in several thousand years. Sherman, for instance, crossed the Chattahoochee, which was held by Johnston, in 1864, in the same way that Alexander crossed the Hydaspes in the year 326 B. C., by feinting at one flank and crossing at the other.

The Vicksburg campaign gave great fame to General Grant and is really one of the most complete and decisive examples in history. In this campaign, he deliberately crossed the river north of Vicksburg, marched south and crossed again below Vicksburg. Then, relying on the country for supplies, he moved to Jackson, forty-five miles east of Vicksburg, where he interposed between the fractions of the Confederate army under Pemberton and Johnston. He then turned back again toward the Mississippi, drove Pemberton into Vicksburg, established a base of supplies at the North and invested the city. In this case, it is noticeable that the tendency to rate localities at too high a value is shown in Pemberton's retreating to Vicksburg, which was quite certain to be surrendered, instead of joining forces with Johnston to oppose Grant in the interior.

The same point is illustrated by the siege of Petersburg. As soon as Grant's army crossed the James and began this siege the fate of Richmond was sealed, for Grant had a great army and numerous means of extending his fortified lines until they crossed every avenue of approach to Richmond.

Moltke remarked that strategy was nothing more than common sense, but he acknowledged that it was often difficult to decide what was common sense and what was not. He might easily have had our Civil War in his mind. In 1861, the art of war had been greatly complicated by pedantic study, principally by officers of the French school, in attempting to reduce it to an exact science. The true lesson of Napoleon's

A DEFENDER OF THE FEDERAL CAPITAL

AN IDLE GARRISON

Only once were the elaborate fortifications about Washington seriously threatened. That was when the Confederate General Jubal A. Early, with a force of 10,000 men, marched against the Federal capital in July, 1864, with the intention of capturing it. Reinforcements were rushed to these works and Early retreated. The constant compliance with the clamor at the North that Washington be strongly defended was a serious strategical mistake. The Army of the Potomac was at first superior in number to Lee's army of Northern Virginia. It could have been made overwhelmingly so at the beginning of the war if the troops around Washington had been added to it. Grant demonstrated the wisdom of this policy in 1864 by leaving only a few heavy artillery regiments, the "hundred days' men," and detachments from the Veteran Reserve to defend Washington. He then outnumbered Lee in the field.

campaigns had either been lost or the effect of new conditions had not been appreciated. It seems rather commonplace to say at this time that the first thing to do in war is to decide on your objective, but in the Civil War an incalculable amount of time was wasted, much treasure expended, and many lives were lost in a blind search for an objective. By objective is meant, of course, a point upon which to concentrate the greatest effort, the gaining of which will mean the success or failure of the cause.

In 1862, when the hostile armies opposed each other in front of Washington, McClellan insisted on attacking Richmond instead of Johnston's army. His plan resulted in the transfer of his army to the Peninsula and carried him to within six miles of Richmond with insignificant loss. For this, great credit has been claimed and unfavorable comment made on later campaigns. But McClellan found the undefeated Confederate army at Richmond, and he was weakened by a vast army which had been kept back to guard Washington. Without entering into this great controversy, we may simply say that to fight the foe as far from Richmond as possible would now be considered the correct solution of that problem. It is well known that Lincoln disapproved of McClellan's plan, whether by the counsel of wise military advisers or by his own common sense we know not.

Again, in 1862, when Halleck with much trouble and skill had collected a great army of one hundred thousand men at Corinth, the army was dispersed, contrary to his desire, it appears, and the true objective was lost. The Confederate leader repaired his losses and soon recovered from his serious defeats. At that time the army could have gone anywhere, whether to Vicksburg to open the Mississippi, or to Chattanooga and even to Richmond. This is the opinion of those best qualified to know. Burnside, also, in the fall of 1862, marched away from Lee's army when he went to Fredericksburg.

## WHERE GRANT CROSSED THE JAMES.

When Grant at this point crossed the James and, ignoring the water approaches upon Richmond, proceeded to the investment of Petersburg, Lee was as good as checkmated. For months Grant's brilliant flanking movements had gained him no advantage over his opponent, who persistently remaining on the defensive shifted from one impregnable position to another till at last Grant saw that the railroads were the key to the situation. With Lee's forces entirely disposed for the defense of Richmond, it was but necessary to cut off the communications of the Confederate capital in order to force Lee to come forth and give battle. The investment of Petersburg, successfully prosecuted, would leave but one railroad in the hands of the Confederates. The crossing of the James near Wilcox Landing over the bridge, the remains of which appear in the picture, was the final strategic triumph by which Grant accomplished victory over Lee's army.

So deep-rooted is the idea of choosing a locality as the objective of a campaign instead of a hostile army, that Rosecrans' campaign, in the summer of 1863, has gone into history as the " Campaign for Chattanooga," and it has been claimed by his admirers that the possession of that place was worth what it cost—a heavy defeat at Chickamauga.

In 1864, Grant had authority to lay down a choice of objective, which he had already announced in 1862. For himself it was clearly Lee's army, and it was intended to be the same with other commands as well. General Sherman, however, was not so clear in his manner of execution as was his chief. His strategy creates a suspicion that it was designed to force Johnston to retreat and to relinquish territory. There was an idea that Johnston would not give up Dalton, which he had strongly fortified, but Sherman's heavy turning movement against his rear forced him to retreat without a battle. The same strategy continued until Atlanta was reached, and still Johnston's army was undefeated, while Sherman had weakened his army by guarding a long line of communication. Judging from this, we are disposed to suspect that Atlanta, rather than Johnston's army, was Sherman's main objective.

Later, the historic " March to the Sea " introduces a novel element into the question, for Sherman abandoned Hood's army as a first objective, and chose Lee's army instead. It will be remembered that Sherman had difficulty in getting consent from Grant, who wanted him to ruin Hood's army first. As it turned out, Sherman marched one thousand miles and was several hundred miles from Lee at the end of the campaign. If Lee's army had been his real objective there were other ways of reaching it: first, by sending his army by sea north from Savannah, as was suggested by Grant, which would have taken two months, say until the end of February, 1865; second, by sending the troops by rail, as Schofield was moved with fifteen thousand men and as Hooker was moved with twenty-three thousand men, and, third, by marching on

[ 128 ]

SHERMAN'S FAMOUS FEINT. RAILROAD BRIDGE OVER THE CHATTAHOOCHEE, 1863

In the foreground we see the formidable defenses behind which Johnston held the railroad bridge over the Chattahoochee against the advance of Sherman upon Atlanta. At this river Sherman exemplified again the strategy of Alexander at the Hydaspes. While Johnston with all his forces save cavalry was lying menacingly at the head of this bridge, Sherman, feinting strongly against his right with Stoneman's cavalry as if determined to gain a crossing, meanwhile quickly shifted the main body of his army to the left of Johnston's position, crossed the river on pontoons and immediately established a *tête du pont* of his own in Johnston's rear capable of withstanding his entire force. There was nothing for Johnston but to retreat upon Atlanta, burning the bridge behind him. In the picture is the bridge as rebuilt by Sherman's engineers, another link in his long line of communication by rail.

Lynchburg by the Knoxville road, which would have been about one-third to one-half the distance actually marched.

Looking upon the war with all the advantage of to-day, it is not difficult to assume that the hopes of both sides rested on two great armies, one in the East and one in the West, and the destruction of either meant the destruction of the other. This clear estimate seems to have come quite naturally and easily to only one man during the war, and that man was Grant. Such a conception clears away a mass of secondary objectives, such as so-called "strategic points" along the coast and west of the Mississippi, which consumed hundreds of thousands of troops and had only a minor effect on the final issue. It must be admitted that Grant used some seventy-five thousand men on secondary objectives which were not successful, in 1864, when these men would have had a great effect either with the armies of Sherman or himself. He probably thought that an army of one hundred and twenty thousand men was large enough for his purposes, but he found it was a mistake.

Equally fallacious with the importance given to "strategic points" was that ascribed to the occupation of territory. The control of Kentucky and Tennessee was given by Grant's Fort Donelson campaign, but the injury inflicted on the Confederate army by the large capture of men at Donelson and Island Number 10 was the real and vital result. The control of territory that was not accompanied by the defeat of the foe often had many disadvantages. Such was the experience of Grant and Sherman, the former in his first advance on Vicksburg, and the latter in the Atlanta campaign.

For the South it was an easier task to decide upon an objective because it was the weaker side and its acts were determined by those of the stronger. The main idea of the strategy of the Southern generals was to divert attention to side issues, to induce the opposing general to weaken his forces at decisive points. Numerous examples of diversions are afforded by Jackson's Valley campaign, in 1862, which kept many

[ 130 ]

### WORK OF THE ENGINEERS AND THE CAVALRY

The great Civil War first introduced the railroad as a strategic factor in military operations. In the upper picture we see the Federal engineers at Vibbard Draw on Long Bridge at Washington busily at work rehabilitating a locomotive for use along the railroad connections of the capital with its army. Extemporized wooden structures of that time seem paltry in comparison with the great steel cranes and derricks which our modern wrecking trains have made familiar. The railroads in control of the North were much better equipped and guarded than those of the South, yet the bold Confederate Cavalry, under such leaders as Stuart, were ever ready for raids to cut communications. How thoroughly they did their work whenever they got the chance, the lower picture tells.

### AFTER A RAID ON THE ORANGE AND ALEXANDRIA RAILROAD

thousand men away from McClellan; Early's march on Washington, and many cavalry raids.

The result of a study of objectives shows that, with good troops, and safe, but not brilliant, generals on both sides, the only way to overthrow the opponent is to attack and defeat his main army.

The long periods of inactivity in the several armies of the North seem to have been largely, but not always, due to the frequent change of commanders. The other causes would take long to analyze. Lee made six campaigns in fourteen months, from May, 1862, to July, 1863, a performance unequaled in history. But McClellan's army was inactive for ten months after Bull Run; Rosecrans' army for five months after Murfreesboro, and Grant's army for four months after Vicksburg, while Grant's army was almost in the same class during its ten months before Petersburg.

The concentration of scattered forces at decisive points, which is technically called in the text-book the use of interior lines, and in more homely phrase, "getting there first with the most men," was often skilfully performed on both a large and small scale. Thus, Johnston joined Beauregard at Bull Run in time to win the battle; Jackson alternately attacked the divided forces of his opponents and neutralized their greatly superior forces, and finally joined Lee for another campaign; Longstreet joined Bragg to win Chickamauga; Ewell joined Breckinridge to defeat Sigel. Many opportunities were lost, even in the very campaigns mentioned, as we see them to-day.

The conduct of pursuits confirms the idea that it is the most difficult operation presented to a general. Johnston after Bull Run, McClellan after Antietam, Meade after Gettysburg, Bragg after Chickamauga, Grant after Chattanooga, and Lee after Fredericksburg practically allowed the defeated enemy to escape without further injury. Lee's pursuit of McClellan in the Seven Days' Battles on the Peninsula and of Meade in

## MILITARY COMMERCE

This view of the magazine wharf at City Point in 1864 reveals the immensity of the transportation problem that was solved by the North in support of its armies in the field. The Federal army in Virginia, unlike the armies of Napoleon, did not forage off the territory which it occupied. Rail and water transportation made possible the bringing of supplies long distances. Whatever point was chosen for the army base quickly became a bustling center, rivaling the activity of any great commercial city, and giving employment to thousands of men whose business it was to unload and forward the arriving stores and ammunition to the army in the field near by.

## CITY POINT, VIRGINIA, JULY, 1864

When Grant finally settled down to the siege of Petersburg, and City Point became the army base, the little village was turned temporarily into a great town. Winter quarters were built in the form of comfortable cabins for the reserve troops and the garrison, and ample hospital buildings were provided. The railroad to Petersburg was controlled and operated by the army for the forwarding of troops and stores. The supply base longest occupied by the Army of the Potomac, City Point, grew up almost in a night. With the coming of peace the importance of the post vanished, and with it soon after the evidences of its aggrandizement.

the operations of October, 1863, had only partial success. Near the end of the war Thomas' pursuit of Hood, after Nashville, showed a much higher efficiency than had yet been reached, and the Appomattox campaign gives the only entirely successful instance in about one hundred years of military history.

The campaigns of Lee and Jackson were models of their kind. Napoleon has said that the general who makes no mistakes never goes to war. The critic of Lee finds it hard to detect mistakes. No general since Hannibal, and perhaps Napoleon, in the last two years of his campaigns, has made war under greater disadvantages and accomplished so much with an inferior force. While all great generals before him inherited a ready-made army, Lee, like Washington, made his own army. He fought soldiers of the same race and generals of the same school as himself. His genius was shown in many ways, but nowhere more than in his ability to calculate chances, even when he was violating the so-called rules of war. He used converging columns which met upon the field of battle; he detached inferior forces against the Federals' rear; he divided his army in the presence of the foe; he uncovered his lines of retreat and fought battles in that position; he did not hesitate to throw his last reserve into the fight.

On two occasions he withdrew his army across the Potomac River, in good order and without loss, in the presence of a powerful hostile army. His use of the ground to compensate for inferior numbers and to hide his movements from the Federals shows how clearly he saw the secrets of Napoleon's generalship, while his battles in the woods were entirely original and his use of entrenchments was effective. The power of the modern fire-arm in the hands of his opponents forced him to accept less decisive results than great soldiers who preceded him. As with other great soldiers, his best success was due to the inefficiency of his opponents in the early days. He was probably the last of the race of generals who, like Napoleon, dominated the field of war by genius alone. He

FORMIDABLE FIELDWORKS IN AN ADVANCE

NEW NECESSITIES OF WARFARE

The increased deadliness of firearms taught the commanders in the Civil War the habit of greatly strengthening every new position occupied with earthworks as formidable as possible. The works in the upper picture were thrown up in a night by the Federals near North Anna River, Virginia, in 1864. It is apparent how they would strengthen the resistance of a small force to larger numbers who might advance across the open upon the position. In the lower picture we see the salient of "Fort Hell," with its ditch and abattis and breastworks constructed of gabions, the result of many days' work of the soldiers in anticipation of attack. This was one of the fortifications about Petersburg, where the construction of fieldworks was developed to the highest point of efficiency.

will be replaced by the safe leader who is never brilliant, but makes no mistakes and at the same time commands the heaviest battalions.

The absence of a broad and comprehensive plan of operations was particularly noticeable on both sides. It never seemed to have been developed in the North until Grant issued his orders for a general advance, in 1864. In the South, Longstreet seems to have prepared a strategic plan for the movement of all Confederate armies after Chancellorsville, but this was not approved. The immense area occupied by the opposing forces, greater than had ever before been occupied in a single war, may be the excuse for this.

Great fame has come to the various generals who each made some well-planned maneuver, which forced the foe to relinquish territory and retreat to a rear position. McClellan before Manassas, Rosecrans before Shelbyville, and Sherman before Dalton did all this, but it is a debatable question whether the final issue was hastened or delayed.

Sherman gained Atlanta with a loss of thirty-two thousand men, and Rosecrans gained Chattanooga with a loss of eighteen thousand men, but the foe was not defeated. On the other hand, Grant, in his year from the Rapidan to Appomattox accomplished the desired result, but with severe losses, it is true.

After all is said, the subject may be narrowed down to the statement that Lee, Jackson, and perhaps Johnston handled inferior forces with as great skill as any commanders since Hannibal and Napoleon.

On the other side it was also an American soldier, even before Sedan and Mukden, who formulated the modern idea of strategy which has been so closely followed in recent wars— to seek out the foe, get close to him, and fight it out by short-arm jolts.

# PART I

## THE FIRST OF THE GREAT CAMPAIGNS

---

# BULL RUN

---

(HERE BEGIN THE CHAPTERS THAT PICTURE BROADLY
THE CAMPAIGNS, FROM BULL RUN TO APPOMATTOX,
CONTINUING THROUGH VOLUME III—EACH OF THE
REMAINING SEVEN VOLUMES IS DEVOTED THROUGH-
OUT TO A SEPARATE PHASE OF WAR-TIME ACTIVITY.)

---

VOLUNTEERS ABOUT TO FACE FIRE AT BULL RUN—
MCCLELLAN'S TROOPS DRILLING NEAR WASHINGTON

### THE TURNING POINT OF THE BATTLE

Across this little stream that was destined to mark the center of the first, and in many respects the most desperate, battle of the Civil War, we see what was left of the bridge after the day had ended in a Federal rout (see "Bull Run," page 142).   On the farther side of Bull Run the Confederates under Beauregard had taken their stand with the stream as a contested barrier between them and McDowell's troops.   At daylight of July 21, 1861, Tyler's division advanced to this bridge.   It was a day of confusion on both sides. First, the Confederates were driven back in disorder by the impetuous onslaught of the Federals.   These were congratulating them-

RUINS OF THE STONE BRIDGE—BULL RUN, VIRGINIA

selves upon a victory, when Johnston's reinforcements from Winchester fell upon the rear of their right, and threw the lines into confusion. Back across the field fled the first memorable Federal rout. The little bridge was soon groaning with the weight of the men struggling to get across it. Finally, in frantic haste, it was destroyed by the Federals to delay the dreaded pursuit. Here Federal engineers are rebuilding the bridge, in order to forward supplies to the army that is some thirty miles to the south in the wooded Virginia country, but dependent on communications with the base at Washington.

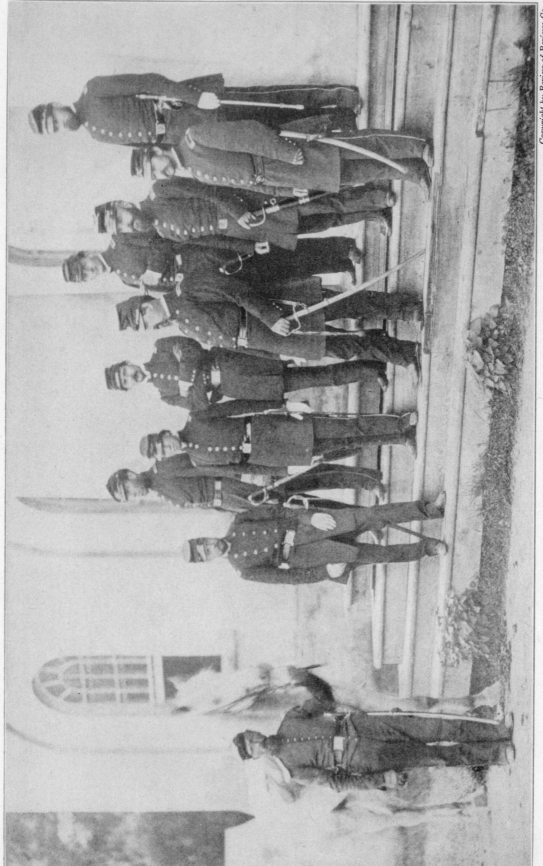

Copyright by Review of Reviews Co.

## THE DEFENDER OF WASHINGTON—GENERAL IRVIN McDOWELL AND HIS STAFF

The man who planned the battle of Bull Run for the Northern Army was Brigadier-General Irvin McDowell, then in command of the forces before Washington. When assured that Patterson would hold Johnston in the Shenandoah, he undertook to advance with his raw and unorganized troops on Beauregard at Manassas. The plan for the battle which he adopted on the night of July 18th was, according to General Sherman, one of the best formed during the entire war. But it failed because, even before he began his attack, Johnston with a good part of his troops had already joined Beauregard at Manassas. After the defeat McDowell was placed in charge of the defenses of Washington on the Virginia side of the Potomac. This picture was taken the next year at General Robert E. Lee's former home in Arlington.

## TROOPS THAT FOUGHT AT BULL RUN—A THREE MONTHS' COMPANY

When Lincoln issued his call for volunteers on the evacuation of Sumter, Rhode Island was one of the first to respond. We here see Company "D" of the First Regiment (organized April, 1861), as it looked during its encampment at Camp Sprague, Washington, from April 24th to July 16th, 1861. The care-free faces of the men lack all the gravity of veterans. In the famous first battle of the war, the regiment was in Burnside's Brigade of Hunter's Division, which marched some miles to the north, crossed Bull Run at Sudley Ford, met the Confederates north of Young's Branch, and drove them south across the stream to the Henry house plateau. Later it yielded to the panic which seized upon the Union army. On August 2, 1861, Company "D" closed its brief career in the conflict that was to fill four years with continuous combat.

# BULL RUN—THE VOLUNTEERS
# FACE FIRE

THERE had been strife, a bloodless, political strife, for forty years between the two great sections of the American nation. No efforts to reconcile the estranged brethren of the same household had been successful. The ties that bound the great sections ·of the country had severed one by one; their contention had grown stronger through all these years, until at last there was nothing left but a final appeal to the arbitrament of the sword—then came the great war, the greatest civil war in the annals of mankind.

For the first time in the nation's history the newly-elected President had entered the capital city by night and in secret, in the fear of the assassin's plots. For the first time he had been inaugurated under a military guard. Then came the opening shots, and the ruined walls of the noble fort in Charleston harbor told the story of the beginnings of the fratricidal war. The fall of Sumter, on April 14, 1861, had aroused the North to the imminence of the crisis, revealing the danger that threatened the Union and calling forth a determination to preserve it. The same event had unified the South; four additional States cast their lot with the seven which had already seceded from the Union. Virginia, the Old Dominion, the first born of the sisterhood of States, swung into the secession column but three days after the fall of Sumter; the next day, April 18th, she seized the arsenal at Harper's Ferry and on the 20th the great navy-yard at Norfolk.

Two governments, each representing a different economic

[A complete record of leading events and the various engagements, giving the troops involved and casualties between January, 1861, and August, 1862, appears on page 344.—THE EDITORS.]

G. T. Beauregard

## THE SOUTHERNER OF THE HOUR IN '61.

Born in New Orleans on May 28, 1818, the Southern leader upon whom at first all eyes were turned, Pierre Gustave Toutant Beauregard, was graduated from the U. S. Military Academy in 1838. Gallant and dashing, he won the brevets of Captain and Major in the war with Mexico and was wounded at Chapultepec. Early in '61 he resigned from the army, and joined the Confederacy, being in command of the Confederate forces in the firing on Fort Sumter in April. Owing to his forceful personality, he became a popular and noted leader in the Confederacy. After the Union defeat at Manassas, he was looked upon as the coming Napoleon. He was confirmed as Major-General in the Confederate army on July 30, 1861, but he had held the provisional rank of Brigadier-General since February 20th, before a shot was fired. After his promotion to Major-General, he commanded the Army of the Mississippi under General A. S. Johnston, whom he succeeded at Shiloh. He defended Charleston, S. C., in 1862–3 and afterward commanded the Department of North Carolina and Southeastern Virginia. He died at New Orleans in 1893.

and political idea, now stood where there had been but one—the North, with its powerful industrial organization and wealth; the South, with its rich agricultural empire. Both were calling upon the valor of their sons.

At the nation's capital all was confusion and disorder. The tramp of infantry and the galloping of horsemen through the streets could be heard day and night. Throughout the country anxiety and uncertainty reigned on all sides. Would the South return to its allegiance, would the Union be divided, or would there be war? The religious world called unto the heavens in earnest prayer for peace; but the rushing torrent of events swept on toward war, to dreadful internecine war.

The first call of the President for troops, for seventy-five thousand men, was answered with surprising alacrity. Citizens left their farms, their workshops, their counting rooms, and hurried to the nation's capital to take up arms in defense of the Union. A similar call by the Southern President was answered with equal eagerness. Each side believed itself in the right. Both were profoundly sincere and deeply in earnest. Both have won the respect of history.

After the fall of Fort Sumter, the two sides spent the spring months marshaling their forces for the fierce conflict that was to follow. President Lincoln had called for three-months' volunteers; at the beginning of July some thirty thousand of these men were encamped along the Potomac about the heights of Arlington. As the weeks passed, the great Northern public grew impatient at the inaction and demanded that Sumter be avenged, that a blow be struck for the Union.

The " call to arms " rang through the nation and aroused the people. No less earnest was the feeling of the South, and soon two formidable armies were arrayed against each other, only a hundred miles apart—at Washington and at Richmond.

The commander of the United States Army was Lieut.-General Winfield Scott, whose military career had begun before most of the men of '61 had been born. Aged and infirm,

YOUNG SOUTHERNERS AT RICHMOND MAKING LIGHT OF WAR

Skylarking before the lens of the Confederate photographer, we see the Boys in Gray just before Bull Run had taught them the meaning of a battle and elated them with the conviction of their own prowess. The young and confident troops on both sides approached this first severe lesson of the war in the same jocular spirit. There is not a serious face in the picture. The man flourishing the sword bayonet and the one with the drawn dagger are marking with mock heroics their bravado toward the coming struggle, while the one with the musket stands debonair as a comic-opera soldier. The pipe-clay cross belt and breast plate, the cock plumes in the "shapo" of the officer, indicate that the group is of a uniformed military organization already in existence at the beginning of the war. There was no such paraphernalia in the outfit of Southern troops organized later, when simplicity was the order of the day in camp.

he remained in Washington. The immediate command of the army was entrusted to Brigadier-General Irvin McDowell.

Another Union army, twenty thousand strong, lay at Martinsburg, Virginia, under the command of Major-General Patterson, who, like General Scott, was a veteran of the War of 1812 and of the Mexican War.

Opposite McDowell, at Manassas Junction, about thirty miles from Washington, lay a Confederate army under Brigadier-General Beauregard who, three months before, had won the homage of the South by reducing Fort Sumter. Opposed to Patterson in the Shenandoah valley was Joseph E. Johnston with a force of nine thousand men. The plans of the President and General Scott were to send McDowell against Beauregard, while Patterson was to detain Johnston in the Valley and prevent him from joining Beauregard. It was confidently believed that, if the two Confederate forces could be kept apart, the "Grand Army" could win a signal victory over the force at Manassas; and on July 16th, with waving banners and lively hopes of victory, amid the cheers of the multitude, it moved out from the banks of the Potomac toward the interior of Virginia. It was a motley crowd, dressed in the varied uniforms of the different State militias. The best disciplined troops were those of the regular army, represented by infantry, cavalry, and artillery. Even the navy was drawn upon and a battalion of marines was included in the Union forces. In addition to the regulars were volunteers from all the New England States, from New York and Pennsylvania and from Ohio, Michigan, and Minnesota, organizations which, in answer to the President's call for troops, had volunteered for three months' service. Many were boys in their teens with the fresh glow of youth on their cheeks, wholly ignorant of the exhilaration, the fear, the horrors of the battle-field. Onward through the Virginia plains and uplands they marched to the strains of martial music. Unused to the rigid discipline of war, many of the men would drop out of line to gather

## ONE OF THE FIRST UNION VOLUNTEER REGIMENTS.

The First Minnesota, a regiment that fought in the flanking column at Bull Run. On April 14, 1861, the day after Sumter's surrender, the Federal Government received an offer of a volunteer regiment from Minnesota, and on April 29, the First Minnesota was mustered into service by Lieutenant W. W. Sanders, U. S. A. Under Colonel Willis A. Gorman, the regiment proceeded to Washington in June and, attached to Franklin's Brigade, Heintzelman's Division of McDowell's Army, at Bull Run gave an excellent account of itself, finally retiring from the field in good order. A record for conspicuous bravery was sustained by the First Minnesota throughout the war, notably its famous charge on the field of Gettysburg, July 2, 1863.

The photograph was taken just before the regiment left Fort Snelling in 1861. In the front line the first from the left is Lieut. Colonel Stephen Miller, the next is Colonel Gorman. On his left hand is Major Dyke and next to him is Adjutant W. B. Leach. Between the last two and behind them is Captain William Colvill, while at the left hand of Adjutant Leach is Captain Mark Downie. At the extreme right of the picture stands General J. B. Sanborn with Lieutenant Sanders (mustering officer) on his right hand, and on Sanders' right is the Honorable Morton S. Wilkinson. Colvill, as Colonel, led the regiment in its Gettysburg charge.

berries or tempting fruits along the roadside, or to refill their canteens at every fresh stream of water, and frequent halts were necessary to allow the stragglers to regain their lines.

After a two days' march, with "On to Richmond" as their battle-cry, the army halted at the quiet hamlet of Centreville, twenty-seven miles from Washington and seven miles from Manassas Junction where lay the waiting Confederate army of similar composition—untrained men and boys. Men from Virginia, from North and South Carolina, from the mountains of Tennessee, from Alabama, Mississippi, and Georgia, even from distant Arkansas, had gathered on the soil of the Old Dominion State to do battle for the Southern cause. Between the two armies flowed the stream of Bull Run, destined to give its name to the first great battle of the impending conflict. The opposing commanders, McDowell and Beauregard, had been long-time friends; twenty-three years before, they had been graduated in the same class at West Point.

Beauregard knew of the coming of the Federal army. The news had been conveyed to him by a young man, a former government clerk at Washington, whose sympathies, however, lay with the cause of the South. He won the confidence of Beauregard. The latter sent him to the capital city bearing a paper with two words in cipher, "Trust Bearer." With this he was to call at a certain house, present it to the lady within, and wait a reply. Traveling all night, he crossed the Potomac below Alexandria, and reached the city at dawn, when the newsboys were calling out in the empty streets the latest intelligence of the army. The messenger rang the doorbell at a house within a stone's throw of the White House and delivered the scrap of paper to the only one in the city to whom it was intelligible. She hurriedly gave the youth his breakfast, wrote in cipher the words, "Order issued for McDowell to march upon Manassas to-night," and giving him the scrap of paper, sent him on his way. That night the momentous bit of news was in the hands of General Beauregard. He instantly wired

EVE OF THE CONFLICT

Stone Church, Centreville, Virginia.—Past this little stone church on the night of July 20, 1861, and long into the morning of the twenty-first marched lines of hurrying troops. Their blue uniforms were new, their muskets bright and polished, and though some faces were pale their spirits were elated, for after their short training they were going to take part, for the first time, in the great game of war. It was the first move of the citizen soldier of the North toward actual conflict. Not one knew exactly what lay before him. The men were mostly from New England and the Middle States. They had left desk and shop and farm and forge, and with the thought in their minds that the war would last for three months the majority had been mustered in. Only the very wise and farseeing had prophesied the immensity of the struggle, and these were regarded as extremists. Their ideas were laughed at. So on they went in long lines down the road in the darkness of the night, chattering, laughing and talking carelessly, hardly realizing in the contagion of their patriotic ardor the grim meaning of real war. The battle had been well planned, but who had had the experience, even among the leaders, to be sure of the details and the absolute carrying out of orders? With the exception of the veterans of the Mexican War, who were regulars, there was not one who had ever maneuvered a thousand men in the field. A lesson lay before them and it was soon to come. The surprising battle that opened early in the morning, and whose results spread such consternation through the North, was really the result of popular clamor. The press and the politicians demanded action, and throughout the South the same confident and reckless spirit prevailed, the same urging to see something done.

President Davis at Richmond and asked that he be reenforced by Johnston's army.

As we have seen, General Scott had arranged that Patterson detain Johnston in the Valley. He had even advised McDowell that " if Johnston joins Beauregard he shall have Patterson on his heels." But the aged Patterson was unequal to the task before him. Believing false reports, he was convinced that Johnston had an army of thirty-five thousand men, and instead of marching upon Johnston at Winchester he led his army to Charleston, twenty miles in the opposite direction. Johnston thereupon was free to join Beauregard at Manassas, and he promptly proceeded to do so.

McDowell's eager troops had rested at Centreville for two days. The time for them to test their mettle in a general engagement was at hand. Sunday, July 21st, was selected as the day on which to offer battle. At half-past two in the morning the sleeping men were roused for the coming conflict. Their dream of an easy victory had already received a rude shock, for on the day after their arrival a skirmish between two minor divisions of the opposing armies had resulted in the retreat of the Union forces after nineteen of their number lay dead upon the plain. The Confederates, too, had suffered and fifteen of their army were killed. But patriotic enthusiasm was too ardent to be quenched by such an incident, and eagerly, in the early dawn of the sultry July morning, they marched toward the banks of the stream on which they were to offer their lives in the cause of their country.

The army moved out in three divisions commanded by Generals Robert O. Tyler, David Hunter, and S. P. Heintzelman. Among the subordinate officers was Ambrose E. Burnside, who, a year and five months later, was to figure in a far greater and far more disastrous battle, not many miles from this same spot; and William T. Sherman, who was to achieve a greater renown in the coming war.

On the Southern side we find equally striking characters.

## PRELUDE TO THE COMBAT—BLACKBURN'S FORD

This crossing of Bull Run, was on July 18, 1861, the scene of a lively prelude to the first great combat. General Daniel Tyler, commanding a division of McDowell's army, pushed a reconnaissance to the north bank of the stream near this Ford. Confederates posted on the opposite bank fired upon Tyler's advance line, driving it back in disorder. Tyler then withdrew "satisfied that the enemy was in force" at this point. This picture was taken the next year, while Rickett's division of the McDowell Corps was encamped at Manassas.

## A THREE MONTHS' REGIMENT—THE THIRD CONNECTICUT

The Third Connecticut was present on the field of Bull Run. The men had enlisted in April, 1861, and their time was all but up in July, for they were three months' men. Their drilling had taken place for a short time in their home State and afterward in the camps around Washington. They were mostly artisans and farmer boys with a sprinkling of mill hands and men of business from the larger towns. The regiment was attached to Tyler's division, of McDowell's army, and suffered little in the battle. The total losses, including deaths from sickness, in this regiment, which was mustered out at the end of its service, amounted to five all told. It goes without saying, however, that many re-enlisted and again went to the front, where they stayed until the conflict ended.

General Joseph E. Johnston was not held by Patterson in the Valley and with a portion of his army had reached Manassas on the afternoon of the 20th. In the Indian wars of Jackson's time Johnston had served his country; like McDowell and Beauregard, he had battled at the gates of Mexico; and like the latter he chose to cast his lot with the fortunes of the South. There, too, was Longstreet, who after the war was over, was to spend many years in the service of the country he was now seeking to divide. Most striking of all was "Stonewall" Jackson, whose brilliant military career was to astonish the world.

The Union plan for this fateful July day was that Tyler should lead his division westward by way of the Warrenton turnpike to a stone bridge that crossed Bull Run, about four miles from Centreville. At the same time the main army under Hunter and Heintzelman was to make a detour of several miles northward through a dense forest to a ford of Bull Run, known as Sudley's Ford. Here they were to cross the stream, march down its right bank and, while Tyler guarded the Stone Bridge, engage the foe on the west side of Bull Run. The plan of the battle was admirably drawn, but the march around to Sudley's Ford was slower than had been expected, and it was ten o'clock before the main army reached the point west of the Stone Bridge. While the Federals were making their plans to attack the Confederate left wing, Generals Beauregard and Johnston were planning an aggressive movement against the left wing of the Federal army. They were to cross Bull Run by fords several miles below the Stone Bridge and attack the Northern troops on the weaker wing of the Union force in an effort to rout them before relief could be sent from the Federal right. The Confederate attack was planned to take place a few hours later than McDowell had decided to move. The Southern troops were preparing to cross the stream when the boom of cannon at the Stone Bridge told that the Federals had taken the aggressive and that the

BULL RUN—BATTLEFIELD OF THE MORNING, JULY 21, 1861

Along Bull Run Creek on the morning of July 21st Tyler's division vigorously attacked from the east the Confederates under Longstreet and Beauregard on the western bank. By this attack McDowell hoped to succeed in falling unexpectedly on the rear of the Confederate left with the force sent on a detour of some three miles to the north. A charge of fresh troops brought forward by Beauregard in person in the late afternoon started the panic of the raw Union volunteers. . . . "Men who had fought courageously an hour before, had become as hares fleeing from pursuing hounds. The confusion was increased and multiplied by the presence among the fugitives of a multitude of panic-stricken picnickers, Congressmen, civilians of every sort, and lavishly dressed women—who had gone out in carriages and carryalls to see the spectacle of a Federal army walking over the Confederates. The Confederates fed fat for days afterward upon the provisions that the picnickers abandoned in their flight."

GENERAL BEAUREGARD'S HEADQUARTERS

The handsome old colonial mansion known as the McLean House was near Manassas station, not far from Blackburn's Ford, the scene of a sharp encounter preliminary to the battle of Bull Run. Tyler's division of McDowell's army, finding the Confederates had retreated from Centreville, attacked near here on the morning of July 18th. A vigorous cannonade opened the action, and a shell landing in the fireplace of the McLean house deprived General Beauregard of his dinner.

weak Confederate left was in danger of being overwhelmed by the superior numbers of the Union right wing. Orders countermanding the command to attack were quickly sent to the Southerners at the lower fords, and preparations were hurriedly made to repulse the attack of the Northern force.

Tyler reached the Stone Bridge before six in the morning and opened fire on a Confederate force under Colonel Evans on the other side of the run. For some time this was kept up, and Evans was much puzzled that the Federals did not attempt to cross the bridge; they merely kept up a desultory fire. The failure of the Union troops to advance led Evans to believe that Tyler's attack was only a feint and that the real attacking force would approach from some other direction. This belief was confirmed when he descried a lengthening line of dust above the tree-tops far in the distance, north of the Warrenton turnpike. Evans was now convinced (and he was right) that the main Union army was marching to Sudley's Ford, three miles above the Stone Bridge, and would reach the field from that direction. Quickly then he turned about with six companies of brave South Carolinians and a battalion of "Louisiana Tigers" and posted them on a plateau overlooking the valley of Young's Branch, a small tributary of Bull Run. Here, not far from the Matthews and Carter houses, he awaited the coming of the Federals.

His force was stationed overlooking the Sudley and Newmarket road and an open field through which the Federal troops would be forced to pass to reach the higher ground held by the Confederates. Two 6-pound howitzers were placed to sweep the field of approach, one at each end of Evans' line of defense.

With guns loaded, and howitzers ready to pour their charges into an advancing force, the Southerners stood and watched the line of dust that arose above the trees. It moved slowly to the westward. Then, where the Sudley road turns to the southward to cross the Sudley Ford, it followed the

## WHERE A FEDERAL VICTORY SEEMED ASSURED

Sudley Church—July 21, 1861.—This Methodist Episcopal church stood a half mile south of the ford by which Hunter and Heintzelman crossed Bull Run. These troops crossed Cat Harpin Run, seen in the foreground, by the ford at the left, and marched southward past the church. A mile farther south Burnside's brigade engaged the Confederate troops led by Colonel Evans. As Evans' men fell back, Johnston deemed the situation "critical." The remains at the right of the picture are of the Sudley Sulphur Spring House.

## THORNTON'S HOUSE—BULL RUN—JULY 21, 1861

This house, which stood some three miles north of the battlefield of the afternoon, marked the northern point of the detour of the divisions of Hunter and Heintzelman. The Confederate Colonel Evans, who held the extreme left of Beauregard's line, and whose suspicions had been aroused, marched upstream with half a brigade and confronted the turning column beyond the turnpike. Instead of deploying a line of battle, Hunter sent successive detached regiments and brigades against it. Evans, heavily reinforced, took up a new position in the rear.

trend of the highway. It reached the crossing of Bull Run, and the line of dust faded as the Federals spread into battle-line behind the expanse of woodland that hid each column from the other's view.

It was nearing ten o'clock. The rays of the summer sun were beating in sweltering heat upon the waiting troops. Those who could find shelter beneath the trees moved from their places into the shade. Heavy banks of storm clouds were gathering on the horizon, giving promise of relief from oppressive warmth. A silence settled over the ranks of the Confederates as they watched the edge of the woodland for the first appearance of the approaching troops.

Suddenly there was a glimmer of the sunlight reflected from burnished steel among the trees. Then, in open battle array, the Federal advance guard, under the command of Colonel Burnside, emerged from the wood on a neighboring hill, and for the first time in the nation's history two hostile American armies faced each other in battle array. At Fort Sumter only the stone walls had suffered; not a drop of human blood was shed. But here was to be a gigantic conflict, and thousands of people believed that here on this field on this day would be decided the fate of the Union and the fate of the Confederacy. The whole country awaited in breathless expectancy the news of this initial conflict, to become known as the battle of Bull Run.

With little delay the battle opened. The Federals had a clear advantage in numbers as their outlying forces came up; but they met with a brave resistance. General Bee, of South Carolina, with two brigades, crossed a valley to the south of Evans in the face of a heavy artillery fire to a point within one hundred yards of the Federal lines. At this short range thousands of shots were fired and many brave men and boys were stretched upon the green. The outcome at this point was uncertain until the Union forces were joined by Heintzelman with heavy reenforcements and by Sherman with a portion of

HERE "STONEWALL" JACKSON WON HIS NAME

Robinson House, Bull Run.—"Stonewall" Jackson won his name near this house early in the afternoon of July 21st. Meeting General Bee's troops retreating in increasing disorder, he advanced with a battery to the ridge behind the Robinson House and held the position until Bee's troops had rallied in his rear. "Look at Jackson standing there like a stone wall," was the sentence that gave birth to his historic nickname. It was General Bee who uttered these words, just before he fell, adding, "Rally on the Virginians."

WHERE THE CONFEDERATES WAVERED

Center of Battle of Morning—July 21, 1861.—North of this house, about a mile, the Confederate Colonel Evans met the columns of Burnside and Porter in their advance south from Sudley Ford. Though reinforced by General Bee, he was driven back at noon to this house in the valley near Young's Branch. Here a vigorous Union charge swept the whole battle to the hill south of the stream. General Bee sent for reinforcements, saying that unless he could be supported "all was lost."

Tyler's division. Bee could now do nothing but withdraw, and in doing so his men fell into great disorder. Cheer after cheer arose from the ranks of the Union army.

Meanwhile, Generals Beauregard and Johnston had remained at the right of their line, near Manassas, nearly four miles from the scene of action, still determined to press their attack on the Federal left if the opportunity was offered. As the morning passed and the sounds of conflict became louder and extended further to the westward, it became evident to the Confederate leaders that the Federals were massing all their strength in an effort to crush the left of the Southern army. Plans for an aggressive movement were then abandoned, the commanders withdrawing all their reserve forces from the positions where they had been held to follow up the Confederate attack, and sending them to the support of the small force that was holding back the Federals. After dispatching troops to threaten the Union left, Johnston and Beauregard galloped at full speed to the scene of the battle. They arrived about noon—at the moment when Bee's brigade was fleeing across the valley from the hail of Federal bullets. As the frightened men were running in the utmost disorder, General Bee, seeing Thomas J. Jackson's brigade calmly waiting the onset, exclaimed to his men, " Look at Jackson; there he stands like a stone wall!" The expression spread to the army and to the world, and that invincible soldier has since been known as " Stonewall " Jackson.

Beauregard and Johnston found it a herculean task to rally the fleeing men and re-form the lines, but they succeeded at length; the battle was renewed, and from noon till nearly three o'clock it raged with greater fury than before. The fight was chiefly for the possession of the plateau called the Henry hill. Up and down the slopes the two armies surged in the broiling sun. Beauregard, like McDowell on the other side, led his men in the thickest of the fight. A bursting shell killed his horse under him and tore the heel from his boot; he mounted

THE STORM CENTER OF THE BATTLE, BULL RUN, JULY 21, 1861

Near where the ruins of this house (the Henry House) are shown, in the middle of the afternoon, the raw, undisciplined volunteers of both sides surged back and forward with the heroism and determined courage of rugged veterans until the arrival of fresh Confederate troops turned the tide, and in the crowning hour of Union victory precipitated the flight and contagious panic. The Union batteries commanded by Ricketts and Griffin had moved across Young's Branch and taken up a position on the Henry Hill. Confederate sharpshooters from bushes, fences and buildings picked off cannoneers and horses. Thirteen Confederate and eleven Federal guns engaged in a stubborn duel till the Confederate regiments swarmed from cover and captured the Union position. The City of Washington was now threatened.

another horse and continued the battle. At half-past two the Confederates had been entirely driven from the plateau, had been pressed back for a mile and a half, and for the second time within three or four hours the Union troops raised the shout of victory.

At three o'clock, while McDowell and his men were congratulating themselves on having won the battle, a faint cheering was heard from a Confederate army far across the hills. It grew louder and nearer, and presently the gray lines were seen marching gallantly back toward the scene of the battle from which they had been driven. The thrilling cry then passed through the Union ranks, "Johnston has come, Johnston has come!" and there was terror in the cry. They did not know that Johnston, with two-thirds of his army, had arrived the day before; but it was true that the remaining third, twenty-three hundred fresh troops, had reached Manassas at noon by rail, and after a forced march of three hours, under the command of Kirby Smith, had just united with the army of Beauregard. It was this that caused the cheering and determined Beauregard to make another attack on the Henry plateau.

The Union men had fought valiantly in this, their first battle, untrained and unused to warfare as they were; they had braved the hail of lead and of bursting shells; they had witnessed their comrades, their friends, and neighbors fall at their feet to rise no more. They nevertheless rejoiced in their success. But with the long march and the five hours' fighting in the scorching July sun they were weary to exhaustion, and when they saw the Confederates again approaching, reenforced with fresh troops, their courage failed and they began to retreat down the hill. With waving colors the Confederates pressed on, opening a volley of musketry on the retreating Federals, and following it with another and another.

In vain McDowell and his officers attempted to rally his panic-stricken men and re-form his lines. Only the regulars,

THE LOST CHANCE. CONFEDERATE FORTIFICATIONS AT MANASSAS.

**Winter 1861-2.** The Confederates did not follow up their success at Bull Run. "Having won the completest and most conspicuous victory of modern times, they set to work to fortify themselves for defence against the enemy they had so disastrously overthrown, precisely as if they had been beaten in the fight, and were called upon to defend themselves against aggression at the hands of an enemy to be feared." It was the lost chance—many military writers aver they could have swept on to Washington. The Federals fully expected them to do so and all was alarm and confusion within the city. The North never quite got over the haunting fear that the Confederate army would some day redeem that error and the defenses of the capital were made well nigh impregnable.

THE ROAD THAT CHANGED HANDS TWICE

**The Orange & Alexandria R. R.** Manassas Station. Part of the eastern defenses constructed by the Confederates after "Bull Run" during the winter of 1861-2. Confederate troops had been withdrawn in March, 1862, as the first move in the spring campaign. This view, taken in August, 1862, after the Union occupation of the abandoned works, looks down the road towards Union Mills ford. At the close of Pope's disastrous campaign against Richmond the railroad again fell into the hands of Lee's army.

about sixteen hundred in number, were subject to the orders of their superiors, and they made a brave stand against the oncoming foe while they covered the retreat of the disorganized mass. On the Henry hill were the two powerful batteries of Griffin and the Ricketts. They had done valiant service while the tide of battle ebbed and flowed. But at last their hour had come. A Confederate regiment, dashing from a neighboring hill, poured in a deadly volley, cut down the cannoneers almost to a man, killed their horses, and captured the guns. A few minutes later General Beauregard rode up to the spot and noticed Captain Ricketts lying on the ground, desperately wounded. The two men had been friends in the years gone by. Beauregard, recognizing his old friend, asked him if he could be of any service. He then sent his own surgeons to care for the wounded captain and detailed one of his staff to make him comfortable when he was carried to Richmond as a prisoner of war.

There is little more to relate of the battle of Bull Run. The Union troops could not be rallied. As they ran down hill and across the plain they became an utterly disorganized mass of frightened men. Some crossed the Stone Bridge, others forded the stream, and all ran panic-stricken toward Centreville, leaving their dead and wounded, their arms and ammunition, in the hands of the victorious Confederates. Some hundreds of civilians, members of Congress and others, had come out from Washington to witness a victory for the Grand Army, and they saw that army scattered in wild flight to escape an imaginary pursuer. The Confederates made no serious effort to follow after them, for the routed Federals had destroyed the Stone Bridge as they passed it in their retreat, and had obstructed the other avenues of pursuit. As darkness settled over the field the Confederates returned to their camps.

McDowell made a desperate effort to check and reorganize his army at Centreville, but he was powerless. The troops refused to listen to any commands; they rushed on and

## THE PRINCIPAL FORT AT CENTREVILLE, 1861-2

This almost circular fort was constructed in the village of Centreville, Va., by the Confederates during the winter of 1861-2. All about it on the North can be seen the quarters in which the Confederate troops wintered after their victory at Bull Run. This picture was taken in March, 1862, when the Federals had occupied the abandoned works. From Centreville McDowell sent a reconnaisance in force July 18, 1861, under General D. Tyler to feel for the Confederate position. A strong force under Longstreet was encountered at Blackburn's Ford and a spirited engagement followed. This was the prelude to the battle of July 21st.

## THE DUMMY GUNS

Here is another well-built field work of the Confederates at Centreville, Va. We are looking north along the line of the earthworks east of the town and can see the abandoned Confederate winter quarters on the left. When the Confederates evacuated this line dummy guns of rough hewn logs were placed in position to deceive the Federals into the belief that the works were still occupied in force. Centreville did not fall into the hands of the Federals until the Peninsula Campaign caused its abandonment. In the lower picture we see the dummy guns in position, and in the upper two of them are lying on the ground.

great numbers of them traveled all night, reaching Washington in the morning.

These raw troops had now received their first baptism of blood and fire. Nearly five hundred of their number were left dead on the field of battle, and fourteen hundred were wounded. The captured and missing brought the Federal loss to nearly three thousand men. The Confederate loss in killed, wounded, and missing was less than two thousand. The Federal forces engaged were nearly nineteen thousand, while the Confederates had more than eighteen thousand men on the field.

The Confederate victory at Bull Run did the South great injury in that it led vast numbers to believe the war was over and that the South had won. Many soldiers went home in this belief, and for months thereafter it was not easy to recruit the Southern armies. The North, on the other hand, was taught a needed lesson—was awakened to a sense of the magnitude of the task before it.

The first great battle of the American Civil War brought joy to the Confederacy and grief to the States of the North. As the Federal troops marched into Washington through a drenching downpour of rain, on July 22d, the North was shrouded in gloom. But the defeated army had not lost its courage. The remnants of the shattered forces were gathered, and from the fragments a mightier host was to be rallied under the Stars and Stripes to meet the now victorious foe on future battle-grounds.

## AFTER BULL RUN—GUARDING THE PRISONERS.

Inside Castle Pinckney, Charleston Harbor, August, 1861.—In these hitherto unpublished Confederate photographs we see one of the earliest volunteer military organizations of South Carolina and some of the first Federal prisoners taken in the war. The Charleston Zouave Cadets were organized in the summer of 1860, and were recruited from among the patriotic young men of Charleston. We see in the picture how very young they were. The company first went into active service on Morris Island, January 1, 1861, and was there on the 9th when the guns of the battery turned back the *Star of the West* arriving with reinforcements for Sumter. The company was also stationed on Sullivan's Island during the bombardment of Sumter, April 12–13, 1861. After the first fateful clash at Bull Run, July 21, 1861, had taught the North that the war was on in earnest, a number of Federal prisoners were brought to Charleston and placed for safekeeping in Castle Pinckney, then

THE PRISONERS—11TH NEW YORK ZOUAVES

garrisoned by the Charleston Zouave Cadets. To break the monotony of guard duty Captain Chichester, some time in August, engaged a photographer to take some pictures about the fort showing his men. Gray uniforms with red stripes, red fatigue caps, and white cross belts were a novelty. The casemates of the fort had been fitted up with bunks and doors as sleeping quarters for the prisoners. Casemate No. 1 was occupied by prisoners from the 11th New York Zouaves, who had been recruited almost entirely from the New York Fire Department. The smaller picture is a nearer view of their quarters, over which they have placed the sign "Hotel de Zouave." We see them still wearing the uniform of the battlefield: wide dark-blue trousers with socks covering the bottoms, red flannel shirts with the silver badge of the New York Fire Department, blue jackets elaborately trimmed with braid, red fez caps with blue tassels, and a blue sash around the waist. Their regiment, the famous "Ellsworth's Zouaves," was posted at Bull Run as a support for Rickett's and Griffin's Batteries during the fierce fighting of the afternoon on the Henry House hill. They gave way before the charge of the Confederates, leaving 48 dead and 75 wounded on the field. About 65 of them were taken prisoners, some of whom we see here a month after the battle. The following October the prisoners were exchanged. At the beginning of the war the possession of prisoners did not mean as much to the South as it did later in the struggle, when exchanges became almost the last resource for recruiting the dwindling ranks. Almost every Southerner capable of bearing arms had already joined the colors.

[ 166 ]

WORK THROWN AWAY—CONFEDERATE ENTRENCHMENTS AT CENTREVILLE

A big gun of the kind now mounted in any of the coast defenses of the United States could have dropped a shot from these entrenchments within a short distance of the heart of Washington. Yet here the Southern army remained after the battle of Bull Run. It is a moot question whether Johnston's victorious troops could ever have reached the Federal capital. Judging from the awful panic into which the city and its defenders had been thrown, the disorganization of army divisions, brigades and regiments due to defeat, perhaps a vigorous Confederate advance might have succeeded. At all events there is no gainsaying that the Confederate batteries could have reached the Virginia shores of the Potomac and from there made a target of the Capitol itself. Later in the war had such a victory been given to either side the very men themselves would have gone forward. Nothing could have stopped them. But the Confederates, like their opponents, had it all to learn. So, content with what they had done, they constructed elaborate defenses around Manassas, then rested. Meanwhile Washington became one huge fortress and the city was surrounded on all sides by fortifications and soldiers at drill. Ceaseless and untiring were the preparations. There is no doubt that in the lull that followed before the opening of the Peninsula Campaign the Federal cause gained momentum. When all was ready and the time ripe for a forward movement the Confederate works at Centreville and Manassas were abandoned. Here we see some Uni'n soldiers viewing the deserted forts.

A SCHOOL FOR SOLDIERS, McCLELLAN'S ARDUOUS TASK

Five days after the disastrous battle of Bull Run, on July 26, 1861, Major-General George B. McClellan was called from his successes in West Virginia to take charge of the raw dispirited troops huddled near Washington. All during the fall and the winter he applied himself to the herculean task of forging the broken regiments and new levies into the powerful weapon that became famous as the Army of the Potomac. Besides, this young leader exerted his abilities as an engineer to devise in all its details the system of defensive works from Alexandria to Georgetown, and employed his unrivaled talents for organization in supplying the newly created army with all the material indispensable for an army in the field. This picture shows the Christmas Day parade of the Second Maine Infantry at Camp James near Washington, 1861. The regiment, with others, took part in the incessant drilling required to give the raw "thinking soldier" the "blind unquestioning obedience" necessary to military success. The Second Maine served in the Army of the Potomac two years and lost 139 men. After Chancellorsville, it was ordered home and the three-year men were transferred to the Twentieth Maine Infantry.

## MAKING AN ARMY—THE TWENTY-SIXTH NEW YORK

Passing before us is a regiment that is yet to taste war in its reality. The regimental drum corps is in position, and, as the marching men step out smartly, the camera catches them as perfectly as would the instantaneous photography of to-day. The scene is within Fort Lyon—one of the outlying defenses of Washington below Alexandria. To the defenses established about the capital came the raw recruits who flocked to the standard of the Union at the call of President Lincoln. Not only were they to serve as defenders of the capital, but here, during the winter of 1861–2, they were made into soldiers for service in the field. McClellan is said to have created an army out of a mob during this period, but the men we see before us—the Twenty-Sixth New York—although green at the game of war when they enlisted, came from stock that makes good soldiers, and from the State which furnished the most men to the Federal cause and suffered the heaviest losses in battle during the struggle. The Twenty-Sixth was one of the two-years regiments and its term of service covered some of the hardest fighting in the war. It went into the battle of Fredericksburg 300 strong, and came out with a loss of 170, nearly sixty per cent.

DRILLING THE 96TH PENNSYLVANIA AT CAMP NORTHUMBERLAND, NEAR WASHINGTON—1861

Along this sloping hillside, well suited for a camp, we see a Federal regiment at its full strength, before bullets and sickness had lowered its numbers to a mere skeleton of its former self. The band is out in front, the men are standing at "shoulder arms;" the Colonel and his Major and Adjutant, mounted on their sleek, well-fed horses, are grouped at one side, conscious that the eye of the camera is upon them. There is an old adage among military men that "a straight shot takes the best." When a freshly joined regiment, recruited to its full strength, reached the army corps to which it had been assigned and which had been for a long time actively engaged, it caused comment that well may be understood. "Hello, here comes a new brigade!" cried a veteran of the Potomac who had seen eight months' continuous service, calling the attention of a companion to a new regiment just marching into camp. "Brigade!" exclaimed the other, "I'll bet my hat it's a division!" There are instances in plenty where a company commander found himself at the head of less than a score of men; where regiments that had started a 1,000 strong could muster but some 200 odd, and where, in a single action, the loss in killed, wounded and missing was over sixty per cent. of those engaged. We begin to understand what war is when we stop to think of this.

## SCOTT—THE FIRST LIEUTENANT-GENERAL AFTER WASHINGTON.

Upon Winfield Scott, hero of the Mexican War, fell the responsibility of directing the Union armies at the outbreak of the Civil War. Sitting here with his staff in Washington, second in command only to President Lincoln, his fine countenance and bearing betoken the soldierly qualities which made him one of the first commanders of his age. In active service for half a century, he had never lost a battle. Born in Petersburg, Virginia, in 1786, he was now in his seventy-fifth year. On his left in the picture stands Colonel E. D. Townsend; on his right, Henry Van Rensselaer. General Scott retired on October 31, 1861.

# FORT HENRY
# AND
# FORT DONELSON

## THE FIRST CLASH WEST OF THE MISSISSIPPI

Near here the citizens of St. Louis saw the first blood spilled in Missouri at the outbreak of the War. By order of Governor Jackson, a camp had been formed in the western suburbs of the city for drilling the militia. It was named in honor of the Governor, and was in command of General D. M. Frost. Captain Nathaniel Lyon was in command of the United States troops at the Arsenal in St. Louis. Lyon, on May 10th, marched nearly five thousand strong, toward Camp Jackson, surrounded it, planted batteries on all the heights over-looking it, and set guards with fixed bayonets and muskets at half cock. Meanwhile the inhabitants of St. Louis had gathered in great crowds in the vicinity, hurrying thither in carriages, baggage-wagons, on horses and afoot. Many of the men had seized their rifles and shotguns and had come too late to the as-sistance of the State troops. Greatly outnumbered by Lyon, General Frost surrendered his command, 689 in all. The prisoners, surrounded by a line of United States soldiers, at half-past five in the afternoon

CAMP JACKSON, ST. LOUIS, MISSOURI, MAY, 1861

were marched out of camp, on the road leading to St. Louis, and halted. After a short wait the ominous silence was suddenly broken by shots from the head of the column. Some of Lyon's soldiers had been pressed and struck by the crowd, and had discharged their pieces. No one was injured. Tranquillity was apparently restored when volley after volley broke out from the rear ranks, and men, women, and children were seen running frantically from the scene. It was said that Lyon's troops were attacked with stones and that two shots were fired at them before they replied. Twenty-eight citizens—chiefly bystanders including women and children—were killed. As Lyon, with his prisoners, marched through the city to the Arsenal, excitement ran high in St. Louis. A clash occurred next day between troops and citizens and it was many weeks before the uproar over Lyon's seizure quieted down. Meanwhile Camp Jackson became a drill-ground for Federal troops, as we see it in the picture.

## WHERE WESTERN SOLDIERS WERE TRAINED BY GRANT

Here, under Ulysses S. Grant, many a Western raw recruit was whipped into shape for active service. Grant, who served under Taylor and Scott, through the Mexican War, had resigned his commission of captain in 1854 and settled in St. Louis. He was among the first to offer his services to his country in 1861. He went to Springfield, Illinois, and Governor Yates gave him a desk in the Adjutant General's office. He soon impressed the Governor with his efficiency and was made drill officer at Camp Butler. Many Illinois regiments, infantry, artillery, and especially cavalry, were organized and trained at Camp Butler under the watchful eye of Grant. By

CAMP BUTLER, NEAR SPRINGFIELD, ILLINOIS, IN 1862

May, 1861, his usefulness had become so apparent that he was made mustering officer and aide, with the complimentary rank of colonel. In June he was appointed Colonel of the Seventh District Regiment, then at Camp Yates on the State Fair Grounds at the western edge of Springfield.   On June 28th this regiment became the Twenty-first Illinois Volunteers, and on July 3d started for northern Missouri.   This photograph was taken in 1862, after Grant had left Camp Butler and was winning laurels for himself as Commander of the District and Army of West Tennessee.

MOUNTING ARTILLERY IN FORT DARLING AT CAMP DEFIANCE

REACHING OUT FOR THE RIVER

These busy scenes were enacted in the late spring of 1861, by five regiments under Brig.-General Swift, who had been ordered by Secretary of War Cameron to occupy Cairo at the junction of the Mississippi and Ohio Rivers and save it from the fate of Sumter, which it was anticipated the Confederate gunboats coming up the Mississippi might visit upon it, and thus gain access to the Ohio. It was tedious work for the men of the Eighth, Ninth, Tenth, Eleventh, and Twelfth Illinois Volunteers, who, began the building of barracks, cleared parade grounds, mounted guns, and threw up fortifications against the attack which never came. In the upper

UNCOMPLETED EARTHWORKS, CAMP DEFIANCE

DRILL GROUNDS OF THE DEFENDERS OF CAIRO, ILL.

pictures the men are at work rushing to completion the unfinished Fort Darling, which was situated to the left of the drill grounds seen in the lower panorama. In the latter we see one of the innumerable drills with which the troops were kept occupied and tuned up for the active service before them. Across the Mississippi was the battery at Bird's Point, on the Missouri shore. This and Fort Darling were occupied by the First and Second Illinois Light Artillery, but their labors were chiefly confined to the prevention of contraband traffic on the river. The troops at Cairo did not see any campaigning till Grant led them to Paducah, Ky., September 5-6, 1861.

# FORT HENRY AND FORT DONELSON

By this brilliant and important victory Grant's fame sprang suddenly into full and universal recognition. President Lincoln nominated him major-general of volunteers, and the Senate at once confirmed the appointment. The whole military service felt the inspiriting event. —*Nicolay and Hay, in "Life of Lincoln."*

THE grasp of a great section of western Kentucky and Tennessee by the Northern armies, the capture of a stronghold that was thought impregnable, the forced surrender of a great army, and the bringing into public notice of a new commander who was destined to outshine all his fellows— these were the achievements of the short, vigorous campaign of Fort Donelson.

There were two great battle-grounds of the Civil War, nearly a thousand miles apart—Virginia and the valley of the great river that divides the continent—and the two definite objects of the Northern armies during the first half of the war period were to capture Richmond and to open the Mississippi. All other movements and engagements were subordinate to the dramas of these two great theaters, incidental and contributory. The South, on the other hand, except for the early threatening of Washington, the Gettysburg campaign, the raid of Morgan in Ohio, and the expeditions of Bragg and Hood into Kentucky and Tennessee, was on the defensive from the beginning of the war to the end.

In the East after the initial engagement at Bull Run "all was quiet along the Potomac" for some months. McClellan had loomed large as the rising hero of the war; but McClellan did not move with the celerity that was expected of him; the North became impatient and demanded that

CAIRO CITIZENS WHO MAY HAVE RECALLED THIS DAY

With his hands thrust in his pockets stands General Grant, next to General McClernand, who is directly in front of the pillar of the Cairo post-office. The future military leader had yet his great name to make, for the photograph of this gathering was taken in September, 1861, and when, later, the whole world was ringing with his praises the citizens who chanced to be in the group must have recalled that day with pride. Young Al Sloo, the postmaster's son, leans against the doorway on Grant's right, and next to him is Bob Jennings; then comes Dr. Taggart, then Thomas, the mason, and Jaques, the butcher. On the extreme right, facing the camera, is young Bill Thomas. Up in the windows sit George Olmstead and Will Smith. In his shirt sleeves, on General McClernand's left, is C. C. Davidson. In the group about him are Benjamin Munn, Fred Theobold, John Maxey, and Phil. Howard. Perhaps these men told their children of the morning that Grant left his headquarters at the St. Charles Hotel and met them here. Who knows?

[A—12]

something be done. But while the public was still waiting there were two occurrences in the West that riveted the attention of the nation, sending a thrill of gladness through the North and a wave of depression over the Southland. These were the fall of Fort Henry and of Fort Donelson.

After Missouri had been saved to the Union in spite of the disaster at Wilson's Creek in August, 1861, a Union army slowly gathered in southern Illinois. Its purpose was to dispute with the Confederates their hold on Kentucky, which had not seceded, and to regain control of the Mississippi. To secure the latter end a flank movement was decided upon—to open the mighty river by moving up the Cumberland and Tennessee—the greatest flanking movement in the history of warfare. It began at Fort Henry and ended at Vicksburg, covered a year and five months, and cost tens of thousands of human lives and millions of dollars' worth of property—but it was successful.

Eastern Kentucky, in the early days of 1862, was also in considerable ferment. Colonel James A. Garfield had driven the Confederate commander, General Humphrey Marshall, and a superior force into the Cumberland Mountains, after a series of slight encounters, terminating at Paintsville on the Big Sandy River, on January 10th. But one later event gave great encouragement to the North. It was the first substantial victory for the Union arms. General Zollicoffer held the extreme Confederate right at Cumberland Gap and he now joined General George B. Crittenden near Mill Springs in central Kentucky. General Buell, in charge of the Army of the Ohio, had placed General George H. Thomas at Lebanon, and the latter promptly moved against this threatening Confederate force. A sharp engagement took place at Logan's Cross Roads near Mill Springs on January 19th. The Confederate army was utterly routed and Zollicoffer was killed. The Union loss was about two hundred and sixty, and the Confederate over twice that number. It was not a great

CAPTAIN CLARK B. LAGOW

DR. JAMES SIMONS.

## WINNING HIS SPURS AT CAIRO.

Few will recognize in this early and unusual photograph the man who at Appomattox, wore plain fatigue dress in striking contrast with the fully uniformed Lee. Here Grant appears in his full-dress Brigadier-General's uniform as he came to Cairo to assume command of a military district including southern Illinois, September 4, 1861. Grasping at once the problems of his new post he began the work of reorganization, assisted by a well-chosen staff. Without waiting for permission from Frémont, his immediate superior, Commander of the Department of the West, Grant pushed forward a

BRIGADIER-GENERAL U. S. GRANT

force and occupied Paducah, Kentucky, before the Confederates, approaching with the same purpose, could arrive. Grant was impatient to drive back the Confederate lines in Kentucky and Tennessee and began early to importune Washington to be allowed to carry out maneuvers. His keen judgment convinced him that these must quickly be made in order to secure the advantage in this outlying arena of the war. Captain Rawlins was made Assistant Adjutant-General by Grant, and lifted from his shoulders much of the routine of the post. Captain Lagow and Captain Hillyer were two of the General's aides-de-camp. Dr. James Simons was Medical Director of the District.

CAPTAIN WILLIAM S. HILLYER

CAPTAIN JOHN A. RAWLINS.

battle, but its effect on the North was most stimulating, and the people first learned to appreciate the abilities of their great general, George H. Thomas.

It was now February, 1862. General U. S. Grant was in command of the Union forces in western Kentucky and Tennessee. The opposing commander was Albert Sidney Johnston, then reputed the ablest general of the South. At Bowling Green, Kentucky, he had thirty thousand men. Believing, perhaps, that he could not hold Kentucky, he determined to save Tennessee for the South and took his stand at Nashville.

On February 2d, 1862, General Grant left Cairo with his army of seventeen thousand men and on transports moved up the Ohio and the Tennessee to attack Fort Henry. Accompanying him was Flag-Officer Foote with his fleet of seven gunboats, four of them ironclads.

Fort Henry was garrisoned by an army of about three thousand men under the command of General Lloyd Tilghman, a brave officer who was destined to give his life for the Confederate cause, the following year, near Vicksburg. It covered about three acres and mounted seventeen heavy guns. Grant's plan of attack was to land his army four miles below the fort, to move across the country and seize the road leading to Fort Donelson, while Foote should move up the river with his fleet and turn his guns on the Confederate batteries.

On February 6th, Foote formed his vessels into two lines, the ironclads—the *Cincinnati,* the *Carondelet,* the *Essex,* and the *St. Louis*—forming a front rank. Slowly and cautiously he approached the fort, firing as he went, the guns on the parapet answering those of the fleet. Several of the Confederate guns were disabled. The fleet was yet unhurt when the first hour had passed. Then a 24-pound shot struck the *Essex,* crashed through her side and penetrated her boiler, instantly killing both her pilots and flooding the vessel from stem to stern with scalding steam. The *Essex,* wholly disabled, drifted

THE UNLUCKY *ESSEX* AFTER FORT HENRY

The thousand-ton ironclad *Essex* received the severest punishment at Fort Henry. Fighting blood surged in the veins of Commander W. D. Porter, son of Admiral David Porter and brother of Admiral David D. Porter. The gunboat which he led into action at Fort Henry was named after the famous *Essex* which his father commanded in the War of 1812. Fifteen of the shots from Fort Henry struck and told upon the *Essex*, the last one penetrating her armor and piercing her middle boiler. Commander Porter, standing among his men directing the fight, was terribly scalded by the escaping steam,

COMMANDER W. D. PORTER

as were twenty-seven others. Wrongly suspected of disloyalty at the outbreak of the war, Commander Porter's conduct during the struggle gave the lie to such calumny. He recovered after Fort Henry, and was made Commodore in July, 1862. Again in command of the *Essex* he attempted unsuccessfully to destroy the dread Confederate ram *Arkansas* at Vicksburg on July 22d. Porter and the *Essex* then joined Farragut's fleet. His shells helped the Union forces to repulse the Confederates at Baton Rouge, August 5th, and he witnessed the blowing up of the *Arkansas* the following day. He died May 1, 1864.

THE *ESSEX* TWO YEARS LATER

down stream, while her companion ships continued their advance and increased their fire.

Presently, a sound exceeding the roar of cannon was heard above the tumult. A great gun in the fort had exploded, killing or disabling every man who served it. A great 10-inch columbiad was also destroyed. Tilghman, seeing that he had no hope of holding the fort, decided to save his army by sending it to Fort Donelson, on the Cumberland River. This he did, reserving fewer than a hundred men to work the guns. He then raised the white flag and surrendered the seventy-eight that remained. Grant had failed to reach the road to Fort Donelson until the Confederates had escaped. The Southerners hastened across the country and added their numbers to the defenders of Donelson—and by so doing they deferred surrender for ten days.

Fort Donelson was a fortified enclosure of a hundred acres that crowned a plateau on the Cumberland River. It was just south of the boundary between Kentucky and Tennessee and close by the little village of Dover, consisting of a court-house, a two-story tavern, and a few houses scattered about. Beneath the bluff and on the river bank were two powerful batteries commanding the approach to the river. Outside the fort and stretching far along the ridges that enclosed it were rifle-pits, lines of logs covered with yellow clay. Farther beyond, the hillsides were covered with felled trees whose interlacing branches were supposed to render the approach of the foe impossible under fire.

At this moment Donelson was held by eighteen thousand men under the command of General John B. Floyd, late Secretary of War in the cabinet of Buchanan. Next to him were Gideon J. Pillow and Simon B. Buckner. The Union army under Grant was divided into three parts under the respective commands of Charles F. Smith, a veteran of the regular army; John A. McClernand, an Illinois lawyer and member of Congress, and Lew Wallace, the future author of "Ben Hur."

## THE GUNBOAT THAT FIRED THE FIRST SHOT AT FORT HENRY

Here, riding at anchor, lies the flagship of Foote, which opened the attack on Fort Henry in the first movement to break the backbone of the Confederacy, and won a victory before the arrival of the army. This gunboat, the *Cincinnati*, was one of the seven flat-bottom iron-clads built by Captain Eads at Carondelet, Missouri, and Mound City, Illinois, during the latter half of 1861. When Grant finally obtained permission from General Halleck to advance the attack upon Fort Henry on the Tennessee River, near the border of Kentucky, Flag Officer Foote started up the river, February 2, 1862, convoying the transports, loaded with the advance detachment of Grant's seventeen thousand troops. Arriving before Fort Henry on

FLAG-OFFICER FOOTE

February 6th, the intrepid naval commander at once began the bombardment with a well-aimed shot from the *Cincinnati*. The eleven heavy guns of the fort responded in chorus, and an iron rain began to fall with telling effect upon the *Cincinnati*, the *Essex*, the *Carondelet*, and the *St. Louis*, which were steaming forward half a mile in advance of the rear division of the squadron. At a range of 1,700 yards the *Cincinnati* opened the engagement. After a little over an hour of heavy firing the colors on Fort Henry were lowered and General Tilghman surrendered it to Flag-Officer Foote. When General Grant arrived an hour later, Foote turned over the fort to him and returned to Cairo with his disabled gunboats.

With waving banners the divisions of Smith and McClernand marched across country on February 12th, arriving at noon and encircling the doomed fort ere nightfall. Smith was stationed on the left and McClernand on the extreme right, near the village of Dover. This left an open space in the center, to be filled by Lew Wallace, who arrived with his division the next day. On the 13th there was a continuous bombardment from morning till night, punctuated by the sharp crack of the sharpshooter's rifle.

The chief action of the day that involved the infantry was an attempt to capture a battery on a hill, near the center of the Confederate line of battle, known as Maney's Battery, commanded by Captain Maney, of Tennessee. This battery had annoyed McClernand greatly, and he delegated his third brigade to capture it. The charge was led by Colonel Morrison of Illinois, and a braver one never was made throughout the whole period of the war. The men who made it were chiefly youths from the farms and workshops of Illinois. With no apparent thought of danger they sallied forth, determined at all hazards to capture the battery on the hill, which stood out in relief against the sky. As they ran up the hill, firing as they went, their numbers were rapidly thinned by the terrific cross-fire from this battery and two others on adjoining hills. Still the survivors pushed on and their deadly fire thinned the ranks of the men at the battery. At length when they came within forty yards of the goal a long line of Confederate musketry beside the battery suddenly burst into flame and a storm of bullets cut down the brave boys of Illinois, with fearful slaughter. Even then they stood for fifteen minutes, returning volley for volley, before retreating. Reaching the foot of the hill, they rallied under the Stars and Stripes, and returned to the assault. Even a third time they charged, but the dry leaves on the ground now caught fire, the smoke stifled them, and they had to retreat. As they returned down the hill, Lew Wallace tells us, "their ears and souls were

## A GALLANT GUNBOAT—THE *ST. LOUIS*.

With the shots from the Confederate batteries ringing and bounding off her iron plates, this gallant gunboat that Foote had chosen for his flag-ship, entered the zone of fire at Fort Donelson. In the confined space of her smoke-filled gun-deck, the river sailors were loading and firing the heavy broadsides as fast as the great guns could be run out and aimed at the frowning line of entrenchments on the river bank. From them the concentrated hail of iron was poured upon her and the marksman-ship was good. Fifty-nine times was this brave vessel struck. But her armored sides withstood the heavy shocks although the plating, dented and bent, bore record of each impact. Nearer and nearer grew the forts as up the narrow channel the flag-ship led the way, the *Louis-ville*, the *Carondelet*, and the *Pittsburgh* belching their fire at the wooded heights, as though endeavoring to attract the attention of the Con-federate gunners to themselves and save the flag-ship from receiving more than her share. Up in the pilot-house the brave man who knew the channel stood at the wheel, his eyes firmly fixed ahead; and on the "texas," as the upper deck was called, within speaking distance of him, stood Foote himself. A great shot, aimed accurately as a minie ball, struck the frail pilot-house. It was as if the vessel's heart was pierced. The wheel was swept away from the pilot's hand and the brave river guide was hurled into the corner, mangled, bleeding and soon to die. Flag Officer Foote did not escape. He fell badly wounded in the leg

THE FLAG-SHIP *ST. LOUIS* VIEWED FROM ASTERN

by a fragment of the shell—a wound from which he never fully re-covered. Helpless now, the current swept the *St. Louis'* bow around, and past her consorts that were still fighting, she drifted down the stream and out of action; later, in convoy of the *Louisville*, she returned to Cairo, leaving the *Carondelet* and *Pittsburgh* to escort the transports. Meanwhile on shore, Grant was earning his first laurels as a soldier in a big battle. The disabling of the gunboats caused the Confederates to make the fatal attack that resulted so disastrously for them. Assail-ing Grant's right wing that held a strong position, on the 15th of February, 19,000 men were hurled against a force 8,000 greater in number. But the repulse was complete. Shattered they retreated to their works, and in the morning of the 16th, the Confederate general, Buckner, surrendered. About 14,000 prisoners were taken. The Federal loss was nearly 3,000, and that of the Southern cause about 1,000 less. For the capture of Fort Donelson Grant was made major-general. The first step to the conquest of the Mississippi had been achieved. In October, 1862, the river fleet was transferred from the Army to the Navy Department, and as there was another vessel in the service, bear-ing the same name the *St. Louis* was renamed the *Baron de Kalb*. At Fort Henry, she went into action lashed to the *Carondelet* on account of the narrowness of the stream; and later again, the gallant gunboat won laurels at Island No. 10, Fort Pillow, Memphis, and Vicksburg.

*LOUISVILLE*—A FIGHTER AT THE FORT

riven with the shrieks of their wounded comrades, upon whom the flames crept and smothered and charred where they lay."

Thus ended the 13th of February. That night the river gunboats, six in number, four of them ironclads, under the command of Andrew H. Foote, arrived. Grant had sent them down the Tennessee to the Ohio and up the Cumberland, to support his army at Fort Donelson. On the 14th, about three in the afternoon, Foote steamed with his four ironclads to a point in the river within four hundred yards of the two powerful batteries on the river bank under the fort and opened fire with his cannon while continuing to advance. The reply from the Confederate batteries was terrific and many of their shots struck home. In a short time the decks of the vessels were slippery with human blood. Foote himself was severely wounded. At length a solid shot struck the pilot house of the flagship and tore away the pilot wheel. At almost the same moment another gunboat was disabled. The two vessels, one of which had been struck fifty-nine times, could no longer be managed; they turned about with the eddies of the river and floated down with the current. The others followed.

The Confederates raised a wild shout of joy at this, their second victory since the coming of the Union army. But what will be the story of the morrow? With the reenforcements brought by Foote, Lew Wallace's division, Grant's army was now swelled to twenty-seven thousand, and in spite of the initial repulse the Federals felt confident of ultimate victory. But a dreary night was before them. The springlike weather had changed. All that fearful night of February 14th there was a fierce, pitiless wind with driving sleet and snow. Thousands of the men, weary of the burden of their overcoats and blankets during the warm preceding days, had thrown them away. Now they spent the night lying behind logs or in ditches or wherever they could find a little protection from the wintry blasts. General Floyd, knowing that Grant's army was much

### THE ADVENTUROUS GUNBOAT *CONESTOGA*

Lying at anchor in the Ohio River this little wooden gunboat is having the finishing touches put to her equipment while her officers and men are impatiently waiting for the opportunity to bring her into action. A side-wheel river steamer originally, she was purchased at Cincinnati by Commander John Rodgers in the spring of 1861 and speedily converted into a gunboat. Her boilers and steam pipes were lowered into the hold and the oaken bulwarks five inches thick which we see were put on her and pierced for guns. She got her first taste of fighting when, at Lucas Bend, she engaged the land batteries and a Confederate gunboat, September 10, 1861. She was present at Fort Henry in the second division of the attacking fleet, and also at Fort Donelson.

### THE *TYLER*

A sister-ship of the *Conestoga*. She was present both at Fort Henry and Fort Donelson.

stronger than his own, decided, after consulting with Pillow and Buckner, to attack the Union right at dawn on the 15th.

The night was spent in preparing for this, and in the morning Pillow with ten thousand men fell upon McClernand, and Buckner soon joined him with an additional force. Toward noon many of McClernand's men ran short of powder and he was forced to recede from his position. Pillow seems then to have lost his head. He felt that the whole Union army was defeated, and though the road to Nashville was open, the Confederates made no attempt to escape. Just then General Grant rode upon the scene. He had been absent all morning down the river consulting Foote, not knowing that the Confederates had planned an escape. This moment, says Lew Wallace, was the crisis in the life of Grant.

Hearing the disastrous news, his face flushed for a moment; he crushed some papers in his hand. Next instant he was calm, and said in his ordinary tone, to McClernand and Wallace, "Gentlemen, the position on the right must be retaken." Then he galloped away to General Smith. In a short time the Union lines were in motion. General Smith made a grand assault on the Confederate outworks and rifle-pits. When his lines hesitated Smith waved his cap on the point of his sword and rode in front, up the hill, in the hottest fire of the foe, toward the rifle-pits—and they were carried. At the same moment Lew Wallace was leading his division up another slope with equal gallantry. Here again the Confederates retired, and the road to Nashville was no longer open. Furthermore, Smith held a position from which he could shell the fort on the inside, and nothing was left to the inmates but surrender or slaughter on the morrow.

A council was held by Floyd, Pillow, and Buckner. Buckner, who was a master in the art of warfare, declared that he could not hold his position for half an hour in the morning. The situation was hopeless. Floyd was under indictment at Washington for maladministration in the Buchanan cabinet.

The Captured Commanders of Forts Henry and Donelson.—It requires as much moral courage to decide upon a surrender, even when odds are overwhelming, as it does physical bravery, in maintaining a useless fight to the death. Brigadier-General Tilghman, who commanded the Confederate Fort Henry on the Tennessee and General Simon Bolivar Buckner in command of the Confederate Fort Donelson —a much stronger position on the Cumberland only a few miles away—were men who possessed this kind of courage. Both had the misfortune to hold untenable positions. Each displayed generalship and sagacity and only gave up to the inevitable when holding out meant nothing but wasted slaughter and the sacrifice of men who had been called upon to exert every human effort. Fort Henry, on the banks of the Tennessee, was held by a few thousand men and strongly armed with twenty guns including one 10-inch Columbiad. But on the 6th of February it fairly lay in the possession of the Federals before a shot had actually been fired, for Grant with 17,000 men had gained the rear of the fortification after his move from Cairo on the 30th of the previous month. The actual reduction of the fort was left to the gunboat flotilla under Flag Officer Foote, whose heavy bombardment began early in the morning. General Tilghman had seen from the first that the position could not be held. He was trapped on all sides, but he would not give way without a display of resistance. Before the firing began, he had sent off most of the garrison and maintained the unequal combat with the gunboats for an hour and a quarter with less than a hundred men, of whom he lost twenty-one. Well did this handful serve the guns on the river bank. One shot struck the gunboat *Essex*, piercing her boilers, and wounding and scalding twenty-eight men. But at last, enveloped on all sides, his retreat cut off —the troops who had been ordered to depart in the morning, some three thousand in number, had reached Fort Donelson, twelve miles away—General Tilghman hauled down his flag, surrendering himself and eighty-four men as prisoners of war. Here we see him—a brave figure of a man—clad in the uniform of a Southern Colonel. There was never the slightest doubt of his courage or of his proper discretion in making this surrender. Only for a short time was he held a prisoner, when he was exchanged and welcomed back with all honor into the ranks of the Confederacy, and given an important command. He did not, however, live long to serve his cause, for shortly after rejoining the army he was killed at the battle of Baker's Creek, Mississippi, on the 16th of May, 1863.

GENERAL LLOYD TILGHMAN.

TWO UNWILLING GUESTS OF THE NORTH

Copyright by Review of Reviews Co.

BUCKNER, THE DEFENDER OF DONELSON

It is not often that on the battlefield ties of friendship are cemented that last a lifetime, and especially is this so between conqueror and conquered. Fort Donelson, that was, in a measure, a repetition of Fort Henry, saw two fighting foes become thus united. It was impossible for the garrison of Fort Donelson to make its escape after the flotilla of gunboats had once appeared in the river, although General Floyd, its senior commander, the former Secretary of War under President Buchanan, had withdrawn himself from the scene tendering the command to General Pillow, who in his turn, after escaping with his own brigade, left the desperate situation to be coped with by General Buckner. Assailed in the rear by an army that outnumbered the defenders of the fort by nearly eight thousand and with the formidable gunboats hammering his entrenchments from the river, Buckner decided to cut his way out in a desperate charge, but being repulsed, saw his men flung back once more into the fort. There was nothing for it but to make terms. On February 16th, in a note to Grant he asked what might be granted him. Here, the coming leader won his nickname of "Unconditional Surrender" Grant. Buckner was informed that the Federal army was about to move upon his works. Hurt and smarting under his position, he sent back a reply that in a few short hours he would, perhaps, have been willing to recall. Yielding to circumstances he accepted what he bluntly pronounced, "ungenerous and unchivalrous terms." But when the capitulation had taken place and nearly fifteen thousand men had surrendered, a greater number than ever before laid down their arms upon the continent, Grant was so generous, that then and there began the friendship that grew as close as if the two men were brothers of the blood. Most of the prisoners were paroled. Each one was allowed to retain his personal baggage, and the officers to keep their side arms. Grant had known Buckner in the Mexican War, and received him after the battle as his guest. For a short time General Buckner was kept a prisoner at Fort Warren until he was exchanged. But the friendship between the two leaders continued. When General Grant, after having been twice President, failed in his business career, Buckner sent him a check, trusting that it might be of use in his time of trouble. Grant, shortly before his death, wrote his old-time comrade and antagonist requesting that Buckner do him the final honors by becoming one of his pallbearers.

He declared that he must not be taken, and that with his Virginia troops he would escape on two little boats that were to arrive from Nashville in the morning. He passed the command to Pillow, and Pillow, declaring that he too would escape, passed it on to Buckner. Floyd and Pillow with their men made good their escape; so did Colonel Forrest, the cavalry leader, and his mounted force.

In the early morning Buckner sent a note to Grant offering to capitulate. The answer is well known. Grant demanded "unconditional surrender," and added, "I propose to move immediately on your works." Buckner was too good a soldier to sacrifice his men in needless slaughter. His men were so worn with eighty-four hours of fighting and watching that many of them had fallen asleep while standing in battle-line and under fire. He accepted the "ungenerous and unchivalrous terms," as he pronounced them, and surrendered Fort Donelson and the army, consisting of at least fourteen thousand men, with all its stores of ammunition. The Union loss was over twenty-eight hundred men. The Confederate loss, killed and wounded, was about two thousand.

The capture of Fort Donelson did three things. First, it opened up the way for the Federal army to penetrate the heart of the western South and gave it control of Kentucky and of western Tennessee. Second, it electrified the North with confident hopes of ultimate success. It was the first great victory for the North in the war. Bull Run had been a moral victory to the South, but the vanquished were weakened scarcely more than the victors. At Donelson, the victors gained control of an extensive territory and captured a noble army which could ill be spared by the South and which could not be replaced. Third, the capture of Donelson forced before the nation a new man—Ulysses S. Grant.

# PART II
## DOWN THE MISSISSIPPI VALLEY

---

# SHILOH
# THE FIRST
# GRAND BATTLE

---

THE PLUCKY LITTLE WOODEN GUNBOAT "TYLER"—ITS FLANKING FIRE ON THE CONFEDERATE TROOPS CHARGING ACROSS THE RAVINE OF DILL'S BRANCH, CLOSE BY THE RIVER, GREATLY ASSISTED HURLBUT, COMMANDER OF THE FEDERAL LEFT, IN HOLDING OFF WITHERS' GALLANT ATTACK

THE DEFENDERS OF GRANT'S LAST LINE AT SHILOH

These heavy guns when this picture was taken had not been moved from the actual position they held in the afternoon of the battle of Shiloh, April 6, 1862. In one of the backward movements of Grant's forces in the afternoon of that day General Prentiss, isolated by the retirement of troops in his flanks, fought till overwhelmed by the Confederates, then surrendered the remnant of his division. Encouraged by this success General Bragg ordered a last desperate charge in an effort to turn the left of the re-formed Federal line. Onward swept the Confederates toward a grim line of batteries, which Colonel Webster, of Grant's staff, had ranged along the top of the bluff from a quarter to a half a mile from Pittsburg Landing. The line of artillery overlooked a deep ravine opening into the

## GUNS THAT HELD THEIR GROUND AT PITTSBURG LANDING

Tennessee River. Into this and up its precipitous side General Withers dashed with two brigades. The gunboats *Tyler* and *Lexington* in the river joined with Webster's batteries upon the ridge and a frightful fire was poured into the ranks of the advancing Confederates. In the face of this, although finding himself unsupported save by Gage's battery, Withers led on his men. The division that he had expected to reenforce him had been withdrawn by the order of General Beauregard. To his men working their way up the slope came the order to retire. General Chalmers, of Withers Division, did not get the word. Down in the ravine his men alone of the whole Confederate army were continuing the battle. Only after nightfall did he retire.

# SHILOH—THE FIRST GRAND BATTLE

No Confederate who fought at Shiloh has ever said that he found any point on that bloody field easy to assail.—*Colonel William Preston Johnston (Son of the Confederate General, Albert Sidney Johnston, killed at Shiloh).*

IN the history of America many battles had been fought, but the greatest of them were skirmishes compared with the gigantic conflicts of the Old World under Marlborough and Napoleon. On the field of Shiloh, for the first time, two great American armies were to engage in a mighty struggle that would measure up to the most important in the annals of Europe. And the pity of it was that the contestants were brethren of the same household, not hereditary and unrelenting enemies.

At Fort Donelson the western South was not slain—it was only wounded. The chief commander of that part of the country, Albert Sidney Johnston, determined to concentrate the scattered forces and to make a desperate effort to retrieve the disaster of Donelson. He had abandoned Bowling Green, had given up Nashville, and now decided to collect his troops at Corinth, Mississippi. Next in command to Johnston was General Beauregard who fought at Bull Run, and who had come from Virginia to aid Johnston. There also came Braxton Bragg, whose name had become famous through the laconic expression, " A little more grape, Captain Bragg," uttered by Zachary Taylor at Buena Vista; Leonidas Polk who, though a graduate of West Point, had entered the church and for twenty years before the war had been Episcopal bishop of Louisiana, and John C. Breckinridge, former Vice President of the United States. The legions of the South were gathered at Corinth until, by the 1st of April, 1862, they numbered forty thousand.

A brilliant Southern leader, whose early loss was a hard blow to the Confederacy. Albert Sidney Johnston was a born fighter with a natural genius for war. A West Pointer of the Class of '26, he had led a strenuous and adventurous life. In the early Indian wars, in the border conflicts in Texas, and in the advance into Mexico, he had always proved his worth, his bravery and his knowledge as a soldier. At the outbreak of the Civil War he had already been brevetted Brigadier-General, and had been commander of the military district of Utah. An ardent Southerner, he made his choice, dictated by heart and conscience, and the Federal authorities

GENERAL A. S. JOHNSTON, C. S. A.

knew the loss they would sustain and the gain that would be given to the cause of the Confederacy. In '61 he was assigned to a district including Kentucky and Tennessee with the rank of General. At once he displayed his gifts as an organizer, but Shiloh cut short a career that would have led him to a high place in fame and history. The early Confederate successes of the 6th of April were due to his leadership. His manner of death and his way of meeting it attested to his bravery. Struck by a minie ball, he kept in the saddle, falling exhausted and dying from the loss of blood. His death put the whole South into mourning.

*Copyright by Review of Reviews Co.*

CAMP OF THE NINTH MISSISSIPPI
The story of this regiment is told on page 201.

To no one who was close to him in the stirring scenes of the early conflict in the West did Grant pay higher tribute than to this veteran of the Mexican War who was his Chief of Staff. He was a man to be relied upon in counsel and in emergency, a fact that the coming leader recognized from the very outset. An artillery officer and engineer, his military training and practical experience made him a most valuable executive. He had also the gift of leading men and inspiring confidence. Always cool and collected in the face of danger, and gifted with a personality that won friends everywhere, the reports of all of his superiors show the trust and confidence that were reposed in him. In

BRIG.-GEN. J. D. WEBSTER

April, 1861, he had taken charge of the fortifications at Cairo, Illinois. He was with Grant at Paducah, at Forts Henry and Donelson, and at Shiloh where he collected the artillery near the Landing that repelled the final Confederate attack on April 6th. He remained Chief of Staff until October, 1862. On October 14th, he was made a Brigadier-General of Volunteers, and was appointed superintendent of military railroads in the Department of Tennessee. Later he was Chief of Staff to General Sherman, and again proved his worth when he was with General Thomas at Hood's defeat before Nashville in December, 1864. On March 13, 1865, he received the brevet of Major-General of Volunteers.

Meantime, the Union army had moved southward and was concentrating at Pittsburg Landing, on the Tennessee River, an obscure stopping place for boats in southern Tennessee, and some twenty miles northeast from Corinth. The name means more now than merely a landing place for river craft. It was clear that two mighty, hostile forces were drawing together and that ere long there would be a battle of tremendous proportions, such as this Western hemisphere had not then known.

General Grant had no idea that the Confederates would meet him at Pittsburg Landing. He believed that they would wait for an attack on their entrenchments at Corinth. The position his army occupied at the Landing was a kind of quadrilateral, enclosed on three sides by the river and several small streams that flow into it. As the early days of April passed there were ominous rumors of the coming storm; but Grant was so sure that Johnston would not attack that he spent the night of the 5th of April at Savannah, some miles down the Tennessee River.

It was Saturday night. For two weeks the Union troops had occupied the undulating tableland that stretched away from the river at the Landing. There was the sound of the plashing streams overflowing from recent rains, there were revelry and mirth around the thousand camp-fires; but there was no sound to give warning of the coming of forty thousand men, who had for two days been drawing nearer with a steady tread, and during this night were deploying around the Union camp, only a mile away. There was nothing to indicate that the inevitable clash of arms was but a few hours in the future.

At the dawn of day on Sunday, April 6th, magnificent battle-lines, under the Confederate battle-flag, emerged from the woods on the neighboring hills within gunshot of the Federal camps. Whether the Union army was really surprised has been the subject of long controversy, which we need not

BRAVE SOUTHERNERS AT SHILOH

In the Southern record of the battle of Shiloh, the name of the Washington Artillery, of New Orleans, stands out in red letters. It was composed of the best blood of the city, the dandies of their day. Here we see the officers of the Fifth Company, in the first year of the war while uniforms were bright, sword-belts pipe-clayed, and buttons glistening. Under the command of Captain W. Irving Hodgson, this company made its name from the very first.

SOUTHERN BOYS IN BATTLE

Here we see plainly shown the extreme youth of some of the enlisted men of the Washington Artillery of New Orleans. Not one of the lads here pictured is within a year of his majority. We hardly realize how young the fighters on both sides were; only their faces and the records can show it. At Shiloh, with Anderson's brigade of brave fighters, these young cannoneers answered to the call. Anderson was first in the second line of battle at the beginning. Before the action was twenty minutes old he was at the front; and with the advance, galloping over the rough ground, came the Washington Artillery.

enter. Certain it is that it was unprepared, and in consequence it fought on the defensive and at a disadvantage throughout the day.

General Hardee's corps, forming the first line of battle, moved against the outlying division of the Union army, which was commanded by General Benjamin Prentiss, of West Virginia. Before Prentiss could form his lines Hardee's shells began bursting around him, but he was soon ready and, though pressed back for half a mile in the next two or three hours, his men fought like heroes. Meanwhile the further Confederate advance under Bragg, Polk, and Breckinridge was extending all along the line in front of the Federal camps. The second Federal force to encounter the fury of the oncoming foe was the division of General W. T. Sherman, which was cut to pieces and disorganized, but only after it had inflicted frightful loss on the Confederate army.

General Grant, as we have noted, spent the night at Savannah, a town nine miles by way of the river from Pittsburg Landing. As he sat at breakfast, he heard the distant boom of cannon and he quickly realized that Johnston's army had attacked his own at the Landing. Instantly he took a boat and started for the scene of the conflict. At Crump's Landing, about half way between the two, General Lew Wallace was stationed with a division of seven thousand men. As Grant passed Crump's Landing, he met Wallace and ordered him to be ready for instant marching when he was called for. When Grant arrived at Pittsburg Landing, about eight o'clock in the morning, he found a tremendous battle raging, and he spent the day riding from one division commander to another, giving directions and cheering them on as best he could.

About two and a half miles from the Landing stood a little log church among the trees, in which for years the simple folk of the countryside had been wont to gather for worship every Sunday morning. But on this fateful Sunday, the demon of war reigned supreme. The little church was known

## UNUNIFORMED BUT FEARLESS SOUTHERN SOLDIERS

A photograph of the Ninth Mississippi taken a few months before it fought at Shiloh. In this military line of coatless men we see as brave a fighting unit as ever, with all the glitter and panoply of war, swept into the tide of battle. Here they stand, uniformed but fearless. Attached to Chalmers' Brigade on the extreme right at the opening of Shiloh these soldiers were commanded by Lieut.-Col. William A. Rankin. They dashed forward in the fierce attack that caused the surrender of Prentiss' division. General Chalmers wrote of the bravery of these Mississippians when attacked in turn next day. "As a last resort, I seized a battle-flag from the color-bearer of the Ninth Mississippi and called them to follow. With a wild shout the whole regiment rallied to the charge, and we drove the enemy back and reoccupied our first position of the morning, which we held until the order of retreat was received." Bragg reported: "Brigadier-General James Chalmers, at the head of the gallant Mississippians, filled—he could not have exceeded—the measure of my expectations."

as Shiloh to all the country around, and it gave its name to the great battle that raged near it on that memorable day.

General Prentiss had borne the first onset of the morning. He had been pressed back half a mile. But about nine o'clock, after being reenforced, he made a stand on a wooded spot with a dense undergrowth, and here he held his ground for eight long hours, until five in the afternoon, when he and a large portion of his division were surrounded and compelled to surrender. Time after time the Confederates rushed upon his position, but only to be repulsed with fearful slaughter. This spot came to be known as the "Hornet's Nest." It was not far from here that the Confederates suffered the irreparable loss of the day. Their noble commander, Albert Sidney Johnston, received his death wound as he was urging his troops to force back Hurlbut's men. He was riding in the center of the fight, cheering his men, when a minie ball cut an artery of his thigh. The wound was not necessarily fatal. A surgeon could easily have saved him. But he thought only of victory and continued in the saddle, raising his voice in encouragement above the din of battle. Presently his voice became faint, a deadly pallor blanched his cheek. He was lifted from his horse, but it was too late. In a few minutes the great commander was dead, from loss of blood.

The death of Johnston, in the belief of many, changed the result at Shiloh and prevented the utter rout or capture of Grant's army. One of Johnston's subordinates wrote: "Johnston's death was a tremendous catastrophe. Sometimes the hopes of millions of people depend upon one head and one arm. The West perished with Albert Sidney Johnston and the Southern country followed." Jefferson Davis afterward declared that " the fortunes of a country hung by a single thread on the life that was yielded on the field of Shiloh."

Beauregard succeeded to the command on the fall of Johnston and the carnage continued all the day—till darkness was falling over the valleys and the hills. The final charge

## THE BOATS THAT TURNED THE TIDE AT SHILOH
## PHOTOGRAPHED A FEW DAYS AFTER THE BATTLE

The assistance rendered by these Tennessee River boats that had been pressed from their peaceful occupations into the service of the army, was of such immense importance as to become a great factor in the turning of the battle tide that saved the Federal cause.   General Grant's headquarters in the early morning of April 6th was some miles from where the fight began.   It was at Savannah, on the Tennessee, and as soon as the cannonade announced the opening of the battle, Grant transferred his headquarters to the *Tigress*, which lies between the other vessels in the photograph.   The steamer on the right is the *Universe*, the largest of the transports present. At one o'clock General Buell, pushing ahead of his troops, reached the river bank, and the two leaders held a conference on the upper deck of the *Tigress*.   It was touch and go whether the troops fighting in the forest, beyond the landing, could hold their ground.   The Confederate General Johnston, in forming his plans, had intended to leave an opening that would tempt the hard-pressed Federal army to retreat down the river.   But, instead, they massed solidly back on Pittsburg Landing, huddled together so closely that brigades, and even regiments, were overlapping.   As soon as Buell's hastening troops came up, the transports were turned into ferry-boats, and all night long they plied across the river loaded within an inch of their gunwales with the reënforcements.   Later, as the picture shows, they brought supplies.

of the evening was made by three Confederate brigades close to the Landing, in the hope of gaining that important point. But by means of a battery of many guns on the bluff of Dill's Branch, aided by the gunboats in the river, the charge was repulsed. Beauregard then gave orders to desist from further attack all along his lines, to suspend operations till morning. When General Bragg heard this he was furious with rage. He had counted on making an immediate grand assault in the darkness, believing that he could capture a large part of the Federal army.

When the messenger informed him of Beauregard's order, he inquired if he had already delivered it to the other commanders. "Yes," was the reply. "If you had not," rejoined the angry Bragg, "I would not obey it. The battle is lost." But Bragg's fears were not shared by his compatriots.

Further mention is due the two little wooden gunboats, *Tyler* and *Lexington,* for their share in the great fight. The *Tyler* had lain all day opposite the mouth of Dill's Branch which flowed through a deep, marshy ravine, into the Tennessee just above the Landing. Her commander, Lieutenant Gwin, was eager for a part in the battle, and when he saw the Confederate right pushing its way toward the Landing, he received permission to open fire. For an hour his guns increased the difficulties of Jackson's and Chalmers' brigades as they made their way to the surrounding of Prentiss. Later on the *Lexington* joined her sister, and the two vessels gave valuable support to the Union cannon at the edge of the ravine and to Hurlbut's troops until the contest ended. All that night, in the downpour of rain, Lieutenant Gwin, at the request of General Nelson, sent shot crashing through the trees in the direction where the Confederates had bivouacked. This completely broke the rest of the exhausted troops, and had a decided effect upon the next day's result.

Southern hopes were high at the close of this first bloody day at Shiloh. Whatever of victory there was at the end of the

THE *LEXINGTON*

## THE GUNBOATS AT SHILOH

In the river near Pittsburg Landing, where the Federal transports lay, were two small gunboats, and what they did during the battle of April 6th makes a separate chapter in the action. In the early morning they were out of sight, though within sound of the continuous firing. How the battle was going, however, was evident. The masses of the blue-clad troops appeared through the trees on the river bank, showing that under the continuous and fierce assaults they were falling back upon the Landing. The *Tyler*, commanded by Lieutenant Gwin, and afterward the *Lexington*, commanded by Lieutenant Shirk, which arrived at four o'clock, strove to keep the Confederate army from the Landing. After the surrender of Prentiss, General Withers set his division in motion to the right toward this point. Chalmers' and Jackson's brigades marched into the ravine of Dill's Branch and into the range of the Federal gunboats and batteries which silenced Gage's battery, the only one Withers had, and played havoc with the Confederate skirmishers. All the rest of the afternoon, until nightfall, the river sailors kept up their continuous bombardment, and in connection with the field batteries on the bank checked General Withers' desperate attempt on the Landing. The dauntless brigade of Chalmers, whose brave Southerners held their ground near the foot of the ravine and maintained the conflict after the battle was ended elsewhere, was swept by the gunboats' fire. When Buell's army, that had been hurrying up to Grant's assistance, reached the battle-field, Gwin sent a messenger ashore in the evening to General Nelson, who had just arrived, and asked in what manner he could now be of service. It was pitch dark; except for the occasional firing of the pickets the armies were resting after the terrific combat. In reply to Gwin's inquiry, General Nelson requested that the gunboats keep on firing during the night, and that every ten minutes an 8-inch shell should be launched in the direction of the Confederate camp. With great precision Gwin followed out this course. Through the forest the shells shrieked and exploded over the exhausted Confederates, showering branches and limbs upon them where they slept, and tearing great gashes in the earth. The result was that they got little rest, and rest was necessary. Slowly a certain demoralization became evident—results that bore fruit in the action that opened on the morrow. Here we see pictured—in the lower part of the page—the captain's gig and crew near the *Lexington*, ready to row their commander out into the stream.

day belonged to the Confederates. They had pressed the Federals back more than a mile and now occupied their ground and tents of the night before. They had captured General Prentiss with some thousands of his men as a result of his brave stand at the "Hornet's Nest."

But their hopes were mingled with grave fears. General Van Dorn with an army of twenty thousand men was hastening from Arkansas to join the Confederate forces at Shiloh; but the roads were bad and he was yet far away. On the other hand, Buell was coming from Nashville to join Grant's army. Should he arrive during the night, the contest of the next day would be unequal and the Confederates would risk losing all that they had gained. Moreover, Beauregard's army, with its long, muddy march from Corinth and its more than twelve hours' continuous fighting, was worn and weary almost to exhaustion.

The Union army was stunned and bleeding, but not disabled, at the close of the first day's battle. Caught unawares, the men had made a noble stand. Though pressed back from their position and obliged to huddle for the night around the Landing, while thousands of their comrades had fallen on the gory field, they had hopes of heavy reenforcements during the night. And, indeed, early in the evening the cry ran along the Union lines that Buell's army had come. The advance guard had arrived late in the afternoon and had assisted Hurlbut in the closing scene on the bluff of Dill's ravine; others continued to pour in during the night. And, furthermore, General Lew Wallace's division, though it had taken a wrong road from Crump's Landing and had not reached the field in time for the fighting of the 6th, now at last had arrived. Buell and Wallace had brought with them twenty-five thousand fresh troops to be hurled on the Confederates on the morning of the 7th. But Van Dorn had not come. The preponderance of numbers now was with the Union army.

Everyone knew that the battle was not over, that the issue

A GALLANT REGIMENT FROM THE HOOSIER STATE

To the Ninth Indiana belongs the banner record, on the Federal side, at bloody Shiloh. It seldom happens to any unit of a fighting force, while still engaged in action, to receive words of thanks and congratulation while still on the firing-line. Flags have been decorated with the medal of honor, individuals have been so rewarded for deeds of bravery and prowess, but to the Ninth Regiment from the Hoosier State fell the unique honor of having the word "well done" given them under fire. General Nelson, on April 7th, rode up and thanked them, and well was it deserved, for they saved the flank of Hazen's brigade by stubborn bravery that has hardly ever been equaled. Posted on the line of a rail fence that offered little or no protection, they held their ground against a force that outnumbered them two to one—able and determined fighters, too, who charged time and again up to the muzzles of their rifles, only to be beaten back by the steady and continuous volleys. Colonel William B. Hazen, in command of the Nineteenth Brigade, two or three times found himself so fiercely assailed that it looked as if the flank would be crumbled in, but the Ninth was there. And when the cost was footed up, it made a sad but gallant showing. The Ninth had suffered the heaviest loss in numbers of any regiment in the Army of the Ohio at that battle. The percentage of officers killed and wounded left many vacancies for promotion; no less than eight positions there were to fill in the depleted companies. And along that thin rail fence, in the battle, one hundred and seventy men had been killed or wounded. The Fourth Division, which General Nelson commanded, points with pride to the scroll of Hazen's Nineteenth Brigade, and first on the list stands the never faltering Ninth. In November it was transferred to the Second Brigade of the Second Division, Fourteenth Corps, Army of the Cumberland, and at Stone's River it lost one hundred and nine men, all told.

must be decided on the coming day, and the weary thousands of both sides sank down on the ground in a drenching rain to get a little rest and to gain a little strength for the desperate struggle that was sure to come on the morrow.

Ten thousand stragglers from the Union army were crouching along the banks of the Tennessee. Like the men at Bull Run, this was their first battle, and they had not the courage to endure the rain of bullets about their ears; but unlike the soldiers at Bull Run, they had fled at the beginning, not at the end, of the day's fighting.

At the break of day on Monday, April 7th, all was astir in both camps on the field of Shiloh, and the dawn was greeted with the roar of cannon. The troops that Grant now advanced into the contest were all, except about ten thousand, the fresh recruits that Wallace and Buell had brought, while the Confederates had not a single company that had not been on the ground the day before. There is every reason to believe that Beauregard would have won a signal victory if neither army had been reenforced during the night. But now under the changed conditions the Confederates were at a great disadvantage, and yet they fought for eight long hours with heroic valor.

The deafening roar of the cannon that characterized the beginning of the day's battle was followed by the rattle of musketry, so continuous that no ear could distinguish one shot from another. Nelson's division of Buell's army was the first to engage the Confederates. Nelson commanded the Federal left wing, with Hardee and Breckinridge immediately opposed to him. The Union center was under the command of Generals McCook and Crittenden; the right wing was commanded by McClernand, with Hurlbut next, while Sherman and Lew Wallace occupied the extreme right. The Confederate left wing was commanded by the doughty Bragg and next to him was General Polk.

Shiloh Church was again the storm center and in it

THE MOUNTED POLICE OF THE WEST

Stalwart horsemen such as these bore the brunt of keeping order in the turbulent regions fought over by the armies in the West. The bugle call, "Boots and Saddles!" might summon them to fight, or to watch the movements of the active Confederates, Van Dorn and Price. It was largely due to their daring and bravery that the Confederate forces were held back from the Mississippi so as not to embarrass the movements of Grant and the gunboats. Of this unattached cavalry of the Army of the Ohio were the men in the upper picture—Company D, Fourth Kentucky Volunteers, enlisted at Louisville, December, 1861.

OFFICERS OF THE FOURTH KENTUCKY CAVALRY

General Beauregard made his headquarters. Hour after hour the columns in blue and gray surged to and fro, first one then the other gaining the advantage and presently losing it. At times the smoke of burning powder enveloped the whole field and hid both armies from view. The interesting incidents of this day of blood would fill a volume. General Hindman of the Southern side had a novel experience. His horse was struck by a bursting shell and torn to a thousand fragments. The general, thrown ten feet high, fell to the ground, but leaped to his feet unhurt and asked for another horse.

Early in the afternoon, Beauregard became convinced that he was fighting a losing battle and that it would be the part of prudence to withdraw the army before losing all. He thereupon sent the members of his staff to the various corps commanders ordering them to prepare to retreat from the field, at the same time making a show of resuming the offensive. The retreat was so skilfully made, the front firing-line being kept intact, that the Federals did not suspect it for some time. Some hours before nightfall the fighting had ceased. The Federals remained in possession of the field and the Confederates were wading through the mud on the road to Corinth.

It was a dreary march for the bleeding and battered Confederate army. An eye-witness described it in the following language:

"I made a detour from the road on which the army was retreating that I might travel faster and get ahead of the main body. In this ride of twelve miles alongside of the routed army, I saw more of human agony and woe than I trust I will ever again be called upon to witness. The retreating host wound along a narrow and almost impassable road, extending some seven or eight miles in length. Here was a line of wagons loaded with wounded, piled in like bags of grain, groaning and cursing; while the mules plunged on in mud and water belly-deep, the water sometimes coming into the wagons. Next came a straggling regiment of infantry, pressing on past the

## BUELL'S TROOPS CROSSING THE BIG BARREN

When the Confederate General Braxton Bragg made his masterly march into Kentucky and succeeded in getting in the rear of General Buell in Middle Tennessee in September, there followed a series of movements that demanded the utmost exertions of the engineers to keep the Federal Army in touch with its base and at the same time to oppose a front to General Bragg. In the first Confederate retreat through Kentucky almost all of the causeways had been destroyed, and when Buell arrived at Bowling Green, which is north of Nashville and on the bank of the Big Barren River, that stream was found to be almost flooding its banks. Here the nineteenth Regiment Michigan Engineers rebuilt the bridge almost at the place where General Mitchell had crossed early in the year. The middle part of the bridge was composed of fourteen pontoons.

[A—14]

## FEDERALS ADVANCING INTO TENNESSEE—1862

Incessantly, through rain or shine, the work on this bridge over the Elk River, near Pulaski, Tennessee, on the Central Alabama Railroad, went on during the months of June and July. The engineers had before them an enormous task. The Federal General Buell's army was short of supplies and ammunition, and the completion of this bridge, and other bridges, was a matter of vital necessity. Supplies had to be brought from Nashville. The roads were heavy with mud and the incessant rains had swollen the streams, making it not only slow but almost impossible for wagon trains to keep in touch with the base. Over the Central Alabama (Nashville and Decatur Railroad) food and other necessities for the army's very exist-

ENGINEERS AND INFANTRY BUSY AT THE ELK RIVER BRIDGE

ence had to be transported. Among those workers who labored uncomplainingly and whose work bore fruit, was the First Regiment, Michigan Engineers, that numbered among its enlisted men mechanics and artisans of the first class. They built this bridge pictured here. Four companies were employed in its construction, aided by an infantry detail working as laborers. The bridge was 700 feet long, 58 feet high, and crossed the Elk River at a point where the water was over 20 feet deep. At the right of the picture three of the engineer officers are consulting together, and to the left a squad of infantry are marching to their position as bridge guards. Here is the daily business of war—to which fighting is the occasional exception.

wagons; then a stretcher borne on the shoulders of four men, carrying a wounded officer; then soldiers staggering along, with an arm broken and hanging down, or other fearful wounds, which were enough to destroy life. And, to add to the horrors of the scene, the elements of heaven marshaled their forces—a fitting accompaniment of the tempest of human desolation and passion which was raging. A cold, drizzling rain commenced about nightfall, and soon came harder and faster, then turned to pitiless, blinding hail. This storm raged with violence for three hours. I passed long wagon trains filled with wounded and dying soldiers, without even a blanket to shelter them from the driving sleet and hail, which fell in stones as large as partridge eggs, until it lay on the ground two inches deep.

"Some three hundred men died during that awful retreat, and their bodies were thrown out to make room for others who, although wounded, had struggled on through the storm, hoping to find shelter, rest, and medical care."

Why the Federals made no attempt to pursue the retreating foe has never been satisfactorily explained. It is not improbable that Grant, had he ordered an immediate and vigorous pursuit, could have captured Beauregard's entire army. But he and all his advisers seemed to rest on their laurels and to be content with the day's work.

The news of these two fearful days at Shiloh was astounding to the American people. Never before on the continent had there been anything approaching it. Bull Run was a skirmish in comparison with this gigantic conflict. The losses on each side exceeded ten thousand men. General Grant tells us that after the second day he saw an open field so covered with dead that it would have been possible to walk across it in any direction stepping on dead bodies, without a foot touching the ground. American valor was tried to the full on both sides at Shiloh, and the record shows that it was equal to the test.

# PART II
### DOWN THE MISSISSIPPI VALLEY

---

# NEW MADRID
# ISLAND No. 10
# NEW ORLEANS

---

CAIRO IN 1862—ON THE EXTREME RIGHT IS THE CHURCH WHERE FLAG-OFFICER FOOTE PREACHED A SERMON AFTER THE FALL OF FORT HENRY—NEXT HE LED THE GUNBOATS AT ISLAND NO. 10.

# NEW MADRID AND ISLAND NO. 10

IT has been truly said that without the American navy, insignificant as it was in the early sixties, the North could hardly have succeeded in the great war. The blockade was necessary to success, and without the navy the blockade would have been impossible. It may further be said that without the gunboats on the winding rivers of the middle West success in that quarter would have been equally impossible. It was these floating fortresses that reduced Fort Henry and that gave indispensable aid at Fort Donelson. At Shiloh, when at the close of the first day's conflict the Confederates made a wild, impetuous dash on the Union camp, it was the two little wooden gunboats that aided in preserving the camp from capture or complete demoralization.

We have now to relate a series of operations down the Mississippi, in which the gunboats were the alpha and omega and almost all that falls between them. The creator of the fleet of gunboats with which we now have to deal was that master-builder, James B. Eads. It was on August 7, 1861, that Eads signed a contract with the Government to build and deliver seven ironclads, each one hundred and seventy-five feet long, fifty-one feet wide, drawing six feet of water, and carrying thirteen guns. In a week or two four thousand men were at work on the contract; sawmills were busy in five States cutting the timber; machine shops and iron foundries in several cities were running day and night. The places of building were Carondelet, near St. Louis, and Mound City, Illinois.

But the time was too short. The boats were unfinished at the end of sixty-five days. The Government refused to pay for them. And the builder, Eads—what did he do? He went ahead and used up his own fortune to finish those gunboats,

On the night of April 4, 1862, the Confederate garrison of the battery on Island No. 10, peering through the darkness out on the Mississippi, caught sight of the flicker of flames from the smoke-stacks of a steamer proceeding down the river. They knew at once that the attempt of the Federal gunboats to pass down to the support of General Pope's crossing of the river below had begun. The men on shore leaped to their guns, and the crash of cannon and the rattle of musketry broke forth across the bosom of the river. Aiming through the darkness at the luminous tops of the smoke-stacks the gunners poured in their vindictive fire, but the Confederates had elevated their guns too high and only two of their shots sped home. The *Carondelet*, for it was she, held on her way, and her commander, Henry Walke, would not permit his men to send a single answering shot. Walke had begged to be the first to take his vessel by the dreaded batteries on Island No. 10. In the pilot-house he directed the daring attempt, catching glimpses of the tortuous channel amid the fitful lightning of a storm which suddenly descended on the river and added the reverberations of Heaven to those of the battery below. At one moment the *Carondelet*

COMMANDER HENRY WALKE

grazed the bank of the island itself, but hastily backing off, made good her escape past a dreaded floating battery below the Island, which offered little opposition. She arrived at New Madrid without a man having received a single scratch. The *Carondelet* and her commander had made good, and the next morning lay ready to support the army after having achieved one of the greatest feats in the record of the inland navy. On April 6th, her elated and plucky crew captured and spiked the guns of the battery opposite Point Pleasant, an event which convinced the Confederates that Island No. 10 must be evacuated. That very night, encouraged by the success of the *Carondelet*, Commander Thompson, with the *Pittsburgh*, ran by the disheartened gunners on Island No. 10 and joined Commander Walke. The crossing of Pope's forces then proceeded, and the Confederates, in full retreat, were hemmed in by Paine's division and surrendered, before dawn of April 8th. Colonel Cook's troops cut off in their retreat from Island No. 10, were also compelled to surrender. The daring of Commander Walke in the face of this great danger had accomplished the first step in the opening of the Mississippi since the expedition left Cairo.

THE *CARONDELET*—FIRST TO RUN THE GANTLET AT ISLAND NO. 10

then handed them over to the Government and waited for his pay until after they had won their famous victories down the river.

Their first commander was Andrew H. Foote, who was called "the 'Stonewall' Jackson of the West." He had won fame in the waters of the Orient and had spent years in the suppression of the slave trade. Like "Stonewall" Jackson, he was a man of deep religious principles. On the Sunday after the fall of Fort Henry he preached a sermon in a church at Cairo. The next year the aged admiral lay sick in New York. His physician dreaded to tell him that his illness would be fatal, but did so. "Well," answered the admiral, "I am glad to be done with guns and war."

We must get to our story. Fort Henry and Fort Donelson had fallen. General Polk had occupied Columbus, Kentucky, a powerful stronghold from which one hundred and fifty cannon pointed over the bluff. But why hold Columbus in its isolation when Henry and Donelson were lost? So thought the good bishop-general and he broke camp on February 25, 1862, transferring one hundred and thirty of his big guns to Island No. 10, and rolling the remainder down the one hundred and fifty foot embankment into the Mississippi. That nothing might be left for the foe, he burned eighteen thousand bushels of corn and five thousand tons of hay, and when the Federals reached Columbus on March 4th they found only charred remains.

Island No. 10 was situated at the upper bend of a great double curve of the Mississippi, about forty miles below Columbus. It had been strongly fortified by General Beauregard, but Beauregard was called to Corinth and Shiloh and he turned the command over to General Mackall with about seven thousand men. It was confidently believed by its defenders that this fortified island would be the final stopping place of all hostile vessels on the great river, that none could pass it without being blown out of the water by the powerful batteries.

# THE RETREAT DOWN THE RIVER.

The Flag-ship of the Confederate Fleet at Island No. 10.—Below the dreaded battery at Island No. 10, lay Commodore George N. Hollins, with his flag-ship, the *McRae* and seven other Confederate gunboats, holding in check the Federal troops chafing to cross the river and get at the inferior force of the enemy on the other side. This opposing fleet was further strengthened by a powerful floating battery which could be pushed about by the gunboats and anchored at the most effective points. When the *Carondelet* accomplished her daring feat of passing Island No. 10 on the night of April 4th, creeping stealthily by this boasted battery and cutting it off from its convoys, the men who manned it cut loose from their moorings and drifted down to the protection of Commodore

COMMODORE GEORGE N. HOLLINS,
C.S.N.

Hollins' vigilant fleet. All was at once activity on board the Confederate vessels. Commodore Hollins did not court a meeting to try conclusions with the powerful Eads gunboats and the mortar boats, which he supposed were all making their way down upon him. The flag at the masthead of the *McRae* quickly signaled the order to weigh anchor, and the Confederate squadron, dropping slowly downstream, confined its activities to storming Pope's batteries on the Missouri shore below New Madrid. Farragut, threatening New Orleans, had caused the withdrawal of every available Confederate gunboat from the upper river, and the remaining river defense fleet under Commodore Hollins was not equal to the task of standing up to the determined and aggressive attempt of the Federals to seize and hold possession of the upper Mississippi.

THE *McRAE*

Below this island, a few miles, was the town of New Madrid on the Missouri shore, held also by the Confederates and protected by heavy guns behind breastworks.

On the west bank of the river, General John Pope commanded a Federal army of twenty thousand men. His object was to capture New Madrid. First he occupied Point Pleasant, twelve miles below, erected batteries and cut off supplies from New Madrid. He then slowly approached the town and meantime sent to Cairo for siege-guns. They arrived on the 12th of March, and all through the next day the cannonading was incessant. At night it ceased, and as Pope was about to renew the attack he discovered that the town had been abandoned during the night. The Confederates had not even delayed to destroy the supply stores, and they fell into the hands of the besiegers, together with all the guns and some thousands of small arms.

Island No. 10 was now isolated, indeed. Above it the river was aswarm with Federal gunboats; below it and along the Missouri shore was Pope's army. Southward was Reelfoot Lake, and eastward were impenetrable swamps. The only possible way of escape was by a road to the southward between the river and Reelfoot Lake to Tiptonville. But the brave defenders of the island were not ready to give up or to flee. They determined to remain and dispute the possession of the river at all hazards. At this time the river was very high. The whole wooded peninsula made by the great bend was covered with water. Houses, fences, trees—every movable thing—had been swept down the current.

General Pope's great desideratum was to secure boats to ferry his army across the river that he might capture Island No. 10. But the threatening cannon on the island forbade, in language without words, any attempt to pass them. The overflow of water on the peninsula was deep enough to float the transports, but a dense forest six miles in width prevented any such passage. At length a novel plan was devised—to cut a

## THE FLAG–OFFICER'S GOOD–BYE

The decks of this staunch gunboat, the *Benton*, we e crowded on the morning of May 9, 1862, by her officers and men waiting solemnly for the appearance of Commodore A. H. Foote. The *Benton* had been his flag-ship in the operations around Island No. 10 and Fort Pillow; but the wound he had received at Fort Donelson continued to undermine his health until now, supported by Captain Phelps, he feebly made his way on deck to bid good-bye to his brave and faithful comrades and resign his command to Captain Charles H. Davis. At sight of him the old tars swung their hats and burst into loud huzzas, which quickly gave place to moist eyes and saddened countenances, as Foote, with tears trickling down his cheeks, addressed to them some simple, heartfelt words of farewell. The men leaned forward to catch every syllable uttered by the beloved commander's failing voice. An hour later the *De Soto* dropped down to the *Benton*. Foote was assisted to the transport's deck by his successor, Captain Davis, and Captain Phelps. Sitting in a chair on her guards, his breast filled with emotion, he gazed across the rapidly widening space separating him forever from the *Benton*, while the men on her deck continued to look longingly after him, till distance and tears hid each from the other's sight.

channel through the forest. Six hundred skilled engineers were in the army and they were soon at work in relays of three hundred. After cutting off the trees above the water they cut the stumps beneath the water and just above the ground by means of hand-saws attached to pivots. After nineteen days of vigorous toil a channel was cut through the forest six miles long, fifty feet wide, and four and a half feet deep. The flat-bottomed transports could pass through this channel and they quickly did so—quickly, because the river was falling and the opportunity would soon pass. They were soon safely lodged at New Madrid without having come within range of the heavy guns of Island No. 10.

But the ironclad gunboats—what could be done with them? They drew too much water to be taken through the newly-made channel. Above the fortified island lay the Eads fleet, as it should be called (for the patriotic engineer still owned it in part), restless, eager for a fight. There were the *Benton,* the flag-ship, the *Carondelet,* the *St. Louis,* the *Cincinnati,* the *Pittsburgh,* the *Mound City,* and eleven mortar-boats. But these vessels could do something: they could shoot, and they did on March 17th. On that day they trained their guns on the island; for nine long hours the boom of cannon was continuous. The results were slight. Beauregard, who had not yet departed for Corinth, wired to Richmond that his batteries were not damaged and but one man was killed.

General Pope was sorely in need of a gunboat or two to silence a number of batteries guarding the Tiptonville road, on the east side of the river. Could he get possession of that road the last hope of escape from the island would be lost and ere long its defenders must surrender. Pope believed it possible for the gunboats to run the gantlet of the batteries of Island No. 10. But Foote thought it impossible, in the face of the mouths of half a hundred cannon that yawned across the channel. He refused to force anyone to so perilous an undertaking, and the commanders of the vessels all agreed

## A VETERAN OF MANY RIVER FIGHTS

The *St. Louis* was the earliest of the Eads iron-clad gunboats to be completed and is first mentioned in despatches on January 14, 1862, when with the *Essex* and *Tyler* she engaged the Confederate batteries at Columbus, Kentucky. The *St. Louis*, commanded by Lieutenant Leonard Paulding, participated in the capture of Fort Henry, going into action lashed to the *Carondelet*. At Fort Donelson she was Foote's flagship. She was struck seven times. Island No. 10, Fort Pillow, Memphis—at all these places the *St. Louis* distinguished herself. On October 1, 1862, the *St. Louis* was renamed the *Baron de Kalb*. All through the Vicksburg operations the *De Kalb* saw service with Admiral Porter. On July 13, 1863, after the fall of Vicksburg, she was sunk by a torpedo in the Yazoo River. This photograph was a gift to the present owner from James B. Eads, the builder.

with him that the running of the batteries was too great a risk, except one—Henry Walke, commander of the *Carondelet*.

"Are you willing to try it with your vessel?" asked Foote, of Commander Walke, in the presence of the other officers. "Yes," answered Walke, and it was agreed that the *Carondelet* should attempt to run the batteries. The next few days were spent in preparing the vessel for the ordeal. Chains, hawsers, and cables were wound around the pilot-house and other vulnerable parts of the vessel. A coal barge loaded with coal and hay was lashed to the side where there was no iron protection for the magazine. The steam escape was led through the wheel-house so as to avoid the puffing sound through the smokestack. The sailors were armed to resist boarding parties, and sharpshooters were placed on board.

The night of April 4th was chosen for this daring adventure. At ten o'clock the moon had set and the sky was overcast with dark clouds. The *Carondelet* began her perilous journey in total darkness. But presently a terrific thunderstorm swept up the river and the vivid flashes of lightning rendered it impossible for the gunboat to pass the island unseen. Presently when near the hostile island the vessel was discovered. Next moment the heavy guns began to roar, as if to answer the thunders of the sky; the flashes from the burning powder commingled with the vivid lightning, the whole presenting a scene of indescribable grandeur.

The *Carondelet* was saved, chiefly, no doubt, through the fact that she ran so near the island that the great guns could not be sufficiently depressed, and they overshot the mark. About midnight the gunboat reached New Madrid uninjured.

Two nights later the *Pittsburgh* ran the gantlet of Island No. 10. The two vessels soon reduced the batteries along the east bank of the river to silence. Pope's army crossed and occupied the Tiptonville road. The Confederate garrison of seven thousand men could only surrender, and this they did, while the second day's battle was raging at Shiloh—April 7, 1862.

## A GUNBOAT OF FIGHTING FAME, THE CAIRO

The first engagement of the *Cairo*, a third-rate ironclad of 512 tons, mounting six 42-pounders, six 32-pounders, three 8-inch guns and one 12-lb. howitzer, was under the command of Lieutenant N. C. Bryant on February 19th, in the Cumberland River in Tennessee. At Clarksville with the gunboat *Conestoga* the *Cairo* engaged three forts, capturing the town. On May 10th the *Cairo*, still commanded by Lieutenant Bryant, participated in the action at Fort Pillow and the river combat with the Confederate "River Defense" fleet. While being rammed the *Cincinnati* was so injured that she sank. The *Mound City* also was injured and three of the Confederate vessels were disabled. Once more the *Cairo*, on June 6th, with four other ironclad gunboats and two of the Ellet rams, engaged the Confederate flotilla off the city of Memphis. On December 12, 1862, the *Cairo*, then under the command of Lieutenant T. O. Selfridge, was destroyed by a torpedo in the Yazoo River.

# NEW ORLEANS—THE ENTERING WEDGE WHERE THE NAVY HELPED THE ARMY

### By James Barnes

**T**HE capture of Forts Jackson and St. Philip and the surrender of New Orleans was the first great blow that the Confederacy received from the south. Coming but two months after the fall of Fort Donelson, it was the thunderous stroke on the wedge that started the ensuing separation of the seceding States into two halves. It was the action that shortened the war by months, if not by years; and though performed by the navy alone, its vital connection with the operations of the army in the West and along the great highway of the Mississippi was paramount. The military history of the war could not be written without touching upon it. The inborn genius of President Lincoln was never more clearly shown than when, on November 12, 1861, he ordered a naval expedition to be fitted out for the capture of New Orleans, the real key to the Mississippi; and never was clearer judgment proved than by the appointment of Captain David G. Farragut to the supreme command as flag-officer. To his fleet was attached a mortar flotilla under Commander David D. Porter, and here again was found the right man for the hour.

All through November, December and early January of 1862, the preparations were hurried without waste of energy. On the 2d of February, Farragut sailed from Hampton Roads, with orders to rendezvous at Key West, where Porter's mortar-boats were to join him. Such vessels as could be spared

## THE STEAM FRIGATE *BROOKLYN*

The Vessel that Followed the Flagship Past the Forts at New Orleans. When David Glasgow Farragut chose the *Hartford* as the ship to fly his flag, he picked out a craft that for her type (a steam frigate of the second class) was as fine as could be found in any navy in the world; and as much could be said for the *Brooklyn*, the second ship of the center division. She marked the transition period between sail and steam. Her tall masts were the inheritance of former days; her engines were merely auxiliary factors, for she could sail with all her canvas set and the proper wind to drive her faster than she could steam under the best conditions. Here we see her with royal, top-gallant sails, top-sails, and courses clewed up, and her funnel lowered to a level with her bulwarks. In passing the forts at New Orleans, she presented no such appearance—her upper yards had been sent down, and with her engines doing their utmost, her funnel belching smoke, she swept slowly on into the line of fire. The first division, composed of eight vessels under command of Captain Theodorus Bailey on the *Cayuga*, was ahead. But every gunner in Fort Jackson and in Fort St. Philip had been told to "look out for the *Hartford* and the *Brooklyn*." It was dark, but the fire-rafts, the soaring shells, and the flames from the guns afloat and ashore made everything as bright as day. By some mistake, the reports that were first sent to Washington of the passing of the forts contained an erroneous plan. It was the first or discarded drawing, showing the fleet in two divisions abreast. This was afterwards changed into the three-division plan in which Captain Bailey with the *Cayuga* led. It was not until four years after the closing of the war that this mistake was rectified, and many of the histories and contemporary accounts of the passing of the forts are entirely in error. The center division was composed of only three vessels, all of them steam frigates of the first class: the *Hartford*, flying Farragut's flag, under Commander Wainwright; the *Brooklyn*, under Captain T. T. Craven, and the *Richmond*, under Commander J. Alden. In the first division were also the steam sloops-of-war *Pensacola* and *Mississippi*, and they already had been under fire for twenty minutes when the center division neared Fort Jackson. The flagship (really the ninth in line) steered in close to the shore, but was obliged to sheer across the stream in an attempt to dodge a fire-raft that was pushed by the Confederate tug *Mosher*. It was a daring act performed by a little crew of half a dozen men, and as a deed of desperate courage has hardly any equal in naval warfare. The *Mosher* all but succeeded in setting the flag-ship in flames, and was sunk by a well-directed shot. The *Brooklyn*, after a slight collision with the *Kineo*, one of the vessels of Bailey's division, and almost colliding with the hulks in the obstructions, was hit by the ram *Manassas* a glancing blow—a little more and this would have sunk her, as both her inner and outer planking were crushed. But, like the flag-ship, she succeeded in passing safely.

[A—15]

from the blockade, whose pinch upon the South Atlantic ports had already begun to be felt, were detached to aid the expedition. No such great plans and actions could be carried on in secrecy. Almost from its incipiency, the object of all this preparation became known throughout the South. Every effort was made by the Confederate military commanders to strengthen the defenses at New Orleans, which consisted of the formidable forts St. Philip and Jackson that faced one another, the former on the north bank and the latter on the south bank of the river below the city. Once these were passed, New Orleans would fall. Not only were the forts strengthened, but every effort was made by the Confederates to gain supremacy afloat; and in this they all but succeeded. In addition to the formidable obstructions placed in the river, the iron-clad ram, *Manassas*, was strengthened and further protected to prepare her for conflict. The *Louisiana*, then building at New Orleans, was rushed toward completion. If she had been ready, perhaps New Orleans would have told a different story, for she was designed to be the most powerful ironclad of her day—4,000 tons rating and mounting sixteen heavy guns, well protected by armor. Up the river, at Memphis, the *Arkansas* was being prepared for active service; and on the various tributaries were being built several iron-clad vessels.

No ship in Farragut's fleet possessed any more powers of resistance than the old wooden walls of Nelson's time. Against this attacking fleet were the well-placed guns ashore, seventy-four in Fort Jackson and fifty-two pieces of ordnance in Fort St. Philip. The garrisons were made up of about seven hundred well-trained cannoneers apiece. As Admiral Porter has observed, "Assuming upon the general concession of military men that one gun in a fort was equal to about three afloat, and considering the disadvantage of a contrary three-and-a-half-knot current to the Federal vessels (with additional channel obstructions of fire-rafts and

## THE *RICHMOND*

The Third Ship of the Center Division at the Passing of the Forts.—There was a current in the Mississippi that had to be taken into account in estimating the time that Farragut's fleet would be under fire from the forts. The larger vessels were all so slow when under steam that, taking the rule that "a fleet is no faster than the slowest ship," caused them literally to crawl past the danger points. The *Richmond* was the slowest of them all. Just as she neared the passageway through the obstructions her boilers began to foam, and she could just about stem the current and no more. The vessels of the third division passed her; but at last, with her bow pointed up the river, she was able to engage Fort Jackson. Opening with her port batteries, she hammered hard at the fort, and with small loss got by, followed by the little gunboat *Sciota* that had equal good fortune. When day dawned, the *Richmond* crept up to the anchored fleet and reported. It was feared at first that she had been lost or sunk. The battle of New Orleans was probably the most successful, and certainly the boldest, attempt ever made to match wooden ships against forts at close range. Although the Confederate gunboats were inferior to the Federal fleet, they also have to be taken into consideration for their brave and almost blind assault. If they had been assisted by the unfinished ironclads they might have borne different results, for the *Louisiana*, owing to her unfinished condition never entered the fight. She was considered to be more powerful than the *Merrimac*. Certainly her armament would prove it, for she mounted two 7-inch rifles, three 9-inch shell guns, four 8-inch smooth-bores, and seven 100-pounder rifles—in all sixteen guns. At the city of New Orleans was an unfinished ironclad that was expected to be even more powerful than the *Louisiana*. Only the arrival of Farragut's fleet at this timely hour for the Federal cause prevented her from being finished. It was believed by her builders—and apparently, in view of the immunity of ironclads, with reason—that not only could the *Mississippi* drive the Federal fleet out of the river, but that she would be able to paralyze the whole of the wooden navy of the North, and might possibly go so far as to lay the Northern Atlantic cities under contribution. In order to prevent her from falling into the Federal hands she, like the *Louisiana*, was set on fire and drifted a wreck down the stream. Commander J. Alden, of the *Richmond*, was on the quarterdeck throughout the action and had seen to it that his vessel, like the others, was prepared in every way to render the chances of success more favorable. Cables were slung over the side to protect her vulnerable parts, sand bags and coal had been piled up around her engines, hammocks and splinter-nettings were spread and rigged, and as the attempt to run the forts would be at night, no lights were allowed. Decks and gun-breeches were whitewashed to make them more visible in the darkness. Farragut's orders had concluded with the following weighty sentence: "I shall expect the most prompt attention to signals and verbal orders either from myself or the Captain of the fleet, who, it will be understood in all cases, acts by my authority." The *Richmond* lost two men killed and four men wounded in the action.

chains), the odds were greatly in favor of the Confederate defenses."

The defenders of the old city, New Orleans, were confident that the fleet would never pass. On the 16th of April, the mortar-boats were in position along what was, owing to the bend of the river, really the southern bank (one division, on the first day, was across the river), and in the morning they opened, each vessel firing at the rate of one shell every ten minutes. Organized into three divisions, they were anchored close to the shore, the furthest up stream, only 2,850 yards from Fort Jackson, and 3,680 from Fort St. Philip. They were near a stretch of woods and their tall masts—they were mostly schooners—were dressed with branches of trees in order to disguise their position from the Confederate guns. For almost eight days, at varying intervals even at night, the twenty boats of this flotilla rained their hail of death and destruction on the forts. Brave and hardy must have been the men who stood that terrific bombardment! The commanders of the Confederate forts bore witness to the demoralization of both the men and defenses that ensued. Nearly every shell of the many thousand fired lodged inside the works; magazines were threatened, conflagrations started, and destruction was reaped on all sides. Long after the memorable day of the 24th of April when the fleet swept past, Colonel Edward Higgins, the brave defender of Fort Jackson, wrote as follows:

"I was obliged to confine the men most rigidly to the casemates, or we should have lost the best part of the garrison. A shell, striking the parapet over one of the magazines, the wall of which was seven feet thick, penetrated five feet and failed to burst. If that shell had exploded, the work would have ended.

"Another burst near the magazine door, opening the earth and burying the sentinel and another man five feet in the same grave.

"The parapet and interior of the fort were completely

David G. Farragut, Who Commanded the Fleets at New Orleans. No man ever succeeded in impressing his own personality and infusing his confidence and enthusiasm upon those under his command better than did David Glasgow Farragut. In drawing up the plans and assuming the responsibility of what seemed to be a desperate and almost foolhardy deed, Farragut showed his genius and courage. His attack was not a blind rush, trusting to suddenness for its effect; it was a well-studied, well-thought-out plan. Nothing was neglected "which prudence could suggest, foresight provide, or skill and science devise." Farragut was well aware of the results that

DAVID GLASGOW FARRAGUT

THE MAN WHO DARED

would follow. The control of the lower Mississippi, if complete, would have enabled the Confederate Government to draw almost unlimited supplies from the vast country to the west of the river, and undoubtedly would have prolonged the war. The failure of Farragut's plan and his defeat would have meant a most crushing blow to the North. But in his trust in his officers and his own fearless courage there was small chance of failure. Calm and collected he went through the ordeal, and when safe above the forts he saw Bailey's vessels waiting, and one by one his other ships coming up, he knew that his stupendous undertaking was a success.

The whole of the North rose in elation at the news of the capture of New Orleans; but the surrender of the city at the mouth of the river did not mean complete possession. From Vicksburg southward, the long line of the river and the land on either side was yet in the possession of the Confederates. Baton Rouge and Natchez surrendered on demand. On May 29th, transports carrying the troops of General Williams came down the river after a reconnaissance at Vicksburg. Farragut was anchored off the town of Baton Rouge. He reported to Williams that a body of irregular Confederate cavalry had fired into one of his boats, wounding an officer and two men, and that he had been compelled to open his batteries upon the shore. Williams at once occupied the town in force.

A FLAGSHIP IN UNFRIENDLY WATERS

The *Hartford* Lying Close to the Levee at Baton Rouge

honeycombed, and the large number of sand bags with which we were supplied alone saved us from being blown to pieces a hundred times, our magazine doors being much exposed.

"On the morning of the 24th, when the fleet passed, the terrible precision with which the formidable vessels hailed down their tons of bursting shell upon the devoted fort made it impossible for us to obtain either rapidity or accuracy of fire, and thus rendered the passage comparatively easy."

Although all the foregoing proves the accuracy and value of the mortar fire, it alone could not reduce the forts. They had to be passed to lay the city at the mercy of the fleet. But there were the obstructions yet to deal with. 'Twas a brave deed that was done by the two gunboats, *Itasca* and *Pinola*, which, after great difficulties, broke the great link-chain that, buoyed by logs and hulks, closed up the channel. General M. L. Smith, the engineer of the department, in his report, in referring to the fall of New Orleans, wrote, "While the obstruction existed, the city was safe; when it was swept away, as the defenses then existed, it was in the enemy's power."

By 2 o'clock A.M. in the morning of the 24th, the intrepid Lieutenant Caldwell, who had suggested the expedition of the two gunboats that had broken up the obstruction, returned to the fleet after a daring survey of the channel, and the flag-ship hoisted the appointed signal. In two divisions, the fleet passed through the broken barriers and steamed into the zone of fire. It was an enfilading fire, as soon the guns of both forts were brought into play. There is not space here to go into the details of the naval battle that followed with the bravely fought Confederate gunboats and the ram *Manassas*. That belongs to naval history. There were deeds of prowess performed by vessels that flew either flag; there were small separate actions whose relating would make separate stories in themselves. Amid burning fire-rafts and a continuous roar from the opposing forts, the first division of the fleet under the command of Captain Theodorus Bailey held its course,

Coaling Farragut's Fleet at Baton Rouge. If "a ship without a captain is like a man without a soul," as runs an old naval saying, a vessel dependent upon steam power with empty bunkers is as a man deprived of heart-blood, nerves, or muscles; and a few days after New Orleans, Farragut's vessels faced a serious crisis. Captain A. T. Mahan has summed it up in the following words: " . . . The maintenance of the coal supply for a large squadron, five hundred miles up a crooked river in a hostile country, was in itself no small anxiety, involving as it did carriage of the coal against the current, the provision of convoys to protect the supply vessels against guerillas, and the employment of pilots, few of whom were to be found, as they naturally favored the enemy, and had gone away. The river was drawing near the time of lowest water, and the flag-ship herself got aground under very critical circumstances, having had to take out her coal and shot, and had even begun on her guns, two of which were out when she floated off." Many of the up-river gunboats could burn wood, and so, at a pinch and for a short time, could the smaller steamers with Farragut. But the larger vessels required coal, and at first there was not much of it to be had, although there were some colliers with the fleet and more were dispatched later. In the two pictures of this page we are shown scenes along the levee in 1862, at Baton Rouge, and out in the river, a part of the fleet. The vessel with sails let down to dry is the sloop-of-war *Mississippi;* ahead of her and a little inshore, about to drop her anchor, is one of the smaller steamers that composed the third division of the fleet. Nearby lies a mortar schooner and a vessel laden with coal. Baton Rouge, where Farragut had hoisted his flag over the arsenal, was policed by a body of foreigners employed by the municipal authority. The mayor had declared that the guerilla bands which had annoyed the fleet were beyond his jurisdiction, saying that he was responsible only for order within the city limits. There was some coal found in the city belonging to private owners, and the lower picture shows the yards of Messrs. Hill and Markham, who, through the medium of Mr. Bryan, the Mayor, opened negotiations with Farragut for its sale.

his ship, the *Cayuga*, leading the van. The second division, under the fleet's commander, followed. The powerful steam ram, *Manassas,* had struck the *Brooklyn,* doing some slight damage. But when the *Mississippi* turned her wooden prow upon her, in order to avoid being turned over like a log, the ram took to the shore, where her crew escaped. Subsequently, having received two broadsides from the *Mississippi*, she slid off the bank and drifted in flames down with the current.

By daybreak nine of the Confederate vessels that had fought so gallantly and dauntlessly were destroyed. The forts lay some five miles downstream. The little batteries that protected the outskirts of the city were silenced. On the 25th, New Orleans lay powerless under Farragut's guns. The dreaded *Louisiana* was set on fire and blew up with tremendous explosion. Another, and still more powerful ironclad, the *Mississippi* (not to be confused with the vessel in Farragut's fleet of the same name), suffered the same fate. She had been launched only six days before. On the 27th, Porter, who was down the river, demanded the surrender of the forts; and General Duncan, the Confederate commander-in-chief, accepted the terms on the 28th. At 2.30 P.M. on that day, Fort St. Philip and Fort Jackson were formally delivered, and the United States flag was hoisted over them. On May 1st, General Butler arrived and the captured city was handed over to the army. The wedge having been driven home, the opening of the Mississippi from the south had begun.

# PART II

## DOWN THE MISSISSIPPI VALLEY

———

# FORT PILLOW
# AND
# MEMPHIS

———

THE CONFEDERATE RAM "GENERAL PRICE"—ACCIDENTALLY STRUCK BY HER CONSORT "GENERAL BEAUREGARD" AT THE BATTLE OF MEMPHIS, RUN ASHORE, AND CAPTURED BY THE FEDERALS

# FORT PILLOW AND MEMPHIS

There can be no denying the dash and spirit with which this attack was made. It was, however, the only service of value performed by this irregular and undisciplined force. At Memphis, a month later, and at New Orleans, the fleet proved incapable of meeting an attack and of mutual support. There were admirable materials in it, but the mistake of withdrawing them from strict military control and organization was fatal. On the other hand, although the gunboats engaged fought gallantly, the flotilla as an organization had little cause for satisfaction in the day's work.—*A. T. Mahan, in "The Gulf and Inland Waters."*

The boats I have purchased are illy adapted for the work I shall require of them; it is not their strength upon which I rely, but upon the audacity of our attack, for success.—*Colonel Charles Ellet, Jr., in a letter to the Secretary of War.*

THE Western gunboat flotilla had done wonderful work in the space of two months, February to April, 1862. It had captured Fort Henry; it had made possible the taking of Fort Donelson, with its vast equipment and fourteen thousand men; it had secured to General Pope's army the surrender of Island No. 10—all within the eight weeks. But there were more strongholds to conquer and the heaviest battle was still in the future. Fort Pillow with its frowning cannon lay eighty miles or more below New Madrid, and eighty miles still farther down the great river was Memphis. Fort Pillow, and Fort Randolph, just below, must now be attacked in order to open the river to Vicksburg.

A few days after the surrender of Island No. 10, the gunboat fleet turned toward Fort Pillow. About this time General Pope was called with most of his army to Shiloh and Corinth, as Beauregard had been before, and the gunboats with a small portion of the land forces were left to fight their way down the

Federal Floating Mortar Battery at Fort Pillow. There would have been no engagement at Fort Pillow had it not been for the continued annoyance inflicted upon that position by the curious little craft—one of which we see tied up to the wharf in the lower picture. Secure in the knowledge that Beauregard's presence with a large force at Corinth had precluded the Federal land attack, General Villepigue awoke one morning to the sound of bursting shells which a Federal mortar boat was rapidly dropping over his ramparts. Every day thereafter, Flag-Officer Foote continued to pay compliments to Fort Pillow by sending down a mortar boat towed by a gunboat of the type seen in the picture. There was nothing for the Confederates to do but take to their bomb-proofs, so long as the Federal gunners continued the bombardment. At last General Villepigue, chafing under the damage done to his works, called urgently upon the Confederate flotilla to come up and put an end to the mortar boats. Early on the morning of May 10, 1862, the day after Flag-Officer Foote went North, leaving Captain Davis in charge of the Federal flotilla, the *Cincinnati* towed mortar No. 16 down to

GENERAL J. B. VILLEPIGUE

THE DEFENDER OF FORT PILLOW

the usual position for shelling the fort, and then tied up to the edge of the stream to protect her. The mortar fired her first shot at five o'clock. One hour and a half later the eight rams of the Confederate River Defense fleet suddenly and unexpectedly appeared bearing down upon the *Cincinnati*. The latter quickly slipped her moorings, and opened her bow guns upon the approaching vessels. One of these, the *General Bragg*, passed quickly above the Federal ironclad, turned and struck her a violent blow on the starboard quarter. After that the *Bragg* disappeared down the river, but the *General Price* and the *Sumter* continued the attack. One struck the *Cincinnati* again, but the other received a shot through her boilers from the *Benton*, and this ended her part of the fight. The wounded *Cincinnati* was helped to the shore and sunk. The other Federal ironclad had now come upon the scene and the *mêlée* became general. The *General Van Dorn* rammed the *Mound City* so severely that she was compelled to run on the Arkansas shore. After that the Confederate rams returned to Fort Pillow and the half hour's thrilling fight was over.

BOATS THAT BROUGHT ON THE BATTLE

river alone. For two weeks the fleet bombarded Fort Pillow at long range. On May 9th, Flag-Officer Foote, whose wound received at Fort Donelson had not healed, asked to be relieved, and Captain Charles H. Davis, a man of well-known skill and bravery, was appointed in his place. The day after the retirement of Foote a Confederate fleet, known as the "River Defense," under the command of Captain J. E. Montgomery, came up and offered battle. Among them was a powerful side-wheel steam ram, the *General Bragg,* which made for the *Cincinnati.* The latter opened fire, but the shots could not drive the antagonist off. Presently the onrushing vessel struck the *Cincinnati* on the starboard side and penetrated the shell-room, rendering the ironclad almost helpless. Before the wounded vessel could get away she was rammed by two other Confederate boats, the *General Price* and the *Sumter.* Meanwhile the *Carondelet* had come to the rescue of the *Cincinnati,* firing as fast as she could load. At last the *Sumter* was struck by a 50-pound Dahlgren shot from the *Carondelet* and completely disabled. Her steam-chest was penetrated and the steam instantly poured out upon all parts of her casemate. The men ran for life, some leaping into the water and some falling on the deck, victims of the scalding steam. The *General Van Dorn,* one of the most agile of the Confederate vessels, partially disabled the *Mound City* by ramming her amidships with fearful force.

The smoke of battle had enveloped the whole scene in a dense cloud. There was a lull in the firing, and when the smoke cleared away the Confederate fleet was seen drifting slowly down the stream to Fort Pillow, and the battle was over.

For two or three days after this battle long-range firing was kept up, the Union fleet lying a mile or more up the river, the Confederate vessels being huddled under the guns of Fort Pillow.

On the 4th of June, great clouds of smoke were seen to arise from the fort, and terrific explosions accompanying

THE VESSEL WITH THE ARMED PROW.  THE FEDERAL RAM *VINDICATOR*

An excellent example of the steam rams as developed from the ideas of Charles Ellet, Jr., adding a new chapter to the history of naval warfare.  As far back as the siege of Sebastopol, in 1854, Charles Ellet—being then in Europe—proposed a plan to the Russians to equip their blockaded fleet with rams.  The plan was not adopted, and in 1855 he published a pamphlet outlining his idea and said, in proposing it to the United States Government, "I hold myself ready to carry it out in all its details whenever the day arrives that the United States is about to become engaged in a naval contest."  It was not until after the appearance of the *Merrimac* at Hampton Roads and the danger to Foote's fleet on the Mississippi from Confederate rams that Ellet was given the opportunity to try his various projects and commissioned to equip several rams at Cincinnati.  The project was regarded as a perilous one.  Had it not been for Ellet's extraordinary personal influence he would never have been able to obtain crews for his rams, as they were entirely unarmored with the exception of the pilot-house, but Ellet had reasoned correctly that the danger from collision was immensely against the vessel struck, while the danger from shot penetrating a vital part of the approaching ram he proved was reduced to an unappreciable fraction.  He contented himself, therefore, with strengthening the hulls of the river steamers which he purchased, filling the bows with solid timbers and surrounding the boilers with a double tier of oak twenty-four inches thick.  At Memphis the rams had their first trial and it resulted in complete vindication of Ellet's theories.  It was a vindication, however, which cost Ellet his life.  He was mortally wounded in the fight at Memphis while in command of the *Queen of the West*.

told the story. The Confederates were evacuating the place and destroying their magazines before departing. The next morning the Federals clambered up the bluff to the site of the fort and found only smoking ruins. Even the earthen breastworks had been torn to pieces by the fearful powder explosions. Fort Randolph was likewise abandoned. The great river, while not yet rolling "unvexed to the sea," was now open as far as Memphis, whither the River Defense fleet had retreated, some eighty miles below Fort Pillow, and thither steered the Federal gunboats in search of their recent antagonists.

Down the glassy river the Union fleet glided on June 5th. The banners were waving. The men were as gay as if they were going to a picnic. In the evening they came within gunshot of Memphis and anchored for the night, not far from the supposed spot where, more than three hundred years before, De Soto had first cast his eyes on the rolling tide of the Mississippi.

The Federal flotilla on the Mississippi had, some days before, been reenforced by four small steam rams under the command of Colonel Charles Ellet, Jr. Ellet was not by profession a military man, but a distinguished civil engineer. He had convinced the Government of the value of the steam ram as a weapon of war, and was given a colonel's commission and authority to fit out a fleet of rams. His vessels were not armed. He cooperated with, but was not under the direction of, Flag-Officer Davis. His "flag-ship" was the *Queen of the West* and the next in importance was the *Monarch*, commanded by his younger brother, Alfred W. Ellet.

It was understood by all that a ferocious river-battle was necessary before the Federals could get control of the city on the hill. It is true that Memphis was not fortified, but it was defended by the fleet which the previous month had had its first taste of warfare at Fort Pillow and now lay at the foot of the bluffs ready to grapple with the coming foe. The vessels, eight in number, were not equal to those of the Union fleet. They

PILOT W. J. AUSLINTY

PILOT DAVID HEINER

PILOT CHARLES ROSS

HEROES OF THE WHEEL–HOUSE

THE UNARMORED CONNING TOWER

Look into these six keen eyes which knew every current and eddy, every snag and sandbar of the Mississippi. To the hands of men like these the commanders of the Federal gunboats owed the safe conduct of their vessels. No hearts more fearless nor hands more steady under fire were brought into the fighting on either side. Standing silently at the wheel, their gaze fixed on the familiar countenance of the river before them, they guided the gunboats through showers of shell. Peering into the murky night, they felt their way through shallow channels past watchful batteries whose first shot would be aimed against the frail and unprotected pilot house.

There was no more dangerous post than the pilot house of a gunboat, standing as a target for the gunners, who knew that to disable the pilot was to render the vessel helpless to drift hither and yon or to run aground to be riddled full of holes. After the Inland Fleet passed from the control of the army to that of the navy the pilots of all the gunboats except Ellet's rams were brevetted acting masters or masters' mates and wore the uniform of the navy. Their services and bravery were fully recognized by the commanders, and their intimate knowledge of the river admitted them to conferences in which the most secret and difficult naval movements were planned. A river pilot knew when he could take his vessel over sandbars and inundated shallows where soundings would have turned back any navigating officer of the navy. Such valuable men were never safe. Even when passing up and down apparently peaceful reaches of the river the singing of some sharpshooters' bullet would give sudden warning that along the banks men were lying in wait for them. The mortality among the pilots during the war speaks volumes for the simple heroism of these silent men.

THE TARGET OF THE SHARPSHOOTERS

carried but two guns each, except one, which carried four. It was therefore a brave thing for Captain Montgomery to lay down the gage of battle to a fleet far stronger than his own. But he and his men did not falter. They moved up the swift current and opened the battle of Memphis, one of the most hotly contested naval battles ever fought in American waters.

It was the 6th of June, 1862, and one of the most charming days that Nature ever gives. As the sun rose over the eastern hills the people of the city gathered along the bluff in thousands, standing in dark silhouette against the sky, to watch the contest, and one can imagine how their emotion rose and fell as the tide of battle ebbed and flowed on the river below.

It was at 5:00 A.M. that Montgomery moved up the stream and fired the first gun. At this opening Colonel Ellet sprang forward on the hurricane deck, waved his hat, and shouted to his brother: "Round out and follow me. Now is our chance."

The *Queen* instantly moved toward the Confederate fleet; the Federal ironclads followed, but already both fleets were engaged in a brisk cannonade and the smoke was so dense that the *Queen* was soon lost to view. The daring little vessel plunged on through the waves. She was headed for the *General Lovell*, almost in the center of the Confederate line of battle. The *Queen* struck her antagonist squarely on the side and cut her almost in two. The wounded vessel groaned and lurched, and in a few minutes she sank, with many of her devoted crew, beneath the dark waters of the river.

Soon after this the *Queen* was rammed by the *General Beauregard* and a little later when the *Beauregard* and the *General Price* were making for the *Monarch,* the *Beauregard* missed her aim and struck her comrade, the *General Price,* tearing off her wheel and putting her out of service. The *Queen* fought with desperation and in the *mêlée* Colonel Ellet, her commander, received a pistol shot in the knee. He fell on the deck and, unable to rise, continued to give orders to his men while lying prone on his ship. But the *Queen* was now dis-

## A SHIP THAT FOUGHT THE FEVER

Grateful, indeed, were the Federal soldiers, in their advance from Cairo down the Mississippi, when this spacious river steamer, with its roomy cabins and wide decks, about which played the cooling breezes of the Mississippi, was added to the fleet. The Confederates were still to be encountered, but a more subtle enemy had already attacked the army. Fever and dysentery had fastened upon the unacclimated Northerners both afloat and ashore, and threatened to kill off more of them than could possibly be done by the men who strove with them for the possession of the river. When Island No. 10 was abandoned by the Confederates, they sank a gunboat and six transports, which they were compelled to leave behind. General Pope soon had the transports raised and in commission on the Federal side. None of them was more highly prized than the *Red Rover*, which we see here converted into the hospital ship of the Mississippi Squadron, commanded by Lieutenant W. R. Wells. Such floating hospitals quickly came into use by both the army and the navy along the Mississippi. Out on the bosom of the river the fever-stricken men on the shady decks grasped that chance of life which would have been denied them tossing in tents on shore, where the beating sun by day and the miasma from the bottom-lands by night, coupled with imperfect drainage, made recovery almost impossible.

abled, after her crash with the *Beauregard,* and Ellet ordered that she be headed for the Arkansas shore.

The next scene in this exciting drama came when the *Beauregard,* after disabling the *Queen,* made for the *Monarch* with like design. But the *Monarch* was the more agile. She evaded the blow, and dexterously whirling about, struck the *Beauregard* on the bow with terrific force, tearing a great hole beneath the water line. The *Beauregard,* disabled also by the gunboats, began to sink and the men on her decks fluttered handkerchiefs or any white thing at hand in token of surrender.

The *Monarch,* however, had determined to add one more to her list of trophies. There was the *Little Rebel,* the Confederate flag-ship, on whose deck Captain Montgomery had stood with unfaltering courage in the midst of Federal gun-shots. The *Monarch* now turned her prow to the *Little Rebel* and put on full steam. The latter, conscious of her inability to stand before the little fighting monster, fled toward the Arkansas shore. The race was a hot one; the *Monarch* gained rapidly, but ere she could strike the *Little Rebel,* the latter ran aground in the shallow water. Her commander and her crew leaped into the water, and they swam to shore and escaped into the forest.

The *Monarch* then steamed back to the middle of the river and rounded out her day's work by doing a deed of mercy. The *Beauregard* was still above water, but was settling rapidly, and her faithful crew, knowing that they had done all they could for the cause for which they fought, were still waving their white flags. The *Monarch* rescued them and towed the sinking *Beauregard* to shallow water, where she sank to her boiler deck.

Four of the Confederate gunboats had now been destroyed and the remaining four turned down the river and made a desperate effort to escape. But the Union fleet closed in on them and three of them turned to the Arkansas shore in the hope that the crews might make their escape. In the lead was the *General*

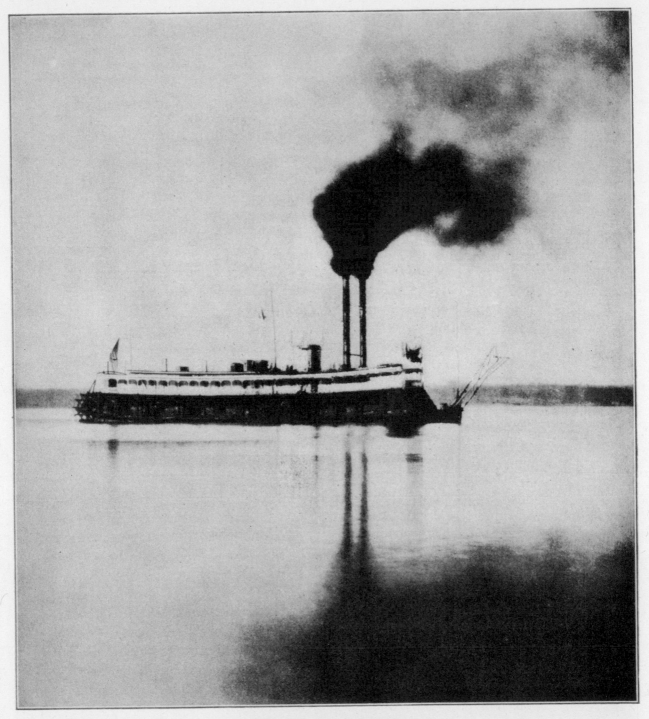

## A RANGER OF THE RIVER

This little "tinclad" is typical of the so-called Mosquito Fleet, officially known as "Light Drafts," which rendered a magnificent minor service in the river operations of the navy. Up narrow tributaries and in and out of tortuous and shallow bayous, impassable for the larger gunboats, these dauntless fighting craft pushed their way, capturing Confederate vessels twice their size, or boldly engaging the infantry and even the field-batteries of the enemy, which were always eagerly pressing the shores to annoy the invading fleet. To Flag-Officer Davis, during his command on the Mississippi, the Federals owed the idea of these light-draft stern-wheel vessels, most of which were ordinary river steamers purchased and altered to suit the purposes of the navy. Covered to a height of eleven feet above the water line with railroad iron a half to three-quarters of an inch thick, and with their boilers still further protected, they were able to stand up to the fire of even moderate-sized guns. Many a gun in the Confederate fleets and forts was silenced by the well-directed fire of the two light bow-rifles with which some of the tinclads were equipped.

*M. Jeff. Thompson.* In a few minutes she had reached the goal and her officers and men leaped from the deck and ran for the protection of the woods. A moment later a shell exploded on her deck, set her on fire and she was burned to the water's edge. Closely following the *Jeff. Thompson* were the *Bragg* and the *Sumter,* and the crews of both escaped in like manner to the swamps and forests of Arkansas. Of all the eight Confederate gunboats the *General Van Dorn* alone evaded her pursuers and made her escape down the river.

The battle of Memphis, one of the fiercest of its kind on record, lasted but an hour and a quarter. The Confederate killed and wounded were never accurately reported. On the Union side there were four wounded, and with one the wound proved fatal—Colonel Ellet. His shattered knee refused to heal, and two weeks later, in the arms of his wife and daughter, the famous engineer breathed his last. His body was carried to Philadelphia and laid to rest at Laurel Hill, after being given a state funeral at Independence Hall.

The view of the battle of Memphis from the bluffs, on which the whole population of the city had gathered, was one of indescribable grandeur. Every house in the city and for miles around quivered with the explosions of burning powder. At times the smoke of the battle was so dense that scarcely a vessel could be seen by the spectators on the hill; but a continuous roar of artillery arose from the hidden surface of the river, while the impingement of the vessels crashing together sounded like a titanic battle of the elements.

There were a few Union sympathisers among the onlookers, but the great majority of them were Confederates, and when they saw their ships go down they broke into wails and lamentations. Sorrowfully they witnessed, before noon of that day, the Stars and Bars lowered from the City Hall and replaced by the Stars and Stripes, which floated over Memphis to the end of the war.

FIGHTING WESTERNERS—THE SECOND WISCONSIN CAVALRY

GENERAL C. C. WASHBURN (ORGANIZER OF THE SECOND WISCONSIN CAVALRY) AND STAFF

Wisconsin sent ninety thousand of her sons into the struggle, and her infantry and cavalry won records "East" and also in the minor, but by no means inglorious, operations west of the Mississippi. In Missouri and Arkansas they protected the inhabitants from outlaw bands and resisted the raids of the Confederates, helping the Union forces on the other side finally to gain possession of the river.

SHERMAN AND HIS OFFICERS—MEMPHIS, 1862

This photograph was taken during the summer of 1862, after Grant had made General Sherman commander of the Third Division of the Army of Tennessee, and shows the coming great marshal at Memphis, grouped with his staff and other officers. In the party are: Captain John T. Taylor; Major J. H. Hammond; Captain Lewis M. Dayton; Colonel Ezra Taylor; Captain J. Condit Smith; Captain James W. Shirk, U. S. N.; Colonel T. K. Smith; Major W. H. Hartshorn; Colonel W. H. H. Taylor; Major W. D. Sanger, and Captain James C. McCoy. Sherman had little to do at Memphis during the summer and autumn of 1862. On December 20th he left the city for the Yazoo River to take part in Grant's first movement against Vicksburg.

## THE CITY ONLY A SIEGE COULD TAKE—VICKSBURG, MISSISSIPPI

The evacuation of Fort Pillow and Fort Randolph and the capture of New Orleans by Farragut left Vicksburg the main point on the Mississippi strongly defended by the Confederates, after the spring of 1862. The Federal government was most anxious for its possession. It is eight hundred miles from Memphis to New Orleans; and Vicksburg, about half way between the two, is the strongest natural position on the river. The batteries which the Confederate engineers placed on the bluffs were too high above the stream for the guns of the Federal fleet to reach them. The little Mississippi city remained the chief hope of the Confederates in holding its eastern and western territory together. With Vicksburg lost, the Confederacy would be definitely parted.

On June 28, 1862, Farragut, who had arrived with war vessels and a mortar fleet about ten days before, started to run the Vicksburg batteries with twelve ships, covered by the guns of the mortar flotilla. All but three got past with a loss of fifteen killed and thirty wounded. Above the town Farragut found some of the Ellet rams, and on the 1st of July Flag-Officer Davis and the river gunboats arrived. The Federal forces of the upper and lower Mississippi had joined hands. But Farragut was convinced that Vicksburg could not be taken without help of the army. Therefore orders on July 20th to return down the river were very welcome. Davis returned to Helena. Vicksburg's danger of Federal capture was reduced to a nullity, for the time being.

On July 24th the fleet under Farragut and the troops that had occupied the position on the river bank opposite Vicksburg under the command of General Thomas Williams went down the river, Farragut proceeding to New Orleans and Williams once more to Baton Rouge. The latter had withdrawn from his work of cutting the canal in front of Vicksburg, and a few days after his arrival at Baton Rouge the Confederate General Van Dorn sent General J. C. Breckinridge to seize the post. On the morning of August 5, 1862, the Federal forces were attacked. Williams, who had with him only about twenty-five hundred men, soon found that a much larger force was opposed to him, Breckinridge having between five and six thousand men. The brunt of the early morning attack fell upon the Indiana and Michigan troops, who slowly fell back before the fierce rushes of the bravely led men in gray. At once, Williams ordered Connecticut, Massachusetts, and Wisconsin regiments to go to their relief, sending at the same time two sections of artillery to his right wing. The Federal gunboats *Katahdin* and *Kineo* opened fire on Breckinridge's lines

THE FEDERAL DEFENDER OF
BATON ROUGE

at a signal from General Williams, who indicated their position. For almost two hours the battle raged fiercely, the firing being at short range and the fighting in some cases hand-to-hand. The Twenty-first Indiana regiment having lost all its field officers, General Williams placed himself at its head, exposing himself repeatedly, and refusing all pleadings to go to the rear. As he was bravely leading his men, he was killed almost instantly by a bullet that passed through his chest; and the Federal forces, concentrating, fell back on the outskirts of the town. The Confederates, who had also suffered heavily, fell back also, retreating to their camp. The action was a drawn fight, but in the loss of the brave veteran of the Mexican War who had led them the land forces of the lower Mississippi sustained a severe blow. General Williams' body was sent to New Orleans on an artillery transport which was sunk in collision with the *Oneida* off Donaldsonville, Louisiana, a few days after the battle. Baton Rouge was abandoned by the Federals on August 20th. Breckinridge had previously retired to Port Hudson.

THE ARTILLERY TRANSPORT THAT WAS SUNK OFF DONALDSONVILLE, LOUISIANA, WITH GENERAL WILLIAMS' BODY ON BOARD.—AUGUST, 1862

# PART III
## THE STRUGGLE FOR RICHMOND

---

# YORKTOWN:
# UP THE
# PENINSULA

---

GUNS MARKED "GEN. MAGRUDER, YORKTOWN"
IN THE POSITIONS WHERE THEY DEFIED
McCLELLAN'S ARMY A MONTH

## THE SUPERFLUOUS SIEGE

The Mortar Battery that Never Fired a Shot. By his much heralded Peninsula Campaign, McClellan had planned to end the war in a few days. He landed with his Army of the Potomac at Fortress Monroe, in April, 1862, intending to sweep up the peninsula between the York and James rivers, seize Richmond at one stroke, and scatter the routed Confederate army into the Southwest. At Yorktown, he was opposed by a line of fortifications that sheltered a force much inferior in strength to his own. For a whole month McClellan devoted all the energies of his entire army to a systematic siege. Its useless elaboration is well illustrated by Battery No. 4, one of fifteen batteries planted to the south and southeast of Yorktown. The ten monster 13-inch siege mortars, the complement of No. 4, had just been placed in position and were almost ready for action. It was planned to have them drop shells on the Confederate works, a mile and a half distant. Just a day before this could be done, Yorktown was evacuated, May 4, 1862.

## THE ELABORATE DEFENSES

Advanced Section, Three Mortars of Union Battery, No. 4.    Looking due north and showing the same three mortars pictured in the preceding views.    The photograph shows (1) the stockade built above the excavations as a protection from attack by Confederate infantry; (2) the ammunition that would have been used the next day if the Confederates had not evacuated, and (3) the temporary bridge crossing the narrow branch that runs into a northern arm of Wormley's Creek at this point.    By this bridge communication was held with the batteries to the west.    The heavy stockade was intended to forestall any attempt of the Confederate infantry to rush the battery.    The mortars shown in this photograph are 13-inch sea-coast mortars and exceeded in weight any guns previously placed in siege batteries.    The first of these mortars was landed at daybreak on April 27th and the whole battery was ready to open bombardment in a week's time.

# THE PENINSULA CAMPAIGN

A SHATTERED and discomfited army were the hosts of McDowell when they reached the banks of the Potomac, after that ill-fated July Sunday at Bull Run. Dispirited by the sting of defeat, this motley and unorganized mass of men became rather a mob than an army. The transformation of this chaos of demoralization into the trained, disciplined, and splendid troops of the Grand Army of the Potomac, was a problem to challenge the military genius of the century.

Fresh from his victories in the mountains of West Virginia, imbued with the spirit of Carnot, that "military discipline is the glory of the soldier and the strength of armies," General George Brinton McClellan began the task of transmuting the raw and untutored regiments into fighting men who were to bear the brunt of the conflict, until the victory should be theirs at Appomattox. Never, since the days of Baron Steuben at Valley Forge, had the American " citizen soldier " received such tuition in the art of war. It was a gigantic attempt; but with the flower of the youth of the North, the winning personality of a popular and efficient commander, in whom lived the enthusiasm of the creator and master whose soul was in his work—all deeply imbued with patriotism—there sprang up as if by magic, in the vacant fields about the capital city, battalions of infantry, batteries of artillery, and squadrons of cavalry.

Washington has become a camp. Day after day the trains bring from the shops and farms the inexperienced sons of the Northland. All during the summer and autumn months, the new recruits continue to march through the streets, with flags flying and bands playing. They come, two hundred thousand strong, that the " Young Napoleon " may forge them into a

HOW PICK AND SHOVEL SERVED

Rear Section, Seven Mortars, of Union Battery No. 4. In order to make it impossible for Confederate sharpshooters to pick off the gunners, the batteries were placed in elaborate excavations. At No. 4 the entire bank of Wormley's Creek was dug away. General McClellan personally planned the location of some of these batteries for the purpose of silencing the Confederate artillery fire.

WASTED TRANSPORTATION

Both Sections of Union Battery No. 4. The heavy barge at the landing transported the ten huge mortars, with their ammunition, all the way from Fortress Monroe up the York River and Wormley's Creek to the position of the battery. There they were laboriously set up, and, without firing a shot, were as laboriously removed. On the day of the evacuation the six batteries equipped were in condition to throw one hundred and seventy-five tons of metal daily into the Confederate defenses around Yorktown.

weapon, which later in the hands of the "Hammerer" will beat down the veterans of Lee before Richmond.

The autumn days come and go. The frosty nights have come. The increasing army continues its drill within the defenses. There are no indications of the forces moving. As if by instinct the men begin the construction of log huts for shelter from the cold of the coming winter.

"All's quiet along the Potomac." The winter months wear on and Public Opinion is growing restless. "Why does not the army move?" Across the country, thirty miles away, at Manassas, is the Confederate army, flushed with its July victory, under the command of General Joseph E. Johnston.

It was the 8th of March, 1862. As the Union army looked toward Manassas, down along the horizon line, clouds of smoke were seen ascending. It was from the burning huts. The Confederates were abandoning Manassas. Johnston was evacuating his camp. The next day orders came for the Army of the Potomac to move. Through the morning mists was heard the bustle of activity. Across the Long Bridge the troops took up the line of march, the old structure shaking under the tread of the passing hosts. Filled with the spirit of action, the men were jubilant at the prospect. But this buoyancy was of short duration. There was the Virginia mud, yellow and sticky, into which the feet of man and horse sank till it was almost impossible to extricate them. Throughout the day the muddy march continued. At night the bivouac was made in the oozy slime, and not till the day after, near evening, were the deserted fortifications of Manassas reached. McClellan was putting his army to a test.

Next morning the two days' return march to Washington began. The rain fell in sheets and it was a wet and bedraggled army that sought the defenses of the capital.

The strategic eye of the commander had detected two routes to the coveted capital of the Confederacy. One lost many of its possibilities by the Confederate retreat from

## "LITTLE MAC" PREPARING FOR THE CAMPAIGN—A ROYAL AIDE

A picture taken in the fall of 1861, when McClellan was at the headquarters of General George W. Morell (who stands at the extreme left), commanding a brigade in Fitz John Porter's Division. Morell was then stationed on the defenses of Washington at Minor's Hill in Virginia, and General McClellan was engaged in transforming the raw recruits in the camps near the national capital into the finished soldiers of the Army of the Potomac. "Little Mac," as they called him, was at this time at the height of his popularity. He appears in the center between two of his favorite aides-de-camp—Lieut.-Cols. A. V. Colburn and N. B. Sweitzer—whom he usually selected, he writes, "when hard riding is required." Farther to the right stand two distinguished visitors—the Prince de Joinville, son of King Louis Phillippe of France, and his nephew, the Count de Paris, who wears the uniform of McClellan's staff, on which he was to serve throughout the Peninsula Campaign (see page 115). He afterwards wrote a valuable "History of the Cival War."

Manassas.  The other was determined on.  Soon the Potomac will swarm with every description of water craft.  It is to be the prelude to another drama on the military stage.  On the placid river there come canal-boats, flat-bottoms, barges, three-decked steamers, and transatlantic packets.

On shore, the cities of tents are being deserted.  The army is massing toward the piers of Alexandria.  It is a glorious day of awakening spring, this 17th of March, 1862.  From the heights above Alexandria a beautiful spectacle is seen.  Armed men cover the hillside and the plain; columns of soldiers, with guns flashing in the sunlight, march and countermarch; thousands of horsemen with shining arms fill the meadows to the right; to the left are many batteries; beyond these, a long line of marching men stretch from the hills to the streets of Alexandria; regimental bands play familiar tunes, and flags and banners are waving over all.  It is a magnificent pageant—a far different scene from that, three years hence, when many of these depleted, war-worn regiments, with tattered flags, will pass in grand review through the avenues of the capital.

Here upon this assortment of transports, without confusion and with the precision of a well-oiled machine, one hundred and twenty-one thousand men, with all the equipment for war, including fourteen thousand horses and mules, forty-four batteries, wagons, pontoon bridges, and boats are loaded.  It comprises a fleet of four hundred vessels.  On board men are swarming like ants; they unmoor from the landings and lazily float down the river.  The unfinished dome of the Capitol fades away in the distance.  The men gather in little knots and can but conjecture as to their destination.

Swinton tells us that it was an undertaking which " for economy and celerity of movement is without a parallel on record."  This vast army with its entire equipage was transferred in about two weeks a distance of two hundred miles without the loss of a man, from the scene of its preparation at Washington to the Flanders of the Civil War.

## McCLELLAN'S HEADQUARTERS BEFORE YORKTOWN

Camp Winfield Scott, near Wormley's Creek. General McClellan was a stickler for neatness. His headquarters were models of military order. The guard always wore white gloves, even in the active campaign. Here we see the general's chargers with their grooms, the waiting orderlies and the sentry standing stiffly at support arms. At the left is the guardhouse with stacked muskets.

## THE TENTED MEADOW

Overlooking the camp from near McClellan's headquarters. Little hardships had these troops seen as yet. Everything was new and fresh, the horses well fed and fat, the men happy and well sheltered in comfortable tents.

The army had already been divided into four corps, commanded, respectively, by Generals McDowell, Sumner, Heintzelman, and Keyes, but at the last moment McDowell had been detached by President Lincoln. The van was led by General Hamilton's division of the Third Corps. On the afternoon of the second day the first transports entered Chesapeake Bay. In the shadowy distance, low against the sky-line, could be descried the faint outlines of the Virginia shore. The vessels passed toward Hampton Roads where a short time before had occurred the duel of the ironclads, the *Monitor* and *Merrimac*. To the right was Old Point Comfort, at whose apex stood the frowning walls of Fortress Monroe.

The first troops landed in a terrible storm of thunder and lightning. The sea became rough; great billows were breaking on the beach; cables broke, allowing vessels to grate against each other or drift helplessly from the docks. The landing was made in an unpitying storm. Shelter was unavailable, and there was no abatement of the gale with the night.

Then came the order to march. At the command the men gathered, and in the darkness, with the incessant rain beating in their faces, with but the lightning's flash to guide them, they crossed the bridge toward Hampton. Here, in an open field, with neither tents nor fire, with water standing in pools, preparations for the night were made. The following morning some pitched their tents under the guns of Fortress Monroe while others found tenting places amid the charred ruins of the once aristocratic village of Hampton. But the cold, dreary rains were unceasing. Transport after transport continued to unload its human freight. Day after day the men stood shivering about their tents. Wet and cheerless, but patient, they awaited the coming of their magnetic chief.

General McClellan reached Fortress Monroe on April 2d. The Confederate capital was yet seventy miles away, on the northern side of the James. The route of approach lay along the narrow neck of land between the James and the York.

### NATURE'S AID TO THE DEFENDERS

Confederate magazines at the southeastern end of Yorktown. Tons of powder, shot and shell could be carried from this fastness in perfect safety to the guns on the heights, behind which the Confederate artillerymen stood and so long successfully defied the besiegers.

### WHENCE THE DEFENSE WAS DIRECTED

Headquarters of General Magruder in Yorktown. This pre-Revolutionary dwelling was on the main street, and here the young commander planned so cleverly the disposition of his 15,000 men—not nearly enough to man the defenses of the city—that McClellan, with nearly 100,000, was held in check.

# Yorktown—Up the Peninsula ❖ ❖ ❖ ❖

This peninsula, marshy and thickly wooded, is from seven to fifteen miles in width, cut by smaller streams into which the tides roll. The task before the army was not an easy one.

Again the splendidly equipped and matchlessly trained Army of the Potomac was ready to move. Out from the camp at Hampton, from under the gun-bristling fort, the advance was made in two divisions along the mud-filled roads of the Peninsula. The troops marched with the precision of veterans. It was a bright April day, but the progress made was slow. Under the weight of unaccustomed burdens in the toilsome march, the men soon fell out of line and began to straggle. The warm sun and the wearisome tramp prompted many to lighten their burdens by throwing away some of their apparel. Soon the entire route was lined with an endless and reckless profusion of overcoats, blankets, parade-coats, and shoes. "Contraband" negroes were reaping a rich harvest, gathering up the discarded articles. Less than five miles was covered this first day. That night the rain came again and the soldiers who had thrown away their clothing found it a night of suffering. The morning march began in the rain. By the time Big Bethel was reached the water was coming down in torrents. The roads were cut till they were veritable rivers of mud. Along this wretched way stumbled and plodded horse and man.

Saturday afternoon, April 5th, the Federal advance guard on the right, consisting of Porter's division of Heintzelman's Third Corps, suddenly came to a river. It was the Warwick, a sluggish stream, nearly cutting the Peninsula from Yorktown to the James, a distance of thirteen and a half miles. Beyond the river was a line of trenches and forts, defended by a Confederate army. General Magruder had been stationed on the Peninsula with about eight thousand men. At the approach of McClellan reenforcements were hastened to him. The Union right wing was in front of Yorktown, the left at Lee's Mills. Now for the first time in the campaign the Union army found its way disputed. A flash of fire blazed

## THE COSTLIEST RAMPART EVER BUILT

Confederate Breastworks to the South and Southeast of Yorktown, Reenforced with Cotton. This device was used once before, in the War of 1812, by the defenders of New Orleans. Before the end of the Civil War, cotton was worth $1.00 a pound, gold. It is safe to say that no fortification was ever built of material so expensive. These cotton bales were used to protect the gunners serving the 8-inch Columbiad at the parapet. The gun in the center, though of archaic pattern, was deemed worth wrecking by the Confederates when they evacuated the position to fall back upon Richmond.

## FORTIFICATIONS OF TWO WARS

Earthworks of the Revolution Used in the Civil War. The ditch, dug by Cornwallis in 1781, was deepened by Magruder in 1862. The higher earthworks to the left are also of Revolutionary origin. The sand-bag ramparts were added by the Confederates as further protection for guns and gunners, and as coverings to the magazines, one of which shows at the left of the picture.

from the rifle-pits. It was returned with equal force and here on the historic soil of Yorktown men of North and South stood opposed, where eighty-one years before their fathers had stood together in the making of the Nation.

The defense confronting the Army of the Potomac was a strong one. Dams, protected by batteries and rifle-trenches, had been built in the river. Yorktown itself was fortified by a line of continuous earthworks, while across the York was Gloucester, also strongly fortified and garrisoned. The force defending the line comprised eleven thousand men, soon to be augmented by the army of General Johnston, who was assigned to the chief command on the Peninsula.

At Lee's Mills General Smith, of Keyes' corps, sent to make a reconnaissance by General McClellan, detected a seeming weak spot in the fortifications. Here would be the logical point to break the Confederate line. General Smith was ordered to send his men across the river. Accordingly four companies of "Green Mountain Boys," under cover of a heavy artillery fire from a battery of eighteen guns, plunged into the Warwick. The water reached above the waist-line, but they waded across the stream, emerging on the other side, and charged the Confederate rifle-pits. Eight additional companies came to their support. For one hour the Union troops held the trenches. The Confederates, after being driven to a redoubt, received reenforcements, reformed, and made a counter-charge. The Vermont soldiers were driven back by a galling fire, many being killed or wounded in recrossing the stream. The attempt to force the line could not succeed, since the condition of the roads and the low, boggy land rendered it impossible to use light artillery. It could not be brought close enough to do effective work.

Preparation for a protracted siege was now begun. Streams were bridged; corduroy roads constructed; a depot of supplies established. Facing the Confederate works, a parallel line extending from before Yorktown to the Warwick, a

RAMPARTS THAT BAFFLED McCLELLAN. (Hasty fortifications of the Confederates at Yorktown.) It was against such fortifications as these, which Magruder had hastily reenforced with sand-bags, that McClellan spent a month preparing his heavy batteries. Magruder had far too few soldiers to man his long line of defenses properly, and his position could have been taken by a single determined attack. This rampart was occupied by the Confederate general, D. H. Hill, who had been the first to enter Yorktown in order to prepare it for siege. He was the last to leave it on the night of May 3, 1862.

WRECKED ORDNANCE. (Gun exploded by the Confederates on General Hill's rampart, Yorktown.) Although the Confederates abandoned 200 pieces of ordnance at Yorktown, they were able to render most of them useless before leaving. Hill succeeded in terrorizing the Federals with grape-shot, and some of this was left behind. After the evacuation the ramparts were overrun by Union trophy seekers. The soldier resting his hands upon his musket is one of the Zouaves whose bright and novel uniforms were so conspicuous early in the war. This spot was directly on the line of the British fortification of 1781.

ANOTHER VOICELESS GUN. (Confederate ramparts southeast of Yorktown.) A 32-pounder Navy gun which had been burst, wrecking its embrasure. The Federal soldier seated on the sand-bags is on guard-duty to prevent camp-followers from looting the vacant fort.

THE MISSING RIFLE. (Extensive sand-bag fortifications of the Confederates at Yorktown.) The shells and carriage were left behind by the Confederates, but the rifled gun to which they belonged was taken along in the retreat. Such pieces as they could not remove they spiked.

GUNS THE UNION LOST AND RECOVERED. (A two-gun Confederate battery in the entrenchments south of Yorktown.) The near gun is a 32-pounder navy; the far one, a 24-pounder siege-piece. More than 3,000 pieces of naval ordnance fell into the hands of the Confederates early in the war, through the ill-advised and hasty abandonment of Norfolk Navy Yard by the Federals. Many of these guns did service at Yorktown and subsequently on the James River against the Union.

THE CONFEDERATE COMMAND OF THE RIVER. (Battery Magruder, Yorktown.) Looking north up the river, four of the five 8-inch Columbiads composing this section of the battery are visible. The grape-shot and spherical shells, which had been gathered in quantities to prevent the Federal fleet from passing up the river, were abandoned on the hasty retreat of the Confederates, the guns being spiked. The vessels in the river are transport ships, with the exception of the frigate just off shore.

distance of four miles, was thrown up. Fourteen batteries and three redoubts, armed with the heaviest ordnance—some of the guns throwing two hundred pounds—were put in place.

Surrounding Yorktown were open fields. But the Federal troops could not remain there because of the shells from the batteries. The siege lasted less than thirty days and it rained on twenty of them. Violent thunderstorms rapidly succeeded one another. The Northern soldier, whether digging trenches, on the picket line, or standing guard, had to endure the fury of these storms. At night his bed might be in a pool of water. Sickness became prevalent, thousands were in the hospitals and many graves were dug in the marshy lowlands.

At last all was in readiness for the attack. The weather had cleared. The bombardment of Yorktown was about to begin. The shells were in position. Batteries capable of throwing sixty shells a minute were ready to belch forth.

Saturday morning, May 3d, Battery No. 1, opposite Yorktown, began its cannonading. The army waited in intense expectation of the grand spectacle. On Sunday, it was surmised, the great guns would play upon the works and ere the set of sun the victorious arms of the North would enter the historic town and unfurl the Stars and Stripes where the Father of his Country had placed them four-score years before.

Early Sunday morning a bright light from behind the Confederate works was seen by the Union pickets. A desultory cannonading had continued during the night and toward morning the firing was at times intense. The Sabbath dawned fair and warm, but no Southerners were to be seen. The Union men in the rifle-pits crept up to the very lines where but yesterday glinted the Confederate guns. The works had been abandoned. Under the cover of night the defenses had been evacuated, with masterly skill, as at Manassas. The troops were even now in full retreat toward Williamsburg.

Soon the Federals were in hot pursuit. General Stoneman with cavalry and horse artillery followed along the Wil-

## AN UNPRECEDENTED SIEGE BATTERY

Federal Battery No. 1 Before Yorktown.—Never before had so heavy a siege battery been mounted. It was placed half a mile farther down the York River than Battery No. 4. From its six Parrott guns, five 100-pounders and one 200-pounder, it could at a single firing drop 700 pounds of shot and shell upon the fortifications and landing at Yorktown, two miles away. It opened up on May 1, 1862, with such telling effect that the evacuation of the town was greatly hastened, occurring two days later. These Parrott guns were in many cases failures. The reinforcement of the breach was not properly placed to stand the heavy charges and many burst, killing the artillerymen and wrecking everything in close vicinity. The life of these guns was short.

## THE PRIDE OF UNION BATTERY NUMBER ONE

A 200-pounder Parrott Gun.—This, at the time, mammoth piece of ordnance stood in the center of Battery No. 1, which was located on the west bank of the York River at the mouth of Wormley's Creek. The range of the battery was upstream toward Yorktown, and this huge Parrott gun in the very center of the battery was much relied upon by the Federals to do heavy damage. Here we see how carefully McClellan's engineers did their work. The wickerwork bastions were reinforced by tiers of sand bags. Well-constructed wooden stands were made for the gunners to facilitate the loading and swabbing. This battery was near the Farenholdt House.

liamsburg road, which was littered with the debris of a retreating army. Six miles from Williamsburg the pursuing cavalrymen came to a sudden halt. The rear guard of the Confederates had been overtaken. On the brow of the hill, in full view, was a Southern cavalry regiment, belonging to the famous brigade of J. E. B. Stuart. A quick passage of arms resulted. The advancing force pressed close but the resistance was stubborn. Stuart's men were covering the retreat of the main column toward the entrenchments of Williamsburg, which were reached by four o'clock.

Night came upon the marching troops, who all the day had been trudging the flooded roads of the Peninsula. The rain had fallen in torrents during the greater part of March. The cavalry prepared to bivouac in the rain-soaked fields in front of the Confederate works. All during the evening and even into the night the forces of Sumner and Hooker, floundering in the mud, were arriving on the scene of the next day's battle. It was a drenched and bedraggled army that slept on its arms that night.

Early in the morning the troops were again in motion. The approach to Williamsburg is along a narrow ridge, from either side of which flow the tributaries of the York and the James. At the junction of two roads stood the main defense of the fortified town. It was Fort Magruder with its bastioned front. To its right and left were a dozen redoubts for the placing of field artillery. In front of its half-mile of earthen wall ran a ditch full of water. In front of this and to the right was an open field, made so by the felling of trees, and beyond were the woods in which the army had bivouacked.

It was scarcely day when the attacking Confederate force emerged into the edge of the timber-strewn field. At once there burst from the wooded cover a vigorous fire. It was answered by the Confederate infantry and every gun in reach. The Federal troops, creeping through the slashes, steadily advanced. Heavy shot crashed amid the fallen timber,

### SILENT AFTER TWO DAYS' WORK

Union Battery No. 1, Two Miles Below Yorktown.—This section of the Parrott guns was in the peach orchard of the Farenholdt House. Never had so heavy a battery been set up before in siege work. McClellan hoped by it to silence the "impregnable" water batteries of the Confederates by dropping shot and shell upon Yorktown wharf and within the defenses on the bluff. After two days of action it was rendered useless by the evacuation of Yorktown, and had to be transported up the river after the change of the base. The Farenholdt mansion, a handsome old Colonial structure, was just in the rear of this battery, and from its roof the work of the shells could be clearly observed. The good shots were cheered and the men stationed here were in holiday mood—no Confederate fire could reach them.

### THE SCENE OF YORKTOWN'S ONLY SURRENDER

Moore's House, about a Mile Southeast of the Town.—Near here, in 1781, Cornwallis laid down his arms to Washington and in this house the terms of the surrender which established the independence of America were drawn up. The damage to the house is the effect of the Revolutionary guns and not those of McClellan. The guns of Battery No. 1 fired their heavy shells over this house. Near here also many of the Continentals were buried, and across their graves and the old camp of Cornwallis's beleaguered troops the messengers of destruction hurtled through the air. The Federal fleet was anchored near where the Comte de Grasse's ships lay at the time of the surrender.

plowing the earth as it struck or, rebounding, tore through the branches of the wood in the rear. Slowly the Federals made their way across the field, targets for the Confederate sharpshooter. Two Union batteries, those of Webber and Bramhall, advanced to within seven hundred yards of the fort and began to play upon its walls.

Meanwhile there was seen emerging from a little ravine on the Union left a swarm of Confederates who opened at once a terrific fire. Giving their characteristic yell, they charged upon the Federals, pushing them back until the edge of the wood was again reached. There the Northerners halted, making a stand. Fresh troops came to their relief but they were insufficient. It seemed as if the Federals must give way. Both armies fought tenaciously. Neither would yield. The contest grew desperate. The Union brigades were being shattered. The last charges were made with ammunition taken from the cartridge boxes of fallen comrades.

Meanwhile "Fighting Phil" Kearny was hastening with his regiments over the bottomless roads of the Peninsula. They came most opportunely, and took the places of Hooker's tired and hungry men, who retreated in good order, leaving on the tree-strewn field seventeen hundred of their comrades, who had gone down before the Confederate fire.

On the York River side there had been no fighting during the early part of the day. But about noon, General Hancock, "the Superb," took his men near the river's bank and occupied two Confederate redoubts. Planting his batteries in these new positions, he began throwing shells into Fort Magruder. This new move of the Federals at once attracted the attention of the Confederates, and General Jubal A. Early, with the Fifth and Twenty-third North Carolina and the Twenty-fourth and Thirty-eighth Virginia regiments, was sent to intercept Hancock's movements. At the bank of a small stream, the Carolina regiments under General D. H. Hill halted to form in line. The intrepid Early did not wait,

THE DOOR TO YORKTOWN

Sallyport in the Center of the Southwestern Line of Entrenchments.—This commanded the road leading past Yorktown to Williamsburg, upon which the Confederates fell back as McClellan advanced after the evacuation. This view looks into the town and toward the river. The advancing Federals entered the city from the other side. The inhabitants, who had first hidden in their homes, flocked to the street corners as regiment after regiment swept into the town with colors flying and bands playing. Out through this gate the detachment marched in pursuit of the retreating Confederates, who made a strong stand at Williamsburg.

THE TOWN McCLELLAN THOUGHT WORTH A SIEGE

Near the Center of Yorktown.—Far from being the almost impregnable fortified city which McClellan appeared to think it, Yorktown was but a small village, to which the occupation by Cornwallis in 1781 had given an exaggerated strategic importance. It consisted chiefly of a single street, seen in the picture. Here a group of residents had gathered after the evacuation curious for a sight of the entering Union troops. A most remarkable thing to be noticed is the unharmed condition of most of the houses. The casualties among noncombatants were almost nothing. The food supply at this time was plentiful, the South as a whole had not begun to feel the pinch of hunger that it endured so bravely and so unflinchingly during the dark days of '64.

but riding at the head of the Twenty-fourth Virginia, rushed into the attack. Up across the field the column swept. On the crest of the hill stood Hancock's men—sixteen hundred strong—waiting for the charge. In front of his soldiers, with drawn sword, stood the man who later would display a similar courage on the field of Gettysburg. On came the Southerners' rush. The sword of Hancock gleamed in the light. Quick and decisive came the order to charge, and the trained soldiers, with the coolness of veterans, hurled themselves upon the Confederate column. Down by the stream, the gallant McRae of the Fifth North Carolina, seeing what was happening, dashed forward to take part in the fight. The Northern musketry fire sang in the afternoon air. So close did the opposing columns come to each other that the bayonets were used with deadly effect. The slaughter of the Fifth North Carolina regiment was appalling. The lines of the South began to waver, then broke and fled down the hill, leaving over five hundred men on the bloody field.

Now the sound of battle began to grow fainter in front of Fort Magruder. The Confederates were falling back behind its protecting walls. The Federal troops, wet and weary and hungry, slept on the field with their fallen comrades, and Hancock held undisputed sway during the starless night.

But it was not too dark for Longstreet's command to retreat once more in the direction of Richmond. It was a perilous road through the flat, swampy lowlands, with rain falling at every step of the way as they hastened toward the Chickahominy. The Union troops, too, had reason to remember this night as one of greatest suffering.

The next morning dawned in all the beauty of early May. The dead lay half buried in the mud. Many of the wounded had not yet been taken to the hospitals. But Williamsburg, the ancient capital of the Old Dominion, soon echoed with the tread of the hostile army as it swept through its quaint streets to the sound of martial music.

### THE GUNS THAT DID NOT TAKE THE TOWN

Federal Ordnance Ready for Transportation from Yorktown.—The artillery thus parked at the rear of the lower wharf was by no means all that McClellan deemed necessary to overcome the resistance at Yorktown. In the center are the Parrott guns. In the background, at the upper wharf, are the transports ready for the embarkation of the troops. The little mortars in the foreground were known as coehorns. They could be lifted by half a dozen men and transported by hand to any part of the entrenchments. Their range was only a few hundred yards, but with small charges they could quite accurately drop shells at almost a stone's throw. During the siege of Petersburg they were used by both armies. Here we see troops and artillery ready for the forward move. The Louisiana Tigers had been encamped here before McClellan's army took possession.

### LOADING THE TRANSPORTS

The Lower Wharf at Yorktown.—The steamer *Robert Morris* ready to depart, waiting for the embarkation of that portion of the Army of the Potomac which went up the York River to the mouth of the Pamunkey from Yorktown, May 6th, after the evacuation. Already the dismantling of both the Confederate and the Federal forts had begun. One sees gun-carriages, mortars, and tons of shot and shell, ready to be taken up the river for the operations against Richmond.

"ON TO RICHMOND!" NEAR CUMBERLAND, VIRGINIA, MAY, 1862. With Confederate opposition at Yorktown and Williamsburg broken down, the Army of the Potomac was now ready for the final rush upon Richmond. The gathering of the Union army of forty thousand men at White House, near Cumberland, was felt to be the beginning of the expected victorious advance. That part of the army not at York-town and Williamsburg was moved up the Peninsula as fast as the conditions of the road would permit. After the affair at Williamsburg the troops there joined the main army before the advance to the Chickahominy. Here we see but part of that camp—the first to be established on a large scale, in the Peninsula campaign—looking north at the bend of the Pamunkey.

THE FAR-STRETCHING ENCAMPMENT. (Cumberland Landing.) Three quarters of a mile from the landing, looking north toward the river. The distance is obscured by the haze of smoke from thousands of camp-fires. Every bit of dried wood had been collected and consumed, and standing timber was felled in all directions.

WHERE SUPPLIES WERE LANDED AT CUMBERLAND. The south bank of the Pamunkey, looking northwest across the lower camp. In this bend of the river was gathered the nondescript fleet of transports, steamers, barges, and schooners that conveyed Federal army supplies up to this point from Fortress Monroe, via York River.

HEADQUARTERS UNDER CANVAS. (Cumberland, May, 1862.) A photograph from a tree-top. Although a long distance from home, McClellan's army presented in the early days of its march up the Peninsula much of the panoply of war. The camera caught a cluster of officers' tents, probably the headquarters of a division or corps.

*Copyright by Patriot Pub. Co.*

ON THE BANKS OF THE PAMUNKEY. (Looking south from Cumberland Landing.) The ground here slopes down directly to the river. The supplies for the camps farther up the river were hauled along a well-traveled road which bisected this stretch of encampment. This road, called New Kent Road, was the main highway of the region and led to Richmond.

A VISTA OF THE FEDERAL CAMP. The Army of the Potomac waiting for the expected victorious advance on the Confederate capital. Yorktown had been evacuated on May 4th and Williamsburg abandoned on May 5th to the Union forces. During the week following, the divisions of Franklin, Sedgwick, Porter, and Richardson, after some opposition, gathered on the banks of the Pamunkey, the southern branch of the York River. Thence they marched toward White House, which—after communication with the divisions that had been fighting at Williamsburg, was established—became headquarters for the whole army. This panoramic view shows a part of the encampment.

IDLE DAYS AT CUMBERLAND. The farm-lands occupied by the impatient, waiting army were soon stripped of fences for firewood. The men sat idly about, discussing the situation. Everyone expected to be in Richmond before the end of June, and no one dreamed that the great campaign would come to nothing.

WAITING FOR ORDERS TO MOVE. (Cumberland, May, 1862.) During the ten days of inaction the soldiers rested after their heavy labors on the elaborate fortifications before Yorktown. The Confederate general, Magruder, had completely deceived McClellan as to the number of men under his command. The siege delayed the army a month.

THE CITY OF TENTS. The Army of the Potomac encamped in readiness for the forward movement on Richmond. These comfortable canvas houses were transported by the army wagons. The Confederates had no such complete shelter during the spring of 1862, which was remarkable for the inclemency of the weather.

[A—18]

HEADQUARTERS OF GENERAL McCLELLAN. (White House on the Pamunkey.) This house, the residence of W. H. F. Lee, son of General R. E. Lee, looked east over the river, which flows south at this point. It was burned in June, 1862, when the Federal army base was changed to the James River by order of General McClellan.

THE FORT THAT STOPPED A PANIC

In May, 1862, the news spread throughout Richmond that a Federal fleet of ironclads, led by the dread *Monitor*, was advancing up the James River. Panic at once seized upon the Confederate capital. The Government archives were shipped to Columbia, South Carolina, and every preparation was made to evacuate the city should the expedition against it succeed in passing up the James. Meanwhile the Confederate forces were working at Drewry's Bluff to establish a battery that would command the river. Earthworks were thrown up and guns were hastily gotten into position seven miles below Richmond. Sailing vessels were sunk in the channel; torpedoes were anchored, and every possible obstruction opposed to the approaching ironclads. When the *Monitor* and the *Galena* arrived they did not attempt to run the gantlet, and Richmond breathed freely again. These works ultimately formed Fort Darling.

In the foreground of the picture we see what a mass of missiles were hurled into the fort, at the heads of the doughty defenders of Richmond. The *Monitor*, the *Galena*, and the gunboats—when Fort Darling opened on them to dispute the passage of the river, May 15, 1862—responded with a rain of projectiles in an effort to silence the Confederate battery and make it possible to proceed up the James. The fort was not silenced, and the gunboats, thoroughly convinced of its strength, did not again seriously attempt to pass it. Fort Darling held the water approach to Richmond until the fall of Petersburg made it necessary for the Confederates to evacuate their capital. This picture was taken in April, 1865, after the fort had been abandoned, and while it was occupied by the First Connecticut Heavy Artillery. The cabin seen in the picture was the quarters of the regimental chaplain.

THE SHOWER OF SHOT AND SHELL

# PART III
## THE STRUGGLE FOR RICHMOND

———

# FAIR
# OAKS

———

A HAVEN FOR THE WOUNDED—THE "SEVEN PINES" FARM-HOUSE SERVING AS A HOSPITAL
FOR HOOKER'S DIVISION, SHORTLY AFTER THE BATTLE OF MAY 30—JUNE 1, 1862

### BRIDGING THE MORASS

From the necessity of getting an army across such barriers as this Chickahominy morass arise the most difficult problems of the army engineer. Here is shown Woodbury's Bridge, across the Chickahominy, named after its builder, which was flanked on either side by bottom lands, in some places forming a swamp stretching nearly a mile back from the stream proper. In the depths of this morass, surrounded by multitudes of reptiles, breathing the stagnant air, shrouded in a pall of mist, and accompanied by an immense orchestra of double-bass bullfrogs, the soldiers worked for weeks constructing causeways and bridges for the advance of the army toward Richmond, in 1862. The cutting of dams above, and the heavy rains, several times swept away the half-finished constructions, likewise the reserve material which had been gathered at immense cost in labor.

## A VICTORY OVER SWAMP AND FLOOD

Here we see the Fifth New Hampshire Infantry, reenforced by details from the Sixty-fourth New York and from the Irish Brigade, at work in the swamp strengthening the upper bridge across the Chickahominy so as to enable Sumner's troops to cross. The bridge had been completed on the night of May 29, 1862, and Colonel Cross, of the Fifth New Hampshire, was the first man to ride over it. The heavy rains on the night of May 30th had so loosened the supports that when Sumner led his troops across on the afternoon of May 31st only the weight of the cautiously marching column kept the logs in place. Sumner named it the Grapevine Bridge because of its tortuous course. It enabled his troops to turn the tide at Fair Oaks and ward off Federal defeat on the first day. After they had crossed much of the Grapevine Bridge was submerged by the rising flood of the Chickahominy.

## THE GUNS THAT GOT THERE.

Mud, according to Napoleon, is the fifth important element in war. Here we see the guns of Pettit's Battery, Company B, First New York Artillery, which had just conquered in a contest with mud. On the night of May 30th the swollen Chickahominy had swept away most of the recently constructed bridges. Some of the Federal Artillery had managed to get across, but the soil was so water-soaked that it was almost impossible to move the guns which were needed for the battle of the two following days. During the night of May 31st Pettit's command dragged their guns through the mud up from the river to Richardson's division on the right of the Federal line near the railroad; caisson and gun carriage had sunk to the very hubs, as their condition shows. Of all the artillery that had been ordered up these were the only guns able to answer at the dawn of June 1st.

## THE BELATED BATTERIES

Regulars Who Arrived Too Late at Fair Oaks. One can well imagine the feelings of the men and officers of these companies of the United States Artillery—Companies C, G, B and L of the reserve, who on the 31st of May could hear the battle raging on the south side of the flooded Chickahominy. The presence of regular troops in the early part of the war always steadied the volunteers. No men were so eager to bring their guns into action as these cannoneers. In the lower picture, to the left, we see part of Captain Robertson's batteries, Companies B and L, drawn up in a cornfield. Before the battle of Fair Oaks he had been attached to General Stoneman's cavalry column operating most of the time in the vicinity of New

Bridge, where the Artillery Reserve camp was at length established. To the right we see Batteries C and G (Gibson's) of the Third United States Artillery ready for action which was not renewed. McClellan's fatal pause had just begun, and here the artillery men so much needed during the two days' fighting are standing idly by, where they had been robbed by the river of the anticipated chance to distinguish themselves and with no further compensation for their disappointment than the diversion of having their pictures taken. Weeks of waiting were to follow before these batteries were to be again needed to do their share in holding back Lee's forces during the advance in the Seven Days' battles. Robertson's guns were in the thick of it at Gaines' Mill and the captain was complimented by General Porter for that day's work.

GIBSON'S BATTERY—ARTILLERY RESERVE

CAPTAIN GIBSON AND OFFICERS OF THE BATTERY THAT BORE HIS NAME

ROBERTSON'S BATTERY—ARTILLERY RESERVE

# FAIR OAKS OR SEVEN PINES

The Confederates, although decidedly successful on their right, had been, it is true, rudely checked on their left; but, in the battle considered as a whole, they not only had not been beaten, but they had driven their antagonists from their entrenchments in one part of the field, and they had guns, small arms, and colors to show as the trophies of their victory. The net result of the battle, in spite of the captured trophies, was undoubtedly favorable to the Federal arms. . . . It remained for General McClellan to utilize the forces at his disposal, to lead his large army of brave men, all of whom were devoted to him, to the achievement of the success which it would seem was really at this period of the campaign within his grasp.—*John C. Ropes, "The Story of the Civil War," Part II, The Campaigns of 1862.*

WITH Yorktown and Williamsburg inscribed upon its victorious banners, the Army of the Potomac took up again its toilsome march from Cumberland Landing toward the Confederate capital on the James. Its route lay along the Pamunkey, a sluggish stream, whose junction with the Mattapony forms the York. Not all the troops, however, were at Cumberland Landing and McClellan had first to bring up the remainder of his forces from Yorktown and Williamsburg. Some came by water up the York, some by land. The march was a picturesque one, through a magnificent country arrayed in all the gorgeousness of a Virginia spring, with its meadows of green set between the wooded hills. Dotted here and there could be seen the mansions of planters, with their slave quarters in the rear. The progress was necessarily slow, for the roads were next to impassable and the rains still continued at intervals.

It was the 16th of May, 1862, when the advanced corps reached White House, the ancestral home of the Lees. On

## TWO KEEPERS OF THE GOAL

The North expected General McClellan to possess himself of this citadel of the Confederacy in June, 1862, and it seemed likely the expectation would be realized. In the upper picture we get a near view of the State House at Richmond, part of which was occupied as a Capitol by the Confederate Congress during the war. In this building were stored the records and archives of the Confederate Government, many of which were

**THE GOAL—THE CONFEDERATE CAPITOL**

lost during the hasty retreat of President Davis and his cabinet at the evacuation of Richmond, April, 1865. Below, we see the city of Richmond from afar, with the Capitol standing out boldly on the hill. McClellan was not destined to reach this coveted goal, and it would not have meant the fall of the Confederacy had he then done so. When Lincoln entered the building in 1865, the Confederacy had been beaten as much by the blockade as by the operations of Grant and Sherman with vastly superior forces.

*Copyright by Patriot Pub. Co.*

### THE SPIRES OF RICHMOND

Here are the portraits of the two military leaders who were conspicuous in the Confederate attack upon McClellan's camp at Fair Oaks. General D. H. Hill did most of the fierce fighting which drove back the Federals on the first day, and only the timely arrival of Sumner's troops enabled the Federals to hold their ground. Had they failed they would have been driven into the morasses of the Chickahominy, retreat across which would have been difficult as the bridges were partly submerged by the swollen stream. After General Johnston was wounded, General G. W. Smith was in command during the second day's fighting.

**GENERAL G. W. SMITH, C. S. A.**

**GENERAL D. H. HILL, C. S. A.**

every side were fields of wheat, and, were it not for the presence of one hundred thousand men, there was the promise of a full harvest. It was here that General McClellan took up his headquarters, a distance of twenty-four miles from Richmond.

In the Confederate capital a panic had seized the people. As the retreating army of Johnston sought the environs of Richmond and news of the invading hosts was brought in, fear took possession of the inhabitants and many wild rumors were afloat as to the probable capture of the city. But it was not a fear that Johnston would not fight. The strategic policy of the Southern general had been to delay the advance of the Northern army. Fortunately for him, the rainy weather proved a powerful ally. The time had now come when he should change his position from the defensive to the offensive. The Army of Northern Virginia had been brought to bay, and it now turned to beat off the invaders and save its capital.

On the historic Peninsula lay two of the greatest and most splendid armies that had ever confronted each other on the field of battle. The engagement, now imminent, was to be the first in that series of contests, between the Army of the Potomac and the Army of Northern Virginia, ending three years thereafter, at Appomattox, when the war-worn veterans of gray should lay down their arms, in honor, to the war-worn veterans of blue.

The Union advance was retarded by the condition of the weather and the roads. Between McClellan's position at White House and the waiting Confederate army lay the Chickahominy, an erratic and sluggish stream, that spreads itself out in wooded swamps and flows around many islands, forming a valley from half a mile to a mile wide, bordered by low bluffs. In dry weather it is but a mere brook, but a moderate shower will cause it to rise quickly and to offer formidable opposition to any army seeking its passage. The valley is covered with trees whose tops reach to the level of

## FROM CAPTAIN TO BREVET MAJOR-GENERAL

John C. Tidball, Who Won His Spurs on the Peninsula. There is hardly a despatch that concerns the doings of the artillery in the Peninsula Campaign that does not mention the name of the gallant officer we see here leaning against his mud-spattered gun. Tidball's battery was the first to try for the position of honor on the artillery firing line and the last to retire. He was a graduate of West Point, class of '48, and like all West Pointers, was imbued with the slogan and motto of that cradle of soldiers, "Duty, Valor, Patriotism." He was appointed captain in '61 and given command of four rifled 10-pounder Parrotts and two 12-pounder smoothbores. Through the heavy roads he kept his guns well to the fore throughout all of the Peninsula Campaign. For his participation in the skirmish at New Bridge he was thrice mentioned in despatches. But previous to this he had been reported for gallantry at Blackburn's Ford in the first battle of Bull Run, his guns being the last of Barry's battery to limber up and retire in order. It was on the 23d of May that Tidball's guns swept the Confederate troops from New Bridge on the banks of the Chickahominy. His firing was so accurate and his men so well drilled that the discharge of his guns was spoken of as being so rapid as to be almost continuous. At Gaines' Mill Tidball and his guns won laurels. The artillery had begun the battle at about 11 o'clock, and it was their fight until nearly 3 o'clock in the afternoon of June 27th, when the fighting became general. The batteries were well in front and occupied a dangerous position, but despite the vigor of the attack the guns stayed where they were. General Sykes reported of the artillery this day: "The enemy's attack was frustrated mainly through the services of Captain Reade and Captain Tidball." Tidball emerged from the action with a brevet of major. He was brevetted lieut.-colonel for gallantry at Antietam on September 17th. At Gettysburg he commanded a brigade of horse artillery which he led in the Wilderness campaign, also, and was brevetted brigadier-general on August 1, 1864, brevetted major-general for gallant and meritorious services at Fort Stedman and Fort Sedgwick in the Petersburg campaign, and confirmed as a brigadier-general at the end of the war.

the adjacent highlands, thus forming a screen from either side. The bridges crossing it had all been destroyed by the retreating army except the one at Mechanicsville, and it was not an easy task that awaited the forces of McClellan as they made their way across the spongy soil.

The van of the Union army reached the Chickahominy on May 20th. The bridge was gone but the men under General Naglee forded the little river, reaching the plateau beyond, and made a bold reconnaissance before the Confederate lines. In the meantime, newly constructed bridges were beginning to span the Chickahominy, and the Federal army soon was crossing to the south bank of the river.

General McClellan had been promised reenforcements from the north. General McDowell with forty thousand men had started from Fredericksburg to join him north of the Chickahominy. For this reason, General McClellan had thrown the right wing of his army on the north of the river while his left would rest on the south side of the stream. This position of his army did not escape the eagle eye of the Confederate general, Joseph E. Johnston, who believed the time had now come to give battle, and perhaps destroy the small portion of the Union forces south of the river.

Meanwhile, General " Stonewall " Jackson, in the Shenandoah, was making threatening movements in the direction of Washington, and McDowell's orders to unite with McClellan were recalled.

The roads in and about Richmond radiate from that city like the spokes of a wheel. One of these is the Williamsburg stage-road, crossing the Chickahominy at Bottom's Bridge, only eleven miles from Richmond. It was along this road that the Federal corps of Keyes and Heintzelman had made their way. Their orders were " to go prepared for battle at a moment's notice " and " to bear in mind that the Army of the Potomac has never been checked."

Parallel to this road, and about a mile to the northward,

## THE ADVANCE THAT BECAME A RETREAT

Here, almost within sight of the goal (Richmond), we see McClellan's soldiers preparing the way for the passage of the army and its supplies. The soil along the Chickahominy was so marshy that in order to move the supply trains and artillery from the base at White House and across the river to the army, corduroy approaches to the bridges had to be built. It was well that the men got this early practice in road-building. Thanks to the work kept up, McClellan was able to unite the divided wings of the army almost at will.

## "REGULARS" NEAR FAIR OAKS—OFFICERS OF McCLELLAN'S HORSE ARTILLERY BRIGADE

These trained soldiers lived up to the promise in their firm-set features. Major Hays and five of his Lieutenants and Captains here—Pennington, Tidball, Hains, Robertson and Barlow—had, by '65, become general officers. From left to right (standing) are Edm. Pendleton, A. C. M. Pennington, Henry Benson, H. M. Gibson, J. M. Wilson, J. C. Tidball, W. N. Dennison; (sitting) P. C. Hains, H. C. Gibson, Wm. Hays, J. M. Robertson, J. W. Barlow; (on ground) R. H. Chapin, Robert Clarke, A. C. Vincent.

runs the Richmond and York River Railroad. Seven miles from Richmond another highway intersects the one from Williamsburg, known as the Nine Mile road. At the point of this intersection once grew a clump of seven pines, hence the name of "Seven Pines," often given to the battle fought on this spot. A thousand yards beyond the pines were two farmhouses in a grove of oaks. This was Fair Oaks Farm. Where the Nine Mile road crossed the railroad was Fair Oaks Station.

Southeast of Seven Pines was White Oak Swamp. Casey's division of Keyes' corps was stationed at Fair Oaks Farm. A fifth of a mile in front lay his picket line, extending crescent shape, from the swamp to the Chickahominy. Couch's division of the same corps was at Seven Pines, with his right wing extending along the Nine Mile road to Fair Oaks Station. Heintzelman's corps lay to the rear; Kearney's division guarded the railroad at Savage's Station and Hooker's the approaches to the White Oak Swamp. This formed three lines of defense. It was a well-wooded region and at this time was in many places no more than a bog. No sooner had these positions been taken, than trees were cut to form abatis, rifle-pits were hastily dug, and redoubts for placing artillery were constructed. The picket line lay along a dense growth of woods. Through an opening in the trees, the Confederate army could be seen in force on the other side of the clearing.

The plans of the Confederate general were well matured. On Friday, May 30th, he gave orders that his army should be ready to move at daybreak.

That night the "windows of heaven seemed to have been opened" and the "fountains of the deep broken up." The storm fell like a deluge. It was the most violent storm that had swept over that region for a generation. Throughout the night the tempest raged The thunderbolts rolled without cessation. The sky was white with the electric flashes. The earth was thoroughly drenched. The lowlands became a

CUSTER AND HIS CLASSMATE—NOW A CONFEDERATE PRISONER

Friends and even relatives who had been enlisted on opposite sides in the great Civil War met each other during its vicissitudes upon the battle-field. Here, caught by the camera, is one of the many instances. On the left sits Lieutenant J. B. Washington, C. S. A., who was an aide to General Johnston at Fair Oaks. Beside him sits Lieutenant George A. Custer, of the Fifth U. S. Cavalry, aide on McClellan's staff, later famous cavalry general and Indian fighter. Both men were West Point graduates and had attended the military academy together. On the morning of May 31, 1862, at Fair Oaks, Lieutenant Washington was captured by some of General Casey's pickets. Later in the day his former classmate ran across him and a dramatic meeting was thus recorded by the camera.

morass. From mud-soaked beds the soldiers arose the next morning to battle.

Owing to the storm the Confederates did not move so early as intended. However, some of the troops were in readiness by eight o'clock. Hour after hour the forces of Longstreet and Hill awaited the sound of the signal-gun that would tell them General Huger was in his position to march. Still they waited. It was near noon before General Hill, weary of waiting, advanced to the front, preceded by a line of skirmishers, along the Williamsburg road. The Union pickets were lying at the edge of the forest. The soldiers in the pits had been under arms for several hours awaiting the attack. Suddenly there burst through the woods the soldiers of the South. A shower of bullets fell beneath the trees and the Union pickets gave way. On and on came the lines of gray in close columns. In front of the abatis had been planted a battery of four guns. General Naglee with four regiments, the Fifty-sixth and One hundredth New York and Eleventh Maine and One hundred and fourth Pennsylvania, had gone forward, and in the open field met the attacking army. The contest was a stubborn one. Naglee's men charged with their bayonets and pressed the gray lines back again to the edge of the woods. Here they were met by a furious fire of musketry and quickly gave way, seeking the cover of the rifle-pits at Fair Oaks Farm. The Confederate infantrymen came rushing on.

But again they were held in check. In this position, for nearly three hours the Federals waged an unequal combat against three times their number. Then, suddenly a galling fire plowed in on them from the left. It came from Rains' brigade, which had executed a flank movement. At the same time the brigade of Rodes rushed toward them. The Federals saw the hopelessness of the situation. The officers at the batteries tried to spike their guns but were killed in the attempt. Hastily falling back, five guns were left to be turned on them

[ 290 ]

THE SLAUGHTER FIELD AT FAIR OAKS

Over this ground the fiercest fighting of the two days' battle took place, on May 31, 1862. Some 400 soldiers were buried here, where they fell, and their hastily dug graves appear plainly in the picture. In the redoubt seen just beyond the two houses was the center of the Federal line of battle, equi-distant, about a mile and a half, from both Seven Pines and Fair Oaks. The entrenchments near these farm dwellings were begun on May 28th by Casey's Division, 4th Corps. There was not time to finish them before the Confederate attack opened the battle, and the artillery of Casey's Division was hurriedly placed in position behind the incomplete works.

THE UNFINISHED REDOUBT

In the smaller picture we see the inside of the redoubt at the left background of the picture above. The scene is just before the battle and picks and shovels were still busy throwing up the embankments to strengthen this center of the Federal defense. Casey's artillery was being hurriedly brought up. In the background General Sickles' Brigade appears drawn up in line of battle. When the Confederates first advanced Casey's artillery did telling work, handsomely repelling the attack early in the afternoon of May 31st. Later in the day Confederate sharpshooters from vantage points in neighboring trees began to pick off the officers and the gunners and the redoubt had to be relinquished. The abandoned guns were turned against the retreating Federals.

Copyright by Patriot Pub. Co.

THE "REDHOT BATTERY"

On the afternoon of May 31st, at Fair Oaks, the Confederates were driving the Federal soldiers through the woods in disorder when this battery (McCarthy's) together with Miller's battery opened up with so continuous and severe a fire that the Federals were able to make a stand and hold their own for the rest of the day. The guns grew so hot from constant firing that it was only with the greatest care that they could be swabbed and loaded. These earthworks were thrown up for McCarthy's Battery, Company C, 1st Pennsylvania Artillery, near Savage's Station. The soldiers nicknamed it the "Redhot Battery."

in their retreat. This move was not too soon. In another minute they would have been entirely surrounded and captured. The gray lines pressed on. The next stand would be made at Seven Pines, where Couch was stationed. The forces here had been weakened by sending relief to Casey. The situation of the Federals was growing critical. At the same time General Longstreet sent reenforcements to General Hill. Couch was forced out of his position toward the right in the direction of Fair Oaks Station and was thus separated from the main body of the army, then in action.

The Confederates pushed strongly against the Federal center. Heintzelman came to the rescue. The fight waged was a gallant one. For an hour and a half the lines of blue and gray surged back and forth. The Federals were gradually giving way. The left wing, alone, next to the White Oak Swamp, was holding its own.

At the same time over at Fair Oaks Station whither Couch had been forced, were new developments. He was about to strike the Confederate army on its left flank, but just when the guns were being trained, there burst across the road the troops of General G. W. Smith, who up to this time had been inactive. These men were fresh for the fight, superior in number, and soon overpowered the Northerners. It looked for a time as if the whole Union army south of the Chickahominy was doomed.

Over at Seven Pines the center of McClellan's army was about to be routed. Now it was that General Heintzelman personally collected about eighteen hundred men, the fragments of the broken regiments, and took a decided stand at the edge of the timber. He was determined not to give way. But this alone would not nor did not save the day. To the right of this new line of battle, there was a rise of ground. From here the woods abruptly sloped to the rear. If this elevation were once secured by the Confederates, all would be lost and rout would be inevitable. The quick eye of General

## A VETERAN OF THREE WARS

General Silas Casey at Fair Oaks. Three years before General Lee had left West Point, Silas Casey had been graduated. He was fifty-four years old when the war began. Active service in two exacting campaigns had aged him in appearance, but not in efficiency. He had been with General Worth at Florida in the Seminole War and under Scott at Mexico and had fought the Indians on the Pacific Coast. At Fair Oaks the old veteran's division, after fighting bravely through the woods, was driven back, for it received the whole brunt of the first Confederate attack. The bravely advancing Confederates had gained possession of his camp before supports could reach him.

GENERAL SILAS CASEY

## TWO LEADERS OF THE FOREFRONT

In the center of this group sits General Naglee. At Fair Oaks his troops had rushed to arms in the dark gloom of that cloudy day, the 31st of May. The woods before his forces were filled with sharpshooters, and back of them, massing on his front, came overpowering numbers. Fighting stubbornly, contesting every inch, General Naglee was driven back to the protection of McCarthy's battery near Savage's Station. Twice during the action had Naglee placed himself personally at the head of his men in the firing line. General Stoneman is handing a note to an orderly. Before the battle of Fair Oaks, he had conducted the successful raids against the railroad. At Hanover Court House Stoneman's riders were opposed to those of the great Stuart.

GENERAL NAGLEE AND THE CAVALRY GENERAL STONEMAN AT FAIR OAKS

Keyes took in the situation. He was stationed on the left; to reach the hill would necessitate taking his men between the battle-lines. The distance was nearly eight hundred yards. Calling on a single regiment to follow he made a dash for the position. The Southern troops, divining his intention, poured a deadly volley into his ranks and likewise attempted to reach this key to the situation. The Federals gained the spot just in time. The new line was formed as a heavy mass of Confederates came upon them. The tremendous Union fire was too much for the assaulting columns, which were checked. They had forced the Federal troops back from their entrenchments a distance of two miles, but they never got farther than these woods. The river fog now came up as the evening fell and the Southern troops spent the night in the captured camps, sleeping on their arms. The Federals fell back toward the river to an entrenched camp.

Meanwhile at Fair Oaks Station the day was saved, too, in the nick of time, for the Federals. On the north side of the Chickahominy were stationed the two divisions of Sedgwick and Richardson, under command of General Sumner. Scarcely had the battle opened when McClellan at his headquarters, six miles away, heard the roar and rattle of artillery. He was sick at the time, but he ordered General Sumner to be in readiness. At this time there were four bridges across the river—two of them were Bottom's Bridge and the railroad bridge. To go by either of these would consume too much time in case of an emergency. General Sumner had himself constructed two more bridges, lying between the others. The heavy flood of the preceding night, which was still rising, had swept one of these partially away. In order to save time, he put his men under arms and marched them to the end of the upper bridge and there waited throughout the greater part of the afternoon for orders to cross. Before them rolled a muddy and swollen stream, above whose flood was built a rude and unstable structure. From the other side

Not long after this picture was taken, the names of most of these men were mentioned in despatches. Against Major D. H. Van Valkenburgh, the gallant soldier leaning on his saber, his arm thrust into his coat, was written, "killed in action at Fair Oaks." He helped to make the name of the First New York Light Artillery a proud one; and next to him stands Major Luther Kieffer. Perhaps the youngest, who is standing next, is Adjutant Rumsey, who by firing his guns so continuously helped save the wing of the Second Army Corps. He was wounded but recovered. Next to him, looking straight at the camera, is Lieut.-Colonel Henry E. Turner; and standing nearest to the tent is Major C. S. Wainright, who won his spurs at Williamsburg, and again proved the metal he was made of at Fair Oaks. Seated in the camp chair is Colonel Guilford T. Bailey, who later died beside his guns. It rained during the days that preceded Fair Oaks. It was the treacherous River Chickahominy that helped to baffle the

FIGHTING OFFICERS OF THE FIRST NEW YORK LIGHT ARTILLERY

well-laid plans of the Federal commander. Well did the Confederate leaders know that with the downpour then falling the stream would rise. Not immediately, but within the next few hours it would gain strength until at last it became a sweeping torrent. All this proved true; only a part of McClellan's army had crossed the river when the Confederates moved to attack, May 31st. Let the Prince de Joinville, who was a spectator, describe the guns that helped to save the day. "They are not those rifled cannon, the objects of extravagant admiration of late, good for cool firing and long range; these are the true guns for a fight—12-pound howitzers (Napoleons), the old pattern, throwing round projectiles or heavy charges of grape and canister. The simple and rapid discharging of these pieces makes terrible havoc in the opposing ranks. In vain Johnston sends against this battery his best troops—those of South Carolina, the Hampton legion among others, in vain he rushes on it himself; nothing can shake the line!"

TWENTY-POUND PARROTT RIFLED GUNS OF THE FIRST NEW YORK

could be distinctly heard the roar of battle. The fate of the day and of the Army of the Potomac rested upon these men at the end of the bridge.

The possibility of crossing was doubted by everyone, including the general himself. The bridge had been built of logs, held together and kept from drifting by the stumps of trees. Over the river proper it was suspended by ropes attached to trees, felled across the stream.

At last the long-expected order to advance came. The men stepped upon the floating bridge. It swayed to and fro as the solid column passed over it. Beneath the men was the angry flood which would engulf all if the bridge should fall. Gradually the weight pressed it down between the solid stumps and it was made secure till the army had crossed. Had the passage been delayed another hour the flood would have rendered it impassable.

Guided by the roar of battle the troops hurried on. The artillery was left behind in the mud of the Chickahominy. The steady, rolling fire of musketry and the boom of cannon told of deadly work in front. It was nearly six o'clock before Sedgwick's column deployed into line in the rear of Fair Oaks Station. They came not too soon. Just now there was a lull in the battle. The Confederates were gathering themselves for a vigorous assault on their opponents' flaming front. Their lines were re-forming. General Joseph E. Johnston himself had immediate command. President Jefferson Davis had come out from his capital to witness the contest. Rapidly the Confederates moved forward. A heavy fusillade poured from their batteries and muskets. Great rents were made in the line of blue. It did not waver. The openings were quickly filled and a scorching fire was sent into the approaching columns. Again and again the charge was repeated only to be repulsed. Then came the order to fix bayonets. Five regiments—Thirty-fourth and Eighty-second New York, Fifteenth and Twentieth Massachusetts and Seventh Michigan

SUMNER IN THE FIELD—A GENERAL FULL OF YEARS AND HONORS.

Not many men distinguished in the war could look back upon forty-two years of actual service at the outbreak of hostilities.  But such was the case with General Edwin V. Sumner.  He stands above in the Peninsula Campaign, at St. Peter's church, near New Kent Court House, Virginia, not far from White House Landing.  In this sacred edifice George Washington had worshiped.  When this picture was taken Sumner was one year past the age when generals of the present day are deemed too old for service.  Commanding the Second Army Corps in the Peninsula Campaign, he was twice wounded; and again, leading his men at Antietam, once more he was struck.  He fought again at Fredericksburg, but died from the effects of his wounds in March, 1863.  The group above from the left, includes Maj. A. M. Clark, Volunteer A. D. C.; Lieut.-Col. J. H. Taylor, A. G.; Capt. F. N. Clarke, Chief of Artillery; General Sumner; Lieut.-Col. J. F. Hammond, Medical Director; Captain Pease, Minnesota Volunteers, Chief Commissary; Capt. Gabriel Grant.

—pushed to the front. Into the woods where the Confederates had fallen back the charge was made. Driving the Southern lines back in confusion, these dashing columns saved the day for the Army of the Potomac.

Night was now settling over the wooded field. Here and there flashes of light could be seen among the oaks, indicating a diligent search for the wounded. General Johnston ordered his troops to sleep on the field. A few minutes later he was struck by a rifle-ball and almost immediately a shell hit him, throwing him from his horse, and he was borne off the field. The first day of the battle was over.

The disability of the Southern commander made it possible for the promotion of a new leader upon whom the fortunes of the Army of Northern Virginia would soon rest. This was General Robert E. Lee; although the immediate command for the next day's contest fell upon General G. W. Smith. Early Sunday morning the battle was again in progress. The command of Smith, near Fair Oaks Station, advanced down the railroad, attacking Richardson, whose lines were north of it and were using the embankment as a fortification. Longstreet's men were south of the railroad. The firing was heavy all along this line, the opposing forces being not more than fifty yards from each other. For an hour and a half the musketry fire was intensely heavy. It was, indeed, a continuous roar. The line of gray could not withstand the galling fire and for the first time that day fell back. But the Union line had been broken, too. A brief lull ensued. Both sides were gathering themselves for another onslaught. It was then that there were heard loud shouts from the east of the railroad.

There, coming through the woods, was a large body of Federal troops. They were the men of Hooker. They formed a magnificent body of soldiers and seemed eager for the fray. Turning in on the Williamsburg road they rapidly deployed to the right and the left. In front of them was an open field, with a thick wood on the other side. The Confederates had

AIMING THE GUNS AT FAIR OAKS.

Here we see the beginning of the lull in the fighting of the second day at Fair Oaks, which it has been asserted led to a fatal delay and the ruin of McClellan's Peninsula Campaign. The first day's battle at Fair Oaks, May 31, 1862, was decidedly a Federal reverse which would have developed into a rout had not Sumner, crossing his troops on the perilous Grapevine Bridge, come up in time to rally the retreating men. Here we see some of them within the entrenchments at Fair Oaks Station on the Richmond, & York River Railroad. The order will soon come to cease firing at the end of the second day's fighting, the result of which was to drive the Confederates back to Richmond. McClellan did not pursue. The heavy rainstorm on the night of May 30th had made the movement of artillery extremely difficult, and McClellan waited to complete the bridges and build entrenchments before advancing. This delay gave the Confederates time to reorganize their forces and place them under the new commander, Robert E. Lee, who while McClellan lay inactive effected a junction with "Stonewall" Jackson. Then during the Seven Days' Battles Lee steadily drove McClellan from his position, within four or five miles of Richmond, to a new position on the James River. From this secure and advantageous water base McClellan planned a new line of advance upon the Confederate Capital. In the smaller picture we see the interior of the works at Fair Oaks Station, which were named Fort Sumner in honor of the General who brought up his Second Corps and saved the day. The camp of the Second Corps is seen beyond the fortifications to the right.

FORT SUMNER, NEAR FAIR OAKS

posted themselves in this forest and were waiting for their antagonists. The Federals marched upon the field in double-quick time; their movements became a run, and they began firing as they dashed forward. They were met by a withering fire of field artillery and a wide gap being opened in their ranks. It immediately filled. They reached the edge of the woods and as they entered its leafy shadows the tide of battle rolled in with them. The front line was lost to view in the forest, except for an occasional gleam of arms from among the trees. The din and the clash and roar of battle were heard for miles. Bayonets were brought into use. It was almost a hand-to-hand combat in the heavy forest and tangled slashings. The sound of battle gradually subsided, then ceased except for the intermittent reports of small arms, and the second day's fight was over.

The Confederate forces withdrew toward Richmond. The Federal troops could now occupy without molestation the positions they held the previous morning. The forest paths were strewn with the dead and the dying. Many of the wounded were compelled to lie under the scorching sun for hours before help reached them. Every farmhouse became an improvised hospital where the suffering soldiers lay. Many were placed upon cars and taken across the Chickahominy. The dead horses were burned. The dead soldiers, blue and gray, found sometimes lying within a few feet of each other, were buried on the field of battle. The two giants had met in their first great combat and were even now beginning to gird up their loins for a desperate struggle before the capital of the Confederacy.

PART III

THE STRUGGLE FOR RICHMOND

# IN THE
# SHENANDOAH
# VALLEY

JUNE, 1862—McCLELLAN'S MEN DRILLING WITHIN FIVE MILES OF RICHMOND,
IGNORANT OF JACKSON'S MOVEMENTS FROM THE VALLEY, SO SOON TO RESULT
IN THEIR REPULSE—RICHARDSON'S ENTRENCHMENTS SOUTH OF FORT SUMNER

## MEN JACKSON COULD AFFORD TO LOSE

These two hundred Confederate soldiers captured the day after "Stonewall" Jackson's victory at Front Royal, were an insignificant reprisal for the damage done to the Federal cause by that dashing and fearless Confederate leader. When Richmond was threatened both by land and water in May, 1862, Johnston sent Jackson to create a diversion and alarm the Federal capital. Rushing down the Valley of the Shenandoah, his forces threatened to cut off and overwhelm those of General Banks, who immediately began a retreat. It became a race between the two armies down the Valley toward Winchester and Harper's Ferry. Forced marches, sometimes as long as thirty-five miles a day, were the portion of both during the four weeks in which Jackson led his forces after the retreating

CONFEDERATE PRISONERS CAPTURED IN THE SHENANDOAH

Federals, engaging them in six actions and two battles, in all of which he came off victorious. Just after these prisoners were taken, Banks was driven back to the Potomac. Once more a panic spread through the North, and both the troops of Banks and McDowell were held in the vicinity of Washington for its defense. But Jackson's purpose was accomplished. He had held Banks in the Shenandoah Valley until McClellan's Peninsula Campaign was well advanced. Then again by forced marches his men disappeared up the Valley to join Lee in teaching the overconfident Union administration that Richmond was not to be won without long and costly fighting. But a year later the Confederacy lost this astonishing military genius.

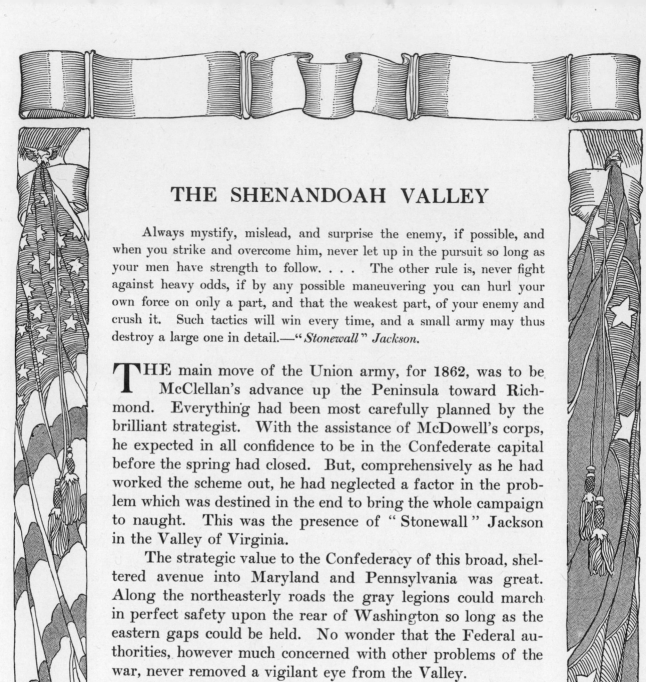

# THE SHENANDOAH VALLEY

Always mystify, mislead, and surprise the enemy, if possible, and when you strike and overcome him, never let up in the pursuit so long as your men have strength to follow. . . . The other rule is, never fight against heavy odds, if by any possible maneuvering you can hurl your own force on only a part, and that the weakest part, of your enemy and crush it. Such tactics will win every time, and a small army may thus destroy a large one in detail.—*"Stonewall" Jackson.*

THE main move of the Union army, for 1862, was to be McClellan's advance up the Peninsula toward Richmond. Everything had been most carefully planned by the brilliant strategist. With the assistance of McDowell's corps, he expected in all confidence to be in the Confederate capital before the spring had closed. But, comprehensively as he had worked the scheme out, he had neglected a factor in the problem which was destined in the end to bring the whole campaign to naught. This was the presence of " Stonewall " Jackson in the Valley of Virginia.

The strategic value to the Confederacy of this broad, sheltered avenue into Maryland and Pennsylvania was great. Along the northeasterly roads the gray legions could march in perfect safety upon the rear of Washington so long as the eastern gaps could be held. No wonder that the Federal authorities, however much concerned with other problems of the war, never removed a vigilant eye from the Valley.

Jackson had taken possession of Winchester, near the foot of the Valley, in November, 1861. He then had about ten thousand men. The Confederate army dwindled greatly during the winter. At the beginning of March there were but forty-five hundred men. With Banks and his forty thousand now on Virginia soil at the foot of the Valley, and Fremont's

## "STONEWALL" JACKSON
## AT WINCHESTER
### 1862

It is the great good fortune of American hero-lovers that they can gaze here upon the features of Thomas Jonathan Jackson precisely as that brilliant Lieutenant-General of the Confederate States Army appeared during his masterly "Valley Campaign" of 1862. Few photographers dared to approach this man, whose silence and modesty were as deep as his mastery of warfare. Jackson lived much to himself. Indeed, his plans were rarely known even to his immediate subordinates, and herein lay the secret of those swift and deadly surprises that raised him to first rank among the world's military figures. Jackson's ability and efficiency won the utter confidence of his ragged troops; and their marvelous forced marches, their contempt for privations if under his guidance, put into his hands a living weapon such as no other leader in the mighty conflict had ever wielded.

army approaching the head, why should the Federal commander even think about this insignificant fragment of his foe? But the records of war have shown that a small force, guided by a master mind, sometimes accomplishes more in effective results than ten times the number under a less active and able commander.

The presence of Banks compelled Jackson to withdraw to Woodstock, fifty miles south of Winchester. If McClellan ever experienced any anxiety as to affairs in the Valley, it seems to have left him now, for he ordered Banks to Manassas on March 16th to cover Washington, leaving General Shields and his division of seven thousand men to hold the Valley. When Jackson heard of the withdrawal, he resolved that, cut off as he was from taking part in the defense of Richmond, he would do what he could to prevent any aggrandizement of McClellan's forces.

Shields hastened to his station at Winchester, and Jackson, on the 23d of March, massed his troops at Kernstown, about three miles south of the former place. Deceived as to the strength of his adversary, he led his weary men to an attack on Shields' right flank about three o'clock in the afternoon. He carried the ridge where the Federals were posted, but the energy of his troops was spent, and they had to give way to the reserves of the Union army after three hours of stubborn contest. The Federal ranks were diminished by six hundred; the Confederate force by more than seven hundred. Kernstown was a Union victory; yet never in history did victory bring such ultimate disaster upon the victors.

At Washington the alarm was intense over Jackson's audacious attack. Williams' division of Banks' troops was halted on its way to Manassas and sent back to Winchester. Mr. Lincoln transferred Blenker's division, nine thousand strong, to Fremont. These things were done at once, but they were by no means the most momentous consequence of Kernstown. The President began to fear that Jackson's goal was

McDOWELL AND McCLELLAN—TWO UNION LEADERS WHOSE
PLANS "STONEWALL" JACKSON FOILED

In General McClellan's plan for the Peninsula Campaign of 1862, General McDowell, with the First Army Corps of 37,000 men, was assigned a most important part, that of joining him before Richmond. Lincoln had reluctantly consented to the plan, fearing sufficient protection was not provided for Washington. By the battle of Kernstown, March 23d, in the Valley of Virginia, Jackson, though defeated, so alarmed the Administration that McDowell was ordered to remain at Manassas to protect the capital. The reverse at Kernstown was therefore a real triumph for Jackson, but with his small force he had to keep up the game of holding McDowell, Banks, and Frémont from reënforcing McClellan. If he failed, 80,000 troops might move up to Richmond from the west while McClellan was approaching from the North. But Jackson, on May 23d and 25th, surprised Banks' forces at Front Royal and Winchester, forcing a retreat to the Potomac. At the news of this event McDowell was ordered not to join McClellan in front of Richmond.

Washington. After consulting six of his generals he became convinced that McClellan had not arranged proper protection for the city. Therefore, McDowell and his corps of thirty-seven thousand men were ordered to remain at Manassas. The Valley grew to greater importance in the Federal eyes. Banks was made entirely independent of McClellan and the defense of this region became his sole task. McClellan, to his great chagrin, saw his force depleted by forty-six thousand men. There were now four Union generals in the East operating independently one of the other.

General Ewell with eight thousand troops on the upper Rappahannock and General Johnson with two brigades were now ordered to cooperate with Jackson. These reenforcements were badly needed. Schenck and Milroy, of Fremont's corps, began to threaten Johnson. Banks, with twenty thousand, was near Harrisonburg.

The Confederate leader left General Ewell to watch Banks while he made a dash for Milroy and Schenck. He fought them at McDowell on May 8th and they fled precipitately to rejoin Fremont. The swift-acting Jackson now darted at Banks, who had fortified himself at Strasburg. Jackson stopped long enough to be joined by Ewell. He did not attack Strasburg, but stole across the Massanutten Mountain unknown to Banks, and made for Front Royal, where a strong Union detachment was stationed under Colonel Kenly. Early on the afternoon of May 23d, Ewell rushed from the forest. Kenly and his men fled before them toward Winchester. A large number were captured by the cavalry before they had gotten more than four miles away.

Banks at Strasburg realized that Jackson was approaching from the rear, the thing he had least expected and had made no provision for. His fortifications protected his front alone. There was nothing to be done but retreat to Winchester. Even that was prevented by the remarkable speed of Jackson's men, who could march as much as thirty-five

## THE GERMAN DIVISION SENT AGAINST JACKSON

Blenker's division, composed of three brigades of German volunteers, was detached from the Army of the Potomac in March, 1862, to assist Frémont in his operations against Jackson. The German troops were but poorly equipped, many of them carrying old-pattern Belgian and Austrian muskets. When they united with Frémont he was obliged to rearm them with Springfield rifles from his own stores. When the combined forces met Jackson and Ewell at Cross Keys, five of Blenker's regiments were sent forward to the first attack. In the picture Brigadier-General Louis Blenker is standing, with his hand on his belt, before the door. At his left is Prince Felix Salm-Salm, a Prussian military officer, who joined the Federal army as a colonel of volunteers. At the right of Blenker is General Stahel, who led the advance of the Federal left at Cross Keys.

miles a day. On May 24th, the Confederates overtook and struck the receding Union flank near Newtown, inflicting heavy loss and taking many prisoners. Altogether, three thousand of Banks' men fell into Jackson's hands.

This exploit was most opportune for the Southern arms. It caused the final ruin of McClellan's hopes. Banks received one more attack from Ewell's division the next day as he passed through Winchester on his way to the shelter of the Potomac. He crossed at Williamsport late the same evening and wrote the President that his losses, though serious enough, might have been far worse "considering the very great disparity of forces engaged, and the long-matured plans of the enemy, which aimed at nothing less than entire capture of our force." Mr. Lincoln now rescinded his resolution to send McDowell to McClellan. Instead, he transferred twenty thousand of the former's men to Fremont and informed McClellan that he was not, after all, to have the aid of McDowell's forty thousand men.

Fremont was coming from the west; Shields lay in the other direction, but Jackson was not the man to be trapped. He managed to hold Fremont while he marched his main force quickly up the Valley. At Port Republic he drove Carroll's brigade of Shields' division away and took possession of a bridge which Colonel Carroll had neglected to burn. Fremont in pursuit was defeated by Ewell at Cross Keys. Jackson immediately put his force of twelve thousand over the Shenandoah at Port Republic and burned the bridge. Safe from the immediate attack by Fremont, he fell upon Tyler and Carroll, who had not more than three thousand men between them. The Federals made a brave stand, but after many hours' fighting were compelled to retreat. Jackson emerged through Swift Run Gap on the 17th of June, to assist in turning the Union right on the Peninsula, and Banks and Shields, baffled and checkmated at every move, finally withdrew from the Valley.

# THE
# SEVEN DAYS'
# BATTLES

VIEW ON THE JAMES, THE RIVER TO WHICH McCLELLAN DECIDED TO
SWING HIS BASE ON THE FIRST OF THE SEVEN DAYS, JUNE 26, 1862—NOT
SIX WEEKS BEFORE, THE GUN SHOWN HAD HELPED TO REPEL THE UNION
GUNBOATS THAT ENDEAVORED TO OPEN McCLELLAN'S WAY TO RICHMOND

# THE SEVEN DAYS' BATTLES

McClellan's one hope, one purpose, was to march his army out of the swamps and escape from the ceaseless Confederate assaults to a point on James River where the resistless fire of the gunboats might protect his men from further attack and give them a chance to rest. To that end, he retreated night and day, standing at bay now and then as the hunted stag does, and fighting desperately for the poor privilege of running away.

And the splendid fighting of his men was a tribute to the skill and genius with which he had created an effective army out of what he had described as "regiments cowering upon the banks of the Potomac, some perfectly raw, others dispirited by recent defeat, others going home." Out of a demoralized and disorganized mass reenforced by utterly untrained civilians, McClellan had within a few months created an army capable of stubbornly contesting every inch of ground even while effecting a retreat the very thought of which might well have disorganized an army. —*George Cary Eggleston, in "The History of the Confederate War."*

GENERAL LEE was determined that the operations in front of Richmond should not degenerate into a siege, and that the Army of Northern Virginia should no longer be on the defensive. To this end, early in the summer of 1862, he proceeded to increase his fighting force so as to make it more nearly equal in number to that of his antagonist. Every man who could be spared from other sections of the South was called to Richmond. Numerous earthworks soon made their appearance along the roads and in the fields about the Confederate capital, giving the city the appearance of a fortified camp. The new commander in an address to the troops said that the army had made its last retreat.

Meanwhile, with the spires of Richmond in view, the Army of the Potomac was acclimating itself to a Virginia summer. The whole face of the country for weeks had been a

JOHNSTON AND LEE—A PHOTOGRAPH OF 1869.

These men look enough alike to be brothers. They were so in arms, at West Point, in Mexico and throughout the war. General Joseph E. Johnston (on the left), who had led the Confederate forces since Bull Run, was wounded at Fair Oaks. That wound gave Robert E. Lee (on the right) his opportunity to act as leader. After Fair Oaks, Johnston retired from the command of the army defending Richmond. The new commander immediately grasped the possibilities of the situation which confronted him. The promptness and completeness with which he blighted McClellan's high hopes of reaching Richmond showed at one stroke that the Confederacy had found its great general. It was only through much sifting that the North at last picked military leaders that could rival him in the field.

veritable bog. Now that the sweltering heat of June was coming on, the malarious swamps were fountains of disease. The polluted waters of the sluggish streams soon began to tell on the health of the men. Malaria and typhoid were prevalent; the hospitals were crowded, and the death rate was appalling.

Such conditions were not inspiring to either general or army. McClellan was still hoping for substantial reenforcements. McDowell, with his forty thousand men, had been promised him, but he was doomed to disappointment from that source. Yet in the existing state of affairs he dared not be inactive. South of the Chickahominy, the army was almost secure from surprise, owing to well-protected rifle-pits flanked by marshy thickets or covered with felled trees. But the Federal forces were still divided by the fickle stream, and this was a constant source of anxiety to the commander. He proceeded to transfer all of his men to the Richmond side of the river, excepting the corps of Franklin and Fitz John Porter. About the middle of June, General McCall with a force of eleven thousand men joined the Federal army north of the Chickahominy, bringing the entire fighting strength to about one hundred and five thousand. So long as there remained the slightest hope of additional soldiers, it was impossible to withdraw all of the army from the York side of the Peninsula, and it remained divided.

That was a brilliant initial stroke of the Confederate general when he sent his famous cavalry leader, J. E. B. Stuart, with about twelve hundred Virginia troopers, to encircle the army of McClellan. Veiling his intentions with the utmost secrecy, Stuart started June 12, 1862, in the direction of Fredericksburg as if to reenforce " Stonewall " Jackson. The first night he bivouacked in the pine woods of Hanover. No fires were kindled, and when the morning dawned, his men swung upon their mounts without the customary bugle-call of " Boots and Saddles." Turning to the east, he surprised and captured a Federal picket; swinging around a corner of the road, he

THE FLEET THAT FED THE ARMY

*Copyright by Patriot Pub. Co.*

THE ABANDONED BASE

White House, Virginia, June 27, 1862.—Up the James and the Pamunkey to White House Landing came the steam and sailing vessels laden with supplies for McClellan's second attempt to reach Richmond. Tons of ammunition and thousands of rations were sent forward from here to the army on the Chickahominy in June, 1862. A short month was enough to cause McClellan to again change his plans, and the army base was moved to the James River. The Richmond and York Railroad was lit up by burning cars along its course to the Chickahominy. Little was left to the Confederates save the charred ruins of the White House itself.

suddenly came upon a squadron of Union cavalry. The Confederate yell rent the air and a swift, bold charge by the Southern troopers swept the foe on.

They had not traveled far when they came again to a force drawn up in columns of fours, ready to dispute the passage of the road. This time the Federals were about to make the charge. A squadron of the Confederates moved forward to meet them. Some Union skirmishers in their effort to get to the main body of their troops swept into the advancing Confederates and carried the front ranks of the squadron with them. These isolated Confederates found themselves in an extremely perilous position, being gradually forced into the Federal main body. Before they could extricate themselves, nearly every one in the unfortunate front rank was shot or cut down.

The Southern cavalrymen swept on and presently found themselves nearing the York River Railroad—McClellan's supply line. As they approached Tunstall's Station they charged down upon it, with their characteristic yell, completely surprising a company of Federal infantry stationed there. These at once surrendered. Telegraph wires were cut and a tree felled across the track to obstruct the road. This had hardly been done before the shriek of a locomotive was heard. A train bearing Union troops came thundering along, approaching the station. The engineer, taking in the situation at a glance, put on a full head of steam and made a rush for the obstruction, which was easily brushed aside. As the train went through a cut the Confederates fired upon it, wounding and killing many of the Federal soldiers in the cars.

Riding all through a moonlit night, the raiders reached Sycamore Ford of the Chickahominy at break of day. As usual this erratic stream was overflowing its banks. They started to ford it, but finding that it would be a long and wearisome task, a bridge was hastily improvised at another place where the passage was made with more celerity. Now,

ELLERSON'S MILL—WHERE HILL ASSAULTED.

Not until after nightfall of June 26, 1862, did the Confederates of General A. P. Hill's division cease their assaults upon this position where General McCall's men were strongly entrenched. Time after time the Confederates charged over the ground we see here at Ellerson's Mill, near Mechanicsville. Till 9 o'clock at night they continued to pour volleys at the position, and then at last withdrew. The victory was of little use to the Federals, for Jackson on the morrow, having executed one of the flanking night marches at which he was an adept, fell upon the Federal rear at Gaines' Mill.

THE WASTE OF WAR

Railroad trains loaded with tons of food and ammunition were run deliberately at full speed off the embankment shown in the left foreground. They plunged headlong into the waters of the Pamunkey. This was the readiest means that McClellan could devise for keeping his immense quantity of stores out of the hands of the Confederates in his hasty change of base from White House to the James after Gaines' Mill. This was the bridge of the Richmond and York River Railroad, and was destroyed June 28, 1862, to render the railroad useless to the Confederates.

on the south bank of the river, haste was made for the confines of Richmond, where, at dawn of the following day, the troopers dropped from their saddles, a weary but happy body of cavalry.

Lee thus obtained exact and detailed information of the position of McClellan's army, and he laid out his campaign accordingly. Meanwhile his own forces in and about Richmond were steadily increasing. He was planning for an army of nearly one hundred thousand and he now demonstrated his ability as a strategist. Word had been despatched to Jackson in the Shenandoah to bring his troops to fall upon the right wing of McClellan's army. At the same time Lee sent General Whiting north to make a feint of joining Jackson and moving upon Washington. The ruse proved eminently successful. The authorities at Washington were frightened, and McClellan received no more reenforcements. Jackson now began a hide-and-seek game among the mountains, and managed to have rumors spread of his army being in several places at the same time, while skilfully veiling his actual movements.

It was not until the 25th of June that McClellan had definite knowledge of Jackson's whereabouts. He was then located at Ashland, north of the Chickahominy, within striking distance of the Army of the Potomac. McClellan was surprised but he was not unprepared. Seven days before he had arranged for a new base of supplies on the James, which would now prove useful if he were driven south of the Chickahominy.

On the very day he heard of Jackson's arrival at Ashland, McClellan was pushing his men forward to begin his siege of Richmond—that variety of warfare which his engineering soul loved so well. His advance guard was within four miles of the Confederate capital. His strong fortifications were bristling upon every vantage point, and his fond hope was that within a few days, at most, his efficient artillery, for which the Army of the Potomac was famous, would be

## THE BRIDGE THAT STOOD

The force under General McCall was stationed by McClellan on June 19, 1862, to observe the Meadow and Mechanicsville bridges over the Chickahominy which had only partially been destroyed. On the afternoon of June 26th, General A. P. Hill crossed at Meadow Bridge, driving the Union skirmish-line back to Beaver Dam Creek. The divisions of D. H. Hill and Longstreet had been waiting at Mechanicsville Bridge (shown in this photograph) since 8 A.M. for A. P. Hill to open the way for them to cross. They passed over in time to bear a decisive part in the Confederate attack at Gaines' Mill on the 27th.

## DOING DOUBLE DUTY

Here are some of McClellan's staff-officers during the strenuous period of the Seven Days' Battles. One commonly supposes that a general's staff has little to do but wear gold lace and transmit orders. But it is their duty to multiply the eyes and ears and thinking power of the leader. Without them he could not direct the movements of his army. There were so few regular officers of ripe experience that members of the staff were invariably made regimental commanders, and frequently were compelled to divide their time between leading their troops into action and reporting to and consulting with their superior.

belching forth its sheets of fire and lead into the beleagured city. In front of the Union encampment, near Fair Oaks, was a thick entanglement of scrubby pines, vines, and ragged bushes, full of ponds and marshes. This strip of woodland was less than five hundred yards wide. Beyond it was an open field half a mile in width. The Union soldiers pressed through the thicket to see what was on the other side and met the Confederate pickets among the trees. The advancing column drove them back. Upon emerging into the open, the Federal troops found it filled with rifle-pits, earthworks, and redoubts. At once they were met with a steady and incessant fire, which continued from eight in the morning until five in the afternoon. At times the contest almost reached the magnitude of a battle, and in the end the Union forces occupied the former position of their antagonists. This passage of arms, sometimes called the affair of Oak Grove or the Second Battle of Fair Oaks, was the prelude to the Seven Days' Battles.

The following day, June 26th, had been set by General "Stonewall" Jackson as the date on which he would join Lee, and together they would fall upon the right wing of the Army of the Potomac. The Federals north of the Chickahominy were under the direct command of General Fitz John Porter. Defensive preparations had been made on an extensive scale. Field works, heavily armed with artillery, and rifle-pits, well manned, covered the roads and open fields and were often concealed by timber from the eye of the opposing army. The extreme right of the Union line lay near Mechanicsville on the upper Chickahominy. A tributary of this stream from the north was Beaver Dam Creek, upon whose left bank was a steep bluff, commanding the valley to the west. This naturally strong position, now well defended, was almost impregnable to an attack from the front.

Before sunrise of the appointed day the Confederate forces were at the Chickahominy bridges, awaiting the arrival of Jackson. To reach these some of the regiments had

THE RETROGRADE CROSSING

Copyright by Patriot Pub. Co.

LOWER BRIDGE ON THE CHICKAHOMINY

Woodbury's Bridge on the Chickahominy. Little did General D. F. Woodbury's engineers suspect, when they built this bridge, early in June, 1862, as a means of communication between the divided wings of McClellan's army on the Chickahominy that it would be of incalculable service during battle. When the right wing, under General Fitz John Porter, was engaged on the field of Gaines' Mill against almost the entire army of Lee, across this bridge the division of General Slocum marched from its position in the trenches in front of Richmond on the south bank of the river to the support of Porter's men. The battle lasted until nightfall and then the Federal troops moved across this bridge and rejoined the main forces of the Federal army. Woodbury's engineers built several bridges across the Chickahominy, but among them all the bridge named for their commander proved to be, perhaps, the most serviceable.

marched the greater part of the night. For once Jackson was behind time. The morning hours came and went. Noon passed and Jackson had not arrived. At three o'clock, General A. P. Hill, growing impatient, decided to put his troops in motion. Crossing at Meadow Bridge, he marched his men along the north side of the Chickahominy, and at Mechanicsville was joined by the commands of Longstreet and D. H. Hill. Driving the Union outposts to cover, the Confederates swept across the low approach to Beaver Dam Creek. A murderous fire from the batteries on the cliff poured into their ranks. Gallantly the attacking columns withstood the deluge of leaden hail and drew near the creek. A few of the more aggressive reached the opposite bank but their repulse was severe.

Later in the afternoon relief was sent to Hill, who again attempted to force the Union position at Ellerson's Mill, where the slope of the west bank came close to the borders of the little stream. From across the open fields, in full view of the defenders of the cliff, the Confederates moved down the slope. They were in range of the Federal batteries, but the fire was reserved. Every artilleryman was at his post ready to fire at the word; the soldiers were in the rifle-pits sighting along the glittering barrels of their muskets with fingers on the triggers. As the approaching columns reached the stream they turned with the road that ran parallel to the bank.

From every waiting field-piece the shells came screaming through the air. Volley after volley of musketry was poured into the flanks of the marching Southerners. The hillside was soon covered with the victims of the gallant charge. Twilight fell upon the warring troops and there were no signs of a cessation of the unequal combat. Night fell, and still from the heights the lurid flames burst in a display of glorious pyrotechnics. It was nine o'clock when Hill finally drew back his shattered regiments, to await the coming of the morning. The Forty-fourth Georgia regiment suffered most in the fight;

## THE FIGHT FOR THE WAGON TRAINS

Three times General Magruder led the Confederates against this position on June 29, 1862, and was as many times repulsed in his attempt to seize the supplies which McClellan was shifting to his new position. Here we see the peaceful morning of that day. Allen's farmhouse in the foreground stands just back from the Williamsburg Road, along which the Federal wagon trains were attempting to move toward Savage's Station. The corps of Sumner and Heintzelman are camped in the background. At dusk of the same day, after Magruder's attacks, the camp was hastily broken and the troops, to avoid being cut off, were marching swiftly and silently toward Savage's Station, leaving behind large quantities of supplies which fell into the hands of the eager Confederates.

[A—21]

three hundred and thirty-five being the dreadful toll, in dead and wounded, paid for its efforts to break down the Union position. Dropping back to the rear this ill-fated regiment attempted to re-form its broken ranks, but its officers were all among those who had fallen. Both armies now prepared for another day and a renewal of the conflict.

The action at Beaver Dam Creek convinced McClellan that Jackson was really approaching with a large force, and he decided to begin his change of base from the Pamunkey to the James, leaving Porter and the Fifth Corps still on the left bank of the Chickahominy, to prevent Jackson's fresh troops from interrupting this great movement. It was, indeed, a gigantic undertaking, for it involved marching an army of a hundred thousand men, including cavalry and artillery, across the marshy peninsula. A train of five thousand heavily loaded wagons and many siege-guns had to be transported; nearly three thousand cattle on the hoof had to be driven. From White House the supplies could be shipped by the York River Railroad as far as Savage's Station. Thence to the James, a distance of seventeen miles, they had to be carried overland along a road intersected by many others from which a watchful opponent might easily attack. General Casey's troops, guarding the supplies at White House, were transferred by way of the York and the James to Harrison's Landing on the latter river. The transports were loaded with all the material they could carry. The rest was burned, or put in cars. These cars, with locomotives attached, were then run into the river.

On the night of June 26th, McCall's Federal division, at Beaver Dam Creek, was directed to fall back to the bridges across the Chickahominy near Gaines' Mill and there make a stand, for the purpose of holding the Confederate army. During the night the wagon trains and heavy guns were quietly moved across the river. Just before daylight the operation of removing the troops began. The Confederates were

## A VAIN RIDE TO SAFETY

During the retreat after Gaines' Mill, McClellan's army was straining every nerve to extricate itself and present a strong front to Lee before he could strike a telling blow at its untenable position. Wagon trains were struggling across the almost impassable White Oak Swamp, while the troops were striving to hold Savage's Station to protect the movement. Thither on flat cars were sent the wounded as we see them in the picture. The rear guard of the Army of the Potomac had hastily provided such field hospital facilities as they could. We see the camp near the railroad with the passing wagon trains in the lower picture. But attention to these wounded men was, perforce, secondary to the necessity of holding the position. Their hopes of relief from their suffering were to be blighted. Lee was about to fall upon the Federal rear guard at Savage's Station. Instead of to a haven of refuge, these men were being railroaded toward the field of carnage, where they must of necessity be left by their retreating companions.

## THE STAND AT SAVAGE'S STATION

Here we see part of the encampment to hold which the divisions of Richardson, Sedgwick, Smith, and Franklin fought valiantly when Magruder and the Confederates fell upon them, June 29, 1862. Along the Richmond & York River Railroad, seen in the picture, the Confederates rolled a heavy rifled gun, mounted on car-wheels. They turned its deadly fire steadily upon the defenders. The Federals fought fiercely and managed to hold their ground till nightfall, when hundreds of their bravest soldiers lay on the field and had to be left alone with their wounded comrades who had arrived on the flat cars.

equally alert, for about the same time they opened a heavy fire on the retreating columns. This march of five miles was a continuous skirmish; but the Union forces, ably and skilfully handled, succeeded in reaching their new position on the Chickahominy heights.

The morning of the new day was becoming hot and sultry as the men of the Fifth Corps made ready for action in their new position. The selection of this ground had been well made; it occupied a series of heights fronted on the west by a sickle-shaped stream. The battle-lines followed the course of this creek, in the arc of a circle curving outward in the direction of the approaching army. The land beyond the creek was an open country, through which Powhite Creek meandered sluggishly, and beyond this a wood densely tangled with undergrowth. Around the Union position were also many patches of wooded land affording cover for the troops and screening the reserves from view.

Porter had learned from deserters and others that Jackson's forces, united to those of Longstreet and the two Hills, were advancing with grim determination to annihilate the Army of the Potomac. He had less than eighteen thousand men to oppose the fifty thousand Confederates. To protect the Federals, trees had been felled along a small portion of their front, out of which barriers protected with rails and knapsacks were erected. Porter had considerable artillery, but only a small part of it could be used. It was two o'clock, on June 27th, when General A. P. Hill swung his division into line for the attack. He was unsupported by the other divisions, which had not yet arrived, but his columns moved rapidly toward the Union front. The assault was terrific, but twenty-six guns threw a hail-storm of lead into his ranks. Under the cover of this magnificent execution of artillery, the infantry sent messages of death to the approaching lines of gray.

The Confederate front recoiled from the incessant outpour of grape, canister, and shell. The heavy cloud of battle

## A GRIM CAPTURE

The Second and Sixth Corps of the Federal Army repelled a desperate attack of General Magruder at Savage Station on June 29th. The next day they disappeared, plunging into the depths of White Oak Swamp, leaving only the brave medical officers behind, doing what they could to relieve the sufferings of the men that had to be abandoned. Here we see them at work upon the wounded, who have been gathered from the field. Nothing but the strict arrest of the stern sergeant Death can save these men from capture, and when the Confederates occupied Savage's Station on the morning of June 30th, twenty-five hundred sick and wounded men and their medical attendants became prisoners of war. The Confederate hospital facilities were already taxed to their full capacity in caring for Lee's wounded, and most of these men were confronted on that day with the prospect of lingering for months in the military prisons of the South. The brave soldiers lying helpless here were wounded at Gaines' Mill on June 27th and removed to the great field-hospital established at Savage's Station. The photograph was taken just before Sumner and Franklin withdrew the rear-guard of their columns on the morning of June 30th.

smoke rose lazily through the air, twisting itself among the trees and settling over the forest like a pall. The tremendous momentum of the repulse threw the Confederates into great confusion. Men were separated from their companies and for a time it seemed as if a rout were imminent. The Federals, pushing out from under the protection of their great guns, now became the assailants. The Southerners were being driven back. Many had left the field in disorder. Others threw themselves on the ground to escape the withering fire, while some tenaciously held their places. This lasted for two hours. General Slocum arrived with his division of Franklin's corps, and his arrival increased the ardor of the victorious Federals.

It was then that Lee ordered a general attack upon the entire Union front. Reenforcements were brought to take the place of the shattered regiments. The engagement began with a sharp artillery fire from the Confederate guns. Then the troops moved forward, once more to assault the Union position. In the face of a heavy fire they rushed across the sedgy lowland, pressed up the hillside at fearful sacrifice and pushed against the Union front. It was a death grapple for the mastery of the field. General Lee, sitting on his horse on an eminence where he could observe the progress of the battle, saw, coming down the road, General Hood, of Jackson's corps, who was bringing his brigade into the fight. Riding forward to meet him, Lee directed that he should try to break the line. Hood, disposing his men for the attack, sent them forward, but, reserving the Fourth Texas for his immediate command, he marched it into an open field, halted, and addressed it, giving instructions that no man should fire until ordered and that all should keep together in line.

The forward march was sounded, and the intrepid Hood, leading his men, started for the Union breastworks eight hundred yards away. They moved at a rapid pace across the open, under a continually increasing shower of shot and shell. At every step the ranks grew thinner and thinner. As they

THE TANGLED RETREAT

Through this well-nigh impassable morass of White Oak Swamp, across a single long bridge, McClellan's wagon trains were being hurried the last days of June, 1862. On the morning of the 30th, the rear-guard of the army was hastily tramping after them, and by ten o'clock had safely crossed and destroyed the bridge. They had escaped in the nick of time, for at noon "Stonewall" Jackson opened fire upon Richardson's division and a terrific artillery battle ensued for the possession of this, the single crossing by which it was possible to attack McClellan's rear. The Federal batteries were compelled to retire but Jackson's crossing was prevented on that day by the infantry.

reached the crest of a small ridge, one hundred and fifty yards from the Union line, the batteries in front and on the flank sent a storm of shell and canister plowing into their already depleted files. They quickened their pace as they passed down the slope and across the creek. Not a shot had they fired and amid the sulphurous atmosphere of battle, with the wing of death hovering over all, they fixed bayonets and dashed up the hill into the Federal line. With a shout they plunged through the felled timber and over the breastworks. The Union line had been pierced and was giving way. It was falling back toward the Chickahominy bridges, and the retreat was threatening to develop into a general rout. The twilight was closing in and the day was all but lost to the Army of the Potomac. Now a great shout was heard from the direction of the bridge; and, pushing through the stragglers at the river bank were seen the brigades of French and Meagher, detached from Sumner's corps, coming to the rescue. General Meagher, in his shirt sleeves, was leading his men up the bluff and confronted the Confederate battle line. This put a stop to the pursuit and as night was at hand the Southern soldiers withdrew. The battle of Gaines' Mill, or the Chickahominy, was over.

When Lee came to the banks of the little river the next morning he found his opponent had crossed over and destroyed the bridges. The Army of the Potomac was once more united. During the day the Federal wagon trains were safely passed over White Oak Swamp and then moved on toward the James River. Lee did not at first divine McClellan's intention. He still believed that the Federal general would retreat down the Peninsula, and hesitated therefore to cross the Chickahominy and give up the command of the lower bridges. But now on the 29th the signs of the movement to the James were unmistakable. Early on that morning Longstreet and A. P. Hill were ordered to recross the Chickahominy by the New Bridge and Huger and Magruder were sent in hot pursuit of the Federal forces. It was the brave Sumner who covered the

MAJOR MEYERS AND LIEUTENANTS STRYKER AND NORTON, 10TH PENN. RESERVES

THREE GROUPS

OF McCLELLAN'S

FIGHTING OFFICERS

COLONEL A. V. COLBURN, COLONEL D. B. SACKETT, AND GENERAL JOHN SEDGWICK

PHOTOGRAPHED

THE MONTH AFTER

THE SEVEN DAYS' BATTLES

COLONEL JAMES H. CHILDS AND OFFICERS, FOURTH PENNSYLVANIA CAVALRY

march of the retreating army, and as he stood in the open field near Savage's Station he looked out over the plain and saw with satisfaction the last of the ambulances and wagons making their way toward the new haven on the James.

In the morning of that same day he had already held at bay the forces of Magruder at Allen's Farm. On his way from Fair Oaks, which he left at daylight, he had halted his men at what is known as the "Peach Orchard," and from nine o'clock till eleven had resisted a spirited fire of musketry and artillery. And now as the grim warrior, on this Sunday afternoon in June, turned his eyes toward the Chickahominy he saw a great cloud of dust rising on the horizon. It was raised by the troops of General Magruder who was pressing close behind the Army of the Potomac. The Southern field-guns were placed in position. A contrivance, consisting of a heavy gun mounted on a railroad car and called the "Land Merrimac," was pushed into position and opened fire upon the Union forces. The battle began with a fine play of artillery. For an hour not a musket was fired. The army of blue remained motionless. Then the mass of gray moved across the field and from the Union guns the long tongues of flame darted into the ranks before them. The charge was met with vigor and soon the battle raged over the entire field. Both sides stood their ground till darkness again closed the contest, and nearly eight hundred brave men had fallen in this Sabbath evening's battle. Before midnight Sumner had withdrawn his men and was following after the wagon trains.

The Confederates were pursuing McClellan's army in two columns, Jackson closely following Sumner, while Longstreet was trying to cut off the Union forces by a flank movement. On the last day of June, at high noon, Jackson reached the White Oak Swamp. But the bridge was gone. He attempted to ford the passage, but the Union troops were there to prevent it. While Jackson was trying to force his way across the stream, there came to him the sound of a desperate battle being

[ 332 ]

## HEROES OF MALVERN HILL

Brigadier-General J. H. Martindale (seated) and his staff, July 1, 1862. Fitz John Porter's Fifth Corps and Couch's division, Fourth Corps, bore the brunt of battle at Malvern Hill where the troops of McClellan withstood the terrific attacks of Lee's combined and superior forces. Fiery "Prince John" Magruder hurled column after column against the left of the Federal line, but every charge was met and repulsed through the long hot summer afternoon. Martindale's brigade of the Fifth Corps was early called into action, and its commander, by the gallant fighting of his troops, won the brevet of Major-General.

## THE NAVY LENDS A HAND

Officers of the *Monitor* at Malvern Hill. Glad indeed were the men of the Army of the Potomac as they emerged from their perilous march across White Oak Swamp to hear the firing of the gunboats on the James. It told them the Confederates had not yet pre-empted the occupation of Malvern Hill, which General Fitz John Porter's Corps was holding. Before the battle opened McClellan went aboard the *Galena* to consult with Commodore John Rodgers about a suitable base on the James. The gunboats of the fleet supported the flanks of the army during the battle and are said to have silenced one of the Confederate batteries fought not more than two miles away, but he was powerless to give aid.

Longstreet and A. P. Hill had come upon the Federal regiments at Glendale, near the intersection of the Charles City road, guarding the right flank of the retreat. It was Longstreet who, about half-past two, made one of his characteristic onslaughts on that part of the Union army led by General McCall. It was repulsed with heavy loss. Again and again attacks were made. Each brigade seemed to act on its own behalf. They hammered here, there, and everywhere. Repulsed at one place they charged at another. The Eleventh Alabama, rushing out from behind a dense wood, charged across the open field in the face of the Union batteries. The men had to run a distance of six hundred yards. A heavy and destructive fire poured into their lines, but on they came, trailing their guns. The batteries let loose grape and canister, while volley after volley of musketry sent its death-dealing messages among the Southerners. But nothing except death itself could check their impetuous charge. When two hundred yards away they raised the Confederate yell and rushed for Randol's battery.

Pausing for an instant they deliver a volley and attempt to seize the guns. Bayonets are crossed and men engage in a hand-to-hand struggle. The contending masses rush together, asking and giving no quarter and struggling like so many tigers. Darkness is closing on the fearful scene, yet the fighting continues with unabated ferocity. There are the shouts of command, the clash and the fury of the battle, the sulphurous smoke, the flashes of fire streaking through the air, the yells of defiance, the thrust, the parry, the thud of the clubbed musket, the hiss of the bullet, the spouting blood, the death-cry, and beneath all lie the bodies of America's sons, some in blue and some in gray.

While Lee and his army were held in check by the events of June 30th at White Oak Swamp and the other battle at

Again we see the transports and supply schooners at anchor—this time at Harrison's Landing on the James River. In about a month, McClellan had changed the position of his army twice, shifting his base from the Pamunkey to the James. The position he held on Malvern Hill was abandoned after the victory of July 1, 1862, and the army marched to a new base farther down the James, where the heavy losses of men and supplies during the

*Copyright by Patriot Pub. Co.*

THE SECOND ARMY BASE

Seven Days could be made up without danger and delay. Harrison's Landing was the point selected, and here the army recuperated, wondering what would be the next step. Below we see the historic mansion which did service as General Porter's headquarters, one of McClellan's most efficient commanders. For his services during the Seven Days he was made Major-General of Volunteers. McClellan was his lifelong friend.

WESTOVER HOUSE: HEADQUARTERS OF GENERAL FITZ JOHN PORTER, HARRISON'S LANDING

Glendale or Nelson's Farm, the last of the wagon trains had arrived safely at Malvern Hill. The contest had hardly closed and the smoke had scarcely lifted from the blood-soaked field, when the Union forces were again in motion toward the James. By noon on July 1st the last division reached the position where McClellan decided to turn again upon his assailants. He had not long to wait, for the Confederate columns, led by Longstreet, were close on his trail, and a march of a few miles brought them to the Union outposts. They found the Army of the Potomac admirably situated to give defensive battle. Malvern Hill, a plateau, a mile and a half long and half as broad, with its top almost bare of woods, commanded a view of the country over which the Confederate army must approach. Along the western face of this plateau there are deep ravines falling abruptly in the direction of the James River; on the north and east is a gentle slope to the plain beneath, bordered by a thick forest. Around the summit of the hill, General Mc-Clellan had placed tier after tier of batteries, arranged like an amphitheater. Surmounting these on the crest were massed seven of his heaviest siege-guns. His army surrounded this hill, its left flank being protected by the gunboats on the river.

The morning and early afternoon were occupied with many Confederate attacks, sometimes formidable in their nature, but Lee planned for no general move until he could bring up a force that he considered sufficient to attack the strong Federal position. The Confederate orders were to advance when the signal, a yell, cheer, or shout from the men of Armistead's brigade, was given.

Late in the afternoon General D. H. Hill heard some shouting, followed by a roar of musketry. No other general seems to have heard it, for Hill made his attack alone. It was gallantly done, but no army could have withstood the galling fire of the batteries of the Army of the Potomac as they were massed upon Malvern Hill. All during the evening, brigade after brigade tried to force the Union lines. The gunners

## ON DARING DUTY

Lieut.-Colonel Albert V. Colburn, a favorite Aide-de-Camp of General McClellan's.—Here is the bold soldier of the Green Mountain State who bore despatches about the fields of battle during the Seven Days. It was he who was sent galloping across the difficult and dangerous country to make sure that Franklin's division was retreating from White Oak Swamp, and then to carry orders to Sumner to fall back on Malvern Hill. Such were the tasks that constantly fell to the lot of the despatch bearer. Necessarily a man of quick and accurate judgment, perilous chances confronted him in his efforts to keep the movements of widely separated divisions in concert with the plans of the commander. The loss of his life might mean the loss of a battle; the failure to arrive in the nick of time with despatches might mean disaster for the army. Only the coolest headed of the officers could be trusted with this vital work in the field.

stood coolly and manfully by their batteries. The Confederates were not able to make concerted efforts, but the battle waxed hot nevertheless. They were forced to breast one of the most devastating storms of lead and canister to which an assaulting army has ever been subjected. The round shot and grape cut through the branches of the trees and the battle-field was soon in a cloud of smoke. Column after column of Southern soldiers rushed up to the death-dealing cannon, only to be mowed down. The thinned and ragged lines, with a valor born of desperation, rallied again and again to the charge, but to no avail. The batteries on the heights still hurled their missiles of death. The field below was covered with the dead and wounded of the Southland.

The gunboats in the river made the battle scene more awe-inspiring with their thunderous cannonading. Their heavy shells shrieked through the forest, and great limbs were torn from the trees as they hurtled by in their outburst of fury.

Night was falling. The combatants were no longer distinguishable except by the sheets of flame. It was nine o'clock before the guns ceased their fire, and only an occasional shot rang out over the bloody field of Malvern Hill.

The courageous though defeated Confederate, looking up the next day through the drenching rain to where had stood the embrasured wall with its grim batteries and lines of blue, that spoke death to so many of his companions-in-arms, saw only deserted ramparts. The Union army had retreated in the darkness of the night. But this time no foe harassed its march. Unmolested, it sought its new camp at Harrison's Landing, where it remained until August 3d, when, as President Lincoln had been convinced of the impracticability of operating from the James River as a base, orders were issued by General Halleck for the withdrawal of the Army of the Potomac from the Peninsula.

The net military result of the Seven Days was a disappointment to the South. Although thankful that the siege of

## AVERELL—THE COLONEL WHO BLUFFED AN ARMY.

Colonel W. W. Averell and Staff.—This intrepid officer of the Third Pennsylvania Cavalry held the Federal position on Malvern Hill on the morning of July 2, 1862, with only a small guard, while McClellan completed the withdrawal of his army to Harrison's Landing.  It was his duty to watch the movements of the Confederates and hold them back from any attempt to fall upon the retreating trains and troops.  A dense fog in the early morning shut off the forces of A. P. Hill and Longstreet from his view.  He had not a single fieldpiece with which to resist attack.  When the mist cleared away, he kept up a great activity with his cavalry horses, making the Confederates believe that artillery was being brought up.  With apparent reluctance he agreed to a truce of two hours in which the Confederates might bury the dead they left on the hillside the day before.  Later, with an increased show of unwillingness, he extended the truce for another two hours.  Just before they expired, Frank's Battery arrived to his support, with the news that the Army of the Potomac was safe.  Colonel Averell rejoined it without the loss of a man.

[A—22]

Richmond had been raised, the Southern public believed that McClellan should not have been allowed to reach the James River with his army intact.

"That army," Eggleston states, "splendidly organized, superbly equipped, and strengthened rather than weakened in morale, lay securely at rest on the James River, within easy striking distance of Richmond. There was no knowing at what moment McClellan might hurl it again upon Richmond or upon that commanding key to Richmond—the Petersburg position. In the hands of a capable commander McClellan's army would at this time have been a more serious menace than ever to the Confederate capital, for it now had an absolutely secure and unassailable base of operations, while its fighting quality had been improved rather than impaired by its seven days of battling."

General Lee's own official comment on the military problem involved and the difficulties encountered was: "Under ordinary circumstances the Federal army should have been destroyed. Its escape was due to the causes already stated. Prominent among these is the want of correct and timely information. This fact, attributable chiefly to the character of the country, enabled General McClellan skilfully to conceal his retreat and to add much to the obstructions with which nature had beset the way of our pursuing columns; but regret that more was not accomplished gives way to gratitude to the Sovereign Ruler of the Universe for the results achieved."

Whatever the outcome of the Seven Days' Battle another year was to demonstrate beyond question that the wounding of General Johnston at Fair Oaks had left the Confederate army with an even abler commander. On such a field as Chancellorsville was to be shown the brilliancy of Lee as leader, and his skilful maneuvers leading to the invasion of the North. And the succeeding volume will tell, on the other hand, how strong and compact a fighting force had been forged from the raw militia and volunteers of the North.

OFFICERS OF THE THIRD PENNSYLVANIA CAVALRY

## AFTER THE SEVEN DAYS

Within a week of the occupation of Harrison's Landing, McClellan's position had become so strong that the Federal commander **no** longer anticipated an attack by the Confederate forces. General Lee saw that his opponent was flanked on each side by a creek **and** that approach to his front was commanded by the guns in the entrenchments and those of the Federal navy in the river. Lee therefore deemed it inexpedient to attack, especially as his troops were in poor condition owing to the incessant marching and fighting of the Seven Days. Rest was what both armies needed most, and on July 8th the Confederate forces returned to the vicinity of Richmond. McClellan scoured the country before he was satisfied of the Confederate withdrawal. The Third and Fourth Pennsylvania cavalry made a reconnaisance to Charles City Court House and beyond, and General Averell reported on July 11th that there were no Southern troops south of the lower Chickahominy. His scouting expeditions extended in the direction of Richmond and up the Chickahominy.

CHARLES CITY COURT HOUSE, VIRGINIA, JULY, 1862

GEN. W. H. C. WHITING

## WHERE JACKSON'S MEN SCORED

From this old ruin, Gaines' Mill, the momentous battle of June 27, 1862, took its name, and on the ridge known as Turkey Hill, a mile to the southeast, the men of the First Maryland Confederate regiment won glory for themselves and their cause. "Stonewall" Jackson's corps at the end of a rapid march had arrived in the middle of the afternoon. After a brief rest, it was hurled against the Federal center on Turkey Hill. A battery defending the position poured a rapid fire upon the ranks of the attackers. The Confederates wavered, broke, and "regiment after regiment rushed back in utter dis-

COL. BRADLEY T. JOHNSON

order." General Winder was then ordered to send his brigade forward and he found, as he advanced, several regiments waiting to join him, among them the First Maryland Infantry

headed by Colonel Bradley T. Johnson. The new line swept forward. The Federal battery on Turkey Hill, which Johnson was ordered to take, limbered up and fled. The Union troops were finally driven from their lost position. Meanwhile on Jackson's extreme right General Whiting's division was making what proved to be the fiercest charge of the Seven Days' Battles. The Southern troops came on with tremendous impetus, scattering some of their own regiments that were retreating in disorder. The Texan brigades of Hood and Law bore the brunt of the desperate and vain effort of the Federals to drive Whiting back. Finally General Hood and the Fourth Texas broke the line in the center of Morell's division and seized the guns.

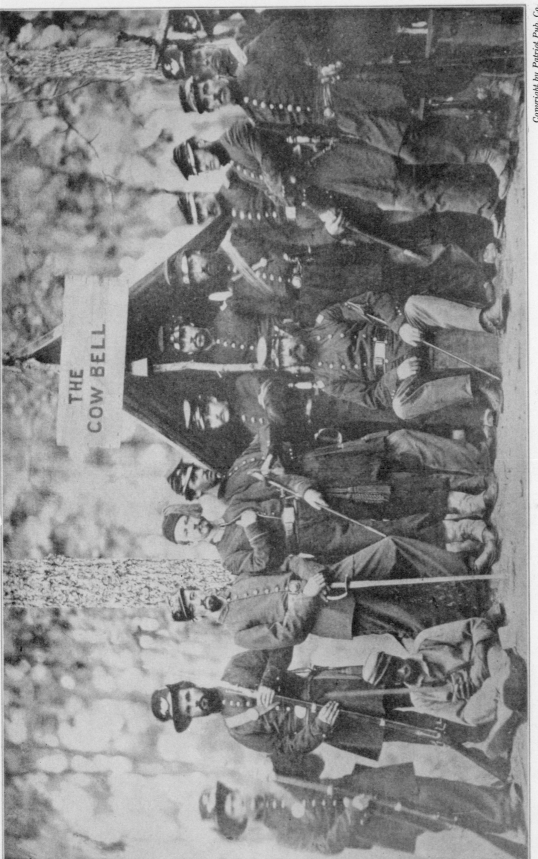

THE COW BELL

## THE STEADY MEN AT GAINES' MILL

Officers of a stalwart Irish regiment which gloriously distinguished itself at Gaines' Mill, the third battle in its career. We see them here at Camp Cass on Arlington Heights, where they had been waiting all winter near Washington for a sight of active service. This regiment was organized as the Ninth Massachusetts Infantry in April, 1861. It was not till almost a year later that, joining McClellan's forces on the Peninsula, it jumped immediately into the thick of things at Hanover Court House and Mechanicsville. Battles came fast and furious during the Seven Days' struggle, and, with Morell's division of the Fifth Corps, this regiment sustained the fierce assault of "Stonewall" Jackson's troops at Turkey Hill. Its total loss that day was 231, including six line officers killed. Four days later at Malvern Hill its Colonel, Thomas Cass, fell mortally wounded. The regiment was commanded thenceforth by Colonel Patrick R. Guiney, and throughout the war gave abundant evidence of the valor of the Irish soldier.

BUILDING WINTER QUARTERS

# VI

# ENGAGEMENTS OF THE CIVIL WAR

# ENGAGEMENTS OF THE CIVIL WAR
## WITH LOSSES ON BOTH SIDES
### DECEMBER, 1860—AUGUST, 1862

CHRONOLOGICAL summary and record of historical events, and of important engagements between the Union and the Confederate armies, in the Civil War in the United States, showing troops participating, losses and casualties, collated and compiled by George L. Kilmer from the official records of the Union and Confederate armies filed in the United States War Department. Minor engagements are omitted; also some concerning which statistics, especially Confederate, are not available.

### PRELIMINARY EVENTS FROM THE SECESSION OF SOUTH CAROLINA TO THE BOMBARDMENT OF FORT SUMTER.

**DECEMBER, 1860.**

20.—Ordinance of Secession adopted by South Carolina.

**JANUARY, 1861.**

9.—U. S. Steamer *Star of the West* fired upon in Charleston harbor by South Carolina troops.
Mississippi seceded.
10.—Florida seceded.
11.—Alabama seceded.
19.—Georgia seceded.
26.—Louisiana seceded.

**FEBRUARY, 1861.**

1.—Texas seceded.
4.—"Confederate States of America" provisionally organized at Montgomery, Ala.
9.—Jefferson Davis elected provisional President of the Confederate States of America.
18.—Jefferson Davis inaugurated President of the Confederate States at Montgomery, Ala.

**MARCH, 1861.**

4.—Abraham Lincoln inaugurated President of the United States at Washington.

**APRIL, 1861.**

12 and 13.—Bombardment of Fort Sumter, S. C. *Union* 1st U. S. Art. *Confed.* S. C. Art. No casualties.
14.—Evacuation of Fort Sumter, S. C., by U. S. Losses: *Union* 1 killed, 5 wounded by premature explosion of cannon in firing a salute to the United States flag.
17.—Virginia adopted the ordinance of secession, subject to popular vote.
19.—Riots in Baltimore, Md. *Union* 6th Mass., 27th Pa. *Baltimoreans*, Citizens of Baltimore. Losses: *Union* 4 killed, 36 wounded. Citizens, 12 killed.
23.—Co. A 8th U. S. Infantry captured at San Antonio, Tex., by a company of organized citizen volunteers.

**MAY, 1861.**

6.—Arkansas seceded.
10.—Camp Jackson, Mo., occupied by Mo. militia, seized by *Union* 1st, 3d, and 4th Mo. Reserve Corps, 3d Mo. Vols. 639 militiamen taken prisoners.
11.—St. Louis, Mo. Collision of *Union* 5th Mo., U. S. Reserves, with citizens of St. Louis. Losses: *Union* 4 killed. *Citizens* 27 killed.
20.—North Carolina seceded.
24.—Col. E. Elmer Ellsworth, 11th N. Y. Vols., killed by a civilian while removing a Southern flag from the roof of the Marshall House, Alexandria, Va.

## THE THREATENED FORT

Fort Pickens, guarding the entrance to Pensacola Bay, 1861. Never was a perilous position more gallantly held than was Fort Pickens by Lieutenant A. J. Slemmer and his little garrison from January to May, 1861. A large force of Confederates were constantly menacing the fort. Slemmer discovered a plot to betray the fort into the hands of a thousand of them

on the night of April 11th. Attempts to seize the fort by Confederates gathered in force for the purpose were held off only by the timely arrival of gunboats with reënforcements from the North. All the efforts to take Fort Pickens failed and it remained in the hands of the Federals throughout the war. In the lower picture we see one of the powerful Confederate batteries at Fort McRee, which fired on Pickens from across the channel.

*Copyright by Review of Reviews Co.*

# Engagements of the Civil War

## JUNE, 1861.

**1.**—Fairfax C. H., Va. *Union*, Co. B 2d U. S. Cav. *Confed.*, Va. Vols. Losses: *Union* 1 killed, 4 wounded. *Confed.* 1 killed, 14 wounded.

**3.**—Philippi, W. Va. *Union*, 1st W. Va., 14th and 16th Ohio, 7th and 9th Ind. *Confed.*, Va. Vols. Losses: Union 2 wounded. *Confed.* 15 killed, wounded (*).

**10.**—Big Bethel, Va. *Union*, 1st, 2d, 3d, 5th, and 7th N. Y., 4th Mass. Detachment of 2d U. S. Artil. *Confed.*, 1st N. C., Randolph's Battery, Va. Infantry and Cavalry. Losses: *Union* 16 killed, 34 wounded. *Confed.* 1 killed, 7 wounded.

**13.**—Romney, W. Va. *Union*, 11th Ind. *Confed.*, Va. Vols. Losses: *Union* 1 wounded. *Confed.* 2 killed, 1 wounded.

**17.**—Vienna, Va. *Union*, 1st Ohio. *Confed.*, 1st S. C. Losses: *Union* 5 killed, 6 wounded. *Confed.* 6 killed.
—Booneville, Mo. *Union*, 2d Mo. (three months') Volunteers, Detachments 1st, Totten's Battery Mo. Light Artil. *Confed.*, Mo. Militia. Losses: Union 3 killed, 8 wounded. *Confed.* (*).
—Edwards Ferry, Md. *Union*, 1st Pa. *Confed.*, Va. Vols. Losses: *Union* 1 killed, 4 wounded. *Confed.* 15 killed.

**26.**—Patterson Creek or Kelley's Island, Va. *Union*, 11th Ind. *Confed.*, Va. Vols. Losses: *Union* 1 killed, 1 wounded. *Confed.* 7 killed, 2 wounded.

**27.**—Mathias Point, Va. *Union*, Gunboats *Pawnee* and *Freeborn*. *Confed.*, Va. Vols. Losses: *Union* 1 killed, 4 wounded.

## JULY, 1861.

**2.**—Falling Waters, Md., also called Haynesville or Martinsburg, Md. *Union*, 1st Wis., 11th Pa. *Confed.*, Va. Vols. Losses: *Union* 8 killed, 15 wounded. *Confed.* 31 killed, 50 wounded.

**5.**—Carthage or Dry Forks, Mo. *Union*, 3d and 5th Mo., one battery of Mo. Artil. *Confed.*, Mo. State Guard. Losses: *Union* 13 killed, 31 wounded. *Confed.* 30 killed, 125 wounded, 45 prisoners.
—Newport News, Va. *Union*, 1 Co. 9th N. Y. *Confed.*, Stanard's Va. Battery, La. Battalion, Crescent Rifles, Collins'

Cav. Troop. Losses: *Union* 6 wounded. *Confed.* 2 killed, 1 wounded.

**6.**—Middle Creek Fork or Buckhannon, W. Va. *Union*, One Co. 3d Ohio. *Confed.*, 25th Va. Losses: *Union* 1 killed, 6 wounded. *Confed.* 7 killed.

**7.**—Great Falls, Md. Losses: *Union* 2 killed. *Confed.* 12 killed.

**10.**—Laurel Hill or Bealington, W. Va. *Union*, 14th Ohio, 9th Ind. *Confed.*, 20th Va. Losses: *Union* 2 killed, 6 wounded.

**10.**—Monroe Station, Mo. Losses: *Union* 3 killed. *Confed.* 4 killed, 20 wounded, 75 prisoners.

**11.**—Rich Mountain, W. Va. *Union*, 8th, 10th, and 13th Ind., 19th Ohio. *Confed.*, Gen. Jno. C. Pegram's command. Losses: *Union* 11 killed, 35 wounded. *Confed.* 60 killed, 140 wounded, 100 prisoners.

**13.**—Carrick's Ford, W. Va. *Union*, Gen. Geo. B. McClellan's command. *Confed.*, Gen. R. E. Lee's command. Losses: *Union* 13 killed, 40 wounded. *Confed.* 20 killed, 10 wounded, 50 prisoners. *Confed.* Gen. R. S. Garnett killed.

**16.**—Millsville or Wentzville, Mo. Losses: *Union* 7 killed, 1 wounded. *Confed.* 7 killed.

**17.**—Fulton, Mo. Losses: *Union* 1 killed, 15 wounded.
—Scarey Creek, W. Va. Losses: *Union* 9 killed, 38 wounded.
—Martinsburg, Mo. Losses: *Union* 1 killed, 1 wounded.

**18.**—Blackburn's Ford, Va. *Union*, 1st Mass., 2d and 3d Mich., 12th N. Y., Detachment of 2d U. S. Cav., Battery E 3d U. S. Artil. *Confed.*, 5th, 11th N. C., 2d, 3d, 7th S. C., 1st, 7th, 11th, 17th, 24th Va., 7th La., 13th Miss. Losses: *Union* 19 killed, 38 wounded. *Confed.* 15 killed, 53 wounded.

**21.**—Bull Run or Manassas, Va. *Union*, 2d Me., 2d N. H., 2d Vt., 1st, 4th, and 5th Mass., 1st and 2d R. I., 1st, 2d, and 3d Conn., 8th, 11th, 12th, 13th, 16th, 18th, 27th, 29th, 31st, 32d, 35th, 38th, and 39th N. Y., 2d, 8th, 14th, 69th, 71st, and 79th N. Y. Militia, 27th Pa., 1st, 2d, and 3d Mich., 1st and 2d Minn., 2d Wis., 1st and 2d Ohio, Detachments of 2d, 3d, and 8th U. S. Regulars, Battalion of Marines, Batteries D, E, G, and M, 2d

* No record found.

## MAJOR ROBERT ANDERSON AND FAMILY

This Federal major of artillery was summoned on April 11, 1861, to surrender Fort Sumter and the property of the government whose uniform he wore. At half-past four the following morning the boom of the first gun from Fort Johnson in Charleston Harbor notified the breathless, waiting world that war was on. The flag had been fired on, and hundreds of thousands of lives were to be sacrificed ere the echoes of the great guns died away at the end of four years into the sobs of a nation whose best and bravest, North and South, had strewn the many battlefields. No wonder that the attention of the civilized world was focussed on the man who provoked the first blow in the greatest conflict the world has ever known. He was the man who handled the situation at the breaking point. To him the North looked to preserve the Federal property in Charleston Harbor, and the honor of the National flag. The action of the South depended upon his decision. He played the part of a true soldier, and two days after the first shot was fired he led his little garrison of the First United States Artillery out of Sumter with the honors of war.

# Engagements of the Civil War

U. S. Artil., Battery E, 3d Artil., Battery D, 5th Artil., 2d R. I. Battery, Detachments of 1st and 2d Dragoons. *Confed.*, 6th, 7th, 8th La., 7th, 8th Ga., 1st Ark., 2d, 3d Tenn., 2d, 3d, 4th, 5th, 7th, 8th S. C., Hampton's Legion, 5th, 6th, 11th N. C., 1st Md., 2d, 11th, 13th, 17th, 18th Miss., 4th, 5th, 6th Ala., 1st, 2d, 4th, 5th, 7th, 8th, 10th, 11th, 13th, 17th, 18th, 19th, 24th, 27th, 28th, 33d, 49th Va., 1st, 30th Va. Cavalry, Harrison's Battalion. Losses: *Union* 481 killed, 1,011 wounded, 1,210 missing and captured. *Confed.* 387 killed, 1,582 wounded, 13 missing. *Confed.* Brig.-Gens. Bee and Bartow killed.

22.—Forsyth, Mo. Losses: *Union* 3 wounded. *Confed.* 5 killed, 10 wounded.

24.—Blue Mills, Mo. Losses: *Union* 1 killed, 12 wounded.

26.—Lane's Prairie, near Rolla, Mo. Losses: *Union* 3 wounded. *Confed.* 1 killed, 3 wounded.

27.—Fort Fillmore and San Augustine Springs, N. Mex. 7th U. S. Inft. and 3d U. S. Mounted Rifles, in all 400 men, captured by Confederates commanded by Col. John R. Baylor.

### AUGUST, 1861.

2.—Dug Springs, Mo. *Union*, Steele's Battalion, 2d U. S. Infantry, Stanley's Cav. Troop, Totten's Battery. *Confed.*, Rains' Mo. State Guard. Losses: *Union* 4 killed, 37 wounded. *Confed.* 40 killed, 41 wounded.

5.—Athens, Mo. *Union*, Home Guards, 21st Mo. Vol. *Confed.* (\*). Losses: *Union* 3 killed, 8 wounded. *Confed.* 14 killed, 14 wounded.
—Point of Rocks, Md. *Union*, 28th N. Y. *Confed.* (\*) Losses: *Confed.* 3 killed, 2 wounded.

7.—Hampton, Va. *Union*, 20th N. Y. Losses: *Confed.* 3 killed, 6 wounded.

8.—Lovettsville, Va. *Union*, 19th N. Y. Losses: *Confed.* 1 killed, 5 wounded.

10.—Wilson's Creek, Mo., also called Springfield and Oak Hill. *Union*, 6th and 10th Mo. Cav., 2d Kan. Mounted Vols., one Co. of 1st U. S. Cav., 1st Ia., 1st Kan., 1st, 2d, 3d, and 5th Mo., Detachments of 1st and 2d U. S. Regulars, Mo. Home Guards, 1st Mo. Light Artil., Battery F 2d U. S. Artil. *Confed.*, 1st, 3d, 4th, 5th Mo. State Guard, Graves' Infantry, Bledsoe's Battery, Cawthorn's Brigade, Kelly's Infantry, Brown's Cavalry, Burbridge's Infantry, 1st Cavalry, Hughes', Thornton's, Wingo's, Foster's Infantry, Rives', Campbell's Cavalry, 3d, 4th, 5th Ark., 1st Cavalry, Woodruff's, Reid's Battery, 1st, 2d Mounted Riflemen, South Kansas-Texas Mounted Regiment, 3d La. Losses: *Union* 223 killed, 721 wounded, 291 missing. *Confed.* 265 killed, 800 wounded, 30 missing. *Union* Brig.-Gen. Nathaniel Lyon killed.
—Potosi, Mo. *Union*, Mo. Home Guards. Losses: *Union* 1 killed. *Confed.* 2 killed, 3 wounded.

17.—Brunswick, Mo. *Union*, 5th Mo. Reserves. Losses: *Union* 1 killed, 7 wounded.

19.—Charleston or Bird's Point, Mo. Losses: *Union* 1 killed, 6 wounded. *Confed.* 40 killed.

20.—Hawk's Nest, W. Va. Losses: *Union* 3 wounded. *Confed.* 1 killed, 3 wounded.

26.—Cross Lanes or Summerville, W. Va. Losses: *Union* 5 killed, 40 wounded, 200 captured.

27.—Ball's Cross Roads, Va. Losses: Union 1 killed, 2 wounded.

28 and 29.—Fort Hatteras, N. C. *Union*, 9th, 20th, and 89th N. Y. and Naval force. *Confed.* North Carolina troops under Col. W. F. Martin. Losses: *Union* 1 killed, 2 wounded. *Confed.* 5 killed, 51 wounded, 715 prisoners.

31.—Munson's Hill, Va. Losses: *Union* 2 killed, 2 wounded.

### SEPTEMBER, 1861.

1.—Bennett's Mills, Mo. Losses: *Union* 1 killed, 8 wounded.

2.—Dallas, Mo. Losses: *Union* 2 killed.
—Dry Wood or Ft. Scott, Mo. Losses: *Union* 4 killed, 9 wounded.

10.—Carnifex Ferry, W. Va. *Union*, 9th, 10th, 12th, 13th, 28th, and 47th Ohio. *Confed.*, Gen. J. B. Floyd's command. Losses: *Union* 17 killed, 141 wounded. *Confed.* (\*).

11.—Lewinsville, Va. *Union*, 19th Ind., 3d Vt., 79th N. Y., 1st U. S. Chasseurs, Griffin's Battery, detachment of Cavalry. *Confed.*, 13th Va., Rosser's Bat-

\* No record found.

THE LAST LETTER

COLONEL EPHRAIM ELMER ELLSWORTH

One of the First to Fall.   The shooting of this young patriot profoundly shocked and stirred the Federals at the opening of the war.   Colonel Ellsworth had organized a Zouave regiment in Chicago, and in April, 1861, he organized another from the Fire Department in New York City.   Colonel Ellsworth, on May 24, 1861, led his Fire Zouaves to Alexandria, Virginia, seized the city, and with his own hands pulled down a Southern flag floating over the Marshall House.   Descending the stairs with the flag in his hand, he cried, "Behold my trophy!"   "Behold mine!" came the reply from the proprietor of the hotel, James T. Jackson, as he emptied a shotgun into Ellsworth's breast.   Jackson was immediately shot dead by Private Brownell.

MARSHALL HOUSE, ALEXANDRIA, VIRGINIA, 1861

# Engagements of the Civil War

tery, detachments of Cavalry. Losses: *Union* 6 killed, 8 wounded.

**12 and 13.**—Cheat Mountain, W. Va. *Union,* 13th, 14th, 15th, and 17th Ind., 3d, 6th, 24th, and 25th Ohio, 2d W. Va. *Confed.,* Va. Vols. commanded by Gen. W. W. Loring. Losses: *Union* 9 killed, 12 wounded, 60 missing. *Confed.* (*).

**12 to 20.**—Lexington, Mo. *Union,* 23d Ill., 8th, 25th, and 27th Mo., 13th and 14th Mo. Home Guards, Berry's and Van Horne's Mo. Cav., 1st Ill. Cav. *Confed.,* Parsons' and Rains' Divisions, Bledsoe's, Churchill's, Guibor's, Kelly's, Kneisley's and Clark's batteries. Losses: *Union* 42 killed, 108 wounded, 1,624 missing and captured. *Confed.* 25 killed, 75 wounded.

**13.**—Booneville, Mo. *Union,* Mo. Home Guards. *Confed.,* Gen. Price's Mo. State Guard. Losses: *Union* 1 killed, 4 wounded. *Confed.* 12 killed, 30 wounded.

**14.**—Confederate Privateer *Judah* destroyed near Pensacola, Fla., by the U. S. Flagship *Colorado.* Losses: *Union* 3 killed, 15 wounded.

**15.**—Pritchard's Mills, Md., or Darnestown, Md. *Union,* detachments 13th Mass., 28th Pa., 9th N. Y. Battery. *Confed.* Losses: *Union* 1 killed, 3 wounded. *Confed.* (estimate) 18 killed, 25 wounded.

**17.**—Morristown, Mo. *Union,* 5th, 6th, 9th Kan. Cav., 1st Kan. Battery. *Confed.* Losses: *Union* 2 killed, 6 wounded. *Confed.* 7 killed.
—Blue Mills, Mo. *Union,* 3d Ia. *Confed.,* Mo. State Guard. Losses: *Union* 11 killed, 39 wounded. *Confed.* 12 killed, 63 wounded.

**19.**—Barboursville, Ky. *Union,* Ky. Home Guards. *Confed.,* Gen. F. K. Zollicoffer's brigade. Losses: *Union* 1 killed, 1 wounded. *Confed.* 2 killed, 3 wounded.

**23.**—Romney or Hanging Rock, W. Va. *Union,* 4th and 8th Ohio. *Confed.,* 77th and 114th Va., 1 battery Art. Losses: *Union* 3 killed, 50 wounded. *Confed.* 35 killed.

**25.**—Kanawha Gap, W. Va. *Union,* 1st Ky., 34th Ohio. *Confed.* Losses: *Union* 4 killed, 9 wounded. *Confed.* 20 killed, 50 wounded.

**25 and 27.**—Alamosa, near Ft. Craig, N. Mex. *Union,* Capt. Mink's Cavalry. *Confed.,* Capt. Coopwood's Tex. Scouts. Losses: *Union.** *Confed.* 2 killed, 8 wounded.

## OCTOBER, 1861.

**3.**—Greenbrier, W. Va. *Union,* 24th, 25th, and 32d Ohio, 7th, 9th, 13th, 14th, 15th, and 17th Ind., Battery G, 4th U. S. Artil., Battery A 1st Mich. Artil. *Confed.,* Va. Vols. of Gen. W. W. Loring's command. Losses: *Union* 8 killed, 32 wounded. *Confed.* 100 killed, 75 wounded.

**9.**—Santa Rosa, Fla. *Union,* 6th N. Y., Co. A 1st U. S. Artil., Co. H 2d U. S. Artil., Co.'s C and E 3d U. S. Inft. *Confed.,* 9th and 10th Miss., 1st Ala., 1st Fla. and 5th Ga. Losses: *Union* 14 killed, 29 wounded. *Confed.* 17 killed, 39 wounded, 30 captured.

**13.**—Wet Glaze, or Monday's Hollow, Mo. *Union,* 13th Ill., 1st Mo. Battalion, Fremont Battalion, Mo. Cav. *Confed.** Losses: *Confed.* 67 killed (estimate).

**14.**—Underwood's Farm (12 miles from Bird's Point), Mo. *Union,* 1st Ill. Cav. *Confed.,* 1st Miss. Cav. Losses: *Union* 2 killed, 5 wounded. *Confed.* 1 killed, 2 wounded.

**15.**—Big River Bridge, near Potosi, Mo. *Union,* 40 men of the 38th Ill. *Confed.,* 2d, 3d Miss. Cav. Losses: *Union* 1 killed, 6 wounded, 33 captured. *Confed.* 5 killed, 4 wounded.

**16.**—Bolivar Heights, Va. *Union,* detachments of 28th Pa., 3d Wis. and 6th Mo. Cavalry. *Confed.,* detachments commanded by Col. Turner Ashby. Losses: *Union* 4 killed, 7 wounded.

**17 to 21.**—Fredericktown and Ironton, Mo. *Union,* 21st, 33d, and 38th Ill., 8th Wis., 1st Ind. Cav., Co. A 1st Mo. Light Artil. *Confed.,* Mo. State Guard. Losses: *Union* 7 killed, 41 wounded. *Confed.* 200 killed, wounded, and missing (estimate).

**21.**—Ball's Bluff, also called Edwards Ferry, Harrison's Landing, Leesburg, Va. *Union,* 15th, 20th Mass. 40th N. Y., 71st Pa., Battery I, 1st U. S., B, R. I. Artil. *Confed.,* 13th, 17th, 18th Miss., 8th Va., 3 co.'s Va. Cavalry. Losses: *Union* 49 killed, 158 wounded, and 714 missing.

* No record found.

## A WESTERN LEADER—MAJOR–GENERAL FRANK P. BLAIR, JR., AND STAFF

One of the most interesting characters in Missouri at the outbreak of the war was Frank P. Blair, Jr., of St. Louis, a Member of Congress. When Governor Jackson refused to obey President Lincoln's proclamation and call out troops, Mr. Blair immediately raised a regiment of three-months men (the First Missouri Infantry) which later became the First Missouri Light Artillery. The First Missouri, under Colonel Blair, assisted Captain Lyon, U. S. A., in the capture of Camp Jackson, May 10, 1861. When, through Blair's influence, Lyon was made brigadier-general and placed in command of the Federal forces in Missouri, Governor Jackson and General Sterling Price at once ordered the militia to prepare itself for service on the Southern side, knowing that Lyon and Blair would quickly attack them. The First Missouri regiment accompanied General Lyon when he went to Booneville and dispersed over a thousand volunteers who had gathered there to enlist under the Confederacy, June 17th. This affair at Booneville practically made it impossible for Missouri to secede from the Union. Colonel Blair was promoted to brigadier-general in August, 1862, and was made major-general the following November.

(This photograph was taken when General Blair was at the head of the Seventeenth Army Corps in 1864–65. The composition of his staff was announced November 9, 1864, from Smyrna Camp Ground, Georgia. In the picture the general is seated in the armchair; on his right is Assistant Inspector-General A. Hickenlooper; on his left Assistant Adjutant-General C. Cadle, Jr. Standing are three of his aides-de-camp: from right to left, Logan Tompkins, William Henley, and G. R. Steele.)

# Engagements of the Civil War

Confed., 33 killed, 115 wounded, and 1 missing. *Union* Acting Brig.-Gen. E. D. Baker killed.

**23.—**West Liberty, Ky. *Union,* 2d Ohio, Konkle's Battery, Laughlin's Cavalry. *Confed.,* Capt. May's command. Losses: *Union* 2 wounded. *Confed.* 10 killed, 5 wounded.

**25.—**Springfield, Mo. "Zagonyi's Charge." *Union,* Fremont's Body Guard and White's Prairie Scouts. *Confed.\** Losses: *Union* 18 killed, 37 wounded. *Confed.* 106 killed (estimate).

**26.—**Romney or Mill Creek Mills, W. Va. *Union,* 4th and 8th Ohio, 7th W. Va., Md. Volunteers, 2d Regt. of Potomac Home Guards and Ringgold (Pa.) Cav. *Confed.,* Va. Vols. commanded by Gen. J. B. Floyd. Losses: *Union* 2 killed, 15 wounded. *Confed.* 20 killed, 15 wounded, 50 captured.

—Saratoga, Ky. *Union,* 9th Ill. *Confed.,* Capt. Wilcox's Cavalry. Losses: *Union* 4 wounded. *Confed.* 8 killed, 17 wounded.

## NOVEMBER, 1861.

**7.—**Belmont, Mo. *Union,* 22d, 27th, 30th, and 31st Ill., 7th Ia., Battery B 1st Ill. Artil., 2 companies 15th Ill. Cav. *Confed.,* 13th Ark., 11th La., 2d, 12th, 13th, 15th, 21st, 22d, 154th (Senior) Tenn. Watson's, Stewart's La. Art., Smith's Miss. Battery, Hamilton's siege Battery. Losses: *Union* 90 killed, 173 wounded, 235 missing. *Confed.* 261 killed, 427 wounded, 278 missing.

—Galveston Harbor, Tex. U. S. Frigate *Santee* burned the *Royal Yacht.* Losses: *Union* 1 killed, 8 wounded. *Confed.* 3 wounded.

—Port Royal, S. C. Capture of Fort Beauregard and Fort Walker (Confederate). *Union,* Du Pont's fleet, 17 vessels, and 3 brigades of land forces under Gen. Thomas W. Sherman. *Confed.,* 3 vessels under Flag-officer Josiah Tattnall, and 1 brigade of land forces under Gen. Thomas F. Drayton. Losses: *Union* 8 killed, 23 wounded. *Confed.* 11 killed, 48 wounded, 7 missing.

**8.—**Seizure of Jas. M. Mason and John Slidell, *Confed.* Commissioners to Europe on board of British steamer *Trent,* by U. S. steamer *San Jacinto.*

**9.—**Piketown or Ivy Mountain, Ky. *Union,* 33d Ohio and Col. Metcalf's Ky. Vols. *Confed.,* Col. J. S. Williams' command. Losses: *Union* 6 killed, 24 wounded. *Confed.* 18 killed, 45 wounded, 200 captured.

**10.—**Guyandotte, W. Va. *Union,* 9th Va. Vols. *Confed.,* Jenkins' Cav. Losses: *Union* 7 killed, 20 wounded. *Confed.* 3 killed, 10 wounded.

**12.—**Occoquan River and Pohick Church, Va. *Union,* 2d, 3d, 5th Mich., 37th N. Y., 4th Me., 2 cos. 1st N. Y. Cav., Randolph's and Thompson's Batteries U. S. Art. *Confed.,* outposts of Gen. Beauregard's command. Losses: *Union* 3 killed, 1 wounded.

**23.—**Ft. Pickens, Pensacola, Fla. *Union,* Cos. C and E 3d U. S. Inft., Cos. G and I 6th N. Y., Batteries A, F, and L 1st U. S. Artil., and C, H, and K 2d U. S. Artil. *Confed.,* Gen. Braxton Bragg's command in Fort McRee and numerous shore batteries. Losses: *Union* 5 killed, 7 wounded. *Confed.* 5 killed, 93 wounded.

**26.—**Drainesville, Va. *Union,* 1st Pa. Cav. *Confed.,* Stuart's Va. Cav. Losses: *Union* 1 wounded. *Confed.* 2 killed, 4 captured.

## DECEMBER, 1861.

**3.—**Salem, Mo. *Union,* 1st Battalion Mo. Cav. *Confed.,* Freeman's and Turner's Cav. Losses: *Union* 3 killed, 9 wounded. *Confed.* 16 killed, 20 wounded.

**4.—**Anandale, Va. *Union,* 45th N. Y. *Confed.,* Va. Cav. Losses: *Union* 1 killed, 14 missing. *Confed.* 3 killed, 2 missing.

**13.—**Camp Allegheny or Buffalo Mountain, W. Va. *Union* 9th and 13th Ind., 25th and 32 Ohio, 2d W. Va., *Confed.,* 12th Ga., 25th, 31st and 52d Va., Lee's and Miller's Art. Losses: *Union* 20 killed, 107 wounded. *Confed.* 20 killed, 98 wounded.

**17.—**Rowlett's Station, also called Munfordsville or Woodsonville, Ky. *Union,* 32d Ind. *Confed.,* Col. Terry's Texas Rangers. Losses: *Union* 10 killed, 22 wounded. *Confed.* 33 killed, 50 wounded.

**18.—**Milford, also called Shawnee Mound, or Blackwater, Mo. *Union,* 8th Ia., 7th

* No record found.

## FIRST FOOTHOLD ON THE SOUTHERN COAST.—THE FIFTIETH PENNSYLVANIA

Although the 12,600 troops under Brigadier-General Thomas W. Sherman took no part in the bombardment of the forts at Port Royal in November, 1861, their work was cut out for them when the abandoned works had to be occupied and rendered adequate for the defense of the Federal naval base here established upon the Southern coast. Particularly active in these operations was the brigade of General Stevens. We see him with his staff at his headquarters, an old Colonial mansion near Hilton Head. The Fiftieth Pennsylvania in Stevens Brigade won its first laurels in the campaigning and fighting which followed upon the conquest of Port Royal.

### GENERAL ISAAC I. STEVENS AND STAFF

# Engagements of the Civil War

Mo., 22d Ind., 1st Ia. Cav., Detach. 4th U. S. Cav., 1st Mo. Cav., 2 Batteries of 1st Mo. Lt. Artil. *Confed.*, Rains' Division. Losses: *Union* 2 killed, 8 wounded. *Confed.* 1,300 captured.

20.—Drainesville, Va. *Union*, 1st, 6th, 9th, 10th, and 12th Pa. Reserve Corps, 1st Pa. Artil., 1st Pa. Cav. *Confed.*, 1st Ky., 10th Ala., 6th S. C., 11th Va., Cutt's Art. Losses: *Union* 7 killed, 61 wounded. *Confed.* 43 killed, 143 wounded.

28.—Sacramento, Ky. *Union*, 3d Ky. Cav. *Confed.*, Forrest's Tenn. Cav. Losses: *Union* 8 killed, 8 captured. *Confed.* 2 killed, 3 wounded.

—Mt. Zion and Hallsville, Mo. *Union*, Birge's Sharpshooters, 3d Mo. Cav. *Confed.** Losses: *Union* 5 killed, 63 wounded. *Confed.* 25 killed, 150 wounded.

## JANUARY, 1862.

4.—Bath, Va. *Union,* 39th Ill. *Confed.*, Col. Loring's command. Losses: *Union* 3 killed, 3 wounded, 8 captured. *Confed.* 4 wounded.

7.—Hanging Rock Pass, Va. *Union*, parts of the 4th, 5th, 7th, 8th Ohio, 14th Ind., detachments of cavalry, Baker's and Daum's batteries. *Confed.*, Col. Monroe's Va. Vols. Losses: *Confed.* 15 killed.

8.—Charleston, Mo. *Union*, 10th Ia., 20th Ill., detachment Tenn. Cav. *Confed.** Losses: *Union* 8 killed, 16 wounded.

10.—Middle Creek, near Paintsville, Ky. *Union*, 14th, 22d Ky., 2d Va. Cav., 1st Ky. Cav., Squadron Ohio Cav. *Confed.*, 5th Ky., 29th, 54th Va., Ky. Mounted Rifles, 2 cos. dismounted Cav. Losses: *Union* 2 killed, 25 wounded. *Confed.* 11 killed, 15 wounded.

19 and 20.—Mill Springs, Ky., also called Logan's Cross Roads, Fishing Creek, Somerset and Beech Grove. *Union*, 9th Ohio, 2d Minn., 4th Ky., 10th Ind., 1st Ky. Cav. *Confed.*, 17th, 19th, 20th, 25th, 28th, 29th Tenn., 16th Ala., 15th Miss., Saunder's Cavalry, Bledsoe's Battery. Losses: *Union* 38 killed, 194 wounded. *Confed.* 190 killed, 160 wounded. *Confed.* Gen. F. K. Zollicoffer killed.

## FEBRUARY, 1862.

6.—Fort Henry, Tenn. *Union*, Gunboats *Essex, Carondelet, St. Louis, Cincinnati, Conestoga, Tyler,* and *Lexington.* *Confed.*, 10th, 48th, 51st Tenn., 15th Ark., 4th Miss., 27th Ala., B. 1st Tenn. Art. Culbertson's and Crain's Art., Milner's and Milton's Cavalry. Losses: *Union* 40 wounded. *Confed.* 5 killed, 11 wounded.

8.—Roanoke Island, N. C. *Union*, 21st, 23d, 24th, 25th and 27th Mass., 10th Conn., 9th, 51st, and 53d N. Y., 9th N. J., 51st Pa., 4th and 5th R. I., U. S. Gunboats *Southfield, Delaware, Stars and Stripes, Louisiana, Hetzel, Commodore Perry, Underwriter, Valley City, Commodore Barney, Hunchback, Ceres, Putnam, Morse, Lockwood, Seymour, Granite, Brinker, Whitehead, Shawseen, Pickett, Pioneer, Hussar, Vidette, Chasseur.* *Confed.*, 2d, 7th, 8th, 17th, 19th, 26th, 27th, 28th, 31st, 33d, 35th, 37th, 46th, 59th N. C., Brem's, Latham's, Whitehurst's N. C. Art., Gunboats *Seabird, Curlew, Ellis, Beaufort, Raleigh, Fanny, Forrest.* Losses: *Union* 35 killed, 200 wounded. *Confed.* 16 killed, 39 wounded, 2,527 taken prisoners.

10.—Elizabeth City, or Cobb's Point, N. C. *Union*, Gunboats *Delaware, Underwriter, Louisiana, Seymour, Hetzel, Shawseen, Valley City, Putnam, Commodore Perry, Ceres, Morse, Whitehead,* and *Brinker.* *Confed.*, " Mosquito fleet " commanded by Commodore W. F. Lynch, and comprising the vessels engaged at Roanoke Island on the 8th, except the *Curlew.* Losses: *Union* 3 killed.

13.—Bloomery Gap, Va. *Union*, Gen. Lander's Brigade. *Confed.*, 31st, 67th, 89th Va. Losses: *Union* 11 killed, 5 wounded. *Confed.* 13 killed, 65 missing.

14–16.—Fort Donelson, or Dover, Tenn. *Union*, Gunboats *Carondelet, Pittsburgh, Louisville, St. Louis, Tyler,* and *Conestoga,* 17th and 25th Ky., 11th, 25th, 31st, and 44th Ind., 2d, 7th, 12th and 14th Iowa, 1st Neb., 58th and 76th Ohio, 8th and 13th Mo., 8th Wis., 8th, 9th, 11th, 12th, 17th, 18th, 20th, 28th, 29th, 30th, 31st, 41st, 45th, 46th, 48th, 49th, 57th, and 58th Ill., Batteries B and D 1st Ill.

* No record found.

[ 356 ]

### THE 10-INCH COLUMBIAD AT FORT WALKER, HILTON HEAD, SOUTH CAROLINA

The Capture of the Confederate forts at Port Royal, South Carolina. On the 29th of October, 1861, there sailed from Hampton Roads the most formidable squadron ever fitted out in American waters—men-of-war commanded by Flag-Officer Samuel F. Du Pont in the *Wabash*, and army transports with a force of twelve thousand men under General Thomas W. Sherman, bound for Port Royal Harbor, twenty miles north of the mouth of the Savannah River. On November 1st, off Hatteras, a severe gale was encountered and for a time the fleet was much scattered, but by the 4th it was again united at the bar outside Port Royal Harbor over which the *Wabash* led the way. The harbor fortifications which had been erected by the Confederates were no small affairs. Fort Walker on Hilton Head Island was two miles and a half across the entrance from Fort Beauregard. Each had at least twenty guns of different caliber. On November 7th the Federal fleet attacked in close action. The men on shore were scarcely able to reply to the terrific broadsides of the main body of the big fleet as it passed back and forth through the harbor entrance, while other vessels outside enfiladed the forts. At the third round of the ships the Confederates could be seen leaving Fort Walker and before half-past two in the afternoon Commander Rodgers had planted the Federal flag on the ramparts. Before sunset Fort Beauregard was likewise deserted. This victory placed in possession of the North one of the finest harbors of the Southern coast. In the lower picture we see the ferry over the Coosaw River, near Port Royal, showing on the opposite shore the site of the Confederate batteries seized and demolished by General I. I. Stevens, January 1, 1862.

### FERRY ACROSS THE COOSAW, PORT ROYAL

Art., D and E 2d Ill. Artil., four cos. Ill. Cav., Birge's Sharpshooters and six gunboats. *Confed.*, 2d, 8th Ky., 1st, 3d, 4th, 20th, 26th Miss., 27th Ala., 3d, 10th, 18th, 26th, 30th, 42d, 48th, 49th, 50th, 53d Tenn., 7th Tex., 15th Ark., 36th, 50th, 51st, 56th Va., Forrest's Cavalry, 9th Tenn. Battalion Colm's Battalion. Losses: *Union* 500 killed, 2,108 wounded, 224 missing. *Confed.* 231 killed, 1,534 wounded, 13,829 prisoners (estimated). *Union* Maj.-Gen. John A. Logan wounded.

17.—Sugar Creek, or Pea Ridge, Ark. *Union,* 1st, 6th Mo., 3d Ill. Cav. *Confed.*, Bowen's Mo. Battalion. Losses: *Union* 13 killed, 15 wounded.

21.—Ft. Craig, or Valverde, N. Mex. *Union,* 1st N. Mex. Cav., 2d Col. Cav., Detachments of 1st, 2d, and 5th N. Mex., and of 5th, 7th, and 10th U. S. Inft., Hill's and McRae's Batteries. *Confed.*, 2d, 4th, 5th, 7th Tex. Cavalry, Teel's Art. Losses: *Union* 62 killed, 140 wounded. *Confed.* 36 killed, 150 wounded.

26.—Keetsville, Mo. *Union,* 6th Mo. Cav. *Confed.*, Ross' Texas Rangers. Losses: *Union* 2 killed, 1 wounded. *Confed.* 3 killed, 1 missing.

## MARCH, 1862.

1.—Pittsburg Landing, Tenn. *Union,* 32d Ill. and U. S. Gunboats *Lexington* and *Tyler. Confed.*, Gen. Daniel Ruggles' command. Losses: *Union* 5 killed, 5 wounded. *Confed.* 20 killed, 200 wounded.

6, 7, and 8.—Pea Ridge, Ark., including engagements at Bentonville, Leetown, and Elkhorn Tavern. *Union,* 25th, 35th, 36th, 37th, 44th, and 59th Ill., 2d, 3d, 12th, 15th, 17th, 24th, and Phelps' Mo., 8th, 18th, and 22d Ind., 4th and 9th Iowa, 3d Iowa Cav., 3d and 15th Ill. Cav., 1st, 4th, 5th, and 6th Mo. Cav., Batteries B and F 2d Mo. Light Artil., 2d Ohio Battery, 1st Ind. Battery, Battery A 2d Ill. Artil. *Confed.*, 1st, 2d Mo. State Guard, Greene's Brigade, 1st, 2d, 3d, 4th, 5th, 6th Mo., 4th, 14th, 16th, 17th, 19th, 21st, 22d Ark., 1st, 2d Ark. Mounted Rifles, 3d La., 3 Indian regiments, Wade's, Guibor's, Bledsoe's, Teel's, Clark's, MacDonald's, Hart's, Provence's, Gaines' and Good's batteries, 1st Mo. Cavalry, Shel-

by's Cavalry, 3d, 4th, 6th, 11th Tex. Cavalry. Losses: *Union* 203 killed, 972 wounded, 174 missing. *Confed.* 800 to 1,000 killed and wounded, 200 to 300 m i s s i n g and captured (estimated). *Union* Brig.-Gen. Asboth and Actg. Brig.-Gen. Carr wounded. *Confed.* Brig.-Gen. B. McCulloch and Actg. Brig.-Gen. James McIntosh killed.

8.—Near Nashville, Tenn. *Union,* 4th Ohio Cav. *Confed.*, Morgan's Ky. Cav. Losses: *Union* 1 killed, 2 wounded. *Confed.* 4 killed, 2 wounded.

—Hampton Roads, Va. *Union,* 20th Ind., 7th and 11th N. Y., Gunboats *Minnesota, Congress, Zouave,* and *Cumberland. Confed.*, Ram *Virginia (Merrimac).* Losses: *Union* 261 killed, 108 wounded. *Confed.* 7 killed, 17 wounded. *Confed.* Commodore Buchanan, wounded.

9.—Hampton Roads, Va. First battle between iron-clad warships. *Union, The Monitor. Confed.,* Ram *Virginia.* Losses: *Union* Capt. J. L. Worden, wounded.

14.—Jacksborough, Big Creek Gap, Tenn. *Union,* 2d E. Tenn. *Confed.*, 1st E. Tenn. Cav. Losses: *Union* 2 wounded. *Confed.* 5 killed, 15 wounded, 15 missing.

11.—Paris, Tenn. *Union,* 1 Battalion 5th Ia. Cav., Bulliss' Mo. Art. *Confed.*, King's Mounted Rifles. Losses: *Union* 5 killed, 3 wounded. *Confed.* 10 wounded.

13-14.—New Madrid, Mo. Bombardment and capture by Gen. Jno. Pope's command. *Union,* 10th and 16th Ill., 27th, 39th, 43d, and 63d Ohio, 3d Mich. Cav., 1st U. S. Inft., Bissell's Mo. Engineers. *Confed.*, 1st Ala., 40th C. S., 46th, 55th Tenn., Heavy Art. Corps. Losses: *Union* 51 wounded. *Confed.* 100 wounded.

14.—Newberne, N. C. *Union,* 51st N. Y., 8th, 10th, and 11th Conn., 21st, 23d, 24th, 25th, and 27th Mass., 9th N. J., 51st Pa., 4th and 5th R. I. *Confed.*, 7th, 26th, 33d, 35th N. C. Losses: *Union* 91 killed, 466 wounded. *Confed.* 64 killed, 106 wounded, 413 captured.

16.—Pound Gap, Tenn. *Union,* Detachs. of 22d Ky., 40th and 42d Ohio Vols., and 1st Ohio Cav. *Confed.*, 21st Va. Losses: *Confed.* 7 killed.

18.—Salem, or Spring River, Ark. *Union,* Detachments 6th Mo., 3d Ia. Cav.

THE GARDEN OF A SOUTHERN MANSION

Here we see the garden of the manor house of John E. Seabrook on Edisto Island, off the Carolina coast. It is now in possession of the Federal troops, but the fine old house was unharmed, and the garden, although not in luxuriant bloom, gives an idea of its own beauty. In the distance are seen the slave quarters, and some of the old plantation servants have mingled with the troops when the picture was being taken. Observe the little colored boy saluting on the pedestal against which leans a Federal officer.

THE SOUTHERN NAVAL BASE OF THE BLOCKADING SQUADRON OF THE NORTH

The Transformation Wrought at Hilton Head by the Naval Engineers. Hilton Head became the base of supplies and the most important part of the blockade, for it was within a few hours' steaming of the ports of entry that the South depended upon in gaining supplies from the outer world, Savannah, Charleston, and Wilmington. After the Federal occupation it was turned into a busy place. Colliers were constantly landing and supplies of all kinds being sent out from here to the blockading vessels kept at sea.

Confed.* Losses: *Union* 4 killed, 18 wounded. *Confed.* 100 killed, wounded, and missing (estimated).

**22.**—Independence or Little Santa Fé, Mo. *Union,* 2d Kan. Cav. *Confed.,* Quantrell's Irregulars. Losses: *Union* 1 killed, 2 wounded. *Confed.* 7 killed.

**23.**—Winchester or Kearnstown, Va. *Union,* 1st W. Va., 84th and 110th Pa., 5th, 7th, 8th, 29th, 62d, and 67th Ohio, 7th, 13th, and 14th Ind., 39th Ill., 1st Ohio Cav., 1st Mich. Cav., 1st W. Va. Artil., 1st Ohio Artil., Co. E 4th U. S. Artil. *Confed.,* 2d, 4th, 5th, 21st, 23d, 27th, 33d, 37th, 42d Va. 1st Va. (Irish) Battalion, Pleasant's, Chew's, Lanier's Va. batteries, 7th Va. Cavalry. Losses: *Union* 103 killed, 440 wounded, 24 missing. *Confed.* 80 killed 342 wounded, 269 prisoners.

**26.**—Humansville, Mo. *Union,* Battalion Mo. Cav. *Confed.,* Col. Frazier's command. Losses: *Union* 12 wounded. *Confed.* 15 killed, 20 wounded.

**26, 27, and 28.**—Apache Cañon, or Glorietta, near Santa Fé, N. Mex. *Union,* 1st and 2d Colo. Cav. *Confed.,* 2d, 4th, 5th, and 7th Tex. Cavalry, Teel's Art. Losses: *Union* 32 killed, 75 wounded, 35 missing. *Confed.* 36 killed, 60 wounded, 93 missing.

**28.**—Warrensburg, Mo. *Union,* 1st Ia. Cav. *Confed.,* Col. Parker's command. Losses: *Union* 1 killed, 2 wounded. *Confed.* 15 killed and wounded, 15 missing.

## APRIL, 1862.

**5.**—Warwick and Yorktown Roads, Va. *Union,* Advance of 4th Corps, Army of Potomac, towards Yorktown. *Confed.* Gen. J. B. Magruder's command. Losses: *Union* 3 killed, 12 wounded. *Confed.* 1 killed, 10 wounded.

**5-May 4.**—Siege of Yorktown, Va. *Union,* Army of Potomac, Gen. Geo. B. McClellan. *Confed.,* Army commanded by Gen. Joseph E. Johnston.

**6 and 7.**—Shiloh or Pittsburg Landing, Tenn. *Union,* Army of Western Tennessee, commanded by Maj.-Gen. U. S. Grant, as follows: 1st Div., Maj.-Gen. J. A. McClernand; 2d Div., Maj.-Gen. C. F. Smith; 3d Div., Brig.-Gen. Lew Wallace; 4th Div., Brig.-Gen. S. A. Hurlburt; 5th Div., Brig.-Gen. W. T. Sherman; 6th Div., Brig.-Gen. B. M. Prentiss. Army of the Ohio commanded by Maj.-Gen. D. C. Buell, as follows: 2d Div., Brig.-Gen. A. McD. Cook; 4th Div., Brig.-Gen. W. Nelson; 5th Div., Brig.-Gen. T. L. Crittenden, 21st Brigade of the 6th Div., Gunboats *Tyler* and *Lexington.* *Confed.,* Army of the Mississippi, commanded by Gen. Albert Sidney Johnston, as follows: 1st Corps, Maj.-Gen. Leonidas Polk; 2d Corps, Maj.-Gen. Braxton Bragg; 3d Corps, Maj.-Gen. Wm. J. Hardee; Reserve Corps, Brig.-Gen. John C. Breckinridge; Forrest's, Wharton's and Clanton's Cavalry. Losses: *Union* 1,754 killed, 8,408 wounded, 2,885 captured. *Confed.* 1,728 killed, 8,012 wounded, 959 captured. *Union* Brig.-Gen. W. T. Sherman and W. H. L. Wallace wounded and B. M. Prentiss captured. *Confed.* Gen. A. S. Johnston and Brig.-Gen. A. H. Gladden killed; Maj.-Gen. W. S. Cheatham and Brig.-Gens. C. Clark, B. R. Johnson, and J. S. Bowen wounded.

**7 and 8.**—Island No. 10, Tenn., captured. *Union,* Maj.-Gen. Pope's command and the Navy, under Flag-officer Foote. *Confed.,* Brigade of Infantry and Battalion Art., commanded by Gen. J. P. McCown, 7 gunboats, under Flag-officer Hollins. Losses: *Union* 17 killed, 34 wounded, 3 missing. *Confed.* 30 killed and wounded. Captured, 2,000 to 5,000 (*Union* and *Confed.* estimates).

**10 and 11.**—Ft. Pulaski, Ga., Siege and capture. *Union,* 6th and 7th Conn., 3d R. I., 46th and 48th N. Y., 8th Maine, 15th U. S. Inft., Crew of U. S. S. *Wabash.* *Confed.,* 5 companies heavy art., commanded by Col. C. H. Olmstead. Losses: *Union* 1 killed. *Confed.* 4 wounded, 360 prisoners.

**14.**—Montevallo, Mo. *Union,* 2 cos. 1st Iowa Cav. *Confed.** Losses: *Union* 2 killed, 4 wounded. *Confed.* 22 captured.

**16.**—Whitemarsh or Wilmington Island, Ga. *Union,* 8th Mich., Battery of R. I. Light Artil. *Confed.,* 13th Ga. Losses: *Union* 10 killed, 35 wounded. *Confed.* 4 killed, 15 wounded.

—Lee's Mills, Va. *Union,* 3d, 4th, and 6th Vt., 3d N. Y. Battery and Battery of 5th U. S. Artil. *Confed.,* Gen. J. B. Ma-

* No record found.

THE CLOSING OF SAVANNAH, APRIL 12, 1862

This terrific punishment was inflicted upon the nearest angle of the fort by the thirty-six heavy rifled cannon and the mortars which the Federals had planted on Big Tybee Island, and by the gunboats which had found a channel enabling them to get in the rear of the fort. We get a more distant view of the angle in the lower picture. Fort Pulaski had been effectually blockaded since February, 1862, as a part of the Federal plan to establish supreme authority along the Atlantic coast from Wassaw Sound, below Savannah, north to Charleston. On April 10, 1862, General Hunter demanded the surrender of Fort Pulaski and when it was refused opened the bombardment. For two days the gallant garrison held out and then finding the fort untenable, surrendered. This enabled the Federal Government effectually to close Savannah against contraband traffic.

FORT PULASKI AT THE ENTRANCE TO SAVANNAH RIVER

gruder's division, Yorktown garrison. Losses: *Union* 35 killed, 129 wounded. *Confed.* 20 killed, 75 wounded, 50 captured.

**17 to 19.**—Falmouth and Fredericksburg, Va. *Union,* Gen. McDowell's Army. *Confed.,* Gen. Field's Brigade. Losses: *Union* 7 killed, 16 wounded. *Confed.* 3 killed, 8 captured.

**18 to 28.**—Forts Jackson and St. Philip, and the capture of New Orleans, La. *Union,* Commodore Farragut's fleet of gunboats, and mortar boats under Commander D. D. Porter. *Confed.,* Gen. Mansfield Lovell's army, fleet of gunboats. Losses: *Union* 36 killed, 193 wounded. *Confed.* 185 killed, 197 wounded, 400 captured.

**19.**—Camden, N. C., also called South Mills. *Union,* 9th and 89th N. Y., 21st Mass., 51st Pa., 6th N. H. *Confed.,* 3d Ga., McComas' Art., 1 co. Cavalry. Losses: *Union* 12 killed, 98 wounded. *Confed.* 6 killed, 19 wounded.

**25.**—Fort Macon, N. C. *Union,* U. S. Gunboats *Daylight, State of Georgia, Chippewa,* the Bark *Gemsbok,* and Gen. Parke's division. *Confed.,* Garrison commanded by Col. M. J. White. Losses: *Union* 1 killed, 11 wounded. *Confed.* 7 killed, 18 wounded, 450 captured.

**26.**—Neosho, Mo. *Union,* 1st Mo. Cav. *Confed.,* Watie's Stand Cherokee Regiment. Losses: *Union* 3 killed, 3 wounded. *Confed.* 2 killed, 5 wounded.

—In front of Yorktown, Va. *Union, 3* companies 1st Mass. *Confed.** Losses: *Union* 4 killed, 12 wounded. *Confed.* 14 captured.

**29.**—Bridgeport, Ala. *Union,* 3d Div. Army of the Ohio. *Confed.* Leadbetter's Division. Losses: *Confed.* 72 killed and wounded, 350 captured.

**—to June 10.**—Siege of Corinth, Miss. *Union,* Gen. Halleck's Army. *Confed.,* Army commanded by Gen. Beauregard.

## MAY, 1862.

**1.**—Camp Creek, W. Va. *Union,* Co. C., 23d Ohio. *Confed.,* Detachment 8th Va. Cav. Losses: *Union* 1 killed, 21 wounded. *Confed.* 1 killed, 12 wounded.

**4.**—Evacuation of Yorktown, Va., by Confederate Army under Gen. Joseph E. Johnston.

**5.**—Lebanon, Tenn. *Union,* 1st, 4th, and 5th Ky. Cav., Detachment of 7th Pa. *Confed.,* Col. J. H. Morgan's Ky. Cavalry. Losses: *Union* 6 killed, 25 wounded. *Confed.* 66 prisoners.

—Lockridge Mills or Dresden, Ky. *Union,* 5th Iowa Cav. *Confed.,* 6th Confederate Cav. Losses: *Union* 4 killed, 16 wounded, 71 missing.

—Williamsburg, Va. *Union,* 3d and 4th Corps, Army of the Potomac. *Confed.,* Gen. James Longstreet's, Gen. D. Hill's Division of Gen. Joseph E. Johnston's army, J. E. B. Stuart's Cavalry Brigade. Losses: *Union* 456 killed, 1,400 wounded, 372 missing. *Confed.* 1,000 killed, wounded, and captured.

**7.**—West Point or Eltham's Landing, Va. *Union,* 16th, 27th, 31st, and 32d N. Y., 95th and 96th Pa., 5th Maine, 1st Mass. Artil., Battery D 2d U. S. Artil. *Confed.,* Gen. Wade Hampton's Brigade, Gen. J. B. Hood's Texan Brigade. Losses: *Union* 49 killed, 104 wounded, 41 missing. *Confed.* 8 killed, 40 wounded.

—Somerville Heights, Va. *Union,* 13th Ind. *Confed.* Maj. Wheat's La. Battalion. Losses: *Union* 3 killed, 5 wounded, 21 missing.

**8.**—McDowell or Bull Pasture, Va. *Union,* 25th, 32d, 75th, and 82d Ohio, 3d W. Va., 1st W. Va. Cav., 1st Conn. Cav., 1st Ind. Battery. *Confed.,* 12th Ga., 10th, 21st, 23d, 25th, 31st, 37th, 42d, 44th, 48th, 52d, 58th, Va., 1st Va. (Irish) Battalion. Losses: *Union* 28 killed, 225 wounded, 3 missing. *Confed.* 75 killed, 424 wounded and missing.

**9.**—Elk River, Ala. *Union,* 1st Ky. Cav. *Confed.,* Texas Rangers. Losses: *Union* 5 killed, 7 wounded. *Confed.* 45 missing.

—Norfolk, Va. Evacuated by the Confederates.

—Farmington, Miss. *Union,* Gen. Plummer's Brigade, Army of the Mississippi. *Confed.,* Gen. Ruggles' Division. Losses: *Union* 16 killed, 148 wounded, 192 missing. *Confed.* 8 killed, 189 wounded, 110 missing.

**10.**—Plum Point, near Fort Pillow, Tenn. Gunboat battle. *Union,* Gunboats *Cincinnati, Carondelet, Benton, Pittsburg, St. Louis,* and *Mound City. Confed.,* eight rams of the River Defense Fleet.

* No record found.

OHIO SOLDIERS WHO FOUGHT UNDER GARFIELD FOR KENTUCKY

The Forty-second Ohio Infantry was one of the regiments that helped to settle the position of Kentucky in the issue between the States. A large Southern element was contained within its borders although it had not joined the Confederacy, and in order to obtain recruits for their army, and to control the great salt works, lead-mines, and lines of railway, the Confederate authorities sent General Humphrey Marshall with a small force into eastern Kentucky in November, 1861. General Buell promptly formed a brigade from the Army of the Ohio, put it in command of James A. Garfield, Colonel of the Forty-second Ohio, with orders to drive General Marshall from the State. This was accomplished by the engagement at Middle Creek, January 10, 1862. This photograph was taken in 1864 while the regiment was stationed at Plaquemine, Louisiana.

General John Charles Frémont (1813–1890). Already a famous explorer and scientist, the first presidential candidate of the Republican party (in 1856), Frémont, at the outbreak of the war, hastened home from Europe to take command of the newly created Western Department. He was born in Savannah, Georgia. His father was a Frenchman and his mother a Virginian, and his temperament was characterized by all the impetuosity of such an ancestry. Upon his arrival in St. Louis he found things in great confusion. The Missourians were divided in sentiment and the home guards were unwilling to reënlist. The U. S. Treasurer at St. Louis had

GENERAL FRÉMONT (ON THE RIGHT) AND
MRS. FRÉMONT

$300,000 in his hands, and Frémont called upon him for a portion of it to enable him to enlist men in the Federal cause. The Treasurer refused, but upon Frémont's threatening to take $100,000 without further ceremony, the funds were turned over. With about four thousand troops, Frémont seized Cairo, and by various demonstrations checked the aggressive attitude of the Confederates on the Kentucky and Tennessee borders, and of the Southern sympathizers in Missouri. Before he was transferred out of the West in November, 1861, Frémont had raised an army of fifty-six thousand men, and was already advancing upon an expedition down the Mississippi.

Losses: *Union* 4 wounded. *Confed.* 2 killed, 1 wounded.

—Norfolk and Portsmouth, Va., occupied by Union forces under Gen. Wool.

**11.**—Confederate Ram *Virginia* destroyed in Hampton Roads by her commander, to prevent capture.

**15.**—Fort Darling, James River, Va. *Union,* Gunboats *Galena, Port Royal, Naugatuck, Monitor,* and *Aroostook. Confed.* Garrison in Fort Darling. Losses: *Union* 12 killed, 14 wounded. *Confed.* 7 killed, 8 wounded.

—Chalk Bluffs, Mo. *Union,* 1st Wis. Cav. *Confed.,* Col. Jeffers' command. Losses: *Union* 2 killed, 5 wounded. *Confed.* 11 killed, 17 wounded.

**15, 16, and 18.**—Princeton, W. Va. *Union,* Gen. J. D. Cox's Division. *Confed.,* Gen. Humphrey Marshall's command. Losses: *Union* 33 killed, 69 wounded, 27 missing. *Confed.* 2 killed, 14 wounded.

**17.**—In front of Corinth, Miss. *Union,* Gen. M. L. Smith's Brigade. *Confed.,* Outposts of Gen. Beauregard's army. Losses: *Union* 10 killed, 31 wounded. *Confed.* 12 killed.

**19.**—Searcy Landing, Ark. *Union,* 17th Mo., 4th Mo. Cav., 2 cos. 4th Ia. Cav. *Confed.\** Losses: *Union* 75 killed, 32 wounded. *Confed.* 150 killed, wounded, and missing.

**23.**—Lewisburg, Va. *Union,* 36th, 44th Ohio, 2d W. Va. Cav. *Confed.* 22d, 45th Va., 1 battalion 8th Va. Cav., Finney's Battalion. Losses: *Union* 14 killed, 60 wounded. *Confed.* 40 k i l l e d, 66 wounded, 100 captured.

—Front Royal, Va. *Union,* 1st Md., Detachments of 29th Pa., Capt. Mapes' Pioneers, 5th N. Y. Cav., and 1st Pa. Artil. *Confed.,* 1st Md., Wheat's La. Battalion, 6th, 7th, 8th La. Losses: *Union* 32 killed, 122 wounded, 750 missing. *Confed.\**

**23 and 24.**—Ellison's Mills, Mechanicsville, and New Bridge, Va. *Union,* 33d, 49th, 77th N. Y., 7th Me., 4th Mich., Tidball's Battery. *Confed.,* 8th, 9th, 10th Ga., part of 1st and 4th Va. Cav., 5th La., battery La. Art., squadron La. Cav. Losses: *Union* 7 killed, 30 wounded. *Confed.* 27 killed, 35 wounded, 43 captured.

**24 to 31.**—Retreat of Gen. N. P. Banks' command (*Union*) from Strasburg, Va., down the Shenandoah Valley, including Middletown and Newtown the 24th, Winchester the 25th, Charlestown the 28th, and Harper's Ferry the 24th to 30th. *Confed.,* Stonewall Jackson's command, including the troops engaged at Front Royal the 23d. Losses: *Union* 62 killed, 243 wounded, 174 missing. *Confed.* 68 killed, 329 wounded (includes losses at Front Royal the 23d).

**27.**—Hanover C. H., Va. *Union,* 12th, 13th, 14th, 17th, 25th, and 44th N. Y., 62d and 83d Pa., 16th Mich., 9th and 22d Mass., 5th Mass. Artil., 2d Maine Artil., Battery F 5th U. S. Artil., 1st U. S. Sharpshooters. *Confed.,* Gen. L. O'B. Branch's N. C. Brigade. Losses: *Union* 53 killed, 344 wounded. *Confed.* 200 killed and wounded, 730 prisoners.

**30.**—Booneville, Miss. *Union,* 2d Ia., 2d Mich. Cav. *Confed.\** Losses: *Confed.* 2,000 prisoners.

—Corinth, Miss. Evacuation by Confederate army under Gen. Beauregard. Occupation by Union troops of Gen. Halleck's command. End of siege begun April 29. Losses: (No detailed report on file.)

—Front Royal, Va. *Union,* 4th, 8th Ohio, 14th Ind., detachment 1st R. I. Cav. *Confed.,* 8th La., 12th Ga., Ashby's Va. Cav. Losses: *Union* 8 killed, 7 wounded. *Confed.* 156 captured.

**31 and June 1.**—Seven Pines and Fair Oaks, Va. *Union,* 2d Corps, 3d Corps, and 4th Corps, Army of the Potomac. *Confed.,* Army commanded by Gen. Joseph E. Johnston, as follows: Gen. James Longstreet's Division; Gen. D. H. Hill's Division; Gen. Benjamin Huger's Division; Gen. G. W. Smith's Division. Losses: *Union* 790 killed, 3,627 wounded, 647 missing. *Confed.* 980 killed, 4,749 wounded, 405 missing. *Union* Brig.-Gen'ls O. O. Howard, Naglee, and Wessells wounded. *Confed.* Brig.-Gen. Hatton killed, Gen. J. E. Johnston and Brig.-Gen. Rodes wounded, Brig.-Gen. Pettigrew captured.

**JUNE, 1862.**

**3.**—Legare's Point; S. C. *Union,* 28th Mass., 8th Mich., 100th Pa. *Confed.,*

* No record found.

The Last Struggle for the River. The fall of Vicksburg was imminent in July, 1863, and seeing this the Confederates determined to make one last herculean effort to retain a hold upon the Mississippi and prevent the Confederacy from being divided. General Holmes collected a force of about nine thousand Confederates and advanced through Arkansas upon Fort Curtis, the principal defense of Helena. There General Prentiss opposed him with a garrison of but 4,129. In the early dawn of July 4, 1863, Holmes hurled his forces upon the battlements of Fort Curtis. He was met with a resistance entirely beyond his expectations. Not only were the Confederates mowed down by the fire from the fort, but the gunboat *Tyler* lying in the river enfiladed the columns pouring through the ravines to support the attack. It was impossible to withstand the deadly rain of shell and shrapnel, and the order was given to withdraw. On the field were left two thousand dead and wounded Confederates.

GENERAL SAMUEL RYAN CURTIS

Most of the dead were buried by the victorious Federals, and more than a thousand wounded were taken prisoners.

Fort Curtis was named for General Samuel Ryan Curtis, who assumed command of the Federal District of Southwest Missouri at the close of 1861. The battle at Pea Ridge, or Elkhorn, Arkansas, near the Missouri border, March, 1862, was a Confederate reverse and was followed by the transfer of the principal Confederate commands which fought there to other fields, leaving Curtis in control. After a stubbornly contested march across Arkansas he arrived on the Mississippi, July 13, 1862, and began to fortify Helena. From that time it was held by the Federals undisputed until the attack of General Holmes. The day of the repulse at Fort Curtis, Vicksburg surrendered to Grant; Port Hudson, Louisiana, on the east bank, yielded to Banks five days later, after a siege of six weeks, and the Mississippi passed forever from the control of the Confederacy.

*From the Meserve Collection.*

FORT CURTIS, HELENA, ARKANSAS

# Engagements of the Civil War

24th S. C., Charleston, S. C., Battalion. Losses: *Union* 5 wounded. *Confed.* 17 wounded.

**3 to 5.**—Fort Pillow, Tenn. Evacuation by Confederates and occupation by Union troops commanded by Col. G. A. Fitch.

**5.**—Tranter's Creek, N. C. *Union,* 24th Mass., Co. I 3d N. Y. Cav. Avery's Battery Marine Art. *Confed.* Losses: *Union* 7 killed, 11 wounded.

**6.**—Memphis, Tenn. *Union,* U. S. Gunboats *Benton, Louisville, Carondelet, Cairo,* and *St. Louis;* and Rams *Monarch* and *Queen of the West. Confed.,* River Defense fleet of 8 gunboats. Losses: *Confed.* 80 killed and wounded, 100 captured.

—Harrisonburg, Va. *Union,* 1st N. J. Cav., 1st Pa. Rifles, 60th Ohio, 8th W. Va. *Confed.,* 1st Md. and 58th Va. Losses: *Union* 63 missing. *Confed.* 17 killed, 50 wounded. *Confed.* Gen. Turner Ashby killed.

**8.**—Cross Keys or Union Church, Va. *Union,* 8th, 39th, 41st, 45th, 54th, and 58th N. Y., 2d, 3d, 5th, and 8th W. Va., 25th, 32d, 55th, 60th, 73d, 75th, and 82d Ohio, 1st and 27th Pa., 1st Ohio Battery. *Confed.,* Winder's, Trimble's, Campbell's, Taylor's brigades, 4 Va. batteries of "Stonewall" Jackson's command. Losses: *Union* 125 killed, 500 wounded. *Confed.* 42 killed, 230 wounded. *Confed.* Brig.-Gens. Stuart and Elzey wounded.

**9.**—Port Republic, Va. *Union,* 5th, 7th, 29th, and 66th Ohio, 84th and 110th Pa., 7th Ind., 1st W. Va., Batteries E 4th U. S. and A and L 1st Ohio Artil. *Confed.,* Winder's, Campbell's, Fulkerson's, Scott's, Elzey's, Taylor's brigades, 6 Va. batteries. Losses: *Union* 67 killed, 361 wounded, 574 missing. *Confed.* 88 killed, 535 wounded, 34 missing.

**10.**—James Island, S. C. *Union,* 97th Pa., 2 cos. 45th Pa., 2 cos. 47th N. Y., Battery E 3d U. S. Art. *Confed.,* 47th Ga. Losses: *Union* 3 killed, 19 wounded. *Confed.* 17 killed, 30 wounded.

**14.**—Tunstall's Station, Va. Stuart's Va. Cav. fire into railway train. Losses: *Union* 4 killed, 8 wounded.

**16.**—Secessionville or Fort Johnson, James Island, S. C. *Union,* 46th, 47th, and 79th N. Y., 3d R. I., 3d N. H., 45th, 97th, and 100th Pa., 6th and 7th Conn., 8th Mich., 28th Mass., 1st N. Y. Engineers, 1st Conn. Artil., Battery E 3d U. S. and I 3d R. I. Artil., Co. H 1st Mass. Cav. *Confed.,* Garrison troops commanded by Gen. N. G. Evans. Losses: *Union* 85 killed, 472 wounded, 138 missing. *Confed.* 51 killed, 144 wounded.

**17.**—St. Charles, White River, Ark. *Union,* 43d and 46th Ind., U. S. Gunboats *Lexington, Mound City, Conestoga,* and *St. Louis. Confed.,* Gunboats *Maurepas* and *Pontchartrain,* 114 soldiers and sailors commanded by Lieut. Joseph Fry. Losses: *Union* 105 killed, 30 wounded. *Confed.* 155 killed, wounded, and captured.

**—and 18.**—Evacuation of Cumberland Gap, Tenn., by Confederates of Gen. C. L. Stevenson's command, and occupation by Gen. G. W. Morgan's Federal division.

**18.**—Williamsburg Road, Va. *Union,* 16th Mass. *Confed.* Losses: *Union* 17 killed, 28 wounded, 14 captured. *Confed.* 5 killed, 9 wounded.

**25.**—Oak Grove, Va., also called Kings School House and The Orchards. *Union,* Hooker's and Kearney's Divisions of the Third Corps, Palmer's Brigade of the Fourth Corps, and part of Richardson's Division of the Second Corps. *Confed.,* Armistead's brigade. Losses: *Union* 51 killed, 401 wounded, 64 missing. *Confed.* 65 killed, 465 wounded, 11 missing.

**26 to 29.**—Vicksburg, Miss. U. S. Fleet, under command of Commodore Farragut, passed the Confederate land batteries, under the cover of bombardment by Commodore Porter's fleet of mortar boats.

**26 to July 1.**—The Seven Days' Battles, in front of Richmond, Va., including engagements known as Mechanicsville or Ellerson's Mills on the 26th, Gaines' Mills or Cold Harbor on the 27th, Garnett's and Golding's Farms on the 28th, Peach Orchard and Savage Station on the 29th, White Oak Swamp, also called Charles City Cross Roads, Glendale or Nelson's Farm or Frayser's Farm, New Market Road on the 30th, and Malvern Hill or Crew's Farm on July 1st. *Union*—Army of the Potomac, Maj.-Gen. Geo. B. McClellan commanding. Losses: First Corps, Brig.-Gen. Geo. A.

* No record found.

[366]

BRIGADIER–GENERAL
NATHANIEL LYON

These fearless leaders by their prompt and daring actions at the outbreak of the war kept Missouri within the Union. Captain Nathaniel Lyon, U. S. A., a veteran of the Mexican War, had been on duty in Kansas during the "free soil" riots and knew what it was to see a State torn by dissension. At the outbreak of the war he was in command of the United States arsenal at St. Louis. Franz Sigel, a Prussian refugee, had settled in St. Louis in 1858, and in May, 1861, raised the Union Third Missouri Infantry and became its colonel. Under Lyon he helped to capture Camp Jackson, St. Louis, where General Frost was drilling a small body of volunteer state militia. On June 1, 1861, the command of the Federal Department of the West was given to Lyon, who had been

MAJOR–GENERAL
FRANZ SIGEL

made brigadier-general, and Governor Jackson, calling for fifty thousand troops "to repel the invasion of the State" left the capital for Booneville, June 14th. Lyon followed, dispersed the militia on the 17th, and other Confederate troops, under McCulloch, at Dug Springs, on August 2d. Meanwhile he had sent Sigel with twelve hundred men into southwestern Missouri, and on July 5th that intrepid leader

MAJOR–GENERAL
JOHN C. BRECKINRIDGE

fought the battle of Carthage. Greatly outnumbered, he finally retreated to Springfield, where he arrived on July 13th, and was later joined by Lyon. McCulloch had been joined by General Price, and although their forces now outnumbered his own five to one, Lyon determined to risk a battle. He met and attacked the Confederates at Wilson's Creek, August 10, 1861, where he was killed.

While the Federals were striving to keep the territory west of the Mississippi in the Union, John Cabell Breckinridge, who had been the youngest Vice President of the United States, resigned from the national Senate in October, 1861, to join the Confederacy. He formed an encampment at Hazel Green, Kentucky, and his personality drew many recruits to the Southern army in that much-divided State. President Davis gave him a commission as brigadier-general in November, 1861, and he was appointed to the command of a brigade in the Second Kentucky division under General Buckner. At the battle of Shiloh Breckinridge commanded the reserve

corps consisting of three brigades, two of which he led in the struggle on April 6, 1862. General Johnston placed him south of the Peach Orchard, and he became engaged about one o'clock in the afternoon. When the Confederate army retired Breckinridge formed the rear-guard. After Shiloh Breckinridge was made major-general and in the break-up of the vast Western army he went to Louisiana, where he attempted, but failed, to drive General Williams from Baton Rouge on August 5th. Breckinridge took prominent part also at Stone's River, Chickamauga, Chattanooga, in the Shenandoah campaign of 1864, and at Cold Harbor.

# Engagements of the Civil War

McCall's Div. 253 killed, 1,240 wounded, 1,581 missing.

Second Corps, Maj.-Gen. E. V. Sumner, 187 killed, 1,076 wounded, 848 missing.

Third Corps, Maj.-Gen. S. P. Heintzelman, 189 killed, 1,051 wounded, 833 missing.

Fourth Corps, Maj.-Gen. E. D. Keyes, 69 killed, 507 wounded, 201 missing.

Fifth Corps, Maj.-Gen. Fitz-John Porter, 620 killed, 2,460 wounded, 1,198 missing.

Sixth Corps, Maj.-Gen. W. B. Franklin, 245 killed, 1,313 wounded, 1,179 missing.

Cavalry, Brig.-Gen. George Stoneman, 19 killed, 60 wounded, 97 missing.

Engineer Corps, 2 wounded, 21 missing.

Total, 1,734 killed, 8,062 wounded, 6,053 missing.

*Confed.*—Army of Northern Virginia, Gen. R. E. Lee commanding. Losses:

Maj.-Gen. Huger's Division, 187 killed, 803 wounded, 360 missing.

Maj.-Gen. J. B. Magruder's command, 258 killed, 1,495 wounded, 30 missing.

Maj.-Gen. James Longstreet's Division, 763 killed, 3,929 wounded, 239 missing.

Maj.-Gen. A. P. Hill's Division, 619 killed, 3,251 wounded.

Maj.-Gen. T. J. Jackson's command, 966 killed, 4,417 wounded, 63 missing.

Maj.-Gen. T. H. Holmes' Division, 2 killed, 52 wounded.

Maj.-Gen. J. E. B. Stuart's Cavalry, 15 killed, 30 wounded, 60 missing.

Artillery, Brig.-Gen. W. N. Pendleton, 10 killed, 34 wounded.

Total, 2,820 killed, 14,011 wounded, 752 missing.

## JULY, 1862.

**1.**—Booneville, Miss. *Union,* 2d Ia., 2d Mich. Cav. *Confed.,* Gen. Chalmers' Cav. Losses: *Union* 45 killed and wounded. *Confed.* 17 killed, 65 wounded.

**4 to 28.**—Gen. Morgan's raid in Kentucky.

**6.**—Grand Prairie, near Aberdeen, Ark. *Union,* detachment of the 24th Ind. *Confed.** Losses: *Union* 1 killed, 21 wounded. *Confed.* 84 killed, wounded, and missing (estimate).

**7.**—Bayou Cache, also called Cotton Plant, Round Hill, Hill's Plantation, and Bayou de View. *Union,* 11th Wis., 33d Ill., 8th Ind., 1st Mo. Light Artil., 1st Ind. Cav., 5th and 13th Ill. Cav. *Confed.,*

Gen. A. Rust's command. Losses: *Union* 7 killed, 57 wounded. *Confed.* 110 killed, 200 wounded.

**9.**—Tompkinsville, Ky. *Union,* 9th Pa. Cav. *Confed.,* Morgan's Cav. Losses: *Union* 4 killed, 6 wounded. *Confed.* 10 killed and wounded.

**12.**—Lebanon, Ky. *Union,* 28th Ky., Lebanon Home Guards. *Confed.,* Col. John H. Morgan's Kentucky Cav. Losses: *Union* 2 killed, 65 prisoners.

**13.**—Murfreesboro', Tenn. *Union,* 9th Mich., 3d Minn., 4th Ky. Cav., 7th Pa. Cav., 1st Ky. Battery. *Confed.,* Gen. N. B. Forrest's Cav. Losses: *Union* 33 killed, 62 wounded, 800 missing. *Confed.* 50 killed, 100 wounded.

**15.**—Near Vicksburg, Miss. *Union,* Gunboats *Carondelet, Queen of the West, Tyler,* and *Essex. Confed.,* Ram *Arkansas.* Losses: *Union* 13 killed, 36 wounded. *Confed.* 5 killed, 9 wounded.

—Fayetteville, Ark. *Union,* detachments of 2d Wis., 3d Mo., 10th Ill., and Davidson's Battery. *Confed.,* Gen. Rains' command. Losses: *Confed.* 150 captured.

**17.**—Cynthiana, Ky. *Union,* 18th Ky., 7th Ky. Cav., Cynthiana, Newport, Cincinnati, and Bracken Co. Home Guards (Morgan's Raid). *Confed.,* Morgan's Cav. Losses: *Union* 17 killed, 34 wounded. *Confed.* 8 killed, 29 wounded.

**18.**—Memphis, Mo. *Union,* 2d Mo., 11th Mo. Cav. *Opponents,* Porter's independent forces. Losses: *Union* 83 killed and wounded. Porter's loss, 23 killed.

**21.**—Hartsville Road, near Gallatin, Tenn. *Union,* detachments 2d Ind., 4th, 5th Ky., 7th Pa. Cav. *Confed.,* Morgan's Cav. Losses: *Union* 30 killed, 50 wounded, 75 captured. *Confed.**

—Nashville Bridge, Tenn. *Union,* 2d Ky. *Confed.,* Forrest's Cav. Losses: *Union* 3 killed, 97 captured. *Confed.**

**25.**—Courtland Bridge and Trinity, Ala. *Union,* 10th Ky., 10th Ind., 31st Ohio. *Confed.,* Armstrong's Cav. Losses: *Union* 2 killed, 16 wounded, 138 captured. *Confed.* 3 killed, 5 wounded.

**28.**—Moore's Mills, Mo. *Union,* 9th Mo., 3d Ia. Cav., 2d Mo. Cav., 3d Ind. Battery. *Opponents,* Porter's independent forces. Losses: *Union* 13 killed, 55 wounded. Porter's loss, 30 killed, 100 wounded.

* No record found.

THEATRE OF
VIRGINIA CAMPAIGNS

SCALE OF MILES

0    25    50    75    100

# The Photographic History
## of The Civil War

---

TWO VOLUMES IN ONE.
Two Years of Grim War

THEATRE OF
**SOUTHWESTERN
CAMPAIGNS**

SCALE OF MILES
0    25    50    75    100

## THE CHURCH WHERE THE VETERAN ARMIES CLASHED

The shot-holes in the little Dunker church of Antietam, and the dead in Blue and Gray as they lay after the battle-smoke had lifted, mark the center of the bloodiest single day's fighting in the Civil War. Here the grand armies of the North and South faced one another on September 17, 1862. At sunrise the action began; by 4 o'clock in the afternoon it was over, and the dead and wounded numbered twenty-three thousand five hundred. The preponderance of the army under McClellan, with his eighty-seven thousand men, was offset by the presence of three great Confederate leaders whose names had already rung round the world—Lee, Jackson, and Longstreet—with numbers less than half those opposed to them. On the 18th the armies lay exhausted; and on the 19th Lee abandoned his invasion of the North.

# The Photographic History of The Civil War

*Complete and Unabridged*

TWO VOLUMES IN ONE.

*Volume 1*
The Opening Battles
*Two Years of Grim War

TEXT BY

HENRY W. ELSON
Professor of History, Ohio University

PHOTOGRAPH DESCRIPTIONS BY

JAMES BARNES
Author of "Naval Actions of 1812" and "David G. Farragut"

THE BLUE & GREY PRESS

# CONTENTS

# Contents

## Part IV

## Part V

# FOREWORD TO VOLUME II

IT is the central act in the great American war drama, and the one of highest suspense, that is presented by Volume II of THE PHOTOGRAPHIC HISTORY. Volume III will be found to cover the period between the first move against Lee by Grant (May, 1864), and Appomattox—a series of battles bitterly contested, but properly described in the volume-title as "DECISIVE," since it had then become only a question of time, with skill and bravery so conspicuous on either side, before the weight of Northern resources and organization would inevitably crush the impoverished Confederacy. But prior to the unifying under Grant of the Federal military force in May, 1864, and subsequent to McClellan's Peninsula Campaign (with which Volume I closes), the actions form a veritable "tug-of-war," a giant struggle of veteran armies, the result of which no contemporary observer could determine. This is the period covered by the present volume—the combats of matched armies, while Federal and Confederate hoped alike, each praying for the triumph of the cause to which he had pledged his soul and body.

Each of the remaining seven volumes of THE PHOTOGRAPHIC HISTORY—IV to X—deals with a special side of the conflict: cavalry, soldier life, the navy, forts and artillery, prisons and hospitals, with other important phases being separately treated.

———

# CEDAR MOUNTAIN—POPE'S ADVANCE IS CHECKED

———

PICKETS ON RESERVE—ACROSS THIS WHEATFIELD
THE UNION CHARGE WAS SWEPT BACK BY
"STONEWALL" JACKSON

## WHERE THE COMMANDER HEARD THE CANNONADING

The Hudson farmhouse, with its mossy shingles, vines, and aged locust trees, suggests anything but the storm-center of a nation at war. Yet it was here that General John Pope set up his headquarters while his eight thousand trained soldiers under General Banks sped toward Gordonsville, to strike the first blow of what the new general had promised would be a series of victories. As this picture was taken, the New York *Herald* wagon stands plainly in view to the left of the porch; the newspaper correspondents prepared to despatch big "stories." John Pope was the leader whose swift success in capturing New Madrid and

## POPE'S HEADQUARTERS DURING THE BATTLE OF CEDAR MOUNTAIN

Island Number Ten in the Mississippi campaign formed a brilliant contrast, in the popular mind, to the failure of the Eastern armies in their attempt upon Richmond. Pope himself proclaimed, "I have come to you from the West, where we have always seen the backs of our enemies." So he set out for the front with "headquarters in the saddle." He could not know what the world later learned—that Robert E. Lee and "Stonewall" Jackson were generals before whose genius few opponents, however brave, could make headway. And so it was too late when Pope heard the cannonading from the Hudson house on the 9th of August.

## A HALT ON THE DAY OF BATTLE

The 9th of August, 1862. A sultry day in old Virginia. The brook rippling toward the Rappahannock cools the hoofs of the battery horses at halt, tired with rushing their heavy guns south from Culpeper Court House. The cannoneers lolling on horseback and caisson-seats look as if they too like to rest in the shade. Some gaze at the lucky wagoners across the creek, at ease while their horses feed. Least war-like of all seems the queer wagon to the right. They stare at it, and the civilian beside it, and at his companion wielding the

## FEDERAL ARTILLERY NEARING CEDAR MOUNTAIN

clumsy apparatus for that newly discovered art—photography.   Little do the actors in this quiet interlude imagine that by half-past two this afternoon the Federal batteries will plunge into range of a flaring crescent two miles long—"Stonewall" Jackson's guns; that those guns will roar destruction upon them for three hours without ceasing; and that before another sun rises, two thousand of Pope's army will lie dead and wounded beside thirteen hundred men in gray, upon the battle-ground of Cedar Mountain.

## McDOWELL'S HEADQUARTERS

Manassas, July 8, 1862.   General McDowell, who had been so unfortunate in the first great battle of the war, was made commander of the Third Corps of the newly created Army of Virginia under Pope.   McDowell had his headquarters at Manassas.   He moved southward during this month with Pope's army toward Gordonville.   But Lee, by his brilliant and daring tactics, drove the Federal troops back until a three-days' battle was fought in the vicinity of the residence which the camera has preserved for us in this picture.   McDowell once more had the chagrin of seeing a beaten army falling back on Washington.

A ROUGH–HEWN CAUSEWAY (See facing page)

## THE ARMY'S HANDY MEN

The Federal army, under Pope, in its advance against Lee needed much more than well drilled regiments of soldiers. Indeed, during the forward march the engineer corps was the busiest division of the army. Artillery battalions and provision trains had to have bridges to cross the numerous streams flowing into the Potomac and the Chesapeake. Three pictures on this page and the preceding show us the men at their work in that summer of long ago. The polka-dot shirt of the foreman (page 14), the roughly hewn timbers cut from the banks, the improvised derrick, the piers built in the middle of the stream around which the water is now rippling, the quiet trees on the banks—all these features stand out as clearly as they did in August of 1862, as the engineer corps was working on the north fork of the Rappahannock, near Sulphur Springs. The pictures are of the same bridge from different points of view.

## CROSSING THE RAPPAHANNOCK

# CEDAR MOUNTAIN

*The Army of Virginia, under Pope, is now to bear the brunt of Lee's assault, while the Army of the Potomac is dismembered and sent back whence it came, to add in driblets to Pope's effective.—Colonel Theodore A. Dodge, U.S.A., in "A Bird's-Eye View of the Civil War."*

GENERAL GEORGE B. McCLELLAN, with all his popularity at the beginning, had failed in his Peninsula campaign to fulfil the expectations of the great impatient public of the North. At the same time, while the Army of the Potomac had as yet won no great victories, the men of the West could triumphantly exhibit the trophies won at Donelson, at Pea Ridge, at Shiloh, and at Island No. 10. The North thereupon came to believe that the Western leaders were more able than those of the East. This belief was shared by the President and his Secretary of War and it led to the determination to call on the West for help.

The first to be called was General John Pope, who had won national fame by capturing New Madrid and Island No. 10 on the Mississippi River. In answer to a telegram from Secretary Stanton, Pope came to Washington in June, 1862. The secretary disclosed the plans on which he and President Lincoln had agreed, that a new army, to be known as the Army of Virginia, was to be created out of three corps, then under the respective commands of Generals McDowell, N. P. Banks, and John C. Fremont. These corps had been held from the Peninsula campaign for the purpose of protecting Washington.

Pope demurred and begged to be sent back to the West, on the ground that each of the three corps commanders was his senior in rank and that his being placed at their head would

A BREATHING SPELL

Federal Encampment at Blackburn's Ford on Bull Run, July 4, 1862. When McClellan went to the Peninsula in March of 1862 he had expected all of McDowell's Corps to be sent him as reënforcement before he made the final advance on Richmond. But the brilliant exploits of Jackson in the Shenandoah required the retention of all the troops in the vicinity of Washington. A new army, in fact, was created to make the campaign which Lincoln had originally wanted McClellan to carry out. The command was given to General John Pope, whose capture of Island No. 10 in the Mississippi had brought him into national importance. The corps of Banks, Frémont, and McDowell were consolidated to form this new army, called the "Army of Virginia." General Frémont refused to serve under his junior, and his force was given to Franz Sigel, who had won fame in 1861 in Missouri. This picture was taken about two weeks after the reorganization was completed. The soldiers are those of McDowell's Corps. They are on the old battle-field of Bull Run, enjoying the leisure of camp life, for no definite plans for the campaign have yet been formed.

WHERE JACKSON STRUCK

Cedar Mountain, Viewed from Pope's Headquarters. On the side of this mountain Jackson established the right of his battle line, when he discovered at noon of August 9th that he was in contact with a large part of Pope's army. He had started from Gordonsville, Pope's objective, to seize Culpeper Court House, but the combat took place in the valley here pictured, some five miles southwest of Culpeper, and by nightfall the fields and slopes were strewn with more than three thousand dead and wounded.

doubtless create a feeling against him. But his protests were of no avail and he assumed command of the Army of Virginia on the 26th of June. McDowell and Banks made no protest; but Fremont refused to serve under one whom he considered his junior, and resigned his position. His corps was assigned to General Franz Sigel.

The new commander, General Pope, on the 14th of July, issued an address to his army that was hardly in keeping with his modesty in desiring at first to decline the honor that was offered him. "I have come to you from the West," he proclaimed, "where we have always seen the backs of our enemies —from an army whose business it has been to seek the adversary and to beat him when found. . . . Meantime I desire you to dismiss from your minds certain phrases which I am sorry to find much in vogue among you. I hear constantly of . . . lines of retreat and bases of supplies. Let us discard such ideas. . . . Let us look before us and not behind."

The immediate object of General Pope was to make the capital secure, to make advances toward Richmond, and, if possible, to draw a portion of Lee's army away from McClellan. His first objective was Gordonsville. From this town, not far from the base of the Blue Ridge Mountains, there was a railroad connecting it with Richmond—a convenient means of furnishing men and supplies to the Confederate army. Pope decided to occupy the town and destroy the railroad. To this end he ordered Banks to Culpeper and thence to send all his cavalry to Gordonsville, capture the town and tear up ten or fifteen miles of the railroad in the direction of Richmond. But, as if a prelude to the series of defeats which General Pope was to suffer in the next six weeks, he failed in this initial movement. The sagacious Lee had divined his intention and had sent General "Stonewall" Jackson with his and General Ewell's divisions on July 13th, to occupy Gordonsville. Ewell arrived in advance of Jackson and held the town for the Confederates.

[ 22 ]

## IN THE LINE OF FIRE

Where the Confederate General Winder was killed at Cedar Mountain. It was while directing the movements of four advance batteries that General Winder was struck by a shell, expiring in a few hours. Jackson reported: "It is difficult within the proper reserve of an official report to do justice to the merits of this accomplished officer. Urged by the medical director to take no part in the movements of the day because of the enfeebled state of his health, his ardent patriotism and military pride could bear no such restraint. Richly endowed with those qualities of mind and person which fit an officer for command and which attract the admiration and excite the enthusiasm of troops, he was rapidly rising to the front rank of his profession."

In the campaign we are describing Jackson was the most active and conspicuous figure on the Confederate side. He rested at Gordonsville for two weeks, recuperating his health and that of the army, which had been much impaired in the malarial district of the Peninsula. The fresh mountain air blowing down from the Blue Ridge soon brought back their wonted vigor. On July 27th A. P. Hill was ordered to join him, and the Confederate leader now had about twenty-five thousand men.

The movement on Gordonsville was exactly in accordance with Jackson's own ideas which he had urged upon Lee. Although believing McClellan to be in an impregnable position on the Peninsula, it was not less evident to him that the Union general would be unable to move further until his army had been reorganized and reenforced. This was the moment, he argued, to strike in another direction and carry the conflict into the Federal territory. An army of at least sixty thousand should march into Maryland and appear before the National Capital. President Davis could not be won over to the plan while McClellan was still in a position to be reenforced by sea, but Lee, seeing that McClellan remained inactive, had determined, by sending Jackson westward, to repeat the successful tactics of the previous spring in the Shenandoah valley. Such a move might result in the recall of McClellan.

And so it happened. No sooner had Halleck assumed command of all the Northern armies than the matter of McClellan's withdrawal was agitated and on August 3d the head of the Army of the Potomac, to his bitter disappointment, was ordered to join Pope on the Rappahannock. Halleck was much concerned as to how Lee would act during the Federal evacuation of the Peninsula, uncertain whether the Confederates would attempt to crush Pope before McClellan could reenforce him, or whether McClellan would be attacked as soon as he was out of his strong entrenchments at Harrison's Landing.

## THE LEADER OF THE CHARGE

The Hero of the Federal Attack. General Samuel W. Crawford, here seen with his staff, at Cedar Mountain led a charge on the left flank of the Confederate forces that came near being disastrous for Jackson. At about six o'clock the brigade was in line. General Williams reported: "At this time this brigade occupied the interior line of a strip of woods. A field, varying from 250 to 500 yards in width, lay between it and the next strip of woods. In moving across this field the three right regiments and the six companies of the Third Wisconsin were re-ceived by a terrific fire of musketry. The Third Wisconsin especially fell under a par-tial flank fire under which Lieut.-Colonel Crane fell and the regiment was obliged to give way. Of the three remaining regiments which continued the charge (Twenty-eighth New York, Forty-sixth Pennsylvania, and Fifth Connecticut) every field-officer and every adjutant was killed or disabled. In the Twenty-eighth New York every com-pany officer was killed or wounded; in the Forty-sixth Pennsylvania all but five; in the Fifth Connecticut all but eight." It was one of the most heroic combats of the war.

COL. ALFRED N. DUFFIÉ

A Leader of Cavalry. Colonel Alfred N. Duffié was in command of the First Rhode Island Cavalry, in the Cavalry Brigade of the Second Division of McDowell's (Third) Corps in Pope's Army of Virginia. The cavalry had been used pretty well during Pope's advance. On the 8th of August, the day before the battle of Cedar Mountain, the cavalry had pro-ceeded south to the house of Dr. Slaughter. That night Duffié was on picket in advance of General Crawford's troops, which had come up during the day and pitched camp. The whole division came to his support on the next day. When the infantry fell back to the protection of the batteries, the cavalry was ordered to charge the advancing Confederates. "Officers and men behaved admirably, and I cannot speak too highly of the good conduct of all of the brigade," reported General Bayard. After the battle the cavalry covered the retreat of the artillery and ambulances. On August 18th, when the retreat behind the Rappahannoc was ordered, the cavalry again checked the Confederate advance. During the entire campaign the regiment of Colonel Duffié did yeoman's service.

The latter of the two possibilities seemed the more probable, and Pope was therefore ordered to push his whole army toward Gordonsville, in the hope that Lee, compelled to strengthen Jackson, would be too weak to fall upon the retiring Army of the Potomac.

The Union army now occupied the great triangle formed roughly by the Rappahannock and the Rapidan rivers and the range of the Blue Ridge Mountains, with Culpeper Court House as the rallying point. Pope soon found that the capturing of New Madrid and Island No. 10 was easy in comparison with measuring swords with the Confederate generals in the East.

On August 6th Pope began his general advance upon Gordonsville. Banks already had a brigade at Culpeper Court House, and this was nearest to Jackson. The small settlement was the meeting place of four roads by means of which Pope's army of forty-seven thousand men would be united. Jackson, informed of the advance, immediately set his three divisions in motion for Culpeper, hoping to crush Banks, hold the town, and prevent the uniting of the Army of Virginia. His progress was slow. The remainder of Banks's corps reached Culpeper on the 8th. On the morning of the 9th Jackson finally got his troops over the Rapidan and the Robertson rivers. Two miles beyond the latter stream there rose from the plain the slope of Slaughter Mountain, whose ominous name is more often changed into Cedar. This "mountain" is an isolated foothill of the Blue Ridge, some twenty miles from the parent range, and a little north of the Rapidan. From its summit could be seen vast stretches of quiet farmlands which had borne their annual harvests since the days of the Cavaliers. Its gentle slopes were covered with forests, which merged at length into waving grain fields and pasture lands, dotted here and there with rural homes. It was here on the slope of Cedar Mountain that one of the most severe little battles of the war took place.

## THE FIRST CLASH

Battlefield of Cedar Mountain, August 9, 1862. Here the Confederate army in its second advance on Washington first felt out the strength massed against it. After Lee's brilliant tactics had turned McClellan's Peninsula Campaign into a fiasco, the Confederate Government resolved to again take the offensive. Plans were formed for a general invasion of the North, the objective points ranging from Cincinnati eastward to the Federal capital and Philadelphia. Immediately after Washington got wind of this, Lincoln (on August 4th) issued a call for three hundred thousand men; and all haste was made to rush the forces of McClellan from the Peninsula and of Cox from West Virginia to the aid of the recently consolidated army under Pope. On August 9, 1862, the vanguards of "Stonewall" Jackson's army and of Pope's intercepting forces met at Cedar Mountain. Banks, with the Second Corps of the Federal army, about eight thousand strong, attacked Jackson's forces of some sixteen thousand. The charge was so furious that Jackson's left flank was broken and rolled up, the rear of the center fired upon, and the whole line thereby thrown into confusion. Banks, however, received no reenforcements, while Jackson received strong support. The Federal troops were driven back across the ground which they had swept clear earlier in the afternoon.

The Battle of Cedar Mountain, August 9, 1862. The lower picture was taken the day after the battle that had raged for a brief two hours on the previous evening. After an artillery fire that filled half the afternoon, the advanced Federal cavalry was pressed back on the infantry supporting the batteries. Banks underestimated the strength of the Confederates. Instead of sending to Pope for reenforcements, he ordered a charge on the approaching troops. The Confederates, still feeling their way, were unprepared for this movement and were thrown into confusion. But at the moment when the Federal charge was about to end in success, three brigades of A. P. Hill in reserve were called up. They forced the Federals to retrace their steps to the point where the fighting began. Here the Federal retreat, in turn, was halted by General Pope with reenforcements. The Confederates moving up their batteries, a short-range artillery fight was kept up until midnight. At daylight it was found that Ewell and Jackson had fallen back two miles farther up the mountain. Pope advanced to the former Confederate ground and rested, after burying the dead. The following morning the Confederates had disappeared. The loss to both armies was almost three thousand in killed, wounded and missing. The battle had accomplished nothing.

On the banks of Cedar Run, seven miles south of Culpeper and but one or two north of the mountain, Banks's cavalry were waiting to oppose Jackson's advance. Learning of this the latter halted and waited for an attack. He placed Ewell's batteries on the slope about two hundred feet above the valley and sent General Winder to take a strong position on the left. So admirably was Jackson's army stationed that it would have required a much larger force, approaching it from the plains, to dislodge it. And yet, General Banks made an attempt with an army scarcely one-third as large as that of Jackson.

General Pope had made glowing promises of certain success and he well knew that the whole North was eagerly watching and waiting for him to fulfil them. He must strike somewhere and do it soon—and here was his chance at Cedar Mountain. He sent Banks with nearly eight thousand men against this brilliant Southern commander with an army three times as large, holding a strong position on a mountain side.

Banks with his infantry left Culpeper Court House on the morning of August 9th and reached the Confederate stronghold in the afternoon. He approached the mountain through open fields in full range of the Confederate cannon, which presently opened with the roar of thunder. All heedless of danger the brave men ran up the slope as if to take the foe by storm, when suddenly they met a brigade of Ewell's division face to face and a brief, deadly encounter took place. In a few minutes the Confederate right flank began to waver and would no doubt have been routed but for the timely aid of another brigade and still another that rushed down the hill and opened fire on the Federal lines which extended along the eastern bank of Cedar Run.

Meanwhile the Union batteries had been wheeled into position and their deep roar answered that of the foe on the hill. For two or three hours the battle continued with the utmost fury. The ground was strewn with dead and dying

SURVIVORS OF THE FIGHTING TENTH

When Crawford's troops were driven back by A. P. Hill, he halted on the edge of a wheatfield, where he was reenforced by the Tenth Maine. For nearly half an hour it held its own, losing out of its 461 officers and men 173 in killed and wounded. A few days after the battle some survivors had a picture taken on the exact spot where they had so courageously fought. The remains of the cavalry horses can be seen in the trampled field of wheat. From left to right these men are: Lieutenant Littlefield, Lieutenant Whitney, Lieut.-Colonel Fillebrown, Captain Knowlton, and First-Sergeant Jordan, of Company C.

THE HOUSE WELL NAMED

Slaughter's house, overlooking the scene of carnage of Cedar Mountain, stood on the northern slope in the rear of the position taken by the Confederate troops under General Ewell. The brigades of Trimble and Hayes were drawn up near this house, at some distance from the brigade of Early. After the battle the whole of Jackson's army was drawn up on the slopes near it.

THE FUGITIVES

Virginia Negroes following Pope's soldiers in their retreat from Cedar mountain. From the beginning of the war Negroes had been a subject of debate. Even before Bull Run, on May 26, 1861, General B. F. Butler had declared that all fugitive slaves would be considered as contraband of war. Congress, however, decided in August that all slaves confiscated should be held subject to the decision of the United States courts. In April of 1862, General Hunter, at Hilton Head, South Carolina, declared that all slaves in his military department were "forever free," but a week later Lincoln annulled the proclamation. Hunter, however, raised a storm by organizing a regiment of fugitive slaves. It was only before Cedar Mountain—to be precise, on July 22, 1862—that "all National commanders were ordered

FOLLOWERS OF POPE'S RETREAT

to employ as many Negroes as could be used advantageously for military and naval purposes, paying them for their labor and keeping a record as to their ownership as a basis on which compensation could be made in proper cases." Ten days after the battle, Greeley published his famous letter to Lincoln, "The Prayer of Twenty Millions." On September 22, 1862, the Emancipation Proclamation was issued, and on January 1, 1863, the final proclamation was made that "Negroes would be received into the military and naval service of the United States Corps." This picture was taken about the time Greeley's letter was published—less than two weeks after the battle of Cedar Mountain had been fought.

and human blood was poured out like water. But the odds were too great and at length, as the shades of evening were settling over the gory field, Banks began to withdraw the remnant of his troops. But he left two thousand of his brave lads—one fourth of his whole army—dead or dying along the hillside, while the Confederate losses were in excess of thirteen hundred.

The dead and wounded of both armies lay mingled in masses over the whole battle-field. While the fighting continued, neither side could send aid or relief to the maimed soldiers, who suffered terribly from thirst and lack of attention as the sultry day gave place to a close, oppressive night.

General Pope had remained at Culpeper, but, hearing the continuous cannonading and knowing that a sharp engagement was going on, hastened to the battle-field in the afternoon with a fresh body of troops under General Ricketts, arriving just before dark. He instantly ordered Banks to withdraw his right wing so as to make room for Ricketts; but the Confederates, victorious as they had been, refused to continue the contest against the reenforcements and withdrew to the woods up the mountain side. Heavy shelling was kept up by the hard-worked artillerymen of both armies until nearly midnight, while the Federal troops rested on their arms in line of battle. For two days the armies faced each other across the valley. Then both quietly withdrew. Pope's first battle as leader of an Eastern army had resulted in neither victory nor defeat.

## PART I
### THE RISE OF LEE

---

# THE SECOND BATTLE AT
# BULL RUN

---

THE UNION RETREAT—SIGEL'S CORPS RECROSSING THE
RAPPAHANNOCK, AUGUST 19, 1862

## THE RAILROAD AS AN

The Federals are clearing up the railroad, the Confederate damage to which compelled Pope to fall back in order to retard Lee's advance toward Washington. "Stonewall" Jackson, who knew every foot of the Manassas region, did not despatch Ewell's forces with Stuart's cavalry to fall upon Catlett's Station and Manassas Junction for nothing. At Manassas the Confederates captured a million dollars' worth of army reserve supplies, seriously crippling Pope's movements for the remainder of the campaign. Meanwhile Jackson, pressing forward, united with Ewell and threatened Pope's exposed flank. The purpose of the advance of Jackson to give battle to Pope

## ELEMENT IN WARFARE

near Manassas and Bull Run was to prevent the concentration of a heavy Federal force between his column and Longstreet's, then more than a day's march distant. The crippling of his railroad communication and the seizure of his stores were not in themselves sufficient to do this. In the pictures we see the work-trains of the Military Railroad removing the wreckage, gathering up débris to be used in repairing the road and its rolling-stock, and the tracks being relaid and guarded by the soldiers. Before Pope could reestablish his railroad communication, Lee's clever maneuvers drew the Federals into the disastrous battle of Second Bull Run.

[B]

## AN IMPORTANT PART OF THE WAR GAME

A problem for the practical railroad man. It takes all kinds of people to make up a world and it takes all kinds of men to make up an army. In the volunteer forces that fought in the ranks of both North and South were men of every calling, every profession, mechanics, artisans, artificers, men familiar with machine-shop practice as well as the men of field and plow, and the thinking soldier whose hand was as ready with the pen as with the sword. Was an engine-driver needed, or a farrier or carpenter, the colonel of a regiment had but to shout. But so important did the lines of communication by railway become to both armies that separate com-

**REPAIRING AFTER THE CONFEDERATE RAID ON POPE'S LINE OF MARCH**

mands of practical engineers, trackmen, and wreckers had to be organized and maintained. Train-wrecking seems a cruel act of deliberate vandalism, yet it is part of warfare. When penetrating the enemy's country over unpatroled and ill-guarded routes, the engine-driver might expect any time to see just ahead of him, and too late to call for brakes, the misplaced rail or the broken culvert that would hurl him and his train, laden sometimes with human freight, into river-bed or deep abyss. War leads to strenuous life and deeds of daring, and upon no force was the labor and the danger harder than the men of the track and throttle.

# SECOND BATTLE OF BULL RUN

The battle was indeed one of which General Lee had good reason to be proud. It would be hard to find a better instance of that masterly comprehension of the actual condition of things which marks a great general than was exhibited in General Lee's allowing our formidable attack, in which more than half the Federal army was taking part, to be fully developed and to burst upon the exhausted troops of Stonewall Jackson, while Lee, relying upon the ability of that able soldier to maintain his position, was maturing and arranging for the great attack on our left flank by the powerful corps of Longstreet.—*John C. Ropes, in "The Army Under Pope."*

THE battle of Cedar Mountain was but a prelude to the far greater one that was to take place three weeks later on the banks of the little stream that had given its name, the year before, to the first important battle of the war; and here again the result to be registered was similar to that of the preceding year—a result that brought dismay to the people of the North and exultation to the adherents of the Southern cause. The three intervening weeks between the battles of Cedar Mountain and the Second Bull Run were spent in sparring, in marshaling the armed hosts, in heavy skirmishing and getting position for a final decisive struggle.

Two events of this period invite special attention. The respective heroes were J. E. B. Stuart, the daring Southern cavalry leader, and "Stonewall" Jackson. The victim in each case was General Pope. Before relating these incidents, however, we must take a general view of the field. General Pope's headquarters at this moment were at Culpeper, with a large part of his army, but he had left much of his personal baggage and many of his private papers at Catlett's, a station on the Orange and Alexandria Railroad between Culpeper and

THE UNHEEDED WARNING

Here we see Catlett's Station, on the Orange & Alexandria Railroad, which Stuart's cavalry seized in a night sortie on August 22, 1862. The damage done was not severe. Stuart was unable to burn the loaded wagon-trains surrounding the station and had to content himself with capturing horses, which he mounted with wounded Federal soldiers; he escaped at four the next morning, driven off by the approach of a superior force. Pope, at the time, was in possession of the fords of the Rappahannock, trying to check the Confederate advance toward the Shenandoah.

CATLETT'S STATION

At Manassas Junction, as it appeared in the upper picture on August 26, 1862, is one of the great neglected strategic points in the theater of the war. Twenty-five miles from Alexandria and thirty miles in a direct line from Washington, it was almost within long cannon-shot from any point in both the luckless battles of Bull Run. It was on the railway route connecting with Richmond, and at the junction of the railway running across the entrance to the Shenandoah Valley and beyond the Blue Ridge, through Manassas Gap. The Confederates knew its value,

Stuart's raid, however, so alarmed General Halleck that he immediately telegraphed Pope from Washington: "By no means expose your railroad communication with Alexandria. It is of the utmost importance in sending your supplies and reinforcements." Pope did not fall back upon his railroad communication, however, until after Jackson had seized Manassas Junction. and after the first battle of Bull Run built the fortifications which we see in the upper picture, to the left beyond the supply-cars on the railroad. Pope, after the battle of Cedar Mountain, should have covered it, extending his lines so as to protect it from Jackson's incursion through Thoroughfare Gap; instead he held the main force of his army opposing that of Lee.

Manassas Junction, while his vast store of army supplies was at the latter place.

Pope's great source of uncertainty lay in the fact that he did not know whether Lee would move against him or would follow McClellan in the latter's retreat from the Peninsula; nor did he know when the reenforcements promised from McClellan's army would reach him. Meanwhile Lee had decided to let McClellan depart in peace and to advance against Pope, with the whole Confederate army. To this end Longstreet was ordered to the scene and with his corps he reached Gordonsville on August 13th.

A few days later the two Confederate generals, Lee and Longstreet, ascended to the top of Clark's Mountain, from which, through powerful field-glasses, they obtained a good view of Culpeper, about twelve miles away. They saw that Pope's position was weak and determined to attack him without delay. Lee ordered his army to cross the Rapidan. He also sent a courier to gallop across the country with an important dispatch to General Stuart, disclosing his plans. It was now that General Pope met fortune; he captured the courier and learned of Lee's plans. Pope knew that he was not in position to meet Lee's army at Culpeper, and he withdrew from that place and took up a strong position behind the Rappahannock. Lee had strained every nerve to get at his antagonist before the latter left Culpeper and before he could be reenforced by McClellan's army. But sudden rains changed the Rappahannock from a placid stream into a rushing torrent. The Confederates were delayed and meantime the reenforcements from the Peninsula began to reach Pope's army. General Reno with a part of Burnside's corps was on the ground by August 14th. One week later came Generals Kearny and Reynolds —both splendid leaders, both destined to give their lives for their country within a year—to join the Army of Virginia with some thousands of additional fighters from the Army of the Potomac.

## WHERE THE THUNDERBOLT FELL

The havoc wrought by the Confederate attack of August 26th on the Federal supply depot at Manassas Junction is here graphically preserved. When Jackson arrived at sunset of that day at Bristoe's Station, on the Orange & Alexandria Railroad, he knew that his daring movement would be reported to Pope's forces by the trains that escaped both north and south. To save themselves, the troops that had already marched twenty-five miles had to make still further exertions. Trimble volunteered to move on Manassas Junction; and, under command of Stuart, a small force moved northward through the woods. At midnight it arrived within half a mile of the Junction. The Federal force greeted it with artillery fire, but when the Confederates charged at the sound of the bugle the gunners abandoned the batteries to the assaulters. Some three hundred of the small Federal garrison were captured, with the immense stores that filled the warehouses to overflowing. The next morning Hill's and Taliaferro's divisions arrived to hold the position. The half-starved troops were now in possession of all that was needed to make them an effective force. Jackson was now in position to control the movements of the Federal army under Pope.

Lee was completely thwarted in his purpose of attacking Pope before his reenforcements arrived. But he was not idle. He sent the dauntless cavalry leader, J. E. B. Stuart, to make a raid around the Union army. Stuart did this effectively, and this was the first of the two notable events of these weeks of sparring. Crossing the Rappahannock at Waterloo Bridge with fifteen hundred mounted men as bold and dauntless as himself, Stuart dashed up the country, riding all day and all night. After the coming of night on the evening of the 22d, in the midst of a torrential rainstorm, while the darkness was so intense that every man was guided by the tread of his brother horsemen, Stuart pounced upon the Federals near Catlett's Station, overpowered the astonished guard, captured nearly two hundred prisoners, scattering the remainder of the troops stationed there far and wide in the darkness, and seized Pope's despatch-book with his plans and private papers. Stuart took also several hundred fine horses and burned a large number of wagons laden with supplies. Among his trophies was a fine uniform cloak and hat which were the personal property of General Pope. These were exchanged on the following day for General Stuart's plumed hat which a few days before had been left behind by that officer when surprised by Federal troops.

Stuart's bold raid proved a serious misfortune for the Union army. But Lee had far greater things in store. His next move was to send Jackson to Pope's rear with a large part of the Confederate army. Stealthily Jackson led his army westward, shielded by the woods, the thickets, and the low hills of the Blue Ridge. It was a quiet rural community through which he passed. The great majority of the simple country folk had never seen an army, though it is true that for many days the far-away boom of cannon had reached their ears from the valley of the Rapidan. Now here was a real army at their very doors. Nor was it a hostile army, for their sympathies were Southern. With baskets and armfuls of

A START TOO LONG DELAYED

Where the troops of General McClellan, waiting near the round-house at Alexandria, were hurried forward to the scene of action where Pope was struggling with Jackson and Ewell. Pope had counted upon the assistance of these reënforcements in making the forward movement by which he expected to hold Lee back. The old bogey of leaving the National Capital defenseless set up a vacillation in General Halleck's mind and the troops were held overlong at Alexandria. Had they been promptly forwarded, "Stonewall" Jackson's blow at Manassas Junction could not have been struck. At the news of that disaster the troops were hurriedly despatched down the railroad toward Manassas. But Pope was already in retreat in three columns toward that point, McDowell had failed to intercept the Confederate reënforcements coming through Thoroughfare Gap, and the situation had become critical. General Taylor, with his brigade of New Jersey troops, was the first of McClellan's forces to be moved forward to the aid of Pope. At Union

BRIGADIER–GENERAL
GEORGE W. TAYLOR

Mills, Colonel Scammon, commanding the First Brigade, driven back from Manassas Junction, was further pressed by the Confederates on the morning of August 27th. Later in the day General Taylor's brigade arrived by the Fairfax road and, crossing the railroad bridge, met the Confederates drawn up and waiting near Manassas Station. A severe artillery fire greeted the Federals as they emerged from the woods. As General Taylor had no artillery, he was obliged either to retire or charge. He chose the latter. When the Confederate cavalry threatened to surround his small force, however, Taylor fell back in good order across the bridge, where two Ohio regiments assisted in holding the Confederates in check. At this point, General Taylor, who had been wounded in the retreat, was borne past in a litter. Though suffering much, he appealed to the officers to prevent another Bull Run. The brigade retired in good order to Fairfax Court House, where General Taylor died of his wounds a short time afterward.

bread and pies and cakes they cheered as best they could the tattered and hungry men on the march.

General Lee in the meantime had kept Longstreet in front of Pope's army on the Rappahannock to make daily demonstrations and feints and thus to divert Pope's attention from Jackson's movements and lead him to believe that he was to be attacked in front. The trick was eminently successful. "Stonewall" Jackson suddenly, on August 26th, emerged from the Bull Run Mountains by way of the Thoroughfare Gap and marshaled his clans on the plains of Manassas, but a few miles from the site of the famous battle of the year before.

Pope had taken alarm. He was astonished to find Jackson in his rear, and he had to decide instantly between two courses—to abandon his communications with Fredericksburg on the one hand, or with Alexandria and Washington on the other. He decided to keep in touch with Washington at all hazards. Breaking his camp on the Rappahannock, he hastened with all speed to lead his forces toward Manassas Junction, where he had stored vast quantities of provisions and munitions of war. But he was too late to save them. Jackson had been joined by Stuart and his cavalry. On the evening of the 26th they were still some miles from Manassas and Trimble was sent ahead to make sure the capture before Pope's army could arrive. Through the darkness rode these same hardy men who had a few nights before made their bold raid on Catlett's Station. Before midnight they reached Manassas. They met little opposition. The guard was overpowered. The spoils of this capture were great, including three hundred prisoners, one hundred and seventy-five horses, ten locomotives, seven long trains of provisions, and vast stores and munitions of war.

Next morning the weary and hungry foot soldiers of Jackson's army came upon the scene and whatever else they did they feasted as only hungry men can. An eye-witness wrote, "To see a starving man eating lobster-salad and

## AN UNREALIZED OPPORTUNITY

Here might have been won a Federal victory that would have precluded defeat at Second Bull Run. The corps of General Heintzelman, consisting of the divisions of Hooker and Kearny, was the next detachment of McClellan's forces to arrive to the aid of Pope. On the 28th of August, Heintzelman had pushed forward to Centreville, entering it soon after "Stonewall" Jackson's rear-guard had retired. Instead of pursuing, Heintzelman drew up his forces east of Cub Run, which we see in the picture. Jackson's forces, now in a precarious position, fell back toward Thoroughfare Gap to form a junction with Longstreet's Corps, which Lee had sent forward. The battle was commenced on the west somewhat feebly by Generals McDowell and Sigel. By night-fall the Confederate left had been driven back fully a mile.

MAJOR–GENERAL SAMUEL P. HEINTZELMAN AND STAFF

drinking Rhine wine, barefooted and in tatters, was curious; the whole thing was incredible."

The amazement at the North when the news of the capture of Manassas became known cannot be described. But the newspapers belittled it, declaring that it was merely a bold raid and that for any large force to get between Pope's army and Washington before Pope became aware of the attempt was simply impossible.

Jackson had done an astonishing thing. But his position was precarious, nevertheless. Pope was moving toward him with a far larger army, recently augmented by Heintzelman's corps from the Army of the Potomac, while Fitz John Porter with an additional force was not far off. It is true that Longstreet was hastening to the aid of Jackson, but he had to come by the same route which had brought Jackson— through Thoroughfare Gap—and Pope thought he saw a great opportunity. If he could only detain Longstreet at the gap, why should he not crush Jackson with his superior numbers? To this end he sent orders to Porter, to McDowell, and to Kearny and others whose forces were scattered about the country, to concentrate during the night of the 27th and move upon Jackson. McDowell sent Ricketts with a small force—too small—to prevent Longstreet from passing through Thoroughfare Gap, and hastened to join the main army against Jackson. But that able commander was not to be caught in a trap. He moved from Manassas Junction by three roads toward the old battle-field of Bull Run and by noon on the 28th the whole corps was once more united between Centreville and Sudley Spring. Late in the day he encountered King's division of McDowell's corps near the village of Groveton, and a sharp fight was opened and kept up till an hour after dark. The Confederates were left in possession of the field.

The following day, August 29th, was the first of the two days' battle, leaving out of account the fight of the evening

## THE TWICE–WON FIELD

Sleeping on their arms on the night of August 29th, the Federal veterans were as confident of having won a victory as were the raw troops in the beginning of the first battle of Bull Run. But the next day's fighting was to tell the tale. General Ewell had been wounded in the knee by a minie ball in the severe fight at Groveton and was unable to lead his command; but for the impetuosity of this commander was substituted that of Longstreet, nicknamed 'the War-Horse,'' whose arrival in the midst of the previous day's en-

MAJOR–GENERAL R. S.
EWELL

MAJOR–GENERAL JAMES
LONGSTREET

gagement had cost the Federals dear On the morning of the second day Longstreet's batteries opened the engagement. When the general advance came, as the sun shone on the parallel lines of glittering bayonets, it was Longstreet's men bringing their muskets to "the ready" who first opened fire with a long flash of flame. It was they who pressed most eagerly forward and, in the face of the Federal batteries, fell upon the troops of General McDowell at the left and drove them irresistibly back. Although the right Federal wing, in command of General Heintzelman, had not given an inch, it was this turning of the left by Longstreet which put the whole Federal army in retreat, driving them across Bull Run. The Confederates were left in possession of the field, where lay thousands of Federal dead and wounded, and Lee was free to advance his victorious troops into the North unmolested.

THE BATTLE–FIELD OF SECOND BULL RUN (MANASSAS), AUGUST 29–30, 1862

before and the desultory fighting of the preceding ten days. General Pope was still hopeful of crushing Jackson before the arrival of Longstreet, and on the morning of the 29th he ordered a general advance across Bull Run. As the noon hour approached a wild shout that arose from Jackson's men told too well of the arrival of Longstreet. Far away on the hills near Gainesville could be seen the marching columns of Longstreet, who had passed through the gap in safety and who was now rushing to the support of Jackson. The Confederate army was at last to be reunited. Jackson was greatly relieved. Pope had lost his opportunity of fighting the army of his opponent in sections.

The field was almost the same that the opposing forces had occupied a year and a month before when the first great battle of the war was fought. And many of them were the same men. Some who had engaged in that first conflict had gone home and had refused to reenlist; others had found soldiers' graves since then—but still others on both sides were here again, no longer the raw recruits that they were before, but, with their year of hard experience in the field, they were trained soldiers, equal to any in the world.

The two armies faced each other in a line nearly five miles long. There was heavy fighting here and there along the line from the early morning hours, but no general engagement until late in the afternoon. The Union right pressed hard against the Confederate left and by ten o'clock had forced it back more than a mile. But the Confederates, presently reenforced in that quarter, hurled heavy masses of infantry against the Union right and regained much that it had lost. Late in the afternoon fresh regiments under Kearny and Hooker charged the Confederate left, which was swept back and rolled in upon the center. But presently the Southern General Hood, with his famous Texan brigade, rushed forward in a wild, irresistible dash, pressed Kearny back, captured one gun, several flags and a hundred prisoners. Night then closed over

[48]

## THE FIGHTING FORTY–FIRST

"C" Company of the Forty-first New York after the Second Battle of Bull Run, August 30, 1862. When the troops of Generals Milroy and Schurz were hard pressed by overpowering numbers and exhausted by fatigue, this New York regiment, being ordered forward, quickly advanced with a cheer along the Warrenton Turnpike and deployed about a mile west of the field of the conflict of July 21, 1861. The fighting men replied with answering shouts, for with the regiment that came up at the double quick galloped a battery of artillery. The charging Confederates were held and this position was assailed time and again. It became the center of the sanguinary combat of the day, and it was here that the "Bull-Dogs" earned their name. Among the first to respond to Lincoln's call, they enlisted in June, '61, and when their first service was over they stepped forward to a man, specifying no term of service but putting their names on the Honor Roll of "For the War."

BRIG.-GEN. RUFUS KING

Brigadier-General King, a division commander in this battle, was a soldier by profession, and a diplomatist and journalist by inheritance—for he was a graduate of West Point, a son of Charles King, editor of the New York *American* in 1827, and a grandson of the elder Rufus, an officer of the Revolution and Minister to the Court of St. James. He had left the army in 1836 to become Assistant Engineer of the New York & Erie Railroad, a post he gave up to become editor of the *Daily Advertiser*, and subsequently of the Milwaukee *Sentinel*. At the outbreak of the war Lincoln had appointed him Minister to Rome, but he asked permission to delay his departure, and was made a Brigadier-General of Volunteers. Later he resigned as Minister, and was assigned to McDowell's corps. At the battle of Manassas, in which the Forty-first New York earned honor, he proved an able leader. In 1867 he was again appointed as Minister of the United States to Italy.

the scene and the two armies rested on their arms until the morning.

The first day's battle is sometimes called the battle of Groveton, but usually it is considered as the first half of the second battle of Bull Run. It was a formidable conflict in itself. The Union loss was at least forty-five hundred men, the Confederate was somewhat larger. Over the gory field lay multitudes of men, the blue and the gray commingled, who would dream of battlefields no more. The living men lay down among the dead in order to snatch a little rest and strength that they might renew the strife in the morning.

It is a strange fact that Lee and Pope each believed that the other would withdraw his army during the night, and each was surprised in the morning to find his opponent still on the ground, ready, waiting, defiant. It was quite certain that on this day, August 30th, there would be a decisive action and that one of the two armies would be victor and the other defeated. The two opposing commanders had called in their outlying battalions and the armies now faced each other in almost full force, the Confederates with over fifty thousand men and the Union forces exceeding their opponents by probably fifteen thousand men. The Confederate left wing was commanded by Jackson, and the right by Longstreet. The extreme left of the Union army was under Fitz John Porter, who, owing to a misunderstanding of orders, had not reached the field the day before. The center was commanded by Heintzelman and the right by Reno.

In the early hours of the morning the hills echoed with the firing of artillery, with which the day was opened. Porter made an infantry attack in the forenoon, but was met by the enemy in vastly superior numbers and was soon pressed back in great confusion. As the hours passed one fearful attack followed another, each side in turn pressing forward and again receding. In the afternoon a large part of

[50]

## THE ADVANCE THAT BECAME A RETREAT

The Stone Bridge across Bull Run.   When the Federal army silently put Bull Run between itself and Lee on the night of August 30, 1862, Pope's attempt to capture Richmond was turned into a Confederate advance upon Washington.   Lee, on discovering Pope's position at Centreville on the next day, sent "Stonewall" Jackson to turn the Federal right.   Crossing Bull Run at Sudley Ford, Jackson advanced along a country road till he reached the Little River Turnpike, on which the troops bivouacked for the night.   On September 1st he was met near Chantilly by Reno and Kearney, who had been sent by Pope to intercept him.   A fierce encounter followed in a drenching rainstorm.   The brilliant bayonet charge by Birney, in command of the division of General Philip Kearney, who had just fallen, drove back the Confederates, and Birney held the field that night.   The next morning orders came from General Halleck for the broken and demoralized army of Pope to fall back within the defenses of Washington.   Large quantities of Federal stores were left to fall into the hands of Lee, which were of great use in his advance into Maryland.

[B]

the Union army made a desperate onslaught on the Confederate left under Jackson. Here for some time the slaughter of men was fearful. It was nearing sunset. Jackson saw that his lines were wavering. He called for reenforcements which did not come and it seemed as if the Federals were about to win a signal victory. But this was not to be. Far away on a little hill at the Confederate right Longstreet placed four batteries in such a position that he could enfilade the Federal columns. Quickly he trained his cannon on the Federal lines that were hammering away at Jackson, and opened fire. Ghastly gaps were soon cut in the Federal ranks and they fell back. But they re-formed and came again and still again, each time only to be mercilessly cut down by Longstreet's artillery. At length Longstreet's whole line rushed forward, and with the coming of darkness, the whole Union front began to waver.

General Lee, seeing this, ordered the Confederates in all parts of the field to advance. With wild, triumphant yells they did so. It was now dark and there was little more fighting; but Lee captured several thousand prisoners. Pope retreated across Bull Run with the remnant of his army and by morning was ensconced behind the field-works at Centreville.

There was no mistaking the fact that General Pope had lost the battle and the campaign. He decided to lead his army back to the entrenchments of Washington. After spending a day behind the embankments at Centreville, the retreat was begun. Lee's troops with Jackson in the advance pursued and struck a portion of the retreating army at Chantilly.

It was late in the afternoon of September 1st. The rain, accompanied by vivid lightning and terrific crashes of thunder, was falling in torrents as Stuart's horsemen, sent in advance, were driven back by the Federal infantry. Jackson now pushed two of A. P. Hill's brigades forward to ascertain the condition of the Union army. General Reno was protecting Pope's right flank, and he lost no time in proceeding against Hill. The latter was promptly checked, and both forces took

## FAIRFAX COURT HOUSE, VIRGINIA

Pope's retirement from the field of Bull Run gave the famous Confederate cavalry leader, J. E. B. Stuart, a splendid opportunity for the kind of warfare he most delighted in. No sooner had the Federals started than Stuart was following them. Ascertaining that their main body was at Centreville and Fairfax Court House, he planned to make an attack on the pike between the two places. A section of the famous Washington Artillery took position just after dark on August 31st, within range of a road completely filled with a continuous stream of Federal army wagons making their way toward the Court House. A few rounds from the Confederate guns threw "everything into confusion, and such commotion, upsetting, collisions, and smash-ups were rarely ever seen." Stuart bivouacked that night near Chantilly, and after Jackson came up on September 1st, tried to force his way down the pike toward Fairfax Court House. But the Federals were too strong in number at that point. The next day (September 2d) Halleck sent word to Pope to bring his army back to Washington. Stuart then promptly took possession of Fairfax Court House, after a sharp skirmish with some of Sumner's departing troops.

position for battle. One side and then the other fell back in turn as lines were re-formed and urged forward. Night fell and the tempest's fury increased. The ammunition of both armies was so wet that much of it could not be used. Try as they would the Confederates were unable to break the Union line and the two armies finally withdrew. The Confederates suffered a loss of five hundred men in their unsuccessful attempt to demoralize Pope in his retreat, and the Federals more than a thousand, including Generals Stevens and Kearny.

General Kearny might have been saved but for his reckless bravery. He was rounding up the retreat of his men in the darkness of the night when he chanced to come within the Confederate lines. Called on to surrender, he lay flat on his horse's back, sank his spurs into its sides, and attempted to escape. Half a dozen muskets were leveled and fired at the fleeing general. Within thirty yards he rolled from his horse's back dead.

The consternation in Washington and throughout the North when Pope's defeated army reached Arlington Heights can better be imagined than described. General Pope, who bore the brunt of public indignation, begged to be relieved of the command. The President complied with his wishes and the disorganized remnants of the Army of Virginia and the Army of the Potomac were handed to the " Little Napoleon " of Peninsula fame, George B. McClellan.

The South was overjoyed with its victory—twice it had unfurled its banner in triumph on the battlefield at Manassas by the remarkable strategy of its generals and the courage of its warriors on the firing-line. Twice it had stood literally on the road that led to the capital of the Republic, only by some strange destiny of war to fail to enter its precincts on the wave of victory.

# PART I
## THE RISE OF LEE

---

# ANTIETAM—THE
# INVASION OF THE NORTH

---

THE FIRST STAND
OF "STONEWALL'S" MEN

## McCLELLAN'S LAST ADVANCE

This splendid landscape photograph of the pontoon bridge at Berlin, Maryland, was taken in October, 1862. On the 26th McClellan crossed the Potomac here for the last time in command of an army. Around this quiet and picturesque country the Army of the Potomac bivouacked during October, 1862, leaving two corps posted at Harper's Ferry to hold the outlet of the Shenandoah Valley. At Berlin (a little village of about four hundred inhabitants), McClellan had his headquarters during the reorganization of the army, which he considered necessary after Antietam. The many reverses to the Federal arms since the beginning of the war had weakened the popular hold of the Lincoln Administration, and there was constant political pressure for an aggressive move against Lee. McClellan, yielding at last to this demand, began advancing his army into Virginia. Late on the night of November 7th, through a heavy rainstorm, General Buckingham, riding post-

## THE CROSSING AFTER ANTIETAM

haste from Washington, reached McClellan's tent at Rectortown, and handed him Stanton's order relieving him from command. Burnside was appointed his successor, and at the moment was with him in the tent. Without a change of countenance, McClellan handed him the despatch, with the words: "Well, Burnside, you are to command the army." Whatever may have been McClellan's fault, the moment chosen for his removal was most inopportune and ungracious. His last advance upon Lee was excellently planned, and he had begun to execute it with great vigor—the van of the army having reached Warrenton on November 7th, opposed only by half of Lee's army at Culpeper, while demonstrations across the gaps of the Blue Ridge compelled the retention of Jackson with the other half in the Shenandoah Valley. Never before had the Federal military prospect been brighter than at that moment.

# ANTIETAM, OR SHARPSBURG

At Sharpsburg (Antietam) was sprung the keystone of the arch upon which the Confederate cause rested.—*James Longstreet, Lieutenant-General C.S.A., in " Battles and Leaders of the Civil War."*

A BATTLE remarkable in its actualities but more wonderful in its possibilities was that of Antietam, with the preceding capture of Harper's Ferry and the other interesting events that marked the invasion of Maryland by General Lee. It was one of the bloodiest and the most picturesque conflicts of the Civil War, and while it was not all that the North was demanding and not all that many military critics think it might have been, it enabled President Lincoln to feel that he could with some assurance issue, as he did, his Emancipation Proclamation.

Lee's army, fifty thousand strong, had crossed the Potomac at Leesburg and had concentrated around Frederick, the scene of the Barbara Frietchie legend, only forty miles from Washington. When it became known that Lee, elated by his victory at Second Bull Run, had taken the daring step of advancing into Maryland, and now threatened the capital of the Republic, McClellan, commanding the Army of the Potomac, pushed his forces forward to encounter the invaders. Harper's Ferry, at the junction of the Potomac and the Shenandoah rivers, was a valuable defense against invasion through the Valley of Virginia, but once the Confederates had crossed it, a veritable trap. General Halleck ordered it held and General Lee sent " Stonewall " Jackson to take it, by attacking the fortress on the Virginia side.

Jackson began his march on September 10th with secret instructions from his commander to encompass and capture the

## LEE LOCKS THE GATES

Sharpsburg, Maryland, September 17, 1862. There were long minutes on that sunny day in the early fall of 1862 when Robert E. Lee, at his headquarters west of Sharpsburg, must have been in almost entire ignorance of how the battle went. Outnumbered he knew his troops were; outfought he knew they never would be. Longstreet, Hood, D. B. Hill, Evans, and D. R. Jones had turned back more than one charge in the morning; but, as the day wore on, Lee perceived that the center must be held. Sharpsburg was the key. He had deceived McClellan as to his numerical strength and he must continue to do so. Lee had practically no reserves at all. At one time General Longstreet reported from the center to General Chilton, Lee's Chief of Staff, that Cooke's North Carolina regiment—still keeping its colors at the front—had not a cartridge left. None but veteran troops could hold a line like this, supported by only two guns of Miller's battery of the Washington Artillery. Of this crisis in the battle General Longstreet wrote afterward: "We were already badly whipped and were holding our ground by sheer force of desperation." Actually in line that day on the Confederate side were only 37,000 men, and opposed to them were numbers that could be footed up to 50,000 more. At what time in the day General Lee must have perceived that the invasion of Maryland must come to an end cannot be told. He had lost 20,000 of his tired, footsore army by straggling on the march, according to the report of Longstreet, who adds: "Nearly one-fourth of the troops who went into the battle were killed or wounded." At dark Lee's rearward movement had begun.

Federal garrison and the vast store of war material at this place, made famous a few years before by old John Brown. To conceal his purpose from the inhabitants he inquired along the route about the roads leading into Pennsylvania. It was from his march through Frederick that the Barbara Frietchie story took its rise. But there is every reason to believe that General Jackson never saw the good old lady, that the story is a myth, and that Mr. Whittier, who has given us the popular poem under the title of her name, was misinformed. However, Colonel H. K. Douglas, who was a member of Jackson's staff, relates, in "Battles and Leaders of the Civil War," an interesting incident where his commander on entering Middletown was greeted by two young girls waving a Union flag. The general bowed to the young women, raised his hat, and remarked to some of his officers, "We evidently have no friends in this town." Colonel Douglas concludes, "This is about the way he would have treated Barbara Frietchie."

On the day after Jackson left Frederick he crossed the Potomac by means of a ford near Williamsport and on the 13th he reached Bolivar Heights. Harper's Ferry lies in a deep basin formed by Maryland Heights on the north bank of the Potomac, Loudon Heights on the south bank, and Bolivar Heights on the west. The Shenandoah River breaks through the pass between Loudon and Bolivar Heights and the village lies between the two at the apex formed by the junction of the two rivers.

As Jackson approached the place by way of Bolivar Heights, Walker occupied Loudon Heights and McLaws invested Maryland Heights. All were unopposed except McLaws, who encountered Colonel Ford with a force to dispute his ascent. Ford, however, after some resistance, spiked his guns and retired to the Ferry, where Colonel Miles had remained with the greater portion of the Federal troops. Had Miles led his entire force to Maryland Heights he could no doubt have held his ground until McClellan came to his relief.

A REGIMENT THAT FOUGHT AT SOUTH MOUNTAIN—THE THIRTY-FIFTH NEW YORK

Here sits Colonel T. G. Morehead, who commanded the 106th Pennsylvania, of the Second Corps. At 7.20 A.M. the order came to advance, and with a cheer the Second Corps—men who for over two years had never lost a gun nor struck a color—pressed forward. But again they were halted. It was almost an hour later when Sedgwick's division, with Sumner at the head, crossed the Antietam. Arriving nearly opposite the Dunker church, it swept out over the cornfields. On it went, by Greene's right, through the West Woods; here it met the awful counter-stroke of Early's reënforced division and, stubbornly resisting, was hurled back with frightful loss.

COLONEL T. G. MOREHEAD
A HERO OF SEDGWICK'S CHARGE

Early in the morning of September 17, 1862, Knap's battery (shown below) got into the thick of the action of Antietam. General Mansfield had posted it opposite the north end of the West Woods, close to the Confederate line. The guns opened fire at seven o'clock. Practically unsupported, the battery was twice charged upon during the morning; but quickly substituting canister for shot and shell, the men held their ground and stemmed the Confederate advance. Near this spot General Mansfield was mortally wounded while deploying his troops. About noon a section of Knap's battery was detached to the assistance of General Greene, in the East Woods.

KNAP'S BATTERY, JUST AFTER THE BLOODY WORK AT ANTIETAM

But General Halleck had ordered him to hold Harper's Ferry to the last, and Miles interpreted this order to mean that he must hold the town itself. He therefore failed to occupy the heights around it in sufficient strength and thus permitted himself to be caught in a trap.

During the day of the 14th the Confederate artillery was dragged up the mountain sides, and in the afternoon a heavy fire was opened on the doomed Federal garrison. On that day McClellan received word from Miles that the latter could hold out for two days longer and the commanding general sent word: "Hold out to the last extremity. If it is possible, reoccupy the Maryland Heights with your entire force. If you can do that I will certainly be able to relieve you. . . . Hold out to the last." McClellan was approaching slowly and felt confident he could relieve the place.

On the morning of the 15th the roar of Confederate artillery again resounded from hill to hill. From Loudon to Maryland Heights the firing had begun and a little later the battle-flags of A. P. Hill rose on Bolivar Heights. Scarcely two hours had the firing continued when Colonel Miles raised the white flag at Harper's Ferry and its garrison of 12,500, with vast military stores, passed into the hands of the Confederates. Colonel Miles was struck by a stray fragment of a Confederate shell which gave him a mortal wound. The force of General Franklin, preparing to move to the garrison's relief, on the morning of the 15th noted that firing at the Ferry had ceased and suspected that the garrison had surrendered, as it had.

The Confederate Colonel Douglas, whose account of the surrender is both absorbing and authoritative, thus describes the surrender in "Battles and Leaders of the Civil War":

"Under instructions from General Jackson, I rode up the pike and into the enemy's lines to ascertain the purpose of the white flag. Near the top of the hill I met General White and staff and told him my mission. He replied that Colonel Miles had been mortally wounded, that he was in command and

[62]

## THE FIRST TO FALL

This photograph was taken back of the rail fence on the Hagerstown pike, where "Stonewall" Jackson's men attempted to rally in the face of Hooker's ferocious charge that opened the bloodiest day of the Civil War—September 17, 1862. Hooker, advancing to seize high ground nearly three-quarters of a mile distant, had not gone far before the glint of the rising sun disclosed the bayonet-points of a large Confederate force standing in a cornfield in his immediate front. This was a part of Jackson's Corps which had arrived during the morning of the 16th from the capture of Harper's Ferry and had been posted in this position to surprise Hooker in his advance. The outcome was a terrible surprise to the Confederates. All of Hooker's batteries hurried into action and opened with canister on the cornfield. The Confederates stood bravely up against this fire, and as Hooker's men advanced they made a determined resistance. Back and still farther back were Jackson's men driven across the open field, every stalk of corn in which was cut down by the battle as closely as a knife could have done it. On the ground the slain lay in rows precisely as they had stood in ranks. From the cornfield into a small patch of woods (the West Woods) the Confederates were driven, leaving the sad result of the surprise behind them. As the edge of the woods was approached by Hooker's men the resistance became stronger and more stubborn. Nearly all the units of two of Jackson's divisions were now in action, and cavalry and artillery were aiding them. "The two lines," says General Palfrey, "almost tore each other to pieces." General Starke and Colonel Douglas on the Confederate side were killed. More than half of Lawton's and Hays' brigades were either killed or wounded. On the Federal side General Ricketts lost a third of his division. The energy of both forces was entirely spent and reënforcements were necessary before the battle could be continued. Many of Jackson's men wore trousers and caps of Federal blue, as did most of the troops which had been engaged with Jackson in the affair at Harper's Ferry. A. P. Hill's men, arriving from Harper's Ferry that same afternoon, were dressed in new Federal uniforms—a part of their booty—and at first were mistaken for Federals by the friends who were anxiously awaiting them.

desired to have an interview with General Jackson. . . . I conducted them to General Jackson, whom I found sitting on his horse where I had left him. . . . The contrast in appearances there presented was striking. General White, riding a handsome black horse, was carefully dressed and had on untarnished gloves, boots, and sword. His staff were equally comely in costume. On the other hand, General Jackson was the dingiest, worst-dressed and worst-mounted general that a warrior who cared for good looks and style would wish to surrender to.

"General Jackson . . . rode up to Bolivar and down into Harper's Ferry. The curiosity in the Union army to see him was so great that the soldiers lined the sides of the road. . . . One man had an echo of response all about him when he said aloud: 'Boys, he's not much for looks, but if we'd had him we wouldn't have been caught in this trap.'"

McClellan had failed to reach Harper's Ferry in time to relieve it because he was detained at South Mountain by a considerable portion of Lee's army under D. H. Hill and Longstreet. McClellan had come into possession of Lee's general order, outlining the campaign. Discovering by this order that Lee had sent Jackson to attack Harper's Ferry he made every effort to relieve it.

The affair at Harper's Ferry, as that at South Mountain, was but a prelude to the tremendous battle that was to follow two days later on the banks of the little stream called Antietam Creek, in Maryland. When it was known that Lee had led his army across the Potomac the people were filled with consternation—the people, not only of the immediate vicinity, but of Harrisburg, of Baltimore, of Philadelphia. Their fear was intensified by the memory of the Second Bull Run of a few weeks earlier, and by the fact that at this very time General Bragg was marching northward across Kentucky with a great army, menacing Louisville and Cincinnati.

As one year before, the hopes of the North had centered in George B. McClellan, so it was now with the people of the

THE THRICE–FOUGHT GROUND

The field beyond the leveled fence is covered with both Federal and Confederate dead. Over this open space swept Sedgwick's division of Sumner's Second Corps, after passing through the East and entering the West Woods. This is near where the Confederate General Ewell's division, reënforced by McLaws and Walker, fell upon Sedgwick's left flank and rear. Nearly two thousand Federal soldiers were struck down, the division losing during the day more than forty per cent. of its entire number. One regiment lost sixty per cent.—the highest regimental loss sustained. Later the right of the Confederate line crossed the turnpike at the Dunker church (about half a mile to the left of the picture) and made two assaults upon Greene, but they were repulsed with great slaughter. General D. R. Jones, of Jackson's division, had been wounded. The brave Starke who succeeded him was killed; and Lawton, who followed Starke, had fallen wounded.

RUIN OF MUMMA'S HOUSE, ANTIETAM

A flaming mansion was the guidon for the extreme left of Greene's division when (early in the morning) he had moved forward along the ridge leading to the East Woods. This dwelling belonged to a planter by the name of Mumma. It stood in the very center of the Federal advance, and also at the extreme left of D. H. Hill's line. The house had been fired by the Confederates, who feared that its thick walls might become a vantage-point for the Federal infantry. It burned throughout the battle, the flames subsiding only in the afternoon. Before it, just across the road, a battery of the First Rhode Island Light Artillery had placed its guns. Twice were they charged, but each time they were repulsed. From Mumma's house it was less than half a mile across the open field to the Dunker church. The fence-rails in the upper picture were those of the field enclosing Mumma's land, and the heroic dead pictured lying there were in full sight from the burning mansion.

East. They were ready to forget his failure to capture Richmond in the early summer and to contrast his partial successes on the Peninsula with the drastic defeat of his successor at the Second Bull Run.

When McClellan, therefore, passed through Maryland to the scene of the coming battle, many of the people received him with joy and enthusiasm. At Frederick City, he tells us in his " Own Story," he was " nearly overwhelmed and pulled to pieces," and the people invited him into their houses and gave him every demonstration of confidence.

The first encounter, a double one, took place on September 14th, at two passes of South Mountain, a continuation of the Blue Ridge, north of the Potomac. General Franklin, who had been sent to relieve Harper's Ferry, met a Confederate force at Crampton's Gap and defeated it in a sharp battle of three hours' duration. Meanwhile, the First and Ninth Army Corps, under Burnside, encountered a stronger force at Turner's Gap seven miles farther up. The battle here continued many hours, till late in the night, and the Union troops were victorious. General Reno was killed. Lee's loss was nearly twenty-seven hundred, of whom eight hundred were prisoners. The Federals lost twenty-one hundred men and they failed to save Harper's Ferry.

Lee now placed Longstreet and D. H. Hill in a strong position near Keedysville, but learning that McClellan was advancing rapidly, the Confederate leader decided to retire to Sharpsburg, where he could be more easily joined by Jackson.

September 16th was a day of intense anxiety and unrest in the valley of the Antietam. The people who had lived in the farmhouses that dotted the golden autumn landscape in this hitherto quiet community had now abandoned their homes and given place to the armed forces. It was a day of marshaling and maneuvering of the gathering thousands, preparatory to the mighty conflict that was clearly seen to be inevitable. Lee had taken a strong position on the west bank of Antietam

WHERE NUMBERS TOLD

Here, in the old sunken road connecting the Hagerstown and the Keedysville Turnpikes, lies the mute testimony of the stubbornness with which the Confederates stood their ground in the most heroic resistance of the day. North of this sunken road was the original position of the Confederate center under General D. H. Hill when the battle opened at dawn. As the fighting reached flood-tide, Hill sent forward the brigades of Colquitt, Ripley, and McRae to the assistance of Jackson at the left. "The men (says Hill) advanced with alacrity, secured a good position, and were fighting bravely when Captain Thompson, Fifth North Carolina, cried out: 'They're flanking us!' This cry spread like an electric shock along the ranks, bringing up vivid recollections of the flank fire at South Mountain. In a moment they broke and fell to the rear." Rallied again at the sunken road, the forces of Hill now met the combined attack of the divisions of French and Richardson of Sumner's Corps,

MAJOR-GENERAL I. B. RICHARDSON

freshly come on the field. It was resistance to the death; reënforced by the division of Anderson, Hill's men, in the face of the deadly fire poured upon them in the sunken road, bravely assumed the offensive in a determined effort to flank the Federal forces to both left and right. Seizing a vantage-point on higher ground to the left, the Federals drove them back; while on the right Barlow, changing front with his two regiments, poured in a rapid fire, capturing three hundred prisoners and two standards. Then came the direct assault; swept by the enfilading fire from both sides, the remnant of the brave men in the sunken road was driven back, leaving the "bloody lane" behind them. It was not an easy victory for the Federals. The determined fire of the Confederates had brought down a heavy harvest, among which was numbered General Richardson, mortally wounded, who had handled his division in this sanguinary contest with his usual valor and skill.

[B]

Creek a few miles from where it flows into the Potomac. He made a display of force, exposing his men to the fire of the Federal artillery, his object being to await the coming of Jackson's command from Harper's Ferry. It is true that Jackson himself had arrived, but his men were weary with marching and, moreover, a large portion of his troops under A. P. Hill and McLaws had not yet reached the field.

McClellan spent the day arranging his corps and giving directions for planting batteries. With a few companions he rode along the whole front, frequently drawing the fire of the Confederate batteries and thus revealing their location. The right wing of his army, the corps of Generals Hooker, Mansfield, and Sumner, lay to the north, near the village of Keedysville. General Porter with two divisions of the Fifth Corps occupied the center and Burnside was on the left of the Union lines. Back of McClellan's lines was a ridge on which was a signal station commanding a view of the entire field. Late on the afternoon of the 16th, Hooker crossing the Antietam, advanced against Hood's division on the Confederate left. For several hours there was heavy skirmishing, which closed with the coming of darkness.

The two great armies now lay facing each other in a grand double line three miles in length. At one point (the Union right and the Confederate left) they were so near together that the pickets could hear each other's tread. It required no prophet to foretell what would happen on the morrow.

Beautiful and clear the morning broke over the Maryland hills on the fateful 17th of September, 1862. The sunlight had not yet crowned the hilltops when artillery fire announced the opening of the battle. Hooker's infantry soon entered into the action and encountered the Confederates in an open field, from which the latter were presently pressed back across the Hagerstown pike to a line of woods where they made a determined stand. Hooker then called on General Mansfield to come to his aid, and the latter quickly did so, for he had led

THE HARVEST OF "BLOODY LANE"

Here, at "Bloody Lane" in the sunken road, was delivered the most telling blow of which the Federals could boast in the day's fighting at Antietam, September 17, 1862. In the lower picture we see the officers whose work first began to turn the tide of battle into a decisive advantage which the Army of the Potomac had every reason to expect would be gained by its superior numbers. On very citadel of the center. Meagher's Irish Brigade had fought its way to a crest from which a plunging fire could be poured upon the Confederates in the sunken road. Meagher's ammunition was exhausted, and Caldwell threw his force into the position and continued the terrible combat. When the Confederates executed their flanking movement to the left, Colonel D. R.

the Federal right Jackson, with a bare four thousand men, had taken the fight out of Hooker's eighteen thousand in the morning, giving ground at last to Sumner's fresh troops. On the Federal left, Burnside (at the lower bridge) failed to advance against Longstreet's Corps, two-thirds of which had been detached for service elsewhere. It was at the center that the forces of French and Richardson, skilfully fought by their leaders, broke through the Confederate lines and, sweeping beyond the sunken road, seized the

BRIGADIER-GENERAL CALDWELL AND STAFF

Cross, of the Fifth New Hampshire, seized a position which exposed Hill's men to an enfilading fire. (In the picture General Caldwell is seen standing to the left of the tree, and Colonel Cross leans on his sword at the extreme right. Between them stands Lieut.-Colonel George W. Scott, of the Sixty-first New York Infantry, while at the left before the tent stands Captain George W. Bulloch, A.C.S. General Caldwell's hand rests on the shoulder of Captain George H. Caldwell; to his left is seated Lieutenant C. A. Alvord.)

his corps across the Antietam after dark the night before. Mansfield, however, a gallant and honored veteran, fell mortally wounded while deploying his troops, and General Alpheus S. Williams, at the head of his first division, succeeded to the command.

There was a wood west of the Sharpsburg and Hagerstown turnpike which, with its outcropping ledges of rock, formed an excellent retreat for the Confederates and from this they pushed their columns into the open fields, chiefly of corn, to meet the Union attacks. For about two hours the battle raged at this point, the lines swaying to and fro, with fearful slaughter on both sides. At length, General Greene, who commanded a division of the fallen Mansfield's corps, gained possession of part of the coveted forest, near a little white church, known as the Dunker's Chapel. This was on high ground and was the key to the Confederate left wing. But Greene's troops were exposed to a galling fire from D. H. Hill's division and he called for reenforcements.

General Sumner then sent Sedgwick's division across the stream and accompanied the troops to the aid of their hard-pressed comrades. And the experience of this body of the gallant Second Corps during the next hour was probably the most thrilling episode of the whole day's battle. Sedgwick's troops advanced straight toward the conflict. They found Hooker wounded and his and Williams' troops quite exhausted. A sharp artillery fire was turned on Sedgwick before he reached the woods west of the Hagerstown pike, but once in the shelter of the thick trees he passed in safety to the western edge. Here the division found itself in an ambush. Heavy Confederate reenforcements—ten brigades, in fact—Walker's men, and McLaws', having arrived from Harper's Ferry—were hastening up, and they not only blocked the front, but worked around to the rear of Sedgwick's isolated brigades. Sedgwick was wounded in the awful slaughter that followed, but he and Sumner finally extricated their men with

## THE BLUNDER AT THE BRIDGE

Burnside's Bridge, as it was called after Antietam, bears the name of a noted Federal general—not because of the brilliant maneuver which he vainly tried to execute in his efforts to cross it, but rather because of the gallant resistance offered here by the Confederates. General Toombs, with two Georgia regiments (the Second and the Twentieth) stood off a greatly superior force during the 16th and the greater part of the 17th of September. This bridge (on the road from Sharpsburg to Porterstown and Rohersville) was not forced till late in the afternoon, when Burnside, after a series of delays and ineffectual attempts, managed to throw his troops across Antietam Creek. The battle, however, was then practically decided. Toombs' forces saved the Confederate right wing—to him Lee and Longstreet gave the highest praise.

a loss of two thousand, over three hundred left dead on the ghastly field. Franklin now sent forward some fresh troops and after obstinately fighting, the Federals finally held a corn-field and most of the coveted wood over which the conflict had raged till the ground was saturated with blood.

Before the close of this bloody conflict on the Union right another, almost if not quite as deadly, was in progress near the center. General French, soon joined by General Richardson, both of Sumner's corps, crossed the stream and made a des-perate assault against the Southerners of D. H. Hill's divis-ion, stationed to the south of where the battle had previously raged—French on a line of heights strongly held by the Con-federates, Richardson in the direction of a sunken road, since known as "Bloody Lane." The fighting here was of a most desperate character and continued nearly four hours. French captured a few flags, several hundred prisoners, and gained some ground, but he failed to carry the heights. Richardson was mortally wounded while leading a charge and was suc-ceeded by General Hancock; but his men finally captured Bloody Lane with the three hundred living men who had re-mained to defend it. The final Federal charge at this point was made by Colonel Barlow, who displayed the utmost brav-ery and self-possession in the thickest of the fight, where he won a brigadier-generalship. He was wounded, and later carried off the field. The Confederates had fought desperately to hold their position in Bloody Lane, and when it was captured it was filled with dead bodies. It was now about one o'clock and the infantry firing ceased for the day on the Union right, and center.

Let us now look on the other part of the field. Burnside held the Federal left wing against Lee's right, and he remained inactive for some hours after the battle had begun at the other end of the line. In front of Burnside was a triple-arched stone bridge across the Antietam, since known as "Burnside's Bridge." Opposite this bridge, on the slope which extends to a

[72]

## SHERRICK'S HOUSE

In three distinct localities the battle waxed fierce from dawn to dusk on that terrible day at Antietam, September 17, 1862. First at the Federal right around the Dunker church; then at the sunken road, where the centers of both armies spent themselves in sanguinary struggle; lastly, late in the day, the struggle was renewed and ceased on the Sharpsburg road. When Burnside finally got his troops in motion, Sturgis' division of the Ninth Corps was first to cross the creek; his men advanced through an open ravine under a withering fire till they gained the opposite crest and held it until reënforced by Wilcox. To their right ran the Sharpsburg road, and an advance was begun in the direction of the Sherrick house.

The fighting along the Sharpsburg road might have resulted in a Confederate disaster had it not been for the timely arrival of the troops of General A. P. Hill. His six brigades of Confederate veterans had been the last to leave Harper's Ferry, remaining behind Jackson's main body in order to attend to the details of the surrender. Just as the Federal Ninth Corps was in the height of its advance, a cloud of dust on Harper's Ferry road cheered the Confederates to redoubled effort. Out of the dust the brigades of Hill debouched upon the field. Their fighting blood seemed to have but mounted more strongly during their march of eighteen miles. Without waiting for orders, Hill threw his men into the fight and the progress of the Ninth Corps was stopped. Lee had counted on the arrival of Hill in time to prevent any successful attempt upon the Confederate right held by Longstreet's Corps, two-thirds of which had been detached in the thick of the fighting of the morning, when Lee's left and center suffered so severely. Burnside's delay at the bridge could not have been more fortunate for Lee if he had fixed its duration himself. Had the Confederate left been attacked at the time appointed, the outcome of Antietam could scarcely have been other than a decisive victory for the Federals. Even at the time when Burnside's tardy advance began, it must have prevailed against the weakened and wearied Confederates had not the fresh troops of A. P. Hill averted the disaster.

GENERAL A. P. HILL, C. S. A.

## AFTER THE ADVANCE

In the advance along the Sharpsburg road near the Sherrick house the 79th New York "Highlanders" deployed as skirmishers. From orchards and cornfields and from behind fences and haystacks the Confederate sharpshooters opened upon them, but they swept on, driving in a part of Jones' division and capturing a battery just before A. P. Hill's troops arrived. With these reënforcements the Confederates drove back the brave Highlanders from the suburbs of Sharpsburg, which they had reached. Stubborn Scotch blood would permit only a reluctant retreat. Sharp fighting occurred around the Sherrick house with results seen in the lower picture. Night closed the battle, both sides exhausted.

high ridge, were Confederate breastworks and rifle-pits, which commanded the bridge with a direct or enfilading fire. While the Federal right was fighting on the morning of the 17th, McClellan sent an order to Burnside to advance on the bridge, to take possession of it and cross the stream by means of it. It must have been about ten o'clock when Burnside received the order as McClellan was more than two miles away.

Burnside's chief officer at this moment was General Jacob D. Cox (afterward Governor of Ohio), who had succeeded General Reno, killed at South Mountain. On Cox fell the task of capturing the stone bridge. The defense of the bridge was in the hands of General Robert Toombs, a former United States senator and a member of Jefferson Davis' Cabinet. Perhaps the most notable single event in the life of General Toombs was his holding of the Burnside Bridge at Antietam for three hours against the assaults of the Federal troops. The Confederates had been weakened at this point by the sending of Walker to the support of Jackson, where, as we have noticed, he took part in the deadly assault upon Sedgwick's division. Toombs, therefore, with his one brigade had a heavy task before him in defending the bridge with his small force, notwithstanding his advantage of position.

McClellan sent several urgent orders to advance at all hazards. Burnside forwarded these to Cox, and in the fear that the latter would be unable to carry the bridge by a direct front attack, he sent Rodman with a division to cross the creek by a ford some distance below. This was accomplished after much difficulty. Meanwhile, in rapid succession, one assault after another was made upon the bridge and, about one o'clock, it was carried, at the cost of five hundred men. The Confederates fell back. A lull in the fighting along the whole line of battle now ensued.

Burnside, however, received another order from McClellan to push on up the heights and to the village of Sharpsburg. The great importance of this move, if successful, was

## THE FLOOD–TIDE OF THE FEDERAL ADVANCE

This Lutheran church on Main Street, to the east of Sharpsburg, marked the end of the Federal assault upon Lee's position at Antietam, as the little church of the non-resistant Dunkers to the north of the town had marked its beginning in the early morning. About three o'clock in the afternoon Burnside's skirmishers advanced to the first cross-street beyond this church, threatening the town itself. Out on the hills beyond the town, Main Street becomes the Shepherdstown road, and along this were arriving and hurrying through the town the anxiously awaited forces of A. P. Hill. From that moment the Federals got no nearer Sharpsburg. Hill drove them back steadily beyond the church, recapturing the battery which they had wrested from the troops of Jones and which had done damage to the little church as well as to the Confederates. Hill's men, taking Rodman's division in flank, poured in a fire in which Rodman met his death. Panic among his troops was averted only by Scammon, who (leading Cox's division) checked Hill for a breathing space; but Burnside's forces were steadily pushed back until at nightfall they lay discomfited, holding the bridge on the banks of Antietam creek, which he had wrested from Toombs' two Georgia regiments.

that it would cut Lee out from his line of retreat by way of Shepherdstown.

After replenishing the ammunition and adding some fresh troops, Cox advanced at three o'clock with the utmost gallantry toward Sharpsburg. The Confederates disputed the ground with great bravery. But Cox swept all before him and was at the edge of the village when he was suddenly confronted by lines in blue uniforms who instantly opened fire. The Federals were astonished to see the blue-clad battalions before them. They must be Union soldiers; but how did they get there? The matter was soon explained. They were A. P. Hill's division of Lee's army which had just arrived from Harper's Ferry, and they had dressed themselves in the uniforms that they had taken from the Federal stores.

Hill had come just in time to save Lee's headquarters from capture. He checked Cox's advance, threw a portion of the troops into great confusion, and steadily pressed them back toward the Antietam. In this, the end of the battle, General Rodman fell mortally wounded. Cox retired in good order and Sharpsburg remained in the hands of the Confederates.

Thus, with the approach of nightfall, closed the memorable battle of Antietam. For fourteen long hours more than one hundred thousand men, with five hundred pieces of artillery, had engaged in titanic combat. As the pall of battle smoke rose and cleared away, the scene presented was one to make the stoutest heart shudder. There lay upon the ground, scattered for three miles over the valleys and the hills or in the improvised hospitals, more than twenty thousand men. Horace Greeley was probably right in pronouncing this the bloodiest day in American history.

Although tactically it was a drawn battle, Antietam was decisively in favor of the North inasmuch as it ended the first Confederate attempt at a Northern invasion. General Lee realized that his ulterior plans had been thwarted by this engagement and after a consultation with his corps commanders

## THE MEDIATOR

President Lincoln's Visit to the Camps at Antietam, October 8, 1862.   Yearning for the speedy termination of the war, Lincoln came to view the Army of the Potomac, as he had done at Harrison's Landing.   Puzzled to understand how Lee could have circumvented a superior force on the Peninsula, he was now anxious to learn why a crushing blow had not been struck.   Lincoln (after Gettysburg) expressed the same thought: "Our army held the war in the hollow of their hand and they would not close it!"   On Lincoln's right stands Allan Pinkerton, the famous detective and organizer of the Secret Service of the army.   At the President's left is General John A. McClernand, soon to be entrusted by Lincoln with reorganizing military operations in the West.

he determined to withdraw from Maryland. On the night of the 18th the retreat began and early the next morning the Confederate army had all safely recrossed the Potomac.

The great mistake of the Maryland campaign from the standpoint of the Confederate forces, thought General Longstreet, was the division of Lee's army, and he believed that if Lee had kept his forces together he would not have been forced to abandon the campaign. At Antietam, he had less than forty thousand men, who were in poor condition for battle while McClellan had about eighty-seven thousand, most of whom were fresh and strong, though not more than sixty thousand were in action.

The moral effect of the battle of Antietam was incalculably great. It aroused the confidence of the Northern people. It emboldened President Lincoln to issue five days after its close the proclamation freeing the slaves in the seceded states. He had written the proclamation long before, but it had lain inactive in his desk at Washington. All through the struggles of the summer of 1862 he had looked forward to the time when he could announce his decision to the people. But he could not do it then. With the doubtful success of Federal arms, to make such a bold step would have been a mockery and would have defeated the very end he sought.

The South had now struck its first desperate blow at the gateways to the North. By daring, almost unparalleled in warfare, it had swung its courageous army into a strategical position where with the stroke of fortune it might have hammered down the defenses of the National capital on the south and then sweep on a march of invasion into the North. The Northern soldiers had parried the blow. They had saved themselves from disaster and had held back the tide of the Confederacy as it beat against the Mason and Dixon line, forcing it back into the State of Virginia where the two mighty fighting bodies were soon to meet again in a desperate struggle for the right-of-way at Fredericksburg.

[78]

PART I
THE RISE OF LEE

————

# FREDERICKSBURG
# DISASTER FOR A NEW UNION LEADER

————

THE MILL ACROSS THE RIVER

## FREDERICKSBURG

### A PHOTOGRAPH TAKEN JUST AFTER THE BATTLE OF DECEMBER, 1862

Two magnificent armies faced one another here in the middle of December, 1862. Along the ground we see spread before us on the east side of the Rappahannock—the famous Stafford Heights—the men in blue were massed in a long line of camps. In the town were scattered forces of Confederate troops, and along the river front each house was a temporary citadel; even cannon frowned from the windows. The winding river, now unbridged and at high water, separated the Army of Northern Virginia under Lee from the Army of the Potomac under Burnside. Fredericksburg, deserted by women, children, the aged, and the infirm, lay helpless before the Federal guns. But along the hill against the horizon stretched Lee's army, under able generals, in an impregnable position. Between it and the town lay open ground with a few scattered houses. Stretching across the river we can see the ruins of the bridges. For a month Burnside had waited for pontoons to enable him to cross in force. On a foggy morning after their arrival, the 11th of December, a landing was effected. The fierce fire of 147 guns from Stafford Heights played havoc among the houses. The sharpshooters that had bothered the pontoniers were driven back, and soon all the Confederate forces had gathered along the ridge a mile to the west of the town. By the 12th the Federal army had crossed and deployed for battle.

## THE DEATH-TRAP ON TELEGRAPH ROAD

Here Sumner's right grand division of the Army of the Potomac exemplified an implicit obedience of orders more magnificent even than that of the "Six Hundred" at Balaklava. Advancing along the Telegraph Road, seen at the right of the picture, the divisions of French and Hancock, already depleted by cruel artillery fire, charged up Marye's Heights, the eminence at the center of the picture. There a blinding flash of flame first disclosed the ambuscade in the sunken road. Ranged in ranks, first four and then six men deep, the Confederates kept up a continuous volleying against which no troops could stand. First the divisions of French and Hancock went down before it—then that of Howard. To the left the supporting divisions of Sturgis and Getty shared the efforts of their comrades with like result. Griffin's and Humphreys' divisions followed later—all to no avail. Six desperate charges were made upon Cobb's and Kershaw's troops. When darkness put an end to the slaughter, seven thousand Federal killed and wounded lay at the foot of Marye's Heights.

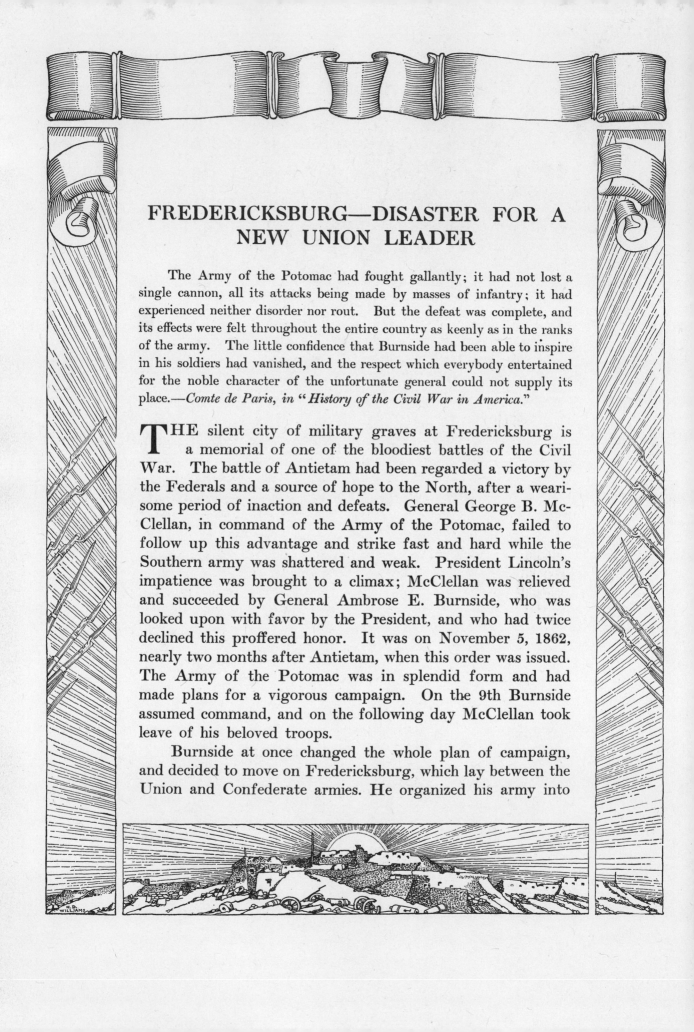

# FREDERICKSBURG—DISASTER FOR A NEW UNION LEADER

The Army of the Potomac had fought gallantly; it had not lost a single cannon, all its attacks being made by masses of infantry; it had experienced neither disorder nor rout. But the defeat was complete, and its effects were felt throughout the entire country as keenly as in the ranks of the army. The little confidence that Burnside had been able to inspire in his soldiers had vanished, and the respect which everybody entertained for the noble character of the unfortunate general could not supply its place.—*Comte de Paris, in "History of the Civil War in America."*

THE silent city of military graves at Fredericksburg is a memorial of one of the bloodiest battles of the Civil War. The battle of Antietam had been regarded a victory by the Federals and a source of hope to the North, after a wearisome period of inaction and defeats. General George B. McClellan, in command of the Army of the Potomac, failed to follow up this advantage and strike fast and hard while the Southern army was shattered and weak. President Lincoln's impatience was brought to a climax; McClellan was relieved and succeeded by General Ambrose E. Burnside, who was looked upon with favor by the President, and who had twice declined this proffered honor. It was on November 5, 1862, nearly two months after Antietam, when this order was issued. The Army of the Potomac was in splendid form and had made plans for a vigorous campaign. On the 9th Burnside assumed command, and on the following day McClellan took leave of his beloved troops.

Burnside at once changed the whole plan of campaign, and decided to move on Fredericksburg, which lay between the Union and Confederate armies. He organized his army into

## THE SECOND LEADER AGAINST RICHMOND

Major-General Ambrose Everett Burnside was a West Point graduate, inventor of a breech-loading rifle, commander of a brigade in the first battle of Bull Run, captor of Roanoke Island and Newberne (North Carolina), and commander of the Federal left at Antietam. He was appointed to the command of the Army of the Potomac and succeeded General George B. McClellan on November 8, 1862. He was a brave soldier, but was an impatient leader and inclined to be somewhat reckless. He pressed rapidly his advance against Lee and massed his entire army along Stafford Heights, on the east bank of the Rappahannock, opposite Fredericksburg. According to General B. B. Franklin (who commanded the left grand division of the army), the notion that a serious battle was necessary to Federal control of the town "was not entertained by any one." General Sumner (who led the advance of Burnside's army) held this opinion but he had not received orders to cross the river. Crossing was delayed nearly a month and this delay resulted in the Federal disaster on December 13th. This put an abrupt end to active operations by Burnside against Lee. This picture was taken at Warrenton, November 24th, on the eve of the departure of the army for its march to Fredericksburg.

three grand divisions, under Generals Sumner, Hooker, and Franklin, commanding the right, center, and left, and moved his troops from Warrenton to Falmouth. A delay of some two weeks was due to the failure of arrival of the pontoons. In a council of war held on the night of December 10th the officers under Burnside expressed themselves almost unanimously as opposed to the plan of battle, but Burnside disregarded their views and determined to carry out his original plans immediately. After some delay and desultory fighting for two days, the crossing of the army was effected by the morning of December 13th. By this time General Robert E. Lee, commanding the Confederates, had his army concentrated and entrenched on the hills surrounding the town. In their efforts to place their bridges the Federals were seriously hindered by the firing of the Confederate sharpshooters— "hornets that were stinging the Army of the Potomac into a frenzy." The Confederate fire continued until silenced by a heavy bombardment of the city from the Federal guns, when the crossing of the army into Fredericksburg was completed without further interference.

The forces of Lee were in battle array about the town. Their line stretched for five miles along the range of hills which spread in crescent shape around the lowland where the city lay, surrounding it on all sides save the east, where the river flowed. The strongest Confederate position was on the slopes of the lowest hill of the range, Marye's Heights, which rose in the rear of the town. Along the foot of this hill there was a stone wall, about four feet in height, bounding the eastern side of the Telegraph road, which at this point runs north and south, being depressed a few feet below the surface of the stone wall, thus forming a breastwork for the Confederate troops. Behind it a strong force was concealed, while higher up, in several ranks, the main army was massed, stretching along the line of hills. The right wing, consisting of thirty thousand troops on an elevation near Hamilton's Cross-

## THE BUSY BASE OF THE ARMY OF THE POTOMAC

Aquia Creek Landing, Virginia, February, 1863. In the movements of Burnside and Hooker along the Rappahannock in the winter of 1862–3 this point became the base of supplies for the Army of the Potomac. Transports and supply-ships from Alexandria were bringing down troops, food, clothing, arms, ammunition, and artillery, and unloading them at the pontoon piers, such as shown in this picture, whence they were forwarded along the line of the Richmond, Fredericksburg & Potomac Railroad to general headquarters at Falmouth Station. The position at Aquia Creek had been occupied alternately by the Federal and Confederate forces from the beginning of the war. Federal troops landed here in August, 1862, before the second battle of Bull Run. After Lee's brilliant victory at Chancellorsville, which drove Hooker in defeat north of the Rappahannock, the great Confederate leader pressed boldly forward. The Federal base of supplies remained at Aquia Creek until Hooker's army marched toward the upper Potomac in pursuit, ing of the Fredericksburg and Potomac Railroad, was commanded by "Stonewall" Jackson. The left, on Marye's Heights and Marye's Hill, was commanded by the redoubtable Longstreet. The Southern forces numbered about seventy-eight thousand.

Into the little city below and the adjoining valleys, the Federal troops had been marching for two days. Franklin's Left Grand Division of forty thousand was strengthened by two divisions from Hooker's Center Grand Division, and was ordered to make the first attack on the Confederate right under Jackson. Sumner's Right Grand Division, also reenforced from Hooker's forces, was formed for assault against the Confederate's strongest point at Marye's Hill.

All this magnificent and portentous battle formation had been effected under cover of a dense fog, and when it lifted on that fateful Saturday there was revealed a scene of truly military grandeur. Concealed by the somber curtain of nature the Southern hosts had fixed their batteries and entrenched themselves most advantageously upon the hills, and the Union legions, massed in menacing strength below, now lay within easy cannon-shot of their foe. The Union army totaled one hundred and thirteen thousand men. After skirmishing and gathering of strength, it was at length ready for the final spring and the death-grapple.

When the sun's rays broke through the fog during the forenoon of December 13th, Franklin's Grand Division was revealed in full strength in front of the Confederate right, marching and countermarching in preparation for the coming conflict. Officers in new, bright uniforms, thousands of bayonets gleaming in the sunshine, champing steeds, rattling gun-carriages whisking artillery into proper range of the foe, infantry, cavalry, batteries, with officers and men, formed a scene of magnificent grandeur which excited the admiration even of the Confederates. This maneuver has been called the grandest military scene of the war.

## THE DETAINED GUNS

Fredericksburg, February, 1863. In the foreground, looking from what is approximately the same position as the opening picture, are three guns of Tyler's Connecticut battery. It was from all along this ridge that the town had suffered its bombardment in December of the previous year. Again the armies were separated by the Rappahannock River. There was a new commander at the head of the Army of the Potomac—General Hooker. The plundered and deserted town now held by the Confederates was to be made the objective of another attack. The heights beyond were once more to be assaulted; bridges were to be rebuilt. But all to no purpose. This ground of much contention was deserted some time before Lee advanced to his invasion of Pennsylvania. Very slowly the inhabitants of Fredericksburg

PONTOON–BOATS IN TRANSIT

had returned to their ruined homes. The town was a vast Federal cemetery, the dead being buried in gardens and backyards, for during its occupancy almost every dwelling had been turned into a temporary hospital. After the close of the war these bodies were gathered and a National Cemetery was established on Willis' Hill, on Marye's Heights, the point successfully defended by Lee's veterans.

Heavy pontoon-boats, each on its separate wagon, were sometimes as necessary as food or ammunition. At every important crossing of the many rivers that had to be passed in the Peninsula Campaign the bridges had been destroyed. There were few places where these streams were fordable. Pontoons, therefore, made a most important adjunct to the Army of the Potomac.

Yet with all this brave show, we have seen that Burnside's subordinate officers were unanimous in their belief in the rashness of the undertaking. Enthusiasm was sadly lacking. The English military writer, Colonel Henderson, has explained why this was so:

And yet that vast array, so formidable of aspect, lacked that moral force without which physical power, even in its most terrible form, is but an idle show. Not only were the strength of the Confederate position, the want of energy of preliminary movements, the insecurity of their own situation, but too apparent to the intelligence of the regimental officers and men, but they mistrusted their commander. Northern writers have recorded that the Army of the Potomac never went down to battle with less alacrity than on this day at Fredericksburg.

The first advance began at 8:30 in the morning, while the fog was still dense, upon Jackson's right. Reynolds ordered Meade with a division, supported by two other divisions under Doubleday and Gibbon, to attack Jackson at his weakest point, the extreme right of the Confederate lines, and endeavor to seize one of the opposing heights. The advance was made in three lines of battle, which were guarded in front and on each flank by artillery which swept the field in front as the army advanced. The Confederates were placed to have an enfilading sweep from both flanks along the entire front line of march. When Reynolds' divisions had approached within range, Jackson's small arms on the left poured in a deadly fire, mowing down the brave men in the Union lines in swaths, leaving broad gaps where men had stood.

This fire was repeated again and again, as the Federals pressed on, only to be repulsed. Once only was the Confederate line broken, when Meade carried the crest, capturing flags and prisoners. The ground lost by the Confederates was soon recovered, and the Federals were forced to retire. Some of the charges made by the Federals during this engagement were heroic in the extreme, only equaled by the opposition met

## THE FLAMING HEIGHTS

This photograph from the Fredericksburg river-bank recalls a terrible scene. On those memorable days of December 11 and 12, 1862, from these very trenches shown in the foreground, the ragged gray riflemen saw on that hillside across the river the blue of the uniforms of the massed Federal troops. The lines of tents made great white spaces, but the ground could hardly be seen for the host of men who were waiting, alas! to die by thousands on this coveted shore. From these hills, too, burst an incessant flaming and roaring cannon fire. Siege-guns and field artillery poured shot and shell into the town of Fredericksburg. Every house became a target, though deserted except for a few hardy and venturesome riflemen. There was scarcely a dwelling that escaped. Ruined and battered and bloody, Fredericksburg three times was a Federal hospital, and its backyards became little cemeteries.

A TARGET AT FREDERICKSBURG FOR THE FEDERAL GUNS

from the foe. In one advance, knapsacks were unslung and bayonets fixed; a brigade marched across a plowed field, and passed through broken lines of other brigades, which were retiring to the rear in confusion from the leaden storm.

The fire became incessant and destructive; many fell, killed or wounded; the front line slackened its pace, and without orders commenced firing. A halt seemed imminent, and a halt in the face of the terrific fire to which the men were exposed meant death; but, urged on by regimental commanders in person, the charge was renewed, when with a shout they leaped the ditches, charged across the railroad, and upon the foe, killing many with the bayonet and capturing several hundred prisoners. But this was only a temporary gain. In every instance the Federals were shattered and driven back. Men were lying dead in heaps, the wounded and dying were groaning in agony. Soldiers were fleeing; officers were galloping to and fro urging their lines forward, and begging their superior officers for assistance and reenforcement.

A dispatch to Burnside from Franklin, dated 2:45, was as follows: " My left has been very badly handled; what hope is there of getting reenforcements across the river?" Another dispatch, dated 3:45, read: " Our troops have gained no ground in the last half hour."

In their retreat the fire was almost as destructive as during the assault. Most of the wounded were brought from the field after this engagement, but the dead were left where they fell. It was during this engagement that General George D. Bayard was mortally wounded by a shot which had severed the sword belt of Captain Gibson, leaving him uninjured. The knapsack of a soldier who was in a stooping posture was struck by a ball, and a deck of cards was sent flying twenty feet in the air. Those witnessing the ludicrous scene called to him, " Oh, deal me a hand!" thus indicating the spirit of levity among soldiers even amid such surroundings. Another soldier sitting on the ground suddenly leaped high above the

## THE BRIDGES THAT A BAND OF MUSIC THREATENED

At Franklin Crossing, on the Rappahannock, occurred an incident that proves how little things may change the whole trend of the best-laid plans. The left Union wing under the command of General Franklin, composed of the First Army Corps under General Reynolds, and the Sixth under General W. S. Smith, was crossing to engage in the battle of Fredericksburg. For two days they poured across these yielding planks between the swaying boats to the farther shore. Now, in the crossing of bridges, moving bodies of men must break step or even well-built structures might be threatened. The colonel of one of the regiments in General Devens' division that led the van ordered his field music to strike up just as the head of the column swept on to the flimsy planking; before the regiment was half-way across, unconsciously the men had fallen into step and the whole fabric was swaying to the cadenced feet. Vibrating like a great fiddlestring, the bridge would have sunk and parted, but a keen eye had seen the danger. "Stop that music!" was the order, and a staff officer spurred his horse through the men, shouting at top voice. The lone charge was made through the marching column: some jumped into the pontoons to avoid the hoofs; a few went overboard; but the head of the column was reached at last, and the music stopped. A greater blunder than this, however took place on the plains beyond. Owing to a misunderstanding of orders, 37,000 troops were never brought into action; 17,000 men on their front bore the brunt of a long day's fighting.

heads of his comrades as a shell struck the spot, scooping a wheelbarrowful of earth, but the man was untouched.

Entirely independent of the action in which the Left Grand Division under Franklin was engaged against the right wing of the Confederate line, Sumner's Right Grand Division was engaged in a terrific assault upon the works on Marye's Heights, the stronghold of the Confederate forces. Their position was almost impregnable, consisting of earthworks, wood, and stone barricades running along the sunken road near the foot of Marye's Hill. The Federals were not aware of the sunken road, nor of the force of twenty-five hundred under General Cobb concealed behind the stone wall, this wall not being new work as a part of the entrenchments, but of earlier construction. When the advance up the road was made they were harassed by shot and shell and rifle-balls at every step, but the men came dashing into line undismayed by the terrific fire which poured down upon them.

The Irish Brigade, the second of Hancock's division, under General Meagher, made a wonderful charge. When they returned from the assault but two hundred and fifty out of twelve hundred men reported under arms from the field, and all these were needed to care for their wounded comrades. The One Hundred and Sixteenth Pennsylvania regiment was new on the field of battle, but did fearless and heroic service. The approach was completely commanded by the Confederate guns. Repeatedly the advance was repulsed by well-directed fire from the batteries.

Once again Sumner's gallant men charged across a railroad cut, running down one side and up the other, and still again attempted to escape in the same manner, but each time they were forced to retire precipitately by a murderous fire from the Confederate batteries. Not only was the Confederate fire disastrous upon the approach and the successive repulses by the foe, but it also inflicted great damage upon the masses of the Federal army in front of Marye's Hill.

[ 92 ]

## MEN WHO CHARGED ON MARYE'S HEIGHTS

Officers of the famous "Irish Brigade," which lost more than 41 per cent. of its strength in the first assault at Marye's Heights. The "Irish Brigade" (consisting of the Twenty-eighth Massachusetts, the Sixty-third, Sixty-ninth, and Eighty-eighth New York, and the One Hundred and Sixteenth Pennsylvania) was commanded by General Thomas F. Meagher and advanced in Hancock's division to the first assault on December 13, 1862. At Antietam this brigade had spent its ammunition at the sunken road and then retired in splendid order. Again, in the charge at Marye's, the lines of the Irish soldiers were "beautifully and rapidly formed," and they moved steadily up the ridge until within a few yards of another and more deadly sunken road, the unexpected fire from which mowed them down. Of the 1,315 men which Meagher led into battle, 545 fell in that charge. Hancock's entire command sustained that day a loss of 40.2 per cent., the second highest percentage of any division in any one engagement in the war. After the charge on Marye's Heights it numbered only 2,800 men. This group was photographed at Harrison's Landing, on the James River, in July, 1862.

The Confederates' effective and successful work on Marye's Hill in this battle was not alone due to the natural strength of their position, but also to the skill and generalship of the leaders, and to the gallantry, courage, and well-directed aim of their cannoneers and infantry.

Six times the heroic Union troops dashed against the invulnerable position, each time to be repulsed with terrific loss. General Couch, who had command of the Second Corps, viewing the scene of battle from the steeple of the court-house with General Howard, says: "The whole plain was covered with men, prostrate and dropping, the live men running here and there, and in front closing upon each other, and the wounded coming back. I had never before seen fighting like that, nothing approaching it in terrible uproar and destruction."

General Howard reports that Couch exclaimed: "Oh, great God! see how our men, our poor fellows, are falling!" At half-past one Couch signaled Burnside: "I am losing. Send two rifle batteries."

The point and method of attack made by Sumner was anticipated by the Confederates, careful preparation having been made to meet it. The fire from the Confederate batteries harassed the Union lines, and as they advanced steadily, heroically, without hurrah or battle-cry, the ranks were cut to pieces by canister and shell and musket-balls. Heavy artillery fire was poured into the Union ranks from front, right, and left with frightful results. Quickly filling up the decimated ranks they approached the stone wall masking the death-trap where General Cobb lay with a strong force awaiting the approach. Torrents of lead poured into the bodies of the defenseless men, slaying, crushing, destroying the proud army of a few hours before. As though in pity, a cloud of smoke momentarily shut out the wretched scene but brought no balm to the helpless victims of this awful carnage. The ground was so thickly strewn with dead bodies as seriously to impede the movements of a renewed attack. These repeated assaults in such good

[94]

## THE SUMMIT OF SLAUGHTER

Marye's House marked the center of the Confederate position on the Heights, before which the Federals fell three deep in one of the bravest and bloodiest assaults of the war. The eastern boundary of the Marye estate was a retaining wall, along which ran a sunken road; on the other side of this was a stone wall, shoulder high, forming a perfect infantry parapet. Here two brigades of Confederates were posted and on the crest above them were the supporting batteries, while the slope between was honeycombed with the rifle-pits of the sharpshooters, one of which is seen in the picture. Six times did the Federals, raked by the deadly fire of the Washington Artillery, advance to within a hundred yards of the sunken road, only to be driven back by the rapid volleys of the Confederate infantry concealed there. Less than three of every five men in Hancock's division came back from their charge on these death-dealing heights. The complete repulse of the day and the terrific slaughter were the barren results of an heroic effort to obey orders.

order caused some apprehension on the part of General Lee, who said to Longstreet after the third attack, " General, they are massing very heavily and will break your line, I am afraid." But the great general's fears proved groundless.

General Cobb was borne from the field mortally wounded, and Kershaw took his place in the desperate struggle. The storm of shot and shell which met the assaults was terrific. Men fell almost in battalions; the dead and wounded lay in heaps. Late in the day the dead bodies, which had become frozen from the extreme cold, were stood up in front of the soldiers as a protection against the awful fire to shield the living, and at night were set up as dummy sentinels.

The steadiness of the Union troops, and the silent, determined heroism of the rank and file in these repeated, but hopeless, assaults upon the Confederate works, were marvelous, and amazed even their officers. The real greatness in a battle is the fearless courage, the brave and heroic conduct, of the men under withering fire. It was the enlisted men who were the glory of the army. It was they, the rank and file, who stood in the front, closed the gaps, and were mowed down in swaths like grass by cannon and musket-balls.

After the sixth disastrous attempt to carry the works of the Confederate left it was night; the Federal army was repulsed and had retired; hope was abandoned, and it was seen that the day was lost to the Union side. Then the shattered Army of the Potomac sought to gather the stragglers and care for the wounded. Fredericksburg, the beautiful Virginia town, was a pitiable scene in contrast to its appearance a few days before. Ancestral homes were turned into barracks and hospitals. The charming drives and stately groves, the wonted pleasure grounds of Colonial dames and Southern cavaliers, were not filled with grand carriages and gay parties, but with war horses, soldiers, and military accouterments. Aside from desultory firing by squads and skirmishers at intervals there was no renewal of the conflict.

## THE FATEFUL CROSSING

From this, the Lacy House, which Sumner had made his headquarters, he directed the advance of his right grand division of the Army of the Potomac on December 11, 1862. Little did he dream that his men of the Second Corps were to bear the brunt of the fighting and the most crushing blow of the defeat on the 13th. Soon after three o'clock on the morning of the 11th the columns moved out with alacrity to the river bank and before daybreak, hidden at first by the fog, the pontoniers began building the bridges. Confederate sharpshooters drove off the working party from the bridge below the Lacy House and also from the middle bridge farther down. As the mist cleared, volunteers ferried themselves over in the boats and drove off the riflemen. At last, at daybreak of the 12th, the town of Fredericksburg was occupied, but the whole of another foggy day was consumed in getting the army concentrated on the western shore. Nineteen batteries (one hundred and four guns) accompanied Sumner's troops, but all save seven of these were ordered back or left in the streets of Fredericksburg. Late on the morning of the 13th the confused and belated orders began to arrive from Burnside's headquarters across the river; one was for Sumner to assault the Confederate batteries on Marye's Heights. At nightfall Sumner's men retired into Fredericksburg, leaving 5,444 dead or dying on the field. "Oh, those men, those men over there! I cannot get them out of my mind!" wailed Burnside in an agony of failure. Yet he was planning almost in the same breath to lead in person his old command, the Ninth Corps, in another futile charge in the morning. On the night of the 14th, better judgment prevailed and the order came to retire across the Rappahannock.

Here, on the heights behind Fredericksburg, Lee's veterans who had fought at Antietam opposed the Army of the Potomac under its new commander. Had Lee been given his choice he could not have selected a more advantageous position. Burnside's futile attempts to wrest these heights from the Confederates cost him 12,653 men in killed, wounded, and missing. On the heights behind Fredericksburg, Lee's soldiers, working night and day, had thrown up a double line of strong entrenchments and constructed a road to facilitate the transfer of troops behind the defenses. Everything that the engineering talent of the Confederacy could suggest had been done. By the time Burnside moved his 113,000 troops against the 78,000 of Lee, Jackson, and Longstreet on December 13, 1862, Marye's Heights had been made impregnable. Four months later, in the Chancellorsville campaign (May 3, 1863), Sedgwick's men fought over this same ground and carried the position. But then the main body of Lee's army was hotly engaged with Hooker and the Heights were not strongly defended. This photograph of Willis's Hill (just south of Marye's) was taken after Sedgwick occupied the position in 1863. Willis's Hill was, with great appropriateness, made a National Cemetery at Fredericksburg after the war.

WILLIS'S HILL,

NEAR MARYE'S HEIGHTS

[B]

## THE PLANS THAT FAILED

From his headquarters at the Phillips house, Burnside directed the disastrous maneuvers of his army during the battle of December 13th.   On December 9th Burnside called his generals together and persisted in his plan for a direct assault upon Lee, who was strongly entrenched in a position of his own choosing.   The slaughter at Marye's Heights on the 13th proved him in the wrong.   Nevertheless, Burnside on the field that night gave orders to renew the attack the next morning.   Returning to the Phillips house about 1 A.M., he found among the others Colonel Rush C. Hawkins, who had come at the request of Generals Willcox, Humphreys, Meade, and Getty, who had all faced that terrible fire on Telegraph Road.   A conference ensued in the presence of Sumner, Hooker, and Franklin, and Burnside was at last dissuaded.

## THE UNLUCKY HEADQUARTERS

The ruins of the Phillips house stand as an aftermath of Burnside's unfortunate career at the head of the Army of the Potomac. The wisest decision that he made in that house was in the early morning of December 14th—not to renew the attack. In the old mansion he had formed the fatal plan of direct assault. Here also he issued his order for the famous "mud march" by which, in the dead of winter, he sought to retrieve failure by putting his army in motion to flank Lee, January 21, 1863. All his efforts had come to naught, and not one of his generals longer agreed with him. His resignation from the command followed on January 26th. In February the Phillips house was set on fire; and in the picture on the preceding page the photographer has caught the Federals (now commanded by Hooker) trying to extinguish the flames.

The bloody carnage was over, the plan of Burnside had ended in failure, and thousands of patriotic and brave men, blindly obedient to their country's command, were the toll exacted from the Union army. Burnside, wild with anguish at what he had done, walking the floor of his tent, exclaimed, "Oh, those men—those men over there," pointing to the battlefield, "I am thinking of them all the time." In his report of the battle to Washington, Burnside gave reasons for the issue, and in a manly way took the responsibility upon himself, and most highly commended his officers and men. He said, "For the failure in the attack I am responsible, as the extreme gallantry, courage, and endurance shown by them [officers and men] were never excelled."

President Lincoln's verdict in regard to this battle is adverse to the almost unanimous opinion of the historians. In his reply, December 22d, to General Burnside's report of the battle, he says, "Although you were not successful, the attempt was not an error, nor the failure other than an accident." Burnside, at his own request, was relieved of the command of the Army of the Potomac, however, on January 25, 1863, and was succeeded by General Hooker. The Union loss in killed, wounded, and missing was 12,653, and the Confederates lost 5,377.

After the battle the wounded lay on the field in their agony exposed to the freezing cold for forty-eight hours before arrangements were effected to care for them. Many were burned to death by the long, dead grass becoming ignited by cannon fire. The scene witnessed by the army of those screaming, agonizing, dying comrades was dreadful and heartrending. Burnside's plan had been to renew the battle, but the overwhelming opinion of the other officers prevailed. The order was withdrawn and the defeated Union army slipped away under the cover of darkness on December 15th, and encamped in safety across the river. The battle of Fredericksburg had passed into history.

# PART I
## THE RISE OF LEE

---

# CHANCELLORSVILLE AND JACKSON'S FLANKING MARCH

---

READY TO COVER THE RAPPAHANNOCK—THE 150TH PENNSYLVANIA,
THREE WEEKS BEFORE THE BATTLE OF CHANCELLORSVILLE

## WAR'S HEAVIEST LABOR

Here a construction corps is rebuilding the railroad bridge across Bull Run. The men are armed with crowbars and axes, and in the constant wielding of such peaceful implements throughout the war many who never fired a musket became expert in the occupations of peace. This photograph was taken in March, 1863, while Hooker was reëstablishing railway communications to make possible his contemplated advance toward Gordonsville, Virginia, with the expectation of driving Lee back upon Richmond. During the previous year, in the disastrous campaign of Pope, most of the bridges along the Orange & Alexandria Railroad had been destroyed and much of the line torn up. In order to flank Lee's position at Fredericksburg, it was imperative for the Army of the Potomac to abandon its base at Aquia Creek and draw supplies overland from Alexandria. In the spring Hooker was pushing the railroad repairs.

## RAPID REPAIRS

This picture of the almost completed bridge across Bull Run shows how thoroughly the work was done—and how quickly, for the photograph was taken in March, 1863, only a short time after that on the opposite page. The hopes of Hooker and his army ran high; rested and heavily reinforced, it again outnumbered Lee's Army of Northern Virginia. It seemed certain that such a superior force must at last wrest a decisive victory from the Confederates. Hooker's plan of campaign was excellent. Demonstrating strongly against Lee's right, he intended to cross the fords of the Rappahannock and Rapidan with his main body and, flanking Lee by the left, draw him from his fastness at Fredericksburg to battle on the open plain. Cavalry was to be sent two weeks in advance of the infantry to sweep around in Lee's rear toward Gordonsville and cut his communications, to compel a retreat upon Richmond. But it was not Lee who retreated after Chancellorsville!

# CHANCELLORSVILLE AND JACKSON'S FLANKING MARCH

The interval of two months between the battles of Chancellorsville and Gettysburg was for the South—notwithstanding the irreparable loss it sustained in the death of Jackson—the brightest period of the Civil War. But its brightness was that of a false and treacherous light. The over-confidence born of the victory of Chancellorsville carried the Army of Northern Virginia against the impregnable front of the Federal lines at Gettysburg; and it was the victory of Gettysburg that sustained the Army of the Potomac in its desperate wrestling in the Wilderness, and in gaining the point of vantage from which it finally started on the arduous, decisive, and fateful race to Appomattox.—*Major John Bigelow, Jr., U.S.A., in "The Campaign of Chancellorsville."*

THE Rappahannock River flows out of the hills at the foot of the Blue Ridge Mountains in a southeasterly course. Falmouth is on the north bank, about a mile from Fredericksburg, which lies on the opposite shore. Along the banks of this peaceful river were fought some of the most important battles of the Civil War. This region was the scene of the conflict of Fredericksburg, December 12–13, 1862, and the later battle of May 1–5, 1863. Chancellorsville is a little over two miles south of the river and about ten miles west of Fredericksburg.

After the Fredericksburg campaign the Union forces encamped at Falmouth for the winter, while Lee remained with the Southern army on the site of his successful contest at Fredericksburg. Thus the two armies lay facing each other within hailing distance, across the historic river, waiting for the coming of spring. Major-General Joseph Hooker, popularly known as "Fighting Joe" Hooker, who had succeeded Burnside in command of the Army of the Potomac, soon had

A MAN OF WHOM MUCH WAS EXPECTED

General Joseph Hooker.   A daring and experienced veteran of the Mexican War, Hooker had risen in the Civil War from brigade commander to be the commander of a grand division of the Army of the Potomac, and had never been found wanting.   His advancement to the head of the Army of the Potomac, on January 26, 1863, was a tragic episode in his own career and in that of the Federal arms. Gloom hung heavy over the North after Fredericksburg.   Upon Hooker fell the difficult task of redeeming the unfulfilled political pledges for a speedy lifting of that gloom.   It was his fortune only to deepen it.

the troops on a splendid campaign footing by a positive and vigorous method of reorganization, and aroused them to enthusiastic loyalty.

It was the month of April, and field and woodland had begun to put on the bright colors of spring. There was activity about the Federal army headquarters that indicated a renewal of hostilities. The hospitals had been well cleared, the forces had been recruited, ammunition and arms replenished and put in order, horses groomed and well fed, uniforms renewed, and the Army of the Potomac was in excellent condition to advance against its foe. President Lincoln had visited the camp, and reviewed the army, thrilling the men with his inspiring presence and personality. It was well known that he had a very deep concern in the welfare of the soldiers. After the review he asked, "What will become of all these men when the war is over?" His parting admonition to Hooker was this wise advice, "In your next battle, put in all your men." By a strange fatality that is just what Hooker failed to do, and a great misfortune overtook his army.

Hooker abandoned Burnside's method of organization. Under "Fighting Joe," instead of three grand divisions, there were seven army corps, each under a major-general, and a cavalry corps. At this time the Union forces aggregated between one hundred and twenty-five and one hundred and thirty thousand men; Lee's forces were estimated at about sixty thousand. Hooker's corps commanders were: Reynolds, in command of the First; Couch, the Second; Sickles, the Third; Meade, the Fifth; Sedgwick, the Sixth; Howard, the Eleventh; Slocum, the Twelfth, and Stoneman, who was in command of the cavalry corps.

Hooker conceived a plan of campaign which was ingenious and masterful, and had he carried it out there would have been a different story to tell about Chancellorsville. The plan was to deploy a portion of the army to serve as a decoy to Lee, while the remainder of the host at the same time

## NEW LEADERS AND NEW PLANS

General Joseph Hooker and his Staff. These were the men whose work it was, during the winter after Fredericksburg, to restore the *esprit du corps* of the Army of the Potomac. The tireless energy and magnetic personality of Hooker soon won officers from their disaffection and put an end to desertions—which had been going on at the rate of two hundred per day before he took command. By spring everything seemed propitious for an aggressive campaign, the plans for which were brilliantly drawn and at first vigorously carried out, giving truth to Lincoln's expressed belief that Hooker was "a trained and skilful soldier." In that remarkable letter of admonition to Hooker upon assuming command, Lincoln added: "But beware of rashness, beware of rashness; with energy and with sleepless vigilance go forward and give us victories." By some strange fate it was not rashness but quite the contrary which compassed the failure of "Fighting Joe" Hooker at Chancellorsville. His first forward advance was executed with his usual bold initiative. Before Lee could fully divine his purpose, Hooker with thirty-six thousand men was across his left flank in a favorable position, with the main body of his army at hand ready to give battle. Then came Hooker's inexplicable order to fall back upon Chancellorsville. That very night, consulting in the abandoned Federal position, Lee and Jackson formed the plan which drove Hooker back across the Rappahannock in ignominious defeat.

occupied the vicinity of Chancellorsville, a country mansion, in the center of the wilderness that stretched along the Rappahannock.

The movement of the army began on the 27th of April when Sedgwick was sent east of Fredericksburg with a large force to attract the attention of the Confederates. Another force was left in camp to give the appearance that the main army was still there, while in fact it was secretly being moved to Chancellorsville. The strategy was carried out successfully. On April 30th the army, except a force under Sedgwick composing the First, Third, and Sixth Corps, was concentrated on Lee's left flank, the entire field and its approaches being commanded by the Fifth, Eleventh, and Twelfth Corps, part of the Second Corps, and Stoneman's cavalry of the Army of the Potomac. Victory seemed assured. Hooker, in an order issued on that day, said, "Now the enemy must flee shamefully or come out of his defenses to accept battle on our own ground, to his certain destruction." The contemplated field of battle was high ground about half way between this plateau and the Chancellor house. The Federal army was not yet in position on this open and favorably located field. At eleven o'clock in the morning Hooker started the movement of the army to the point where he intended it to be in line of battle at two o'clock on the afternoon of May 1st.

Lee was a great general and a master in strategy. He had learned of Hooker's plan and, paying but little attention to Sedgwick, had collected his forces and turned to face Hooker. By a rapid night march he met the Union army before it had reached its destination. He was pushed back, however, by Sykes, of Meade's corps, who occupied the position assigned to him. Meade was on the left, and Slocum on the right, with adequate support in the rear. All was in readiness and most favorable for the "certain destruction" of the Confederates predicted by "Fighting Joe" when, to the amazement and consternation of all his officers, Hooker

## LEADERS OF THE FRUITLESS RAID

Major-General George Stoneman and Staff; photographed in April, 1863, a month before it fell to the lot of these gallant cavalry officers to lead ten thousand sabers on a daring but futile expedition. Sweeping around in the rear of the Confederate army, it was their intention to cut Lee's railroad communication with Richmond. According to Hooker's plan, this advance movement was to begin April 13th, two weeks before that of his main army, but heavy rains delayed the expedition until the 27th and Hooker's whole force set out simultaneously with the cavalry. Thus Stoneman's work was wasted, for the Army of the Potomac was defeated and in full retreat before the cavalry could strike. On the 5th of May Stoneman recalled his detachments and, leaving his headquarters at Louisa Court House, rejoined the army at Falmouth on the 8th. The most daring raid of the expedition was performed by Colonel Kilpatrick, with his Second New York Cavalry. Dashing across the country, he passed within two and a half miles of Richmond, creating great consternation. Turning down the peninsula, he ended his long ride at Gloucester Point, which was garrisoned by the Federals. With great boldness the regiment rode forth from this refuge. Eluding the Confederates and repulsing a strong force, it rebuilt a bridge and returned safely to Falmouth on June 3d, bringing two hundred prisoners, forty wagons, and a thousand contraband slaves. Hooker, dissatisfied with what the cavalry had accomplished, removed Stoneman from his command.

ordered the whole army to retire to the position it had occupied the day before, leaving the advantage to his opponents.

Lee quickly moved his army into the position thus relinquished, and began feeling the Federal lines with skirmishers and some cannonading during the evening of May 1st. By the next morning the two armies were in line of battle.

The danger in which the Confederate army now found itself was extreme. One large Federal army was on its front, while another was at its rear, below Fredericksburg. But Lee threw the hopes of success into one great and decisive blow at Hooker's host. Dividing an army in the face of the foe is extremely dangerous and contrary to all accepted theories of military strategy; but there comes a time when such a course proves the salvation of the legions in peril. Such was the case at Chancellorsville on May 2, 1863.

At 7 A.M. the cannonading began its death-song and was soon followed by infantry demonstrations, but without serious results. The action was continued. Early in the afternoon, Hooker by a ruse was beguiled into the belief that Lee's army was in full retreat. What Hooker had seen and believed to be a retreat was the marching of Jackson's forces, about twenty-six thousand strong, from the battlefield. What he did not see, however, was that, after a few miles, Jackson turned abruptly and made for the right flank of the Federal host, the Eleventh Corps, under Howard. It was after half-past five when Jackson broke from the woods into which he had marched in a paralyzing charge upon the unprepared troops of Howard.

The approach of this Confederate force was first intimated to the Federals by the bending of shrubbery, the stampede of rabbits and squirrels, and the flocks of birds in wild flight, as before a storm. Then appeared a few skirmishers, then a musket volley, and then the storm broke in all its fury—the war scream, the rattling musketry, the incessant roar of cannon. The Confederates fought heroically. The knowledge

## THE CORPS THAT STOOD ALONE

Major-General John Sedgwick and Staff. Sedgwick's Sixth Corps alone and unaided executed the most successful maneuver during the Chancellorsville battles of May 1–4, 1863. For two days Sedgwick had been keeping up a strong demonstration against Lee's extreme right below Fredericksburg. On the night of May 2d, after Jackson had routed the entire Eleventh Corps, came the order from Hooker for Sedgwick to move forward toward Chancellorsville, "attack and destroy any forces met with on the march," then fall upon Lee's rear. By midnight the Sixth Corps was in motion and at dawn advanced against Marye's Heights. Only after a fierce uphill fight was that bloody field won from Early's 9,000 Confederates. At night, forced back by Lee, he established communication with Hooker, but could get no definite orders. Next morning word came not to attack unless Hooker did likewise. But Hooker's inactivity encouraged Lee to send heavy forces to crush the Sixth Corps. All the afternoon, cut off from help, the corps fought off assault after assault till nightfall of May 4th. Then, upon the receipt of orders, Sedgwick retired north of the Rappahannock.

SICKLES REVIEWS HIS EIGHTEEN THOUSAND TROOPS, UNAWARE OF JACKSON'S FLANKING MARCH

The photograph, presented one-half above and one-half below, is a reflection of history in the very making. It was at midnight on May 1, 1863, that Lee and Jackson sat on two cracker-boxes before their fire in the abandoned Union camp, and conceived the audacious idea of flanking the Federals. It was 5.30 the next morning that Jackson formed his devoted veterans in column, then bade his last farewell to his chief, and rode into the tangled forest. And it was the same morning that a Union photographer made this picture of Major-General Daniel E. Sickles reviewing his Third Corps of the Army of the Potomac, 18,000 horse, foot, and artillery—all unsuspecting that a couple of miles distant 31,000 in gray were pushing across their front and around to the unprotected rear of the Union encampment: The confidence of the Federals was only natural. Who would have suspected that Lee, with less than 45,000 men, all told, would deliberately have detached more than two-thirds of them in the face of Hooker's encamped 70,000? But Lee was a military genius, and genius knows when to dare—especially with a leader in the field like "Stonewall" Jackson, no less secret than swift. And so it befell that when the Confederate column was spied passing over a bare hill about a mile and a half from the left of Sickles's line, General Hooker supposed that such a movement could mean only a retreat. He ordered a pursuit. This drew a division away from a point where soon it was sorely needed. For Jackson's Corps, having passed around the Federal right, formed in battle-line, burst through the woods in the rear of the unsuspecting Federals, and drove them in utter rout. It was a piece of strategy as daring as it was masterly.

"STONEWALL" JACKSON—TWO WEEKS BEFORE HIS MORTAL WOUND

The austere, determined features of the victor of Chancellorsville, just as they appeared two weeks before the tragic shot that cost the Confederacy its greatest Lieutenant-General—and, in the opinion of sound historians, its chief hope for independence. Only once had a war photograph of Jackson been taken up to April, 1863, when, just before the movement toward Chancellorsville, he was persuaded to enter a photographer's tent at Hamilton's Crossing, some three miles below Fredericksburg, and to sit for his last portrait. At a glance one can feel the self-expression and power in this stern worshiper of the God of Battles; one can understand the eulogy written by the British military historian, Henderson: "The fame of 'Stonewall' Jackson is no longer the exclusive property of Virginia and the South: it has become the birthright of every man privileged to call himself an American."

[B]

that "Old Jack" was on the field was inspiration enough for them. The charge was so precipitous, so unexpected and terrific that it was impossible for the Federals to hold their lines and stand against the impact of that awful onslaught which carried everything before it. The regiments in Jackson's path, resisting his advance, were cut to pieces and swept along as by a tidal wave, rolled up like a scroll, multitudes of men, horses, mules, and cattle being piled in an inextricable mass. Characteristic of Jackson's brilliant and unexpected movements, it was like an electric flash, knocking the Eleventh Corps into impotence, as Jackson expected it would. This crowning and final stroke of Jackson's military genius was not impromptu, but the result of his own carefully worked-out plan, which had been approved by Lee.

General Hooker was spending the late afternoon hours in his headquarters at the Chancellor house. To the eastward there was considerable firing, where his men were carrying out the plan of striking Lee in flank. Jackson was retreating, of that he was sure, and Sickles, with Pleasanton's cavalry and other reenforcements, was in pursuit. Everything seemed to be going well. About half-past six the sounds of battle grew suddenly louder and seemed to come from another direction. A staff-officer went to the front of the house and turned his field-glass toward the west.

"My God, here they come!"

At the startled cry Hooker sprang upon his horse and dashed down the road. He encountered portions of the Eleventh Corps pouring out of the forest—a badly mixed crowd of men, wagons, and ambulances. They brought the news that the right wing was overwhelmed. Hurriedly Hooker sought his old command, Berry's division of the Third Corps, stationed in support of the Eleventh. "Forward, with the bayonet!" he commanded.

An officer who witnessed the scene says the division advanced with a firm and steady step, cleaving the multitude

WILDERNESS CHURCH—THE SCENE OF JACKSON'S SECOND RUSH

The shots that riddled the roof of this humble meeting-house were fired on an evening of triumph and panic. Beyond the church, as the sun sank low on May 2d, stretched the main Union line, Howard's Eleventh Corps. The troops had stacked their arms and lay at ease. Supper was cooking. Suddenly bugle-calls came from the west. Then a roar of human voices swept the forest. A double battle-line in gray burst from the woods, ran over the gunners, and shattered the divisions into fragments. Gallant Federal officers did their best to re-form their lines. With the little church at about the center, a stand was made by five thousand men of Schurz's division, with some of Devens'—but without respite Jackson gave the call to advance. After twenty minutes of furious fighting, the Confederate battle-flag flew in the clearing. It was then that the fugitives from the Eleventh Corps came in sight.

# Chancellorsville and Jackson's Flanking March

May
1863

of disbanded Federals as the bow of a vessel cleaves the waves of the sea. It struck the advance of the Confederates obliquely and checked it, with the aid of the Twelfth Corps artillery.

A dramatic, though tragic, feature of the rout was the charge of the Eighth Pennsylvania cavalry, under Major Keenan, in the face of almost certain death, to save the artillery of the Third Corps from capture. The guns rested upon low ground and within reach of the Confederates. The Federals had an equal opportunity to seize the artillery, but required a few minutes to prepare themselves for action. The Confederate advance must be checked for these few moments, and for this purpose Keenan gallantly led his five hundred cavalrymen into the woods, while his comrades brought the guns to bear upon the columns in gray. He gained the necessary time, but lost his life at the head of his regiment, together with Captain Arrowsmith and Adjutant Haddock, who fell by his side.

The light of day had faded from the gruesome scene. The mighty turmoil was silenced as darkness gathered, but the day's carnage was not ended. No camp-fires were lighted in the woods or on the plain. The two hostile forces were concealed in the darkness, watching through the shadows, waiting for—they knew not what. Finally at midnight the order "Forward" was repeated in subdued tones along the lines of Sickles' corps. Out over the open and into the deep, dark thicket the men in blue pursued their stealthy advance upon the Confederate position. Then the tragedies of the night were like that of the day, and the moon shed her peaceful rays down upon those shadowy figures as they struggled forward through the woods, in the ravines, over the hillocks. The Federals, at heavy loss, gained the position, and the engagement assumed the importance of a victory.

It was on this day that death robbed the South of one of her most beloved warriors. After darkness had

[118]

Within an hour after Jackson's sudden and deadly charge, his men captured Dowdall's Tavern. Here Howard, commander of the Eleventh Corps, now fleeing before the Confederate rush, was holding his headquarters when the blow fell. The trenches in the picture below were the goal in a race between Jackson's men and the men of Williams's Federal division. This had been sent to support Sickles and

DOWDALL'S TAVERN

tried too late to recover the position that it had left, unaware of the Confederate flanking movement. Jackson captured two hundred men of the One Hundred and Twenty-eighth Pennsylvania as they tried to get to their places. Williams after falling back finally checked the Confederates, aided by Barry of the Third Corps and fresh artillery. As night fell, Jackson with his staff ventured on his last reconnaissance. The picture on the

right shows the tangled wood through which he passed and the fury of the fire that lopped off the stunted trees. Through a fatal mischance, some Confederates stationed along the road to the north of this spot fired upon what they thought to be a Federal scouting party—and there mortally wounded their own general. Jackson had turned back along the road itself, and his men had orders to fire upon any advance from the Federal position. The next day, with a cry of "Remember Jackson!" the line in gray again swept forward, and by nine in the morning had carried the rude breastworks in the left-hand picture. Hooker withdrew his entire army. Yet the Confederate victory lacked the completeness that would have been expected with Jackson in the saddle; and the Confederacy had lost one of its greatest captains.

WHERE THE FEDERALS MADE A STAND
SOUTH OF THE "PLANK ROAD"

TREES SHATTERED BY THE FIRING NEAR
THE SPOT WHERE JACKSON FELL

overspread the land, Jackson, accompanied by members of his staff, undertook a reconnaissance of the Federal lines. He was planning a night attack. He came upon a line of Union infantry lying on its arms and was forced to turn back along the plank road, on both sides of which he had stationed his own men with orders to fire upon any body of men approaching from the direction of the Federal battle-lines. The little cavalcade of Confederate officers galloped along the highway, directly toward the ambuscade, and apparently forgetful of the strict orders left with the skirmishers. A sudden flash of flame lighted the scene for an instant, and within that space of time the Confederacy was deprived of one of its greatest captains—Jackson was severely wounded, and by his own men and through his own orders. When the news spread through Jackson's corps and through the Confederate army the grief of the Southern soldiers was heartbreaking to witness. The sorrow spread even into the ranks of the Federal army, which, while opposed to the wounded general on many hard-fought battle-grounds, had learned to respect and admire " Stonewall " Jackson.

The loss of Jackson to the South was incalculable. Lee had pronounced him the right arm of the whole army. Next to Lee, Jackson was considered the ablest general in the Confederate army. His shrewdness of judgment, his skill in strategy, his lightning-like strokes, marked him as a unique and brilliant leader. Devoutly religious, gentle and noble in character, the nation that was not to be disunited lost a great citizen, as the Confederate army lost a great captain, when a few days later General Jackson died.

That night orders passed from the Federal headquarters to Sedgwick, below Fredericksburg, eleven miles away. Between him and Hooker stood the Confederate army, flushed with its victories of the day. Immediately in his front was Fredericksburg, with a strong guard of Southern warriors. Beyond loomed Marye's Heights, the battle-ground on which

## THE DEMOLISHED HEADQUARTERS

From this mansion, Hooker's headquarters during the battle of Chancellorsville, he rode away after the injury he received there on May 3d, never to return. The general, dazed after Jackson's swoop upon the right, was besides in deep anxiety as to Sedgwick. The latter's forty thousand men had not yet come up. Hooker was unwilling to suffer further loss without the certainty of his coöperation. So he decided to withdraw his army. The movement was the signal for increased artillery fire from the Confederate batteries, marking the doom of the old Chancellor house. Its end was accompanied by some heart-rending scenes. Major Bigelow thus describes them: "Missiles pierced the walls or struck in the brickwork; shells exploded in the upper rooms, setting the building on fire; the chimneys were demolished and their fragments rained down upon the wounded about the building. All this time the women and children (including some slaves) of the Chancellor family, nineteen persons in all, were in the cellar. The wounded were removed from in and around the building, men of both armies nobly assisting one another in the work."

Burnside had in the preceding winter left so many of his brave men in the vain endeavor to drive the Confederate defenders from the crest.

The courageous Sedgwick, notwithstanding the formidable obstacles that lay on the road to Chancellorsville, responded immediately to Hooker's order. He was already on the south side of the river, but he was farther away than Hooker supposed. Shortly after midnight he began a march that was fraught with peril and death. Strong resistance was offered the advancing blue columns as they came to the threshold of Fredericksburg, but they swept on and over the defenders, and at dawn were at the base of the heights. On the crest waved the standards of the Confederate Washington Artillery. At the foot of the slope was the stone wall before which the Federals had fought and died but a few months before, in the battle of Fredericksburg. Reenforcements were arriving in the Confederate trenches constantly. The crest and slopes bristled with cannon and muskets. The pathways around the heights were barricaded. The route to the front seemed blocked; still, the cry for help from Hooker was resounding in the ears of Sedgwick

Gathering his troops, he attacked directly upon the stone wall and on up the hillside, in the face of a terrific storm of artillery and musketry. The first assault failed; a flank movement met with no better success; and the morning was nearly gone when the Confederates finally gave way at the point of the bayonet before the irresistible onset of men in blue. The way to Chancellorsville was open; but the cost to the Federals was appalling. Hundreds of the soldiers in blue lay wrapped in death upon the bloody slopes of Marye's Heights.

It was the middle of the afternoon, and not at daybreak, as Hooker had directed, when Sedgwick appeared in the rear of Lee's legions. A strong force of Confederates under Early prevented his further advance toward a juncture with Hooker's army at Chancellorsville. Since five o'clock in the

## THE STONE WALL AT FREDERICKSBURG

Behind the deadly stone wall of Marye's Heights after Sedgwick's men had swept across it in the gallant charge of May 3, 1863.   This was one of the strongest natural positions stormed during the war.   In front of this wall the previous year, nearly 6,000 of Burnside's men had fallen, and it was not carried.   Again in the Chancellorsville campaign Sedgwick's Sixth Corps was ordered to assault it.   It was defended the second time with the same death-dealing stubbornness but with less than a fourth of the former numbers—9,000 Confederates against 20,000 Federals.   At eleven o'clock in the morning the line of battle, under Colonel Hiram Burnham, moved out over the awful field of the year before, supported to right and left by flanking columns.   Up to within twenty-five yards of the wall they pressed, when again the flame of musketry fire belched forth, laying low in six minutes 36.5 per cent. of the Fifth Wisconsin and the Sixth Maine.   The assailants wavered and rallied, and then with one impulse both columns and line of battle hurled themselves upon the wall in a fierce hand-to-hand combat.   A soldier of the Seventh Massachusetts happened to peer through a crack in a board fence and saw that it covered the flank of the double line of Confederates in the road.   Up and over the fence poured the Federals and drove the Confederates from the heights.

morning the battle had been raging at the latter place, and Jackson's men, now commanded by Stuart, though being mowed down in great numbers, vigorously pressed the attack of the day while crying out to one another " Remember Jackson," as they thought of their wounded leader.

While this engagement was at its height General Hooker, leaning against a pillar of the Chancellor house, was felled to the ground, and for a moment it was thought he was killed. The pillar had been shattered by a cannon-ball. Hooker soon revived under the doctor's care and with great force of will he mounted his horse and showed himself to his anxious troops. He then withdrew his army to a stronger position, well guarded with artillery. The Confederates did not attempt to assail it. The third day's struggle at Chancellorsville was finished by noon, except in Lee's rear, where Sedgwick fought all day, without success, to reach the main body of Hooker's army. The Federals suffered very serious losses during this day's contest. Even then it was believed that the advantage rested with the larger Army of the Potomac and that the Federals had an opportunity to win. Thirty-seven thousand Union troops, the First, and three-quarters of the Fifth Corps, had been entirely out of the fight on that day. Five thousand men of the Eleventh Corps, who were eager to retrieve their misfortune, were also inactive.

When night came, and the shades of darkness hid the sights of suffering on the battlefield, the Federal army was resting in a huge curve, the left wing on the Rappahannock and the right on the Rapidan. In this way the fords across the rivers which led to safety were in control of the Army of the Potomac. Lee moved his corps close to the bivouacs of the army in blue. But, behind the Confederate battle-line, there was a new factor in the struggle in the person of Sedgwick, with the remnants of his gallant corps, which had numbered nearly twenty-two thousand when they started for the front, but now were depleted by their terrific charge upon Marye's Heights

THE WORK OF ONE SHELL

Part of the Havoc Wrought on Marye's Heights by the Assault of Sedgwick on May 3, 1863.   No sooner had they seized the stone wall than the victorious Federals swarmed up and over the ridge above, driving the Confederates from the rifle-pits, capturing the guns of the famous Washington Artillery which had so long guarded the Heights, and inflicting slaughter upon the assaulting columns.   If Sedgwick had had cavalry he could have crushed the divided forces of Early and cleared the way for a rapid advance to attack Lee's rear.   In the picture we see Confederate caisson wagons and horses destroyed by a lucky shot from the Second Massachusetts' siege-gun battery planted across the river at Falmouth to support Sedgwick's assault.   Surveying the scene stands General Herman Haupt, Chief of the Bureau of Military Railways, the man leaning against the stump.   By him is W. W. Wright, Superintendent of the Military Railroad.   The photograph was taken on May 3d, after the battle.   The Federals held Marye's Heights until driven off by fresh forces which Lee had detached from his main army at Chancellorsville and sent against Sedgwick on the afternoon of the 4th.

COPYRIGHT, 1911, REVIEW OF REVIEWS CO.

## OVER THE RUINED TOWN

Here stand the Federal cannoneers at their posts on the last morning of the Chancellorsville struggle, ready to open fire with their 32-pounders against the fateful Marye's Heights across the river—where Sedgwick and his gallant Sixth Corps were to pluck the only shred of victory that remained to the beaten Army of the Potomac at the close of Hooker's futile and costly campaign. On the night of May 2d came the order to advance. The men of the Sixth Corps, already drawn up in battle, slept on their arms till dawn, ready to push forward and play their part in the conflict, the distant heavy booming of which had shaken the air as they had stood all day impatiently waiting. The troops of the Sixth Corps marched out across the plain from the river at four o'clock in the morning; and as they reached the eastern part of Fredericksburg the Confederate batteries opened upon them from above, while the skirmishers rose in swarms before them and poured volley after volley into their ranks, the conflict being hottest around a large mansion

FEDERAL BATTERY BEFORE FREDERICKSBURG, MAY 3, 1863

in the town, where both sides dodged behind the garden-fence of the outhouses and fought furiously. For a brief interval the Federals were held in check, but the rifled guns on Stafford Heights were already hurling their huge shells across the river and the wide valley, to burst in the Confederate works on the ridge before which Sedgwick's men waited for the order to charge. Field batteries were unlimbered and these added their iron hail to the hammering that was being inflicted on Marye's Heights, where so many brave Federals had lost their lives the previous December. At half-past ten Sedgwick, seeing that the Heights could be taken only by direct assault, ordered General Newton to command the charge, and the two commanders anxiously watched for the outcome of another hurling of flesh and blood up the slope against the sunken road which held such bitter memories. The columns went forward as coolly as did Pickett's men at Gettysburg, closing up ranks as men fell, till they swept over the hilltop, and Marye's Heights was won.

and the subsequent hard and desperate struggle with Early in the afternoon.

Lee was between two fires—Hooker in front and Sedgwick in the rear, both of whose forces were too strong to be attacked simultaneously. Again the daring leader of the Confederate legions did the unexpected, and divided his army in the presence of the foe, though he was without the aid of his great lieutenant, " Stonewall " Jackson.

During the night Lee made his preparations, and when dawn appeared in the eastern skies the movement began. Sedgwick, weak and battered by his contact with Early on the preceding afternoon, resisted bravely, but to no avail, and the Confederates closed in upon him on three sides, leaving the way to Banks's Ford on the Rappahannock open to escape. Slowly the Federals retreated and, as night descended, rested upon the river bank. After dark the return to the northern side was begun by Sedgwick's men, and the Chancellorsville campaign was practically ended.

The long, deep trenches full of Federal and Confederate dead told the awful story of Chancellorsville. If we gaze into these trenches, which by human impulse we are led to do, after the roar and din of the carnage is still, the scene greeting the eye will never be forgotten. Side by side, the heroes in torn and bloody uniforms, their only shrouds, were gently laid.

The Union loss in killed and wounded was a little over seventeen thousand, and it cost the South thirteen thousand men to gain this victory on the banks of the Rappahannock. The loss to both armies in officers was very heavy.

The two armies were weary and more than decimated. It appeared that both were glad at the prospect of a cessation of hostilities. On the night of May 5th, in a severe storm, Hooker conveyed his corps safely across the river and settled the men again in their cantonments of the preceding winter at Falmouth. The Confederates returned to their old encampment at Fredericksburg.

# BATON ROUGE—AN ARSENAL RECAPTURED

HOMES DESTROYED TO CLEAR THE WAY FOR
FORTS—BATON ROUGE, 1862

ON THE MISSISSIPPI

As the Federal forces gradually recovered the Mississippi for the Union,
many troops were necessary to hold
its banks. Whole regiments were detached from the main army for this
purpose. The Thirteenth Connecticut
was organized in November, 1861, and
belonged to Grover's division of the
Nineteenth Army Corps. Here a portion of the regiment is seen drawn up
on the banks of the Mississippi, in
Louisiana. From their neat appearance and white gloves they have evidently been on headquarters duty, and
possibly have been in recent touch
with the quartermaster's stores; their
uniforms are in fine condition and their
caps brand new. After its service in
the vicinity of the Mississippi, where
the regiment had taken part in the
operations against Port Hudson and
the capture of Donaldsonville and the
constant fighting and skirmishing in
western Louisiana, the Thirteenth
Connecticut went on the ill-fated Red
River expedition and bore itself bravely at Monett's Bluff and Cane River
Crossing. The men from Connecticut
assisted the Michigan and Wisconsin
woodsmen in building the famous dam
at Alexandria that released the imprisoned gunboats. During July and
August the seasoned veterans enjoyed
a well-earned furlough after their
arduous campaign, and upon its expi-
ration they returned to duty and were
attached to Sheridan's Army of the
Shenandoah, for service in the East.

[B]

## PATROLLING THE RIVER

To split the Confederacy apart was the Federal aim in the fall of 1862. It was necessary to the possession and command of the great waterway of the Mississippi that a constant patrol should be established after it was opened, and for this purpose, aside from the heavily armored gunboats, there was maintained a fleet of light-draught stern- and side-wheel vessels. This vessel (pictured by the Southern photographer Lytle) is No. 8 of the lightly armored "tin-clads." It was by means of these vessels of light draught that the shallow tributaries could be used as highways for the transportation of troops and supplies. The fleet or flotilla was at first really a division of the army. The crews were a miscellaneous lot of artillery-men and drafts made up from regiments in the service along the river. The early organization caused great confusion. In numerous cases naval officers in command of vessels were given military rank. Captain Foote found that he ranked only as a colonel, and that every brigadier could interfere with him. In November, 1861, he received the appointment of flag-officer that gave him the same rank as a major-general, and put him above the orders of any except the commander of the department; still he commanded soldiers, and it was not until late in the year of 1861 that any trained naval men of the rank and file were placed on the river gunboats.

## THE CAMP THAT BECAME A BATTLE-FIELD

The Federal Camp at Baton Rouge, Photographed Before the Battle of August 5, 1862. When the operations in the vicinity of Vicksburg had come to an end the Second Brigade (under the command of General Thomas Williams) of the Department of the Gulf once more went into camp at Baton Rouge, pitching tents within the limits of the city. On the 5th the Confederates under General J. C. Breckinridge attacked in two divisions in the early morning, their movements being hidden by a very dense fog. At first the Confederates were most successful and they seized a camp that lay in front of the Union battle-line. But the Federals soon advanced; the Confederates made three charges upon them but were finally driven back in much disorder. General Williams was killed. Baton Rouge was evacuated shortly after. The town was not burned on account of its many public institutions.

WHERE THE HOSPITALS FURNISHED REËNFORCEMENTS

The Federal Camp Banks, at Baton Rouge, near the Penitentiary, taken in late July, 1862. This is another view of what was soon to become a battle-field. We are looking down at the camp of the Seventh Vermont and the Twenty-first Indiana; on the extreme right is the camp of Nims' battery. This point was attacked fiercely, as it was supposed to be held by regiments much depleted by sickness, but at the first alarm the men in the hospitals picked up their rifles and fell into line. After General Williams' death the command devolved upon Colonel Cahill, of the Ninth Connecticut, an Irish regiment. By evening the Confederates had abandoned the ground that they had won in the fight.

### THE BREAD–LINE AT BATON ROUGE

This picture was taken just at the close of the war in 1865.   It is a remarkable and interesting picture.   The Verandah House, the building shown on the left, is where General W. T. Sherman stopped in 1859, when he was Superintendent of the Louisiana Seminary of Learning and Military Academy.   The group of colored people lining the sidewalk are waiting for their issue of rations.   The skill of Lytle, the photographer, is shown by the fact that the man walking is hardly blurred and the mule's ears in the foreground might have been taken by an instantaneous shutter.   The view below shows the home of the Union soldiers who remained in Baton Rouge from its occupation on May 12, 1862.   Brigadier-General Thomas Williams had been assigned from Butler's force at New Orleans to assist Farragut to clear the Mississippi.   Williams' headquarters was Baton Rouge, but during most of May, June, and July he was in the vicinity of Vicksburg operating in conjunction with Farragut's fleet.   When he arrived at Baton Rouge at the end of July the barracks was almost a hospital, for half the men were on the sick-list.

THE COURT HOUSE AT BATON ROUGE

The Parade of a Part of a Regiment of Federal Troops at Baton Rouge. It would take a long search to find a finer body of men than these trained and seasoned veterans here drawn up in line. The campaign on the lower Mississippi was a survival of the fittest in more ways than one. Sickness was rife, and only those in the best condition and the hardiest kept in trim for active service. In many cases regiments could muster only 120 men. Camp fevers and the threat of the yellow scourge were always present. The returns of the regiments employed in the vicinity of New Orleans show a startling mortality. The Thirteenth Connecticut lost by disease 160 men. The Twenty-first Indiana, whose casualty list in the battle of Baton Rouge was 126, lost twice that number from sickness. A larger proportion of sick to killed and wounded prevailed in the Fourteenth Maine and the Seventh Vermont—the former losing 332 and the latter 407.

DRESS–PARADE OF FEDERAL TROOPS AT BATON ROUGE

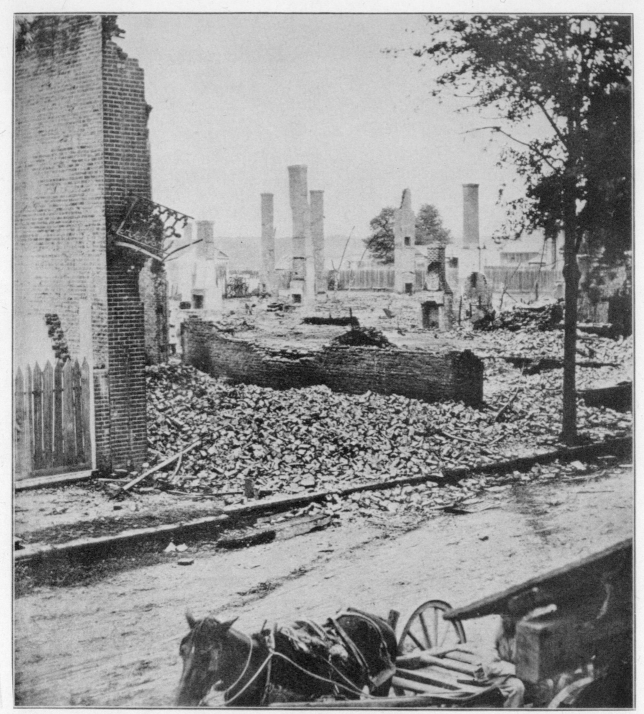

BY ORDER OF THE COMMANDING OFFICER

Buildings in Line of Fire Condemned and Destroyed at Baton Rouge by Order of Colonel Halbert E. Paine. This view was photographed by Mr. Lytle after the drawn battle of the 5th of August, 1862, when the Federals had retreated from their outer camps and had concentrated on the Arsenal grounds between the cemetery and the river bank, at the northwestern end of the town. In order that the houses should not afford protection to any attacking party, those in the immediate vicinity (on the southeastern flank of the fortified Arsenal) were set on fire and razed to the ground. In this picture the heavy stockade that surrounded the garrison is plainly visible, as is also the roof of one of the barracks. Nevertheless, although the Federal troops were never attacked in their stronghold, General Butler determined to concentrate his forces in New Orleans, and Baton Rouge was abandoned.

# PART II
## OPENING THE MISSISSIPPI

———

# THE ASSAULT
# ON CORINTH

———

PUSHING THROUGH TENNESSEE, 1862
UNION BRIDGE OVER THE ELK RIVER AT PULASKI

THE RUSE OF THE WHISTLES

The Tishomingo Hotel was an old hostelry forming practically the railway station at Corinth, Miss., and here was played a little comedy by way of prelude to the tragic spectacle that was to happen on this very scene. After the battle of Shiloh, General Beauregard retreated to Corinth, where soon the Confederate army numbered about eighty thousand men. Halleck, who had assumed command in person, after a little delay started in pursuit at the head of the largest army ever assembled west of the Alleghanies, numbering more than 135,000 effective men. But the great forces did not come to decisive blows; Halleck, as usual, did not act with energy. For more than a month he went on gathering still more reenforcements, planning and organizing, all the time closing in slowly on Corinth. It was expected that a conclusive battle would soon take place, but Beauregard did not risk the test of arms. Keeping his intentions absolutely secret, he decided to evacuate. This plan was carried out with great cleverness; his army with its stores and munitions

THE GUARDED TRACK, CORINTH, MISSISSIPPI, 1862

boarded the assembled railway trains on the night of May 29, 1862, and the roads to the southward were filled with wagons and marching troops. But along the Confederate front the watch-fires burned brightly; and Halleck's army, waiting within earshot, heard sounds of commotion—the tooting of locomotive whistles and, with every fresh clear blast, loud cheers. It was rumored through the Federal camp that strong Confederate reenforcements were arriving. Into the gray of the morning this continued. The troops awoke with the nervous expectancy of battle, but before them lay a deserted town. The whistling and the cheering had covered Beauregard's retreat. The "movement of artillery" that had been reported had been some old wagons driven round in a circle. General Pope was sent in pursuit of the wily Confederate leader, but failed to force him to a stand. The evacuation had opened the Tennessee River, and finally resulted in giving the Federals the control of the Mississippi from Cairo to Memphis.

## WHERE TRAGEDY FOLLOWED COMEDY AT CORINTH

Across the road, at the extreme right, against Battery Robinett, frowning above the camp, the Confederates charged on October 4th with terrible results, some of which are shown in the picture following. Only a short distance down the track from the old hotel and railway station shown in the preceding picture, the photographer had aimed his camera to take this view. Months had passed since over this very ground had swept two charges memorable in the annals of the Civil War. On the left of the picture is Battery Williams. Over this foreground the Confederates bravely advanced in the attempt to take two positions. By firmly holding his ground, General Rosecrans leaped at once into national fame.

## THE DAY AFTER THE MAGNIFICENT ASSAULT THAT FAILED

As the camera snapped, October 5, 1862, every object in this picture was a tragedy. Directly in the foreground lies a Confederate soldier who had swept along in the grand and terrible charge against the ramparts of Battery Robinett, to fall within fifty yards of the goal. Even nearer the battery lies the battle-charger of the colonel of the Texas Brigade. And to the left has been reverently laid the body of Colonel Rogers himself—the brave leader who leaped from his dying horse, seized the colors, and on foot dashed up the parapet straight into the last charge of grape-shot. "Then," writes one of the Federal defenders (General John Crane, the adjutant of the Seventeenth Wisconsin), "we learned who it was—Colonel William P. Rogers, of the Second Texas. General Rosecrans asked us to uncover his face; he said, 'He was one of the bravest men that ever led a charge. Bury him with military honors and mark his grave so that his friends may claim him.'" Colonel Rogers is said to have been the fifth standard-bearer to fall in that last desperate charge of the Texas Brigade.

# CORINTH—ROSECRANS HOLDS FIRM

This battle finally relieved Grant from his anxiety as to the possession of the territory he commanded. After Corinth, he had 48,500 men, and the arrival of reenforcements soon placed him in position for attack. —*Colonel W. C. Church, U. S. V., in " Ulysses S. Grant."*

THE appalling carnage at Pittsburg Landing, on the Tennessee, awakened the North and the South to a fuller sense of the magnitude of the war. The South had suffered a double disaster—the loss of the battle and the loss of General Albert Sidney Johnston. But the Federal victory was not decisive. The Union forces had found their adversaries worthy of their steel and had paid dearly for what they had won.

The Confederate troops after the battle of Shiloh under General Beauregard, who had assumed command of the Army of the Mississippi on the death of Johnston, had been led to the little railroad center in Mississippi, Corinth, where they were recovering their lost organization and strength.

Western Tennessee and the adjoining counties of Mississippi, the territory in which the armies of the Confederacy and the Union were operating, were unfavorable to successful military movements in force. Dense forests covered the region, and the soil was marshy and soft, stretching away in gently rolling hills. The small creeks, abundant about Corinth, are for the most part sluggish and their water unfit for drinking purposes.

Three great railroad systems penetrated the region, offering an excellent and expeditious method of transportation to whichever army was in control of the strategic point on the steel highways—and this important point at the junction of two of the roads was Corinth, which Beauregard now occupied,

GENERAL EARL VAN DORN, C.S.A.

## THE CONFEDERATE COMMANDER AT CORINTH

General Earl Van Dorn was born in Mississippi in 1821; he was graduated from West Point in 1842, and was killed in a personal quarrel in 1863. Early in the war General Van Dorn had distinguished himself by capturing the steamer "Star of the West" at Indianola, Texas. He was of a tempestuous nature and had natural fighting qualities. During the month of August he commanded all the Confederate troops in Mississippi except those under General Price, and it was his idea to form a combined movement with the latter's forces and expel the invading Federals from the northern portion of his native State and from eastern Tennessee. The concentration was made and the Confederate army, about 22,000 men, was brought into the disastrous battle of Corinth. Brave were the charges made on the entrenched positions, but without avail.

## THE CONFEDERATE SECOND IN COMMAND

General Sterling Price was a civilian who by natural inclination turned to soldiering. He had been made a brigadier-general during the Mexican War, but early allied himself with the cause of the Confederacy. At Pea Ridge, only seven months before the battle of Corinth, he had been wounded. Of the behavior of his men, though they were defeated and turned back on the 4th, he wrote that it was with pride that sisters and daughters of the South could say of the officers and men, "My brother, father, fought at Corinth." And nobly they fought indeed. General Van Dorn, in referring to the end of that bloody battle, wrote these pathetic words: "Exhausted from loss of sleep, wearied from hard marching and fighting, companies and regiments without officers, our troops—let no one censure them—gave way. The day was lost."

GENERAL STERLING PRICE, C.S.A.

and upon which the Federal authorities cast longing glances as soon as the present campaign had begun.

However, it became clear to Beauregard that although his opponent did not immediately pursue, it would be impossible to hold Corinth. Soon after Shiloh the Union army was re-enforced to more than double the strength it had been before. Four days after the battle, General H. W. Halleck arrived at the Landing and took command in person; ten days later General John Pope, who had captured Island No. 10, on April 7th, joined his army to that at the Landing, and this, with other reenforcements, raised the number to a hundred thousand.

Beauregard had been joined by Van Dorn and Sterling Price from beyond the Mississippi, but, although the rolls showed now a force of over one hundred and twelve thousand he could not muster much more than fifty thousand men at any time and he prepared to give up Corinth whenever the great Northern force should move against it. About the 1st of May the movement of the Federal hosts, reorganized and now consisting of the Army of the Tennessee under General Thomas, the Army of the Ohio under Buell, and the Army of the Mississippi under Pope, began. Grant was second in command of the whole force, under Halleck. Slowly and cautiously, entrenching at every night halt, Halleck moved upon Corinth, guarding always against attack. He arrived before the town on May 25th. He met with but slight resistance. But Beauregard, although he had thrown up entrenchments and was maintaining a bold front, stealthily prepared to evacuate the town and save his army. Troops, provided with three days' cooked rations, manned the trenches confronting the Federal line, waiting for the order to advance. The Confederate soldiers had no inkling of the intentions of their leader. As the days passed and the command to attack was not given, the men behind the breastworks became restless.

Meanwhile, the patients in the hospitals within the town were being hurried away, and with great trainloads of stores

### BEFORE THE SOD HID THEM

The Gathered Confederate Dead Before Battery Robinett—taken the morning after their desperate attempt to carry the works by assault. No man can look at this awful picture and wish to go to war. These men, a few hours before, were full of life and hope and courage. Without the two last qualities they would not be lying as they are pictured here. In the very foreground, on the left, lies their leader, Colonel Rogers, and almost resting on his shoulder is the body of the gallant Colonel Ross. We are looking from the bottom of the parapet of Battery Robinett. Let an eye-witness tell of what the men saw who looked toward the houses on that bright October day, and then glanced along their musket-barrels and pulled the triggers: "Suddenly we saw a magnificent brigade emerge in our front; they came forward in perfect order, a grand but terrible sight. At their head rode the commander, a man of fine physique, in the prime of life—quiet and cool as though on a drill. The artillery opened, the infantry followed; notwithstanding the slaughter they were closer and closer. Their commander [Colonel Rogers] seemed to bear a charmed life. He jumped his horse across the ditch in front of the guns, and then on foot came on. When he fell, the battle in our front was over."

were sent south over the Mobile and Ohio Railroad. On the night of the 29th, the preparations for the evacuation of the town by the Confederates were completed. Most of the troops were withdrawn from the trenches to the railroad, and there instructed concerning the part they were to play in the strategy to deceive the Federals.

Late that night a train rolled into the station, and the Federal pickets heard a lusty cheer arise from the Confederate ranks. Other trains followed, and the sounds of exuberation increased. Word quickly spread through the Federal camps that heavy reenforcements had come to the Confederates. The Northerners spent the early morning hours preparing to resist the attack they expected would be made with the coming of dawn.

At break of day the Federals, waiting in battle-line, could see no signs of life in the pits confronting them. The pickets crept forward to investigate. A thunderous explosion shook the town. It was the destruction of the last of the Confederate stores. The Southerners had evacuated the village, and Corinth, with all its strategic advantage, with its command of the great railroads connecting the Mississippi valley with the Atlantic coast and with the Gulf of Mexico, fell into the hands of the North. Both of the great armies were quickly broken up. Halleck, in possession of Corinth, looked to Chattanooga as the next objective, and Buell led the Army of the Ohio back to middle Tennessee as a preliminary move in that direction.

In the midsummer, Halleck was made general-in-chief of all the Northern armies and went to Washington. He left Grant in control of the West. Meantime, Beauregard was relieved of the command of the Confederate Army of the Mississippi and it was handed over to General Bragg. Leaving a portion of his army in Mississippi with Van Dorn and Price, Bragg began, late in August, his famous expedition into Kentucky, pursued by Buell with the Army of the Ohio. A part of the Federal Army of the Mississippi remained at Corinth,

## THE BATTERY THAT CONTROLLED THE RIGHT OF WAY

Battery Williams, that can just be seen at the left of the picture, controlled the cutting through which the Memphis & Charleston Road ran on its way between Corinth and the Mississippi. It faced the right flank of Fort Robinett, distant about half a mile. During the action of October 4th, when the gallant Texans bravely assailed Battery Robinett, Battery Williams with all its guns was playing steadily upon the Confederate left flank, and so closely did they follow that brave and brilliant charge that two shells from the battery landed inside the Federal earthworks and burst there. Most of the houses seen in the mid-distance are barracks erected by the Fifty-seventh and Fifty-second Illinois Infantry. It was directly from this ground, in front of the railway station, that the Confederate advance took place. A short distance to the left of the freight-house stood a small cottage. General Rosecrans. as he rode along the Federal line, noticed that the porch and windows were filled with Confederates, who were firing at long range at the batteries. Immediately he ordered two field-pieces to open upon the dwelling with grape and canister. Hardly a man escaped alive. The town suffered severely from the fire of both Confederate and Federal artillery, but most of the inhabitants had retreated to their cellars and no casualties were reported. Note the bales of precious cotton gathered from some storehouse, worth almost their weight in gold before the war was over.

[B]

where there were immense military stores, under the command of General William S. Rosecrans. After inflicting a defeat on Sterling Price, September 19th, in a severe combat at Iuka, Mississippi, Rosecrans was settled snugly at Corinth with two divisions and cavalry of his army, and two divisions of the Federal Army of West Tennessee, in all about twenty-three thousand men. Van Dorn then joined his Army of West Tennessee with Price's Corps, or Army of the West, and decided to make a desperate attempt to capture Corinth. It was a daring venture, for Corinth was well fortified and Rosecrans' army was slightly larger than his own.

The battle of Corinth, October 3-4, 1862, does not compare in magnitude with the greatest battles of the war; but for ferocity of fighting, it was not surpassed by any. Rosecrans did not believe that Van Dorn would attack him, and when the latter appeared in force in the neighborhood on October 3rd he supposed that it was only a feint and that the real object of the Confederate attack was to be Jackson, about sixty miles north, in Tennessee, where Grant's headquarters were, or Bolivar, Tennessee, about forty miles northwest, where Hurlbut's division of Grant's Army of West Tennessee was at that time located.

However, Rosecrans was prepared for any emergency. He sent Colonel Oliver with three regiments to take an advanced position on a hill, near the Chewalla road, to watch the movements of the Confederates. A desultory cannonade was begun and soon Rosecrans sent General McArthur to the front with his brigade. In a short time a sharp battle was raging. Then came a sudden determined Confederate charge by which the Union forces were driven from the hill and two of their heavy guns captured. The Union commander was now convinced that the attack was no feint, but that the purpose of the Southern general was to make a grand assault on Corinth with a view of defeating its defenders and capturing the great stores within its fortifications.

[ 148 ]

## WINTER QUARTERS AT CORINTH

A Photograph Taken During the Federal Occupation, Winter of 1862.   These little cottages—bungalows we should call them—resemble much the summer residences erected by the holiday-makers on the sea-coast at some wintering resort.   Many were built by soldier-carpenters who found time to turn their hands to carpentering, and even to architectural decoration.   All trades were represented in the army, and during a lull in the fighting the men plied their avocations.   Besides the artisans that were of use to the commanding generals—such as mechanics, locomotive engineers, machinists, and farriers—there were tailors and shoemakers, watchmakers and barbers, and all the little trades by which men with time on their hands could turn an honest penny.   Some regiments became renowned for the neatness of their quarters.   It was a matter of prideful boastings.   In this picture a soldier has fashioned a well-cut overcoat out of a gaudy blanket.   These are officers' quarters.   The man smoking the long cigar as he sits on the veranda railing is a captain.   A bearded lieutenant stands on the steps of the second house, and another young officer has apparently adopted for the time a tow-headed child of a Corinth family.

The hours of the afternoon were given to disposing the various divisions of the army to the best advantage for the defense of the town; but it was no easy task because of the annoying Confederate fire from the surrounding hills. Before either side opened a general engagement it was night, and both armies slept on their arms, confident that a fierce battle was in store for the coming day.

The early hours of the night were spent by Rosecrans in rearranging his battle-lines, and before he went to sleep about 3 A.M., his forces had drawn closer to the town. The Federal left, under McKean, rested near Corona College; next in line was Stanley, in support of Battery Robinett, a small fortification mounting three guns; in the center of the battle-line, was Davies, and Hamilton was assigned to the right wing. Thus stood the weary warriors in blue, who had struggled desperately in the terrific heat of the preceding day and were now exhausted. The line was crescent shaped, and covered the northern and western approaches to Corinth, extended a mile in length and rested on the edge of the town. The Confederate divisions, commanded by Lovell, Maury, and Hébert stood arrayed in another great crescent, conforming to the curve of Rosecrans' battle-line. About four o'clock on the morning of the 4th the sleeping village was awakened by the shells that shrieked over the housetops and fell bursting in the streets.

During the night a Confederate battery had been planted a few hundred yards from the Union lines, opposite Stanley's position, and now opened with several Parrott guns. Little damage was done, except that the teamsters, sutlers, and other non-combatants were kept in a ferment of excitement. No reply was made till near daylight, when a Union battery opened on the Confederate guns, and the latter were silenced and disabled in a few minutes. Indian summer had descended over the land, bringing its enervating heat from which the soldiers of both armies suffered. The sun peeped over the eastern hills, and its rays were soon beating down upon the bivouacs.

[ 150 ]

PHOTOGRAPHERS OF THE WESTERN ARMIES

The Civil War was the first great war to be photographed.  The art had just arisen.  The daguerreotype had been superseded by the tintype, and the wet-plate method (still in vogue in the best portrait galleries) was then in the height of its excellence.  It is a fortunate thing in recording the history of the time that the camera was in existence.  In Corinth there was a firm of photographers occupying a little wooden shack in the outskirts of the town.  They did a thriving business during the occupancy by the Confederates and by the Federals.  George Armstead was a wonderful photographer—rivaling Brady at his best.  In the picture he is standing back to the left, near where some of his negatives are printing in the sun; in front of the shop a drummer-boy stands with folded arms near the civilians who loll against the post.   What would we not give for a nearer glimpse of the samples of Armstead's work on the right of the doorway! The little frame of portrait tintypes on the other side would also give us to-day a thrill of interest.   They are the only relics, perhaps, of men who lie in far-off graves—duplicates of the only mementoes that their people, who are now old, possess.   In turning the pages of this volume many will exclaim, "Look, there he is!"

During the day the temperature rose to ninety-four degrees in the shade.

Soon after daybreak the skirmishers of both sides began with scattering shots, which presently came thicker and faster; the batteries came into play, and shells were falling and bursting all around. So it continued until half-past nine. Then came a sudden and amazing change in the whole aspect of the battle. A vast column of gleaming bayonets was seen to flash from the woods east of the Memphis and Charleston Railroad; long lines of determined, gray-clad troops of Price's divisions quickly formed and began to march swiftly and steadily along the Purdy road, toward Davies and Hamilton, behind whom lay the town of Corinth. Presently the great column took the shape of a wedge as it moved impetuously forward.

General Rosecrans was prepared for the charge. He had skilfully planned to entice the Confederates to attack at a point where his carefully placed batteries and infantry could sweep the road with direct, cross, and enfilading fires. There was an outburst from the Federal guns. Gaps were torn in the moving gray column, but they were instantly filled and the lines moved on with great steadiness. A gently sloping hill led up to the Federal position. As Price's troops began the ascent, volley after volley of grape, canister, and shell were poured into their ranks, but still they marched on with a valor not surpassed by Leonidas and his Spartans at Thermopylæ.

Colonel Sweeny, who commanded a brigade of Davies' division on that memorable 4th of October, gives a vivid picture of this remarkable charge:

An ominous silence took place for a few moments, when a sharp rattling of musketry was heard, accompanied by heavy volleys, and the enemy's columns burst from the woods in front and to the right, driving the sharpshooters before them and following close upon their heels. Colonel Burke's regiment fought like heroes and disputed every inch of ground as they fell back on my position. I cautioned my men, who were lying on the ground, to reserve their fire until the enemy got within

## OHIO TROOPS ON THE BATTLE-FIELD OF CORINTH

The Eighty-first Ohio, pictured here drawn up at "parade rest," enlisted in August, 1861; when its term expired in 1864, it reënlisted and served to the end of the war. The youth of these men is very evident; yet when this picture was taken they were already tried and proved veterans. Attached to Sweeney's division of the Sixteenth Army Corps, they fought through most of the actions in Tennessee and Mississippi, but were not present at the time of the Confederate attack on the fortifications we see behind them—Battery Williams to the left, and Battery Robinett to the right. The Eightieth Ohio was present at this action and was attached to the second brigade of the second division of the Army of the Mississippi under Rosecrans. Its commander, Major Lanning, was killed. Well can Ohio be proud of her record in the war; nearly twenty-one thousand men remained in the field and served after their three-years' enlistment had expired, and most of these reënlistments embraced a very large proportion of the original volunteers of '61.

point-blank range, and then fire low and keep perfectly cool. It was a terribly beautiful sight to see the columns advance, in despite of a perfect storm of grape and canister, shell, and rifle-ball; still on they marched and fired, though their ranks were perceptibly thinned at every step. The brigade stood firm as a rock, and the men loaded and fired with the coolness and precision of veterans, when all of a sudden the troops on the right of the redan (a brigade of Hamilton's division) gave way and broke. The First Missouri Artillery, in the redan, and the two pieces on the left of the Fifty-second Illinois limbered up and galloped off in wild confusion through our reserves, killing several of our men and scattering the rest. My line remained still unbroken, pouring deadly volleys into the enemy's ranks, who, taking advantage of the panic on the right, moved their columns obliquely in that direction and charged up to the redan. . . .

I now ordered the line to charge on the enemy, who had by this time gained the crest of the hill in our front. With a shout that was heard through our whole lines the men of the First Brigade rushed upon them. Those who had given way a short time before, being evidently ashamed of the momentary panic that had seized them, seemed determined to wipe out the stain upon their courage by their reckless daring. The foe, reluctant to abandon the advantage they had gained, fought stubbornly for a while, but was finally compelled to give way, retreating in great confusion through the swamps and abatis to the woods, hotly pursued by our men.

In spite of the desperate resistance, the center of the Federal line was penetrated, and Price's troops drove the regiments back into the town, scattering the Union soldiers among the houses. The storming Confederates advanced to the north side of the square and posted themselves around a house close to where General Halleck had maintained his headquarters the summer before. Two field-pieces opened upon them, and the daring Southerners were whirled back, leaving seven of their number dead in the dooryard, after one round of grape and canister. Union troops stationed in the town hurried up and General Sullivan immediately supported the shattered center. His men retook Battery Powell while General Hamilton

## A CAMP MEETING WITH A PURPOSE

There was something of extreme interest taking place when this photograph was taken at Corinth. With arms stacked, the soldiers are gathered about an improvised stand sheltered with canvas, listening to a speech upon a burning question of the hour—the employment of colored troops in the field. A question upon which there were many different and most decided opinions prevailing in the North, and but one nearly universal opinion holding south of Mason and Dixon's line. General Thomas, at the moment this photograph was taken, was addressing the assembled troops on this subject. Some prominent Southeners, among them General Patrick Cleburne, favored the enrollment of Negroes in the Confederate army.

collected his scattered division and charged upon the Confederate left, driving it across an open field over which the recaptured Union artillery hurled a pitiless fire. It was now one o'clock in the afternoon and the battle on the Federal right was over.

The Confederate commanders had planned a general assault, Price and Van Dorn acting in concert, but on different points of Rosecrans' line. Van Dorn delayed in reaching his position, and Price's majestic and thrilling charge had been in progress half an hour or more when the standards of the Army of West Tennessee emerged from the woods, in front of Stanley's division and batteries Robinett and Williams. The Federal troops were eagerly watching affairs on their right, when their attention was called to the gray wave plunging over fallen trees and through growths of underbrush in front of Battery Robinett. A sheet of flame burst from the fort, and the advance line of Confederates was enveloped in smoke, many of its numbers falling dead and wounded. A second storming column appeared, and again the Federal guns smote the daring Confederates. Again and again the courageous Southerners charged until they finally won the ditch surrounding the battery, and after a desperate hand-to-hand fight gained the interior of the fort, the defenders falling back to another position. At the head of the attacking regiments stood Colonel W. P. Rogers of the Second Texas regiment of Maury's division.

The Southerners had almost gained this important point in the Federal line, when a burst of flame appeared in Battery Williams, and two shells hurtled across the intervening space and fell into the Confederate ranks. Simultaneously, Fuller's Ohio brigade of Stanley's division and the Eleventh Missouri appeared in the rear of the fort where they had been concealed, and delivered six successive volleys into the gray ranks at the front of the battery. When the smoke cleared the front of the fort was clear of living Confederates. They could not stand the terrific storm of lead and iron. Many of them fell to rise

PROVOST MARSHAL'S HEADQUARTERS AT CORINTH

During the occupation of a town where soldiers were in predominance, there was one man who was responsible for the conduct of the troops, and also for the practical government and policing of the streets, and the control of the inhabitants' actions. Such was the provost marshal. He was head constable, police-court judge, health department, and general almoner. Negroes from the outlying districts had flocked, as usual, into Corinth in nondescript wagons drawn by oxen and mules, and sometimes both, as we see here pictured.

FOOD FOR POWDER

Give a glance at these seventeen men, who, for some reason that we cannot tell, have chosen to stand before the camera and be "taken." Note one thing first—there is not one smiling face nor one look of the holiday soldier about this little group. Able, grim, stern-hearted veterans—their faces show it. Among them all there is not a single merry-maker. These men have faced death often, they have seen their comrades die. They have looked across the sights of their muskets at the ragged men in gray, and peered through the enveloping smoke to see if their shots have told. These are not the machine-made soldiers of the European armies. They are the development of the time and hour. The influence of emigration is plainly shown. Here is a Scotchman—

FEDERAL TROOPS AT CORINTH

An old soldier of the Queen, perhaps, who knew the Mutiny and the Crimea. Here are Swedes and Germans, Irish and French; but, predominating, is the American type—the Yankee, and the man of many blends from the mid-West and the North woods. There are two or three regulars standing in the center—artillerymen with bell buttons. On the extreme right are two men of the saber, with short jackets. Beyond them is the battle-field of October. It is now winter, but these men saw that field shrouded in battle smoke. They saw Price and Van Dorn's brave troops come yelling and charging across the railway track and the road beyond up to the very guns of Battery Robinett, which we see rising like a mound or hillock beyond the line of the railway shed.

no more. The others began to waver. Then came a panic. They broke and fled in great disorder. Volley after volley was fired at the fleeing men. They were now pursued by the victors, across ravines, over hills, and among the fallen trees. Many threw away their guns and surrendered, others escaped, and still others gave their lives for the cause in which they believed. Fifty-six bodies of brave Confederates were found in a space of a few rods about Battery Robinett and were buried in one pit. Among them was Colonel Rogers, who had fallen while planting his battle-flag on the parapet. The wild shouts of the victorious Federals rang through the streets of Corinth, above the moaning of the wounded and dying. By two o'clock Rosecrans was convinced that the Confederate generals did not intend to make another attack and were retreating in force, but his troops were too weary to follow after on that day.

Later in the afternoon McPherson arrived with four regiments sent by Grant, and these were ordered to begin the pursuit at daylight the next morning. Meanwhile, Hurlbut with his division was hastening from Bolivar to the Confederate rear. On the night of the 4th he bivouacked on the west bank of the Hatchie River near Davis' Bridge, right in the path of Van Dorn. The following morning General Ord arrived and took command of the Federal forces.

Owing to a number of mishaps and delays Rosecrans never overtook the Confederate army, but when Van Dorn's advance guard attempted to seize the Hatchie bridge on the morning of the 5th, it was most spiritedly attacked and driven off by Ord, who was severely wounded. Although the Confederates greatly outnumbered their opponents, Van Dorn, fearful of Rosecrans in his rear, moved down the east bank of the Hatchie, crossed six miles below, and made his way to Holly Springs. On these three October days the Federals lost over twenty-five hundred and the Confederates forty-eight hundred. Of these over two thousand had been captured by Rosecrans and Ord.

[ 160 ]

# PART II
## OPENING THE MISSISSIPPI

---

# THE MIDWINTER COMBAT
# AT STONE'S RIVER

---

THE MURFREESBORO COURTHOUSE UNDER GUARD—1863

THE SINEWS OF WAR

This busy scene along the Nashville wharf on December 18, 1862, gives a clear idea of the magnitude of the preparations at the Federal army base thirteen days before the battle opened around Murfreesboro, at which point Bragg was threatening Nashville. Rosecrans could not move forward to attack him without supplies, and the river steamers which played so important a part in all the military operations in the West were hurrying up the Cumberland heavily loaded with the munitions and sustenance that made possible the coming battles. The first boat completely visible in the picture at the right is the " Mercury," a famous Ohio River packet at the time. Next to her lies the " Lizzie Martin," and then the " Palestine," another Ohio racer. She has a hole stove in her prow just above the water-line, and the ship's carpenter in his yawl is busily repairing it. Confederate batteries constantly menaced the Federal transports as they plied up and down the rivers. The renowned Tom Napier sometimes scared and captured a vessel with his dummy wooden guns.

SUPPLY STEAMERS AT NASHVILLE, DECEMBER, 1862

Beyond the "Palestine" lie the "Reveillie," the "Irene," the "Belle Peoria" (a famous Mississippi boat from St. Louis), and last the "Rob Roy"—all discharging their tons of freight, paid for by the Government at war-time prices. On the snow-covered wharf are piled barrels of whiskey (the standard brand familiarly known as "Cincinnati rot-gut," distilled for the Government's own use), while the roustabouts are rolling ashore barrels of sugar and hogsheads of molasses to be mixed with the coffee which weary soldiers are to brew for themselves in the field. There are thousands of barrels of flour still to be unloaded. In symmetrical piles lie myriad boxes each stencilled "Pilot bread from U. S. Government Bakery, Evansville, Ind." Many an old Confederate knew the taste of this hard-tack and had to depend upon capturing a supply of it to stay his hunger. Confederate prisoners in their confinement watched many such scenes as this, wondering what newcomers would be added to their numbers during the ensuing campaign.

[B]

CONFEDERATES WHO FOUGHT THE GUNS AT STONE'S RIVER

The Washington Artillery, mustered in at New Orleans, was one of the crack military organizations of the Confederacy. In this rare picture a Confederate photographer has caught a jolly group of them, confident and care-free, whiling away the hours in camp. The photograph was taken the year before the battle of Stone's River. Ere that conflict the youngsters had received their baptism of fire at Shiloh and had acquitted themselves like men. Their gallant force was attached to Anderson's First Brigade and then to General Samuel Jones's Corps, of Bragg's army. At the battle of Stone's River they fought in Breckinridge's division of Hardee's Corps. It was they who made the daring rush to plant their batteries on the hill, and suffered so severely from the galling fire of

MEN OF THE FAMOUS WASHINGTON ARTILLERY

Mendenhall's Federal guns across the river.   On that hard-fought battlefield they were differently occupied than in the picture.   Their deeds in the swift moments of the conflict were not acted out to the accompaniment of a merry tune; each man played  his part amid the roar of cannon and the clash of arms, and many paid the piper with his life for that awful music.   Even in the confident  poses and smiling faces of the picture are apparent all the dash and spirit which they displayed later at Stone's River.   This brave Con- federate organization distinguished itself on all the fields where it fought.   Not till Chancellorsville did it ever lose a gun; in that en- gagement five  pieces were captured from it, when Sedgwick's 20,000 wrested Marye's Heights from the 9,000 Lee had left there.

# STONE'S RIVER, OR MURFREESBORO

As it is, the battle of Stone's River seems less clearly a Federal victory than the battle of Shiloh. The latter decided the fall of Corinth; the former did not decide the fall of Chattanooga. Offensively it was a drawn battle, as looked at from either side. As a defensive battle, however, it was clearly a Union victory.—*John Fiske in "The Mississippi Valley in the Civil War."*

THE battle of Corinth developed a man—William S. Rosecrans—whose singular skill in planning the battle, and whose dauntless courage in riding between the firing-lines at the opportune moment, drew the country's attention almost as fully as Grant had done at Fort Donelson. And at this particular moment the West needed, or thought it needed, a man. The autumn months of 1862 had been spent by Generals Bragg and Buell in an exciting race across Kentucky, each at the head of a great army. Buell had saved Louisville from the legions of Bragg, and he had driven the Confederate Army of the Mississippi from the State; but he had not prevented his opponent from carrying away a vast amount of plunder, nor had he won decisive results at the battle of Perryville, which took place October 8, 1862, four days after the battle of Corinth. Thereupon the Federal authorities decided to relieve Buell of the Army of the Ohio and to give it to General Rosecrans.

On October 30, 1862, Rosecrans assumed command at Nashville of this force, which was now designated as the Army of the Cumberland. Bragg had concentrated his army at Murfreesboro, in central Tennessee, about thirty miles southeast of Nashville and a mile east of a little tributary of the Cumberland River called Stone's River. Here occurred, two months later, the bloodiest single day's battle in the West,

THE GUARDED DEPOT—STEVENSON IN 1862

This little Alabama town first became the subject of a war photograph during General Buell's campaign. It sprang into strategic importance as a base of supplies, and in order to hold it Buell sent forward Colonel A. S. Barker, who began the construction of extensive defenses, pressing into service some five hundred Negroes. Barker succeeded in completing two large redoubts and seven lockhouses; so defensible was the position made that during Hood's invasion of Tennessee it was not attacked by the Confederates.

THE STRENGTHENED FORTS

This picture of Fort Barker, at Stevenson, shows the care with which the Federals defended this advance base. In this fort, which was about 150 feet square, there were barbette platforms for seven guns and an extensive magazine, and bomb-proof. Fort Mitchell, south of the station on the other side of the railroad, was equally strong. The two forts guarded the approach from the north.

which has taken the double name of the town and the river. Beside the winding little stream ran the turnpike to Nashville and the Nashville and Chattanooga Railroad.

Bragg had the advantage in cavalry. In addition to Wheeler's command there were the troops of Forrest and Morgan, who acted independently of the Army of the Mississippi, now known as the Army of Tennessee. These men, with several hundred horsemen, raided through the country, regardless of mud, snow, or ice, and at one time threatened Nashville, the Federal supply-depot. They tore up railroads, burned bridges, and left a trail of destruction in their wake. One night, early in December, Morgan pounced upon the town of Hartsville, overpowered the guard of several hundred Federal troops, captured and carried them to Murfreesboro.

Christmas day, in 1862, was passed by Bragg's army in whatever festivities the little town of Murfreesboro could afford. The fratricidal strife that was draining both the North and the South was forgotten for the moment. A general belief had circulated in the Confederate camps that the Federal commander, harassed on every side by the raiders, would have enough to do to keep his army intact, and would not make a general advance on Bragg. But soon there was a different story to tell. On the day after Christmas, the news reached the little town that the Federal army had emerged from Nashville, that it was headed directly for Murfreesboro, and that a great battle was imminent.

The battle-ground toward which the Federal army was marching was broken and heavily wooded, with an occasional open field, and gentle rises on which artillery and infantry could be posted. But cavalry was practically useless in this rough country. Stone's River, which ran through the battle-ground, was tortuous in its channel and shallow; its banks were fringed with clumps of cedar brakes. Numerous turnpikes converged at the little town of Murfreesboro from the surrounding towns; the principal highway being the Nashville

## LEADERS OF A GALLANT STAND AT STONE'S RIVER

General William P. Carlin and Staff. Early in the war Carlin made a name for himself as colonel of the Thirty-eighth Illinois Infantry, which was stationed at Pilot Knob, Mossouri, and was kept constantly alert by the raids of Price and Jeff Thompson. Carlin rose rapidly to be the commander of a brigade, and joined the forces in Tennessee in 1862. He dis- tinguished himself at Perryville and in the advance to Murfreesboro. At Stone's River his brigade, almost surrounded, repulsed an overwhelming force of Confederates. This picture was taken a year after that battle, while the brigade was in winter quarters at Ringgold, Georgia. The band-stand was built by the General's old regiment.

turnpike, which, after crossing the river, took the general direction of its course for some distance.

General Bragg did not lose a moment in marshaling his army into well-drawn battle-lines. His army was in two corps with a cavalry division under General Wheeler, Forrest and Morgan being on detached service. The left wing, under General Hardee, and the center, under Polk, were sent across Stone's River, the right wing, a division under John C. Breckinridge, remaining on the eastern side of the stream to guard the town. The line was three miles in length, and on December 30th the Federal host that had come from Nashville stood opposite, in a parallel line. It was also in three sections. The left wing, opposite Breckinridge, was commanded by Thomas L. Crittenden, whose brother was a commander in the Confederacy. They were sons of the famous United States senator from Kentucky, John J. Crittenden. The Federal center, opposite Polk, was commanded by George H. Thomas, and the right wing, opposing the Confederate left, was led by Alexander McD. McCook, one of the well-known "Fighting McCook" brothers. The effective Federal force was about forty-three thousand men; the Confederate army numbered about thirty-eight thousand. That night they bivouacked within musket range of each other and the camp-fires of each were clearly seen by the other as they shone through the cedar groves that interposed. Thus lay the two great armies, ready to spring upon each other in deadly combat with the coming of the morning.

Rosecrans had permitted McCook to thin out his lines over too much space, while on that very part of the field Bragg had concentrated his forces for the heaviest attack. The plans of battle made by the two opposing commanders were strikingly similar. Rosecrans' plan was to throw his left wing, under Crittenden, across the river upon the Confederate right under Breckinridge, to crush it in one impetuous dash, and to swing around through Murfreesboro to the Franklin road and

## MEN WHO LEARNED WAR WITH SHERMAN

The Twenty-first Michigan Infantry. In the Murfreesboro campaign, the regiment, detached from its old command, fought in the division of Brigadier-General "Phil" Sheridan, a leader who became scarcely less renowned in the West than Sherman and gave a good account of himself and his men at Stone's River. Most of the faces in the picture are those of boys, yet severe military service has already given them the unmistakable carriage of the soldier. The terrible field of Chickamauga lay before them, but a few months in the future; and after that, rejoining their beloved "Old Tecumseh," they were to march with him to the sea and witness some of the closing scenes in the struggle.

cut off the Confederate line of retreat. Bragg, on the other hand, intended to make a similar dash upon the Union right, pivot upon his center, press back McCook upon that center, crumpling the Federals and seizing the Nashville turnpike to cut off Rosecrans' retreat toward Nashville. Neither, of course, knew of the other's plan, and much would depend on who would strike first.

At the early light of the last day of the year the Confederate left wing moved upon the Union right in a magnificent battle-line, three-quarters of a mile in length and two columns deep. At the same time the Confederate artillery opened with their cannon. McCook was astonished at so fierce and sudden a charge. The gallant Patrick Cleburne, one of the ablest commanders in the Southern armies, led his division, which had been brought from the Confederate right, in the charge. The Federal lines were ill prepared for this sudden onslaught, and before McCook could arrange them several batteries were overpowered and eleven of the heavy guns were in the hands of the Confederates.

Slowly the Union troops fell back, firing as they went; but they had no power to check the impetuous, overwhelming charge of the onrushing foe. McCook's two right divisions, under Johnson and Jeff. C. Davis, were driven back, but his third division, which was commanded by a young officer who had attracted unusual attention at the battle of Perryville—Philip H. Sheridan—held its ground. At the first Confederate advance, Sill's brigade of Sheridan's division drove the troops in front of it back into their entrenchments, and in the charge the brave Sill lost his life.

While the battle raged with tremendous fury on the Union right, Rosecrans was three miles away, throwing his left across the river. Hearing the terrific roar of battle at the other end of the line, Rosecrans hastened to begin his attack on Breckinridge hoping to draw a portion of the Confederate force away from McCook. But as the hours of the forenoon

## FIGHTERS IN THE WEST

This picture of Company B of the Twenty-first Michigan shows impressively the type of men that the rough campaigning west of the Alleghanies had molded into veterans. These were Sherman's men, and under the watchful eye and in the inspiring presence of that general thousands of stalwart lads from the sparsely settled States were becoming the very bone and sinew of the Federal fighting force. The men of Sherman, like their leader, were forging steadily to the front. They had become proficient in the fighting which knows no fear, in many hard-won combats in the early part of the war. Greater and more magnificent conflicts awaited those who did not find a hero's grave.

passed he was dismayed as he noted that the sound of battle was coming nearer, and he rightly divined that his right wing was receding before the dashing soldiers of the South. He ordered McCook to dispute every inch of the ground; but Mc-Cook's command was soon torn to pieces and disorganized, except the division of Sheridan.

The latter stood firm against the overwhelming numbers, a stand that attracted the attention of the country and brought him military fame. He checked the onrushing Confederates at the point of the bayonet; he formed a new line under fire. In his first position Sheridan held his ground for two hours. The Confederate attack had also fallen heavily on Negley, who was stationed on Sheridan's left, and on Palmer, both of Thomas' center. Rousseau commanding the reserves, and Van Cleve of Crittenden's forces were ordered to the support of the Union center and right. Here, for two hours longer the battle raged with unabated fury, and the slaughter of brave men on both sides was appalling. Three times the whole Confederate left and center were thrown against the Union divisions, but failed to break the lines. At length when their cartridge boxes were empty Sheridan's men could do nothing but retire for more ammunition, and they did this in good order to a rolling plain near the Nashville road. But Rousseau of Thomas' center was there to check the Confederate advance.

It was now past noon, and still the battle roar resounded unceasingly through the woods and hills about Murfreesboro. Though both hosts had struggled and suffered since early morning, they still held to their guns, pouring withering volleys into each other's ranks. The Federal right and center had been forced back at right angles to the position they had held when day dawned; and the Confederate left was swung around at right angles to its position of the morning. The Federal left rested on Stone's River, while Bragg's right was on the same stream and close to the line in blue. Meantime, Rosecrans had massed his artillery on a little hill over-

## AN UNCEASING WORK OF WAR

In the picture the contraband laborers often pressed into service by Federals are repairing the "stringer" track near Murfreesboro after the battle of Stone's River. The long lines of single-track road, often involving a change from broad-gauge to narrow-gauge, were entirely inadequate for the movement of troops in that great area. In these isolated regions the railroads often became the supreme objective of both sides. When disinclined to offer battle, each struck in wild raids against the other's line of communication. Sections of track were tipped over embankments; rails were torn up, heated red-hot in bonfires, and twisted so that they could never be used again. The wrecking of a railroad might postpone a maneuver for months, or might terminate a campaign suddenly in defeat. Each side in retreat burned its bridges and destroyed the railroad behind it. Again advancing, each had to pause for the weary work of repair.

looking the field of action. He had also re-formed the broken lines of the right and center and called in twelve thousand fresh troops. Then, after a brief lull, the battle opened again and the ranks of both sides were torn with grape and canister and bursting shells.

In answer to Bragg's call for reenforcements came Breckinridge with all but one brigade of his division, a host of about seven thousand fresh troops. The new Confederate attack began slowly, but increased its speed at every step. Suddenly, a thundering volley burst from the line in blue, and the front ranks of the attacking column disappeared. Again, a volley tore through the ranks in gray, and the assault was abandoned.

The battle had raged for nearly eleven hours, when night enveloped the scene, and the firing abated slowly and died away. It had been a bloody day—this first day's fight at Stone's River—and except at Antietam it had not thus far been surpassed in the war. The advantage was clearly with the Confederates. They had pressed back the Federals for two miles, had routed their right wing and captured many prisoners and twenty-eight heavy guns. But Rosecrans determined to hold his ground and try again.

The next day was New Year's and but for a stray fusillade, here and there, both armies remained inactive, except that each quietly prepared to renew the contest on the morrow. The renewal of the battle on January 2nd was fully expected on both sides, but there was little fighting till four in the afternoon. Rosecrans had sent General Van Cleve's division on January 1st across the river to seize an elevation from which he could shell the town of Murfreesboro. Bragg now sent Breckinridge to dislodge the division, and he did so with splendid effect. But Breckinridge's men came into such a position as to be exposed to the raking fire of fifty-two pieces of Federal artillery on the west side of the river. Returning the deadly and constant fire as best they could, they stood the storm of shot and shell for half an hour when they retreated to a place

## ALONG THE HAZARDOUS ADVANCE FROM MURFREESBORO

Portion of the Bridgeport Bridge from Long Island to the East Bank of the Tennessee. The island, 1,232 feet at this point, divides the stream opposite Bridgeport, Alabama. The Union troops crossed at four points (at all of which the river was very wide), the division of Reynolds to the north of Bridgeport by means of captured boats, while that of Brannan crossed on rafts. The main crossing of McCook's Corps was at Caperton's Ferry, where the one complete pontoon-bridge had been laid. The army was all across by September 10th, but even greater difficulties now confronted it. The greatest of these obstacles were the steeps of Raccoon Mountain—the towering heights of Lookout Mountain rising before them, almost impassable to wagons and destitute of water. Beyond these, Missionary Ridge and a succession of lesser ranges must be crossed before Bragg's railroad connections with Atlanta could be struck at Dalton. Yet the trains which had already been brought across the Cumberland Mountains into Tennessee must ever be carried forward, loaded with twenty-five days' supplies and ammunition enough for the two great battles that were to follow.

of safety, leaving seventeen hundred of their number dead or wounded on the field. That night the two armies again lay within musket shot of each other. The next day brought no further conflict and during that night General Bragg moved away to winter quarters at Shelbyville, on the Elk River.

Murfreesboro, or Stone's River, was one of the great battles of the war. The losses were about thirteen thousand to the Federals and over ten thousand to the Confederates. Both sides claimed victory—the South because of Bragg's signal success on the first day; the North because of Breckinridge's fearful repulse at the final onset and of Bragg's retreating in the night and refusing to fight again. A portion of the Confederate army occupied Shelbyville, Tennessee, and the larger part entrenched at Tullahoma, eighteen miles to the southeast.

Six months after the battle of Stone's River, the Federal army suddenly awoke from its somnolent condition—a winter and spring spent in raids and unimportant skirmishes—and became very busy preparing for a long and hasty march. Rosecrans' plan of campaign was brilliant and proved most effective. He realized that Tullahoma was the barrier to Chattanooga, and determined to drive the Confederates from it.

On June 23, 1863, the advance began. The cavalry, under General Stanley, had received orders to advance upon Shelbyville on the 24th, and during that night to build immense and numerous camp-fires before the Confederate stronghold at Shelbyville, to create the impression that Rosecrans' entire army was massing at that point. But the wily leader of the Federals had other plans, and when Stanley, supported by General Granger, had built his fires, the larger force was closing in upon Tullahoma.

The stratagem dawned upon Bragg too late to check Rosecrans' plans. Stanley and Granger made a brilliant capture of Shelbyville, and Bragg retired to Tullahoma; but finding here that every disposition had been made to fall upon his rear, he continued his southward retreat toward Chattanooga.

# PART II
## OPENING THE MISSISSIPPI

---

# THE SIEGES OF VICKSBURG
# AND PORT HUDSON

---

CONFEDERATE FORTS THAT HELD THE STEEP RIVER-BANKS
AT PORT HUDSON, 1863

FEDERAL GUNS AND A CONFEDERATE CAMERA

The Second, Fourth, and Sixth Massachusetts Light Artillery at Baton Rouge, in May, 1862, photographed by Lytle, of the Confederate Secret Service. When Farragut's fleet, after the capture of New Orleans, moved up the Mississippi on May 2d, General Williams, with fourteen hundred men, including two sections of Everett's (Sixth) battery, accompanied it. The ambitious plan was the opening of the Mississippi and the establishment of communication with the Federal forces to the north. Occupying Baton Rouge, the expedition pushed on to Vicksburg. Here Farragut's guns could not be sufficiently elevated to silence the batteries on the bluff,

THE FIRST BATTERIES SENT AGAINST VICKSBURG

in the face of which Williams could not land.  After three weeks on the crowded transports, the men were returned to Baton Rouge and went into camp.  On the 20th of June, General Williams again set out for Vicksburg with four regiments and Nims's (Second) and Everett's (Sixth) Massachusetts batteries.  At Ellis's Bluff, and again at Grand Gulf, the troops drove off the Confederate field-batteries that opened on the gunboats.  But at Vicksburg no effective land attack could be made and the troops, whose numbers had been reduced by overwork, malaria, and scurvy from thirty-two hundred to but eight hundred fit for duty, returned to Baton Rouge.

FORWARDING THE RAW RECRUITS—CAIRO

In the fall of 1862 all the available river-steamers were busy transporting newly organized regiments from Cairo to Memphis to take part in the independent expedition against Vicksburg, which had been proposed by Major-General John A. McClernand and in command of which he had been placed by secret orders from Lincoln and Stanton. Not even Grant was informed of this division of authority. McClernand, who was influential in the West, raised in Indiana, Illinois, and Iowa some thirty regiments of volunteers, two-thirds of which had been forwarded to Cairo and Memphis by November 10th, and at the latter place were being drilled into shape by Sherman. Both Sherman and Grant supposed that they were the promised reënforcements for the expedition which they had planned together. On December 12th Sherman was ready to move, and on the 19th transports arrived at Memphis and the embarkation of the troops began. Next day they moved down the river, convoyed by Porter's fleet. On the 26th Sherman landed thirteen miles up the Yazoo River and advanced to Chickasaw Bluffs, where on the 29th he assaulted the defenses of Vicksburg to the north. The news of the failure of Grant's land expedition at Oxford had reached McClernand instead of Sherman, and as the latter general emerged from the swamps with his defeated divisions, McClernand, on New Year's Day, met him at the mouth of the Yazoo and superseded him in command.

FEDERAL TRANSPORTS ON THE MISSISSIPPI
ONE SMOKESTACK DAMAGED BY CONFEDERATE FIRE FROM THE RIVER BANK

## WHERE GRANT'S CAMPAIGN WAS HALTED

The Courthouse at Oxford, Mississippi.   The second attempt to capture Vicksburg originated with Grant. Since he had sprung into fame at Fort Donelson early in 1862, he had done little to strengthen his reputation; but to all urgings of his removal Lincoln replied: "I can't spare this man; he fights."   He proposed to push southward through Mississippi to seize Jackson, the capital.   If this could be accomplished, Vicksburg (fifty miles to the west) would become untenable.   At Washington his plan was overruled to the extent of dividing his forces.   Sherman, with a separate expedition, was to move from Memphis down the Mississippi directly against Vicksburg.   It was Grant's hope that by marching on he could unite with Sherman in an assault upon this key to the Mississippi.   Pushing forward from Grand Junction, sixty miles, Grant reached Oxford December 5, 1862, but his supplies were still drawn from Columbus, Kentucky, over a single-track road to Holly Springs, and thence by wagon over roads which were rapidly becoming impassable.   Delay ensued in which Van Dorn destroyed Federal stores at Holly Springs worth $1,500,000.   This put an end to Grant's advance.   In the picture we see an Illinois regiment guarding some of the 1200 Confederate prisoners taken during the advance and here confined in the Courthouse.

## VICKSBURG PROVES IMPREGNABLE

Chickasaw Bayou.   Here rested Sherman's extreme left, December 28, 1862, after a day's advance over bottom-lands of extreme difficulty.   From this point, after sharp skirmishing which discomforted the advancing Federals, at nightfall the Confederates retired to their works on the bluff beyond, confident of being able to repel the assault that was to come. That confidence was not misplaced.   Sherman had miscalculated in two particulars— chiefly in supposing that Grant was close at hand to support him.   Furthermore, he did not know that his movements had been daily reported and that Johnston and Pemberton were fully aware of his strength.   On the very day that Sherman landed on the Yazoo, Pemberton arrived in Vicksburg with reënforcements, bringing the garrison up to twelve thousand, while Sherman supposed that he was to contend with but half that number. Fully prepared for uncompromising defense, the Confederates were bound to win.

## WHERE SHERMAN FAILED

Chickasaw Bluffs. Stretching northeast from Vicksburg, Walnut Hill forms a perfect natural fortress overlooking the bottom-lands toward the Yazoo, rising to a height of two hundred feet, as seen in the picture. In the whole twelve miles between Haynes' Bluff (where Sherman landed) and Vicksburg, there were but five points where troops could pass from the Yazoo through the network of bayous and swamps to attack this bluff, and all these points were commanded by Confederate batteries. Sherman had considerable difficulty in properly posting his troops during the determined skirmishing kept up by the Confederates on the 28th. On the 29th, at noon, he gave the signal for the assault. The two brigades of De Courcy and Blair, together with the Fourth Iowa—six thousand men in all—bore the brunt of the fighting and charged gallantly up to the Confederate works. There, unsupported, they were cut to pieces by the cross-fire that was poured upon them. Sherman, who had lost nearly two thousand, decided that the position was impregnable. A thousand men could have held it against ten times their number.

THE LEADER AT HAYNES' BLUFF

U. S. S. *Choctaw*, resting peacefully at Vicksburg after the surrender. She had led the other gunboats in the attack upon Haynes' Bluff on the Yazoo, simultaneous with Sherman's second demonstration against the defenses northeast of Vicksburg. Grant distracted Pemberton long enough to enable the Federals to concentrate to the south of the city for its final investment. Since the end of January, Grant (again in supreme command) had been working hard with tentative operations, first for the completion of the canal begun by General Williams the previous year, then for the cutting of the levee at Yazoo Pass to flood the bottom-lands and enable gunboats to engage in amphibious warfare.

"WHISTLING DICK"—THE PET OF THE CONFEDERATE GUNNERS

This 18-pounder rifle, made at the Tredegar Iron Works at Richmond, was mounted in the Vicksburg water-batteries overlooking the Mississippi. Porter's fleet was exposed to its fire when it passed down the river on the night of April 16, 1863. From the peculiar sound of its missiles speeding through the air it earned the nickname "Whistling Dick." It was a monster of its time; its fire sunk the Federal gunboat *Cincinnati* on May 28th. Finally it was disabled and silenced by the Federal batteries from across the river.

# VICKSBURG AND PORT HUDSON

On the banks of this, the greatest river in the world, the most decisive and far-reaching battle of the war was fought. Here at Vicksburg over one hundred thousand gallant soldiers and a powerful fleet of gunboats and ironclads in terrible earnestness for forty days and nights fought to decide whether the new Confederate States should be cut in twain; whether the great river should flow free to the Gulf, or should have its commerce hindered. We all know the result—the Union army under General Grant, and the Union navy under Admiral Porter were victorious. The Confederate army, under General Pemberton, numbering thirty thousand men, was captured and General Grant's army set free for operating in other fields. It was a staggering blow from which the Confederacy never rallied.—*Lieutenant-General Stephen D. Lee, C.S.A., at the dedication of the Massachusetts Volunteers' statue at the Vicksburg National Military Park, Vicksburg, Mississippi, November 14, 1903.*

THE Mississippi River, in its lower course, winds like a mighty serpent from side to side along a vast alluvial bottom, which in places is more than forty miles in width. On the eastern bank, these great coils here and there sweep up to the bluffs of the highlands of Tennessee and Mississippi. On these cliffs are situated Memphis, Port Hudson, Grand Gulf, and Vicksburg. The most important of these from a military point of view was Vicksburg, often called the "Gibraltar of the West." Situated two hundred feet above the current, on a great bend of the river, its cannon could command the waterway for miles in either direction, while the obstacles in the way of a land approach were almost equally insurmountable.

The Union arms had captured New Orleans, in the spring of 1862, and Memphis in June of that year; but the Confederates still held Vicksburg and Port Hudson and the two hundred and fifty miles of river that lies between them. The military

## WHERE VICKSBURG'S FATE WAS SEALED

The Battle-field of Champion's Hill. Here on May 16, 1863, Grant crowned his daring maneuver against Vicksburg from the south with complete success. Once across the river below Grand Gulf, after an easy victory at Port Gibson, he was joined by Sherman. The army struck out across the strange country south of the Big Black River and soon had driven Pemberton's southern outposts across that stream. Grant was now on solid ground; he had successfully turned the flank of the Confederates and he grasped the opportunity to strike a telling blow. Pressing forward to Raymond and Jackson, he captured both, and swept westward to meet the astounded Pemberton, still vacillating between attempting a junction with Johnston or attacking Grant in the rear. But Grant, moving with wonderful precision, prevented either movement. On May 16th a battle ensued which was most decisive around Champion's Hill. Pemberton was routed and put to flight, and on the next day the Federals seized the crossings of the Big Black River. Spiking their guns at Haynes' Bluff, the Confederates retired into Vicksburg, never to come out again except as prisoners. In eighteen days from the time he crossed the Mississippi, Grant had gained the advantage for which the Federals had striven for more than a year at Vicksburg.

object of the Federal armies in the West was to gain control of the entire course of the great Mississippi that it might "roll unvexed to the sea," to use Lincoln's terse expression, and that the rich States of the Southwest, from which the Confederacy drew large supplies and thousands of men for her armies, might be cut off from the rest of the South. If Vicksburg were captured, Port Hudson must fall. The problem, therefore, was how to get control of Vicksburg.

On the promotion of Halleck to the command of all the armies of the North, with headquarters at Washington, Grant was left in superior command in the West and the great task before him was the capture of the "Gibraltar of the West." Vicksburg might have been occupied by the Northern armies at any time during the first half of the year 1862, but in June of that year General Bragg sent Van Dorn with a force of fifteen thousand to occupy and fortify the heights. Van Dorn was a man of prodigious energy. In a short time he had hundreds of men at work planting batteries, digging rifle-pits above the water front and in the rear of the town, mounting heavy guns and building bomb-proof magazines in tiers along the hillsides. All through the summer, the work progressed under the direction of Engineer S. H. Lockett, and by the coming of winter the city was a veritable Gibraltar.

From the uncompleted batteries on the Vicksburg bluffs, the citizens and the garrison soldiers viewed the advance division of Farragut's fleet, under Commander Lee, in the river, on May 18, 1862. Fifteen hundred infantry were on board, under command of General Thomas Williams, and with them was a battery of artillery. Williams reconnoitered the works, and finding them too strong for his small force he returned to occupy Baton Rouge. The authorities at Washington now sent Farragut peremptory orders to clear the Mississippi and accordingly about the middle of June, a flotilla of steamers and seventeen mortar schooners, under Commander D. D. Porter, departed from New Orleans and steamed up the river.

THE BRIDGE THE CONFEDERATES BURNED AT BIG BLACK RIVER

THE FIRST FEDERAL CROSSING—SHERMAN'S PONTOONS

The pursuit of Pemberton's army brought McClernand's Corps to the defenses of the Big Black River Bridge early on May 17, 1863. McPherson was close behind. McClernand's division carried the defenses and Bowen and Vaughn's men fled with precipitate haste over the dreary swamp to the river and crossed over and burned the railroad and other bridges just in time to prevent McClernand from following. The necessary delay was aggravating to Grant's forces. The rest of the day and night was consumed in building bridges. Sherman had the only pontoon-train with the army and his bridge was the first ready at Bridgeport, early in the evening.

Simultaneously Farragut headed a fleet of three war vessels and seven gunboats, carrying one hundred and six guns, toward Vicksburg from Baton Rouge. Many transports accompanied the ships from Baton Rouge, on which there were three thousand of Williams' troops.

The last days of June witnessed the arrival of the combined naval forces of Farragut and Porter below the Confederate stronghold. Williams immediately disembarked his men on the Louisiana shore, opposite Vicksburg, and they were burdened with implements required in digging trenches and building levees.

The mighty Mississippi, at this point and in those days, swept in a majestic bend and formed a peninsula of the western, or Louisiana shore. Vicksburg was situated on the eastern, or Mississippi shore, below the top of the bend. Its batteries of cannon commanded the river approach for miles in either direction. Federal engineers quickly recognized the strategic position of the citadel on the bluff; and also as quickly saw a method by which the passage up and down the river could be made comparatively safe for their vessels, and at the same time place Vicksburg " high and dry " by cutting a channel for the Mississippi through the neck of land that now held it in its sinuous course.

While Farragut stormed the Confederate batteries at Vicksburg, Williams began the tremendous task of diverting the mighty current across the peninsula. Farragut's bombardment by his entire fleet failed to silence Vicksburg's cannon-guards, although the defenders likewise failed to stop the progress of the fleet. The Federal naval commander then determined to dash past the fortifications, trusting to the speed of his vessels and the stoutness of their armor to survive the tremendous cannonade that would fall upon his flotilla. Early in the morning of June 28th the thrilling race against death began, and after two hours of terrific bombardment aided by the mortar boats stationed on both banks, Farragut's fleet with

*Vicksburg, taken under fire.*

## THE GATE TO THE MISSISSIPPI

The handwriting is that of Surgeon Bixby, of the Union hospital ship "Red Rover." In his album he pasted this unique photograph from the western shore of the river where the Federal guns and mortars threw a thousand shells into Vicksburg during the siege. The prominent building is the courthouse, the chief landmark during the investment. Here at Vicksburg the Confederates were making their last brave stand for the possession of the Mississippi River, that great artery of traffic. If it were wre ted from them the main source of their supplies would be cut off. Pemberton, a brave and capable officer and a Pennsylvanian by birth, worked unremittingly for the cause he had espoused. Warned by the early attacks of General Williams and Admiral Farragut, he had left no stone unturned to render Vicksburg strongly defended. It had proved impregnable to attack on the north and east, and the powerful batteries planted on the river-front could not be silenced by the fleet nor by the guns of the Federals on the opposite shore. But Grant's masterful maneuver of cutting loose from his base and advancing from the south had at last out-generaled both Pemberton and Johnston. Nevertheless, Pemberton stoutly held his defenses. His high river-battery is photographed below, as it frowned upon the Federals opposite.

the exception of three vessels passed through the raging inferno to the waters above Vicksburg, with a loss of fifteen killed and thirty wounded. On the 1st of July Flag-Officer Davis with his river gunboats arrived from Memphis and joined Farragut.

Williams and his men, including one thousand negroes, labored like Titans to complete their canal, but a sudden rise of the river swept away the barriers with a terrific roar, and the days of herculean labor went for naught. Again Williams' attempt to subdue the stronghold was abandoned, and he returned with his men when Farragut did, on July 24th, to Baton Rouge to meet death there on August 5th when General Breckinridge made a desperate but unsuccessful attempt to drive the Union forces from the Louisiana capital.

Farragut urged upon General Halleck the importance of occupying the city on the bluff with a portion of his army; but that general gave no heed; and while even then it was too late to secure the prize without a contest, it would have been easy in comparison to that which it required a year later.

In the mean time, the river steamers took an important part in the preliminary operations against the city. Davis remained at Memphis with his fleet for about three weeks after the occupation of that city on the 6th of June, meanwhile sending four gunboats and a transport up the White River, with the Forty-sixth Indiana regiment, under Colonel Fitch. The object of the expedition, undertaken at Halleck's command, was to destroy Confederate batteries and to open communication with General Curtis, who was approaching from the west. It failed in the latter purpose but did some effective work with the Southern batteries along the way.

The one extraordinary incident of the expedition was the disabling of the *Mound City,* one of the ironclad gunboats, and the great loss of life that it occasioned. When near St. Charles the troops under Fitch were landed, and the *Mound City* moving up the river, was fired on by concealed batteries

## THE WELL–DEFENDED CITADEL

Behind these fortifications Pemberton, driven from the Big Black River, gathered his twenty-one thousand troops to make the last stand for the saving of the Mississippi to the Confederacy. In the upper picture we see Fort Castle, one of the strongest defenses of the Confederacy. It had full sweep of the river; here "Whistling Dick" (one of the most powerful guns in possession of the South) did deadly work. In the lower picture we see the fortifications to the east of the town, before which Grant's army was now entrenching. When Vicksburg had first been threatened in 1862, the Confederate fortifications had been laid out and work begun on them in haste with but five hundred spades, many of the soldiers delving with their bayonets. The sites were so well chosen and the work so well done that they had withstood attacks for a year. They were to hold out still longer. By May 18th the Federals had completely invested Vicksburg, and Grant and Sherman rode out to Haynes' Bluff to view the open river to the north, down which abundant supplies were now coming for the army. Sherman, who had not believed that the plan could succeed, frankly acknowledged his mistake. But the Mississippi was not yet theirs. Sherman, assaulting the fortifications of Vicksburg, the next day, was repulsed. A second attack, on the 22d, failed and on the 25th Grant settled down to starve Pemberton out.

under the direction of Lieutenant Dunnington.  A 32-pound shot struck the vessel, crashed through the side and passed through the steam-drum.  The steam filled the vessel in an instant.  Many of the men were so quickly enveloped in the scalding vapor that they had no chance to escape.  Others leaped overboard, some being drowned and some rescued through the efforts of the *Conestoga* which was lying near.  While straining every nerve to save their lives, the men had to endure a shower of bullets from Confederate sharpshooters on the river banks.  Of the one hundred and seventy-five officers and men of the *Mound City* only twenty-five escaped death or injury in that fearful catastrophe.  Meanwhile, Colonel Fitch with his land forces rushed upon the Confederate batteries and captured them.  The unfortunate vessel was at length repaired and returned to service.

For some time it had been known in Federal military and naval circles that a powerful ironclad similar to the famous *Monitor* of Eastern waters was being rushed to completion up the Yazoo.  The new vessel was the *Arkansas*.  She and a sister ship were building at Memphis when the capture of that city was anticipated by the destruction of one of them.  The work on the *Arkansas* was far enough advanced for her to be taken to Yazoo City for the finishing touches.  The Union fleet was not unduly terrified by tales of the monster, but nevertheless Farragut and Davis determined to find out what they could about her.  Three vessels were chosen for the reconnaissance— the ironclad *Carondelet,* the wooden *Tyler,* and the Ellet ram *Queen of the West*.  Bravely they steamed up the Yazoo on the morning of July 15th, but before they had gone more than six miles they encountered the *Arkansas,* under the command of Captain Isaac N. Brown, coming down the river.

The *Carondelet,* though supported at a distance by the *Tyler,* fled before her stronger antagonist, being raked from stem to stern, struck several times with solid shot, and saved from destruction only by running into shallow water where

[ 196 ]

## THE WORK OF THE BESIEGERS

Battery Sherman, on the Jackson Road, before Vicksburg. Settling down to a siege did not mean idleness for Grant's army. Fortifications had to be opposed to the formidable one of the Confederates and a constant bombardment kept up to silence their guns, one by one. It was to be a drawn-out duel in which Pemberton, hoping for the long-delayed relief from Johnston, held out bravely against starvation and even mutiny. For twelve miles the Federal lines stretched around Vicksburg, investing it to the river bank, north and south. More than eighty-nine battery positions were constructed by the Federals. Battery Sherman was exceptionally well built—not merely revetted with rails or cotton-bales and floored with rough timber, as lack of proper material often made necessary. Gradually the lines were drawn closer and closer as the Federals moved up their guns to silence the works that they had failed to take in May. At the time of the surrender Grant had more than 220 guns in position, mostly of heavy caliber. By the 1st of July besieged and besiegers faced each other at a distance of half-pistol shot. Starving and ravaged by disease, the Confederates had repelled repeated attacks which depleted their forces, while Grant, reenforced to three times their number, was showered with supplies and ammunition that he might bring about the long-delayed victory which the North had been eagerly awaiting since Chancellorsville.

the *Arkansas* could not follow her. The *Arkansas* was injured also and her brave captain was twice wounded; but, not being disabled, she steamed on and out into the Mississippi, driving the *Tyler* and the *Queen* before her. A few miles above Vicksburg the *Arkansas* ran into the midst of the Federal fleet. She steamed slowly through the maze of hostile vessels, and the tempest of broadsides, returning them with the utmost steadiness, until she was safely lodged under the guns of Vicksburg.

But the day's events were not ended. In the dusk of evening, all of Farragut's fleet accompanied by the ram *Sumter* stole down the river to finish the plucky *Arkansas*. But she changed her position as soon as it was dark and the Union vessels had difficulty in finding her. They came down the river amid the roar of cannon, but only one 11-inch shot struck her as the fleet went by, and down the river, and the broadsides from the *Arkansas* killed five and wounded sixteen of the Union crews. None of Farragut's fleet was ever seen above Vicksburg again. It returned to New Orleans, July 24th.

The *Arkansas* had another fight for her life on July 22d. Commander William D. Porter with the *Essex*, aided by the *Queen of the West,* made the attack. The crew of the *Arkansas* had been reduced by half, but the remainder fought savagely and saved their vessel from destruction.

The month of July had not been favorable to the Federal hopes. Farragut had returned to New Orleans. General Williams had gone with him as far as Baton Rouge. Davis now went with his fleet back to Helena. Halleck was succeeded by Grant. Vicksburg entered upon a period of quiet.

But this condition was temporary. The city's experience of blood and fire had only begun. During the summer and autumn of 1862, the one thought uppermost in the mind of General Grant was how to gain possession of the stronghold. He was already becoming known for his bull-dog tenacity. In the autumn, two important changes took place, but one day apart. On October 14th, General John C. Pemberton

# A GOOD POLITICIAN WHO BECAME A GREAT SOLDIER

## MAJOR–GENERAL JOHN ALEXANDER LOGAN AND STAFF IN VICKSBURG, JULY, 1863

John A. Logan, a War Democrat who left Congress to fight as a private in a Michigan regiment at Bull Run, was one of the mainstays of the Federal cause in the West. A successful lawyer and brilliant orator, he proved to be one of the most successful civilian generals of the war. In Grant's Vicksburg campaign, Logan's soldierly qualities came particularly into prominence. His division of McPherson's Corps distinguished itself in the battle of Raymond, Mississippi, and again at that of Champion's Hill, which sounded the knell of Vicksburg. It was Logan's division that marched in on the Jackson road to take possession of the fallen city, July 4, 1863. For his services in the campaign Logan was made a major-general.

succeeded Van Dorn in command of the defenses of Vicksburg, and on the next day David D. Porter succeeded Davis as commander of the Federal fleet on the upper Mississippi.

So arduous was the task of taking Vicksburg that the wits of General Grant, and those of his chief adviser, General W. T. Sherman, were put to the test in the last degree to accomplish the end. Grant knew that the capture of this fortified city was of great importance to the Federal cause, and that it would ever be looked upon as one of the chief acts in the drama of the Civil War.

The first plan attempted was to divide the army, Sherman taking part of it from Memphis and down the Mississippi on transports, while Grant should move southward along the line of the Mississippi Central Railroad to cooperate with Sherman, his movements to be governed by the efforts of the scattered Confederate forces in Mississippi to block him. But the whole plan was destined to failure, through the energies of General Van Dorn and others of the Confederate army near Grant's line of communication.

The authorities at Washington preferred the river move upon Vicksburg, as the navy could keep the line of communication open. The stronghold now stood within a strong line of defense extending from Haynes' Bluff on the Yazoo to Grand Gulf on the Mississippi, thirty miles below Vicksburg. To prepare for Sherman's attack across the swamps of the Yazoo, Admiral Porter made several expeditions up that tortuous stream to silence batteries and remove torpedoes. In one of these he lost one of the Eads ironclads, the *Cairo*, blown up by a torpedo, and in another the brave Commander Gwin, one of the heroes of Shiloh, was mortally wounded.

Sherman, with an army of thirty-two thousand men, left Memphis on December 20th, and landed a few days later some miles north of Vicksburg on the banks of the Yazoo. On the 29th he made a daring attack in three columns on the Confederate lines of defense at Chickasaw Bayou and suffered a

## INVESTING BY INCHES

Logan's Division undermining the most formidable redoubt in the defenses of Vicksburg. The position was immediately in front of this honeycombed slope on the Jackson road. Upon these troops fell most of the labor of sapping and mining, which finally resulted in the wrecking of the fort so gallantly defended by the veterans of the Third Louisiana. As the Federal lines crept up, the men working night and day were forced to live in burrows. They became proficient in such gopher work as the picture shows. Up to the "White House" (Shirley's) the troops could be marched in comparative safety, but a short distance beyond they were exposed to the Confederate sharpshooters, who had only rifles and muskets to depend on; their artillery had long since been silenced. Near this house was constructed "Coonskin's" Tower; it was built of railway iron and cross-ties under the direction of Second Lieutenant Henry C. Foster, of Company B, Twenty-third Indiana. A backwoodsman and dead-shot, he was particularly active in paying the Confederate sharpshooters in their own coin. He habitually wore a cap of raccoon fur, which gave him his nickname and christened the tower, from which the interior of the Confederate works could be seen.

decisive repulse. His loss was nearly two thousand men; the Confederate loss was scarcely two hundred.

Two hundred feet above the bayou, beyond where the Federals were approaching, towered the Chickasaw Bluffs, to which Pemberton hastened troops from Vicksburg as soon as he learned Sherman's object. At the base of the bluff, and stretching away to the north and west were swamps and forests intersected by deep sloughs, overhung with dense tangles of vines and cane-brakes. Federal valor vied with Confederate pluck in this fight among the marshes and fever-infested jungle-land.

One of Sherman's storming parties, under General G. W. Morgan, came upon a broad and deep enlargement of the bayou, McNutt Lake, which interposed between it and the Confederates in the rifle-pits on the slopes and crest of the bluff. In the darkness of the night of December 28th, the Federal pontoniers labored to construct a passage-way across the lake. When morning dawned the weary pontoniers were chagrined to discover their well-built structure spanning a slough leading in another direction than toward the base of the bluff. The bridge was quickly taken up, and the Federals recommenced their labors, this time in daylight and within sight and range of the Southern regiments on the hill. The men in blue worked desperately to complete the span before driven away by the foe's cannon; but the fire increased with every minute, and the Federals finally withdrew.

Another storming party attempted to assail the Confederates from across a sandbar of the bayou, but was halted at the sight and prospect of overcoming a fifteen-foot bank on the farther side. The crumbling bank was surmounted with a levee three feet high; the steep sides of the barrier had crumbled away, leaving an overhanging shelf, two feet wide. Two companies of the Sixth Missouri regiment volunteered to cross the two hundred yards of exposed passage, and to cut a roadway through the rotten bank to allow their comrades a free

THE FIRST MONUMENT AT THE MEETING PLACE

Independence Day, 1863, was a memorable anniversary of the nation's birth; it brought to the anxious North the momentous news that Meade had won at Gettysburg and that Vicksburg had fallen in the West. The marble shaft in the picture was erected to mark the spot where Grant and Pemberton met on July 3d to confer about the surrender. Under a tree, within a few hundred feet of the Confederate lines, Grant greeted his adversary as an old acquaintance. They had fought in the same division for a time in the Mexican War. Each spoke but two sentences as to the surrender, for Grant lived up to the nickname he gained at Donelson, and Pemberton's pride was hurt. The former comrades walked and talked awhile on other things, and then returned to their lines. Next day the final terms were arranged by correspondence, and the Confederates marched out with colors flying; they stacked their arms and, laying their colors upon them, marched back into the city to be paroled. Those who signed the papers not to fight until exchanged numbered 29,391. The tree where the commanders met was soon carried away, root and branch, by relic-hunters. Subsequently the monument which replaced it was chipped gradually into bits, and in 1866 a 64-pounder cannon took its place as a permanent memorial.

VICKSBURG IN POSSESSION OF THE FEDERALS

path to the bluff beyond. To add to the peril of the crossing, the sandbar was strewn with tangles of undergrowth and fallen trees, and the Confederate shells and bullets were raining upon the ground. Still, the gallant troops began their dash. From the very start, a line of wounded and dead Missourians marked the passage of the volunteers. The survivors reached the bank and desperately sought to dig the roadway. From the shrubbery on the bank suddenly appeared Confederate sharpshooters who poured their fire into the laboring soldiers; the flame of the discharging muskets burned the clothing of the Federals because the hostile forces were so close. Human endurance could not stand before this carnage, and the brave Missourians fled from the inferno. Sherman now found the northern pathway to Vicksburg impassable, and withdrew his men to the broad Mississippi.

Earlier in the same month had occurred two other events which, with the defeat of Chickasaw, go to make up the triple disaster to the Federals. On the 11th, General Nathan Forrest, one of the most brilliant cavalry leaders on either side, began one of those destructive raids which characterize the Civil War. With twenty-five hundred horsemen, Forrest dashed unopposed through the country north of Grant's army, tore up sixty miles of railroad and destroyed all telegraph lines.

Meantime, on December 20th, the day on which Sherman left Memphis, General Van Dorn pounced upon Holly Springs, in Mississippi, like an eagle on its prey, capturing the guard of fifteen hundred men and burning the great store of supplies, worth $1,500,000, which Grant had left there. Through the raids of Forrest and Van Dorn, Grant was left without supplies and for eleven days without communication with the outside world. He marched northward to Grand Junction, in Tennessee, a distance of eighty miles, living off the country. It was not until January 8, 1863, that he heard, through Washington, of the defeat of Sherman in his assault on Chickasaw Bluffs.

[204]

SHIRLEY'S RESIDENCE, "THE WHITE HOUSE"

KEEPING THE MISSISSIPPI
OPEN

Illinois sent into the war Grant, Logan, McClernand, Grierson, and other prominent leaders in the Vicksburg campaign. It was one of the few States which furnished troops in excess of their quota. The Seventy-second Illinois Infantry, whose synonym was "First Board of Trade," together with other Illinois regiments, saw severe active service along the Mississippi and at Vicksburg; it served in General McArthur's division of the Seventeenth Corps, and distinguished itself on November 30th of the following year in the battle of Franklin, Tenn.

BARRACKS OF FIFTH U. S. COLORED HEAVY ARTILLERY

VICKSBURG IN FEDERAL
HANDS

Shirley's "White House," on the Jackson road, stood between the opposing lines; although a target for both sides, it remained practically uninjured. General Lieb's colored regiment was recruited in Louisiana and Mississippi and organized at Vicksburg in August, 1863. It suffered a heavy loss in deaths from fever, being stationed along the river. In the assault on Port Hudson colored troops were first used by the Federals in a general engagement — the First Louisiana Native Guard of the "Corps d'Afrique," organized by General Butler.

HEADQUARTERS 72ND ILLINOIS VOLUNTEERS

Grant and Sherman had no thought of abandoning Vicksburg because of this failure. But a month of unfortunate military dissension over rank in the command of Sherman's army resulted in General John A. McClernand, armed with authority from Washington, coming down from Illinois and superseding Sherman. On January 11, 1864, he captured Arkansas Post, a stronghold on the Arkansas River. But Grant, having authority to supersede McClernand in the general proceedings against Vicksburg, did so, on January 30th, and arguments on military precedence were forgotten.

Grant was determined to lead his Army of the Tennessee below Vicksburg and approach the city from the south, without breaking with his base of supplies up the river. Two projects, both of which were destined to fail, were under way during the winter and spring months of 1863. One of these was to open a way for the river craft through Lake Providence, west of the Mississippi, through various bayous and rivers into the Red River, a detour of four hundred miles.

Another plan was to cut a channel through the peninsula of the great bend of the Mississippi, opposite Vicksburg. For six weeks, thousands of men worked like marmots digging this ditch; but, meantime, the river was rising and, on March 8th, it broke over the embankment and the men had to run for their lives. Many horses were drowned and a great number of implements submerged. The "Father of Waters" had put a decisive veto on the project and it had to be given up. Still another plan that failed was to cut through the Yazoo Pass and approach from the north by way of the Coldwater, the Tallahatchie, and the Yazoo rivers.

Failure with Grant only increased his grim determination. He *would* take Vicksburg. His next plan was destined to bring success. It was to transfer his army by land down the west bank of the Mississippi to a point below the city and approach it from the south and west. This necessitated the running of the batteries by Porter's fleet—an extremely

## THE CONFEDERACY CUT IN TWAIN

The Levee at Vicksburg, February, 1864.   For seven months the Federals had been in possession of the city, and the Mississippi—now open through its entire course—cut off the struggling Confederacy in the East from the South and Southwest, the storehouses of their resources and their main dependence in continuing the struggle.   But even such a blow as this, coming on top of Gettysburg, did not force the brave people of the South to give up the struggle.   In the picture the only remaining warlike signs are the tents on the opposite shore.   But on both sides of the river the Confederates were still desperately striving to reunite their territory.   In the East another year and more of the hardest kind of fighting was ahead; another severing in twain of the South was inevitable before peace could come, and before the muskets could be used to shoot the crows, and before their horses could plough the neglected fields.

GUNS THAT HELPED TO REDUCE PORT HUDSON

This picture is another example of the accuracy and completeness with which Lytle, the Confederate Secret Service photographer at Baton Rouge, recorded the numbers and equipment of the Federal forces operating in Louisiana. This body of artillery first enlisted as the Twenty-first Volunteers in 1861, and sustained the heavy loss of one hundred and twenty-six men while acting as infantry in the battle of Baton Rouge, August 5, 1862. It served with distinction throughout the war, its number of veteran reënlistments being five hundred and three—the largest in any body of Indiana troops. In March, 1863, the regiment was changed to artillery; and in Augur's division of the Nineteenth Corps it accompanied General Banks in his first expedition against Port Hudson, as well as in the final investment of that place. Banks, who had been sent with between fifteen thousand and twenty thousand troops to suc-

FIRST INDIANA HEAVY ARTILLERY, 1863

ceed General Butler in command of the Department of the Gulf, arrived at New Orleans in the middle of December, 1862, with orders from Halleck to advance up the Mississippi, and (in coöperation with Grant) to hold an unbroken line of communication by land from New Orleans to Vicksburg.   When this was accomplished he was to occupy the Red River country as a basis for future operations against Texas.   During the winter, Banks confined his attention to operations west of the Mississippi, with varying success.   Early in March, at the request of Farragut, who had determined to run past the Port Hudson batteries with his fleet, Banks moved forward with about seventeen thousand men to make a demonstration against that place with his artillery.   He did not get near enough to do this, however, and was still building bridges when near midnight of March 14th Farragut's guns began to boom from the river.

## THE LAST STRONGHOLD ON THE MISSISSIPPI

Confederate Fortifications on the bluff overlooking the Mississippi at Port Hudson, Louisiana.    At Port Hudson the east bank of the river rises steeply in a bluff eighty feet high, forming a perfect natural fortress. When Breckinridge failed in his attempt to recapture Baton Rouge in 1862, he retired to Port Hudson, thirty miles farther up the river, and by the middle of August the fortifying of that place was well advanced, the object being to hold the Mississippi between this point and Vicksburg, so that supplies coming from Arkansas by way of the Red River would not be cut off from the Confederacy.    Within the heavy parapets, twenty feet thick, the Confederates mounted twenty siege-guns along the bluff, completely commanding the river.    It was therefore no light task that Farragut took upon himself when on the night of March 14th he attempted to run by these batteries with his fleet.    Five of his seven vessels were disabled, the *Mississippi* running aground and being abandoned and burned by her commander.    Farragut, in the famous *Hartford*, with the *Albatross* lashed to her side, barely escaped running aground under the guns of the batteries in the darkness.    Finally he got safely by, and the object of the gallant fight was accomplished.

## THE WELL–PLANTED BATTERIES

Confederate Siege-gun Mounted in the River Fortifications at Port Hudson.   Twenty of these great pieces thundered at Farragut's fleet till long after midnight on March 14, 1863.   Although the objective was not so important to the Federals as in the famous fight at New Orleans, the engagement at Port Hudson was scarcely less brilliant, and its outcome was more costly to the navy, which lost the valuable steam corvette *Mississippi*, mounting nineteen guns.   The fleet lost 113 men in action.   Farragut had the superiority in number and weight of metal, but this was more than offset by the advantageous position of the Confederates.   A successful shot from the ship could do little more than tear up the earth in the fortifications on the bluff, while every shot from the shore that told might mean the piercing of a boiler or the disabling of a rudder, rendering a ship helpless.   To add to the disadvantages, Farragut's intention was discovered at the outset.   A river steamer approached with flaring lights and tooting whistles and ran through the fleet, up to the *Hartford*, merely bringing the word that Banks was within five miles of Port Hudson.   Thus the fleet was discovered and the Confederates, illuminating the river with piles of blazing pine-knots, trained their guns with deadly precision on the advancing vessels.

[B]

perilous enterprise. The army was divided into four corps, commanded respectively by Sherman, McClernand, McPherson, and Hurlbut. The latter was stationed at Memphis. On March 29th, the movement of McClernand from Milliken's Bend to a point opposite Grand Gulf was begun. He was soon followed by McPherson and a few weeks later by Sherman. It required a month for the army, with its heavy artillery, to journey through the swamps and bogs of Louisiana.

While this march was in progress, something far more exciting was taking place on the river. Porter ran the batteries of Vicksburg with his fleet. After days of preparation the fleet of vessels, protected by cotton bales and hay about the vital parts of the boats, with heavy logs slung near the water-line—seven gunboats, the ram *General Price,* three transports, and various barges were ready for the dangerous journey on the night of April 16th. Silently in the darkness, they left their station near the mouth of the Yazoo, at a quarter past nine. For an hour and a half all was silence and expectancy. The bluffs on the east loomed black against the night sky. Suddenly, the flash of musketry fire pierced the darkness.

In a few minutes every battery overlooking the river was a center of spurting flame. A storm of shot and shell was rained upon the passing vessels. Not one escaped being struck many times. The water of the river was lashed into foam by the shots and shell from the batteries. The gunboats answered with their cannon. The air was filled with flying missiles. Several houses on the Louisiana shore burst into flame and the whole river from shore to shore was lighted with vivid distinctness. A little later, a giant flame leaped from the bosom of the river. A vessel had caught fire. It was the transport *Henry Clay.* It burned to the water's edge, nearly all its crew escaping to other vessels. Grant described the scene as "magnificent, but terrible"; Sherman pronounced it "truly sublime."

By three in the morning, the fleet was below the city and ready to cooperate with the army. One vessel had been

## WITHIN THE PARAPET AT PORT HUDSON IN THE SUMMER OF 1863

These fortifications withstood every attack of Banks' powerful army from May 24 to July 9, 1863. Like Vicksburg, Port Hudson could be reduced only by a weary siege. These pictures, taken within the fortifications, show in the distance the ground over which the investing army approached to the two unsuccessful grand assaults they made upon the Confederate defenders. The strength of the works is apparent. A continuous line of parapet, equally strong, had been thrown up for the defense of Port Hudson, surrounding the town for a distance of three miles and more, each end terminating on the river-bank. Four powerful forts were located at the salients, and the line throughout was defended by thirty pieces of field artillery. Brigadier-General Beall, who commanded the post in 1862, constructed these works. Major-General Frank Gardner succeeded him in command at the close of the year.

THE WELL–DEFENDED WORKS

CONFEDERATE FORTIFICATIONS BEFORE PORT HUDSON

Gardner was behind these defenses with a garrison of about seven thousand when Banks approached Port Hudson for the second time on May 24th. Gardner was under orders to evacuate the place and join his force to that of Johnston at Jackson, Mississippi, but the courier who brought the order arrived at the very hour when Banks began to bottle up the Confederates. On the morning of May 25th Banks drove in the Confederate skirmishers and outposts and, with an army of thirty thousand, invested the fortifications from the eastward. At 10 A.M., after an artillery duel of more than four hours, the Federals advanced to the assault of the works. Fighting in a dense forest of magnolias, amid thick undergrowth and among ravines choked with felled timber, the progress of the troops was too slow for a telling attack. The battle has been described as "a gigantic bushwhack." The Federals at the center reached the ditch in front of the Confederate works but were driven off. At nightfall the attempt was abandoned. It had cost Banks nearly two thousand men.

destroyed, several others were crippled; thirteen men had been wounded, but Grant had the assistance he needed. About a week later, six more transports performed the same feat and ran the batteries; each had two barges laden with forage and rations in tow.

Grant's next move was to transfer the army across the river and to secure a base of supplies. There, on the bluff, was Grand Gulf, a tempting spot. But the Confederate guns showed menacingly over the brow of the hill. After a fruitless bombardment by the fleet on April 29th, it was decided that a more practical place to cross the river must be sought below.

Meanwhile, Sherman was ordered by his chief to advance upon the formidable Haynes' Bluff, on the Yazoo River, some miles above the scene of his repulse in the preceding December. The message had said, "Make a demonstration on Haynes' Bluff, and make all the *show* possible." Sherman's transports, and three of Porter's gunboats, were closely followed by the Confederate soldiers who had been stationed at the series of defenses on the range of hills, and when they arrived at Snyder's Mill, just below Haynes' Bluff, on April 30th, General Hébert and several Louisiana regiments were awaiting them. On that day and the next the Confederates fiercely engaged the Union fleet and troops, and on May 2d Sherman withdrew his forces to the western bank of the Mississippi and hastened to Grant. The feint had been most successful. The Confederates had been prevented from sending reenforcements to Grand Gulf, and Grant's crossing was greatly facilitated.

The fleet passed the batteries of Grand Gulf and stopped at Bruinsburg, six miles below. A landing was soon made, the army taken across on April 30th, and a march to Port Gibson, twelve miles inland, was begun. General Bowen, Confederate commander at Grand Gulf, came out and offered battle. He was greatly outnumbered, but his troops fought gallantly throughout most of the day, May 1st, before yielding

## THE GUN THAT FOOLED THE FEDERALS

A "Quaker gun" that was mounted by the Confederates in the fortifications on the bluff at the river-front before Port Hudson. This gun was hewn out of a pine log and mounted on a carriage, and a black ring was painted around the end facing the river. Throughout the siege it was mistaken by the Federals for a piece of real ordnance. To such devices as this the beleaguered garrison was compelled constantly to resort in order to impress the superior forces investing Port Hudson with the idea that the position they sought to capture was formidably defended. The ruse was effective. Port Hudson was not again attacked from the river after the passing of Farragut's two ships.

## WITHIN "THE CITADEL"

This bastion fort, near the left of the Confederate line of defenses at Port Hudson, was the strongest of their works, and here Weitzel and Grover's divisions of the Federals followed up the attack (begun at daylight of June 14th) that Banks had ordered all along the line in his second effort to capture the position. The only result was simply to advance the Federal lines from fifty to two hundred yards nearer. In front of the "citadel" an advance position was gained from which a mine was subsequently run to within a few yards of the fort.

the field. Port Gibson was then occupied by the Union army, and Grand Gulf, no longer tenable, was abandoned by the Confederates.

Grant now prepared for a campaign into the interior of Mississippi. His first intention was to cooperate with General Banks in the capture of Port Hudson, after which they would move together upon Vicksburg. But hearing that Banks would not arrive for ten days, Grant decided that he would proceed to the task before him without delay. His army at that time numbered about forty-three thousand. That under Pemberton probably forty thousand, while there were fifteen thousand Confederate troops at Jackson, Mississippi, soon to be commanded by General Joseph E. Johnston, who was hastening to that capital.

The Federal leader now determined on the bold plan of making a dash into the interior of Mississippi, beating Johnston and turning on Pemberton before their forces could be joined. This campaign is pronounced the most brilliant in the Civil War. It was truly Napoleonic in conception and execution. Grant knew that his base of supplies at Grand Gulf would be cut off by Pemberton as soon as he moved away from it. He decided, therefore, against the advice of his generals, to abandon his base altogether.

A more daring undertaking could scarcely be imagined. With a few days' rations in their haversacks the troops were to make a dash that would possibly take several weeks into the heart of a hostile country. This was certainly defying fate. When General Halleck heard of Grant's daring scheme he wired the latter from Washington, ordering him to move his army down the river and cooperate with Banks. Fortunately, this order was received too late to interfere with Grant's plans.

As soon as Sherman's divisions joined the main army the march was begun, on May 7th. An advance of this character must be made with the greatest celerity and Grant's army showed amazing speed. McPherson, who commanded the right

FIFTY-ONE PIECES OF ARTILLERY FELL INTO THE HANDS OF THE FEDERALS AT THE SURRENDER OF PORT HUDSON, MANY OF THEM BATTERED INTO SILENCE BY THE LONG BOMBARDMENT KEPT UP BY THREE FEDERAL FIELD-BATTERIES AND AN ENTIRE REGIMENT OF HEAVY ARTILLERY (THE FIRST INDIANA) ON THE FEDERAL SIDE.

THE CONFEDERATES HAD ONLY FIELD-PIECES WITH WHICH TO DEFEND THEIR WORKS AGAINST THE INVESTING ARMY. THE BATTERED GUNS SHOWN IN THE PICTURES WERE MOUNTED IN THE CAMP OF DURYEA'S AND BAINBRIDGE'S BATTERIES. THESE WORKS WERE GARRISONED BY THE FIFTEENTH ARKANSAS CONFEDERATE INFANTRY wing, proceeded toward Jackson by way of Raymond and at the latter place encountered five thousand Confederates, on May 12th, who blocked his way and were prepared for fight. The battle of Raymond lasted two hours. McPherson was completely successful and the Confederates hastened to join their comrades in Jackson.

McPherson lost no time. He moved on toward Jackson, and as the last of his command left Raymond the advance of Sherman's corps reached it. That night, May 13th, Grant ordered McPherson and Sherman to march upon Jackson next morning by different roads, while McClernand was held in the rear near enough to reenforce either in case of need. The rain fell in torrents that night and, as Grant reported, in places the water was a foot deep in the road. But nothing could daunt his determined army. At eleven o'clock in the morning of the 14th, a concerted attack was made on the capital of Mississippi. A few hours' brisk fighting concluded this act of the drama, and the Stars and Stripes were unfurled on the State capitol. Among the spoils were seventeen heavy guns. That night, Grant slept in the house which Johnston had occupied the night before.

Meantime, Johnston had ordered Pemberton to detain Grant by attacking him in the rear. But Pemberton considered it more advisable to move toward Grand Gulf to separate Grant from his base of supplies, not knowing that Grant had abandoned his base. And now, with Johnston's army scattered, Grant left Sherman to burn bridges and military factories, and to tear up the railroads about Jackson while he turned fiercely on Pemberton. McPherson's corps took the lead. Grant called on McClernand to follow without delay. Then, hearing that Pemberton was marching toward him, he called on Sherman to hasten from Jackson. At Champion's Hill (Baker's Creek) Pemberton stood in the way, with eighteen thousand men.

The battle was soon in progress—the heaviest of the

## THE NAVY HELPS ON LAND

A View within Federal Battery No. 10. One of the investing works before Port Hudson. Farragut's fleet of gunboats and mortarboats assisted materially from the river above and below Port Hudson. Guns were also taken ashore from the gunboats and placed in position to assist in the bombardment which quickly laid the little hamlet of Port Hudson in ruins. This battery was situated on a wooded height about a mile to the east of the town; its 9-inch Dahlgren guns were kept warm hurling shells at the Confederate fortifications throughout the siege. Lieutenant Terry, of the "Richmond," was in command of this battery with a detachment from his vessel, which in the effort to run past Port Hudson in March had received a shot in her safety-valves, rendering her engines useless and forcing her to turn back. The "Richmond" mounted twenty such guns as are seen in the picture, besides two heavy rifles.

campaign. It continued for seven or eight hours. The Confederates were defeated with a loss of nearly all their artillery and about half their force, including four thousand men who were cut off from the main army and failed to rejoin it. On the banks of the Big Black River, a few miles westward, the Confederates made another stand, and here the fifth battle of the investment of Vicksburg took place. It was short, sharp, decisive. The Confederates suffered heavy losses and the remainder hastened to the defenses of Vicksburg. They had set fire to the bridge across the Big Black, and Grant's army was detained for a day—until the Confederates were safely lodged in the city.

The Federal army now invested Vicksburg, occupying the surrounding hills. It was May 18th when the remarkable campaign to reach Vicksburg came to an end. In eighteen days, the army had marched one hundred and eighty miles through a hostile country, fought and won five battles, captured a State capital, had taken twenty-seven heavy cannon and sixty field-pieces, and had slain or wounded six thousand men and captured as many more. As Grant and Sherman rode out on the hill north of the city, the latter broke into enthusiastic admiration of his chief, declaring that up to that moment he had felt no assurance of success, and pronouncing the campaign one of the greatest in history.

The great problem of investing Vicksburg was solved at last. Around the doomed city gleamed the thousands of bayonets of the Union army. The inhabitants and the army that had fled to it as a city of refuge were penned in. But the Confederacy was not to yield without a stubborn resistance. On May 19th, an advance was made on the works and the besieging lines drew nearer and tightened their coils. Three days later, on May 22nd, Grant ordered a grand assault by his whole army. The troops, flushed with their victories of the past three weeks, were eager for the attack. All the corps commanders set their watches by Grant's in order to begin

## THE GUNS THAT WORKED AT CLOSE RANGE

In advance of Lieutenant Terry's naval battery, at the edge of another wooded height, stood Federal Battery No. 9 (Cox's), within about 300 yards of the Confederate fortifications, its two 12-pounder rifles doing telling work against the Confederate forts in their front.   The Federals pushed their entrenchments nearest to the works of the defenders at this part of the line—so near that a duplicate of Grant's message to Banks announcing the surrender of Vicksburg was thrown within the Confederate lines on July 7th.   This picture shows the method of constructing field fortifications, the parapet here being revetted with cotton-bales.

the assault at all points at the same moment—ten o'clock in the morning. At the appointed time, the cannon from the encircling lines burst forth in a deafening roar. Then came the answering thunders from the mortar-boats on the Louisiana shore and from the gunboats anchored beneath the bluff. The gunboats' fire was answered from within the bastions protecting the city. The opening of the heavy guns on the land side was followed by the sharper crackle of musketry—thousands of shots, indistinguishable in a continuous roll.

The men in the Federal lines leaped from their hiding places and ran to the parapets in the face of a murderous fire from the defenders of the city, only to be mowed down by hundreds. Others came, crawling over the bodies of their fallen comrades—now and then they planted their colors on the battlements of the besieged city, to be cut down by the galling Confederate fire. Thus it continued hour after hour, until the coming of darkness. The assault had failed. The Union loss was about three thousand brave men; the Confederate loss was probably not much over five hundred.

Grant had made a fearful sacrifice; he was paying a high price but he had a reason for so doing—Johnston with a re-enforcing army was threatening him in the rear; by taking Vicksburg at this time he could have turned on Johnston, and could have saved the Government sending any more Federal troops; and, to use his own words, it was needed because the men " would not have worked in the trenches with the same zeal, believing it unnecessary, as they did after their failure, to carry the enemy's works."

On the north side of the city overlooking the river, were the powerful batteries on Fort Hill, a deadly menace to the Federal troops, and Grant and Sherman believed that if enfiladed by the gunboats this position could be carried. At their request Admiral Porter sent the *Cincinnati* on May 27th to engage the Confederate guns, while four vessels below the town did the same to the lower defenses. In half an hour five

### WHERE MEN WORKED LIKE MOLES

In burrows such as these the Federal soldiers worked incessantly from June 14th until the surrender of Port Hudson in an effort to undermine "the citadel," the strongest fortification in the Confederate lines near the Jackson road. Cotton-bales roped about were used as sap-rollers to protect the men from sharpshooters. The heat under the semi-tropical sun was terrible, drying up the brooks and distilling miasma from the pestilential swamp near by. The illness and mortality among the Federals were enormous, and yet the men worked on the saps uncomplainingly, and by July 7th the central one had been carried within seventeen feet of the ditch of the fort, and a storming party of a thousand volunteers had been organized to assault the works as soon as the two heavily charged mines should be sprung. That very day came the word that Vicksburg had fallen, and the work of the sappers and miners was useless.

### THE SAP AGAINST "THE CITADEL"

of the *Cincinnati's* guns were disabled; and she was in a sinking condition. She was run toward the shore and sank in three fathoms of water.

The army now settled down to a wearisome siege. For six weeks, they encircled the city with trenches, approaching nearer and nearer to the defending walls; they exploded mines; they shot at every head that appeared above the parapets. One by one the defending batteries were silenced. The sappers slowly worked their way toward the Confederate ramparts. Miners were busy on both sides burrowing beneath the fortifications. At three o'clock on the afternoon of June 25th a redoubt in the Confederate works was blown into the air, breaking into millions of fragments and disclosing guns, men, and timber. With the mine explosion, the Federal soldiers before the redoubt began to dash into the opening, only to meet with a withering fire from an interior parapet which the Confederates had constructed in anticipation of this event. The carnage was appalling to behold; and when the soldiers of the Union finally retired they had learned a costly lesson which withheld them from attack when another mine was exploded on July 1st.

Meantime, let us take a view of the river below and the life of the people within the doomed city. Far down the river, two hundred and fifty miles from Vicksburg, was Port Hudson. The place was fortified and held by a Confederate force under General Gardner. Like Vicksburg, it was besieged by a Federal army, under Nathaniel P. Banks, of Cedar Mountain fame. On May 27th, he made a desperate attack on the works and was powerfully aided by Farragut with his fleet in the river. But aside from dismounting a few guns and weakening the foe at a still heavier cost to their own ranks, the Federals were unsuccessful. Again, on June 10th, and still again on the 14th, Banks made fruitless attempts to carry Port Hudson by storm. He then, like Grant at Vicksburg, settled down to a siege. The defenders of Port Hudson proved their courage by enduring every hardship.

[ 224 ]

## THE USES OF ADVERSITY

War brings out more strongly than anything else the truth of the trite old adage that necessity is the mother of invention. In the operations on the James River a locomotive mounted on a flat-boat was used as an extemporized stationary engine for working a pile-driver. The Confederates at Port Hudson put one to as strange a use. Lifted free from the rails and with a belt attached to the driving-wheels, it was used to operate a grist-mill that ground the corn into rough meal, which was their substitute for flour. It did the work in a very satisfactory manner. There were large quantities of grain and corn that had been brought into Port Hudson before it was invested, and the Red River country, as long as it was kept open and accessible, provided the garrison with supplies. But at the time of the investment the Confederate quartermaster was hard put to it to answer the demands made upon him to feed the overworked and hungry men that night and day toiled and slept at the guns. Powder and shell were also running short. Despite the privations suffered by the garrison, they, being used to the climate, suffered less from sickness than did the Federal troops, many detachments of which were encamped along the low-lying and swampy ground that lay at the bend of the river to the north.

## THE CHURCH USED AS A GRANARY

At Vicksburg, during the whole six weeks of the siege, the men in the trenches worked steadily, advancing the coils about the city. Grant received reenforcement and before the end of the siege his army numbered over seventy thousand. Day and night, the roar of artillery continued. From the mortars across the river and from Porter's fleet the shrieking shells rose in grand parabolic curves, bursting in midair or in the streets of the city, spreading havoc in all directions. The people of the city burrowed into the ground for safety. Many whole families lived in these dismal abodes, their walls of clay being shaken by the roaring battles that raged above the ground. In one of these dens, sixty-five people found a home. The food supply ran low, and day by day it became scarcer. At last, by the end of June, there was nothing to eat except mule meat and a kind of bread made of beans and corn meal.

It was ten o'clock in the morning of July 3d. White flags were seen above the parapet. The firing ceased. A strange quietness rested over the scene of the long bombardment. On the afternoon of that day, the one, too, on which was heard the last shot on the battlefield of Gettysburg, Grant and Pemberton stood beneath an oak tree, in front of McPherson's corps, and opened negotiations for the capitulation. On the following morning, the Nation's birthday, about thirty thousand soldiers laid down their arms as prisoners of war and were released on parole. The losses from May 1st to the surrender were about ten thousand on each side.

Three days later, at Port Hudson, a tremendous cheer arose from the besieging army. The Confederates within the defenses were at a loss to know the cause. Then some one shouted the news, "Vicksburg has surrendered!"

The end had come. Port Hudson could not hope to stand alone; the greater fortress had fallen. Two days later, July 9th, the gallant garrison, worn and weary with the long siege, surrendered to General Banks. The whole course of the mighty Mississippi was now under the Stars and Stripes.

# PART III
# THE CRISIS

———

# GETTYSBURG

———

AFTER THE BATTLE—A SHARPSHOOTER

FEELING FOR LEE'S ARMY

Battery D, Second United States Artillery, Going into Action, June 5, 1863. This was part of the reconnaisance in force under Sedgwick, whom Hooker ordered to cross three miles below Fredericksburg on June 3d and find out if Lee's army still held its old position. The cavalry had brought in reports of some new movement by the Army of Northern Virginia, and Hooker believed that another invasion of the North was impending. It was imperative that this should be checked at once. Every effort was made to discover the real position of the Confederates in order to give battle. Lee, on his side, was equally anxious for a decisive engagement. The

THE NORTH AGAIN THREATENED

It was this Virginia village (seventy-five miles from Washington, on the Orange & Alexandria Railroad) that Lee chose as the point of concentration for his forces preparatory to his last daring invasion of the North, which ended at Gettysburg. Culpeper was no stranger to war's alarms. Two brigades of Pleasonton's cavalry were sent off by Hooker on June 7th to definitely determine Lee's position. Riding in the direction of Culpeper, they ran into a similar force of the Confederates under Stuart, which proved too strong for the

## SPARRING BEFORE GETTYSBURG

victory at Chancellorsville had elated the Confederacy with hopes of early recognition by Europe. Exaggerated reports of disaffection at the North led the Government at Richmond to urge an immediate advance. Lee promptly complied. His strongest hope was that he might draw Hooker into a position where the Federals could be advantageously attacked and a blow struck that would end the war. So cleverly was Lee's movement masked by the resistance of Hill's Corps to Howe's division of the Sixth Corps on June 5th that Sedgwick was deceived into reporting that the greater portion of Lee's force still held their old positions.

## CULPEPER COURT HOUSE

Federals. The encounter left no doubt in Hooker's mind that Lee was preparing for an aggressive movement either against Washington or into Maryland. On June 13th it was clear that Lee was massing his forces in the direction of Culpeper. Hooker at once began throwing his lines out toward Culpeper, with the purpose of keeping abreast of Lee by advancing south of the Blue Ridge—and the race for the Potomac was on. This picture was taken in November, 1863, when Culpeper was occupied by the Federals.

## THE HIGH–WATER MARK OF THE CONFEDERACY

Just as we see it here, the Confederates first saw Gettysburg. Down these roads and past these houses they marched to the high-water mark of their invasion of the North. It was quite by accident that the little town became the theater of the crucial contest of the Civil War. On the morning of June 30th Heth's division of General D. H. Hill's Corps was marching upon the town from the west. It came on confidently, expecting no resistance, meaning only to seize a supply of shoes much needed by the footsore Army of Northern Virginia, which had marched triumphantly from Culpeper to the heart of Pennsylvania. Between Heth's men and their goal lay two brigades of Federal cavalry under Buford. Riding into the town from the opposite direction came Major Kress, sent by General Wadsworth to get these same shoes for his division of the Federals. Before the tavern Kress found Buford and explained his errand. "You

## THE LITTLE TOWN OF GETTYSBURG, PENNSYLVANIA

had better return immediately to your command," said Buford. "Why, what is the matter, General?" asked Kress. At that instant a single gun boomed in the distance, and Buford, mounting, replied as he spurred his horse to the gallop, "That's the matter." The world had never seen a finer body of fighting men than Lee's Army of Northern Virginia, then massing rapidly toward Gettysburg. More than seventy-three thousand five hundred strong they came, every man a veteran, contemptuous of adversaries whose superior numbers had never yet been made to count completely against them. In the center of the panorama rises Cemetery Ridge, where the defeated First and Eleventh Federal Corps slept on their arms on the night of July 1st, after having been driven back through the town by the superior forces of Hill and Ewell. The lower eminence to the right of it is Culp's Hill. At the extreme right of the picture stands Round Top.

## THE CRISIS BRINGS FORTH THE MAN

Major-General George Gordon Meade and Staff. Not men, but a man is what counts in war, said Napoleon; and Lee had proved it true in many a bitter lesson administered to the Army of the Potomac. At the end of June, 1863, for the third time in ten months, that army had a new commander. Promptness and caution were equally imperative in that hour. Meade's fitness for the post was as yet undemonstrated; he had been advanced from the command of the Fifth Corps three days before the army was to engage in its greatest battle. Lee must be turned back from Harrisburg and Philadelphia and kept from striking at Baltimore and Washington, and the somewhat scattered Army of the Potomac must be concentrated. In the very first flush of his advancement, Meade exemplified the qualities of sound generalship that placed his name high on the list of Federal commanders.

## GETTYSBURG—WHERE STIRRING DEEDS BROUGHT FORTH IMMORTAL WORDS

This is Gettysburg, the sleepy little Pennsylvania town that leaped into the focus of the world's eye on those scorching death-ridden days of July, 1863, and down the street comes swaying in cadenced steps a marching regiment. We are looking at them just as the inhabitants, gathered here in their quaint old costumes, saw them. Here are the defenders returned again to the place whose name spells victory and glorious memories on their tattered battle-flags. It is the 19th of November, 1863. Lincoln is here to speak those glowing words that every schoolboy knows, and dedicate the National Cemetery, where lie the Blue and Gray, and where their children's children make yearly pilgrimages.

# THE BATTLE OF GETTYSBURG—THE HIGH-WATER MARK OF THE CIVIL WAR

We cannot dedicate—we cannot consecrate—we cannot hallow this ground. The brave men, living and dead, who struggled here have consecrated it, far above our poor power to add or detract. The world will little note, nor long remember what we say here, but it can never forget what they did here. It is for us, the living, rather, to be dedicated here to the unfinished work which they who fought here have thus far so nobly advanced. It is rather for us to be here dedicated to the great task remaining before us—that from these honored dead we take increased devotion to that cause for which they gave the last full measure of devotion—that we here highly resolve that these dead shall not have died in vain—that this nation, under God, shall have a new birth of freedom—and that government of the people, by the people, for the people, shall not perish from the earth.—*Abraham Lincoln, on November 19, 1863, four months after this battle, in his " Gettysburg Address."*

THE military operations of the American Civil War were carried on for the most part south of the Mason and Dixon line; but the greatest and most famous of the battles was fought on the soil of the old Keystone State, which had given birth to the Declaration of Independence and to the Constitution of the United States.

Gettysburg is a quiet hamlet, nestling among the hills of Adams County, and in 1863 contained about fifteen hundred inhabitants. It had been founded in 1780 by James Gettys, who probably never dreamed that his name thus given to the village would, through apparently accidental circumstances, become famous in history for all time.

The hills immediately around Gettysburg are not rugged

ROBERT E. LEE IN 1863

It was with the gravest misgivings that Lee began his invasion of the North in 1863.   He was too wise a general not to realize that a crushing defeat was possible.   Yet, with Vicksburg already doomed, the effort to win a decisive victory in the East was imperative in its importance.   Magnificent was the courage and fortitude of Lee's maneuvering during that long march which was to end in failure.   Hitherto he had made every one of his veterans count for two of their antagonists, but at Gettysburg the odds had fallen heavily against him.   Jackson, his resourceful ally, was no more.   Longstreet advised strongly against giving battle, but Lee unwaveringly made the tragic effort which sacrificed more than a third of his splendid army.

or precipitous; they are little more than gentle swells of ground, and many of them were covered with timber when the hosts of the North and the legions of the South fought out the destiny of the American republic on those memorable July days in 1863.

The village is the radiating point of several important roads, known by the names of the respective towns to which they lead. The one leading directly into the town from the north is known as the Carlisle road. It passes through the village and deflects to the southeast, becoming the Baltimore turnpike. East of the Carlisle road is the Harrisburg road, and west of it the Mummasburg road. This latter crosses a wooded ridge known as Oak Hill, and this hill became the center of operations on the first day of the battle. West of the village about half a mile a Lutheran theological seminary is situated on a ridge which extends north and south and is called Seminary Ridge. Directly south of Gettysburg, almost parallel with Seminary Ridge and about a mile from it, lies Cemetery Ridge. Three miles from the town, Cemetery Ridge culminates in a bold, rocky peak, with steep, rugged slopes several hundred feet in height, which is called Round Top. North of Round Top, and quite near it, is a similar peak about half as high, called Little Round Top. About five hundred yards west of Little Round Top another rugged peak, known as the Devil's Den, rises from the lowland marshes at the junction of a small creek which runs along the western base of Cemetery Ridge, and is known as Plum Run, with a smaller tributary. The Devil's Den is about one hundred feet lower than Little Round Top, and its slopes are covered with huge boulders and seamed with crevasses. The largest of these pits, and the one from which the hill took its name, is on the slope facing toward Little Round Top, and formed a natural breastwork of solid rock.

The valley between Cemetery Ridge and Seminary Ridge was rolling farm-land, with cultivated fields and orchards

HANCOCK, "THE SUPERB"

**Every** man in this picture was wounded at Gettysburg. Seated, is Winfield Scott Hancock; the boy-general, Francis C. Barlow (who was struck almost mortally), leans against the tree. The other two are General John Gibbon and General David B. Birney. About four o'clock on the afternoon of July 1st a foam-flecked charger dashed up Cemetery Hill bearing General Hancock. He had galloped thirteen miles to take command. Apprised of the loss of Reynolds, his main dependence, Meade knew that only a man of vigor and judgment could save the situation. He chose wisely, for Hancock was one of the best all-round soldiers that the Army of the Potomac had developed. It was he who re-formed the shattered corps and chose the position to be held for the decisive struggle.

spreading across the landscape. At the southern end of the valley to the west of Round Top the lowland was covered with heavy timber, and the ground was strewn with huge rocks. Near the northwestern base of the Devil's Den there was a broad wheat-field, with the grain ripening in the summer sun. A short distance to the north of the wheat-field, on a slight elevation, stood the farmhouse and barns of the Trostle farm. To the west and slightly to the south of the Trostle farm the land rises gradually to a low hill which stands midway between the Trostle farm and the crest of Seminary Ridge. On the eastern slope of this hill, and reaching to its crest, there was an extensive peach orchard. The western side of the orchard bordered on the broad Emmitsburg road, which stretched away from Gettysburg to the southwest to Emmitsburg, a short distance over the Maryland line. A mile and a half west of Gettysburg flows Willoughby Run, while at about the same distance on the east and nearly parallel to the run flows a somewhat larger stream called Rock Creek. Between Rock Creek and the northern extremity of Cemetery Ridge is situated Culp's Hill, on whose sides the armies in blue and gray struggled heroically during the three days' fight. The area of the entire battle-ground is something over twenty-five square miles, all of which may be seen at a glance from any one of the five observatories which have since been erected on the ground by the Government.

Lee's army was flushed with victory after Chancellorsville and was strengthened by the memory of Fredericksburg. Southern hopes were high after Hooker's defeat on the Rappahannock, in May, 1863, and public opinion was unanimous in demanding an invasion of Northern soil. On the other hand, the Army of the Potomac, under its several leaders, had met with continual discouragement, and, with all its patriotism and valor, its two years' warfare showed but few bright pages to cheer the heart of the war-broken soldier, and to inspire the hopes of the anxious public in the North.

MUTE PLEADERS IN THE CAUSE OF PEACE

There was little time that could be employed by either side in caring for those who fell upon the fields of the almost uninterrupted fighting at Gettysburg. On the morning of the 4th, when Lee began to abandon his position on Seminary Ridge, opposite the Federal right, both sides sent forth ambulance and burial details to remove the wounded and bury the dead in the torrential rain then falling. Under cover of the hazy atmosphere, Lee was get-

MEN OF THE IRON BRIGADE

ting his whole army in motion to retreat. Many an unfinished shallow grave, like the one above, had to be left by the Confederates. In this lower picture some men of the Twenty-fourth Michigan infantry are lying dead on the field of battle. This regiment—one of the units of the Iron Brigade—left seven distinct rows of dead as it fell back from battle-line to battle-line, on the first day. Three-fourths of its members were struck down.

Leaving General Stuart with ten thousand cavalry and a part of Hill's corps to prevent Hooker from pursuing, Lee crossed the Potomac early in June, 1863, concentrated his army at Hagerstown, Maryland, and prepared for a campaign in Pennsylvania, with Harrisburg as the objective. His army was organized in three corps, under the respective commands of Longstreet, Ewell, and A. P. Hill. Lee had divided his army so as to approach Harrisburg by different routes and to assess the towns along the way for large sums of money. Late in June, he was startled by the intelligence that Stuart had failed to detain Hooker, and that the Federals had crossed the Potomac and were in hot pursuit.

Lee was quick to see that his plans must be changed. He knew that to continue his march he must keep his army together to watch his pursuing antagonist, and that such a course in this hostile country would mean starvation, while the willing hands of the surrounding populace would minister to the wants of his foe. Again, if he should scatter his forces that they might secure the necessary supplies, the parts would be attacked singly and destroyed. Lee saw, therefore, that he must abandon his invasion of the North or turn upon his pursuing foe and disable him in order to continue his march. But that foe was a giant of strength and courage, more than equal to his own; and the coming together of two such forces in a mighty death-struggle meant that a great battle must be fought, a greater battle than this Western world had hitherto known.

The Army of the Potomac had again changed leaders, and George Gordon Meade was now its commander. Hooker, after a dispute with Halleck, resigned his leadership, and Meade, the strongest of the corps commanders, was appointed in his place, succeeding him on June 28th. The two great armies—Union and Confederate—were scattered over portions of Maryland and southern Pennsylvania. Both were marching northward, along almost parallel lines. The Confederates

## THE FIRST DAY'S TOLL

The lives laid down by the blue-clad soldiers in the first day's fighting made possible the ultimate victory at Gettysburg.    The stubborn resistance of Buford's cavalry and of the First and Eleventh Corps checked the Confederate advance for an entire day.    The delay was priceless; it enabled  Meade to concentrate his army upon the heights to the south of Gettysburg, a position which proved impregnable. To a Pennsylvanian, General John F. Reynolds, falls the credit of the determined stand that was made that day.    Commanding the advance of the army, he promptly went to Buford's support, bringing up his infantry and artillery to hold back the Confederates.

## McPHERSON'S WOODS

At the edge of these woods General Reynolds was killed by a Confederate sharpshooter in the first vigorous contest of the day. The woods lay between the two roads upon which the Confederates were advancing from the west, and General Doubleday (in command of the First Corps) was ordered to take the position so that the columns of the foe could be enfiladed by the infantry, while contending with the artillery posted on both roads.    The Iron Brigade under General Meredith was ordered to hold the ground at all hazards.    As they charged, the troops shouted: "If we can't hold it, where will you find the men who can?"    On they swept, capturing General Archer and many of his Confederate brigade that had entered the woods from the other side.    As Archer passed to the rear, Doubleday, who had been his classmate at West Point, greeted him with "Good morning!  I'm glad to see you!"

were gradually pressing toward the east, while the Federals were marching along a line eastward of that followed by the Confederates. The new commander of the Army of the Potomac was keeping his forces interposed between the legions of Lee and the Federal capital, and watching for an opportunity to force the Confederates to battle where the Federals would have the advantage of position. It was plain that they must soon come together in a gigantic contest; but just where the shock of battle would take place was yet unknown. Meade had ordered a general movement toward Harrisburg, and General Buford was sent with four thousand cavalry to intercept the Confederate advance guard.

On the night of June 30th Buford encamped on a low hill, a mile west of Gettysburg, and here on the following morning the famous battle had its beginning.

On the morning of July 1st the two armies were still scattered, the extremes being forty miles apart. But General Reynolds, with two corps of the Union army, was but a few miles away, and was hastening to Gettysburg, while Longstreet and Hill were approaching from the west. Buford opened the battle against Heth's division of Hill's corps. Reynolds soon joined Buford, and three hours before noon the battle was in progress on Seminary Ridge. Reynolds rode out to his fighting-lines on the ridge, and while placing his troops, a little after ten o'clock in the morning, he received a sharpshooter's bullet in the brain. The gallant Federal leader fell dead. John F. Reynolds, who had been promoted for gallantry at Buena Vista in the Mexican War, was one of the bravest and ablest generals of the Union army. No casualty of the war brought more widespread mourning to the North than the death of Reynolds.

But even this calamity could not stay the fury of the battle. By one o'clock both sides had been greatly reenforced, and the battle-line extended north of the town from Seminary Ridge to the bank of Rock Creek. Here for hours the roar

### FEDERAL DEAD AT GETTYSBURG, JULY 1, 1863

All the way from McPherson's Woods back to Cemetery Hill lay the Federal soldiers, who had contested every foot of that retreat until nightfall.   The Confederates were massing so rapidly from the west and north that there was scant time to bring off the wounded and none for attention to the dead.   There on the field lay the shoes so much needed by the Confederates, and the grim task of gathering them began.   The dead were stripped of arms, ammunition, caps, and accoutrements as well—in fact, of everything that would be of the slightest use in enabling Lee's poorly equipped army to continue the internecine strife.   It was one of war's awful expedients.

### SEMINARY RIDGE, BEYOND GETTYSBURG

Along this road the Federals retreated toward Cemetery Hill in the late afternoon of July 1st. The success of McPherson's Woods was but temporary, for the Confederates under Hill were coming up in overpowering numbers, and now Ewell's forces appeared from the north. The First Corps, under Doubleday, "broken and defeated but not dismayed," fell back, pausing now and again to fire a volley at

the pursuing Confederates. It finally joined the Eleventh Corps, which had also been driven back to Cemetery Hill. Lee was on the field in time to watch the retreat of the Federals, and advised Ewell to follow them up, but Ewell (who had lost 3,000 men) decided upon discretion. Night fell with the beaten Federals, reënforced by the Twelfth Corps and part of the Third, facing nearly the whole of Lee's army.

[B]

THE PRICE OF VICTORY

Such scenes as these marked every one of the detached battle-fields at Gettysburg. The lower picture is a result of the first day's fighting near McPherson's Woods, through which the Iron Brigade swept with the cry, "We've come to stay!" The picture above was taken near the spot where the First Minnesota was sacrificed to stem the advance of the Confederates after their victory at the Peach Orchard. Hancock, while patching up a second line to protect Sickles' retreating troops, saw a heavy column of Confederates emerge from a clump of trees and advance toward a weak point in his line. Dashing up to Colonel Colvill, Hancock shouted: "Do

THE MEN WHO "CAME TO STAY"

WHERE A SHELL DROPPED

you see those colors? Take them!" And the First Minnesota, in five minutes, captured the colors and stemmed the advance. Of the 262 officers and men who obeyed that order, half a hundred lay dead on the field and 174 others were wounded. The regiment's total mortality from that charge was 75, more than 28 per cent. of the number engaged—the highest known short of an Indian massacre. The Federals lost at Gettysburg 3,063 killed, 14,492 wounded, and 5,435 missing (Fox's figures). The Confederate loss was 3,903 killed, 18,735 wounded, and 5,425 missing (Livermore's figures). Total loss on both sides, 51,053.

NEAR THE BLOODY ANGLE

of the battle was unceasing. About the middle of the afternoon a breeze lifted the smoke that had enveloped the whole
battle-line in darkness, and revealed the fact that the Federals
were being pressed back toward Gettysburg. General Carl
Schurz, who after Reynolds' death directed the extreme right
near Rock Creek, leaving nearly half of his men dead or
wounded on the field, retreated toward Cemetery Hill, and
in passing through the town the Confederates pursued and captured a large number of the remainder. The left wing, now
unable to hold its position owing to the retreat of the right,
was also forced back, and it, too, took refuge on Cemetery
Hill, which had been selected by General O. O. Howard;
and the first day's fight was over. It was several hours before night, and had the Southerners known of the disorganized
condition of the Union troops, they might have pursued and
captured a large part of the army. Meade, who was still some
miles from the field, hearing of the death of Reynolds, had
sent Hancock to take general command until he himself should
arrive.

Hancock had ridden at full speed and arrived on the field
between three and four o'clock in the afternoon. His presence
soon brought order out of chaos. His superb bearing, his air
of confidence, his promise of heavy reenforcements during the
night, all tended to inspire confidence and to renew hope in the
ranks of the discouraged army. Had this day ended the affair
at Gettysburg, the usual story of the defeat of the Army of
the Potomac would have gone forth to the world. Only the
advance portions of both armies had been engaged; and yet
the battle had been a formidable one. The Union loss was
severe. A great commander had fallen, and the rank and file
had suffered the fearful loss of ten thousand men.

Meade reached the scene late in the night, and chose to
make this field, on which the advance of both armies had accidentally met, the place of a general engagement. Lee had
come to the same decision, and both called on their outlying

## THE CARNAGE OF BLOODY ANGLE

Trostle's House, Sickles' headquarters at the beginning of the second day. The house stood some distance back from the Emmitsburg road, overlooking the Peach Orchard, from which the Confederates finally drove the sturdy men of the Third Corps. Whether or not it was a tactical error for Sickles to post his command along the road so far in advance of the line is a subject of discussion. The result cost many lives, and nearly lost to the Federals the key to their position. Back from the Peach Orchard Sickles' men were driven, past Trostle's House, where Bigelow's Ninth Massachusetts battery made its glorious stand, and near which Sickles himself lost his leg. All the way back to Round Top the ground was strewn with dead.

legions to make all possible speed to Gettysburg. Before morning, nearly all the troops of both armies had reached the field. The Union army rested with its center on Cemetery Ridge, with its right thrown around to Culp's Hill and its left extended southward toward the rocky peak called Round Top. The Confederate army, with its center on Seminary Ridge, its wings extending from beyond Rock Creek on the north to a point opposite Round Top on the south, lay in a great semi-circle, half surrounding the Army of the Potomac. But Lee was at a disadvantage. First, "Stonewall" Jackson was gone, and second, Stuart was absent with his ten thousand cavalry. Furthermore, Meade was on the defensive, and had the advantage of occupying the inner ring of the huge half circle. Thus lay the two mighty hosts, awaiting the morning, and the carnage that the day was to bring. It seemed that the fate of the Republic was here to be decided, and the people of the North and the South watched with breathless eagerness for the decision about to be made at Gettysburg.

The dawn of July 2d betokened a beautiful summer day in southern Pennsylvania. The hours of the night had been spent by the two armies in marshaling of battalions and maneuvering of corps and divisions, getting into position for the mighty combat of the coming day. But, when morning dawned, both armies hesitated, as if unwilling to begin the task of bloodshed. They remained inactive, except for a stray shot here and there, until nearly four o'clock in the afternoon.

The fighting on this second day was chiefly confined to the two extremes, the centers remaining comparatively inactive. Longstreet commanded the Confederate right, and opposite him on the Union left was General Daniel E. Sickles. The Confederate left wing, under Ewell, was opposite Slocum and the Union right stationed on Culp's Hill.

The plan of General Meade had been to have the corps commanded by General Sickles connect with that of Hancock and extend southward near the base of the Round Tops.

[248]

## IN THE DEVIL'S DEN

Upon this wide, steep hill, about five hundred yards due west of Little Round Top and one hundred feet lower, was a chasm named by the country folk "the Devil's Den." When the position fell into the hands of the Confederates at the end of the second day's fighting, it became the stronghold of their sharpshooters, and well did it fulfill its name. It was a most dangerous post to occupy, since the Federal batteries on the Round Top were constantly shelling it in an effort to dislodge the hardy riflemen, many of whom met the fate of the one in the picture. Their deadly work continued, however, and many a gallant officer of the Federals was picked off during the fighting on the afternoon of the second day. General Vincent was one of the first victims; General Weed fell likewise; and as Lieutenant Hazlett bent over him to catch his last words, a bullet through the head prostrated that officer lifeless on the body of his chief.

Sickles found this ground low and disadvantageous as a fighting-place. In his front he saw the high ground along the ridge on the side of which the peach orchard was situated, and advanced his men to this position, placing them along the Emmitsburg road, and back toward the Trostle farm and the wheat-field, thus forming an angle at the peach orchard. The left flank of Hancock's line now rested far behind the right flank of Sickles' forces. The Third Corps was alone in its position in advance of the Federal line. The Confederate troops later marched along Sickles' front so that Longstreet's corps overlapped the left wing of the Union army. The Northerners grimly watched the bristling cannon and the files of men that faced them across the valley, as they waited for the battle to commence.

The boom of cannon from Longstreet's batteries announced the beginning of the second day's battle. Lee had ordered Longstreet to attack Sickles in full force. The fire was quickly answered by the Union troops, and before long the fight extended from the peach orchard through the wheat-field and along the whole line to the base of Little Round Top. The musketry commenced with stray volleys here and there—then more and faster, until there was one continuous roar, and no ear could distinguish one shot from another. Longstreet swept forward in a magnificent line of battle, a mile and a half long. He pressed back the Union infantry, and was seriously threatening the artillery.

At the extreme left, close to the Trostle house, Captain John Bigelow commanded the Ninth Battery, Massachusetts Light Artillery. He was ordered to hold his position at all hazards until reenforced. With double charges of grape and canister, again and again he tore great gaps in the advancing line, but it re-formed and pressed onward until the men in gray reached the muzzles of the Federal guns. Again Bigelow fired, but the heroic band had at last to give way to the increased numbers of the attack, which finally resulted in a hand-

## THE UNGUARDED LINK

Little Round Top, the key to the Federal left at Gettysburg, which they all but lost on the second day —was the scene of hand-to-hand fighting rarely equaled since long-range weapons were invented. Twice the Confederates in fierce conflict fought their way near to this summit, but were repulsed. Had they gained it, they could have planted artillery which would have enfiladed the left of Meade's line, and Gettysburg might have been turned into an overwhelming defeat. Beginning at the right, the Federal line stretched in the form of a fish-hook, with the barb resting on Culp's Hill, the center at the bend in the hook on Cemetery Hill, and the left (consisting of General Sickles' Third Corps) forming the shank to the southward as far as Round Top. On his own responsibility Sickles had advanced a portion of his line, leaving Little Round Top unprotected. Upon this advanced line of Sickles, at the Peach Orchard on the Emmitsburg road, the Confederates fell in an effort to turn what they supposed to be Meade's left flank. Only the promptness of General Warren, who discovered the gap and remedied it in time, saved the key.

to-hand struggle with a Mississippi regiment. Bigelow was wounded, and twenty-eight of his hundred and four men were left on the bloody field, while he lost sixty-five out of eighty-eight horses, and four of six guns. Such was one of many deeds of heroism enacted at Gettysburg.

But the most desperate struggle of the day was the fight for the possession of Little Round Top. Just before the action began General Meade sent his chief engineer, General G. K. Warren, to examine conditions on the Union left. The battle was raging in the peach orchard when he came to Little Round Top. It was unoccupied at the time, and Warren quickly saw the great importance of preventing its occupation by the Confederates, for the hill was the key to the whole battle-ground west and south of Cemetery Ridge. Before long, the engineer saw Hood's division of Longstreet's corps moving steadily toward the hill, evidently determined to occupy it. Had Hood succeeded, the result would have been most disastrous to the Union army, for the Confederates could then have subjected the entire Union lines on the western edge of Cemetery Ridge to an enfilading fire. Warren and a signal officer seized flags and waved them, to deceive the Confederates as to the occupation of the height. Sykes' corps, marching to the support of the left, soon came along, and Warren, dashing down the side of the hill to meet it, caused the brigade under Colonel Vincent and a part of that under General Weed to be detached, and these occupied the coveted position. Hazlett's battery was dragged by hand up the rugged slope and planted on the summit.

Meantime Hood's forces had come up the hill, and were striving at the very summit; and now occurred one of the most desperate hand-to-hand conflicts of the war—in which men forgot that they were human and tore at each other like wild beasts. The opposing forces, not having time to reload, charged each other with bayonets—men assaulted each other with clubbed muskets—the Blue and the Gray grappled in

## THE SECOND DAY'S FIGHT

The battle of Gettysburg was a crescendo of carnage—each day marked by a special climax more dramatic and deadly than the preceding one. That of the second day was the struggle for Little Round Top. It began with the thrilling charge by Longstreet's men of Hood's division. Turning Ward's flank, on they swept from Devil's Den up the ravine between the Round Tops, confident that Little Round Top was undefended. Near the crest Vincent's brigade, posted in the nick of time by General Warren, burst upon them with the bayonet. Up and down the slope the struggling lines undulated, broken rapidly by the trees and boulders into single-handed combats; men and muskets in a moment were scattered all about. Just as Vincent's right was about to be overwhelmed, the 140th New York came upon the crest, led by the gallant young Colonel O'Rorke, who fell dead at the first volley. The regiment, rallied by Vincent, held their ground, but there Vincent, too, was killed. Meanwhile Hazlett's regular battery had

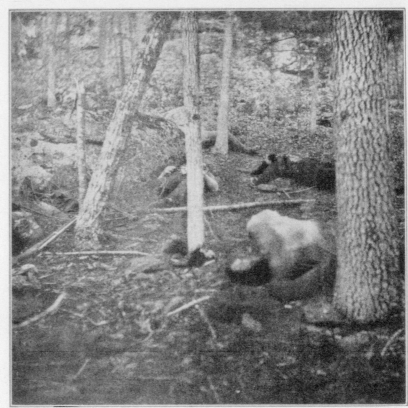

THE BATTLE–FIELD AMID THE TREES

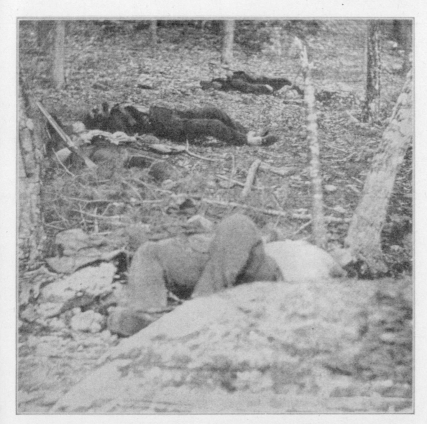

THE WOODED SLOPE OF LITTLE ROUND TOP

dragged its guns with great difficulty to the crest, where Generals Weed and Hazlett soon fell together. Colonel Rice, of the Forty-fourth New York (now in command in place of Vincent), had repulsed the assaults on his right and center. There was a lull, during which the Confederates stole around from the woods and fell with fury on the left of the line. Here Chamberlain's regiment, the Twentieth Maine, rapidly swinging around the rear of the mountain to meet the attack, was forced over the crest. Rallying, they drove back the Confederates in their turn. Twice more the struggling men fought back and forth over the summit, strewing the slopes with the fallen. Then a brigade of the Pennsylvania reserves and one from the Fifth Corps dashed over the hill. Chamberlain's brave men who were left greeted the reënforcements with a shout, dashed forward in a final charge, and drove the Confederates through the valley between the Round Tops. The Twentieth Maine had lost a third of its men and spent its last round of ammunition.

mortal combat and fell dead, side by side. The privates in the front ranks fought their way onward until they fell, the officers sprang forward, seized the muskets from the hands of the dying and the dead, and continued the combat. The furious struggle continued for half an hour, when Hood's forces gave way and were pressed down the hillside. But they rallied and advanced again by way of a ravine on the left, and finally, after a most valiant charge, were driven back at the point of the bayonet.

Little Round Top was saved to the Union army, but the cost was appalling. The hill was covered with hundreds of the slain. Scores of the Confederate sharpshooters had taken position among the crevasses in the Devil's Den, where they could overlook the position on Little Round Top, and their unerring aim spread death among the Federal officers and gunners. Colonel O'Rourke and General Vincent were dead. General Weed was dying; and, as Hazlett was stooping to receive Weed's last message, a sharpshooter's bullet laid him—dead—across the body of his chief.

During this attack, and for some hours thereafter, the battle continued in the valley below on a grander scale and with demon-like fury. Here many thousands were engaged. Sickles' whole line was pressed back to the base of the hill from which it had advanced in the morning. Sickles' leg was shattered by a shell, necessitating amputation, while scores of his brave officers, and thousands of his men, lay on the field of battle when the struggle ceased at nightfall. This valley has been appropriately named the " Valley of Death."

Before the close of this main part of the second day's battle, there was another clash of arms, fierce but of short duration, at the other extreme of the line. Lee had ordered Ewell to attack Cemetery Hill and Culp's Hill on the north, held by Slocum, who had been weakened by the sending of a large portion of the Twelfth Corps to the assistance of the left wing. Ewell had three divisions, two of which were commanded by

MEN WHO HELD LITTLE ROUND TOP

When General Warren discovered the defenseless condition of Little Round Top, he spied the division of Brigadier-General James Barnes marching to the relief of their comrades fighting along the Emmitsburg road. Warren, on his own responsibility, rode over to General Barnes and detached Vincent's brigade, hurrying it back to guard Little Round Top. It was not long before the men of the Forty-fourth New York were engaged in a fierce hand-to-hand combat with the determined Confederates of Hood, worming their way from tree to tree and boulder to boulder, in a running fight up the slope. The men of the Forty-fourth New York were among the finest in the service; they were enlisted from every county in their native State, and were selected in accordance with strict requirements as to fitness. The average age of the regiment was twenty-two; its heaviest battle loss (one hundred and eleven), occurred in the defense of Little Round Top at Gettysburg. The ground seemed impregnable, but the Southerners, rushing on from their victory at "the bloody angle," climbed the slopes in such a desperate onslaught that the Federals, not having time to load, advanced to repel the attack with the bayonet. The hillside after the battle was literally strewn with the dead and wounded. To the prompt and brave work of Vincent's brigade, in which fought the Forty-fourth New York, was due, in part, the fact that Little Round Top was not taken in that first assault. The repulse of the Confederates gave the Federals time to bring up a battery and strengthen the position against the repeated charges of the afternoon.

WHERE THE SECOND DAY'S ATTACK ENDED

Generals Early and Johnson. It was nearly sunset when he sent Early to attack Cemetery Hill. Early was repulsed after an hour's bloody and desperate hand-to-hand fight, in which muskets and bayonets, rammers, clubs, and stones were used. Johnson's attack on Culp's Hill was more successful. After a severe struggle of two or three hours General Greene, who alone of the Twelfth Corps remained on the right, succeeded, after reenforcement, in driving the right of Johnson's division away from its entrenchments, but the left had no difficulty in taking possession of the abandoned works of Geary and Ruger, now gone to Round Top and Rock Creek to assist the left wing.

Thus closed the second day's battle at Gettysburg. The harvest of death had been frightful. The Union loss during the two days had exceeded twenty thousand men; the Confederate loss was nearly equal. The Confederate army had gained an apparent advantage in penetrating the Union breastworks on Culp's Hill. But the Union lines, except on Culp's Hill, were unbroken. On the night of July 2d, Lee and his generals held a council of war and decided to make a grand final assault on Meade's center the following day. Against this decision Longstreet protested in vain. His counsel was that Lee withdraw to the mountains, compel Meade to follow, and then turn and attack him. But Lee was encouraged by the arrival of Pickett's division and of Stuart's cavalry, and Longstreet's objections were overruled. Meade and his corps commanders had met and made a like decision—that there should be a fight to the death at Gettysburg.

That night a brilliant July moon shed its luster upon the ghastly field on which thousands of men lay, unable to rise. Many of them no longer needed help. Their last battle was over, and their spirits had fled to the great Beyond. But there were great numbers, torn and gashed with shot and shell, who were still alive and calling for water or for the kindly touch of a helping hand. Nor did they call wholly in vain. Here and

## THE GROUND THAT WAS REGAINED

The indomitable photographer, Brady, in his famous duster, is sitting amid the battered trees on Culp's Hill, whose scars mark the scene of the recent crucial contest. The possession of the hill at nightfall of July 2d encouraged Lee to renew the general assault next day. This was the extreme right of the Federal position. Hancock, arriving on the afternoon of the first day, had seen its importance and sent a shattered brigade of Doubleday's First Corps to hold it. The marvelous fighting of Longstreet's men on the 2d had laid low 6,000 Federals before the Round Tops at the Federal left, and by nightfall Johnson's division of Ewell's Corps drove the defenders of Culp's Hill from their entrenchments. But Ewell, owing to the darkness, did not perceive the value of his new position. A short musket-shot beyond Culp's Hill, the artillery reserves and the supply trains of the Union army lay almost unprotected. At daylight of the 3d, Johnson's lines were attacked by the Second Massachusetts and the Twentieth Indiana, but these regiments were almost annihilated. But after seven hours of fighting the Confederates retreated.

there in the moonlight little rescuing parties were seeking out whom they might succor. They carried many to the improvised hospitals, where the surgeons worked unceasingly and heroically, and many lives were saved.

All through the night the Confederates were massing artillery along the crest of Seminary Ridge. The sound horses were carefully fed and watered, while those killed or disabled were replaced by others. The ammunition was replenished and the guns were placed in favorable positions and made ready for their work of destruction.

On the other side, the Federals were diligently laboring in the moonlight, and ere the coming of the day they had planted batteries on the brow of the hill above the town as far as Little Round Top. The coming of the morning revealed the two parallel lines of cannon, a mile apart, which signified only too well the story of what the day would bring forth.

The people of Gettysburg, which lay almost between the armies, were awakened on that fateful morning—July 3, 1863—by the roar of artillery from Culp's Hill, around the bend toward Rock Creek. This knoll in the woods had, as we have seen, been taken by Johnson's men the night before. When Geary and Ruger returned and found their entrenchments occupied by the Confederates they determined to recapture them in the morning, and began firing their guns at daybreak. Seven hours of fierce bombardment and daring charges were required to regain them. Every rod of space was disputed at the cost of many a brave man's life. At eleven o'clock this portion of the Twelfth Corps was again in its old position.

But the most desperate onset of the three days' battle was yet to come—Pickett's charge on Cemetery Ridge—preceded by the heaviest cannonading ever heard on the American continent.

With the exception of the contest at Culp's Hill and a cavalry fight east of Rock Creek, the forenoon of July 3d

## THE HEIGHT OF THE BATTLE-TIDE

Near this gate to the local cemetery of Gettysburg there stood during the battle this sign: "All persons found using firearms in these grounds will be prosecuted with the utmost rigor of the law." Many a soldier must have smiled grimly at these words, for this gateway became the key of the Federal line, the very center of the cruelest use of firearms yet seen on this continent. On the first day Reynolds saw the value of Cemetery Hill in case of a retreat. Howard posted his reserves here, and Hancock greatly strengthened the position. One hundred and twenty Confederate guns were turned against it that last afternoon. In five minutes every man of the Federals had been forced to cover; for an hour and a half the shells fell fast, dealing death and laying waste the summer verdure in the little graveyard. Up to the very guns of the Federals on Cemetery Hill, Pickett led his devoted troops. At night of the 3d it was one vast slaughter-field. On this eminence, where thousands were buried, was dedicated the soldiers' National Cemetery.

[B]

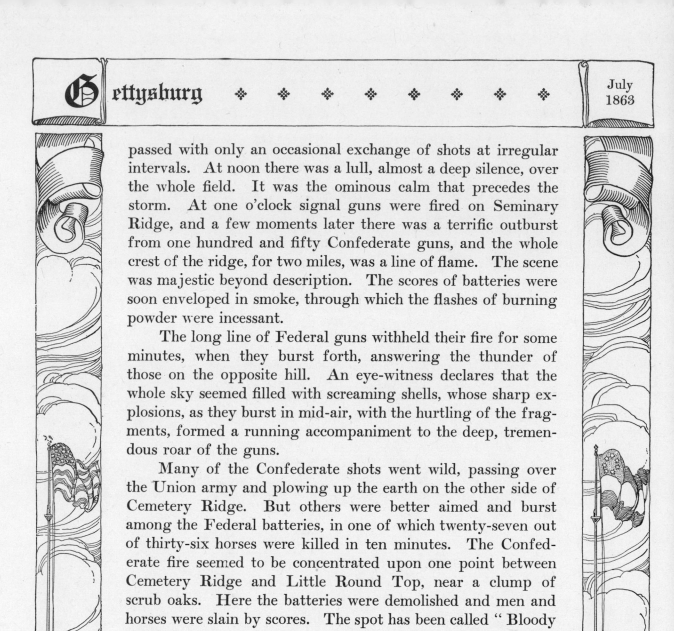

passed with only an occasional exchange of shots at irregular intervals. At noon there was a lull, almost a deep silence, over the whole field. It was the ominous calm that precedes the storm. At one o'clock signal guns were fired on Seminary Ridge, and a few moments later there was a terrific outburst from one hundred and fifty Confederate guns, and the whole crest of the ridge, for two miles, was a line of flame. The scene was majestic beyond description. The scores of batteries were soon enveloped in smoke, through which the flashes of burning powder were incessant.

The long line of Federal guns withheld their fire for some minutes, when they burst forth, answering the thunder of those on the opposite hill. An eye-witness declares that the whole sky seemed filled with screaming shells, whose sharp explosions, as they burst in mid-air, with the hurtling of the fragments, formed a running accompaniment to the deep, tremendous roar of the guns.

Many of the Confederate shots went wild, passing over the Union army and plowing up the earth on the other side of Cemetery Ridge. But others were better aimed and burst among the Federal batteries, in one of which twenty-seven out of thirty-six horses were killed in ten minutes. The Confederate fire seemed to be concentrated upon one point between Cemetery Ridge and Little Round Top, near a clump of scrub oaks. Here the batteries were demolished and men and horses were slain by scores. The spot has been called " Bloody Angle."

The Federal fire proved equally accurate and the destruction on Seminary Ridge was appalling. For nearly two hours the hills shook with the tremendous cannonading, when it gradually slackened and ceased. The Union army now prepared for the more deadly charge of infantry which it felt was sure to follow.

They had not long to wait. As the cannon smoke drifted away from between the lines fifteen thousand of Longstreet's

The Now-or-never Charge of Pickett's Men. When the Confederate artillery opened at one o'clock on the afternoon of July 3d, Meade and his staff were driven from their headquarters on Cemetery Ridge. Nothing could live exposed on that hillside, swept by cannon that were being worked as fast as human hands could work them. It was the beginning of Lee's last effort to wrest victory from the odds that were against him. Longstreet, on the morning of the 3d, had earnestly advised against renewing the battle against the Gettysburg heights. But Lee saw that in this moment the fate of the South hung in the balance; that if the Army of Northern Virginia did not win, it would never again become the aggressor. Pickett's division,

PICKETT—THE MARSHALL NEY OF GETTYSBURG

asked of Longstreet if he should go forward. Longstreet merely bowed in answer. "Sir, I shall lead my division forward," said Pickett at last, and the heavy-hearted Longstreet bowed his head. As the splendid column swept out of the woods and across the plain the Federal guns reopened with redoubled fury. For a mile Pickett and his men kept on, facing a deadly greeting of round shot, canister, and the bullets of Hancock's resolute infantry. It was magnificent—but every one of Pickett's brigade commanders went down and their men fell by scores and hundreds around them. A hundred led by Armistead, waving his cap on his sword-point, actually broke through and captured a battery, Armistead falling beside a gun.

as yet not engaged, was the force Lee designated for the assault; every man was a Virginian, forming a veritable Tenth Legion in valor. Auxiliary divisions swelled the charging column to 15,000. In the middle of the afternoon the Federal guns ceased firing. The time for the charge had come. Twice Pickett

It was but for a moment. Longstreet had been right when he said: "There never was a body of fifteen thousand men who could make that attack successfully." Before the converging Federals the thinned ranks of Confederates drifted wearily back toward Seminary Ridge. Victory for the South was not to be.

MEADE'S HEADQUARTERS ON CEMETERY RIDGE

corps emerged in grand columns from the wooded crest of Seminary Ridge under the command of General Pickett on the right and General Pettigrew on the left. Longstreet had planned the attack with a view to passing around Round Top, and gaining it by flank and reverse attack, but Lee, when he came upon the scene a few moments after the final orders had been given, directed the advance to be made straight toward the Federal main position on Cemetery Ridge.

The charge was one of the most daring in warfare. The distance to the Federal lines was a mile. For half the distance the troops marched gayly, with flying banners and glittering bayonets. Then came the burst of Federal cannon, and the Confederate ranks were torn with exploding shells. Pettigrew's columns began to waver, but the lines re-formed and marched on. When they came within musket-range, Hancock's infantry opened a terrific fire, but the valiant band only quickened its pace and returned the fire with volley after volley. Pettigrew's troops succumbed to the storm. For now the lines in blue were fast converging. Federal troops from all parts of the line now rushed to the aid of those in front of Pickett. The batteries which had been sending shell and solid shot changed their ammunition, and double charges of grape and canister were hurled into the column as it bravely pressed into the sea of flame. The Confederates came close to the Federal lines and paused to close their ranks. Each moment the fury of the storm from the Federal guns increased.

"Forward," again rang the command along the line of the Confederate front, and the Southerners dashed on. The first line of the Federals was driven back. A stone wall behind them gave protection to the next Federal force. Pickett's men rushed upon it. Riflemen rose from behind and hurled a death-dealing volley into the Confederate ranks. A defiant cheer answered the volley, and the Southerners placed their battle-flags on the ramparts. General Armistead grasped the flag from the hand of a falling bearer, and leaped upon the

The prelude to Pickett's magnificent charge was a sudden deluge of shells from 159 long-range Confederate guns trained upon Cemetery Ridge. General Meade and his staff were instantly driven from their headquarters (already illustrated) and within five minutes the concentrated artillery fire had swept every unsheltered position on Cemetery Ridge clear of men. In the woods, a mile and a half distant, Pickett and his men watched the effect of the bombardment, expecting the order to "Go Forward" up the slope (shown in the picture). The Federals had instantly opened with their eighty available guns, and for three hours the most terrific artillery duel of the war was kept up. Then the Federal fire slackened, as though the batteries were silenced. The Confederates' artillery ammunition also was now low. "For God's sake, come on!" was the word to Pickett. And at Longstreet's reluctant nod the commander led his 14,000 Virginians across the plain in their tragic charge up Cemetery Ridge.

## WHERE PICKETT CHARGED

In that historic charge was Armistead, who achieved a momentary victory and met a hero's death. On across the Emmitsburg road came Pickett's dauntless brigades, coolly closing up the fearful chasms torn in their ranks by the canister. Up to the fence held by Hays' brigade dashed the first gray line, only to be swept into confusion by a cruel enfilading fire. Then the brigades of Armistead and Garnett moved forward, driving Hays' brigade back through the batteries on the crest. Despite the death-dealing bolts on all sides, Pickett determined to capture the guns; and, at the order, Armistead, leaping the fence and waving his cap on his sword-point, rushed forward, followed by about a hundred of his men. Up to the very crest they fought the Federals back, and Armistead, shouting, "Give them the cold steel, boys!" seized one of the guns. For a moment the Confederate flag waved triumphantly over the Federal battery. For a brief interval the fight raged fiercely at close quarters. Armistead was shot down beside the gun he had taken, and his men were driven back. Pickett, as he looked around the top of the ridge he had gained, could see his men fighting all about with clubbed muskets and even flag-staffs against the troops that were rushing in upon them from all sides. Flesh and blood could not hold the heights against such terrible odds, and with a heart full of anguish Pickett ordered a retreat. The despairing Longstreet, watching from Seminary Ridge, saw through the smoke the shattered remnants drift sullenly down the slope and knew that Pickett's glorious but costly charge was ended.

GENERAL L. A. ARMISTEAD, C.S.A.

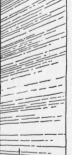

wall, waving it in triumph. Almost instantly he fell among the Federal troops, mortally wounded. General Garnett, leading his brigade, fell dead close to the Federal line. General Kemper sank, wounded, into the arms of one of his men.

Pickett had entered a death-trap. Troops from all directions rushed upon him. Clubbed muskets and barrel-staves now became weapons of warfare. The Confederates began surrendering in masses and Pickett ordered a retreat. Yet the energy of the indomitable Confederates was not spent. Several supporting brigades moved forward, and only succumbed when they encountered two regiments of Stannard's Vermont brigade, and the fire of fresh batteries.

As the remnant of the gallant division returned to the works on Seminary Ridge General Lee rode out to meet them. His demeanor was calm. His features gave no evidence of his disappointment. With hat in hand he greeted the men sympathetically. " It was all my fault," he said. " Now help me to save that which remains."

The battle of Gettysburg was over. The cost in men was frightful. The losses of the two armies reached fifty thousand, about half on either side. More than seven thousand men had fallen dead on the field of battle.

The tide could rise no higher; from this point the ebb must begin. Not only here, but in the West the Southern cause took a downward turn; for at this very hour of Pickett's charge, Grant and Pemberton, a thousand miles away, stood under an oak tree on the heights above the Mississippi and arranged for the surrender of Vicksburg.

Lee could do nothing but lead his army back to Virginia. The Federals pursued but feebly. The Union victory was not a very decisive one, but, supported as it was by the fall of Vicksburg, the moral effect on the nation and on the world was great. The period of uncertainty was ended. It required but little prophetic vision to foresee that the Republic would survive the dreadful shock of arms.

## THE MAN WHO HELD THE CENTER

Headquarters of Brigadier-General Alexander S. Webb. It devolved upon the man pictured here (booted and in full uniform, before his headquarters tent to the left of the picture) to meet the shock of Pickett's great charge. In command of three Pennsylvania regiments (the Seventy-First, Seventy-Second, and One Hundred and Sixth) of Hancock's Second Corps, Webb was equal to the emergency. Stirred to great deeds by the example of a patriotic ancestry, he felt that upon his holding his position depended the out-come of the day. His front had been the focus of the Confederate artillery fire. Batteries to right and left of his line were practically silenced. Young Lieutenant Cushing, mortally wounded, fired the last serviceable gun and fell dead as Pickett's men came on. Wheeler's First New York Battery dashed up to take Cushing's place and was captured by the men of Armistead. Webb at the head of the Seventy-second Pennsylvania fought back the on-rush, posting a line of slightly wounded in his rear. Webb himself fell wounded but his command checked the assault till Hall's brilliant charge turned the tide at this point.

THE GOLDEN OPPORTUNITY

The Potomac from Berlin Heights, July, 1863. Instead of a wall of steel in his rear, as might have happened, Lee met only open roads in his retreat after Gettysburg. After the failure of Pickett's charge, Lee and his generals began rallying their troops behind the guns as a protection against the counter-charge which all felt sure was bound to come. Hancock, lying in an ambulance, severely wounded, argued that as he had been struck by a ten-penny nail the Confederate ammunition must be exhausted. His deduction was correct, but although he summoned his waning strength to dictate an approval of the charge, should it be ordered, no advance was made. Meade could have sent forward an entire corps (Sedgwick's) which had not been engaged. By the afternoon of July 4th, Lee's shattered forces were in full retreat toward the Potomac, beyond which lay safety.

## THE LEISURELY PURSUIT

Meade's army crossing the Potomac at Berlin, eighteen days after the battle of Gettysburg. Lincoln never ceased to regret that he had not gone in person to Gettysburg to push the pursuit of Lee. Not till July 5th did Meade put his army in motion to follow the Confederates, who had marched all afternoon and all night in the pouring rain, impeded with heavy trains of ammunition which might easily have been captured. Lee found the pontoon bridges which he had left at Falling Waters destroyed by a Federal raiding party sent by General French from Frederick, and drew up his army for the battle that he anticipated must be fought before recrossing the Potomac. Not till the night of July 13th did Meade determine upon an attack. Meanwhile Lee had gained the time necessary to repair his bridges and retreat into Virginia. Meade could not follow directly. Only after a long march through the neighborhood of Harper's Ferry did he get his army across. Before he could strike the Confederates again, Lee was strongly posted along the line of the Rapidan.

# CHAPTER ONE

———

## PART IV
## ALONG THE TENNESSEE

———

# CHICKAMAUGA—A
# CONFEDERATE VICTORY

———

1864
UNION STOREHOUSES AT BRIDGEPORT, TENNESSEE RIVER

LEE & GORDON'S MILLS ON THE CHICKAMAUGA, SEPTEMBER, 1863

Dozing in the autumn sunlight of 1863, this obscure building, bearing by chance the patronymics of two great Southern generals, was suddenly to mark a strategic point in the most sanguinary of the battles of the West. It stood on the west branch of Chickamauga Creek, which flowed through the fertile valley between Missionary Ridge and Pigeon Mountain. Through the passes of the one the Federals under Rosecrans were advancing on September 12th, while the Confederates under Bragg held the approaches at the other. Between them flowed the little stream, undoubtedly the scene of some prehistoric conflict, for the Indians had named it Chickamauga, "River of Death." In 1863 the word was about to be written into American history to designate a two-days' battle in which the South lost more in killed and wounded than at Gettysburg and the North almost the same number as at Chancellorsville. The storm center

## THE BLOODIEST BATTLE-FIELD OF THE WAR

of the mighty conflict had shifted to the West. After Gettysburg the Army of Northern Virginia and the Army of the Potomac lay warily watching each other, each disinclined to become the aggressor. Lincoln had been urging Rosecrans to move his Army of the Cumberland on from Murfreesboro and attack Bragg's entrenched position in south central Tennessee so as to prevent Bragg from detaching troops to raise the siege of Vicksburg. At last, on June 24, 1863, he took the initiative, and then, with what is considered by some military writers the war's masterpiece of strategy, he drove Bragg out of Tennessee into Georgia. Rosecrans' advance was in Bragg's abandoned works around Tullahoma on July 3d and in Chattanooga on September 9th, all without a battle. Burnside, with the Army of the Ohio, captured Knoxville on September 3d. But Tennessee was not to be abandoned by the Confederates without a fight.

# CHICKAMAUGA—THE BLOODIEST CONFLICT IN THE WEST

In its dimensions and its murderousness the battle of Chickamauga was the greatest battle fought by our Western armies, and one of the greatest of modern times. In our Civil War it was exceeded only by Gettysburg and the Wilderness; in European history we may compare with it such battles as Neerwinden, or Malplaquet, or Waterloo.—*John Fiske in "The Mississippi Valley in the Civil War."*

THE town of Chattanooga, Tennessee, lies in a great bend of the Tennessee River and within a vast amphitheater of mountains, ranging in a general southwesterly direction, and traversed at intervals by great depressions or valleys. These passes form a natural gateway from the mid-Mississippi valley to the seaboard States. To dislodge the Confederate army under General Bragg from this natural fortress would remove the last barrier to the invading Federals, and permit an easy entry upon the plains of Georgia. The importance of this position was readily apparent to the Confederate Government, and any approach by the Federal forces toward this point was almost certain to be met by stubborn resistance.

Rosecrans' forward movement from Murfreesboro, in the early summer of 1863, forced Bragg over the Cumberland Mountains and across the Tennessee. The Confederate leader destroyed the railroad bridge at Bridgeport and entrenched himself in and around Chattanooga. The advanced portion of the Federal army had made its way as far as Stevenson, Alabama, when circumstances compelled a halt. It was found impossible to transport needed forage and supplies over the terrible roads of eastern Tennessee. Rosecrans could go no

## ON THE WAY TO CHICKAMAUGA

To the Elk River Bridge (near Decherd, Tennessee) the enterprising army photographer who was recording Rosecrans' advance had followed the Army of the Cumberland in July, 1863. The two distinct maneuvers that led to Chickamauga fully sustained the reputation of Rosecrans as one of the greatest strategic generals of the war. The first movement was executed in nine days, during which time the troops struggled with their heavy trains along roads little better than bogs. Torrential rains, such as Tennessee had rarely known before, fell incessantly; the artillery had to be dragged through the mire by hand. Despite such difficulties, Rosecrans succeeded in flanking Bragg, compelling him to retreat from his strong position at Tullahoma. South of that place, on the Nashville & Chattanooga Railroad, this bridge was made the objective of Wilder's mounted infantry, which swept around in Bragg's rear, striking the railroad at Decherd, destroying the commissary depot and cutting the rail connection with Chattanooga. A detachment pushed forward to the bridge, but it was too strongly guarded to be destroyed. The Confederates burnt it in their retreat to Chattanooga, but was rebuilt by Rosecrans; it was completed by the Federal engineers on July 13th.

further until the Nashville and Chattanooga Railroad was repaired as far as Stevenson and Bridgeport, and storage depots established at these and neighboring places. Consequently it was not until August 16th that the movement over the Cumberland Mountains began. Rosecrans had the choice of approaching Chattanooga from the north side of the river, a seventy-mile march through a rough, mountainous country, ill supplied with water and forage, or of crossing the Tennessee on the southwest and moving on the town over Sand and Lookout mountains. He chose the latter for all but a small portion of his force, although it was the more hazardous.

Between August 29th and September 4th Crittenden, Thomas, and McCook got their corps over at various places between Shellmound and Caperton's Ferry. General Granger, with the reserve corps, took charge of the rear. When Crittenden received orders for crossing the river he was commanded to leave the brigades of Hazen and Wagner behind to threaten Chattanooga from the north. For some days Wagner had been shelling the town, and Bragg, fully expecting the early approach of the Army of the Cumberland from this direction, had concentrated his forces at and above Chattanooga. Rosecrans, consequently, was able to accomplish the difficult crossing of the Tennessee without interference.

He found the Confederates in possession of the north end of Lookout Mountain and decided to dislodge his adversary by endangering his line of communication from the south and east. McCook on the Federal right was sent across Lookout Mountain at Winston's Gap, forty-six miles south of Chattanooga to occupy Alpine, east of the mountains. Thomas went to McLemore's Cove, east of Missionary Ridge, while Crittenden, on the left, was stationed in Lookout Valley to keep his eye on Chattanooga. The cavalry was sent forward to destroy the Western and Atlantic Railroad near Dalton, Georgia. On September 8th, before all these moves had been accomplished, Bragg abandoned his stronghold.

[274]

## WHERE THE PONTOONS RAN SHORT

The Railroad Bridge over the Tennessee River at Bridgeport, Alabama, August, 1863.  In the movement against Chattanooga, Rosecrans chose the Tennessee River for his line.   Feinting strongly with Crittenden's command to the north of Bragg's position, he crossed the main body of his army to the south.   There was much impatience in Washington that the movement was not more promptly executed, but serious difficulties delayed it.  It took three weeks to repair the railroad, and on August 25th the first supply-train was pushed through Stevenson, Alabama, where the new commissary base was established.   Meanwhile  the Tennessee, greatly swollen by recent rains, presented a formidable barrier.   There were not enough pontoons, and at Bridgeport Sheridan had to piece out the bridge with trestle-work.

[B]

Crittenden the next day marched around the north end of Lookout and entered the town, while Hazen and Wagner crossed over from the opposite bank of the Tennessee.

Rosecrans believed that Bragg was in full retreat toward Rome, Georgia, and Crittenden, leaving one brigade in Chattanooga, was ordered to pursue. Bragg encouraged his adversary in the belief that he was avoiding an engagement and sent spies as deserters into the Federal ranks to narrate the details of his flight. Meanwhile, he was concentrating at Lafayette, about twenty-five miles south of Chattanooga. Hither General S. B. Buckner, entirely too weak to cope with Burnside's heavy column approaching from Kentucky, brought his troops from Knoxville. Breckinridge and two brigades arrived from Mississippi, while twelve thousand of Lee's veterans, under Lee's most trusted and illustrious lieutenant, Longstreet, were hastening from Virginia to add their numbers to Bragg's Army of Tennessee.

The three corps of the Union army, as we have seen, were now separated over a wide extent of territory by intervening ridges, so intent was Rosecrans on intercepting the vanished Bragg. But the latter, by no means vanished, and with his face toward Chattanooga, considered the position of his antagonist and discovered his own army almost opposite the Federal center. Crittenden was advancing toward Ringgold, and the remoteness of Thomas' corps on his right precluded any immediate union of the Federal forces.

Bragg was quick to grasp the opportunity made by Rosecrans' division of the army in the face of his opponent. He at once perceived the possibilities of a master-stroke; to crush Thomas' advanced divisions with an overwhelming force.

The attempt failed, owing to a delay in the attack, which permitted the endangered Baird and Negley to fall back. Bragg then resolved to throw himself upon Crittenden, who had divided his corps. Polk was ordered to advance upon that portion of it at Lee and Gordon's Mills, but when Bragg came

## THE FIRST TO REACH THE BATTLE-FIELD

General James S. Negley and Staff.   General Negley (standing uncovered in this picture) formed with his division the advance-guard in the forward movement from the Tennessee against Bragg.   This picture (taken at Cove Spring, near Stevenson, Alabama, before the advance) shows the arduous character of the country through which the march was made.   Crossing the Tennessee at Caperton's Ferry, Negley's division pressed forward, and on September 9th held the passes of Lookout Mountain.   Next day, crossing Missionary Ridge, he took up position in McLemore's Cove.   This was destined to become the battle-field of Chickamauga, and here Negley's advance was checked.   Bragg, instead of being in retreat, was concentrating in his front, eager to crush the corps of Thomas, which he knew had come up too confidently, unsupported by the rest of Rosecrans' army.   On the 11th Negley's position became precarious; Bragg was sending against him such a superior force that he was in great danger of losing his train.   With great energy and skill, supported by Baird's division, he succeeded in falling back to a strong position in front of Stevens' Gap without the loss of a single wagon.   Negley, who was made a major-general for his bravery at Stone's River, was censured by the irascible Rosecrans for his supposed disobedience of orders at Chickamauga.   Subsequent investigation completely exonerated him.   With only a handful of his men he had saved fifty guns in the rout of the 20th.

to the front September 13th, expecting to witness the annihilation of the Twenty-first Corps, he found to his bitter disappointment that the bishop-general had made no move and that Crittenden had reunited his divisions and was safe on the west bank of the Chickamauga. Thus his splendid chances of breaking up the Army of the Cumberland were ruined.

When Bragg's position became known to Rosecrans, great was his haste to effect the concentration of his army. Couriers dashed toward Alpine with orders for McCook to join Thomas with the utmost celerity. The former started at once, shortly after midnight on the 13th, in response to Thomas's urgent call. It was a real race of life and death, attended by the greatest hardships. Ignorant of the roads, McCook submitted his troops to a most exhausting march, twice up and down the mountain, fifty-seven miles of the most arduous toil, often dragging artillery up by hand and letting it down steep declines by means of ropes. But he closed up with Thomas on the 17th, and the Army of the Cumberland was saved from its desperate peril.

Crittenden's corps now took position at Lee and Gordon's Mills on the left bank of Chickamauga Creek, and the Federal troops were all within supporting distance. In the Indian tongue Chickamauga means "The River of Death," a name strangely prophetic of that gigantic conflict soon to be waged by these hostile forces throughout this beautiful and heretofore peaceful valley.

The Confederate army, its corps under Generals Polk, D. H. Hill, and Buckner, was stationed on the east side of the stream, its right wing below Lee and Gordon's Mills, and the left extending up the creek toward Lafayette. On the Federal side Thomas was moved to the left, with Crittenden in the center and McCook on the right. Their strength has been estimated at fifty-five to sixty-nine thousand men. On the 18th, Longstreet's troops were arriving from Virginia, and by the morning of the 19th the greater part of the Confederate army

[278]

## THE LEADER OF THE RIGHT WING

General Alexander McD. McCook at Chickamauga.   While Thomas, preceded by Negley, was pressing forward to McLemore's Cove, McCook advanced the right wing of the army to the southward within twenty miles of Lafayette, where Bragg had his headquarters.   Crittenden, meanwhile, with the left wing, was advancing from Chattanooga on the north.   It was the opportunity to strike one of these widely separated corps that Bragg missed.   At midnight on September 13th McCook received the order to hurry back and make junction with Thomas.   Then began a race of life and death over fifty-seven miles of excruciating marching, back across Lookout Mountain and northward through Lookout Valley to Stevens' Gap, where he arrived on the 17th.   After a brief rest the right wing marched through half the night to its designated position on the battle-field, and by the morning of the 18th Rosecrans' army was at last concentrated.   General McCook (of a family that sent a father and five sons into the war) had distinguished himself at Shiloh and Corinth, and with the First Corps of the Army of the Ohio had borne the brunt of the battle at Perryville.   At Stone's River he commanded the right wing of the army, which suffered such severe disaster.   Again at Chickamauga the right wing, after sending reënforcements to Thomas at the left, was driven back in rout.

had crossed the Chickamauga. The two mighty armies were now face to face, and none could doubt that the impending struggle would be attended by frightful loss to both sides.

It was Bragg's intention to send Polk, commanding the right wing, in a flanking movement against the Federal left under Thomas, and thus intervene between it and Chattanooga. The first encounter, at 10 o'clock in the morning of the 19th, resulted in a Confederate repulse, but fresh divisions were constantly pushed forward under the deadly fire of the Federal artillery. The Federals were gradually forced back by the incessant charge of the Confederates; but assailed and assailant fought with such great courage and determination that any decided advantage was withheld from either. Meanwhile, the Federal right was hard pressed by Hood, commanding Longstreet's corps, and a desperate battle ensued along the entire line. It seemed, however, more like a struggle between separate divisions than the clash of two great armies. When night descended the Federals had been forced back from the creek, but the result had been indecisive.

Disaster to the Union army had been averted by the use of powerful artillery when the infantry seemed unable to withstand the onslaught. Rosecrans had assumed the defensive, and his troops had so far receded as to enable the Confederates to form their lines on all the territory fought over on that day. During the night preparations were made in both camps for a renewal of the battle on the following morning, which was Sunday. A fresh disposition of the troops was made by both leaders. Near midnight General Longstreet arrived on the field, and was at once placed in command of the Confederate left, Polk retaining the right. Not all of Longstreet's troops arrived in time for the battle, but Bragg's force has been estimated at fifty-one to seventy-one thousand strong.

Thomas was given command of the Union left, with McCook at his right, while Crittenden's forces occupied the center, but to the rear of both Thomas and McCook. Thomas had

## THE CONFEDERATE LEADER AT CHICKAMAUGA

Major-General Braxton Bragg, C.S.A.   Born, 1815; West Point, 1837; Died, 1876.   Bragg's name before 1861 was perhaps better known in military annals than that of any other Southern leader because of his brilliant record in the Mexican War.   In the Civil War he distinguished himself first at Shiloh and by meritorious services thereafter.   But his delays rendered him scarcely a match for Rosecrans, to say nothing of Grant and Sherman.   Flanked out of two strong positions, he missed the opportunity presented by Rosecrans' widely separated forces  and  failed to crush the Army of the Cumberland in detail, as it advanced to the battle of Chickamauga.   The error cost the Confederates the loss of Tennessee, eventually.

spent the night in throwing up breastworks on the brow of
Snodgrass Hill, as it was anticipated that the Confederates
would concentrate their attack upon his position.

Hostilities began with a general movement of the Confederate right wing in an attempt to flank the Union left. General Bragg had ordered Polk to begin the attack at daybreak,
but it was nearly ten o'clock in the morning before Breckinridge's division, supported by General Cleburne, advanced
upon Thomas' entrenchments. Fighting desperately, the Confederates did not falter under the heavy fire of the Federals,
and it seemed as if the latter must be driven from their position.
Rosecrans, in response to urgent requests for reenforcements,
despatched troops again and again to the aid of Thomas, and
the assault was finally repulsed. Cleburne's division was driven
back with heavy loss, and Breckinridge, unable to retain any
advantage, was forced to defend his right, which was being
seriously menaced. The battle at this point had been desperately waged, both sides exhibiting marked courage and determination. As on the previous day, the Confederates had been
the aggressors, but the Federal troops had resisted all attempts
to invade their breastworks.

However, the fortunes of battle were soon to incline to the
side of the Southern army. Bragg sent Stewart's division forward, and it pressed Reynolds' and Brannan's men back to
their entrenchments. Rosecrans sent Wood word to close up
on Reynolds. Through some misunderstanding in giving or
interpreting this order, General Wood withdrew his division
from its position on the right of Brannan. By this movement
a large opening was left almost in the center of the battle-line.
Johnson's, Hindman's, and Kershaw's divisions rushed into the
gap and fell upon the Union right and center with an impetus
that was irresistible. The Confederate general, Bushrod Johnson, has given us an unforgetable picture of the thrilling event:
" The resolute and impetuous charge, the rush of our heavy
columns sweeping out from the shadow and gloom of the forest

## THE TOO–ADVANCED POSITION

Crawfish Spring, to the South of the Chickamauga Battle-field.    Rosecrans, in concentrating his troops on the 18th of September, was still possessed of the idea that Bragg was covering his retreat upon his railroad connections at Dalton.    Instead, the Confederate commander had massed his forces on the other side of Chickamauga and was only awaiting the arrival of Longstreet to assume the aggressive. On the morning of the 19th, McCook's right wing at Crawfish Spring was strongly threatened by the Confederates, while the real attack was made against the left in an effort to turn it and cut Rosecrans off from a retreat upon Chattanooga.    All day long, brigade after brigade was marched from the right of the Federal line in order to extend the left under Thomas and withstand this flanking movement. Even after nightfall, Thomas, trying to re-form his lines and carry them still farther to the left for the work of the morrow, brought on a sharp conflict in the darkness.    The Confederates had been held back, but at heavy cost.    That night, at the Widow Glenn's house, Rosecrans consulted his generals.    The exhausted Thomas, when roused from sleep for his opinion, invariably answered, "I would strengthen the left."    There seemed as yet to be no crisis at hand, and the council closed with a song by the debonair McCook.

into the open fields flooded with sunlight, the glitter of arms, the onward dash of artillery and mounted men, the retreat of the foe, the shouts of the hosts of our army, the dust, the smoke, the noise of fire-arms—of whistling balls, and grape-shot, and of bursting shell—made up a battle-scene of unsurpassed grandeur. Here, General Hood gave me the last order I received from him on the field, 'Go ahead and keep ahead of everything.'" A moment later, and Hood fell, severely wounded, with a minie ball in his thigh.

Wood's right brigade was shattered even before it had cleared the opening. Sheridan's entire division, and part of Davis' and Van Cleve's, were driven from the field. Longstreet now gave a fine exhibition of his military genius. The orders of battle were to separate the two wings of the opposing army. But with the right wing of his opponents in hopeless ruin, he wheeled to the right and compelled the further withdrawal of Federal troops in order to escape being surrounded. The brave soldier-poet, William H. Lytle, fell at the head of his brigade as he strove to re-form his line. McCook and Crittenden were unable, in spite of several gallant efforts, to rally their troops and keep back the onrushing heroes of Stone's River and Bull Run. The broken mass fled in confusion toward Chattanooga, carrying with it McCook, Crittenden, and Rosecrans. The latter telegraphed to Washington that his army had been beaten. In this famous charge the Confederates took several thousand prisoners and forty pieces of artillery.

Flushed with victory, the Confederates now concentrated their attack upon Thomas, who thus far, on Horseshoe Ridge and its spurs, had repelled all attempts to dislodge him. The Confederates, with victory within their grasp, and led by the indomitable Longstreet, swarmed up the slopes in great numbers, but they were hurled back with fearful slaughter. Thomas was looking anxiously for Sheridan, whom, as he knew, Rosecrans had ordered with two brigades to his support.

## WHERE THE LINES WERE SWEPT BACK

Lee & Gordon's mill, seen in the picture, marked the extreme right of the Federal line on the second day at Chickamauga. From it, northward, were posted the commands of McCook and Crittenden, depleted by the detachments of troops the day before to strengthen the left. All might have gone well if the main attack of the Confederates had continued to the left, as Rosecrans expected. But hidden in the woods, almost within a stone's throw of the Federal right on that misty morning, was the entire corps of Longstreet, drawn up in columns of brigades at half distance—"a masterpiece of tactics," giving space for each column to swing right or left. Seizing a momentous opportunity which would have lasted but thirty minutes at the most, Longstreet hurled them through a gap which, owing to a misunderstanding, had been left open, and the entire Federal right was swept from the field.

But in Longstreet's rout of the right wing Sheridan, with the rest, had been carried on toward Chattanooga, and he found himself completely cut off from Thomas, as the Confederates were moving parallel to him. Yet the indomitable Sheridan, in spite of his terrible experience of the morning, did not give up the attempt. Foiled in his efforts to get through McFarland's Gap, he moved quickly on Rossville and came down the Lafayette road toward Thomas' left flank.

Meanwhile, advised by the incessant roar of musketry, General Gordon Granger, in command of the reserve corps near Rossville, advanced rapidly with his fresh troops. Acting with promptness and alacrity under orders, Granger sent Steedman to Thomas' right.

Directly across the line of Thomas' right was a ridge, on which Longstreet stationed Hindman with a large command, ready for an attack on Thomas' flank—a further and terrible menace to the nearly exhausted general, but it was not all. In the ridge was a small gap, and through this Kershaw was pouring his division, intent on getting to Thomas' rear. Rosecrans thus describes the help afforded to Thomas: " Steedman, taking a regimental color, led the column. Swift was the charge and terrible the conflict, but the enemy was broken."

The fighting grew fiercer, and at intervals was almost hand to hand. The casualties among the officers, who frequently led their troops in person, were mounting higher and higher as the moments passed. All the afternoon the assaults continued, but the Union forces stood their ground. Ammunition ran dangerously low, but Steedman had brought a small supply, and when this was distributed each man had about ten rounds. Finally, as the sun was setting in the west, the Confederate troops advanced in a mighty concourse. The combined forces of Kershaw, Law, Preston, and Hindman once more rushed forward, gained possession of their lost ridge at several points, but were unable to drive their attack home. In many places the Union lines stood firm and both sides

## THE HOUSE WHENCE HELP CAME

Here, at his headquarters, holding the Federal line of retreat at Rossville Gap (the Confederate objective in the battle), General Gordon Granger heard with increasing anxiety the sounds of the conflict, three miles away, growing more and more ominous. Finally, in disobedience of orders, he set in motion his three brigades to the relief of Thomas, pushing forward two of them under Steedman. These arrived upon the field early in the afternoon, the most critical period of the battle, as Longstreet charged afresh on Thomas' right and rear. Seizing a battle-flag, Steedman (at the order of General Granger) led his command in a counter-charge which saved the Army of the Cumberland. This old house at Rossville was built by John Ross, a chief of the Cherokee Indians, and he lived in it till 1832, giving his name to the hamlet. Half-breed descendants of the Cherokees who had intermarried with both whites and Negroes were numerous in the vicinity of Chickamauga, and many of them fought with their white neighbors on the Confederate side.

rested in the positions taken. The plucky Thomas was saved. The onslaught on the Federal left of the battlefield was one of the heaviest attacks made on a single point during the war.

History records no grander spectacle than Thomas' stand at Chickamauga. He was ever afterwards known as "The Rock of Chickamauga." Under the cover of darkness, Thomas, having received word from Rosecrans to withdraw, retired his army in good order to Rossville, and on the following day rejoined Rosecrans in Chattanooga. The battle of Chickamauga, considering the forces engaged, was one of the most destructive of the Civil War. The Union army lost approximately sixteen thousand men, and while the loss to the Confederate army is not definitely known, it was probably nearly eighteen thousand. The personal daring and tenacious courage displayed in the ranks of both armies have never been excelled on any battlefield. The Confederate generals, Helm, Deshler, and Preston Smith were killed; Adams, Hood, Brown, Gregg, Clayton, Hindman, and McNair were wounded. The Federal side lost Lytle. The battle is generally considered a Confederate victory, and yet, aside from the terrible loss of human life, no distinct advantage accrued to either side. The Federal army retained possession of Chattanooga, but the Confederates had for the time checked the Army of the Cumberland from a further occupation of Southern soil.

It is a singular coincidence that the generals-in-chief of both armies exercised but little supervision over the movements of their respective troops. The brunt of the battle fell, for the most part, upon the commanders of the wings. To the subordinate generals on each side were awarded the highest honors. Longstreet, because of his eventful charge, which swept the right wing of the Union army from the field, was proclaimed the victor of Chickamauga; and to General Thomas, who by his firmness and courage withstood the combined attack of the Confederate forces when disaster threatened on every side, is due the brightest laurels from the adherents of the North.

# PART IV
## ALONG THE TENNESSEE

———

# THE BATTLES
# AT CHATTANOOGA

———

ON LOOKOUT MOUNTAIN—1864

## IN THE BELEAGUERED CITY

In the parlor of this little dwelling sat Ulysses S. Grant on the evening of October 23, 1863. Muddy and rain-soaked from his long ride, he was gravely consulting with General Thomas and his officers. The Army of the Cumberland was in a serious predicament, summed up by Thomas' reply to Grant's first order from Nashville: "We will hold the town till we starve." Grant had starved a Confederate army out of Vicksburg; and now Bragg's army, reënforced by troops from Johnston, had settled down before Chattanooga to starve out, in turn, what was then the most important Federal force in the West. Strongly posted on Missionary Ridge and Lookout Mountain and in Chattanooga Valley to the south and southeast of the town, Bragg controlled the railroad, making it impossible for supplies to come over it from Bridgeport, Ala. Everything had to be brought into Chattanooga by wagon-trains over a roundabout route of nearly

## HEADQUARTERS OF GENERAL THOMAS AT CHATTANOOGA

thirty miles.   The passage of wagons over the roads was difficult even in good weather, and they were rapidly becoming impassable from the autumn rains.   Bragg's forces had fallen upon and burned some three hundred Federal wagons, and with those that were left it was impossible to bring in more than the scantiest supplies.   The men had been for weeks on half-rations; all the artillery horses had starved to death; an occasional herd of beef cattle was driven down from Nashville through the denuded country and upon arrival would be aptly characterized by the soldiers as "beef dried on the hoof."   This and hard bread were their only sustenance.   Grant, now in command of all the Federal forces from the Alleghanies to the Mississippi, was first confronted by the necessity of hastening the delivery of supplies.   Either the Army of the Cumberland must be fed or Bragg would regain the ground that had been lost in Tennessee.

[B]

COPYRIGHT, 1911, REVIEW OF REVIEWS CO.

## THE ATTACK THAT HAD TO WAIT

Near this spot General Sherman crossed his advance column in boats on the night of November 23d and captured all the Confederate pickets along the river except one. Grant, after seizing Brown's Ferry and thus opening a new route for his supplies, ordered Sherman to join him by forced marches. Immediately upon arrival the wearied soldiers of the Army of the Tennessee were assigned the task of opening the main attack upon Bragg's line to the southeast of Chattanooga on Missionary Ridge. Grant did not consider the Army of the Cumberland strong enough to attack Bragg alone, and consequently had postponed such a movement until Sherman could come up. By the 23d of November Sherman's divisions lay in camp, concealed behind the hills near the river bank, at the right of this structure, all ready to cross on a pontoon-bridge which had already been laid higher up the stream.

## THE UNEXPECTED VICTORY

The Northeast Slope of Lookout Mountain. This photograph was taken from the hill to the north, where Hooker directed his troops in their "battle above the clouds" on the morning of November 24, 1863. Up this mountain-side Hooker's men fought their way to Pulpit Rock, a height of 2,400 feet. Grant's plan was for nothing more than a demonstration by Hooker to drive the Confederates back from reënforcing their right, where Sherman was to do the heavy work. Hooker's divisions had never before fought together, but with fine ardor they drove Stevenson's six brigades up this slope, and, fighting in the mist, swept them from their entrenchments on the mountain-top. Thus victory first came at the farther end of the line.

# THE BATTLES ON LOOKOUT MOUNTAIN AND MISSIONARY RIDGE

AFTER CHATTANOOGA: "The Confederate lines . . . could not be rebuilt. The material for reconstructing them was exhausted. The blue-crested flood which had broken these lines was not disappearing. The fountains which supplied it were exhaustless. It was still coming with an ever increasing current, swelling higher and growing more resistless. This triune disaster [Vicksburg, Gettysburg, Missionary Ridge] was especially depressing to the people because it came like a blight upon their hopes which had been awakened by recent Confederate victories."—*General John B. Gordon, C. S. A., in "Reminiscences of the Civil War."*

FOLLOWING the defeat of Rosecrans' army at Chickamauga, in September, 1863, Bragg at once took strong positions on Missionary Ridge and Lookout Mountain. From these heights he was able to besiege the entire Army of the Cumberland in Chattanooga and obstruct the main arteries of supply to the Federal troops. Rosecrans was forced to abandon the route along the south bank of the Tennessee River, which led from Bridgeport, in Alabama, and to depend exclusively upon a long and mountainous wagon road on the north side of the river for the transportation of supplies. The Confederate cavalry, crossing the Tennessee above Chattanooga, fell upon the trains entangled in the mud of the Sequatchie valley, destroying in one day three hundred wagons, and killing or capturing about eighteen hundred mules. Within a short time the wisdom of Bragg's plan became apparent; famine threatened the Union army and several thousand horses and mules had already died from starvation. By his relentless vigil, the Confederate leader seemed destined to achieve a greater victory over his opponent than had hitherto attended his efforts in actual conflict.

[ 294 ]

## THE BESIEGED

At this point, where Citico Creek joins the Tennessee, the left of the Eleventh Corps of the Army of the Cumberland rested on the river bank, the limit of the Federal line of defense, east of Chattanooga.   Here, on high ground overlooking the stream, was posted Battery McAloon to keep the Confederates back from the river, so that timber and firewood could be rafted down to the besieged army.   In the chill of  autumn, with scanty rations, the soldiers had a hard time keeping warm, as all fuel within the lines had been consumed.   The Army of the Cumberland was almost conquered by hardship.   Grant feared that the soldiers "could not be got out of their trenches to assume the offensive."   But it was these very men who achieved the most signal victory in the battle of Chattanooga.

Meanwhile, a complete reorganization of the Federal forces in the West was effected. Under the title of the Military Division of the Mississippi, the Departments of the Ohio, the Cumberland, and the Tennessee were united with Grant as general commanding, and Rosecrans was replaced by Thomas at the head of the Army of the Cumberland.

A hurried concentration of the Federal forces was now ordered by General Halleck. Hooker with fifteen thousand men of the Army of the Potomac came rapidly by rail to Bridgeport. Sherman, with a portion of his army, about twenty thousand strong, was summoned from Vicksburg and at once embarked in steamers for Memphis. General Grant decided to assume personal charge of the Federal forces; but before he reached his new command, Thomas, ably assisted by his chief engineer, General W. F. Smith, had begun to act on a plan which Rosecrans had conceived, and which proved in the end to be a brilliant conception. This was to seize a low range of hills known as Raccoon Mountain on the peninsula made by a bend of the river, on its south side and west of Chattanooga, and establish a wagon road to Kelly's Ferry, a point farther down the river to which supplies could be brought by boat from Bridgeport, and at the same time communication effected with Hooker.

A direct line was not only secured to Bridgeport, but Hooker advanced with a portion of his troops into Lookout Valley and after a short but decisive skirmish drove the Confederates across Lookout Creek, leaving his forces in possession of the hills he had gained. The route was now opened between Bridgeport and Brown's Ferry; abundant supplies were at once available and the Army of the Cumberland relieved of its perilous position.

Unlike the condition which had prevailed at Chickamauga, reenforcements from all sides were hastening to the aid of Thomas' army; Hooker was already on the ground; Sherman was advancing rapidly from Memphis, and he arrived in

OPENING "THE CRACKER LINE"

The U. S. S. *Chattanooga* was the first steamboat built by the Federals on the upper Tennessee River.   Had the gunboats on the Ohio been able to come up the Tennessee River nearly three hundred miles, to the assistance of Rosecrans, Bragg could never have bottled him up in Chattanooga.   But between Florence and Decatur, Alabama, Muscle Shoals lay in the stream, making the river impassable.   While Bragg's pickets invested the railroad and river, supplies could not be brought up from Bridgeport; and besides, with the exception of one small steamboat (the *Dunbar*), the Federals had no boats on the river.   General W. F. Smith, Chief Engineer of the Army of the Cumberland, had established a saw-mill with an old engine at Bridgeport for the purpose of getting out lumber from logs rafted down the river, with which to construct pontoons. Here Captain Arthur Edwards, Assistant Quartermaster, had been endeavoring since the siege began to build a steamboat consisting of a flat-bottom scow, with engine, boiler, and stern-wheel mounted upon it. On October 24th, after many difficulties and discouragements had been overcome, the vessel was launched successfully and christened the *Chattanooga*.   On the 29th she made her trial trip.   That very night, Hooker, in the battle of Wauhatchie, definitely established control of the new twelve-mile "Cracker Line" from Kelley's Ferry, which Grant had ordered for the relief of the starving army.   The next day the little *Chattanooga*, with steam up, was ready to start from Bridgeport with a heavy load of the much-needed supplies, and her arrival was anxiously awaited at Kelley's Ferry, where the wagon-trains were all ready to rush forward the rations and forage to Chattanooga.   The mechanics were still at work upon the little vessel's unfinished pilot-house and boiler-deck while she and the two barges she was to tow were being loaded, and at 4 A.M. on November 30th she set out to make the 45-mile journey against unfavorable head-winds.

person on November 15th, while Burnside's forces at Knoxville offered protection to the left flank of the Federal army.

The disposition of the Confederate troops at this time was a formidable one; the left flank rested on the northern end of Lookout Mountain and the line extended a distance of twelve miles across Chattanooga Valley to Missionary Ridge. This position was further strengthened by entrenchments throughout the lowlands. Despite the danger which threatened his army from the converging Union forces, General Bragg determined to attack Burnside and despatched Longstreet with twenty thousand of his best troops to Knoxville. His army materially weakened, the Confederate general continued to hold the same extended position, although his combined force was smaller than had opposed Rosecrans alone at Chickamauga.

On the 23d of November, after a long and fatiguing march over roads almost impassable by reason of continuous rains, Sherman crossed the Tennessee by the pontoon bridge at Brown's Ferry, recrossed it above Chattanooga, and was assigned a position to the left of the main army near the mouth of Chickamauga Creek. Grant had now some eighty thousand men, of whom sixty thousand were on the scene of the coming battle, and, though fearful lest Burnside should be dislodged from his position at Knoxville, he would not be diverted from his purpose of sweeping the Confederates from the front of Chattanooga. It had been Grant's plan to attack on the 24th, but information reached him that Bragg was preparing a retreat. He, therefore, on the 23d, ordered Thomas to advance upon Bragg's center.

Preparations for the movement were made in full view of the Confederates; from the appearance of the troops, clad in their best uniforms, the advance line of the Southern army was content to watch this display, in the belief that the maneuvering army was parading in review. Suddenly, the peaceful pageant turned into a furious charge, before which the

[ 298 ]

## THE WELCOME NEWCOMER

The home-made little steamboat *Chattanooga* was beset with difficulties and dangers on her memorable voyage of November 30th. She made but slow progress against the wind and the rapid current of the tortuous Tennessee. Fearful of breaking a steam pipe or starting a leak, she crawled along all day, and then was enveloped in one of the darkest of nights, out of which a blinding rain stung the faces of her anxious crew. Assistant Quartermaster William G. Le Duc, in command of the expedition, helped the pilot to feel his way through the darkness. At last the camp-fires of the Federals became guiding beacons from the shore and soon the *Chattanooga* tied up safely at Kelley's Ferry. The "Cracker Line" was at last opened—in the nick of time, for there were but four boxes of hard bread left in the commissary at Chattanooga, where four cakes of hard bread and one-quarter of a pound of pork were being issued as a three-days' ration.

Confederate pickets, taken by surprise, retreated from the first line of earthworks, and Thomas, with little loss to either side, captured Orchard Knob, between Chattanooga and Missionary Ridge. From this point, which was almost a mile in advance of the position occupied during the morning, Grant directed the movements of his army on the following day.

The Federal position was of less extent than that occupied by the Confederates. Sherman was in command of the left wing, while Thomas held the center, and "Fighting Joe" Hooker, with the Union right in Lookout Valley, threatened Lookout Mountain. The plan of battle was for Sherman to engage the Confederate right and sever communications between Bragg and Longstreet; Hooker was to carry out an assault on the Southern left flank, and at the same time maintain connection with Bridgeport. With both wings assailed by a superior force, it was believed that Bragg must reenforce these positions and permit Thomas, with overwhelming numbers, to concentrate upon the center.

On the 24th, two distinct movements were in progress. Sherman met with but little opposition in his initial attack upon the Confederate right and promptly seized and occupied the north end of Missionary Ridge. The Confederates, late in the afternoon, fought desperately to regain the hill but were finally repulsed, and Sherman fortified the position he had gained. In the mean time, Hooker, early in the day, had begun his operations against Lookout Mountain. Standing like a lone sentinel above the surrounding valleys, its steep, rocky, and deeply furrowed slopes, rising into a high, palisaded crest, frowned defiance upon the advancing troops, while a well-constructed line of defenses completed the imposing barrier.

Hooker had in addition to his own troops a division of Sherman's army (Osterhaus') which, owing to damage to the pontoon bridge at Brown's Ferry, had been prevented from joining its own leader. As ordered by Hooker, General Geary took his division up the valley to Wauhatchie, crossed the creek

## WHERE AN ARMY GAVE ITS OWN ORDERS

At Missionary Ridge (seen in the distance in the lower picture) the Army of the Cumberland removed forever from Grant's mind any doubt of its fighting qualities. Grant, anxious to develop Bragg's strength, ordered Thomas, on November 23d, to demonstrate against the forces on his front. Moving out as if on parade, the troops under Gordon Granger drove back the Confederates and captured Orchard Knob (or Indian Hill) a day before it had been planned to do so. Still another surprise awaited Grant on the 25th, when from this eminence he watched the magnificent spectacle of the battle of Chattanooga. Thomas' men again pressed forward in what was ordered as a demonstration against Missionary Ridge. Up and over it they drove the Confederates from one entrenchment after another, capturing the guns parked in the lower picture. "By whose orders are those troops going up the hill?" "Old Pap" Thomas, who knew his men better than did Grant, replied that it was probably by their own orders. It was the most signal victory of the day.

### THE CAPTURED CONFEDERATE GUNS

and marched down the east bank, sweeping the Confederate outposts before him. The remainder of the command got across by bridges lower down. Gaining the slopes of the mountain the Federal troops rushed on in their advance. From the high palisaded summit, invisible in the low-hanging clouds, the guns of General Stevenson's brigades poured an iron deluge upon them. But on they went, climbing over ledges and boulders, up hill and down, while the soldiers of the South with musket and cannon tried in vain to check them. Position after position was abandoned to the onrushing Federals, and by noon Geary's advanced troops had rounded the north slope of the mountain and passed from the sight of General Hooker, who was watching the contest from a vantage point to the west. Grant and Thomas from the headquarters on Orchard Knob were likewise eager witnesses of the struggle, although the haze was so dense that they caught a glimpse only now and then as the clouds would rise.

Reenforcements came to the Confederates and they availed nothing. Geary's troops had been ordered to halt when they reached the foot of the palisades, but fired by success they pressed impetuously forward. From its higher position at the base of the cliff Cobham's brigade showered volley after volley upon the Confederate main line of defense, while that of Ireland gradually rolled up the flank. The Federal batteries on Moccasin Point across the river were doing what they could to clear the mountain. The Southerners made a last stand in their walls and pits around the Craven house, but were finally driven in force over rocks and precipices into Chattanooga Valley.

Such was the "battle in the clouds," a wonderful spectacle denied the remainder of Hooker's troops holding Lookout Valley. That general says, "From the moment we had rounded the peak of the mountain it was only from the roar of battle and the occasional glimpses our comrades in the valley could catch of our lines and standards that they knew of the

## THE MEN WHO COMPLETED THE VICTORY

General Hooker and Staff at Lookout Mountain. Hooker's forces of about 9,700 men had been sent from the East to reënforce Rose-crans, but until the arrival of Grant they were simply so many more mouths to feed in the besieged city. In the battle of Wauhatchie, on the night of October 20th, they drove back the Confederates and established the new line of communication. On November 24th they, too, had a surprise in store for Grant. Their part in the triple conflict was also ordered merely as a "demonstration," but they astounded the eyes and ears of their comrades with the spectacular fight by which they made their way up Lookout Mountain. The next day, pushing on to Rossville, the daring Hooker attacked one of Bragg's divisions and forced it into precipitate retreat.

## HOOKER'S CAMP AT THE BASE OF LOOKOUT MOUNTAIN

strife or its progress, and when from these evidences our true condition was revealed to them their painful anxiety yielded to transports of joy which only soldiers can feel in the earliest moments of dawning victory."

By two in the afternoon the clouds had settled completely into the valley and the ensuing darkness put an end to further operations. Hooker established and strengthened a new position and waited for reenforcements, which General Carlin brought from Chattanooga at five o'clock. Until after midnight an irregular fire was kept up, but the Confederates could not break the new line. Before dawn General Stevenson abandoned the summit, leaving behind twenty thousand rations and the camp equipage of his three brigades. Hooker, anticipating this move, sent several detachments to scale the palisades. A party of six men from the Eighth Kentucky regiment, by means of ladders, was the first to reach the summit, and the waving Stars and Stripes greeted the rising sun of November 25th on Lookout Mountain, amid the wild and prolonged cheers of " Fighting Joe's " valiant troops.

The fighting of Sherman and Hooker on the 24th secured to Grant's army a distinct advantage in position. From the north end of Lookout Mountain across Chattanooga Valley to the north end of Missionary Ridge the Union forces maintained an unbroken front.

The morning of the 25th dawned cold, and an impenetrable mist which lay deep in the valleys was soon driven away. From Orchard Knob, a point almost in the center of the united Federal host, General Grant watched the preparations for the battle. At sunrise, Sherman's command was in motion. In his front, an open space intervened between his position and a ridge held by the Confederates, while just beyond rose a much higher hill. Toward the first ridge the attacking column, under General Corse, advanced rapidly and in full view of the foe. For a time it seemed as if the Confederates must recede before the terrific onslaught, but the advance was abruptly

## THE BATTLE–FIELD ABOVE THE CLOUDS

Entrenchments on Lookout Mountain.   Up such rugged heights as these, heavily timbered and full of chasms, Hooker's men fought their way on the afternoon of November 24th.   Bridging Lookout Creek, the troops crossed, hidden by the friendly mist, and began ascending the mountain-sides, driving the Confederates from one line of rifle-pits and then from another.   The heavy musketry fire and the boom of the Confederate battery on the top of the mountain apprised the waiting Federals before Chattanooga that the battle had begun.   Now and again the fitful lifting of the mist disclosed to Grant and Thomas, watching from Orchard Knob, the men of Hooker fighting upon the heights.   Then all would be curtained once more.   At two o'clock in the afternoon the mist became so heavy that Hooker and his men could not see what they were doing, and paused to entrench.   By four o'clock, however, he had pushed on to the summit and reported to Grant that his position was impregnable.   Direct communication was then established and reënforcements sent.

checked after a very close and stubborn struggle, when within a short distance of the entrenchment.

Unmindful of the numbers which opposed him, General Hardee not only succeeded in repulsing the attack, but, assuming the offensive, drove back the forces under General John E. Smith, who had sought to turn his left, and captured several hundred prisoners. The Federals, quickly re-forming their lines, renewed the assault and for several hours the fighting was desperate on both sides. A general advance of the Northern forces had been withheld, awaiting the arrival of Hooker who, under orders from Grant, was sweeping down Chickamauga Valley, and was to operate against the Confederate left and rear, in the expectation that Bragg would further weaken his line by massing at those points. But Hooker's army had been delayed several hours by repairs to the bridge crossing Chattanooga Creek. Although Sherman had failed in his attempt to turn the Confederate right he had forced Bragg to draw heavily upon his center for reenforcements. Grant, satisfied that Hooker was not far off, ordered the signal—six guns fired in rapid succession from the battery on Orchard Knob—for a general advance of Thomas' army upon the Confederate center.

It was now three o'clock in the afternoon. The four division commanders of the Army of the Cumberland, Sheridan, Wood, Baird, and Johnson, gave the word to advance. Between Orchard Knob and the base of Missionary Ridge, a mile away, is a broad valley covered for the most part with heavy timber. This had to be crossed before the entrenchments at the foot of the hill could be assaulted. Scarcely were the Cumberland troops in motion when fifty pieces of artillery on the crest of Missionary Ridge opened a terrific fire upon them. But the onward rush of the Federals was not checked in the slightest degree. The line of entrenchments at the base was carried with little opposition. Most of Breckinridge's men abandoned the ditches as the Federal skirmishers approached

THE PEAK OF VICTORY—THE MORNING AFTER THE BATTLE

Pulpit Rock, the Summit of Lookout Mountain. Before dawn of November 25th, Hooker, anticipating the with-drawal of the Confederates, sent detachments to seize the very summit of the mountain, here 2,400 feet high. Six volunteers from the Eighth Kentucky Regiment scaled the palisades by means of the ladders seen in this picture, and made their way to the top. The rest of the regiment quickly followed; then came the Ninety-sixth Illinois. The rays of the rising sun disclosed the Stars and Stripes floating in triumph from the lofty peak "amid the wild and prolonged cheers of the men whose dauntless valor had borne them to that point."

[B]

and sought refuge up the hill, breaking and throwing into confusion other troops as they passed through.

At the foot of Missionary Ridge Thomas' army had reached its goal. Its orders carried it no further. But, as General Wood has related, "the enthusiasm and impetuosity of the troops were such that those who first reached the entrenchments at the base of the ridge bounded over them and pressed on up the ascent. . . . Moreover the entrenchments were no protection against the artillery on the ridge. To remain would be destruction—to return would be both expensive in life, and disgraceful. Officers and men, all seemed impressed with this truth. . . . Without waiting for an order the vast mass pressed forward in the race for glory, each man anxious to be the first on the summit. . . . Artillery and musketry could not check the impetuous assault. The troops did not halt to fire. To have done so would have been ruinous. Little was left to the commanders of the troops than to cheer on the foremost—to encourage the weaker of limb and to sustain the very few who seemed to be faint-hearted."

Midway up the slope was a small line of rifle-pits, but these proved of no use in stemming the Federal tide. In the immediate front, however, Major Weaver of the Sixtieth North Carolina rallied a sufficient number of the demoralized Confederates to send a well-directed and effective fire upon the advancing troops. At this point the first line of oncoming Federals was vigorously repulsed, and thrown back to the vacated Confederate trenches. General Bragg, noticing this, rode along the ridge to spread his good news among the troops, but he had not gone far when word was brought that the right flank was broken and that the Federal standard had been seen on the summit. A second and a third flag appeared in quick succession. Bragg sent General Bate to drive the foe back, but the disaster was so great that the latter was unable to repair it. Even the artillery had abandoned the infantry. The Confederate flank had gone, and within an hour of the start from

THE FLANKING PASS

The Gap in Missionary Ridge at Rossville.   Through this Georgia mountain-pass runs the road to Ringgold.   Rosecrans took advantage of it when he turned Bragg's flank before the battle of Chickamauga; and on November 25, 1863, Thomas ordered Hooker to advance from Lookout Mountain to this point and strike the Confederates on their left flank, while in their front he (Thomas) stood ready to attack.   The movement was entirely successful, and in a brilliant battle, begun by Hooker, Bragg's army was swept from Missionary Ridge and pursued in retreat to Georgia.

THE SKIRMISH LINE

Multiply the number of these men by ten, strike out the tents, and we see vividly how the advancing line of Thomas' Army of the Cumberland appeared to the Confederates as they swept up the slope at Missionary Ridge to win the brilliant victory of November 25th.   This view of drilling Federal troops in Chattanooga preserves the exact appearance of the line of battle only a couple of months before the picture was taken.   The skirmishers, thrown out in advance of the line, are "firing" from such positions as the character of the ground makes most effective.   The main line is waiting for the order to charge.

## CONQUERING THE CURRENT

The "Suck" in the Tennessee River below Chattanooga. Through this narrow gorge in Raccoon Mountain the water rushes with such force that vessels cannot stem the current under their own steam. The little *Chattanooga* could not be rendered the customary assistance of windlass and shore-lines while Bragg's forces invested the river, consequently she could ascend it only so far as Kelly's Ferry. In the picture one of the river steamers is being warped through this difficult part of the stream.

THE RIVER OPENED

The success of the little *Chattanooga* spurred the Federal saw-mill at Bridgeport to renewed activity. Captain Edwards' shipyard was greatly enlarged after the defeat of Bragg,
and in a remarkably short time thirteen staunch transports and four light-draft gunboats
were built. Their trial trips during the spring and summer of 1864 were watched with interest because of the difficulties of navigation at "the Suck," where the current of the Tennessee River prevented the small craft from ascending under their own steam.

THE READY RIVER ROUTE

Here, waiting to get through the "Suck," below Chattanooga, are some of the light-draft river steamers which enabled Grant to establish communications almost immediately after his successful encounter with Bragg.   The smoke of the Chattanooga battles had scarely cleared away when the two little steamboats then at the disposal of the Federals were loaded with supplies for Burnside, besieged in Knoxville.   They were to steam up the Tennessee, abreast of the troops, as far as the mouth of the Holston River, so that their freight might reach Burnside's famished troops as soon as the reënforcements drove off Longstreet.   When this was done the river steamers plying between Knoxville and Chattanooga were kept busy and the former became a secondary base.   Preparations for the Spring campaign were now set afoot.   There were two objectives in Grant's mind.   General Joseph E. Johnston had succeeded Bragg in

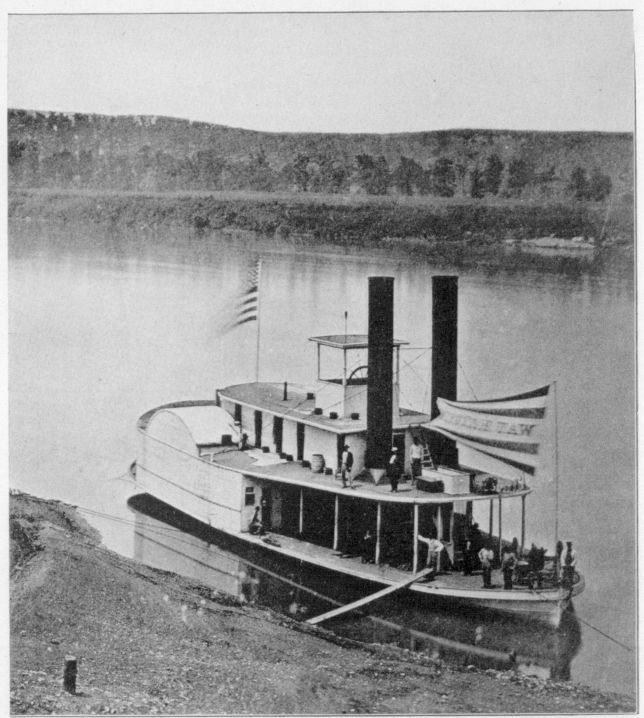

FEDERAL TRANSPORTS IN THE TENNESSEE, WINTER OF 1863–4

command of the Confederate forces, and to vanquish his army and obtain possession of Atlanta were the important things. But Grant looked further into the future. An expedition against Mobile was seriously considered, and from Nashville, to which place Grant had returned, the telegraph wires were kept busy. Every effort was made to strengthen the Federal positions and prepare for the important movements that were to follow. Early in January, 1864, the Commander-in-Chief, with his staff, returned to Chattanooga, and, boarding one the little river steamers, proceeded up the Tennessee as far as its junction with the Clinch River, up to which point the tedious repairs of the railroad from Knoxville to Chattanooga had progressed. From Knoxville Grant and his staff rode out over the frozen and difficult road to inspect the line of communication from Cumberland Gap that it was necessary to abandon or improve.

PREPARING FOR PERMANENT OCCUPATION

Bragg was now definitely driven from Tennessee, and his beaten army lay in winter quarters at Dalton, Georgia, holding the railroad to Atlanta. Longstreet had failed at Knoxville, and after a winter of hardship in the unfriendly mountain regions was to make
his way back to Lee for the final struggle. This bridge was the last link in the connection by rail between Nashville and Chattanooga, and the Federal engineers at once set about rebuilding it so that trains might be run into the latter city, which was now made

MILITARY RAILROAD BRIDGE OVER CHATTANOOGA CREEK, DECEMBER, 1863

a military post. The original structure was destroyed by Bragg September 7, 1863, when he withdrew from Chattanooga, outflanked by Rosecrans. Grant had saved the Army of the Cumberland and Chattanooga, and Sherman had pressed forward to the relief of Burnside at Knoxville, driving off Longstreet. Chattanooga and Knoxville, now occupied by the Federals, were to become new bases for still greater and more aggressive operations by Sherman against the Confederate army in Georgia the following year.

## COUNTRY HARD TO HOLD

Whiteside Valley, Tennessee. Over such difficult ground as this the Army of the Cumberland had to make its way in the Chattanooga campaign. Therein lay one valid reason why the Confederates were not sooner swept from eastern Tennessee, as President Lincoln and the War Department at Washington impatiently expected. Only the men who marched over the mountain roads knew to the full the hardships that the task involved. Railroad communications were constantly threatened and interrupted and, when this happened, the daily bread of the soldiers must be hauled in groaning wagon-trains by long, roundabout routes over the almost impassable mountain roads. On these roads points open to attack had to be properly guarded. Even the crude bridges shown in the picture must be commanded by protecting blockhouses or the army might be without food for days.

## COMMUNICATION COMPLETED

Railroad Bridge Across the Ravine of Running Water at Whiteside, Tennessee. In this picture stands one of the most notable of the almost incredible achievements of army engineers in the Civil War. Between Whiteside and Wauhatchie the railroad on its way in Chattanooga curves southward almost along the boundary of Alabama, and the destroyed bridge at Whiteside had to be replaced before trains could be run into Chattanooga, which was to be held as a Federal military post and base for future operations in Georgia. Here, fourteen miles from Chattanooga, the engineers built this four-tier trestle-bridge, 780 feet long and 116 feet high in the center, completing the work in a remarkably short time toward the close of 1863. Plans for Sherman's Atlanta campaign were already formulating and it was necessary that this bridge in its isolated position should be strongly held. The camp of the Federal detachment constantly on guard here is seen in the picture, and two of the four double-cased blockhouses, which served as refuges from any attack.

Orchard Knob the crest of Missionary Ridge was occupied by Federal troops. Sheridan did not stop here. He went down the eastern slope, driving all in front of him toward Chickamauga Creek. On a more easterly ridge he rested until midnight, when he advanced to the creek and took many prisoners and stores.

While the Army of the Cumberland accomplished these things, Hooker was advancing his divisions at charging pace from the south. Cruft was on the crest, Osterhaus in the eastern valley, and Geary in the western—all within easy supporting distance. Before Cruft's onrush the left wing of Bragg's army was scattered in all directions from the ridge. Many ran down the eastern slope into Osterhaus' column and the very few who chose a way of flight to the west, were captured by Geary. The bulk of them, however, fell back from trench to trench upon the crest until finally, as the sun was sinking, they found themselves surrounded by Johnson's division of the Army of the Cumberland. Such was the fate of Stewart's division; only a small portion of it got away.

On the Confederate right Hardee held his own against Sherman, but with the left and center routed and in rapid flight Bragg realized the day was lost. He could do nothing but cover Breckinridge's retreat as best he might and order Hardee to retire across Chickamauga Creek.

Thus ended the battle of Chattanooga. Bragg's army had been wholly defeated, and, after being pursued for some days, it found a resting place at Dalton among the mountains of Georgia. The Federal victory was the result of a campaign carefully planned by Generals Halleck and Grant and ably carried out by the efforts of the subordinate generals.

The losses in killed and wounded sustained by Grant were over fifty-eight hundred and those of Bragg about sixty-six hundred, four thousand being prisoners. But the advantage of the great position had been forever wrested from the Southern army.

# PART V

---

# ENGAGEMENTS
# OF THE CIVIL WAR

---

THE SIEGE OF CHARLESTON, JULY–SEPTEMBER, 1863.
A BREACHING BATTERY IN THE MARSHES.  BELOW
ARE FEDERAL MORTARS ON MORRIS ISLAND,
TURNED AGAINST SUMTER

# ENGAGEMENTS OF THE CIVIL WAR

## WITH LOSSES ON BOTH SIDES

### AUGUST, 1862—APRIL, 1864

CHRONOLOGICAL summary and record of historical events, and of important engagements between the Union and the Confederate armies, in the Civil War in the United States, showing troops participating, losses and casualties, collated and compiled by George L. Kilmer from the official records of the Union and Confederate armies filed in the United States War Department. Minor engagements are omitted; also some concerning which statistics, especially Confederate, are not available.

### AUGUST, 1862.

**3.**—Jonesboro', L'Anguille Ferry, Ark. *Union,* 1st Wis. Cav.; *Confed.,* Parsons' Texas Rangers. Losses: *Union,* 11 killed, 33 wounded, 21 missing; *Confed.**

**5.**—Baton Rouge, La. *Union,* 14th Me., 6th Mich., 7th Vt., 21st Ind., 30th Mass., 9th Conn., 4th Wis., 2d, 4th, and 6th Mass. Batteries; *Confed.,* Four brigades under command of Gen. John C. Breckinridge, Semmes' Battery and Pond's Partisan Rangers. Losses: *Union,* 82 killed, 255 wounded, 34 missing; *Confed.,* 84 killed, 316 wounded, 78 missing; *Union,* Brig.-Gen. Thomas Williams killed.

—Malvern Hill, Va. *Union,* Portion of Hooker's Div., Third Corps, and Richardson's Div., Second Corps and Cavalry, Army of the Potomac; *Confed.,* Divisions of Longstreet, McLaws, Jones, and Ripley, Army of Northern Virginia, Gen. R. E. Lee commanding. Losses: *Union,* 3 killed, 11 wounded; *Confed.,* 100 captured.

**6.**—Kirksville, Mo. *Union,* Detachments commanded by Col. John McNeil, 2d Mo. Cav.; *Opponents,* Porter's independent forces. Losses: *Union,* 28 killed, 60 wounded (estimated); Porter's loss, 128 killed, 200 wounded (estimated).

—Matapony or Thornburg, Va. *Union,* Gen. John Gibbons' Brigade; *Confed.,* Stuart's Cav. Losses: *Union,* 1 killed, 12 wounded, 72 missing; *Confed.**

**9.**—Cedar Mountain, Va., also called Slaughter Mountain, Southwest Mountain, Cedar Run, and Mitchell's Station. *Union,* Second Corps, Maj.-Gen. Banks; Third Corps, Maj.-Gen. McDowell; Army of Virginia, under command of Maj.-Gen. Pope; *Confed.,* Army commanded by Gen. T. J. ("Stonewall") Jackson as follows: Gen. C. S. Winder's Division; Gen. R. S. Ewell's Division; Gen. A. P. Hill's Division. Losses: *Union,* 450 killed, 660 wounded, 290 missing; *Confed.,* 229 killed, 1,047 wounded, 31 missing; *Union,* Brig.-Gens. Augur, Carroll, and Geary wounded; *Confed.,* Brig.-Gen. C. S. Winder killed.

**10 to 13.**—Grand River, Lee's Ford, Chariton River, Walnut Creek, Compton Ferry, Switzler's Mills, and Yellow Creek, Mo. *Union,* 9th Mo. Cav.; *Opponents,* Poindexter's Independent forces. Losses: *Union,* 5 wounded. Poindexter lost 150 men killed and wounded, 100 captured [estimated].

**11.**—Independence, Mo. *Union,* 7th Mo. Cav.; *Confed.,* Col. J. T. Hughes' command. Losses: *Union,* 26 killed, 30 wounded, 256 missing; *Confed.**

**12.**—Gallatin, Tenn. *Union,* 28th Ky. (4 co's) surrendered to Morgan's Cavalry.

**16.**—Lone Jack, Mo. *Union,* 7th Mo. Cav.; *Confed.,* Col. Cockrell's Cav. Losses: *Union,* 43 killed, 54 wounded, 73 missing; *Confed.,* 118 killed and wounded.

* No record found.

## THE GENERAL–IN–CHIEF IN 1862

Major-General Henry Wager Halleck; born 1814; West Point 1839; died 1872. Sherman credits Halleck with having first discovered that Forts Henry and Donelson, where the Tennessee and the Cumberland Rivers so closely approach each other, were the keypoints to the defensive line of the Confederates in the West. Succeeding Fremont in November, 1861, Halleck, importuned by both Grant and Foote, authorized the joint expedition into Tennessee, and after its successful outcome he telegraphed to Washington: "Make Buell, Grant, and Pope major-generals of volunteers and give me command in the West. I ask this in return for Donelson and Henry." He was chosen to be General-in-Chief of the Federal Armies at the crisis created by the failure of McClellan's Peninsula Campaign. Halleck held this position from July 11, 1862, until Grant, who had succeeded him in the West, finally superseded him at Washington.

# Engagements of the Civil War

**19.**—Clarksville, Tenn. *Union*, 71st Ohio (5 co's) surrendered to Confederates commanded by Col. A. R. Johnson. Losses: *Union*, 350 captured.

**22 to 25.**—Skirmishes on the Rappahannock at Waterloo Bridge, Lee Springs, Freeman's Ford and Sulphur Springs, Va. *Union*, Milroy's Brigade, Army of Virginia; *Confed.*, Gen. Longstreet's command. Losses: *Confed.*, 27 killed, 94 wounded; *Union*, Brig.-Gen. Bohlen killed.

**23.**—Big Hill, Madison Co., Ky. *Union*, 3d Tenn. (Houk's Battalion), 7th Ky. Cav.; *Confed.*, 1st La. Cav. Losses: *Union*, 120 killed, wounded, and missing (estimate); *Confed.*, 4 killed, 12 wounded.

**23 to Sept. 1.**—Pope's Campaign in Virginia. *Union*, Army of Virginia, commanded by Gen. John Pope; *Confed.*, Army of Northern Virginia, commanded by Gen. R. E. Lee. Losses: *Union*, 1747 killed, 8452 wounded, and 4623 missing; *Confed.*, 1090 killed, 6154 wounded.

**25 and 26.**—Fort Donelson and Cumberland Iron Works, Tenn. *Union*, 71st Ohio (4 co's), 5th Ia. Cav.; *Confed.*, Col. Woodward's command. Losses: *Union*, 31 killed and wounded; *Confed.*, 30 killed and wounded.

**27.**—Bull Run Bridge, Va. *Union*, 11th and 12th Ohio, 1st, 2d, 3d, and 4th N. J.; *Confed.*, Part of Gen. "Stonewall" Jackson's command. Losses:* *Union*, Brig.-Gen. G. W. Taylor mortally wounded.
—Kettle Run, Va. *Union*, Maj.-Gen. Hooker's Div. of Third Corps; *Confed.*, Ewell's Division of Jackson's Corps. Losses: *Union*, 300 killed and wounded; *Confed.*, 300 killed and wounded.

**28 and 29.**—Groveton and Gainesville, Va. *Union*, First Corps, Maj.-Gen. Sigel, Third Corps, Maj.-Gen. McDowell, Army of Virginia, Hooker's and Kearny's Divisions of Third Corps and Reynolds' Division of First Corps, Army of Potomac, Ninth Corps, Maj.-Gen. Reno, Buford's cavalry brigade (Second Corps); *Confed.*, Army of Northern Virginia commanded by Gen. Robert E. Lee, as follows: Right Wing, Gen. James Longstreet's Corps; Left Wing, Gen. T. J. Jackson's Corps; Cavalry Division, Gen. J. E. B. Stuart. Casualties included in those given for the campaign, Aug. 23 to Sept. 1.
—McMinnville, Tenn. *Union*, 18th Ohio (2 co's) 9th Mich. (1 co); *Confed.*, Forrest's Cav. Losses: *Union*, 9 wounded; *Confed.*, 12 killed, 41 wounded.

**30.**—Second Battle of Bull Run or Manassas, Va. Same troops as engaged at Groveton and Gainesville on the 28th and 29th, with the addition of Porter's Fifth Corps (*Union*). Casualties included as above.
—Bolivar, Tenn. *Union*, 20th, 78th Ohio, 2d Ill. Cav. (4 co's), 11th Ill Cav. (2 co's) 9th Ind. Battery; *Confed.*, Armstrong's Cavalry. Losses: *Union*, 5 killed, 18 wounded, 64 missing. *Confed.*, 100 killed and wounded (estimate).
—Richmond, Ky. *Union*, 12th, 16th, 55th, 66th, 69th and 71st Ind., 95th Ohio, 18th Ky., 6th and 7th Ky. Cav., Batteries D and G Mich. Art.; *Confed.*, Four brigades under Generals Kirby Smith and Patrick Cleburne. Losses: *Union*, 200 killed, 700 wounded, 4000 missing; *Confed.*, 250 killed, 500 wounded.

## SEPTEMBER, 1862

**1.**—Britton's Lane, Tenn. *Union*, 20th and 30th Ill., 4th Ill. Cav., Foster's (Ohio) Cav., Battery A 2d Ill. Art. *Confed.*, Gen. F. C. Armstrong's command. Losses: *Union*, 5 killed, 51 wounded, 52 missing; *Confed.*, 179 killed, 100 wounded. (Union Report.)
—Chantilly, Va. *Union*, McDowell's Corps, Army of Virginia. Hooker's and Kearny's Divisions of Third Corps, Army of Potomac, Reno's Ninth Corps; *Confed.*, "Stonewall" Jackson's Corps. Losses: *Union*, 1300 killed, wounded, and missing; *Confed.*, 800 *killed*, wounded, and missing; *Union*, Maj.-Gen. Kearny and Brig.-Gen. Stevens killed.

**6.**—Washington, N. C. *Union*, 24th Mass., 1st N. C., 3d N. Y. Cav.; *Confed.*, Gen. J. G. Martin's command. Losses: *Union*, 7 killed, 47 wounded; *Confed.*, 30 killed, 100 wounded.

**10.**—Fayetteville, W. Va. *Union*, 34th, 37th Ohio, 4th W. Va.; *Confed.*, Gen. W. W. Loring's command. Losses: *Union*, 13 killed, 80 wounded.

* No record found.

[ 322 ]

## A DARING MOVE OF SEPTEMBER, 1862

Ruins of the Bridge at Harper's Ferry, Virginia. Lee had invaded Maryland. Boldly dividing his army, which was but two-thirds as strong as that of McClellan, who was confronting him with seventy-five thousand men, he sent the swift and silent Jackson to capture Harper's Ferry, renowned as the place where John Brown was captured. Europe, watching with keen interest the progress of the war, was dazzled by the splendid coöperation of the two great Confederate leaders. By the stroke at Harper's Ferry Lee removed an element of danger from his rear, while his advance into Maryland was causing consternation throughout the North. The Federal garrison of twelve thousand five hundred men at Harper's Ferry, out-numbered and out-maneuvered by Jackson, surrendered on September 15th, after a two-days' defense, and Jackson rejoined Lee in Maryland just in time to stem the tide at Antietam.

[B]

# Engagements of the Civil War

**12 to 15.**—Harper's Ferry, Va. *Union,* 39th, 111th, 115th, 125th, and 126th N. Y., 12th N. Y. Militia, 32d, 60th, and 87th Ohio, 9th Vt., 65th Ill., 15th Ind., 1st and 3d Md. Home Brigade, 8th N. Y. Cav., 12th Ill. Cav., 7th Squadron R. I. Cav., five batteries of Artil.; *Confed.,* Gen. T. J. Jackson's Corps; Gen. R. H. Anderson's Division; Gen. J. G. Walker's Division; Gen. Lafayette McLaws' Division. Losses: *Union,* 44 killed, 173 wounded, 12520 missing and captured; *Confed.,* 500 killed and wounded.

**14.**—Turner's and Crampton's Gap, South Mountain, Md. *Union,* First Corps, Maj.-Gen. Hooker; Sixth Corps, Maj.-Gen. Franklin; Ninth Corps, Maj.-Gen. Reno; *Confed.,* Gen. D. H. Hill's Division; Gen. Lafayette McLaws' Division. Losses: *Union,* 443 killed, 1806 wounded. *Confed.,* 500 killed, 2343 wounded, 1500 captured; *Union,* Maj.-Gen. Reno killed; *Confed.,* Brig.-Gen. Garland killed.

**14 to 16.**—Munfordville, Ky. *Union,* 18th U. S. Inft., 28th and 33d Ky., 17th, 50th, 60th, 67th, 68th, 74th, 78th, and 89th Ind., Conkle's Battery, 13th Ind. Artil., and Louisville Provost Guard; *Confed.,* Army of Tennessee, commanded by Gen. Braxton Bragg. Losses: *Union,* 50 killed, 3566 captured and missing; *Confed.,* 714 killed and wounded.

**17.**—Antietam or Sharpsburg, Md. *Union,* Army of the Potomac, commanded by Maj.-Gen. Geo. B. McClellan, as follows: First Corps, Maj.-Gen. Joseph Hooker; Second Corps, Maj.-Gen. E. V. Sumner; Fifth Corps, Maj.-Gen. Fitz-John Porter; Sixth Corps, Maj.-Gen. W. B. Franklin; Ninth Corps, Maj.-Gen. A. E. Burnside; Twelfth Corps, Maj.-Gen. J. K. F. Mansfield, Brig.-Gen. Alpheus Williams; Couch's Div., Fourth Corps; Pleasonton's Cavalry; *Confed.,* Army of Northern Virginia, commanded by Gen. Robert E. Lee, as follows: Maj.-Gen. James Longstreet's Corps; Maj.-Gen. T. J. Jackson's Corps; Reserve Artillery, Gen. W. N. Pendleton, Gen. J. E. B. Stuart's Cavalry. Losses: *Union,* 2010 killed, 9416 wounded, 1043 missing; *Confed.,* total in the campaign, 1890 killed, 9770 wounded, 2304 missing; *Union,* Maj.-Gen. Mansfield killed, Maj.-Gens. Hooker and Richardson, and

Brig.-Gens. Rodman, Weber, Sedgwick, Hartsuff, Dana, and Meagher wounded; *Confed.,* Brig.-Gens. Branch, Anderson, and Starke killed, Maj.-Gen. Anderson, Brig.-Gens. Toombs, Lawton, Ripley, Rodes, Gregg, Armistead, and Ransom wounded.

**19 and 20.**—Iuka, Miss. *Union,* Stanley's and Hamilton's Divisions, Army of the Mississippi, under Maj.-Gen. Rosecrans; *Confed.,* Gen. Sterling Price, Army of the West; Gen. Henry Little's Division, Gen. Frank C. Armstrong's Cavalry. Losses: *Union,* 144 killed, 598 wounded; *Confed.,* 263 killed, 692 wounded, 561 captured; *Confed.,* Brig.-Gens. Little killed and Whitfield wounded.

**20.**—Blackford's Ford, Shepherdstown, Va. *Union,* Fifth Corps, Griffin's and Barnes' Brigades; *Confed.,* Gen. A. P. Hill's Division. Losses: *Union,* 92 killed, 131 wounded, 103 missing; *Confed.,* 33 killed, 231 wounded.

**30.**—Newtonia, Mo. *Union,* 1st Brigade Army of Kansas, 4th Brigade Mo. Militia Cav.; *Confed.,* 3000 Indians under Col. D. H. Cooper, Gen. Shelby's Cav. Losses: *Union,* 50 killed, 80 wounded, 115 missing; *Confed.,* 220 killed, 280 wounded.

## OCTOBER, 1862.

**1.**—Shepherdstown, Va. *Union,* 8th Ill., 8th Penna., 3d Ind. Cav., Pennington's Battery; *Confed.,* Stuart's Cav. Losses: *Union,* 12 wounded; *Confed.,* 60 killed.

**3 and 4.**—Corinth, Miss. *Union,* McKean's, Davies', Hamilton's, and Stanley's Divisions, Army of the Miss.; *Confed.,* Army of West Tennessee, commanded by Gen. Earl Van Dorn, Gen. Price's Corps, and Gen. Mansfield Lovell's Division of Mississippians. Losses: *Union,* 315 killed, 1812 wounded, 232 missing; *Confed.,* 1423 killed, 5692 wounded, 2248 missing. *Union,* Brig.-Gens. Hackleman killed and Oglesby wounded.

**5.**—Metamora, on Big Hatchie River, Miss. *Union,* Hurlburt's and Ord's Divisions; *Confed.,* Rear-Guard of Van Dorn's Army. Losses: *Union,* 500 killed and wounded; *Confed.,* 400 killed and wounded.

**7.**—La Vergne, Tenn. *Union,* Palmer's Brigade; *Confed.,* Outposts of Bragg's

## THE ABANDONED STRONGHOLD

Maryland Heights, in the rear of Harper's Ferry. The Federal retreat from this position on September 13, 1862, sealed the fate of Harper's Ferry. Colonel Ford was dismissed from the service for yielding it so easily. From this commanding hill and from Loudon Heights (on the Virginia side of the Potomac) the Confederate artillery could enfilade the Federal rifle-pits on Bolivar Heights. These can be seen in the opposite picture, rising amid the houses. McClellan had urged that the garrison be withdrawn, as the position could be easily reoccupied. But when one of Lee's despatches fell into his hands, acquainting him with Jackson's daring movement to capture it, he pushed forward rapidly two divisions under Franklin to prevent its fall—but in vain. Jackson's haul of more than twelve thousand prisoners had been equaled only at Fort Donelson.

# Engagements of the Civil War

Army. Losses: *Union,* 5 killed, 9 wounded; *Confed.,* 80 killed and wounded, 175 missing.

**8.**—Perryville, Ky. *Union,* First Corps, Army of the Ohio, Maj.-Gen. McCook, and Third Corps, Brig.-Gen. Gilbert; *Confed.,* Gen. Braxton Bragg's Army, Gen. B. F. Cheatham's and Simon B. Buckner's Divisions, Gen. Joseph Wheeler's Cav. Losses: *Union,* 916 killed, 2943 wounded, 489 missing; *Confed.,* 2500 killed, wounded, and missing. *Union,* Brig.-Gens. J. S. Jackson and Terrill killed; *Confed.,* Brig.-Gens. Cleburne, Wood, and Brown wounded.

**10.**—Harrodsburg, Ky. *Union,* Troops commanded by Lieut.-Col. Boyle, 9th Ky. Cav.; *Confed.,* same as at Perryville. Losses: *Confed.,* 1600 captured.

**17.**—Lexington, Ky. *Union,* Detach. 3d and 4th Ohio Cav.; *Confed.,* Gen. J. H. Morgan's Cav. Losses: *Union,* 4 killed, 24 wounded, 350 missing.

**22.**—Pocotaligo or Yemassee, S. C. *Union,* 47th, 55th, and 76th Penna., 48th N. Y., 6th and 7th Conn., 3d and 4th N. H., 3d R. I., 1st N. Y. Engineers, 1st Mass. Cav., Batteries B, D, and M 1st U. S. Artil. and E 3d U. S. Artil.; *Confed.,* Gen. W. S. Walker's Command. Losses: *Union,* 43 killed, 258 wounded; *Confed.,* 14 killed, 102 wounded.

## NOVEMBER, 1862.

**1.**—Philomont, Va. *Union,* Pleasonton's Cav.; *Confed.,* Stuart's Cav. Losses: *Union,* 1 killed, 14 wounded; *Confed.,* 5 killed, 10 wounded.

**2 and 3.**—Bloomfield and Union, Loudon Co., Va. *Union,* Pleasonton's Cav.; *Confed.,* Stuart's Cav. Losses: *Union,* 2 killed, 10 wounded; *Confed.,* 3 killed, 15 wounded.

**5.**—Barbee's Cross Roads and Chester Gap, Va. *Union,* Pleasonton's Cav.; *Confed.,* Gen. J. E. B. Stuart's Cav. Losses, *Union,* 5 killed, 10 wounded; *Confed.,* 36 killed.

—Nashville, Tenn. *Union,* 16th and 51st Ill., 69th Ohio, 14th Mich., 78th Pa., 5th Tenn. Cav., 7th Pa. Cav.; *Confed.,* Cheatham's Division, Wheeler's Cav. Losses: *Union,* 26 wounded; *Confed.,* 23 captured.

**7.**—Big Beaver Creek, Mo. 10th Ill., two Cos. Mo. Militia Cav.; *Confed.\** Losses: *Union,* 300 captured.

—Marianna, Ark. *Union,* 3d and 4th Iowa, 9th Ill. Cav.; *Confed.\** Losses: *Union,* 3 killed, 20 wounded; *Confed.,* 50 killed and wounded.

**8.**—Hudsonville, Miss. *Union,* 7th Kan. Cav., 2d Iowa Cav.; *Confed.\** Losses: *Confed.,* 16 killed, 185 captured.

**24.**—Beaver Creek, Mo. *Union,* 21st Iowa, 3d Mo. Cav.; *Confed.,* Campbell's Cav. Losses: *Union,* 6 killed, 10 wounded; *Confed.,* 5 killed, 20 wounded.

**28.**—Cane Hill, Boston Mountain, and Boonsboro', Ark. *Union,* 1st Division Army of the Frontier; *Confed.,* Gen. Jno. S. Marmaduke's Cav. Losses: *Union,* 4 killed, 36 wounded; *Confed.,* 75 killed, 300 wounded.

—Hartwood Church, Va. *Union,* 3d Pa. Cav.; *Confed.,* Gen. Hampton's Cav. Losses: *Union,* 4 killed, 9 wounded, 200 missing.

## DECEMBER, 1862.

**5.**—Coffeeville, Miss. *Union,* 1st, 2d, and 3d Cav. Brigades, Army of the Tennessee; *Confed.,* Gen. John C. Pemberton, Army of Vicksburg defense. Losses: *Union,* 10 killed, 64 wounded; *Confed.,* 7 killed, 43 wounded.

**7.**—Prairie Grove or Fayetteville, Ark. *Union,* 1st, 2d, and 3d Divisions Army of the Frontier; *Confed.,* Gen. T. C. Hindman's command, and Gen. Marmaduke's Cav. Losses: *Union,* 167 killed, 798 wounded, 183 missing; *Confed.,* 300 killed, 1200 wounded and missing.

—Hartsville, Tenn. *Union,* 106th and 108th Ohio, 104th Ill., 2d Ind. Cav., 11th Ky. Cav., 13th Ind. Battery; *Confed.,* Gen. Basil Duke's Cav. Brigade, Hanson's Kentucky Infantry, Cobb's Battery. Losses: *Union,* 58 killed, 204 wounded, 1834 captured; *Confed.,* 21 killed, 114 wounded.

**9.**—Dobbin's Ferry, Tenn. *Union,* 35th Ind., 51st Ohio, 8th and 21st Ky., 7th Ind. Battery; *Confed.,* Wheeler's Cav. Losses: *Union,* 5 killed, 48 wounded.

**12 to 18.**—Foster's expedition to Goldsboro', N. C. *Union,* 1st, 2d, and 3d Brigades of First Division and Wessell's

* No record found.

## IN SOUTH CAROLINA

With his foot on the cannon-ball sits Captain Michael J. Donohoe, commanding at the time—1862—Company C of the Third New Hampshire. On the left is Lieutenant Allen, and on the right Lieutenant Cody. At the battle of Secessionville, Captain Donohoe's company was stationed on the left and received the first fire of the Confederate reënforcements. Both lieutenants were wounded. Thus in June, 1862, these gallant officers first came into notice, and Captain Donohoe rose rapidly to the rank of colonel, commanding the Tenth New Hampshire. At Fredericksburg, on December 17, 1862, the Tenth New Hampshire (organized September, 1862) was under fire for the first time and acquitted itself creditably for raw troops. Colonel Donohoe and his regiment were transferred to the Army of the James, where his old regiment, the Third New Hampshire, was distinguishing itself. On September 29, 1864, Colonel Donohoe was wounded while leading his troops at Fort Harrison, near Richmond. His gallantry was mentioned by General Ord in despatches, and he was brevetted brigadier-general September 27, 1864.

# Engagements of the Civil War

Brigade of Peck's Division, Dep't of North Carolina; *Confed.,* Robertson's, Clingman's and Evans' brigades. Losses: *Union,* 90 killed, 478 wounded; *Confed.,* 71 killed, 268 wounded, 400 missing.

**13.**—Fredericksburg, Va. *Union,* Army of the Potomac, Maj.-Gen. Burnside; Right Grand Div., Maj.-Gen. Sumner; Second Corps, Maj.-Gen. Couch; Ninth Corps, Maj.-Gen. Wilcox. Left Grand Div., Maj.-Gen. Franklin; First Corps, Gen. Reynolds; Sixth Corps, Maj.-Gen. W. F. Smith. Center Grand Div., Maj.-Gen. Hooker. Third Corps, Maj.-Gen. Stoneman; Fifth Corps, Maj.-Gen. Butterfield. *Confed.,* Army of Northern Virginia, Gen. Robert E. Lee; First Corps, Gen. Longstreet; Second Corps, "Stonewall" Jackson; Artillery Reserve, Gen. W. N. Pendleton; Gen. Stuart's Cavalry. Losses: *Union,* 1180 killed, 9028 wounded, 2145 missing; *Confed.,* 579 killed, 3870 wounded, 127 missing. *Union,* Brig.-Gens. Jackson and Bayard killed and Gibbon and Vinton wounded; *Confed.,* Brig.-Gen. T. R. R. Cobb killed and Maxcy Gregg wounded.

**14.**—Kinston, N. C. *Union,* 1st, 2d, and 3d Brigades 1st Div. and Wessell's Brigade of Peck's Division, Dep't of North Carolina; *Confed.,* Gen. N. G. Evans' command. Losses: *Union,* 40 killed, 120 wounded; *Confed.,* 50 killed, 75 wounded, 400 missing.

**18.**—Lexington, Tenn. *Union,* 11th Ill. Cav., 5th Ohio Cav., 2d Tenn. Cav.; *Confed.,* Forrest's Cav. Losses: *Union,* 7 killed, 10 wounded, 124 missing. *Confed.,* 7 killed, 28 wounded.

**20.**—Holly Springs, Miss. *Union,* 2d Ill. Cav. (6 co's), 8th Wis., part of 62d Ill.; *Confed.,* Earl Van Dorn's Cav. Losses: *Union,* 9 killed, 39 wounded, 1500 captured.
—Trenton, Tenn. *Union,* Detachments 122d Ill., 7th Tenn. Cav., and convalescents; *Confed.,* Forrest's Cav. Losses: *Union,* 1 killed, 250 prisoners; *Confed.,* 17 killed, 50 wounded.

**21.**—Davis' Mills, Miss. *Union,* Six Cos. 25th Ind., two Cos. 5th Ohio Cav.; *Confed.,* Earl Van Dorn's Cav. Losses: *Union,* 3 wounded; *Confed.,* 22 killed, 50 wounded, 20 missing.

**24.**—Middleburg, Tenn. *Union,* 115 men of 12th Mich.; *Confed.,* Griffith's Texas Brigade. Losses: *Union,* 9 wounded; *Confed.,* 9 killed, 11 wounded.

**25.**—Green's Chapel, Ky. *Union,* Detachment of 4th and 5th Ind. Cav.; *Confed.,* Morgan's Cav. Losses: *Union,* 1 killed; *Confed.,* 9 killed, 22 wounded.

**26.**—Bacon Creek, Ky. *Union,* 91st Ill.; *Confed.,* Morgan's Cav. Losses: *Union,* 3 wounded, 93 captured.

**27.**—Elizabethtown, Ky. *Union,* 91st Ill. 500 men captured by Morgan.
—Dumfries, Va. *Union,* 5th, 7th, and 66th Ohio, 12th Ill. Cav., 1st Md. Cav., 6th Maine Battery; *Confed.,* Stuart's Cav. Losses: *Union,* 3 killed, 8 wounded; *Confed.,* 25 killed, 40 wounded.

**28.**—Bacon Creek, Ky. *Union,* 91st Ill.; Ky. Cav.; *Confed.\** Losses: *Confed.,* 30 killed, 176 wounded, 51 missing.

**28 and 29.**—Chickasaw Bayou, Vicksburg, Miss. *Union,* Thirteenth Army Corps, Maj.-Gen. W. T. Sherman, Brig.-Gens. G. W. Morgan's, Frederick Steele's, M. L. Smith's, and A. J. Smith's Divisions; *Confed.,* Gen. Pemberton's Army, M. L. Smith's and S. D. Lee's Divisions. Losses: *Union,* 191 killed, 982 wounded, 756 missing; *Confed.,* 63 killed, 134 wounded, 10 missing; *Union,* Maj.-Gen. M. L. Smith wounded.

**30.**—Wautauga Bridge and Carter's Station, Tenn. *Union,* 7th Ohio Cav., 9th Pa. Cav.; *Confed.,* Gen. Humphrey Marshall's command. Losses: *Union,* 1 killed, 2 wounded; *Confed.,* 7 killed, 15 wounded, 273 missing.
—Jefferson, Tenn. *Union,* Second Brigade 1st Division Thomas' corps; *Confed.,* Wheeler's Cav. Losses: *Union,* 20 killed, 40 wounded; *Confed.,* 15 killed, 50 wounded.
—Parker's Cross Roads or Red Mound, Tenn. *Union,* 18th, 106th, 119th, and 122d Ill., 27th, 39th, and 63d Ohio, 50th Ind., 39th Iowa, 7th Tenn., 7th Wis. Battery; *Confed.,* Forrest's Cav. Losses: *Union,* 23 killed, 139 wounded, 58 missing; *Confed.,* 50 killed, 150 wounded, 300 missing.

**31 to Jan. 2.**—Murfreesboro' or Stone's River, Tenn. *Union,* Army of the Cumberland, Maj.-Gen. Rosecrans; Right

\* No record found.

[328]

## A NEW ENGLAND REGIMENT IN THE SOUTH

Company F, Third New Hampshire Volunteers. Organized in August, 1861, this regiment first saw active service in South Carolina. Accompanying the famous Port Royal Expedition, by which a Federal foothold was first gained in Southern territory, the regiment was stationed at Hilton Head, November 4, 1861. While Port Royal was being elaborately equipped as a naval and military base, the troops were constantly coöperating with the gunboats in reconnaissances, the ultimate object being operations against Savannah and Charleston. At the beginning of 1862 Confederate troops were found to be massing for the purpose of shutting up the Federals on Port Royal Island, and General Stevens, determining to nip the attempt in the bud, began active operations which were pushed close to both Savannah and Charleston. The Federals succeeded in occupying the southwestern portion of James' Island on the Stono River, after skirmishes at Pocotaglio, St. John's Island, and James' Island. On June 16th a battle took place at Secessionville, within five or six miles of Charleston, in which the Federals were defeated, and in this the Third New Hampshire, under command of Colonel John H. Jackson, established its reputation for gallantry, losing 104 men.

# Engagements of the Civil War

Wing, McCook's Corps; Center, Thomas' Corps; Left Wing, Crittenden's Corps; *Confed.*, Army of the Tennessee, Gen. Braxton Bragg; Leon. Polk's Corps, W. J. Hardee's Corps, Wheeler's Cav. Losses: *Union*, 1533 killed, 7245 wounded, 2800 missing; *Confed.*, 1294 killed, 7945 wounded, 1027 missing. *Union*, Brig.-Gens. Sill killed and Kirk wounded; *Confed.*, Brig.-Gens. Rains and Hanson killed and Chalmers and Adams wounded.

## JANUARY, 1863.

1.—Galveston, Tex. *Union*, Three Cos. 42d Mass., U. S. Gunboats *Westfield, Harriet Lane, Owasco, Sachem, Clifton* and *Coryphæus; Confed.*, Gen. J. B. Magruder's Command, Gunboats *Bayou City* and *Neptune*. Losses: *Union*, 600 killed, wounded, and missing; *Confed.*, 50 killed and wounded.

7 and 8.—Springfield, Mo. *Union*, Mo. Militia, convalescents and citizens; *Confed.*, Marmaduke's Cav. Losses: *Union*, 14 killed, 144 wounded; *Confed.*, 40 killed, 206 wounded and missing. *Union*, Brig.-Gen. Brown wounded.

11.—Fort Hindman, Ark. *Union*, Thirteenth Corps, Maj.-Gen. McClernand; Fifteenth Corps, Maj.-Gen. Sherman and gunboats Mississippi squadron; *Confed.*, Brig.-Gen. T. J. Churchill's command. Losses: *Union*, 129 killed, 831 wounded; *Confed.*, 100 killed, 400 wounded, 5000 prisoners.
—Hartville or Wood's Fork, Mo. *Union*, 21st Iowa, 99th Ill., 3d Iowa Cav., 3d Mo. Cav., Battery L, 2d Mo. Artil.; *Confed.*, Marmaduke's Cav. Losses: *Union*, 7 killed, 64 wounded; *Confed.*, Col. MacDonald killed.

14.—Bayou Teche, La. *Union*, 8th Vt., 16th and 75th N. Y., 12th Conn., 6th Mich., 21st Ind., 1st La. Cav., 4th and 6th Mass. Battery, 1st Maine Battery, and U. S. Gunboats *Calhoun, Diana, Kinsman*, and *Estrella; Confed.*, Gen. Magruder's Command, Gunboat *Cotton*. Losses: *Union*, 10 killed, 27 wounded; *Confed.*, 15 killed. *Union*, Lieut.-Comdr. Buchanan killed. *Confed.*, Gunboat *Cotton* destroyed.

24.—Woodbury, Tenn. *Union*, Second Division Crittenden's Corps; *Confed.*, Gen.

Bragg's Command. Losses: *Union*, 2 killed, 1 wounded; *Confed.*, 35 killed, 100 missing.

30.—Deserted House or Kelly's Store, near Suffolk, Va. *Union*, portion of Maj.-Gen. Peck's forces; *Confed.*, 1st S. C. Losses: *Union*, 24 killed, 80 wounded; *Confed.*, 50 wounded.

31.—Rover, Tenn. *Union*, 4th Ohio Cav.; *Confed.*, 51st Ala., 8th Cav. Losses: *Confed.*, 12 killed, 12 wounded, 300 captured.
—Charleston, S. C. Raid of the *Confed.* Gunboats *Palmetto State* and *Chicora* on the *Union* blockading fleet; *Union, Mercidita, Quaker City*, and *Keystone State, Ottawa, Unadilla, Augusta*, and *Memphis*. Losses: *Union*, 30 killed and wounded.

## FEBRUARY, 1863.

—Fort Donelson or Cumberland Iron Works, Tenn. *Union*, 83d Ill., 2d Ill. Artil., one battalion 5th Iowa Cav.; *Confed.*, Wheeler's, Forrest's, and Wharton's Cav. Losses: *Union*, 16 killed, 60 wounded, 50 missing; *Confed.*, 140 killed, 400 wounded, 130 missing.

24.—Mississippi River below Vicksburg. *Union*, U. S. Gunboat *Indianola; Confed., The Webb* and *Queen of the West*. Losses: *Union*, 1 killed, 1 wounded; *Confed.*, 35 killed.

## MARCH, 1863.

4 and 5.—Thompson's Station, also called Spring Hill and Unionville, Tenn. *Union*, 33d and 85th Ind., 22d Wis., 19th Mich., 124th Ohio, 18th Ohio Battery, 2d Mich. Cav., 9th Pa. Cav., 4th Ky. Cav.; *Confed.*, Earl Van Dorn's Cav. Corps, Forrest's, Martin's, and Jackson's Divisions. Losses: *Union*, 100 killed, 300 wounded, 1306 captured; *Confed.*, 150 killed, 450 wounded.

8.—Fairfax C. H., Va. *Union*, Brig.-Gen. Stoughton and thirty-three men captured by Capt. John S. Mosby (*Confed.*) in a midnight raid.

13 to April 5.—Fort Pemberton, Miss. *Union*, Thirteenth Corps, Brig.-Gen. Ross; Seventeenth Corps, Brig.-Gen. Quimby, U. S. Gunboats *Chillicothe* and

WHERE NEW ORLEANS WAS SAVED, JUNE 28, 1863

Donaldsonville, Louisiana. Within the little Fort Butler (the lower picture), Major J. D. Mullen, at half-past one in the morning of June 28th, with 180 men of the Twenty-eighth Maine, gallantly withstood the assault of 14,000 Confederates sent against the place by General Taylor. By daylight the little garrison, assisted by three gun-boats in the river, completed the repulse. The Confederates retired, leaving behind them, according to Major Mullen's report, 69 dead and 120 prisoners. This prevented Taylor from capturing New Orleans before the capitulation of Port Hudson would permit Banks to detach a sufficient force to drive off the Confederates, who were threatening his communications down the river. New Orleans would undoubtedly have been retaken had Taylor's request for reënforcements not been overruled by Kirby Smith. As it was, Taylor recruited his own forces to about 3,000 and moved against New Orleans in two detachments, getting within twenty-five miles of New Orleans two weeks before Port Hudson surrendered.

*DeKalb; Confed.,* Garrison under Gen. W. W. Loring. Casualties not recorded.

**14.**—Port Hudson, La. *Union,* Maj.-Gen. Banks' troops and Admiral Farragut's fleet; *Confed.,* Gen. Frank Gardner's Command. Losses: *Union,* 65 wounded.

**16 to 22.**—Expedition up Steele's Bayou, and at Deer Creek, Miss. *Union,* 2d Division Fifteenth Corps, Maj.-Gen. Sherman, Gunboat fleet, Admiral Porter: *Confed.,* Troops of Gen. Maury's and Gen. S. D. Lee's commands. Casualties not recorded.

**17.**—Kelly's Ford, Va. *Union,* 1st and 5th U. S. Regulars, 3d, 4th, and 16th Pa., 1st R. I., 6th Ohio, 4th N. Y. Cav., 6th N. Y. Battery; *Confed.,* Stuart's Cav. Losses: *Union,* 9 killed, 35 wounded; *Confed.,* 11 killed, 88 wounded.

**20.**—Vaught's Hill, near Milton, Tenn. *Union,* 105th Ohio, 101st Ind., 80th and 123d Ill., 1st Tenn. Cav., 9th Ind. Battery; *Confed.,* Morgan's Cav. Losses: *Union,* 7 killed, 48 wounded; *Confed.,* 63 killed, 300 wounded.

**22.**—Mt. Sterling, Ky. *Union,* 10th Ky. Cav.; *Confed.,* Morgan's Cav. Losses: *Union,* 4 killed, 10 wounded; *Confed.,* 8 killed, 13 wounded.

**24.**—Danville, Ky. *Union,* 18th and 22d Mich., 1st Ky. Cav., 2d Tenn. Cav., 1st Ind. Battery; *Confed.,* Morgan's Cav.

**25.**—Brentwood, Tenn. *Union,* Detachment 22d Wis. and 19th Mich.; *Confed.,* Forrest's Cav. Losses: *Union,* 1 killed, 4 wounded, 300 captured; *Confed.,* 1 killed, 5 wounded.
—Franklin and Little Harpeth, Tenn. *Union,* 4th and 6th Ky. Cav., 9th Pa. Cav., 2d Mich. Cav.; *Confed.,* Forrest's Cav. Losses: *Union,* 4 killed, 19 wounded, 40 missing.

**28.**—Pattersonville, La. *Union,* Gunboat *Diana* with Detachment of 12th Conn. and 160th N. Y. on board; *Confed.,* Gen. Richard Taylor's Command. Losses: *Union,* 4 killed, 14 wounded, 99 missing.

**30.**—Dutton's Hill or Somerset, Ky. *Union,* 1st Ky. Cav., 7th Ohio Cav., 44th and 45th Ohio Mounted Vol.; *Confed.,* Gen. John Pegram's Command. Losses: *Union,* 10 killed, 25 wounded; *Confed.,* 290 killed, wounded, and missing.

## APRIL, 1863.

**2 and 3.**—Woodbury and Snow Hill, Tenn. *Union,* 3d and 4th Ohio Cav.; *Confed.,* Morgan's Cav. Losses: *Union,* 1 killed, 8 wounded; *Confed.,* 50 killed and wounded.

**7.**—Bombardment Fort Sumter, S. C. *Union,* South Atlantic squadron; *Keokuk, Weehawken, Passaic, Montauk, Patapsco, New Ironsides, Catskill, Nantucket,* and *Nahant; Confed.,* S. C. Art. in Batteries Beauregard, Wagner, and Bee, Fort Sumter and Fort Moultrie. Losses: *Union,* 2 killed, 20 wounded; *Confed.,* 4 killed, 10 wounded.

**10.**—Franklin and Harpeth River, Tenn. *Union,* 40th Ohio and portion of Granger's Cav.; *Confed.,* Forrest's Cav. Losses: *Union,* 100 killed and wounded; *Confed.,* 19 killed, 35 wounded, 83 missing.

**12 to 14.**—Irish Bend and Bisland, La., also called Indian Ridge and Centreville. *Union,* Nineteenth Corps, Grover's, Emory's, and Weitzel's Divisions; *Confed.,* Gen. Richard Taylor's Command, Gunboat *Diana.* Losses: *Union,* 89 killed, 458 wounded, 30 missing; *Confed.**

**12 to May 4.**—Siege of Suffolk, Va. *Union,* Troops of the Army of Virginia and Department of North Carolina; *Confed.,* Gen. James Longstreet's Command. Losses: *Union,* 44 killed, 202 wounded; *Confed.,* 500 killed and wounded, 400 captured.

**17 to May 2.**—Grierson's expedition from La Grange, Tenn., to Baton Rouge, La. *Union,* 6th and 7th Ill. Cav., 2d Iowa Cav.; *Confed.,* detachments of Cav. and Home Guards. Losses: *Union,* 3 killed, 7 wounded, 9 missing; *Confed.,* 100 killed and wounded, 1600 captured (estimated).

**26.**—Cape Girardeau, Mo. *Union,* 32d Iowa, 1st Wis. Cav., 2d Mo. Cav., Batteries D and L 1st Mo. Lt. Artil.; *Confed.,* Marmaduke's Cav. Losses: *Union,* 6 killed, 6 wounded; *Confed.,* 60 killed, 275 wounded and missing.

**27 to May 3.**—Streight's Raid, Tuscumbia, Ala., to Rome, Ga., including skirmishes at Day's Gap, April 30th; Black Warrior Creek, May 1, and Blount's Farm,

* No record found.

[332]

## SUMTER

Searching all history for a parallel, it is impossible to find any defenses of a beleaguered city that stood so severe a bombardment as did this bravely defended and never conquered fortress of Sumter, in Charleston Harbor. It is estimated that about eighty thousand projectiles were discharged from the fleet and the marsh batteries, and yet Charleston, with its battered water-front, was not abandoned until all other Confederate positions along the Atlantic Coast were in Federal hands and Sherman's triumphant army was sweeping in from the West and South. The picture shows Sumter from the Confederate Fort Johnson. The powerful batteries in the foreground played havoc with the Federal fleet whenever it came down the main ship-channel to engage the forts. Protected by almost impassable swamps, morasses, and a network of creeks to the eastward, Fort Johnson held an almost impregnable position; and from its protection by Cummings' Point, on which was Battery Gregg, the Federal fleet could not approach nearer than two miles. Could it have been taken by land assault or reduced by gun-fire, Charleston would have fallen.

May 2. *Union*, 3d Ohio, 51st and 73d Ind., 80th Ill., Mounted Inft., two Cos. 1st Ala. Cav.; *Confed.*, Forrest's *Cav.* Losses: *Union*, 12 killed, 69 wounded. 1466 missing and captured; *Confed.*, 12 killed, 73 wounded.

**27 to May 8.**—Cavalry Raid in Virginia. *Union*, Gen. Stoneman's Corps; *Confed.*, Stuart's Cav., Home Guards and local garrisons. Losses.*
—Grand Gulf, Miss. *Union*, Gunboat fleet; *Confed.*, Gen. Bowen's Command. Losses: *Union*, 26 killed, 54 wounded.

**30.**—Spottsylvania C. H., Va. *Union*, 6th N. Y. Cav.; *Confed.*, Stuart's Cav. *Union*, 58 killed and wounded.

## MAY, 1863.

**1.**—Port Gibson, Miss. (the first engagement in Grant's Campaign against Vicksburg). *Union*, Thirteenth Corps, Maj.-Gen. McClernand, and 3d Division Seventeenth Corps, Maj.-Gen. McPherson; *C o n f e d.*, Gen. Bowen's Command. Losses: *Union*, 130 killed, 718 wounded; *Confed.*, 68 killed, 380 wounded, 384 missing. *Confed.* Brig.-Gen. Tracy killed.

**1 to 4.**—Chancellorsville, Va., i n c l u d i n g battles of Sixth Corps at Fredericksburg and Salem Heights. *Union*, Army of the Potomac, Maj.-Gen. Hooker; First Corps, Maj.-Gen. Reynolds; Second Corps, Maj.-Gen. Couch; Third Corps, Maj.-Gen. Sickles; Fifth Corps, Maj.-Gen. Meade; Sixth Corps, Maj.-Gen. Sedgwick; Eleventh Corps, Maj.-Gen. Howard; Twelfth Corps, Maj.-Gen. Slocum; *Confed.*, Army of Northern Virginia, Gen. R. E. Lee; Second Corps, "Stonewall" Jackson; R. H. Anderson's and McLaws' divisions of Longstreet's First Corps; Pendleton's Art. Battalion; Stuart's Cav. Losses: *Union*, 1512 killed, 9518 wounded, 5000 missing; *Confed.*, 1581 killed, 8700 wounded, 2000 missing. *Union*, Maj.-Gen. Berry and Brig.-Gen. Whipple killed, Devens and Kirby wounded. *Confed.*, Brig.-Gen. Paxton killed, Lieut.-Gen. Jackson, Maj.-Gen. A. P. Hill, Brig.-Gens. Hoke, Nichols, Ramseur, McGowan, Heth, and Pender wounded. Jackson's wound was mortal.

**3.**—Warrenton Junction, Va. *Union*, 1st W. Va. Cav., 5th N. Y. Cav.; *Confed.*, Stuart's Cav. Losses: *Union*, 1 killed, 16 wounded; *Confed.*, 15 wounded.

**4.**—Siege of Suffolk, Va., raised. (See April 12.)

**11.**—Horse Shoe Bend, Ky. *Union*, Detachment commanded by Col. R. T. Jacobs; *Confed.*, Morgan's Cav. Losses: *Union*, 10 killed, 20 wounded, 40 missing; *Confed.*, 100 killed, wounded, and missing.

**12.**—Raymond, Miss. *Union*, Seventeenth Corps, Maj.-Gen. McPherson. *Union*, 66 killed, 339 wounded, 37 missing; *Confed.*, Gen. Gregg's Command. Losses: *Confed.*, 969 killed and wounded.

**14.**—Jackson, Miss. *Union*, Fifteenth Corps, Maj.-Gen. Sherman; Seventeenth Corps, Maj.-Gen. McPherson; *Confed.*, Gen. Jos. E. Johnston's Command. Losses: *Union*, 42 killed, 251 wounded, 7 missing; *Confed.*, 450 killed and wounded.

**16.**—Champion's Hill, Miss. *Union*, Hovey's Div. Thirteenth Corps and Seventeenth Corps; *Confed.*, Army of Defense, commanded by Gen. J. C. Pemberton. Losses: *Union*, 410 killed, 1844 wounded, 187 missing; *Confed.*, 2500 killed and wounded, 1800 missing (estimate). *Confed.*, Gen. Tilghman killed.

**17.**—Big Black River, Miss. *Union*, Carr's and Osterhaus' divisions, Thirteenth Corps, Maj.-Gen. McClernand; *Confed.*, same as at Champion's Hill on the 16th. Losses: *Union*, 39 killed, 237 wounded, 3 missing; *Confed.*, 600 killed and wounded (estimate), 1751 captured.

**18 to July 4.**—Siege of Vicksburg, Miss. *Union*, Army of the Tennessee, commanded by Maj.-Gen. U. S. Grant; Ninth Corps, Thirteenth Corps, Fifteenth Corps, Sixteenth Corps (detachment), and Seventeenth Corps, and gunboat fleet, commanded by Admiral D. D. Porter; *Confed.*, Army of Defense, Gen. J. C. Pemberton. Assault on Fort Hill on May 19th and general assault on the 20th, in which *Confed.* Brig.-Gen. Green was killed; Loring's (portion), Bowen's, Stevenson's, Forney's, Smith's divisions, forces under Gen. J. E. Johnston and 7 river batteries. Losses: Included in the table for July 4.

* No record found.

THE NEVER–SURRENDERED FORT MOULTRIE, BESIEGED APRIL 10–SEPTEMBER 6, 1863

This is no hastily constructed battery, but the remains of a fort older than Sumter itself, as is shown by the brick walls and the permanent emplacement of the guns. It may be that this was the very piece of ordnance from which was fired the first shot that staggered humanity in 1861. Like Sumter, Fort Moultrie never surrendered. Protected by the encroaching sand-banks, it presented no such target as the high brick walls of the more historic fortress. Yet it had its place in history. Eighty-five years before, guns placed here had helped to repel the British fleet, and Sergeant Jasper had nailed to the flagstaff the banner of the new republic. Farther down the harbor the Confederates held permanent positions, the efforts to capture which were costly to the blockading fleet and besieging army. Before Fort Wagner there fell more than two thousand Federal soldiers. On Morris Island, to the south, the Federals had effected lodgment and turned their guns upon Sumter, Moultrie, and Wagner. The breaching batteries they erected in the swamps helped to complete the ruin. Tons of iron and exploding shells rained for months upon the bravely defended positions. The Confederate flags at Moultrie and Sumter, shot away a dozen times, were always replaced; and they waved proudly and defiantly until Charleston was threatened from the rear.

**20 to 28.**—Clendenin's raid, below Fredericksburg, Va. *Union,* 8th Ill. Cav.; *Confed.,* Outposts of Lee's Army. Losses: *Confed.,* 100 prisoners.

**23 to July 8.**—Siege of Port Hudson, La. Losses: *Union,* 708 killed, 3336 wounded, 319 missing; *Confed.,* 176 killed, 447 wounded, 5500 (estimate) captured.

## JUNE, 1863.

**4.**—Franklin, Tenn. *Union,* 85th Ind., 7th Ky. Cav., 4th and 6th Ky. Cav., 9th Pa. Cav., 2d Mich. Cav.; *Confed.** Losses: *Union,* 25 killed and wounded; *Confed.,* 200 killed and wounded.

**5.**—Franklin's Crossing, Rappahannock River, Va. *Union,* 26th N. J., 5th Vt., 15th and 50th N. Y. Engineers, supported by 6th Corps; *Confed.,* Outposts of Gen. R. E. Lee's Army. Losses: *Union,* 6 killed, 35 wounded.

**6 to 8.**—Milliken's Bend, La. *Union,* 23d Iowa and three regts. colored troops, gunboat *Choctaw; Confed.,* Gen. Richard Taylor's Command. Losses: *Union,* 154 killed, 223 wounded, 115 missing; *Confed.,* 125 killed, 400 wounded, 200 missing.

**9.**—Monticello and Rocky Gap, Ky. *Union,* 2d and 7th Ohio Cav., 1st Ky. Cav., 45th Ohio and 2d Tenn. Mounted Inft.; *Confed.,* Morgan's Cav. Losses: *Union,* 4 killed, 26 wounded; *Confed.,* 20 killed, 80 wounded.

—Beverly Ford and Brandy Station, Va. *Union,* Cavalry Corps, Brig.-Gen. Pleasonton, 2d, 3d, and 7th Wis., 2d and 33d Mass., 6th Maine, 86th and 124th N. Y., 1st, 2d, 5th, and 6th U. S. Cav., 2d, 6th, 8th, 9th, and 10th N. Y. Cav., 1st, 3d, 4th, 6th, 11th, and 17th Pa. Cav., 1st Md., 8th Ill., 3d Ind., 1st N. J., 1st Maine Cav., 1st R. I. Cav., and 3d W. Va. Cav., 8th and 12th Ill.* Cav., 1st Mass. Cav., 6th O. Cav., Batteries B and L, 2d U. S. Art., K, 1st U. S. Art., E, 4th U. S. Art., 6th Bat. N. Y. Light Art.; *Confed.,* Stuart's Cav. Losses: *Union,* 421 killed and wounded, 486 missing; *Confed.,* 301 killed and wounded, 184 missing. First true cavalry battle in the East.

**11.**—Middletown, Va. *Union,* 87th Pa., 13th Pa. Cav., Battery L, 5th U. S. Artil.; *Confed.,* Gen. Ewell's Command. Losses: *Confed.,* 8 killed, 42 wounded.

**13 and 15.**—Winchester, Va. *Union,* 2d, 67th and 87th Pa., 18th Conn., 12th W. Va., 110th, 116th, 122d, and 123d Ohio, 3d, 5th, and 6th Md., 12th and 13th Pa. Cav., 1st N. Y. Cav., 1st and 3d W. Va. Cav., Battery L 5th U. S. Artil., 1st W. Va. Battery, Baltimore Battery, one Co. 14th Mass. Heavy Artil.; *Confed.,* Gen. R. S. Ewell's Corps. Losses: *Union,* 95 killed, 443 wounded, and 4443 missing; *Confed.,* 42 killed and 210 wounded.

**14.**—Martinsburg, Va. *Union,* 106th N. Y., 126th Ohio, W. Va. Battery; *Confed.,* Gen. Ewell's Command. Losses: *Union,* 200 missing; *Confed.,* 1 killed, 2 wounded.

**16.**—Triplett's Bridge, Ky. *Union,* 15th Mich., 10th and 14th Ky. Cav., 7th and 9th Mich. Cav., 11th Mich. Battery; *Confed.,* Morgan's Cav. Losses: *Union,* 15 killed, 30 wounded.

**17.**—Aldie, Va. *Union,* Kilpatrick's Cav.; *Confed.,* Stuart's Cav. Losses: *Union,* 24 killed, 41 wounded, 89 missing; *Confed.,* 100 wounded.

—Wassau Sound, Ga. Capture of *Confederate* gunboat *Atlanta* by U. S. ironclad *Weehawken.* Losses: *Confed.,* 1 killed, 17 wounded, 145 prisoners.

**20 and 21.**—La Fourche Crossing, La. *Union,* Detachments 23d Conn., 176th N. Y., 26th, 42d, and 47th Mass., 21st Ind.; *Confed.,* Gen. Richard Taylor's Command. Losses: *Union,* 8 killed, 40 wounded; *Confed.,* 53 killed, 150 wounded.

**21.**—Upperville, Va. *Union,* Pleasonton's Cav.; *Confed.,* Stuart's Cav. Losses: *Union,* 94 wounded; *Confed.,* 20 killed, 100 wounded, 60 missing.

**22.**—Hill's Plantation, Miss. Detachment of 4th Iowa Cav.; *Confed.** Losses: *Union,* 4 killed, 10 wounded, 28 missing.

**23.**—Brashear City, La. *Union,* Detachments of 114th and 176th N. Y., 23d Conn., 42d Mass., 21st Ind.; *Confed.,* Gen. Taylor's Command. Losses: *Union,* 46 killed, 40 wounded, 300 missing; *Confed.,* 3 killed, 18 wounded.

* No record found.

[336]

The lower picture was taken after the war, when relic-hunters had removed the shells, and a beacon light had been erected where once stood the parapet. On September 8, 1863, at the very position in these photographs, the garrison repelled a bold assault with musketry fire alone, causing the Federals severe loss. The flag of the Confederacy floated triumphantly over the position during the whole of the long struggle. Every effort of the Federals to reduce the crumbling ruins into submission was unavailing. It stood the continual bombardment of ironclads until it was nothing but a mass of brickdust, but still the gallant garrison held it.

SCENE OF THE NIGHT ATTACK ON SUMTER, SEPTEMBER 8, 1863

It is strange that despite the awful destruction the loss of lives within the fort was few. For weeks the bombardment, assisted by the guns of the fleet, tore great chasms in the parapet. Fort Sumter never fell, but was abandoned only on the approach of Sherman's army. It had withstood continuous efforts against it for 587 days. From April, 1863, to September of the same year, the fortress was garrisoned by the First South Carolina Artillery, enlisted as regulars. Afterward the garrison was made up of detachments of infantry from Georgia, North Carolina, and South Carolina. Artillerists also served turns of duty during this period.

WHERE BURNSIDE HELD KNOXVILLE, NOVEMBER 17TH TO DECEMBER 4, 1863

This high ground, commanding Fort Sanders across the Holston River, had just been captured by the Confederates when Longstreet learned of Bragg's defeat at Chattanooga and was compelled to abandon the siege of Knoxville. He had bottled up Burnside. In Fort Sanders the Army of the Ohio was bravely holding on till help should come from Grant; they were eating bread made of pure bran, and their sustenance was almost exhausted. Before dawn on November 29, 1863, they repulsed the second assault which Longstreet's superior numbers made upon them. Longstreet, disheartened by constant disagreements with Bragg and without faith in the generalship of his superior, led the expedition, contrary to his judgment, as a forlorn hope, and his officers prosecuted the movement but half-heartedly. Longstreet himself admits that he was not as energetic as was his wont. Delay and misinformation as to the strength of the Federals cost him a thousand men before Fort Sanders. Baffled and discouraged, he finally abandoned the siege.

FORT SANDERS, KNOXVILLE, WHERE LONGSTREET ATTACKED, NOVEMBER 29, 1863

KNOXVILLE, AND TWO BRIDGES IN THE SIEGE. THE LOWER ONE, AT STRAWBERRY PLAINS, WAS DESTROYED FOUR TIMES DURING THE WAR

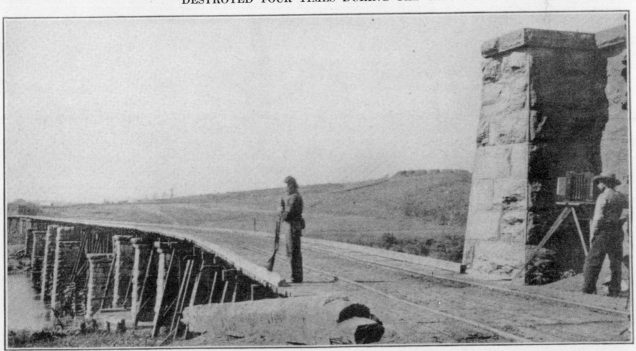

[B]

# Engagements of the Civil War

**23 to July 7.**—Rosecrans' Campaign. Murfreesboro to Tullahoma, Tenn., including Middleton, Hoover's Gap, Beech Grove, Liberty Gap, and Guy's Gap. Army of the Cumberland: Fourteenth, Twentieth, and Twenty-first Corps, Granger's Reserve Corps, and Stanley's Cavalry; *Confed.*, Army of Tennessee, Gen. Braxton Bragg. Losses: *Union*, 84 killed, 473 wounded, 13 missing; *Confed.*, 1634 (estimate) killed, wounded, and captured.

**28.**—Donaldsonville, La., and Fort Butler. *Union*, 28th Maine and convalescents, assisted by gunboats; *Confed.*, Gen. Taylor's Command. Losses: *Confed.*, 39 killed, 112 wounded, 150 missing.

**30.**—Hanover, Pa. *Union*, Kilpatrick's Cavalry Division; *Confed.*, Stuart's Cav. Losses: *Union*, 12 killed, 43 wounded; *Confed.*, 75 wounded, 60 missing.

## JULY, 1863.

**1 to 3.**—Gettysburg, Pa. *Union*, Army of the Potomac, Maj.-Gen. Geo. G. Meade; First Corps, Maj.-Gen. Reynolds; Second Corps, Maj.-Gen. Hancock; Third Corps, Maj.-Gen. Sickles; Fifth Corps, Maj.-Gen. Sykes; Sixth Corps, Maj.-Gen. Sedgwick; Eleventh Corps, Maj.-Gen. Howard; Twelfth Corps, Maj.-Gen. Slocum; Cavalry Corps, Maj.-Gen. Pleasonton, Artillery Reserve under Brig.-Gen. Tyler; *Confed.*, Army of Northern Virginia, Gen. R. E. Lee; First Corps, Gen. Longstreet; Second Corps, Gen. Ewell; Third Corps, Gen. A. P. Hill; Gen. Stuart's Cav., Reserve Artillery under Cols. Walton, Walker, and Brown. Losses: *Union*, 3155 killed, 14529 wounded, 5365 missing; *Confed.*, 3500 killed, 14500 wounded, 13621 missing.

**2 to 26.**—Morgan's raid into Kentucky, Indiana, and Ohio. At Blennerhasset Island, Ohio River (July 19th), the larger part of Morgan's force was killed, wounded, and captured—820 in all. The remainder, with Morgan himself, surrendered July 26th, near New Lisbon, Ohio. *Union*, Detachments of Rosecrans' Army of the Cumberland, Hobson's and Shackleford's Cav., Home Guard, and Militia; *Confed.*, Gen. John H. Morgan's Cav. Corps. Losses: *Union*, 33 killed, 97 wounded, 805 missing; *Confed.*,

about 2500 killed, wounded, and captured.

**4.**—Helena, Ark. *Union*, Maj.-Gen. Prentiss' Division of Sixteenth Corps and gunboat *Tyler*; *Confed.*, Gen. T. H. Holmes' Command, Price's Mo. and Ark. brigades, Marmaduke's and Shelby's Cav. Losses: *Union*, 57 killed, 117 wounded, 32 missing; *Confed.*, 173 killed, 687 wounded, 776 missing.
—Surrender of Vicksburg to Maj.-Gen. U. S. Grant; end of the siege. Losses, during the campaign and including Port Gibson, Raymond, Jackson, Champion's Hill, Big Black River, assaults May 19th and 22d, siege operations and skirmishes: *Union*, 1514 killed, 1395 wounded, 453 missing; *Confed.* (Incomplete) 1260 killed, 3572 wounded, 4227 captured or missing in action, surrendered (including non-combatants attached to the army) 29941.

**4 and 5.**—Bolton and Birdsong Ferry, Miss. *Union*, Maj.-Gen. Sherman's forces; *Confed.*, Gen. Johnston's Command. Losses: *Confed.*, 2000 captured.
—Monterey Gap and Fairfield Pa., and Smithsburg, Md. *Union*, Kilpatrick Cav.; *Confed.*, Hampton's Cav. Losses: *Union*, 30 killed and wounded; *Confed.*, 30 killed and wounded, 100 captured.

**5.**—Lebanon, Ky. *Union*, 20th Ky.; *Confed.*, Morgan's Cav. Losses: *Union*, 9 killed, 15 wounded, 400 missing; *Confed.*, 3 killed, 6 wounded.

**6.**—Hagerstown and Williamsport, Md. *Union*, Buford's and Kilpatrick's Cav., *Confed.*, Stuart's Cav. Losses: *Union*, 33 killed, 87 wounded, 293 missing; *Confed.*, 125 killed, wounded, and missing.

**7 to 9.**—Boonsboro, Md. *Union*, Buford's and Kilpatrick's Cav.; *Confed.*, Gen. Fitzhugh Lee's Cav. Losses: *Union*, 9 killed, 45 wounded.

**8.**—Port Hudson, La. Surrendered by Confederates to Maj.-Gen. Banks. (See May 23.)

**9 to 16.**—Jackson, Miss., including engagements at Rienzi, Bolton Depot, Canton, and Clinton. *Union*, 9th, 13th, 15th, and part of 16th Corps; *Confed.*, Gen. Jos. E. Johnston's Army. Losses: *Union*, 100 killed, 800 wounded, 100 missing; *Confed.*, 71 killed, 504 wounded, 764 missing.

## MISSOURI ARTILLERY IN SHERMAN'S RAID, FEBRUARY, 1864

Battery M, First Missouri Light Artillery, originally in Colonel Frank P. Blair's infantry regiment, marched with Sherman from Vicksburg through Mississippi to Meridian during February, 1864. Sherman, with twenty thousand men and sixty pieces of artillery, was to break up all the railroad communications, so that small Federal garrisons would be able to hold important positions along the Mississippi. The advance corps under the intrepid McPherson left Vicksburg on February 3d and arrived at Meridian on the 8th. It was a precursor of the famous "March to the Sea," but on a smaller scale. The troops destroyed whatever would be of service to the Confederates, who fell back before Sherman, burning provisions and laying waste the country. At Meridian, the great railway center of the Southwest at the time, Sherman accomplished "the most complete destruction of railroads ever beheld." Meantime, General W. S. Smith, with the Federal cavalry force from Memphis, was unable to reach Meridian. Escaping in the night from a dangerous predicament at Okolona on February 22d, he managed to return safely to Memphis by February 25th, after having destroyed a million bushels of corn and many miles of railroad.

**10 to Sept. 6.**—Siege of Fort Wagner, Morris Island, S. C. *Union,* Troops of the Department of the South, under command of Maj.-Gen. Gillmore, and U. S. Navy under Admiral Dahlgren; *Confed.,* Garrison commanded by Gen. W. B. Taliaferro. Losses: *Union,* 1757 killed, wounded, and missing; *Confed.,* 561 killed, wounded, and missing.

—Falling Waters, Md. *Union,* 3d Cav. Division Army of the Potomac; *Confed.,* Army of Northern Virginia, Gen. R. E. Lee. Losses: *Union,* 29 killed, 36 wounded; *Confed.,* 125 killed and wounded, 1500 prisoners. *Confed.,* Maj.-Gen. Pettigrew killed.

**13.**—Yazoo City, Miss. *Union,* Maj.-Gen. Herron's Division and three gunboats; *Confed.,* Detachments of Capt. I. N. Brown. Losses: *Confed.,* 250 captured.

—Jackson, Tenn. *Union,* 9th Ill., 3d Mich. Cav., 2d Iowa Cav., and 1st Tenn. Cav.; *Confed.,* Gen. N. B. Forrest's Cav. Losses: *Union,* 2 killed, 20 wounded; *Confed.,* 38 killed, 150 wounded.

—Donaldsonville, La. *Union,* Advance of Gen. Weitzel's command; *Confed.,* Gen. Green's brigade, Col. Taylor's Cav. Losses: *Union,* 465 killed, wounded, and missing; *Confed.,* 3 killed, 30 wounded.

**13 to 15.**—Draft riots in New York City, in which over 1000 rioters were killed.

**14.**—Elk River, Tenn. *Union,* Advance of the Fourteenth Corps Army of the Cumberland; *Confed.,* Rear Guard of Gen. Bragg's Army in retreat. Losses: *Union,* 10 killed, 30 wounded; *Confed.,* 60 killed, 24 wounded, 100 missing.

—Halltown, Va. *Union,* 16th Pa. and 1st Maine Cav.; *Confed.,* Gen. J. D. Imboden's command. Losses: *Union,* 25 killed and wounded; *Confed.,* 20 killed and wounded.

**16.**—Shepherdstown, Va. *Union,* 1st, 4th, and 16th Pa., 10th N. Y. and 1st Maine Cav.; *Confed.,* Stuart's Cav. Losses: *Confed.,* 25 killed, 75 wounded.

**17.**—Honey Springs, Ind. Ter. *Union,* 2d, 6th, and 9th Kan. Cav., 2d and 3d Kan. Batteries, 2d and 3d Kan. Indian Home Guards; *Confed.,* Col. Cooper's Indians and Tex. Cav. Losses: *Union,* 17 killed, 60 wounded; *Confed.,* 150 killed, 400 wounded.

—Wytheville, W. Va. Union, 34th Ohio, 1st and 2d W. Va. Cav.; *Confed.** Losses: *Union,* 17 killed, 61 wounded; *Confed.,* 75 killed, 125 missing.

**21 to 23.**—Manassas Gap and Chester Gap, Va. *Union,* Cavalry advance and Third Corps Army of the Potomac; *Confed.,* Stuart's Cav. Losses: *Union,* 35 killed, 102 wounded; *Confed.,* 300 killed and wounded.

## AUGUST, 1863.

**1 to 3.**—Rappahannock Station, Brandy Station, and Kelly's Ford, Va. *Union,* Brig.-Gen. Buford's Cav.; *Confed.,* Stuart's Cav. Losses: *Union,* 16 killed, 134 wounded.

**21.**—Quantrill's plunder and massacre of Lawrence, Kan., in which 140 citizens were killed and 24 wounded. Quantrill's loss, 40 killed.

**25 to 30.**—Averell's Raid in W. Va. Losses: *Union,* 3 killed, 10 wounded, 60 missing.

**25 to 31.**—Brownsville, Bayou Metoe, and Austin, Ark. *Union,* Davidson's Cav.; *Confed.,* Marmaduke's Cav. Losses: *Union,* 13 killed, 72 wounded.

**26 and 27.**—Rocky Gap, near White Sulphur Springs, W. Va. *Union,* 3d and 8th W. Va., 2d and 3d W. Va. Cav., 14th Pa. Cav.; *Confed.,* Gen. Samuel Jones' command. Losses: *Union,* 16 killed, 113 wounded; *Confed.,* 156 killed and wounded.

## SEPTEMBER, 1863.

**1.**—Devil's Back Bone, Ark. *Union,* 1st Ark. 6th Mo. Militia, 2d Kan. Cav., 2d Ind. Battery; *Confed.,* Part of Gen. Price's command. Losses: *Union,* 4 killed, 12 wounded; *Confed.,* 25 killed, 40 wounded.

**8.**—Night attack on Fort Sumter, S. C. *Union,* 413 marines and sailors from the South Atlantic Blockading Squadron, led by Commander Stevens, U. S. N. *Confed.,* Garrison of Fort Sumter. Losses: *Union,* 124 killed, wounded, and missing.

**9.**—Cumberland Gap, Tenn. *Union,* Shackleford's Cav.; *Confed.,* Gen. J. W. Frazer's brigade. Losses: *Confed.,* 2000 captured.

* No record found.

## HOLDING THE WESTERN FRONTIER IN '63

Two regiments of fighting men from the Northwest that participated in the rough campaigning of the frontier across the Mississippi in Arkansas in 1863. In the upper picture is the camp of the Twenty-eighth Wisconsin Infantry at Little Rock, and in the lower view the Third Minnesota Infantry, Colonel C. C. Andrews commanding, is drawn up on dress parade in front of the State Capitol. Both organizations fought in the expedition which Major-General Frederick Steele organized at Helena, August 5, 1863, to break up the Confederate army under Price in Arkansas. On the very day that Vicksburg surrendered, July 4th, the Confederate General T. H. Holmes appeared before Helena with a force of over eight thousand. He had telegraphed to his superior, E. K. Smith, on June 15th, "I believe we can take Helena; please let me do it." To which Smith had replied, "Most certainly do it." Holmes hoped to make a new Vicksburg to keep the Mississippi closed from the west bank. Helena was garrisoned by a force less than half as great as that which came against it. Among the defenders were the Twenty-eighth Wisconsin. On the morning of July 4, 1863, under command of Major-General B. M. Prentiss, these Federals repulsed two vigorous assaults, and Holmes, giving up hope of success, returned to Little Rock. This aroused the Federals to the importance of holding Arkansas, and General Frederick Steele collected about twelve thousand men at Helena early in August. The troops left Helena on August 10th, and pushed back the Confederates under General Marmaduke.

THE THIRD MINNESOTA

# Engagements of the Civil War

.6.—Little Rock, Ark. Evacuation by Confederates under Gen. Price. *Union,* Maj.-Gen. .Steele's troops and Davidson's Cav.; *Confed.,* Price's Division, L. M. Walker's and J. S. Marmaduke's Cav.

13.—Culpeper, Va. *Union,* Cavalry Corps, Army of the Potomac; *Confed.,* Stuart's Cav. Losses: *Union,* 3 killed, 40 wounded; *Confed.,* 10 killed, 40 wounded, 75 missing.

—Leet's Tan Yard, near Chickamauga, Ga. *Union,* Wilder's mounted brigade; *Confed.,* Outposts of Gen. Bragg's Army. Losses: *Union,* 50 killed and wounded; *Confed.,* 10 killed, 40 wounded.

19 and 20.—Chickamauga, Ga. Army of the Cumberland, Maj.-Gen. Rosecrans; Fourteenth Corps, Maj.-Gen. Thomas; Twentieth Corps, Maj.-Gen. McCook; Twenty-first Corps, Maj.-Gen. Crittenden; Reserve Corps, Maj.-Gen. Granger; *Confed.,* Army of Tennesseee, Gen. Braxton Bragg; Gen. Polk's Corps, Longstreet's Corps (Army of Northern Virginia); D. H. Hill's Corps, Buckner's Corps, Gen. W. H. T. Walker's Reserve Corps, Forrest's and Wheeler's Cav. Losses: *Union,* 1644 killed, 9262 wounded, 4945 missing; *Confed.,* 2389 killed, 13412 wounded, 2003 missing.

—Blountsville, Tenn. *Union,* Foster's 2d Brigade Cav.; *Confed.,* 1st Tenn. Cav. Losses: *Union,* 5 killed, 22 wounded; *Confed.,* 15 killed, 50 wounded, 100 missing.

—Rockville, Md. *Union,* 11th N. Y. Cav.; *Confed.,* Stuart's Cav. Losses: *Confed.,* 34 killed and wounded.

## OCTOBER, 1863.

3.—McMinnville, Tenn. *Union,* 4th Tenn.; *Confed.,* Detachment of Gen. Bragg's Army. Losses: *Union,* 7 killed, 31 wounded, 350 missing; *Confed.,* 23 killed and wounded.

7.—Near Farmington, Tenn. *Union,* 1st, 3d, and 4th Ohio Cav., 2d Ky. Cav., Long's 2d Cav. Division, and Wilder's Brigade Mounted Inft.; *Confed.,* Wheeler's Cav. Losses: *Union,* 15 killed, 60 wounded; *Confed.,* 10 killed, 60 wounded, 240 missing.

—Blue Springs, Tenn. *Union,* Ninth Corps, Army of the Ohio, and Shackleford's Cav.; *Confed.,* Gen. J. S. Williams' command. Losses: *Union,* 100 killed, wounded, and missing; *Confed.,* 66 killed and wounded, 150 missing.

12 and 13.—Ingham's Mills and Wyatts, Miss. *Union,* 2d Iowa Cav.; *Confed.,* Chalmers' Cav. Losses: *Union,* 45 killed and wounded; *Confed.,* 50 killed and wounded.

—Culpeper and White Sulphur Springs, Va. *Union,* Cavalry Corps Army of the Potomac; *Confed.,* Stuart's Cav. Losses: *Union,* 8 killed, 46 wounded.

—Merrill's Crossing on La Mine Bridge, Mo. *Union,* Mo. Enrolled Militia, 1st Mo. Militia Battery, 1st, 4th, and 7th Mo. Militia Cav.; *Confed.,* Shelby's Cav. Losses: *Union,* 16 killed; *Confed.,* 53 killed, 70 wounded.

14.—Bristoe Station, Va. *Union,* Second Corps, portion of Fifth Corps, 2d Cav. Division, Army of the Potomac; *Confed.,* Divisions of Heth, R. H. Anderson, and A. P. Hill. Losses: *Union,* 51 killed, 329 wounded; *Confed.,* 750 killed and wounded, 450 missing.

15.—McLean's Ford or Liberty Mills, Va. *Union,* 5th, 6th, 7th, and 8th N. J., 151st N. Y., 115th Pa., 4th Bat. Me. Art. and Bat. K. 4th U. S. Art. *Confed.,* Gen. L. L. Lomax's Cav. Brigade. Losses: *Union,* 2 killed, 25 wounded; *Confed.,* 60 killed and wounded.

15 to 18.—Canton, Brownsville, and Clinton, Miss. *Union,* Portion of Fifteenth and Seventeenth Corps; *Confed.,* Gen. W. H. Jackson's command. Losses: *Confed.,* 200 killed and wounded.

18.—Charlestown, W. Va. *Union,* 9th Md.; *Confed.,* Gen. Imboden's command. Losses: *Union,* 12 killed, 13 wounded, 379 missing.

19.—Buckland Mills, Va. *Union,* 3d Division of Kilpatrick's Cav.; *Confed.,* Stuart's Cav. Losses: *Union,* 20 killed, 60 wounded, 100 missing; *Confed.,* 10 killed, 40 wounded.

20 and 22.—Philadelphia, Tenn. *Union,* 45th Ohio Mounted Inft., 1st, 11th, and 12th Ky. Cav., 24th Ind. Battery; *Confed.,* Gen. J. S. Williams' command. Losses: *Union,* 20 killed, 80 wounded, 354 missing; *Confed.,* 15 killed, 82 wounded, 111 missing.

THE MONTH BEFORE MINE RUN, OCTOBER, 1863

Meade's Headquarters at Culpeper, Virginia. In the vicinity of Culpeper Court House, ten miles from the banks of the Rappahannock and thirty miles northwest of Fredericksburg, the Army of the Potomac was encamped after Gettysburg. Meade had followed Lee southward throughout the summer in the hope of striking his army before it had recovered from the blow dealt it in Pennsylvania. But Lee, in great depression and wishing to retire, remained on the defensive; the departure of Longstreet for Chickamauga in September had made him still more wary. Meade's forces had been reduced also by the despatching of two corps, under Hooker, into Tennessee, so he in turn was urged to caution. The fall of 1863 was spent in skilful maneuvers with the flash of battle at Bristoe Station, October 14th, where Warren worsted A. P. Hill, and at Rappahannock Station on November 7th, where the Sixth Corps distinguished itself. At Mine Run, near the old Chancellorsville battle-ground, Lee was strongly entrenched and here the opposing forces came near a general engagement on November 30th, but the moment passed and both sides went into winter quarters. By March, 1864, all was activity at Culpeper; the army awaited its new commander, Grant, who was to lead it again toward Chancellorsville and The Wilderness.

# Engagements of the Civil War

**25.**—Pine Bluff, Ark. *Union,* 5th Kan. and 1st Ind. Cav.; *Confed.,* Gen. Price's command. Losses: *Union,* 11 killed, 27 wounded; *Confed.,* 53 killed, 164 wounded.

**28 and 29.**—Wauhatchie, Tenn. *Union,* Eleventh Corps and 2d Division of Twelfth Corps; *Confed.,* Gen. James Longstreet's Corps. Losses: *Union,* 78 killed, 327 wounded, 15 missing. *Confed.* (estimated) 300 killed, 1200 wounded.

## NOVEMBER, 1863.

**3.**—Grand Coteau, La. *Union,* 3d and 4th Divisions, Thirteenth Corps; *Confed.,* Gen. Green's Cav. Division. Losses: *Union,* 26 killed, 124 wounded, 576 missing; *Confed.,* 60 killed, 320 wounded, 65 missing.

**6.**—Rogersville, Tenn. *Union,* 7th Ohio Cav., 2d Tenn. Mounted Inft., 2d Ill. Battery; *Confed.,* Gens. W. E. Jones and H. L. Giltner's Brigades. Losses: *Union,* 5 killed, 12 wounded, 650 missing; *Confed.,* 10 killed, 20 wounded. —Droop Mountain, Va. *Union,* 10th W. Va., 28th Ohio, 14th Pa. Cav., 2d and 5th W. Va. Cav., Battery B, W. Va. Artil.; *Confed.,* Gen. Echol's Brigade. Losses: *Union,* 31 killed, 94 wounded; *Confed.,* 50 killed, 250 wounded, 100 missing.

**7.**—Rappahannock Station, Va. *Union,* 5th Wis., 5th, 6th Maine, 49th, 119th Pa., 121st N. Y.; *Confed.,* Two brigades of Gen. Jubal Early's command. Losses: *Union,* 419 killed and wounded; *Confed.,* 6 killed, 39 wounded, 1,629 captured or missing. —Kelly's Ford, Va. *Union,* 1st U. S. Sharpshooters, 40th N. Y., 1st and 20th Ind., 3d and 5th Mich., 110th Pa., supported by remainder of Third Corps; *Confed.,* Stuart's Cav. Losses: *Union,* 70 killed and wounded; *Confed.,* 5 killed, 59 wounded, 295 missing.

**14.**—Huff's Ferry, Tenn. *Union,* 111th Ohio, 107th Ill., 11th and 13th Ky., 23d Mich., 24th Mich. Battery; *Confed.,* Wheeler's Cav. Losses: *Union,* 100 killed and wounded.

**16.**—Campbell's Station, Tenn. *Union,* Ninth Corps, 2d Division of Twenty-third Corps, Sanders' Cav.; *Confed.,*

Longstreet's Corps. Losses: *Union,* 31 killed, 211 wounded, and 76 missing; *Confed.,* 570 killed and wounded.

**17 to Dec. 4.**—Siege of Knoxville, Tenn. *Union,* Army of the Ohio, commanded by Maj.-Gen. Burnside; *Confed.,* Gen. Longstreet's Corps, Alexander's Art., Wheeler's Cav. Losses: Complete casualties not recorded. *Union,* 94 killed, 394 wounded, and 207 missing; *Confed.,* (minus the cavalry *) 182 killed, 768 wounded, 192 missing.

**23 to 25.**—Chattanooga, Lookout Mountain, Orchard Knob and Missionary Ridge, Tenn. *Union,* Forces commanded by Maj.-Gen. U. S. Grant, as follows: Fourth and Fourteenth Corps, Army of the Cumberland; Maj.-Gen. Geo. H. Thomas, Eleventh Corps; Geary's Division of the Twelfth Corps; Fifteenth Corps; Smith's Division, Seventeenth Corps, Army of the Tennessee, Maj.-Gen. W. T. Sherman; *Confed.,* Gen. Bragg's command; W. J. Hardee's Corps; Breckinridge's Corps; Art. Reserve, detachments of Cav. Losses: *Union,* 757 killed, 4529 wounded, 330 missing; *Confed.,* 361 killed, 2181 wounded, 6142 missing.

**26 to 28.**—Operations at Mine Run, Va., including Raccoon Ford, New Hope, Robertson's Tavern, Bartlett's Mills, and Locust Grove. *Union,* First Corps, Second Corps, Third Corps, Fifth Corps, Sixth Corps, and 1st and 2d Cav. Divisions Army of the Potomac; *Confed.,* Army of Northern Virginia, Gen. Robert E. Lee. Losses: *Union,* 173 killed, 1099 wounded, 381 missing; *Confed.,* 98 killed, 610 wounded, 1104 missing.

**27.**—Ringgold and Taylor's Ridge, Ga. *Union,* Portions of Twelfth, Fourteenth, and Fifteenth Corps; *Confed.,* Rear Guard of Gen. Bragg's Army on retreat from Chattanooga. Losses: *Union,* 68 killed, 351 wounded; *Confed.,* 50 killed, 200 wounded, 230 missing.

## DECEMBER, 1863.

**1 to 4.**—Ripley and Moscow Station, Miss., and Salisbury, Tenn. *Union,* 2d Brigade Cav. Division of Sixteenth Corps; *Confed.,* Gen. S. D. Lee's command. Losses: *Union,* 175 killed and

* No record found.

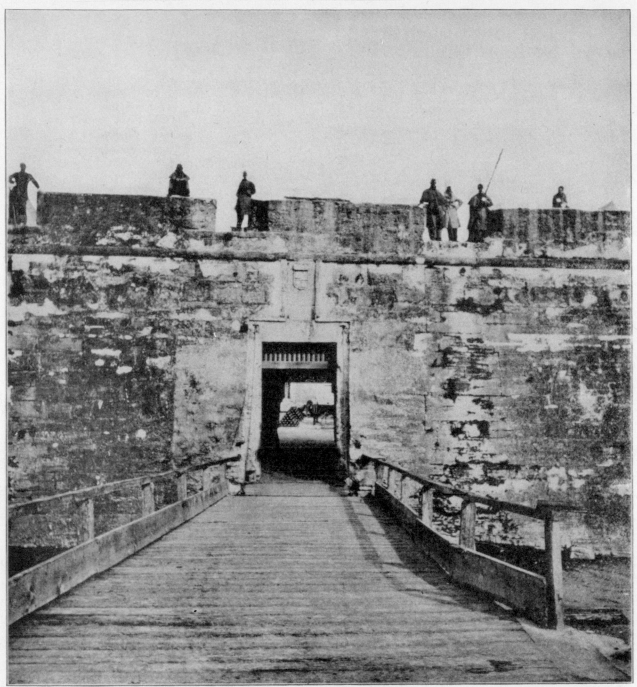

## THE ANCIENT SALLY PORT

Civil War Garrison at the Gate of Fort Marion, St. Augustine, Florida. American guns were first turned against it when Oglethorpe led his expedition from South Carolina against St. Augustine in May, 1740. Its style of architecture tells plainly of its origin and antiquity; it was called by the Spaniards "Castle St. Marcus." When Commander Rodgers brought his flag of truce to St. Augustine, the mayor proposed to turn over the fort to him, but Rodgers instructed him to establish a patrol and guard at the fort and make careful inventories of what it contained. Several good guns had been taken from it by the Confederates, but there still remained three fine army 32-pounders and two 8-inch seacoast howitzers, with a quantity of ammunition. About a fifth of the inhabitants of St. Augustine had fled at the coming of the Federals, but of the 1,500 that remained Commander Rodgers reported that they were "many citizens who are earnestly attached to the Union, a large number who are silently opposed to it, and a still larger number who care very little about the matter."

# Engagements of the Civil War

wounded; *Confed.,* 15 killed, 40 wounded.

**2.**—Walker's Ford, Tenn. *Union,* 65th, 116th, and 118th Ind., 21st Ohio Battery, 5th Ind. Cav., 14th Ill. Cav.; *Confed.,* Wheeler's Cav. Losses: *Union,* 9 killed, 39 wounded; *Confed.,* 25 killed, 50 wounded.

**8 to 21.**—Averell's raid in South-western Va.; *Confed.,* Gen. Jno. D. Imboden's command. Losses: *Union,* 6 killed, 5 wounded; *Confed.,* 200 captured.

**10 to 14.**—Bean's Station and Morristown, Tenn. *Union,* Shackleford's Cav.; *Confed.,* Longstreet's Corps, Martin's Cav. Losses: *Union,* 700 killed and wounded; *Confed.,* 932 killed and wounded, 150 captured.

**19.**—Barren Fork, Ind. Ter. *Union,* 1st and 3d Kan., Indian Home Guards; *Confed.\** Losses: *Confed.,* 50 killed.

**28.**—Charleston, Tenn. *Union,* Detachments of the 2d Mo. and 4th Ohio Cav. guarding wagon train; *Confed.,* Wheeler's Cav. Losses: *Union,* 2 killed, 15 wounded; *Confed.,* 8 killed, 89 wounded, 121 captured.

**30.**—St. Augustine, Fla. *Union,* 10th Conn., 24th Mass.; *Confed.,* 2d Fla. Cav. Losses: *Union,* 4 killed.

—Waldron, Ark. *Union,* 2d Kan. Cav.; *Confed.,* Maj. Gibson's command. Losses: *Union,* 2 killed, 6 wounded; *Confed.,* 1 killed, 8 wounded.

## JANUARY, 1864.

**1 to 10.**—Rectortown and Loudon Heights, Va. *Union,* 1st Md. Cav., Potomac Home Brigade; *Confed.,* Col. J. S. Mosby's command. Losses: *Union,* 29 killed and wounded, 41 missing; *Confed.,* 4 killed, 10 wounded.

**3.**—Jonesville, Va. *Union,* Detachment 16th Ill. Cav., 22d Ohio Battery; *Confed.,* Jones' Cavalry. Losses: *Union,* 12 killed, 48 wounded, 300 missing; *Confed.,* 4 killed, 12 wounded.

**16 and 17.**—D a n d r i d g e, Tenn. *Union,* Fourth Corps and Cav. Division of Army of the Ohio; *Confed.,* Longstreet's command. Losses: *Union,* 150 wounded.

**19 and 24.**—Tazewell, Tenn. *Union,* 34th Ky., 116th and 118th Ind., 11th Tenn. Cav., 11th Mich. Bat'y.; *Confed.,* Longstreet's command. Losses: *Confed.,* 31 killed.

**27.**—Fair Gardens or Kelly's Ford, Tenn. *Union,* Sturgis's Cavalry; *Confed.,* Martin's and Morgan's Cavalry. Losses: *Union,* 100 killed and wounded; *Confed.,* 65 killed, 100 captured.

**28.**—Tunnel Hill, Ga. *Union,* part of Fourteenth Corps; *Confed.,* Outposts of the Army of Tennessee. Losses: *Union,* 2 wounded; *Confed.,* 32 wounded.

**31.**—Smithfield, Va. *Union,* Detachments 99th N. Y., 21st Conn., 20th N. Y. Cav., 3d Pa. Artil., and marines from U. S. Gunboats *Minnesota* and *Smith Briggs; Confed.\** Losses: *Union,* 90 missing.

**29 to Feb. 1.**—Medley, W. Va. *Union,* 1st and 14th W. Va., 23d Ill., 2d Md., Potomac Home Brigade, 4th W. Va. Cav., Ringgold (Pa.) Cav.; *Confed.,* Col. T. L. Rosser's Cav. Losses: *Union,* 10 killed, 70 wounded.

## FEBRUARY, 1864.

**1 to 3.**—Bachelor Creek, Newport Barracks, and New Berne, N. C. *Union,* 132d N. Y., 9th Vt., 17th Mass., 2d N. C., 12th N. Y. Cav., 3d N. Y. Artil.; *Confed.,* Expedition commanded by Gen. Geo. E. Pickett. Losses: *Union,* 16 killed, 50 wounded, 280 missing; *Confed.,* 5 killed, 30 wounded.

**1 to March 8.**—Expedition up the Yazoo River, Miss. *Union,* 11th Ill., 47th U. S. Colored, 3d U. S. Colored Cav., and a portion of Porter's Fleet of gunboats; *Confed.,* Gen. J. E. Johnston's command. Losses: *Union,* 35 killed, 121 wounded. *Confed.,* 35 killed, 90 wounded.

**3 to March 5.**—Expedition from Vicksburg to Meridian, Miss. *Union,* Two Divisions of the Sixteenth and three of the Seventeenth Corps, with the 5th Ill., 4th Iowa, 10th Mo. and Foster's (Ohio) Cav.; *Confed.,* Gen. Polk's command; Loring's and French's divisions, Forrest's and Armstrong's Cav. Losses: *Union,* 56 killed, 138 wounded, 105 miss-

* No record found.

[ 348 ]

## FIGHTING IN FLORIDA—DECEMBER, 1863

A Civil War skirmish took place at St. Augustine, Florida, December 30, 1863, before the quaint old bastions of Fort Marion —the oldest Spanish fort in the Western Hemisphere, and the oldest anywhere outside of Spain. St. Augustine, however, was not disturbed by the one serious attempt that was made to penetrate the interior of Florida. If this could be done, it was throught at Washington that many citizens of the State would flock to the Union cause and could be reconstructed into a State whose electoral vote would be extremely valuable in retaining the Lincoln Administration in power. On February 5, 1864, under orders from General Gillmore, an expedition left Hilton Head and, arriving at Jacksonville, Florida, pushed forward across the State. Rapidly collecting reënforcements from Savannah and Charleston, the Confederate General Finegan met the Federals at Clustee and sharply defeated them February 20, 1864. This put an end to the only effort to invade the State of Florida.

ARTILLERY INSIDE THE FORT

# Engagements of the Civil War

ing; *Confed.*, 503 killed and wounded, 212 captured.

**5.**—Quallatown, N. C. *Union*, Detachment of 14th Ill. Cav.; *Confed.*, 26th N. C. Losses: *Union*, 3 killed, 6 wounded; *Confed.*, 50 captured.

**6.**—Morton's Ford, Va. *Union*, Portion of Second Corps; *Confed.*, Wade Hampton's Cav. Losses: *Union*, 14 killed, 218 wounded, 391 missing; *Confed.*, 100 killed, wounded, and missing.

**9 to 14.**—Barber's Place, St. Mary's River, Lake City, and Gainesville, Fla. *Union*, 40th Mass. Mounted Inft. and Independent (Mass.) Cav.; *Confed.*, Gen. Joseph Finnegan's command. Losses: *Union*, 4 killed, 16 wounded; *Confed.*, 4 killed, 48 wounded.

**10 to 25.**—Gen. Wm. Sooy Smith's Raid from Memphis, Tenn., into Mississippi. *Union*, Smith's Division; *Confed.*, Forrest's Cav. Losses: *Union*, 47 killed, 152 wounded, 120 missing; *Confed.*, 50 wounded, 300 captured.

**14 and 15.**—Waterproof, La. *Union*, 49th U. S. Colored and U. S. Gunboat *Forest Rose; Confed.*, Col. Harrison's command. Losses: *Union*, 8 killed, 14 wounded; *Confed.*, 15 killed.

**20.**—Olustee or Silver Lake, Fla. *Union*, 47th, 48th, and 115th N. Y., 7th Conn., 7th N. H., 40th Mass., 8th and 54th U. S. Colored, 1st N. C. Colored, 1st Mass. Cav., 1st and 3d U. S. Artil., 3d R. I. Artil.; *Confed.*, Colquitt's and Harrison's brigades under Gen. Joseph Finnegan. Losses: *Union*, 193 killed, 1175 wounded, 460 missing; *Confed.*, 940 killed and wounded.

**22.**—Okolona, Miss. *Union*, Smith's Cav.; *Confed.*, Forrest's Cav. Losses: *Union*, 47 killed, 152 wounded, 120 missing; *Confed.**

**25 to 27.**—Buzzard Roost, Tunnel Hill, and Rocky Face, Ga. *Union*, Fourth and Fourteenth Corps and Cavalry Corps Army of the Cumberland; *Confed.*, Troops of Gen. Jos. E. Johnston's command. Losses: *Union*, 17 killed, 272 wounded; *Confed.*, 20 killed, 120 wounded.

**28 to March 4.**—Kilpatrick's and Dahlgren's Raid from Stevensburg, Va., to Richmond. *Union*, Kilpatrick's Cav-

alry; *Confed.*, Cavalry commanded by Gens. G. W. C. Lee, Bradley T. Johnson, and Wade Hampton and Home Guards. Losses: *Union*, 330 killed, wounded, and captured; *Confed.*, 308 killed, wounded, and captured.

### MARCH, 1864.

**14.**—Fort De Russy, La. *Union*, Detachments of Sixteenth and Seventeenth Corps and Porter's Miss. Squadron; *Confed.*, Troops under Gen. Walker's command. Losses: *Union*, 7 killed, 41 wounded; *Confed.*, 5 killed, 4 wounded, 260 prisoners.

**21.**—Henderson Hills, La. *Union*, Detachments of Sixteenth Corps and Cavalry Division Nineteenth Corps; *Confed.*, 2d La. Cav. Losses: *Union*, 1 wounded; *Confed.*, 8 killed, 250 captured.

**24.**—Union City, Tenn. *Union*, 7th Tenn. Cav.; *Confed.*, Forrest's Cav. Losses: *Union*, 450 captured.

**25.**—Fort Anderson, Paducah, Ky. *Union*, 122d Ill., 16th Ky. Cav., 8th U. S. Colored Artil.; *Confed.*, Forrest's Cav. Losses: *Union*, 14 killed, 46 wounded; *Confed.*, 10 killed, 40 wounded.

**26 to 30.**—Longview and Mt. Elba, Ark. *Union*, 28th Wis., 5th Kan. Cav., 7th Mo. Cav.; *Confed.*, Gen. Price's command. Losses: *Union*, 4 killed, 18 wounded; *Confed.*, 12 killed, 35 wounded, 300 captured.

**30.**—Snyder's Bluff, Miss. *Union*, 3d U. S. Colored Cav.; *Confed.*, 3d, 9th Tex. Cav. Losses: *Union*, 16 killed, 3 wounded; *Confed.*, 3 killed, 7 wounded.

### April, 1864.

**1.**—Augusta, Ark. *Union*, 3d Minn., 8th Mo. Cav.; *Confed.*, Gen. Price's command. Losses: *Union*, 8 killed, 16 wounded; *Confed.*, 15 killed, 45 wounded.

—Crump's Hill or Piney Woods, La. *Union*, 14th N. Y. Cav., 2d La., 2d Ill., and 16th Mo. Cav., 5th U. S. Colored Artil.; *Confed.*, Gen. Richard Taylor's command. Losses: *Union*, 20 wounded; *Confed.*, 10 killed, 25 wounded.

* No record found.

THE BASTIONS OF FORT MARION

On one of the bastions of Fort Marion, St. Augustine, a white flag was raised on the evening of March 8, 1862, as Commander C. R. P. Rodgers sailed up the harbor. He had been detached from the expedition sent from the North under command of Flag-Officer Du Pont to recover control of the whole line of seacoast of Georgia, Florida, and Alabama. Florida troops had been the first to seize a Federal fortification, taking possession of Fort Barrancas and the navy yard at Pensacola, January 13, 1861, and Fort Marion, at St. Augustine, was the first fortification in Florida to be surrendered to Federal authority, Flag-Officer Du Pont having seized and garrisoned the abandoned Fort Clinch, at Fernandina, on March 4, 1862. The Confederate troops in Florida abandoned their fortifications

as Du Pont's expedition approached, and at St. Augustine were found the first inhabitants who had remained in their homes.

The citizens of St. Augustine raised the white flag on Fort Marion in answer to the one which Commander Rodgers was bearing as he approached to assure them of pacific intentions. Landing at the wharf, he was soon joined by the mayor and conducted to the city hall, where the municipal authorities were assembled. Rodgers assured them that so long as St. Augustine respected the Federal authority its government would be left in the hands of its citizens, and recommended that the flag of the Union be at once displayed at the fort. The night before a party of women had assembled in front of the barracks in Fort Marion and cut down the flagstaff to prevent its being used to again support the old flag. By order of the mayor, however, the Stars and Stripes were at once hoisted over Fort Marion.

THE OLDEST CHURCH IN AMERICA, 1864

# Engagements of the Civil War

**3.**—Okalona, Ark. *Union,* 27th Wis., 40th Iowa, 77th Ohio, 43d Ill., 1st Mo. Cav., 13th Ill. Cav.; *Confed.,* Gen. Sterling Price's command. Losses: *Union,* 16 killed, 74 wounded; *Confed.,* 75 killed and wounded.

**4.**—Campti, La. 35th Iowa, 5th Minn., 2d and 18th N. Y. Cav., 3d R. I. Cav. Losses: *Union,* 10 killed, 18 wounded; *Confed.,* 3 killed, 12 wounded.

—Elkins' Ferry, Ark. *Union,* 43d Ind., 29th and 36th Iowa, 1st Iowa Cav., Battery E 2d Mo. Light Artil.; *Confed.,* Gen. Sterling Price's command. Losses: *Union,* 5 killed, 33 wounded; *Confed.,* 18 killed, 30 wounded.

**5.**—Roseville, Ark. Seventy-five men of 2d and 6th Kan. Cav. (*Union*) in engagement with guerrillas. Losses: *Union,* 4 killed, 10 wounded; *Confed.,* 6 killed, 20 wounded, 11 captured.

**7.**—Wilson's Farm, La. *Union,* Cavalry of Nineteenth Corps; *Confed.,* Gen. Richard Taylor's command. Losses: *Union,* 14 killed, 39 wounded; *Confed.,* 15 killed, 40 wounded, 100 captured.

**8 and 9.**—Sabine Cross Roads and Pleasant Hill, La. *Union,* Portions of Thirteenth, Sixteenth, and Nineteenth Corps and Cavalry Division of Gen. Banks; *Confed.,* Walker's, Mouton's, and Green's Divisions of Gen. Richard Taylor's command. Losses: *Union,* 300 killed, 1600 wounded, 2100 missing; *Confed.,* 600 killed, 2400 wounded, 500 missing. *Union,* Maj.-Gen. Franklin and Brig.-Gen. Ransom wounded. *Confed.,* Maj.-Gen. Mouton and Brig.-Gen. Parsons killed.

**10 to 13.**—Prairie D'Ann, Ark. *Union,* 3d Division Seventh Corps; *Confed.,* Gen. Price's command. Losses: *Union,* 100 killed and wounded; *Confed.,* 50 killed and wounded.

**12.**—Blair's Landing, La. *Union,* Gen. Kirby Smith's command, Gunboats *Osage* and *Lexington; Confed.,* Gen. Green's Division of Taylor's command. Losses: *Union,* 7 wounded; *Confed.,* 200 killed and wounded.

**13.**—Moscow, Ark. *Union,* 18th Iowa, 6th Kan. Cav., 2d Ind. Battery; *Confed.,* Gen. Price's command. Losses: *Union,* 5 killed, 17 wounded; *Confed.,* 30 killed and wounded.

**13 and 14.**—Paintsville and Half-Mountain, Ky. *Union,* Ky. Volunteers; *Confed.,* Johnson's brigade Ky. Cav. Losses: *Union,* 4 wounded; *Confed.,* 25 killed, 25 wounded.

**15 and 16.**—Liberty P. O., and occupation of Camden, Ark. *Union,* 29th Iowa, 50th Ind., 9th Wis.; *Confed.,* Gen. Sterling Price's command. Losses: *Union,* 255 killed and wounded.

**17 to 20.**—Plymouth, N. C. *Union,* 85th N. Y., 103d Pa., 16th Conn., Gunboats *Southfield* and *Miami; Confed.,* Gen. Hoke's command, iron-clad ram *Albemarle.* Losses: *Union,* 20 killed, 80 wounded, 1500 missing; *Confed.,* 500 killed, wounded, and missing. *Union,* Lieut.-Com. Flusser killed.

**18.**—Poison Springs, eight miles from Camden, Ark. *Union,* 18th Iowa, 79th U. S. Colored, 6th Kan. Cav.; *Confed.,* Shelby's Cav. Losses: *Union,* 204 killed and missing, 97 wounded. *Confed.,* 16 killed, 88 wounded, 10 missing.

**22 and 24.**—Monette's Ferry, Cane River, and Cloutersville, La. *Union,* Portion of Thirteenth, Seventeenth, and Nineteenth Corps; *Confed.,* Gen. Richard Taylor's command. Losses: *Union* (estimate), 350 killed and wounded; *Confed.,* 400 killed and wounded.

**25.**—Marks' Mills, Ark. *Union,* 36th Iowa, 77th Ohio, 43d Ill., 1st Ind. Cav., 7th Mo. Cav., Battery E 2d Mo. Light Artil.; *Confed.,* Troops of Gen. Kirby Smith's command. Losses: *Union,* 100 killed, 250 wounded, 1100 captured; *Confed.,* 41 killed, 108 wounded, 44 missing.

**26.**—Moro Creek, Ark. *Union,* 33d and 40th Iowa, 5th Kan., 2d and 4th Mo., 1st Iowa Cav.; *Confed.,* Troops of Gen. Kirby Smith's command. Losses: *Union,* 5 killed, 14 wounded.

**30.**—Jenkins' Ferry, Saline River, Ark. *Union,* 3d Division of Seventeenth Corps; *Confed.,* Texas, Missouri, and Arkansas troops under Gens. Kirby Smith and Sterling Price. Losses: *Union,* 200 killed, 955 wounded; *Confed.,* 86 killed, 356 wounded.

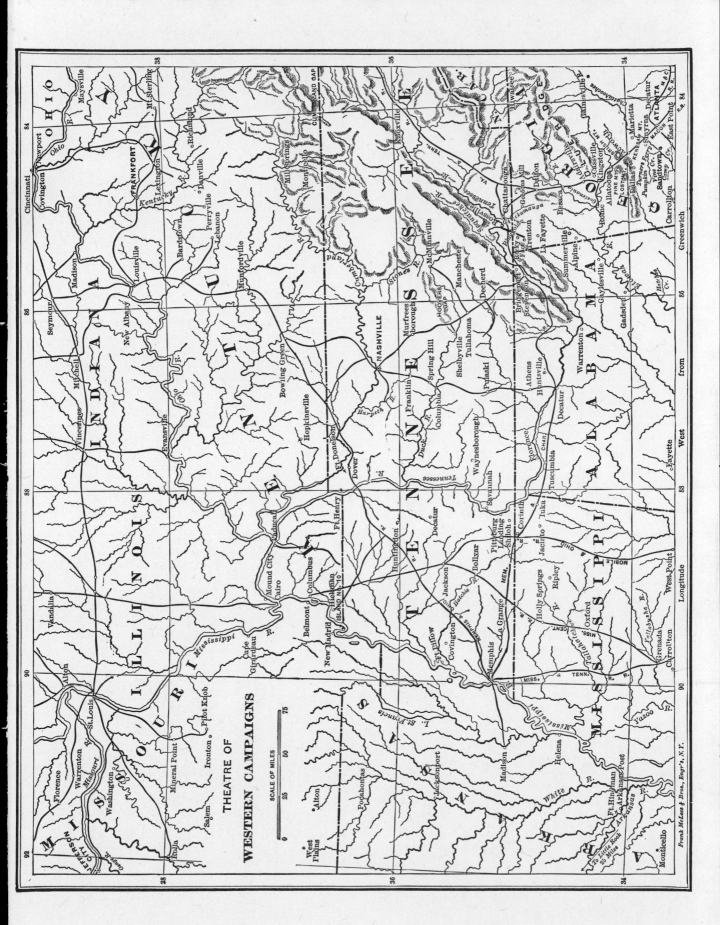

THEATRE OF

WESTERN CAMPAIGNS

SCALE OF MILES
0    25    50    75

Frank McLees & Bros., Engr's, N.Y.